The Myth and Mystery of UFOs

The Myth and Mystery of UFOs

Thomas E. Bullard

UNIVERSITY PRESS OF KANSAS

© 2010 by the University Press of Kansas

Published by the University Press of Kansas (Lawrence, Kansas 66045),
which was organized by the Kansas Board of Regents and is operated and funded by
Emporia State University, Fort Hays State University, Kansas State University,
Pittsburg State University, the University of Kansas, and Wichita State University

Library of Congress Cataloging-in-Publication Data

Bullard, Thomas E. (Thomas Eddie), 1949–
The myth and mystery of UFOs / Thomas E. Bullard.
p.   cm.
Includes bibliographical references and index.
ISBN 978-0-7006-1729-6 (cloth : alk. paper)
1. Unidentified flying objects. I. Title.
TL789.B75 2010
001.942—dc22
2010026289

British Library Cataloguing-in-Publication Data is available.

Printed in the United States of America
10 9 8 7 6 5 4 3 2 1

The paper used in this publication is recycled and contains 30 percent postconsumer waste.
It is acid free and meets the minimum requirements of the American National Standard for
Permanence of Paper for Printed Library Materials Z39.48-1992.

Contents

Acknowledgments

I would like to thank Mary Castner, Mark Rodeghier, and Michael D. Swords for CUFOS, James Carrion for MUFON, Phyllis Galde for *Fate* magazine, Janet Bord for the Fortean Picture Library, and Richard F. Haines, whose help in providing illustrations for this book is greatly appreciated.

I owe especial thanks to Jerome Clark and David M. Jacobs for reading the manuscript and devoting efforts above and beyond the call of duty to whip my unruly writing into shape. A final thank-you goes to my long-suffering editor, Michael J. Briggs, who had to wait far too long for me to finish, but who did so with patience and always a helping hand.

Abbreviations Used in This Book

APRO	Aerial Phenomena Research Organization
AAAS	American Association for the Advancement of Science
BUFORA	British UFO Research Association
CUFOS	Center for UFO Studies
CRIFO	Civilian Research, Interplanetary Flying Objects
CSICOP	Committee for the Scientific Investigation of Claims of the Paranormal
ETH	extraterrestrial hypothesis
FAA	Federal Aviation Administration
FSR	*Flying Saucer Review*
FOIA	Freedom of Information Act
FUFOR	Fund for UFO Research
GEPAN	Groupe d'Etudes des Phénomènes Aérospatiaux non Identifiés
MILABs	military abductions
MUFON	Mutual UFO Network
NARCAP	National Aviation Reporting Center on Anomalous Phenomena
NICAP	National Investigations Committee on Aerial Phenomena
NIDS	National Institute for Discovery Science
NUFORC	National UFO Reporting Center
NDE	near-death experience
SAC	Strategic Air Command

Introduction:
A Mystery of Mythic Proportions

> Being compelled to rely upon such meager information as your
> committee could gain from terrestrial observation, inquiry and the
> truthful reports of the newspapers . . . we are led to the conclusion
> that the phenomenon is not an hallucination caused by too frequent
> and deep porations from mundane schooners. . . . That while the
> aerial visitation may be regarded as a mote to trouble the mind's eye, it
> should not necessarily cause great apprehension or serious alarm.
> —*Davenport (IA) Daily Leader,* April 13, 1897

The skies over O'Hare Airport in Chicago got a little more crowded than usual on November 7, 2006. It was 4:30 P.M. on a cloudy day just before sunset when employees of United Airlines spotted a dark gray, unlighted, elliptical or Frisbee-shaped object over Concourse C, hovering not far below the clouds. The well-defined object stayed in place while United personnel turned out for a look, with grounds crew, mechanics, pilots, and managers viewing the object before it ascended straight up and punched a clear hole into the cloud deck at 1,900 feet. The hole closed within a few minutes. At least a dozen United workers reported the sighting to company officials; accounts also reached the National UFO Reporting Center (NUFORC) and the National Aviation Reporting Center on Anomalous Phenomena (NARCAP).

This strange story almost never made the news at all. First published in the *Chicago Tribune* on January 1, 2007, and already two months old, the tip that something interesting had happened came to reporters via NUFORC. When transportation newsman Jon Hilkevitch made inquiries, United officials said they knew nothing about the sighting and had no record of any unusual incident in the duty manager's log. The Federal Aviation Administration (FAA) gave the same response. Aware that the witnesses contradicted these statements, Hilkevitch filed a Freedom of Information Act (FOIA) request, whereupon the FAA discovered that a United supervisor had called an FAA manager in the airport control tower to ask about the object.

United officials interviewed several witnesses, asked for written reports and drawings, then advised some witnesses not to talk about what they saw. No air traffic controllers observed the object and it did not appear on radar, according to the FAA. The agency planned no further investigations after concluding that a weather condition, abetted by airport lights playing on low clouds, deceived witnesses with the false impression of a saucerlike object.

Accounts differed in some respects: Estimates of size ranged from six to twenty-four feet and the duration of the sighting from a few minutes up to twenty. Some witnesses said the object was spinning, others said it was not; some spoke of the edges as hard and metallic, one said they rippled like a heat mirage. All agreed that the object made no noise and kept a fixed position in the sky before it ascended. The hole punched in the clouds was especially striking and quite unlike the appearance of a jet slicing through the canopy.

The public gave this belated news a warm reception. The article scored more than a million hits during the four days it remained the top story on the *Tribune*'s Web site, while the Associated Press, National Public Radio, CNN, MSNBC, and *Newsweek* picked up the account. Inquiries about the case reached Hilkevitch from as far away as Australia. Some of the witnesses appeared in TV interviews, and in the following weeks hints began to circulate that some passengers witnessed the object and that a video of it existed. In a week the *Tribune* received four hundred e-mails, some to praise the newspaper for serious treatment of a UFO story, some to offer conspiracy theories, some to report unrelated UFO experiences, and some to scoff at the event. The story quickly became a source of amusement: One air traffic controller joked that it was unacceptable for aliens to travel millions of light years only to find their gate occupied, and on the *Tonight Show* Jay Leno poked fun at drunken airport workers.

Any stray object over an airport was proper cause for concern. It might interfere with radar and navigational devices or create a collision risk, but ridicule along with official stonewalling and apparent indifference toward this potential hazard left witnesses frustrated and outraged. Few of them advocated a particular identity for the object. They insisted only that they saw something unusual and it was unlike any aircraft or balloon they had ever seen before. Yet among some witnesses and with the public at large, a sort of default possibility hovered close to mind that this mysterious object was a visitor from space.[1]

The O'Hare incident illustrates in microcosm the curious public career of unidentified flying objects today. Multiple observers describe a strange object in the sky in similar ways, with no more variations in details than different vantage points and honest human error can explain. Such consistency is a hallmark of an objective event, and, moreover, the observers are quality witnesses, people whose jobs require a high level of skill and responsibility, whose testimony would stand tall in a court of law. The observers are on familiar turf and see the sky over O'Hare on a daily basis. They know the way lights and aircraft interact with clouds, but still they are puzzled. They insist with dead seriousness that they saw something out of the ordinary and brave a barrage of derision and denials to say so.

That the observers saw something unusual seems beyond doubt. What they saw remains an open question. Good testimony needs independent support, but lack of radar contact at an airport seems curious, if the object was truly solid. The weather explanation sounds thin, contrived, but at least possible. At the same time, some doubts taint the negative evidence. The FAA says there was no radar contact, but the FAA would not even admit a sighting occurred until a FOIA request pried loose an embarrassing reversal in their story. The airline officials have a similar credibility problem, compounded by their insistence that the witnesses keep their mouths shut. Maybe the secrecy stems from nothing more sinister than snafus and the desire of a corporation to avoid controversy, but with distrust of government running almost as deep as the genetic code, many people translate denials into clues that some shadowy power conspires to cheat the public out of the truth. With aviation safety always a concern and airport security now so stringent that grannies have to remove their tennis shoes for inspection, indifference to a potential threat looks all the more like somebody has something to hide. And who decided that a weather phenomenon was responsible for the sighting? What is the evidence for this conclusion, and does it come from a qualified source?

If the sighting itself is a thing of wonder, the divide between popular and official responses is even more striking. An overwhelming public interest surrounds the story. It draws out comments from people with agendas, strong opinions, eccentric beliefs, and an attraction rooted in personal experience and a desire to share those experiences with others. A million hits breaks the record for any story ever posted on the *Tribune* Web site and confirms the potent grassroots appeal of UFOs. The response of elite and official sources flows in just the opposite direction. Two months pass before news media pick up the story and reporters find out about it only in a roundabout way, aviation authorities apparently solve the case to their satisfaction without even bothering to investigate, and commentators help themselves to a good laugh at the expense of the witnesses. Whenever UFOs are concerned, a similar pattern repeats. The outpouring of enthusiasm from the public seems out of proportion to the particular event, and the ho-hum dismissals of officials, along with the knee-jerk raillery from media figures, seem inappropriate for the honest, good-faith testimonies of the hapless witnesses.

What did the United workers really see? This kind of question rushes to the forefront after every UFO sighting, and the answers round up the usual suspects: Did the twilight play tricks on human eyes, did a scudding cloud catch a beam of light to create a chance illusion, did a weather balloon or military aircraft wander into commercial airspace, did an unearthly spaceship spy on the world's second busiest airport? No solution will satisfy everyone, and no well-substantiated final conclusion is likely ever to emerge. Judging from one UFO case after another, a controversy will spiral outward as facts and interpretations alike become subjects of dispute until, in the end, the questions matter more than the answers.

An Outer and an Inner Mystery

The "story" of the O'Hare UFO is really two stories. One concerns the immediate curiosity about a mysterious object in the sky, what it was and what it was doing there; but fixation on the physical nature of UFOs overlooks an almost equally intriguing human problem. The puzzlement and emotional turmoil of witnesses, the smug and flippant official responses, the intense and widespread public interest play out like stock scenes in a predictable but always engrossing drama. A second story, then, considers the reasons that people respond to the reports in such varied yet standardized ways. Or to frame the question in briefer terms, why are UFOs at once so popular and so despised?

As the O'Hare sighting demonstrates, the public cares about UFOs. They enjoy a favored position in modern culture, with aliens and their spaceships pervasive in movies, TV documentaries, cartoons, advertisements, toys, greeting cards, Halloween costumes, and T-shirts, while aliens have grown so familiar that having a few around the house is no cause for alarm, at least in the form of alien-head banks, cookie jars, and salt-and-pepper shakers.[2] Public recognition of UFOs remains among the highest for any subject in the history of Gallup polls—as high as 96 percent in 1966. To set that number in perspective, consider that only 92 percent recognized the name of Gerald Ford just six months after he left the White House.[3] *Communion*, which recounted horror novelist Whitley Strieber's abduction experiences, became a best seller in 1987. *The X-Files* captivated TV audiences from 1993 to 2001 with its moody atmosphere of sinister conspiracies and unearthly visitation. And where would all-night talk radio be without UFOs? In one sense, these invaders have conquered the world. Far from being limited to North America, UFOs have appeared in all continents and interest is world-wide. As mainstays of popular culture, aliens are versatile enough to scare, intrigue, perplex, entertain, amuse, and sell.

UFOs are matters of experience as well as belief and wonder. Reports sent to NU-FORC average more than three hundred a month.[4] A 1996 Gallup poll found that 12 percent of respondents thought they had seen a UFO, a figure that translates into over thirty million Americans. According to that same poll, about half the population believes that extraterrestrials have visited the earth and nearly three-fourths suspect that the government knows more than it tells about UFOs.[5] Far from being eccentric or marginal people, UFO witnesses register normal scores on psychological tests and come from all walks of life.[6] Among the observers are trustworthy, high-functioning people like the airline pilots and aviation crews of O'Hare, police officers, military personnel, business executives, college professors, and astronomers. Thousands of ordinary citizens join organizations dedicated to UFO study, attend UFO conventions, and make the town of Roswell a major tourist attraction in New Mexico. A Google search on the Internet garners forty-one million returns for "UFO," give or take a few. Thousands of Web sites now join an extensive literature of books, magazines, and proceedings to document evidence and discuss theories.

Despite robust success in mass, popular, and folk culture, UFOs seldom attract a serious glance from scientists, academics, the elite media, or government authorities. The attitudes of opinion-makers with the broadest power and impact usually range from indifference to hostility. Public pronouncements of military officials ever since the 1950s have dismissed UFOs as posing no defense risks, while prominent civilian scientists like astronomers Donald H. Menzel and Carl Sagan proclaim that witnesses misidentify mirages, aircraft, meteors, and other conventional sights.[7] In the consensus view of official science and government, UFOs simply do not exist as a unique and interesting mystery. For the organized community of skeptics (represented by the Committee for Skeptical Inquiry, formerly the Committee for the Scientific Investigation of Claims of the Paranormal, or CSICOP), belief in UFOs is not merely mistaken but dangerous, a pseudoscientific faith that misleads the public and promotes irrationality.[8] The mainstream news media seldom treat the subject kindly. One exception was a sympathetic documentary hosted by ABC News anchor Peter Jennings in February 2005, but even he did not escape reprimand. Deaf to the evidence presented, a writer for *TV Guide* commented, "Jeers to Peter Jennings for squandering his journalistic gravitas on a two-hour report examining the phenomenon of UFOs. [His] prime-time special would have been more at home on the Science Fiction Channel. And it's not exactly like we're running short of newsworthy stories here on Earth."[9]

The habit of rejecting UFOs runs deep. In *The Demon-Haunted World* (1996), Sagan compiled a chapter of letters he received after publishing a skeptical article about UFO abductions in *Parade*, a weekly newspaper supplement magazine. One response described meetings not just with aliens but also with Jesus; a second writer saw aliens and ghosts. Another letter came from a grandmother who stated that she had experienced abductions all her life, and while she offered no explanation for their nature, she insisted that the experiences were quite real. If the claims of the first two letters are easy enough to classify as delusions, the claims of the grandmother deserve no snap judgment. She gives a matter-of-fact report of experiential phenomena as observations calling for explanation, without attempting to press any preconceived notion. Whatever the nature of her experiences, they would seem problematic enough to engage scientific curiosity, yet Sagan passed them by without any curiosity at all.[10]

A similar lack of interest characterizes the response of most academic disciplines to the subject. It has inspired some scholarly publications in religious studies, cultural studies, sociology, anthropology, history, folklore, and especially psychology, but very few in the physical sciences. In fact, the total for all disciplines seems disproportionately small in comparison with the cultural stature of UFOs. The academic environment is typically an unfriendly place for research on UFOs. If they appear in university classrooms, UFOs usually serve as examples of error in observation, reasoning, and belief. The few professors who have offered courses or pursued research with a positive approach have met with ridicule and impediments to their careers.

The experience of Bruce Maccabee, an optical physicist for the U.S. Navy, illustrates that the scientific gate seems barred to UFOs without even a hearing of the evidence. Multiple witnesses, movie footage, and radar tracking combined in UFO sightings at Kaikoura, New Zealand, in 1978 to create an intriguing case. He spent a month in New Zealand interviewing witnesses and analyzing the data. When an article appeared in the *Journal of Atmospheric and Terrestrial Physics* concluding that refracted lights from Japanese squid boats were responsible for the sightings, Maccabee submitted a rebuttal that argued a strong case against mirages in favor of an unidentified phenomenon. The editor rejected his article, saying it contained no "real science," in an apparent demonstration that a study based on extensive investigation did not merit publication if it arrived at an unacceptable answer, while a study based on nothing more than newspaper reports breezed into print as long as its results conformed to proper scientific opinion.[11]

In casual conversation with faculty members over the years, I have heard scholars usually restrained and careful in their judgments suddenly turn opinionated and emotional when UFOs are the topic. These people admit that they know very little about UFOs with one breath then declare with the next that the subject is a silly one and unworthy of attention. The hatchet of distrust falls everywhere—on the reliability of eyewitnesses, dependability of the reports, honesty of the literature recording the reports, and credibility of any explanation or theory if it leaves room for the unconventional. Doubters wrap evidence, interpretation, witness, and proponent alike in deep layers of prejudice. If this informal impression is truly as widespread as it seems, no wonder UFOs remain shunned as a scholarly taboo.

This rejection is entrenched yet relies on tenuous justifications. During the 1950s and 1960s the U.S. Air Force insisted that nothing more than mistaken identities explained UFOs, but poor investigations or no investigations at all undercut the credibility of these repeated assertions.[12] The Air Force funded a study of UFOs at the University of Colorado from 1966 to 1968, and the director, physicist Edward U. Condon, concluded that UFOs were unworthy of further scientific attention.[13] While it circulated in the news as the official verdict, his declaration contradicted the study's actual findings that over one-fourth of the reports investigated, including many of the most detailed and impressive cases, remained unexplained.[14] Menzel and CSICOP skeptics Philip J. Klass, James Oberg, Robert Sheaffer, and Joe Nickell have investigated important UFO cases and found conventional solutions for all of them. The skeptics readily declare that they have solved the UFO mystery, but a close examination of their solutions shows that some are persuasive while others are unconvincing and any rush to close the book on UFOs is premature.[15] By way of contrast, mainstream scientists like Maccabee, Northwestern University astronomer J. Allen Hynek, and University of Arizona atmospheric physicist James McDonald have investigated UFO cases and concluded that a genuine unconventional phenomenon exists.[16] Yet the foregone conviction that there is nothing to the subject bulldozes its way over favorable evidence and covers up shortcomings of the critics.

Reasons for Rejection

So here we have the pretty paradox of UFOs: Though popular with the public and a staple image in everyday life, they cannot even get off the ground as a matter of interest among the scientists and journalists who ought to lead the way in exploring the matter.

Thousands of people have UFO experiences every year but seldom find anyone willing to listen, any acknowledgment that the objects of their puzzlement count as anything more than trivial entertainment or intellectual junk.

How has this darling of the public become such a pariah for the elite? The fault lies not with the evidence, because the evidence has received little serious attention, so the problem takes on a human slant and the issue becomes a question of why the subject provokes such prejudiced responses. This question is intriguing in its own right, but some answers are already on the table.

1. With sufficient information, all UFO reports resolve into conventional phenomena. This oft-repeated argument serves as a cornerstone for opposition to UFOs and gains support from the undeniably high ratio of noise to signal in the reports. While the Air Force claim that they have found satisfactory explanations for 97 percent of cases was overoptimistic, ufologists admit that conventional solutions account for 80 percent or more of reports. Even many unknowns languish in a "gray area" where reports are impressive but the evidence falls short of persuasive. Opponents justify ignoring the residue of unexplained reports with a faith that, given further evidence, an ordinary answer will fall into place for these cases as well.

2. UFOs are hard to study and are uncongenial to the preferred practice of science. They do not fly into the laboratory, submit to experiments, allow observation under controlled conditions, or act in predictable ways. The great majority of UFO evidence is anecdotal when science regards such testimony as scarcely evidential at all. The hoaxes and delusions that plagued the study of alleged psychic phenomena in the nineteenth century admonish modern scientists that witnesses can distort or fabricate facts as well as relate them, while complex conventional events may combine to deceive even the most honest witness and sink investigators into a morass of confusion. Such inherent difficulties load the subject with disincentives for scientists to invest their time in a study.

3. The extravagance of UFO claims far outstrips the supporting evidence. Assertions that the government has known all about UFOs since one crashed at Roswell in 1947; that aliens have abducted thousands if not millions of people; that UFOs make right-angle turns at high speed, bend beams of light, or vanish into thin air; that extraterrestrials can reach the earth in the first place—all clash with the prevailing understanding of physics and history. After sixty years of reports no one has submitted indisputable evidence—no alien body, unearthly fragment of metal, or technologically advanced artifact. Carl Sagan wondered why aliens would converse about religious philosophy but not prove their intelligence with something indisputable like an elegant proof for Fermat's Last Theorem.[17] Lack of ironclad evidence forecloses

not only scientific acceptance of UFOs but apparently scientific interest in them as well.

Beyond problems inherent in the subject matter, less explicit social reasons come to mind as further grounds for rejection.

4. Popular enthusiasm for UFOs has degraded their perceived worth as a serious topic. Too many books, conferences, Web sites, and documentaries implicate UFOs in conspiracy theories, mystical speculations about crop circles, and claims like the Roswell crash is the source of our modern technology. These extravagant assertions excite enthusiasts but leave critical onlookers with reason to think that UFOs belong to the realm of faith and that scientific study is unwarranted. Quality reports and rigorous research suffer collateral damage in the crossfire of dubious claims.

5. The practices of ufologists do more to discredit than support their cause. While some UFO investigators and researchers are admirably painstaking, their work is seldom the most visible. The standards of critical thinking apparent in most popular treatments tend to be lax, and a willingness to tolerate less-than-air-tight cases as adequate proof pervades the field. It also suffers from being too wide open, so that outright charlatans and opportunists can speak as authorities with little or no peer control. The consequent impression of true believers banded together to affirm their beliefs overshadows the subject and turns serious outsiders away.

6. The nonexistence of UFOs has acquired the status of a settled and self-evident fact. Where UFOs are concerned, the proper agnosticism of science has hardened into an atheistic consensus, a certainty that nothing unconventional is involved. Yet close examination suggests that this conclusion belongs to what folklorist David Hufford terms a "tradition of disbelief," where a negative belief comes to appear true simply by being repeated often enough.[18] Faith may sustain negative as readily as positive beliefs, and in the case of UFOs, conviction has supplanted evidence so that the verdict of scientists owes little to science.

7. Confusion of interpretations with facts undercuts perception of UFOs as a genuine scientific problem. A recurrent criticism of UFOs is that they appear too earthbound for space visitors. If taken to mean that the things said about UFOs—the purposes and meanings attributed to them, the associations and speculations imposed on them—seem too firmly rooted in earthly affairs to be truly alien, then this criticism strikes close to the mark. The phenomenon of UFOs has a strangeness all its own; but theories, explanations, and beliefs about UFOs often supplant, mask, or distort the phenomenon with a suspect familiarity. As a result it becomes easy to mistake human ideas for the physical reality and believe that UFOs are nothing more than cultural products.

Distinguishing the Social from the Phenomenal UFO

This last possibility deserves close attention as an answer for what is "wrong" with UFOs. When an account in a book or Web site purports to describe an eyewitness experience, the intention may be honest, but many hands have intervened along the way to complicate the truth. Even with the best of intentions, every participant in reporting, relaying, and recording a UFO account may add to or subtract from the story, slant or revise it, introduce error or distortion, until the final result bears imperfect resemblance to the initial event. The following list suggests how knowledge of a UFO event passes through a series of stages from experience to ultimate historical record:

The Event.—At the bottom lies a possible phenomenon that exists independent of witnesses, the tree that falls in the woods whether anyone hears it or not.

The Experience.—Humans meet the phenomenon for the first time when an individual senses it. The perception may be a sensory and emotional response to an objective event, but not necessarily: a subjective experience based on hallucination, illusion, delusion, fantasy, or error can feel like a real event.

Memory.—Once an experience passes from the senses, the primary evidence that it happened lies in the memory of the witness. Yet memory is not set in stone but a fluid, reconstructive process that personal agendas, outside influence, and subsequent information can distort or falsify.

Understanding.—The fate of an experience depends on how a witness makes sense of it. The process of conception requires an active effort of thought to name, categorize, and relate the memories of an experience to things already known. An experience enters the "UFO" category only when recognized as unconventional, but the passage from perception to conception is fraught with opportunities for bad judgment, erroneous connections, and confusion of conventional sights with something out of the ordinary.

Communication.—To share a personal experience the witness must cast it in the common language of words and images. Descriptive and narrative reports re-create the experience for others but never as a perfect image, always as a version compromised by the limitations and stereotyping tendencies of words.

Social Reception.—UFO reports make their social debut when an audience receives them. Each receiver repeats the process of understanding as he or she formulates a personal version of what the witness relates. The report becomes public property as individuals advocate or dispute various versions and understandings to impose a chosen sense of truth, but these multiple participants recast and reinterpret the report in ways that the witness may never have intended.

Cultural Representation.—The sum of stories and ideas about UFOs comprises the cultural image of the subject. This collective knowledge funds the awareness of people who have not had experiences and the ideas of image-makers in the entertainment industry and popular culture. Cultural narratives link UFO stories and ideas into a suppositional picture of reality, and whether accurate or fanciful, this picture not only shapes many people's impressions and understanding of UFOs but also joins the parts with a sense of coherence that enables willing people to believe that the cultural image is true.

Though the preceding list depicts UFO knowledge as a succession of layers, the relationship of processes might be better visualized as circular rather than vertical. Feedback loops interconnect the various stages so that no witness starts out as a blank slate ready to record a phenomenon. Cultural ideas of how a UFO should look or behave push witnesses to fill the gaps inside a cluster of lights with the perception of a solid framework, and they pull interpreters to forget the full strangeness of a report and recall only elements compatible with nuts-and-bolts technology. Prior conceptions have turned Venus or an airplane into a spaceship many times in the files of UFO cases, and outside social interests like conspiracies or child abuse have drawn UFOs into associations that are heartfelt but empty of an observational basis. Committed to memory, an experience adapts to personal desires and external influences. Written down or spoken aloud, it suffers from the innate ambiguities of words and the readiness of audiences to hear only what they want to hear. Drawn into the social matrix, a report serves the agendas of factions as, for example, when UFO investigators ask leading questions and present a case in terms that conform to desired preconceptions. Coded into schemes of cultural knowledge, UFOs acquire meanings borrowed from traditional cultural themes like the threatening outsider, a coming apocalypse, or saviors from the sky.

The UFOs that soar in social space may little resemble their counterparts in outer space. So many human variables mediate between the cultural representation of an event and the event itself that sound reason exists to doubt, even despair of, meaningful fidelity between the two. A "psychosocial" school takes up the human side of the equation as the full answer, to explain UFOs as nothing more than a tissue of fantasies and illusions based on cultural sources and psychological predispositions. Popular in Europe, this approach finds trenchant English-language advocates in the American skeptic Martin Kottmeyer and writers associated with the British journal *Magonia*.[19] Most psychologists and academics who treat UFOs borrow the psychosocial tenet of cultural influences to explain the specific contents of UFO reports.

Ufologists predictably reject such theories but seldom recognize that human influences channel thoughts and expressions about UFOs onto well-worn paths. It would not stretch the truth too far to say that current knowledge of UFOs is mainly a structure of beliefs about UFOs, more responsive to human concerns, ordered according to cultural patterns, and expressive of ethnocentric assumptions than reflective of a physical phenomenon. Whatever sort of phenomenal fact UFOs may be, the social fact of UFO ideas dominates representations and discussions, and this domination may contribute to prejudice against UFOs as an independent phenomenon. The psychosocial proponents overstate their case when they take legitimate instances of cultural influence as sufficient pretext to dismiss an underlying phenomenon, but they rightly insist that UFOs as we know them present significant psychosocial dimensions. Right or wrong, love them or hate them, psychosocial explanations address a major dimension of the mystery.

A psychosocial idea is the premise of this book: UFOs—as we think of them, understand them, find meaning in them—owe most of their public character to a cultural version, to what human belief puts into them rather than to what observation or scientific study reveals. I will argue that UFO ideas comprise a modern myth, one that has grown out of cultural traditions, psychological predispositions, and social preoccupations, to create a full-blown understanding of this world based on its relationship to others. The means to cast UFOs into human terms include imagery, themes, motifs, narrative structures, and explanatory theories adapted to a UFO context from cultural sources that are sometimes borrowed from traditions and contemporary parallels and are sometimes invented independently as a response to similar situations. The motives for these adaptations address social and psychological functions of UFOs—the purpose they serve proponents and their mirror images, the skeptics.

An orientation toward cultural aspects means this book is less about sights in the sky or the people who see them than about the thoughts and expressions that represent UFOs. This approach does not include attempts to determine the ideas of individuals or their histories of exposure to particular traditions; rather it emphasizes collective knowledge, the accounts, beliefs, theories, speculations, and imaginings that comprise the ufological literature and popular treatments of UFOs. Such an approach runs counter to the goal of ufology to understand the phenomenon and also to current research practices into narrative behavior that concentrate on individual and interpersonal processes rather than the isolated product. Yet this narrow attention has its own value. A conviction underlies this book that comparative study of long-running cultural themes and patterns reveals an important shaping influence on the way people think and talk about UFOs. To grasp these themes and patterns as formal causes serves as a necessary adjunct to understanding both process and product.

Although in agreement with the psychosocial thesis that most UFO thought reflects human rather than phenomenal matters, this book will maintain another, equally important premise—that individual, social, and cultural factors do not tell the whole story, and this story requires an experience with properties of its own for completion. I do not intend to treat UFO evidence in depth or campaign in favor of particular identities for the phenomenon, but only to recognize that the sights and the ideas about them are inseparable. Understanding the phenomenal UFO requires awareness of what cultural influences do to it. Understanding the cultural UFO must reckon with contributions of experience or else both understandings remain oversimplified and partial. The cultural role identified by psychosocial proponents does not have to discredit a genuine phenomenon; rather such influences demonstrate the inescapable fact that UFO thinking inhabits a cultural context where belief restructures our perceptions until UFOs become something less of what they are, something more of what we think they ought to be. A narrow approach that sees only human influences or only nuts-and-bolts spaceships loses sight of the problem as an interlocking whole.

Approaching the Problem

Some clarifications at the outset will smooth the way: Most of us do not know UFOs directly but only through what people say about them—the witness's report of experience, the investigator's account of other people's experiences, the researcher's historical narrative based on the collation and retelling of reports, the ufologist's explanatory and interpretational discussions, theories, disputes, and speculations. All participants speak a cultural language. Its vocabularies and templates build narratives, its meanings structure beliefs and discourse. Even a straightforward eyewitness report is neither pure nor simple because experience itself is a personal story, its makings filtered through acquired expectations and its outcome cast in a cultural mold. In other words, UFO information comes with a caveat—various sorts of human intervention always mediate the truth of this information.

UFOs serve broad human purposes rather than narrow scientific understanding; uncovering those human uses is a job for social and behavioral sciences and humanistic scholarship. Anthropology, psychology, religious studies, and especially folklore scholarship will prove useful. A UFO appeared over O'Hare and a million heads bobbed up to seek more information, in a suggestive demonstration that broad popular interest simmers beneath the surface of official denials and indifference. Ufology represents an exemplary case of unofficial knowledge, of beliefs held and developed by an extensive public independent of—and even in defiance of—recognized social authorities. How such a parallel intellectual universe coexists and competes with the official realm is an aspect of folk culture long investigated by folklorists. They have also studied the legend and related narrative genres that describe encounters with the extranormal. This scholarship into the dynamics of traditional narratives, their processes of variation, disputation, stereotypical ordering, and inclusion of fantastic elements, provides a useful framework of understanding for UFO accounts. Folklore scholarship has explored the functions and meanings of narratives, how jokes and urban legends express fears and tensions current in society, how myths order ideals and beliefs into a coherent narrative map of how the world does and ought to work. All these insights will help make sense of the earthly life of UFOs.

The most audible voices speaking about UFOs belong not to witnesses but to ufologists, the people interested in the subject who in some sense study UFOs. Unlike astronomy or geology or other well-defined disciplines, ufology is slippery and amorphous. Even such a basic issue as the scope of the field lacks widespread agreement. Condon defined a UFO as "the stimulus for a report . . . of something seen in the sky . . . which the observer could not identify as having an ordinary natural origin, and which seemed to him sufficiently puzzling that he undertook to make a report of it."[20] Hynek's definition takes a UFO to be "the reported perception of an object or light seen in the sky . . . which is not only mystifying to the original percipients but remains unidentified after close scrutiny of all available evidence."[21] The first leaves UFOs as a social phenomenon, a sight mysterious in human thought and behavior but otherwise not necessarily unconventional. The second accents the mysteriousness of the object itself, its unconventional qualities sustained even after experts try and fail to explain it. Condon's definition justifies attention to mistaken identities while Hynek's seeks to limit inquiry to the evidence for an unknown phenomenon. This tension between expansive and restrictive inclinations tugs at ufology throughout its history, but the tendency toward enlargement emerges as the clear winner.

UFO story types begin with personal experience accounts. They range from simple descriptions of distant lights or objects to elaborate close-encounter reports, this latter group including observations near enough to reveal a structured craft, interactions between the UFO and earthly objects or persons (such as ground traces, interference with electrical equipment, or injury to humans), and the appearance of UFO occupants.[22] The three most complex stories in the UFO literature describe friendly meetings between humans and aliens (contacts), kidnap of humans by alien beings (abductions), and crashes of UFOs (crash retrievals). These three story types have provoked intensive quests for meaning centered on such emotionally charged possibilities as cosmic salvation, alien hostility, and government deception.

The uncertain boundaries of ufology have allowed it to include far more than current sights in the sky. Historical researchers hunt for evidence of UFO activity in medieval chronicles and nineteenth-century newspapers or reconsider the monuments and literature of the past as indicators that ancient astronauts visited the earth. A UFO connection has formed with suggestive historical events like the Tunguska explosion of 1908, the disappearance of ships and aircraft in the Bermuda Triangle, the apparent mutilation of cattle from the 1970s onward, and the beautiful, increasingly complex crop circles that have appeared in English wheat fields since the 1980s. Even Bigfoot and other mystery monsters become aliens in some proposals. Conspiracy theories have settled into UFO belief as basic tenets and all-purpose axioms of interpretation. The Roswell crash becomes the reason for a secrecy campaign that shapes all of history since 1947 and morphs into claims about government treaties with aliens and plots to take over the world by secret earthly or extraterrestrial groups. The disclosure movement, an effort to force the government to reveal its UFO secrets, and exopolitics, a political program for how life will go on after the public learns about the alien presence, have grown out of the conspiracy premise in ufology. A variety of anomalous occurrences and social concerns have accumulated under the umbrella of ufology, for reasons that range from strong to tenuous.

Not every ufologist welcomes such inclusiveness, and much contention over what is or is not a legitimate piece of the puzzle rives the field. A consensus is so rare among people who identify themselves as ufologists that ufology is more nearly synonymous with the sum of UFO beliefs than with anything like a well-defined academic discipline. In its broadest sense as the study of UFOs and in a narrower sense as promotion of an unconventional identity for them, ufology covers a variety of viewpoints and the reader needs a scorecard to recognize the players. The following list is based on a subjective perception of some key types that participate in UFO conventions, discussions, and literature, along with their interests, perspectives, and agendas. The types are ideals, whereas in reality the characteristics often mix in individualistic ways:

Scientific Ufologists.—For this group UFOs are a phenomenon accessible to rational inquiry. These people pursue in-depth case investigations, critical examination of evidence, comparison of collected data, and rigorous research projects to determine if any UFO reports describe an unknown phenomenon. Scientific ufology aims to prove or disprove an evidential basis for the UFO phenomenon rather than to find meanings in it. Exemplified by Hynek and McDonald, professed by the leading UFO organizations, this scientific approach represents ufology in the purest sense of a scientific or scholarly discipline.

Explorers.—A larger and more impetuous group than the scientific ufologists, explorers care about evidence but only insofar as it supports their beliefs. The explorer is to ufology what Indiana Jones is to archaeology—a treasure hunter eager to bring home the prize rather than a systematic excavator attentive to every detail. UFOs excite these people and motivate them to investigate, research, and debate. They are often the most active members of organizations and are responsible for much of the expansiveness of the field, always plunging toward new avenues of support and quick to draw a connection between other mysteries and UFOs. The critical discipline to give negative evidence its due may get lost in the shuffle as explorers hurry from case to case and from issue to issue in selective pursuit of proof for their chosen theory.

Interested Followers.—This group consists of the consumers rather than the producers of ufology. Here belong the people who join organizations, attend conferences, and read the literature with a keen interest in whatever is going on in the field, but these individuals support rather than contribute directly to investigation and research. This rank and file shapes ufology, since what they want to hear influences speaker selection for conferences and articles published in UFO magazines. The breadth of the field reflects the broad interests of these members.

Activists.—Some people have grown impatient with the gathering of evidence. They regard the existence of UFOs and their extraterrestrial origin as established facts and care only about the implications of alien visitation. Some of these people consider the social consequences of alien contact. Others regard a government "truth embargo" as the real impediment to mainstream recognition for UFOs, then try to wrest UFO information out of recalcitrant agencies or convince Congress to take the initiative. The philosophical and political orientation of activists sets them far apart from the research interests of scientific ufologists.

Specialists.—The people who concentrate on one aspect of ufology are sometimes helpful and sometimes harmful to the field. At the positive end belong people whose prior training or long practical experience equips them to undertake skillful investigations of matters like abductions, Roswell, or ground-trace cases. At the negative end are people who claim expertise and special knowledge of doubtful validity or promote unfounded claims and favorite speculations with the relentless insistence of cranks. With so many conspiracies, wooly theories, and wild claims so prominent in the public image of ufology, the dedication of some specialists to their cause does much damage to the field.

Interlopers.—One type of specialist enters the UFO field for a while, promotes some special interest, and then leaves. Several academic psychologists have studied abductions, but only for their help in illuminating a problem like false memory, and some conspiracy theorists have wrung UFOs for aspects of government secrecy and then moved on. The loyalty of interlopers lies with some other subject, and their UFO commitment lasts only as long as it serves their primary interest.

These groups can be said to participate in ufology since they contribute directly or indirectly to its primary activities and discourse, but ufologists represent the core of a broader population of believers. An extensive penumbra of *passive believers* surrounds the active proponents and advocates. Passive believers may read an occasional UFO article or book, or watch a TV documentary now and then, but UFOs are no more than a casual interest, certainly not a scholarly study, hobby, or obsession. Yet this superficial acquaintance may lead these people to affirm a belief in UFOs for an opinion poll or respond in casual conversation that there is "something to" them, thereby insulating the subject from official hostility and media jests with a widespread social willingness to give UFOs the benefit of the doubt. Believers also include the *metaphysical seekers*, a group recognized by sociologists as engaged in an active quest for satisfying spiritual ties outside of conventional religion and likely to experiment with a succession of alternatives such as UFOs and New Age beliefs.[23] Seekers have little interest in UFO phenomena but listen to messages from the Space Brothers, channelers, or prophets. The cacophonous voices from believers of every stripe sum up popular support for UFOs as real in some sense and a matter of abiding interest.

Skeptics.—To counterbalance the believers, there are the disbelievers, the skeptics and debunkers who attack UFOs as a social delusion. Some active skeptics like Menzel and Klass find conventional solutions for specific cases, and these findings have supported a general skeptical thesis that the only strangeness in UFOs belongs to human error, imagination, and hoaxes. The philosophical objections of skepticism blame the preference for fanciful ideas over rational answers on a widespread, uncritical will to believe, and frown on beliefs like UFOs, creationism, and astrology for corroding social commitment to science and reason. Like ufologists, the skeptics organize to promote their cause and keep close watch on what they regard as the offenses of UFO believers.

Critics.—Also like ufologists, skeptics belong to a larger community. Not all doubts about UFOs lead to blanket rejection but rather to questions about a particular case, bit of evidence, line of argument, or interpretation. The critics who do not reject UFOs as a philosophical creed nevertheless expect convincing evidence and continue to doubt because they have not found sufficient reason to change their minds. Another basis for criticism is an alternate belief, as some conspiracy theorists allege that alien abductions are not alien at all but illusions resulting from government thought-control experiments. The disbelief of skeptics and critics belongs within the circle of UFO discourse as a necessary opposition, an incitement for believers to be aware of their beliefs, a reminder that not everyone shares them, and a challenge to defend the faith. Disbelief maintains the dynamism of belief by sustaining controversy and dispute.

Experiencers.—Alongside believers and disbelievers, but not automatically identifiable with one or the other camp, travels another important group—the people who claim to have witnessed UFOs. Many people trace their interest in UFOs to a personal experience, among them such prominent ufologists as Leonard Stringfield, Richard Hall, Walt Andrus, and Budd Hopkins, though experience does not automatically create converts. Nobel Prize–winning biochemist Kary Mullis had a bizarre abduction-like experience but did not accept UFOs because of it. Many ordinary people without his credentials also compartmentalize the experience, certain that something strange happened but unwilling to commit to any solution. The experience remains memorable and puzzling but without an identity. Folklorists studying supernatural experiences have discovered that a direct question like, "Have you ever seen a ghost?" will likely draw out nothing more than a shake of the head and a denial, whereas an indirect question like, "What do you know about the stranger side of life?" may open up a wealth of memories about apparent psychic and paranormal experiences.[24] In my experience, to ask, "Who has seen a UFO?" usually wins fewer responses than the inquiry, "Who has seen something strange in the sky?" UFOs share with ghosts the status of a socially stigmatized subject, and some people may hedge their opinions to avoid ridicule, but for others the uncertainty expresses a straightforward, well-judged position. For them the implicit social identity that equates UFO with space visitor may specify too much. They may want more evidence or prefer another identity, since one person's spaceship may be another's angel or omen.

Insiders.—A special kind of experiencer has risen to prominence in recent years, an individual who claims privileged information about UFOs. This information usually concerns inside access to military or other governmental sources and serves to confirm allegations like crashes, alien bodies, secret projects, high-level interest, or interaction with extraterrestrials. Insiders typically support the most sensational UFO beliefs, but with claims that are hard to establish and doubtful. The bearers may enjoy a brief period of celebrity within the UFO community then fall into disrepute.

This diverse cast of characters deploys around almost any UFO issue. A well-publicized case like the O'Hare incident brought out scientific ufologists interested primarily in the sighting, but others emphasized the apparent cover-up, and the same story served other interests as subject for meditations on the purpose of UFO visitation or incitement for the government to release its UFO secrets. Different approaches join with varied opinions as a reminder of the inherent heterogeneity of ufology. The range of thinking about UFOs is broad and often surprising, with seemingly foregone conclusions not at all welcomed by everyone. Some ufologists dispute the extraterrestrial hypothesis, some dismiss abductions or Roswell, some are as harsh as skeptics in criticizing evidence or theory, and others argue with passion for some personal notion about the identity or purpose of UFOs.

Many voices have a say in ufology and urge it along different, even opposing directions, but they all shape the discourse. The divisions have grown more acute since the mid-1980s in absence of any one respected authority to speak for the field, and with a proliferation of controversial UFO-related claims to further complicate treating ufology as a unitary whole in any meaningful sense. One solution is to abandon any effort to treat the subject in collective terms and surrender to its inner diversity, though at a cost of rendering discussion cumbersome. Another solution is to favor the best work in the field, perhaps the most scientific and scholarly efforts; but this approach omits so much of what happens in ufology that the result bears little resemblance to reality. A more feasible alternative seeks out representative positions. The breadth of ufological thinking is considerable, but this variety distorts the everyday practice of most participants. Majority opinion typically clusters into a narrow band of understandings of UFOs as mechanical devices, extraterrestrial spaceships known as such by a government that hides the truth. As evidence that these notions enjoy a dominant position, they not only have long historical standing but also underlie the most active trends and interests in current ufology—disclosure, exopolitics, crash-retrievals, and abductions. These same ideas pervade convention lectures, magazine articles, popular books, TV presentations, and images of UFOs in mass and popular culture. Various dissidents prefer a paranormal or evil-government solution, but they tend to be elite or fringe thinkers with a limited following, and even their denials of the extraterrestrial hypothesis still count as recognition of its centrality in ufological thinking.

The idea of extraterrestrial UFOs belongs to the realm of what can best be termed "popular ufology." Critics both inside and outside the field may deride this image as naive or a caricature, but it is representative of how the general public, the mass media, and a majority of people with an interest in the subject understand UFOs. Popular ufology identifies a normative expression of "what ufologists believe" based on ideas that have attracted widespread attention and enthusiasm. The results do not necessarily express the best that the field has to offer, and they include even embarrassing or improbable elements that most serious ufologists reject, such as 1950s contactees or modern-day exopolitics.

Few individuals are likely to subscribe to all the elements of popular ufology, but its broad scope prescribes the content of the field without value judgments and avoids disputes over how to separate fringe from core or mainstream concepts. Such restraint is timely given that the evidence-based, rigorous brand of ufology that Hynek advocated has fallen somewhat out of favor today, or if still paid lip service no longer corresponds to the bulk of ufological activity. Such groups as NARCAP and some individuals continue to practice scientific ufology, but the pursuits that now occupy center stage show less regard to painstaking establishment of an unconventional phenomenon than to attributing meanings and purposes to less-than-firm evidence. If the popular image is unflattering from scientific and scholarly viewpoints, at least it reflects realities rather than ideals.

Another reason to favor popular ufology as the most representative version of the field is the possibility of defining it in objective terms. Prescribing what makes up the best of ufology or its mainstream risks an irreconcilable clash of individual opinions; delineating the popular trends of the field requires only consultations of its literature as a matter of record. Magazines, books, and organizational newsletters document the history of thinking about UFOs, augmented now by a proliferation of Web sites and TV documentaries. Jerome Clark's comprehensive *UFO Encyclopedia* provides a scholarly discussion of many of the topics that have held some sort of place within ufology over six decades. One of the most valuable barometers of the state of affairs in ufology is the annual symposium of the Mutual UFO Network (MUFON). At each convention the speakers cover a cross section of issues in the field, while forty years of symposium proceedings preserve the prevailing interests and changing beliefs from year to year. These sources provide concrete evidence for the subject matter of ufological thought.

Scientific and popular ufology often stand in opposition, the one dedicated to an objective understanding of the phenomenon, the other concerned with subjective understanding of what UFOs mean. This book will usually defer to popular ideas as the only way to manage generalizations about ufology and the best way to uncover the human meanings of UFOs. Not everyone will be happy with this choice, but it represents the field of ufology in its broadest sense and also in terms that are demonstrable and supportable by reference to documentation. At the same time it bears repeating that popular ideas are far from unanimous and not necessarily representative of ufological thinking at its best. Scientific ufology will serve as a necessary check to popular trends, while skeptical explanations, particularly the psychosocial approach, provide a conventional challenge to the unconventional premises of ufology.

A basic task for this book is to distinguish the human contribution to UFO narratives. Comparison of UFO stories with types of narratives not directly associated with UFOs can reveal continuities of human thinking, but useful indications must consist of significant patterns rather than mere isolated likenesses. Perhaps the most telling patterns in human interest lie at the thematic level. A theme implies that multiple clues converge to support a single idea, and a theme of UFO thinking reveals itself when varied descriptive and interpretive texts repeat a similar complex of ideas. Three thematic complexes recur with noteworthy insistence in UFO literature. The extraterrestrial hypothesis and conspiracy theories stand out as favored and fundamental tenets, expressed in some form or other with almost every breath. A third theme draws UFOs into the ongoing cultural love-hate relationship with technology. The expressions are less explicit perhaps than with the other two themes, yet UFO discourse often mirrors some aspect of this ambivalence. Much UFO thinking is structured around these themes, but they extend well beyond ufology. A search for continuities will find the patterns of UFO thought echoed in other contemporary cultural contexts—for example, in an isomorphic relationship between abductions and the recent panic over satanic ritual abuse. Historical antecedents expand this dimension—for example, when representations of witchcraft, Jewish blood sacrifices, or anti-Catholic propaganda from the 1840s share thematic continuities with both abduction and ritual abuse.

These continuities hint that the meanings attributed to UFOs do not emerge as a natural outgrowth of observation but from human needs and concerns. If the same themes form similar complex patterns in various contexts with different content, this recurrence betrays a cultural origin. Such patterns do not belong solely to one set of observations but exist as independent intellectual entities, able to assimilate diverse materials and adapt to different subjects yet still maintain a recognizable integrity. This book will attempt to show that these patterns are not just afterthoughts attached to a factual base but active organizing principles, cultural tools of thought that reshape observational facts to conform to established meanings.

Popular ufology will provide the most detailed evidence for human thought about UFOs. Evidence for the image of the subject outside of ufology will come from all layers of culture. At the folk level are the narratives of witnesses and opinions of everyday citizens, and at the elite level is the treatment of UFOs by scientists, scholars, and the news media. The appearance of UFOs in mass and popular culture holds particular value because imagination has freedom to play with the subject and realize its what-ifs in cartoons, movies, and science fiction literature. A search for comparative material can pursue social issues with evident superficial similarities, like accounts of satanic ritual abuse that share with abductions the claims of kidnap, molestation, fantastic circumstances, and repressed memories. Deeper follow-ups into religion, mythology, and folklore will find suggestive antecedents in traditional interactions with supernatural beings and otherworld journeys. Whether or not these parallels say anything about the nature of UFO experience, they say that similar patterns of thought organize the descriptive expressions of various unrelated subjects, and distinguishing these patterns identifies intersections of culture with UFOs.

The first chapter will argue that thinking about UFOs can be understood as the creation of a myth. This identity does not pass judgment on the reality of the phenomenon but proposes that UFO thinking follows a distinctive strategy for the construction of understanding, one that builds a complex and self-sustaining image of reality but serves human purposes over straightforward historical truth.

Chapter 2 outlines a history to trace how key characteristics of UFO knowledge have emerged and how they have developed into a mythology. Chapter 3 broadens the perspective to examine a "prehistory" of strange sights in the sky, the various eras when those objects were supernatural aerial prodigies, natural anomalies of science, or technological mysteries like the phantom airships of the 1890s. These reports reflect the power of changing expectations to reshape what people see and bring into sharp relief the human contribution to observation.

Each of the next four chapters treats one of the themes of the UFO myth. In the fourth chapter the subject, taken in its broadest form, is the relationship of humans with the otherworld. Far from being a modern invention, the notion of extraterrestrials belongs to ancient cosmologies, philosophical speculations about the plurality of worlds, and scientific debates over canals on Mars and dying planets. Ideas of the modern alien evolved from the supernatural beings of religion, mythology, and folklore, and from travelers' tales that envisioned faraway places as habitations of outlandish creatures. Science fiction carried these principles of the imagination outward to the stars. These prior conceptions not only prepared the way for the extraterrestrial hypothesis but also provided patterns now visible in ufological thinking. The fifth chapter treats the minor theme of the space children—that is, stories of human children imperiled or improved in fantastic ways by contact with beings that are alien in some sense—as a case example of mythic structures organizing UFO narratives even in their smaller aspects.

Chapter 6 considers the extremes of positive and negative expectations associated with UFOs. Fears of invasion in the 1950s have continued in apprehensions over personal safety from abductions, and early concerns about military censorship have escalated from rumors that a super-secret agency hides the Roswell crash to alarms that the government colludes with aliens to create a totalitarian New World Order. These UFO versions parallel concurrent fears, such as Soviet attack in the 1950s and the child abuse panic of the 1980s, and entangle with conspiracy theories that an evil government threatens to destroy liberty and control the world. On the hopeful side, UFOs fulfill the wishes of people who welcome aliens as heavenly saviors. The 1950s contactees preached that Space Brothers came to rescue the earth from cold war dangers, but hope has sprouted as well from the uncongenial soil of abductions as some abductees report not just harrowing experiences but also life-changing encounters that promise to transform all mankind. Such ideas update historical patterns of thought found in apocalyptic and millenarian beliefs, in recurrent scares over subversive outsiders like witches, immigrants, and Communists, and in expectations of a better world that have taken both sacred and secular form over the years.

Chapter 7 recognizes UFO narratives as a theater where tensions between Self and Other play out. UFOs exemplify advanced technology but also echo deep and ongoing social divisions over whether technology is a progressive force beneficial to mankind or a destructive form of hubris. The alien from space is an exemplary Other that embodies earthly misgivings over the value of intellect, whether it leads to the wise and benevolent Space Brothers or the gray, soulless technocrats of abduction accounts. These thematic patterns of UFO thought revive prior conflicts over nature versus culture, the wild versus the tamed, and savagery versus civilization in, for example, the Romantic call for a return to nature and the environmentalist rejection of an overly technological society. Though aliens are the vehicle, they only disguise the fact that important parts of UFO discourse represent not visitors from outside but inner issues like how to define self, our human possibilities, and a proper life for mankind.

The two final chapters wrestle with how to explain UFOs. Chapter 8 examines the reach of psychological, social, and cultural contributions as solutions to the mystery, but chapter 9 reckons the shortcomings of human causes to find a reminder that something is left over after all: that besides the meanings imposed on UFOs, traces of an independent phenomenon remain. In the end a construction of human imagination and cultural meaning cannot explain UFOs, but the answer must factor in experience as essential to understand the origin, shape, and persistence of the UFO stories people tell.

For the sake of truth in advertising and to warn the reader of possible conflicts of interest, I will step out from behind the curtain of scholarly anonymity and declare where I stand. I have never seen a UFO or had any sort of anomalous experience. My awareness of UFOs began through the mass-culture route by watching 1950s science-fiction movies; grew to a fascination as I read anything I could find about the subject in newspapers, magazines, and books; and progressed to a long-term commitment by the 1960s as I became a member of NICAP and APRO, the leading ufological organizations of the era. Years later in graduate school when I needed a dissertation topic, I was fortunate to have my old interest and more fortunate still that the Indiana University Folklore Institute supported research into such a dubious subject. After receiving my doctorate I continued with research into phantom airships and UFO abductions. I have been a member of the Mutual UFO Network (MUFON) and the British UFO Research Organization (BUFORA), and I serve on the board of the J. Allen Hynek Center for UFO Studies (CUFOS) and the Fund for UFO Research (FUFOR). As an insider of sorts I have been privileged to hear experiencers tell their stories and to watch leading ufologists at work, to see the length and breadth of the field, its fine spots and its potholes. I would like to find aliens, all the more so as one of a disappointed generation that expected colonies on the moon and expeditions to Mars by now but found instead that the future was a wasteland of unimaginative politicians.

In the end I side with the believers. My conclusion is not based on personal preference but on familiarity with the evidence. Much of it is sloppy, ambiguous, and unsatisfactory, to be sure; and ufology is a fine mess, crowded with charlatans, true believers, gullibility, and unsubstantiated claims. But for all the human interests and human errors beclouding the subject, I still recognize some substance beneath the clutter. A distinctive and genuinely mysterious phenomenon appears in usually fleeting, sometimes startling glimpses out of the morass of reports. I will not hazard an explanation for UFOs or insist they come from Zeta Reticuli, but I accept J. Allen Hynek's conclusion that "there exists a phenomenon, described by the contents of UFO reports . . . , that is worthy of systematic rigorous study," and "the body of data points to an aspect of the natural world not yet explored by science."[25] I will go further and say that enough threads of coherent experience exist to reject cultural explanations as less than the whole story, though cultural influences contribute much to our interest in the phenomenon even as they do much to confuse our understanding of it. Both sides deserve the serious attention they have never received.

CHAPTER ONE

Who Goes There?
The Myth and the Mystery of UFOs

The earth hath bubbles, as the water has, and these are of them.
—Shakespeare, *Macbeth*

We don't see things as they are; we see things as we are.
—Anaïs Nin

UFOs have come to mean many things to many people. Reports of UFOs, curiosity about their nature and purpose, theories and speculations, disputes and controversies spiral outward until the subject breaks free of narrow scientific considerations. UFOs fly in an atmosphere of implication and possibility as objects of the imagination, subjects for entertainment, humor, commerce, popular belief, and a mystery with something of interest even for people unmoved by aliens or spaceships. One consequence of human interest is human participation in construction of the UFO story. Whether these participants narrate experience or discuss meaning, they relate more than an unvarnished account of a phenomenon. They add and take away, slant and interpret, as they assimilate it into meaningful history. A few illustrations demonstrate how the interplay of the phenomenon with its human treatment leads to a complex and sometimes unequal partnership.

A Gallery of Cases

What's in a Name?—Kenneth Arnold was a traveling salesman for modern times. Thirty-two years old in 1947, he already owned his own company and piloted his small airplane throughout the Pacific Northwest, selling, distributing, and installing fire control equipment. He served customers in remote rural areas, which familiarized him not only with the art of landing in cow pastures but also with most sights in the sky. The afternoon of June 24, 1947, was clear and beautiful as he took off from Chehalis, Washington, on his way to Yakima. Arnold spent an hour searching the glaciers and gorges of Mount Rainier for a crashed military transport plane, turning eastward toward the mountain about 3 P.M. at an altitude of 9,200 feet. Almost as soon as he set this new course a bright flash chilled him with fear that he was about to collide with another aircraft. Instead he spotted a chain of nine flat objects north of Rainier and flying southward. Every few seconds one or more of the objects flipped on its side to reflect the sun, as if it were made of polished metal. Silhouetted against the mountain snow, the objects appeared heel-like, with the rounded edge forward and the rear edge slightly pointed, though one object differed from the rest and seemed crescent in shape. The tailless objects resembled no aircraft he had ever seen, and he suspected some new type of experimental jet, a notion reinforced when he timed their passage as they flew in and out among the mountain peaks from Rainier to Mount Adams and calculated an amazing speed of 1,200 miles per hour (Chuck Yeager would not break the sound barrier for another four months). The objects flew south until out of sight beyond Mount Adams after less than three minutes of observation.[1]

The more he mulled over the speed and appearance of these objects, the more puzzled Arnold became. He talked over his experience with other pilots when he landed in Yakima, and the next morning in Pendleton, Oregon, he told his story to Bill Bequette, a young reporter for the *East Oregonian*. Bequette sent out a report over the United Press wire service and Arnold's sighting landed on front pages all over the country. In trying to describe the flipping, jerking motion of the objects, Arnold compared them to a rock or a saucer skipping across water. Before long news writers condensed this description of motion into a vivid and visually suggestive name for the objects themselves. They became flying saucers, springing full-grown into public awareness as an intriguing new expectation of things to see in the sky.[2]

Arnold's sighting was far from the last. For two weeks flying saucers became a nationwide craze, starting with a few sightings then multiplying into the hundreds on the Fourth of July. Reports increased until the seventh and took a precipitous drop after the eighth, while by mid-month flying saucers had lost their news value and largely disappeared from the public eye.[3] Ufologist Ted Bloecher found some 850 reports in 140 major newspapers around the country, while systematic searches of smaller newspapers have raised the tally to several thousand, largely concentrated into a five-day period.[4]

Throughout the furor newspapers kept up a constant drumbeat of references to flying "saucers" and flying "disks." A great many observers obliged by describing flat, round objects, though they were often seen at such a distance that they appeared as mere specks in the sky, and any designation as a saucer was honorary rather than accurate. Yet many of the best reports also included fine examples of the saucer shape. On July 4 Captain E. J. Smith, a pilot for United Airlines, was about to take off from Boise, Idaho, to Seattle when someone asked him what he thought about flying saucers. "I'll believe them when I see them," he answered; a few minutes later, he did. Just after 9 P.M. Smith and his copilot spotted four large circular objects flying in formation against the evening sky, appearing flat on the bottom and rough on top. A stewardess confirmed the objects before they disappeared to the northwest, then another formation of similar objects appeared on the left for several minutes before flying off. Most of Bloecher's cases where shape is mentioned favor terms like disk, plate, pancake, coin— by any name something like a saucer.[5]

The disk shape had appeared from time to time in illustrations for science fiction and on the cover of magazines like *Popular Science* to depict futuristic aviation designs, but images of round craft enjoyed no special favor in mass or popular culture, and the jet plane or rocket ship image was the odds-on favorite when reports simply reflected widespread cultural expectations. Some ufologists regard Kenneth Arnold standing at the pivot between a saucerless past and a disk-infested future as reason to think a genuine visitation of spaceships began in 1947. Skeptics reject that supposition because a telling "uh-oh" factor spoils the argument—after all, Arnold may have started the flying saucer craze, but he neither saw nor spoke of flying saucers. What he reported were heel-shaped objects, but what the public heard through the press, thanks to a moment of creative license, was an ever-so-suggestive name, and no sooner was it coined than countless descriptions repeated it to the exclusion of all others. This is clearly an odd way for aliens to behave. Skeptic Martin Kottmeyer points out how unlikely it would be for them to reconfigure their spaceships according to popular expectation, yet how natural for fantasies and errors to reflect a novel and exciting cultural belief. To state the case in strongest terms, either UFOs suddenly conformed to the saucer image as soon as it emerged or a new popular belief imposed itself on the observational claims of thousands of people. Kottmeyer argues that taken as a critical test, the 1947 wave demonstrates the direct causative influence of a journalistic error and proves that flying saucers took shape in inner rather than outer space.[6]

Some critics are ready to declare victory at this point and overlook another twist the story has in store. The flying saucers of 1947 represent a stereotype entrenched in the newspaper version where writers insisted on the flying disk image irrespective of observers' statements. Sometimes far down the column in a big-city paper, sometimes only in the small local press do the real observations step out from behind the smooth, shiny saucer image to reveal nuances of individuality at odds with the wording of headlines and leading paragraphs. A few reports describe objects that are not disk shaped at all but cylindrical, conical, spherical, oval, V-shaped, and even resembling a propeller. Some disks include fins, domes, and projections, others present the appearance of a thick or convex disk, a sight like an overturned washtub, or, in the report of a young private pilot flying over North Carolina, a form like a squashed barrel. While most 1947 flying saucers lived up to their given name without need of help, newspaper articles rounded off differences in the remaining accounts until every strange object in the sky became a flying saucer in spite of itself. Yet a reading of what observers actually said reveals a degree of variety within the aerial armada of 1947 and displaces some of the burden of cultural influence from the observers and onto the media, where, then as now, considerable weight truly belongs.[7]

Just for Fun.—When officials worried over weapons of mass destruction during the buildup to war with Iraq in late 2002, they overlooked an even more fearsome danger awaiting our troops at the hands of Saddam Hussein. An alarm sounded on a UFO Web site in mid-December with stories that a U.S. fighter shot down a UFO in 1998 or during the Gulf War of 1990–1991 and the Iraqi military hid the surviving aliens from capture by the Americans. Since then the aliens' technology had provided the Iraqis with advanced weapons capable of defeating any earthly enemy, the most impressive example being a pack of bioengineered scorpions the size of cows. The Russian newspaper *Pravda*, once the staid official voice of the Soviet Union but now effectively a tabloid, picked up the UFO story at the end of January and added a tissue of rumors from Arab journalists and a Russian colonel, who claimed to have examined the wreckage of a circular craft with three seats designed for occupants the size of children. Then came the war, and by miraculous good fortune no soldiers tangled with Saddam's giant scorpions—so far as we know.[8]

Wheels within Wheels.—The Million Man March of October 16, 1995, may have fallen short of its name in terms of actual numbers; estimates of half that total are probably closer to the truth. Yet this vast gathering in Washington more than lived up to its spirit as countless African American men pledged themselves to the spiritual, economic, and social improvement of themselves, their families, and their communities. A social action seemingly so benign in its goals nevertheless met with widespread suspicion because the chief promoter was Louis Farrakhan, head of the Nation of Islam, or Black Muslims, an often inflammatory advocate of racial separatism and a leader forever embroiled in controversy for his extremist views. Farrakhan sees reality in ways all his own. The world reflected in Nation of Islam doctrine is a battleground where oppressive white conspirators hold black people in bondage and an apocalyptic reckoning is nigh when Allah destroys the white race as the source of all evil.

UFOs sailed into the publicity buildup for the upcoming march in a speech by Farrakhan on September 17. Initially enthusiastic listeners fell silent and shifted uneasily in their seats when he announced that his inspiration came from a vision of a UFO flying him to a mother ship, where he received messages from the deceased founder of the Nation of Islam, Elijah Muhammad.[9] Ideas about spaceships had circulated among the leadership of the sect for decades. Elijah Muhammad's mentor and cofounder of the Nation of Islam was Fard Muhammad, who announced in the 1930s that the Japanese had built an enormous airplane called the Mother Plane (or Mother of Planes, Mother Ship, or Mother Wheel), and it would soon release a fleet of smaller airplanes to destroy all white people in America with poison bombs.[10] Elijah Muhammad elaborated on this great airplane, saying in 1965 that this Mother of Planes is

> one-half mile by a half mile and is the largest man-made object in the sky. It is a small human planet made for the purpose of destroying the present world of the enemies of Allah.... The finest brains were used to build it. It is capable of staying in outer space six to twelve months at a time without coming into the earth's gravity. It carried fifteen hundred bombing planes with most deadly explosives—the type used in bringing up mountains on earth. The very same method is to be used in the destruction of this world.[11]

The Mother Plane is oval or circular and the smaller "baby" planes are round; perhaps, Elijah Muhammad said, they are the flying saucers so often reported. As Nation of Islam mythology evolved, it replaced the Japanese with God and a council of twenty-four imams, alternately identified as black scientists and as builders of the great ship. A rebel scientist in this group created the white race by selective breeding and thereby introduced demons into the divine order, an offense the Mother Plane would stamp out in the last days.[12]

The keynote for the Mother Plane was Ezekiel's Wheel in the Bible, its symbolism at once preserved as an eschatological destroyer of evil and reinterpreted to subvert traditional Judeo-Christian meanings. In Nation of Islam doctrine, the Judeo-Christian tradition is inauthentic and evil, the enemy of the black man's true religion, Islam; yet the power of white man's science appears desirable enough to incorporate into the basic creed of the sect. As this creed translates old myths into new, it stakes a claim on the white man's technology as in fact the rightful invention and property of the black man. Nation of Islam doctrine is a fluid synthesis of religious supernaturalism and technological materialism to serve the guiding principles of a movement dedicated to black supremacy and hostility toward the Western worldview. This changing belief system adapts UFOs here as physical objects, there as visionary images, and then again as a reworking of biblical prophecy, while at the same time borrowing UFO sightings as confirmation of belief and UFO abductions as a model for Louis Farrakhan's visions.

Fortune Favors the Prepared Mind . . . and So Do UFOs.—A genuine spaceship flashed through the skies over nine states from the Midwest to the East Coast on the night of March 3, 1968. Two or three gleaming starlike lights began the course and several more appeared by the end. This promising story takes a disappointing turn when the craft proves Soviet rather than extraterrestrial, the *Zond IV* moon probe burning in the upper atmosphere a hundred miles high after an unsuccessful attempt to leave orbit; but reports to the UFO investigative unit of the Air Force, Project Blue Book, offer exceptional insight into eyewitness conceptions and how they leave their mark on descriptions.

About thirty of seventy-eight reports include detailed descriptions, a mixture of accurate, subtly inaccurate, and grossly distorted accounts. Twenty of the witnesses providing extended details reported no sound, and only one thought he heard something. Twelve people suggested outright that the objects were meteors or space debris reentry, and the same number correctly reported straight, uniform motion. Many inaccuracies belong to categories of poor choice of words, like the seventeen references to the lights flying in "formation" when a less suggestive term like "pattern" would serve better, or to typical human difficulties in estimating altitude, speed, and size. The serious inaccuracies are more varied. Seven people claimed to see rocket, cigar, or saucer-shaped objects, six spoke of a change in direction, three called the lights windows, and two implied the lights were attached to a dark body.[13]

When conception goes astray, it can lead an observation very, very far off the mark. A Tennessee witness who watched the reentry with her husband and the local mayor illustrates the potential for extreme error in an account based on misconception. According to her report, they saw a silent, lighted object approach directly toward them.

> It was shaped like a fat cigar. . . . It appeared to have square-shaped windows. . . . For an instant, I thought I caught a glimpse of a metallic look about the fuselage. . . . It appeared to me that the fuselage was constructed of many pieces of flat sheets of metal-like material with a "riveted together look. . . ." The many "windows" seemed to be lit up from the inside of the fuselage with light that was quite bright. . . . From out of the back end . . . came a wide . . . long, reddish-orangish-yellowish stream of dusty fire.[14]

Another fantastic litany of distortions fills a report from Indiana:

> The object flew at about tree-top level and was seen very clearly since it was just a few yards away. All of the observers saw a long jet airplane, looking like a vehicle without wings. It was on fire both in front and behind. All the observers observed many windows. . . . My cousin said "If there had been anybody in the UFO near the windows, I would have seen them."[15]

Here is proof beyond any shadow of a doubt that a spectacular UFO experience does not require the attendance of a spectacular UFO. Sometimes the truth is not out there but in ourselves, in beliefs so powerful they reshape a conventional sight into the image of expectation.

Spirits of the Times.—In modern Western culture mysterious flying or luminous objects and strange beings usually find their way into the UFO file whether or not they fit comfortably within the spaceship category. We face a dearth of credible alternatives now that the supernatural has fallen into disrepute, while UFOs have become acceptable enough to seem inevitable in such a scenario. The fact remains that UFOs represent a cultural category defined by the ideas of our time, place, and background. A reminder of this cultural confinement occurred near Mutare, Zimbabwe, on August 15, 1981. The phenomenology is UFO-like yet ill-suited to the usual notion of alien activity, while the explanation of the witness breaks with a technological solution to express the belief configuration of a traditional culture.

Twenty workers returning from the fields watched a luminous sphere about one and a half meters in diameter roll across the ground. Terrified women gathered their children and fled into the bush. The ball reached an observation tower and seemed to climb the three stories to the top, then appeared to burst into flames. Clifford Muchena, a foreman, rang the fire bell but the luminous ball gathered itself together and descended to the ground again and once more appeared to burst into flames. Muchena saw three men observing the flames and ran toward them, assuming his boss was one of the three. They turned to the sound of Muchena's call, and he realized they were strangers in every sense. Tall and luminous, they wore silver suits, and a power from them caused him to fall to the ground, where he lay until aware that the light and the men were gone.

Muchena had heard of astronauts but had never seen a picture of one and did not credit the claim that anyone had visited the moon. He knew nothing of UFOs. At the same time, he had a ready explanation for the men—they were spirits of his ancestors. When investigator Cynthia Hind pointed out that his ancestors would wear hides and crocodile teeth instead of silvery suits, Muchena considered for a moment. "Yes," he answered, "but times change!"[16]

What a Tangled Web We Weave, without Even Trying to Deceive.—If feverish imaginations tried to dream up a UFO story as convincing as it is astonishing, they could hardly do better than the following: Choose a setting of utmost seriousness. Make it a Strategic Air Command (SAC) base and have the UFO trespass into forbidden airspace one night to hover over a nuclear missile silo. Let's make certain the UFO is spectacular, say an orange-lighted behemoth the size of a football field and close to the ground, lighting up the countryside with an unearthly glow. Alarms from electronic sensors signal an intrusion and Sabotage Alert Teams speed off to investigate. Big men with guns though they are, these soldiers refuse an order to press near the giant disk looming ahead because its presence completely unnerves them. The UFO soon begins to rise and radar picks up the object. Two jet interceptors race to the area, but the UFO suddenly blinks out. The jets circle for a while, but only when they depart does the object light up again. Ascending swiftly into the starry sky, the unknown blip disappears from radar at 200,000 feet. A good story needs a thrilling coda, so envision the next morning when inspection teams check out the missile and discover that the targeting computer underwent some mysterious reprogramming while the UFO hovered nearby.[17]

Just such a story exists not merely at the top of a proponent's wish list but also as part of UFO literature. The location is Malmstrom Air Force Base in Montana and the date is November 7, 1975. Who could ask for more compelling proof of UFO reality? The Malmstrom case has all the answers to beat down every doubt—or would, if the story bore anything like a resemblance to the facts. What the Malmstrom case proves with decisiveness is not the existence of UFOs but the readiness of fictitious UFO tales to spring up and displace the truth.

An intrusion did indeed occur at Malmstrom on this date, along with a series of incursions during late October and early November at other air bases—Loring in Maine, Wurtsmith in Michigan, Minot in North Dakota, and Falconbridge in Ontario.[18] Remarkably little publicity attended these incidents at the time. Montana was rife with UFO activity, and reports of a mystery helicopter hovering over a missile site prompted Air Force officials to cooperate with local law enforcement in investigation of strange lights and apparent cattle mutilations; but the wire services did not pick up stories from the Montana press, and UFO investigators, usually alert to any sort of suggestive activity, largely overlooked an exciting two weeks when UFOs entangled with national security. More than two years passed before the story became national news, and then the source was the *National Enquirer*. During the mid-1970s the notorious tabloid was attempting a serious presentation of UFO reports, but even on its best behavior few serious ufologists took this source very seriously. A Pentagon "leak" was the basis for the article, but its specific places and dates enabled ufologists to try out a new research tool, the Freedom of Information Act (FOIA), and their reward more than repaid the effort.[19]

Documents obtained through FOIA searches confirmed a spectacular series of incidents and led to a flurry of press interest. An article in the Sunday-supplement newspaper magazine, *Parade*, on December 10, 1978, provoked congressional questions. On January 14, 1979, the *New York Times* gave brief coverage to the FOIA findings but said nothing about the SAC base intrusions, focusing instead on the discovery of CIA interest in UFO surveillance over the years. A few days later a *Washington Post* article paid attention to the UFO aspect of the story and discussed the air base intrusions, but despite these revelations, the reporters failed to pursue any further investigations. Only on October 14 did mention of the air base intrusions appear in the *New York Times Magazine*, when it finally considered the story as news fit to print, four years after the fact.[20]

What the documents have to say about the Malmstrom case is at once remarkable and confusing. They confirm UFO sightings, but they spread over a week, from November 3 to November 10, with two tumultuous nights of extensive activity. On the seventh, an officer reported that he heard a sound like a helicopter and looked out a window to see an aircraft with red and white lights hovering ten to fifteen feet off the ground. Later that night alerts from four missile sites described a large red, orange, or yellow object, while at 5:03 A.M., personnel from one Launch Control Facility reported that light from this object illuminated the driveway. About an hour later one security team reported that an object seen through binoculars had lights arranged in no apparent pattern, while another object overhead also bore several small lights. Another team reported a UFO that seemed to extrude a dark tubular formation. All these objects appeared to ascend as the sun rose.

Unusual sightings resumed the following night when radar detected from one to seven objects at altitudes from 9,500 to 15,600 feet, traveling at speeds ranging from almost stationary to 150 knots. Four security teams reported a lighted object at an altitude of 300–1,000 feet and the sounds of a jet. Just before 1:00 A.M. two F-106 interceptors began a search for the intruders but had to remain at high altitude due to mountainous terrain. The fighters broke off their search at 1:50 A.M. after loss of ground radar contact and failure to spot anything from the air. At least one security team reported that, in an apparent cat-and-mouse game, the mystery lights went out when the jets approached and came on again once the jets departed. About 3:00 A.M.

one team reported that the lighted object increased speed to high velocity as it ascended and became indistinguishable from the stars.[21]

The terse military log entries are tantalizing for what they say and tormenting for what they leave out. We can read enough into the stingy details to know that Venus and Jupiter were the intruders in some of the cases, while the report of objects ascending as the sun rises is a classic description of stars or planets fading with the dawn. Earlier reports of intrusions at other air bases led to a heightened level of alert and primed security personnel to be overly vigilant, perhaps also to hear the F-106s as intruder aircraft. The radar reports are less easy to explain, though skeptics suggest that birds were responsible for the contacts. The cat-and-mouse game of the UFO suggests intelligent control and the skeptical solution—that the brightness of the jet exhaust from the interceptors dimmed astronomical bodies as a contrast effect—does not seem very persuasive. One description of the UFO includes several white lights separated from one red light by a distance of fifty yards, but this report leaves more questions than it answers, and no report provides a satisfying depth of description. When researchers asked for further documentation, they received the response that all other reports from the time of the incidents had been destroyed—surely a remarkable if not a criminal course of action, considering the security implications of any sort of intrusion involving these sensitive installations.[22]

Whatever else about the Malmstrom story dangles in uncertainty, there is no mistaking the glaring contrast between the documentary version and the version in UFO literature. No document reports that a security team balked before a UFO the size of a football field or that radar tracked anything to 200,000 feet. Nowhere do we read of interference with Minuteman missiles. Where do these sensational additions come from? The answer lies with filmmaker Linda Moulton Howe, whose research on cattle mutilations led to a prize-winning documentary, *A Strange Harvest*, first broadcast in 1980. She had no interest in mutilations in 1975, but one night her brother phoned her with some intriguing UFO hearsay from Malmstrom. He said that a huge UFO shone a light "brighter than daylight" on one of the missile silos; security guards refused to approach the object; jets attempted to intercept it, but it blinked out until they departed; and targeting information of a missile computer had changed. She later recognized the possible significance of these claims in connection with the concurrent cattle mutilation epidemic in Montana.[23]

Some of these rumors may have stemmed from memories of another intrusion at Malmstrom on March 16, 1967. In this case several security patrols allegedly spotted UFOs in the night, and one or more sizable objects hovered over missile sites. The men of one patrol reported a red glowing object parked just above the gate to a missile site

and a man suffered injury during the encounter, while members of another patrol decided not to fire at a UFO. Ten missiles went off alert in quick succession. Documents
recovered through FOIA requests confirm that a group of ICBMs became inoperable
and no reason for the failure was found despite extensive technical examinations. The
SAC termed the incident "cause for grave concern," but the role of UFOs remains undocumented. The only reference to UFOs describes them as a rumor with no foundation, since a security team questioned about the night of the missile incident asserted
that no unusual aerial activity took place. Most of the information about UFOs origi-
nates with an officer present in one of the missile command centers, but his testimony
came to light only after publicity about the 1975 Malmstrom incidents and remains the
word of a single individual.[24]

The documented aspects of the 1975 Malmstrom case remain intriguing but fragmentary. The most spectacular and clear-cut UFO incidents appear only in the UFO
literature. The documented and undocumented ends of this story fail to meet, but the
rumor of Malmstrom UFOs has settled deeper and deeper into the canon of UFO lore
as an established fact. Lawrence Fawcett and Barry J. Greenwood, two pioneer FOIA
researchers who publicized their findings in Clear Intent (1984), began their chapter
on Malmstrom with the story told by Linda Howe but identified her as the source
and then supplemented the account from recovered documents. Howe readily admitted that her information was hearsay. Those fine lines of distinction have faded with
retellings until the rumor now fronts as the truth in print and on the Internet, even in a
compendium of record like The UFO Evidence, Volume 2, and the UFO Briefing Document, a collection of the "best available evidence" presented to Congress in 1995.[25]

Malmstrom highlights the misfortune that many UFO stories are really two stories, one factual and one distorted with mythic elements. An intriguing account of air
base intrusions by UFOs remains to be told, whether the cause lies with alien invaders or maintainers of nuclear weapons confused by stars or military maneuvers to test
guard personnel for preparedness. The treatments at hand tell another story, one of
newspapers pursuing their own agendas, UFO writers substituting congenial rumors
for less riveting facts, and fictitious events gaining credit as substantive evidence of
alien visitation. In the realm of UFO belief this confusion of fact and fiction is not a
scandal so much as business as usual.

An Impractical Joker.—By 2 A.M. on September 3, 1965, Norman Muscarello's long
walk home was almost over. Eighteen years old and bound for Navy boot camp in three
weeks, he had sold his car and tried to hitchhike back to Exeter, New Hampshire, after
a visit to his girlfriend twelve miles away, but rides were few so late at night and he
walked most of the way. As he passed a field three miles from Exeter, a row of five red

flashing lights slanted at a sixty-degree angle emerged out of the woods and hovered low over the Clyde Russell farmhouse one hundred feet away. The lights flashed in rapid sequence—one, two, three, four, five, four, three, two, one—with only one light visible at a time and the entire cycle completed every two seconds. The brightness lighted up the surrounding area and prevented him from seeing if any solid object was behind the lights, but they remained together as they moved over a field, passed behind a second house and some trees, and then rose again with motions like a fluttering leaf. At one point the lights drew so near that Muscarello dived into a ditch for fear he would be hit. When they flew away into the field again, he ran to the Russell house and knocked on the door, but no one answered. When a car approached he flagged it down and rode to the Exeter police station after observing the lights for some fifteen minutes.

Impressed by Muscarello's agitation, the officer on duty radioed Officer Eugene Bertrand to investigate. At 1 A.M. Bertrand had found a frightened woman motorist stopped on the roadside and she reported that a large light had followed her, but he dismissed the incident; now a little before 3 A.M. he carried Muscarello back to the scene of his sighting. They saw nothing as they walked into the field, but shortly after dogs began to howl and livestock in a barn began to kick, Muscarello shouted and Bertrand turned to see the flashing lights rise from behind some trees. Bertrand described the lights as attached to an object as big as a barn and a hundred feet overhead. "It lit up the entire field, and two nearby houses turned completely red. It stopped, hovered, and turned on a dime." He likened the brightness of the lights to facing automobile headlights at close distance. When first seen, the object appeared to be the size of a baseball at arm's length; he compared the angular size to a grapefruit when the object was nearest. At one point the object approached and Bertrand prepared to draw his revolver but thought better of it. Fearing radiation burns, he pulled Muscarello back to the cruiser. Bertrand radioed the station and another officer, David Hunt, arrived in time to see the red lights as they flew off into the southeast at slow speed and always about a hundred feet above the ground, after being visible some ten minutes. The animals then quieted down again. The lights departed toward the town of Hampton, and a call to the police station from Hampton soon followed as an excited man reported that a UFO was chasing him.

The Exeter close encounter became an instant cornerstone UFO case, supported by the statements of Muscarello and the two police officers, investigated at length by ufologist Raymond E. Fowler and *Saturday Review* columnist John G. Fuller, who published the story of his inquiries in *Incident at Exeter* (1966). Fowler's report is included in the *Congressional Record* after a hearing on UFOs by the House Committee on Armed Services in 1966.[26] Efforts to explain the sighting have been no less diligent.

The Air Force Project Blue Book investigators proposed stars and planets viewed through a temperature inversion but soon dropped this solution in favor of aircraft on maneuvers from nearby Pease Air Force Base. Bertrand and Hunt countered the stars-and-planets explanation by pointing out that the night was clear and the lights were near the ground, while Bertrand had served four years in Air Force refueling operations and knew what aircraft looked like at night. A helicopter could not have been responsible because the UFO was silent, and the military maneuvers in question had ended by 2 A.M. Faced with the officers' objections, the Blue Book staff reclassified the sighting as unidentified. A newspaper reporter offered the answer that an advertising airplane was responsible, but Fowler found that the only aerial advertising company in the area had not flown its airplane between August 21 and September 10—and, anyway, what advertiser would fly so late that the only audience was owls and crickets?[27]

One reader of Fuller's *Incident at Exeter* was Philip J. Klass, an editor for the magazine *Aviation Week and Space Technology*. Klass noted that many of the Exeter-area UFOs reported in the fall of 1965 hovered near power lines and proposed that corona discharges from high-tension cables could explain the sightings. The Muscarello incident occurred near power lines but not over them, and Klass suggested that electric plasmas might separate from the wires and float some distance across the countryside,[28] though these proposals did not meet with support from technical experts. Fuller recorded in his book many Exeter-area UFOs from the autumn of 1965, and another skeptic, Robert Sheaffer, plotted the reported positions of these sightings against the locations of Jupiter and Venus for that season to find a strong correlation. Many UFOs not only shared location but also behaved like planets, slowly rising or setting and twinkling near the horizon. Astronomical bodies are responsible beyond a reasonable doubt for many of Fuller's cases,[29] but the Muscarello sighting stands apart with an abundance of detail that simply does not square with the Jupiter explanation. The planet can account for neither the systematic flashing of a series of lights nor a red color bright enough to bathe the surrounding buildings, while the movement of the UFO from near to far or above and below the surrounding trees bears no resemblance to the rising of a planet. Humans are capable of extremes in observational error, but in this case only by extremes of ignoring some testimony and force-fitting the rest can Jupiter even begin to serve.

Martin Kottmeyer puzzled over the fluttering and yawing motion of the UFO, its perpetual low altitude, its seeming willingness to attract attention, and the scarcity of other UFO reports describing lights with a similar angle and flash pattern. This Exeter object was quite an oddity even for a UFO—but not, he argues, for a kite. All these peculiarities fall into place if a prankster attached five strobe flashers to the string of a

large box kite and carried a battery to power them. A kite straining against the wind
would keep the lights at an angle, while the UFO's fluttering and diving motions are
characteristic of a kite.[30]

This proposal fits some aspects of the reports but raises its own host of objections.
With the road too deserted for Muscarello to hitch a ride, a practical joker chose an
impractical time of day for his pranks. Trees are the bane of the kite flier, but this fool-
hardy prankster was fortunate enough to fly his device over and among them without
any close encounters of the entangling kind. March is the month of kite flying for good
reason—strong and steady winds. According to weather records, a westerly breeze of
only five miles per hour was blowing that night, perhaps not impossible conditions
but certainly challenging for lifting a kite loaded with lights and wires off the ground.
The Exeter UFO changed places quite a bit, and with little wind to help, the operator
would have to run around with superhuman athleticism to shift the kite here and there
over hundreds of yards and finally off into the distance. So much vigorous motion also
would risk calling attention to the prankster in the illumination of his own lights. For
lights strung along the tether line of a kite to present an angle of sixty degrees, observers would have to view the lights from an orientation perpendicular to the plane, with
the kite always to the left or right of the observer. If the observer ever faced the angle
head-on or from the rear, the lights would stack up in a vertical line. This arrangement
never occurs in the reports yet seems unavoidable given the considerable movement of
both object and witnesses. Officer Bertrand's statement that the bottom lights pointed
forward when the object moved raises a final objection. A western wind would bear the
kite east from the tether point, so the uppermost light on the line would point farthest
eastward. Since the UFO moved off to the east, the upper light would lead if the object
were a kite, but Bertrand's description contradicts that expectation. How a solid object
could present the reported configuration is equally baffling, but for a string of reasons
the kite hypothesis fails to fly.[31]

The incident at Exeter leaves three lessons in its wake: newspaper accounts and
even a professional reporter like Fuller are prone to introduce errors, skeptics will
grasp at any solution as long as it is conventional, and some UFO reports hold onto
their strangeness even after critical examination.

The Myth in the Mystery

These examples only begin to enumerate the ways observations blend with ideas to create a human truth distinct from historical truth. The mystery starts with observations,

and whatever their source they ground UFOs on a platform of experience. At the same time, the examples make clear that the phenomenal elements combine with additions and modifications that originate in belief or interpretation. Stereotypes remake the verbal record at the expense of accuracy, fiction mixes with fact, and religious, political, or entertainment motives rewrite the story to serve purposes unrelated to observation. While human observers are quite good on the whole, some few are capable of extreme distortion. Most sobering of all, not even experience is pure but mediated by cultural frameworks so that perceptual and conceptual errors can confuse observation, expectations replace reality with imagined images, preconceptions shape memory and recall of events.

What these instances demonstrate is the possibility, even the likelihood, that human factors will intervene between an event and its representation. Many people have internalized UFOs so that they exist in imagination as if they belonged to the physical world. True or false, a UFO experience remains profoundly personal to some people, memorable or even life-changing. Beliefs—in the sense of propositions taken for true whether or not they are proven so—solidify rumor, observation, and imagining into social and personal facts so that UFOs have real-world consequence whether or not they have a real-world presence. These beliefs work their mischief across the spectrum of UFO thought, attaching unrelated ideas to observations, steering judgment onto prefigured pathways, or gratifying personal wishes and social requirements with fictions tailored to please. The actual event that gave rise to observation risks distortion and remaking several times over between initial perception and eventual communication.

External or interpersonal representations of UFOs typically take the form of texts. The texts may range from narrative testimonies of witnesses about a light in the sky or an eerie abduction to the rhetorical writings of interpreters offering planet of origin, mission statements, and exposés of official cover-ups. Even the nonanecdotal evidence of photographs, radar tracking, and ground traces is not self-evidently out of this world, but it requires textual explications to relate this evidence to UFOs and lay out its provenance. A further growth of texts expands the idea of UFOs for purposes unrelated to observations or their nature, such as entertainment or political discourse. As soon as speakers or writers organize their thinking into a text, they shape memories into a shared language and forms of expression, whereupon texts take on an autonomous life with social dynamics guiding formulation, transmission, adaptation, and variation. The UFO mystery is not synonymous with the textual truths and illusions created in its name, but it is nevertheless inseparable from them.

The narrator or interpreter contributes more than random additions and modifications. Creating a text engages cultural preferences for telling a story and established frameworks of meaning, so that patterns emerge in the human treatment of a phenomenon. Folklorists recognize that categories of narratives seem to reflect basic modes of expression for human concerns. Certain narrative types recur as fundamental or simple forms (*einfache Formen*), structural containers for human expression with similar narrative patterns and social functions.[32] One such form is the legend, a narrative that centers on the events that befall people in stories often concerned with inexplicable occurrences or supernatural confrontations.[33] An experience narrative may be a rough account of a personal encounter or a polished, widely circulated story like the popular urban legends of today, but in either case the narrative casts protagonists as victims rather than heroes, ordinary people going about ordinary business when some out-of-the-ordinary occurrence threatens them. The legend universe is often amoral, the occupants not punished for any crime or sin but simply unlucky, in the wrong place at the wrong time; or if some moral infraction is involved the consequences seem out of proportion to the cause. UFO abduction reports are usually stories of victimization with the captive guilty of nothing more than driving on a lonely midnight road, while even the best of citizens tucked away in their beds awake to find small gray intruders gathered round about. The simple sighting report foregoes the extravagance of close encounters but still preserves the gist of the legend form, that element of a brush with the inexplicable, that transgression of boundaries when the extranormal breaks momentarily into the everyday world.

If the UFO mystery begins with individual experiential texts, the subsequent discussions that add related cases, interpretations, glosses, controversies, and associations also belong within UFO discourse. All such UFO talk integrates into a systematized or partially systematized network to form a loose, protean, but unitary state. Such a cumulative end result also needs a name. The term to recognize this entirety is "myth," even though for many reasons—overuse, banality, multiple definitions, and pejorative connotations, among others—it is in many ways a regrettable choice; yet no alternative will serve half as well.[34]

A dictionary-style definition identifies myth as a traditional genre of sacred narratives that explains origins of the cosmos, mankind, and the moral order. This definition emphasizes religious and intellectual purposes at the expense of social context, while functional anthropologists and sociologists reverse this bias to redefine myth as a model of the way things ought to be or a blueprint to maintain present-day understandings and practices as faithful continuations of the primordial past.[35] The functionalist's center of gravity, so to speak, shifts from myth as textual product to myth as social process, from a story that satisfies curiosity to a master plan for living.

Myths never qualify as paragons of rational thinking. A generalization asserts that myths always present at least one humanly or physically impossible event like meta-morphosis or magic flight.[36] One explanation attributes this strangeness to primitive, prescientific thinking with an anthropomorphized view of the natural world.[37] The storms that toss people about then become fits of divine anger, death enters the world because of a mistake or a bad choice, a bite of an apple best left alone. Another pro-posal traces the origin of myths to the unconscious conflicts of dreams. These conflicts acquire dramatic and narrative form in myths but keep the irrational plot progressions of dreaming.[38] French structural anthropologist Claude Lévi-Strauss proposes that myths resolve contradictions between cultural beliefs and physical reality by serving as ideational go-betweens, mediating opposites on an unconscious level and thereby relieving the dissonance of seemingly irreconcilable ideas. The resulting stories appear fantastic because they serve logical needs rather than realistic representation.[39]

Anthropologists have long contrasted myth with science and rationality as distinc-tive ways of thinking. In Edward B. Tylor's theory of cultural evolution, civilized ra-tionality replaced the savage's metaphorical and animistic understanding of nature.[40] David Bidney argued that "the effectiveness of myth depends upon its acceptance in a given society, irrespective of its rational foundation in fact and experience. . . . It is not the truth-value of an ideal or principle which determines its acceptability by a given society, but rather its relevance to emotional needs, common aspirations, and wish-fulfillment."[41] Lévi-Strauss recasts mythic thinking as logical in process but different in means from scientific thought.[42] Postmodernist theory continues this trend by as-serting that metanarratives underlie the explanations of science. These metanarratives enjoy no special legitimacy and are themselves mythic, thereby undercutting any faith that science approaches absolute truth or holds unique superiority as a way of know-ing. With this shift toward cultural relativism, myth reclaims both its primacy as nar-rative and a sense of falsehood.[43]

Depth psychologists have taken an interest in myths because the appearance of similar stories in diverse cultures offers evidence for universal psychological processes. Freud understood myth as a distorted wish fantasy based on the projection in dreams of universal unconscious conflicts such as the Oedipus complex.[44] C. G. Jung traced myths to archetypal structures of the collective unconscious—in other words, trans-personal patterns shaping human thought found conscious expression in mythic nar-ratives. According to these theories, the close tie of mythic expressions to instinctual or unconscious psychological processes enables myths to distill complex relationships into widespread symbolic forms.[45]

Enlarging the concept of myth beyond narrative genre or social function has been a growth industry for scholars over the years. Following Jung's lead, literary critic

Northrop Frye proposed that myths embody archetypal plots that serve as the organizing basis for any story people tell. The pattern may derive from basic relationships like birth and death, the succession of day and night, or the life cycle. From the seasonal decline of autumn, for example, comes the underlying paradigm of tragedy, where the hero begins at a pinnacle of fortune then falls to destruction through the working out of an internal or external fate.[46] Mythologist Joseph Campbell drew on psychoanalytic theory to explain the plot of the hero's quest as a series of initiation ordeals leading to transformation. The hero myth dramatizes in conscious expression the unconscious conflicts of the psyche as it develops from infancy to adulthood, and since all people share the same developmental tasks, the mythic pattern is universal and eternal.[47] These approaches also serve as reminders that myths are not just vehicles for information but expressions of extraordinary emotional and artistic force. As archetypical forms, myths correspond to basic patterns of the psyche, and by fulfilling those patterns myths tell a story ordered for optimal psychological impact.

Ideas of myth proliferate in popular as well as scholarly thought. One common popular notion defines myth as false belief, another treats myth as the way things should have happened.[48] Both usages recur in *The Myth of the Titanic*, a book that treats many fictitious incidents that have accumulated around this famous disaster. Several iconic scenes never happened or differed significantly from familiar portrayals in literature or the movies, thereby qualifying familiar versions of the sinking as mythic in the simplistic sense of false history. Yet these versions are not simply wrong; they are wrong in a particular way: They deepen from mere error into myth because they retell history to express human ideals. A meaningless accident acquires the shape of purposeful tragedy when essential dramatic roles of heroes and villains emerge, and the necessary hubris enters with a boast that God himself could not sink the ship. The passengers and crew reaffirm cherished civilized values as the men obey the rule of "women and children first," then resign themselves to "be British" and die like gentlemen when no lifeboats remain. Such stories bear repeating whether they happened or not because they are too good not to be true.[49]

A third idea active in common usage applies the term to a body of stories interconnected to portray a fictitious world. William Faulkner invented the mythic southern microcosm of Yoknapatawpha County, where a vivid fabric of social classes and family histories sets a backdrop for literary drama; the expanding universe of *Star Trek* is sometimes called mythic as its technology, aliens, and generations of characters lend depth to a future history of human space-faring. Though altogether a fiction, the *Star Trek* saga piles layer on layer to acquire the density of real life. The same can be said of versatile literary characters like Sherlock Holmes, Tarzan, Superman, and Dracula.

They are so full of possibilities that they outlive their creators, never destitute of an audience and destined to have writers continue their adventures. Not just any theme or actor enjoys such a long life, but the exploratory quest of *Star Trek* and the dark, amoral sexuality of the vampire touch deep, abiding concerns as readily as archetypal characters of classical myth.

Whatever myth explains, reflects, or reinforces how it accomplishes its task is unmistakable—the terms are unremittingly human, always centered within the personal or social sphere. One appealing quality of myth is its comfortable, human-friendly way of thinking. Scientific thought is arduous and unforgiving—it requires exact observation, critical examination, and division of the continuity of nature into analytical units. A scientific theory loses the appearances it describes in symbols and mathematics or, like quantum theory, breaks loose entirely from everyday points of reference. No room remains for easygoing commonsense judgments, no excuse for playing favorites among suppositions. Something impersonal, uncongenial, and undemocratic characterizes scientific thought. It has the stiffness of abstract language, whereas myth flows with the ease of vernacular, an everyday language akin to the *bricolage* of Lévi-Strauss wherein people throw together concrete terms and build lazy, discursive arguments without the step-by-step formality of deduction.[50] Mythic thinking favors analogy, metaphor, and magical causation to associate ideas that by stricter standards seem unrelated. The result is poor in rational rigor but rich in creative imagination, satisfying for emotions and wishes even when wrong about physical reality.

To sum up, the characteristics of myth leads to an eclectic list of more descriptive than definitive value, but unavoidably so. A single clear essence no longer exists for a term with so many popular and scholarly usages. The preceding discussion touches on no more than a few meanings, but it captures the attributes most helpful for understanding the relationship of myth to UFOs:

1. A myth is, at heart, a narrative text about events. The narrative presents a scenario of confrontation, conflict, revelation, or some such incident of inherent dramatic interest. The subject matter can be sacred or secular, but it depicts strange or extraordinary occurrences; not necessarily magical or supernatural events, but at least situations that stand apart from the everyday. These subjects also treat ideals, values, hopes, fears, or mysteries and thereby align with cardinal points of human interest.

2. As a mode of expression myth exchanges an idiosyncratic for a collective representation. The story condenses historical particulars into an exemplary type and crystallizes the account into its essential parts. Myth serves as a fundamental way to tell a story, an archetypal way to represent a character or action. This ability to capture some important relationship, value, or meaning in a concentrated plot or image lends the

product symbolic value and affirms that making myth is creative, artistic work rather than a reporter's job.

3. Myths function to create meanings, express values, and serve social or personal needs. A mythic story looms larger than other stories because it encapsulates fundamental and vital human truths, while close attunement to aesthetic values, social concerns, and primary psychological states affords myths an extraordinary emotional resonance. They are sources of wonder, awe, admiration, excitement, unease, and dread. They also deal in a people-friendly way with important human matters that strict rationalism handles unsatisfactorily or neglects altogether. A combination of intellectual and emotional appeal gains commitment and loyalty for mythic treatments that scientific alternatives seldom enjoy.

4. Myths grow by association of ideas and tend toward inclusiveness, where scientific theory excludes any term not connected by causation or some rigorous mathematical or logical fit. Even when a myth begins with narratives of concrete events, a matrix of extensions grows out of that core to include related events, commentaries, theories, and beliefs. The primary texts about events and the secondary texts of interpretation interconnect to form a system of knowledge. The full myth encompasses this entire network of meanings, wherein the key symbolic elements acquire layers of significance and multiple uses. A mythic system tends toward a wholeness of meanings—that is, the system comes to represent a possible world so dense and well integrated with its own facts and truths that they become self-referencing, sufficiently complete and satisfying for believers to accept as the real world.

5. In creating a belief world, mythmaking sacrifices some part of literal truth for a more coherent and desirable fiction. The process adds features that should be there and removes excess baggage to construct a purposeful whole, somewhat in the way a fine diamond emerges from a rough stone. The jeweler cuts away much of the initial weight, but the remaining gem-quality crystal gains symmetry to maximize sparkle and brilliance. According to social values the tradeoff is advantageous, and so it goes with myth. Mere facts are real but not necessarily important, while the fictions of myth are better—they have been called "realer than real" because they select, arrange, and modify the haphazard incidents of history to become meaningful make-believes, false to the literal truth but true to the world that ought to be, the world as adherents want it to be.

6. An identifiable pattern of events and understandings distinguishes a myth. The subject matter is not necessarily false—after all, the *Titanic* disaster really happened—but something is usually suspect about the treatment. Certain recurrent themes and plots order any story widely identified as mythic; familiar motifs and characters occupy

it. If similar elements turn up in historical, news, or experiential accounts, good reason exists to question the literal accuracy of these accounts. A mythic influence in less evident form may shape a representation whenever ideals, ideology, wishes, beliefs, values, and cultural contaminations intrude into the case. This influence may be subtle, a matter of small degree; but any such sign cautions that mythic ideas have bent historical truth, however slightly, to fit a pattern more or less external to the events described.

7. Myths are more than false belief, but the fact remains that controversy surrounds them. They make claims about the real world, but they are not science; their assertions do not enjoy a consensus. One inescapable property of myth is that it is "only a myth" to someone, and if that "someone" speaks with the authoritative voice of science, any opposing claim about the natural world holds the official status of an untruth. The belief world surrounding a myth embeds particulars in a structure of ideas, a structure massive enough to stand firm against opposing viewpoints, coherent enough to allow lengthy defensive reasoning, and appealing enough to motivate resistance to authority. But a subject like UFOs remains mythic so long as its truth status depends on social negotiations rather than incontrovertible proof, and controversies bind the issue in a tug-of-war between official and unofficial perspectives.

Connecting Myth and UFOs

At first glance nothing seems less compatible with myth than UFOs. They are technological and futuristic rather than sacred and primeval. They call for explanation rather than offer one, and, aside from reports, much of UFO discourse shuffles off narrative form to argue and speculate in academic rather than storytelling style. Yet on closer inspection some affinities reveal the comparison as not at all far-fetched. UFOs are inherently strange and fantastic. They behave in "magical" ways, remain embroiled in controversy, and provoke a sense of awe, mystery, and power. For such reasons UFOs fulfill some basic criteria of myth, though of course these properties by themselves are far from sufficient.

While UFO stories are cause for wonder, something about them seems wondrous in a suspiciously old-fashioned way. Folklorist Stith Thompson's *Motif Index of Folk Literature* catalogs the minimal basic units that persist in tradition and manifest some unusual or striking quality—for instance, a stepmother is not a motif, but a wicked stepmother who treats children with cruelty may be. This index orders the recurrent themes and contents of Western folk narratives, and several categories compare with elements of UFO stories.[51] Motifs that deal with a primordial time when gods

interacted with humans and culture heroes brought knowledge to mankind reappear
in speculations that ancient astronauts visited the earth and founded the first civilizations. Motifs of marvels include otherworld journeys, diminutive supernatural beings,
and the sunless sky of fairyland. The whole premise of extraterrestrial visitation is an
otherworld journey, while UFO aliens are usually pictured as short humanoids and
abductees sometimes describe a subterranean otherworld with a luminous but sunless
sky. Fairy kidnaps and the supernatural lapse of time in fairyland parallel abductions
and missing-time experiences. Even these cursory examples suggest at least casual af-
finity between some UFO representations and typical mythological contents.

One recurrent effort to relate UFOs to myth has treated them as part of an incipi-
ent religion. According to religion scholar John Saliba, UFOs adapt equally well to a
traditional language of signs and demonic activity or to a technological language where
sacred terms translate into ancient astronauts. In either case the story develops around
key religious themes like awe, the otherworld, and salvation. UFO-based religiosity is
overt in contactee groups and covert among abductees, though contactees represent a
peripheral aspect of UFO belief, while abduction remains largely personal without the
emergence of any collective movement.[52] In a view from cultural studies, Jodi Dean,
assistant professor of political science at Hobart and William Smith Colleges, argues
that modern society inhabits a virtual reality created by the media and Internet, where
information overload leaves consensus impossible and authority dead. No longer able
to trust government or science, people negotiate individualized truths based on political rather than scientific criteria. Human exploration of space served as a showcase for
triumphant democracy and Western technology in the 1960s, but UFOs supported a
subversive countervision of outer space already occupied and earthly science trumped
by superior extraterrestrials, of a feckless government unable to protect its citizens and
conspiring to hide its failure. The search for ultimate answers may no longer go by the
name of religion, but the current mythology of conspiracy and distrust fulfills some
of the same purposes, and UFOs serve in this search as modern agents in what is effectively a religious quest.[53]

"Myth" with a dismissive connotation has been entrenched in the vocabulary of
UFO discourse from its beginnings. The most outspoken scientific opponent of the
1950s and 1960s, Harvard astronomer Donald H. Menzel spoke of UFOs as "the modern myth" and "a major myth of the space age" throughout his skeptical career.[54] Aviation historian Curtis Peebles follows this tradition when he casts the UFO myth as
imaginative stories that provide meaning and satisfaction in times of social crisis.[55]
Brandeis University anthropology professors Benson Saler and Charles A. Ziegler
maintain the negative truth value of myth but broaden appreciation for human needs

served by the emergent mythical qualities of Roswell. The story began with the crash of an experimental balloon but grew into tales of flying saucers and aliens to satisfy the wishes and needs of narrators. The Roswell myth comes to life when narrators perform the texts, though the key concern of those performances is not historical truth but persuasion of an audience that one belief or another is true. Religious qualities like a sense of mystery, the idea of superior beings, and a form of salvation that comes by wresting knowledge from a demonized government accumulate around Roswell.[56] This reenchantment of the modern world in a seemingly secular story lends it an extra dimension, an emotional appeal that plumbs true mythic depths.

UFO abductions receive comparable treatment from Terry Matheson, a professor of English literature at the University of Saskatchewan. He concludes that the experiences are emotionally valid but not literal events, rather imaginative constructions based on popular culture, given a feeling of reality by the suggestion-enhancing influences of hypnosis and unwarranted coherency when an external narrator intervenes to lead the witness or rewrite the story. These stories hold inherent fascination and make sense of scattered cultural elements. By repeating age-old accounts of encounters with supernatural beings in technological terms, abductions restore the credibility and relevance of long-standing mythic patterns. The imagery of weak, colorless extraterrestrials with big brains and no emotion or compassion betrays the real concern behind the abduction myth, a fear that modern life dehumanizes humans so that when we look at the aliens, we really see our alienated selves.[57]

Another strand of ufological theorizing identifies the mythic potential of UFOs as their greatest significance. Jung called flying saucers a "modern myth of things seen in the sky," even though he accepted that they might be extraterrestrial spaceships. For him UFOs were important, though whether they were extraterrestrial or hallucinatory, material or imaginative made no difference because their psychological consequence was the same in any case. He saw that rational consciousness dominated the modern psyche and strangled off healthy outlets for the chaotic energies of the unconscious, unleashing those energies to break out in progressively more destructive wars and oppressive social movements like Nazism. The significance of flying saucers belonged to their role in rebalancing the psyche in this time of crisis. Real or imaginary, they symbolized an archetype of wholeness in visionary rumors now emerging from the collective unconscious. These rumors formed the nucleus of a salvation myth, its irrational but insistent growth restoring a place for mystery and wonder in a reformed modern consciousness.[58]

Jung's seminal idea has continued to develop within ufological thinking as one answer for the meaning behind the phenomenon. Independent scholar and journalist

Keith Thompson sees UFOs as subjects for allegories, dualistic narratives with a sur-face story as well as deeper, hidden meanings. On the surface are accounts of space-ships and extraterrestrials, but underneath are the supernatural characters and magical forces of myth. UFOs manifest the protean elusiveness of the mythic imagination, sug-gesting to Thompson that whatever their ontological status, UFOs assume an impor-tant role as objects of belief. Our imagined aliens share our interests and purposes, but this relationship is two-sided, since the strangeness of these beings initiates earthlings into a realm of larger awareness—a mythic union of opposites that compensates for materialism and rationality with a renewed awareness of strangeness and a loosen-ing of familiar boundaries.[59] Philosopher Michael Grosso sees UFOs as bearers of the profound symbolic truth characteristic of myth. In the fetal, frail, sickly aliens of ab-duction accounts he recognizes a collective representation of the near-death experience of mankind, an archetypal image of the human child threatened by dangers of the modern world. Yet the child is also symbolic of the future, so beyond the harrowing initiatory imagery projects the mythic hope of rebirth into a new age.[60]

Even among researchers who accept the physical reality of UFOs, the notion has prospered that their strangeness is the underlying message. Abductee Whitley Strieber and abduction investigators like University of Wyoming psychologist Leo Sprinkle, University of Connecticut psychologist Kenneth Ring, and Harvard psychiatrist John Mack have proposed that UFO encounters are unsettling for a purpose. These encoun-ters disturb the intellectual status quo, break down established boundaries of material-istic, earthbound thought to free consciousness for evolution toward transcendence of rationalistic capabilities, a healthier relationship with nature, and openness to nonhu-man intelligences.[61] Without adopting Jung's system, these theorists share his assess-ment of the mythic symbolism and instrumental role of UFOs.

Other ufologists have carried the Jungian premise farther afield. Jacques Vallee sees conditioning of consciousness through exposure to strangeness as the purpose behind UFOs, fairy encounters, and other types of anomalous experience but externalizes the collective unconscious into a cosmic control system that introduces mysterious phe-nomena into the everyday world and manipulates the development of human society for unknown goals.[62] John Keel also adopts an external controlling force as responsible for multiple anomalous manifestations.[63] Jerome Clark once proposed that the physi-cal aspects of UFOs were psychokinetic creations of the human mind, but, like Jung, he sought meanings outside the physical realm. For Clark, "the UFO mystery is pri-marily subjective and its content primarily symbolic." In other words UFOs belong to the inner space of the psyche, and accounts express in mythic form a contact with the archetypal otherworld.[64]

Clark later repudiated his Jungian leanings to reaffirm an external source for UFOs, but both experimental psychologists and representatives of the psychosocial school carry on the argument that UFOs are human rather than alien inventions. The explanatory variables shift away from unknowns toward conventional answers to a stock of cultural ideas and standard narrative patterns, to prior interests and personal psychological traits. In this view, UFOs amount to false belief, but falsity with full mythic scope. The myth itself receives credit not only for having complex sources and the support of an intricate belief world, but also for having a cultural outgrowth that serves social and psychological functions.

Any lingering strangeness in relating UFOs to myths diminishes with appreciation of how pervasive mythic patterns really are in the structuring of thought and narrative. A growing body of scholarship identifies mythic templates that underlie popular expectations, historical writings, social movements, even news stories in the press and on television.[65] Newspaper accounts of Custer's last stand repeated the "epic of defeat" structure also found in the story of the three hundred Spartans at Thermopylae, popular treatments of the life and death of John F. Kennedy mimic Arthurian legend, and the controversy over abortion often invokes apocalyptic rhetoric.[66] Mythic patterns find an outlet as close to home as the daily news, where despite journalistic striving for objectivity and facts, accounts of Mother Teresa seldom escape some formulaic refrains of the selfless, all-nurturing mother; reports on the misbehavior of celebrities often mirror elements of the disruptive antihero trickster; and descriptions of mundane disasters borrow from the imagery of cosmic cataclysm.[67]

Folklorists and other scholars have long recognized that stereotypical formulations rewrite the life histories of saints, heroic leaders, and wonderworkers.[68] In *The Myth of the Magus*, Cambridge professor of German E. M. Butler delineated a distinctive biographical pattern for the sage or magician. The magus has a supernatural or mysterious origin and a birth announced by signs. Perils menace his infancy, while he later undergoes an initiation and undertakes a faraway journey. He engages in a magical contest and then may face a trial or persecution, leading to a farewell scene before a violent or mysterious death followed by resurrection or ascension.

Butler applied this formula to the lives of Zoroaster, Moses, Solomon, Pythagoras, Apollonius of Tyana, Simon Magus, Christ, Merlin, and Doctor Faust,[69] but it continues to structure life histories into modern times with striking resilience. One example appears in the legendary afterlife that has grown up around the inventor Nikola Tesla (1856–1943). One of the legitimate geniuses of the electrical age, he also qualifies as one of its most colorful characters, an enigmatic eccentric who astounded audiences at the Columbian Exposition of 1893 with lightning bolts sparking from his fingertips. As a youthful immigrant to America he worked for Edison briefly and then became a rival, successfully promoting alternating current over Edison's direct-current system. He engineered the harnessing of Niagara Falls for electrical generation and went out west to perfect a means of transmitting electrical energy through the air. Funded for a time by J. P. Morgan, Tesla's dream of electrifying the world with free energy came to an end when the financier withdrew his support. The inventor accomplished little thereafter but entertained reporters with plans for death rays and grandiose visions of the future until he died in relative poverty.[70]

Even these historically valid parts of Tesla's biography match several key stations in the life of the magus—a career-changing journey (to America and later to Colorado), a magical contest (with the Wizard of Menlo Park), triumphs (for his system of motors and generators that continue to power the world), and a reversal of fortune (loss of financial support for his greatest undertaking) leading to an obscure death but followed by a resurrection of fame. Much of that subsequent fame has depended on the imaginative possibilities of his life rather than its realities. The occultist Margaret Storm preserved supernatural implications of the magus with modern equivalents by identifying Tesla as a visitor from Venus in her book *Return of the Dove* (1959). Other writers have stopped short of attributing outright magical qualities to Tesla while still treating him as a superhuman figure far ahead of his time. He has become entangled with the Philadelphia Experiment, an alleged World War II attempt to make a warship invisible. This effort supposedly tore a hole in the space-time continuum and opened an entry for evil beings now mistaken for aliens.[71] A related notion that Tesla invented a teleportation device threads its way into popular awareness through the recent mainstream movie *The Prestige* (2006), where rivalry between two magicians leads one to consult the inventor for ways to improve his act. Tesla also finds perennial favor with conspiracy theorists. They see him envisioning a better world of boundless energy free for the taking; but greedy plutocrats cared only to collect the electric bill and stopped his work in one more example of vested interests suppressing a revolutionary invention. In conspiracist views Tesla technology has only begun to come into its own. According to various speculations, his death ray forms part of the Star Wars defense system, the secrecy at Area 51 protects tests of his futuristic inventions, and his power broadcast system provided the means to send craft on clandestine missions to Mars as early as the 1930s or 1940s.[72] Nothing like credible evidence supports these fantasies, but they attest to the extraordinary potentials for legend formation inherent in Tesla's extraordinary life.

An early American literary genre, the "captured by Indians" story, enjoyed popularity from the seventeenth to the nineteenth centuries. The narratives had their basis in real experiences, but again and again they assumed the archetypal shape of the hero's journey of initiation, moving from symbolic death to transformation and rebirth. The story begins with forcible separation from familiar surroundings, followed by a ritual ordeal marked by privation, torture, and exposure to savage customs like cannibalism. A captive's transformation proceeds with accommodation to the Indians' way of life, such as eventual relish for seemingly inedible foods, and at last a ritualized adoption as the captive becomes a member of Indian society. The story closes with the captive returned to his or her former culture by escape, rescue, or involuntary repatriation, restored but forever changed by the experience.[73]

Though the Indian threat has vanished, key parts of the captivity narrative pattern revive in media treatments of POWs and the U.S. hostages held by militant Iranians from 1979 to 1981.[74] Two scholarly articles identify UFO abduction narratives as the latest incarnation of the pattern. Both captivity and abduction accounts posit a frontier world where dangerous Others lurk just beyond the boundary, Indians in the wilderness or aliens in space. These Others invade the civilized human realm, attacking suddenly in the night to carry off helpless victims into an unknown and overwhelming environment. The story continues along well-worn paths, with mortification as abductees lose their clothes and autonomy and then terror and torture as they undergo an examination. While abductees do not assimilate into alien society, they respond with familiar ambivalence to the cruelty or indifference of their captors to develop a bond, even a sense of love. The sexual overtones of the captivity narrative echo in the reproductive procedures of abduction accounts, while the old concern over mixing of races returns in the theme of aliens creating hybrids. Like their predecessors, abductees may describe their experience as transformative and return with new knowledge, perspective, and identity, but also with a sense of alienation as if torn between two worlds.[75]

Mythic interventions in historical narratives range from minor to major and seldom displace facts with complete fictions, but the upshot is that patterns and processes external to the events take a hand in shaping narratives of personal experience, collective history, and interpretive understanding. The vulnerability of so many narratives to mythic patterns forewarns that UFO stories are ripe for similar modification. UFOs are uncertain, mysterious, and exotic. They invite wonder and speculation, provoke hope and fear. In short, they constitute a subject fertile for the growth of rumor and legend, prone to join the ranks of accounts where stereotypical fictions compensate for a dearth of facts or conspiracy theories fill in the blanks when reasons are unknown or unsatisfying. The case will follow that much thought about UFOs does indeed depend on mythic patterns.

CHAPTER TWO

The Growth and Evolution of UFO Mythology

Every one who has considered the subject knows full well that a nation without fancy, without some romance, never did, never can, never will hold a great place under the sun.
—Charles Dickens, "Frauds on the Fairies"[1]

Each one, all the millions on earth, stood on the threshold of something strange and tremendous. Inevitable as the rising sun, it would change the lives of all, for good or bad, irrevocably. How it would happen, when it would come, there was still no way of knowing. But one thing was certain, beyond all doubt. The world would never be the same.
—Donald E. Keyhoe, *Flying Saucers: Top Secret*[2]

The visitors are sweeping up from where we buried them under layers of denial and false assurance to deliver what is truly a message from the beyond: There is something more to us and the universe, and it is rich with the potential of the unknown. It will be incredibly hard for us to achieve real relationship with the visitors. But also, I can tell you from experience that there will be wonder. There will be great wonder.
—Whitley Strieber, *Transformation: The Breakthrough*[3]

Kenneth Arnold's report of nine objects skipping over the slopes of Mount Rainier on June 24, 1947, marks the nominal beginning of the UFO era. In a sense his sighting comes as just one among ongoing streams of predecessors and successors, and being chosen as the "first" is as arbitrary as pulling one person out of a line to celebrate the millionth customer of a supermarket. If unidentified flying objects did not begin with Arnold's report, the social debut of UFOs certainly did. His report crystallized a coherent mystery out of random observations, gave it a catchy name and captivated public interest. With beginner's luck he started a craze that has matured into a cultural institution. Since then the UFO myth has grown out of observations and experiences, theories and speculations, media images and quarrels with official authority. Much said about UFOs dwells on conspiracies, New Age hopes, and paranormal phenomena, so that the initial mystery of flying disks branches out into unlikely and unforeseen connections with matters scientific, political, religious, social, cultural, and imaginary.

No few pages can do justice to the history and scope of this myth, only sketch its outline. This chapter follows UFO mythology through four phases distinguished by characteristics of the reported phenomenon and interests of the people pursuing it. The early period, from 1947 to 1963, introduced most UFO story types, motifs, and themes; 1964 to 1975 saw widening tolerance for strangeness and hosted a climax in the conflict between official and unofficial views; emphasis turned to high-profile claims of crashes and abductions during the late 1970s and 1980s; while from the 1990s onward the cultural image and political implications of UFOs became more important than the UFOs themselves.[4]

The Formative Years, 1947–1963

A Phenomenon Takes Shape.—Several thousand flying saucer reports flooded newspapers in the few weeks following Arnold's sighting. The furor came and went like a summer heat wave with no resolution for the nature or purpose of these objects. They began and ended as oddities. Orson Welles, famous for his 1938 *Invasion from Mars* radio broadcast, predicted that the flying saucers would die out as just another silly season fad,[5] and perhaps his word would have stood as their epitaph had not an object like an ice-cream cone appeared over Fort Knox, Kentucky, on the afternoon of January 7, 1948. The pilots of several P-51s flying in the area responded to a request from the base to investigate. Capt. Thomas F. Mantell, the leader of the flight, continued to climb toward the object after his companions gave up the chase for lack of fuel. He radioed a description of the object as metallic and tremendous in size soon before he crashed into a farmer's field. The *New York Times* captioned the story as "Flier Dies Chasing a 'Flying Saucer,'" though the object was probably a high-altitude Skyhook balloon, part of a secret project unknown to local commanders. Mantell likely rose too high and blacked out for lack of oxygen.[6] Within a few years the story would circulate that a hostile saucer shot down the plane with an alien death ray[7], but for the moment flying saucers had simply returned to the news bringing a newfound seriousness, a hint that the lighthearted puzzle of the previous summer was more than a laughing matter after all.

Two other sightings from 1948 helped shape the emergent image of the mystery and became canonical classics for every new enthusiast to learn. On July 24, pilot Clarence S. Chiles and copilot John B. Whitted were flying an Eastern Airlines DC-3 near Montgomery, Alabama. At 2:45 A.M., out of the clear, moonlit sky, a wingless, rocket-like object streaming a trail of fire sped past the aircraft. Chiles watched the object for about ten seconds. He described it as having a blue glow underneath and two rows of brilliantly lighted round windows along the side. Whitted estimated the length of the object at 100 feet and the speed as 700 miles per hour. He depicted the two rows of windows as square. "If you look at one of those fantastic Flash Gordon rocket ships," he was quoted the next day in the *Atlanta Constitution*, "you've got a picture of what we saw."[8] Another pilot, Lt. George F. Gorman, had a dogfight with a small UFO over Fargo, North Dakota, about two hours after dark on October 1. The object, a spherical white light less than a foot in diameter, seemed to circle, turn, rush at Gorman's plane, and then veer off at speeds of several hundred miles per hour, rising and diving over some 10,000 feet of altitude during Gorman's attempts at interception. Explanations for these sightings build strong arguments for a bright meteor and a light-bearing balloon, but the three famous sightings of 1948 established that flying saucers could be any shape or size and gave indication of purpose and control.[9] These reports also reinforced a continuity of flying saucers as a recurrent fixture of observation.

The standard name of flying saucer belied the various shapes reported and became synonymous with spaceships. The Air Force favored the looser, less prejudicial term "unidentified flying object," and it gradually supplanted the older designation in popular usage as well from the mid-1950s onward. In the early years saucers did little more than fly, sometimes in formations or swarms but almost never landing or drawing near or revealing structural features, and seldom making noise or leaving contrails or exhaust. By day the saucers often appeared as silvery disks; by night they gave off an eerie glow in the dark. A spectacular nocturnal case reported by airline pilot William B. Nash and copilot William H. Fortenberry began over Chesapeake Bay in the early evening of July 14, 1952. The two pilots saw half a dozen objects glowing like hot embers rush toward the plane in echelon formation. These coinlike disks slowed, then flipped on edge in unison and reversed their arrangement, then flipped back into a level position and shot off at a sharp angle. Two more objects, faster and brighter than the original six, sped out of the dark, as if late for an appointment, to join the formation and fly away with the group during a performance that lasted some fifteen seconds.[10]

The saucers soared at extraordinary speeds and maneuvered with a seemingly immaterial recklessness that distinguished them from any possible aircraft of the day.

Flying saucers darted in and out of the news during the 1950s, with sightings often increasing during the summer when, in an era before home air-conditioning, people spent hot evenings out of doors. Every two or three years a dramatic flood of sightings attracted widespread attention. These waves—or "flaps" in military jargon—broke out in 1947, 1950, 1952, and 1957 in the United States, 1954 in Europe, and 1954 and 1957 in South America. The waves of 1947 and 1957 played out in two or three weeks; those of 1952 and 1954 surged for several months. The 1954 outbreaks ended an illusion that UFOs were largely made in the USA, and the mystery has lived happily ever after with an international scope.[11] Waves brought spectacular sightings as well as hundreds of reports, such as July 19–20 and 26–27, 1952, when radar at Washington National Airport tracked UFOs flying over the city, even violating restricted airspace over the Capitol and the White House. The impossibly fast and maneuverable objects appeared as orange lights to the naked eye and eluded every jet sent to intercept them. The Air Force dismissed the sightings as consequences of temperature inversions—colder air sandwiched between layers of hot air during a summer heat wave, resulting in unusual reflections of radar and lights from the ground—but the Washington incidents made headlines all over the country and still spark controversy today.[12]

Another wave began in late 1957 and became national news on November 2 with multiple reports from Texas of huge torpedo or egg-shaped objects that hovered close to highways and caused automobile engines to stall. The first incident began with two men near Levelland when the engine of their truck died and its headlights dimmed as a glowing object approached. One man, named Saucedo, to the delight of journalistic wags around the country, dove to the ground as the 200-foot torpedo flew overhead with a roar, a rush of wind, and a sensation of heat. As the object departed to the east, the truck started again and the men phoned the sheriff. Skeptics invoked ball lightning to explain the object and its effects, but similar incidents occurred over a wide area as the UFO wave spread nationwide. Ufologists valued apparent electromagnetic effects as a form of physical proof, evidence that UFOs interfered with earthly electrical systems and motor vehicles.[13]

If saucers were intelligently controlled craft, they might well have occupants. The first occupant report widely publicized as news originated in Flatwoods, West Virginia, on the evening of September 12, 1952. After watching a fireball land or crash on a nearby hill, eight residents and a dog climbed to the top to investigate. They smelled a foul odor and looked at a glowing object until the dog growled at something off to the side. A swing of the flashlight beam revealed a ten-foot-tall monster with glowing eyes, clawed hands, and its head surrounded by a hood shaped like the ace of spades. The dog headed downhill in a hurry with the humans close behind. The sheriff found no monster or saucer but saw traces like skid marks on the ground. Critics have since built a cogent case that the excited witnesses, all but one of them teenagers or children, disturbed a barn owl and panic enlarged the bird to regulation monster size.[14]

Despite Hollywood sanction, tall monsters are scarce in UFO reports and the typical occupant is diminutive in both stature and menace. Occupant reports first became commonplace with the French wave of 1954, and one of the best encounters began for a man named Marius Dewilde after he went outside on the evening of September 10 to see why his dog was barking. An oval, capsulelike object sat astride the railroad track and two entities, three feet tall and dressed in diving suits, waddled toward the craft. As Dewilde tried to intercept the entities, a light from the UFO struck him and he was unable to move until the craft took off. Indentations along the tracks suggested an object weighing several tons had rested there.[15] A few weeks later *Life* magazine published an illustration of an Italian woman's encounter with two smiling little entities half her size as they tried to pull her toward their craft.[16] Reports from South America told of hairy dwarfs from UFOs attacking hunters and passersby, clawing the victims' shirts to shreds and leaving bloody scratches.[17] Neither the diving suit nor belligerence has endured as characteristics of UFO occupants, but a striking souvenir of the 1954 wave is a photograph of a French farmer chalking the image of the entity he saw on the side of a barn. This figure of a dwarfish being with a rounded, hairless head and large eyes resembles the typical entities from countless abduction reports of subsequent years.[18]

Occupant reports multiplied on the home front in 1955, with the most sensational account coming from Kelly, Kentucky, on August 21. Eight adults and three children of the Sutton family were spending Sunday afternoon at home. One young man came back from the well a little before dark saying he saw a flying saucer, but no one paid attention. About 8 o'clock a barking dog announced the approach of a humanoid creature about three and a half feet tall, luminous like a radium watch dial, with a large round head and enormous round glowing eyes. The being walked or floated toward the back door and two men fired guns at the intruder. It flipped over then ran off into the darkness unharmed. A few minutes later another being appeared at a window, and the men shot through the screen. As one man stepped out the door to see if they had hit the entity, a clawed hand reached down from the roof and touched his hair. After shooting this creature off the roof, they blasted another one in a tree. Finding gunfire ineffectual against the invaders, the men retreated into the house, and over the next three hours the women and children became progressively more terrified as the beings, while never hostile, continued to appear at the windows or doors. About 11 P.M. the family fled in two cars to the Hopkinsville sheriff and returned half an hour later with a troop of police, reporters, and curiosity seekers. An extensive search over the next two hours turned up no entities, only holes in the screen and shotgun shells littering the ground. Once the police departed and the Suttons settled down to sleep, the beings returned, one of them looking in at a window close to Mrs. Lankford, the family matriarch. A shot drove the being away but others appeared until around 4:30 A.M. Mrs. Lankford was well respected, and her testimony foreclosed for many people any explanation of the incident as hoax or panic. Skeptics have resorted to owls again, assuming their feathers were covered with luminous fungus; but this sort of owl attack seems unprecedented in natural history or even tall tales, and the sheer unlikelihood that these shy birds would besiege a house for hours amid a barrage of gunfire mires this explanation in a swamp of improbabilities.[19]

Getting a Grip on the Phantom of the Skies.—With the cold war setting in as the saucers began to fly, governmental authorities took keen interest in the observations as possible evidence of Soviet secret weapons. The task of investigating saucers befell the U.S. Air Force, an unwelcome birthday present for a branch of service organized as a separate entity on September 18, 1947. Plans for a saucer study began that same month, and Project Sign opened in January 1948, two weeks after the death of Captain Mantell. The project hired astronomer J. Allen Hynek as a scientific adviser to weed out natural phenomena mistaken for saucers. By late 1948 the subject provoked its typical sharp polarization of opinion as some project members concluded that the saucers were not only real but probably extraterrestrial, while the commanding general of the Air Force, Hoyt S. Vandenberg, rejected this "estimate of the situation" as unproven. A shakeup of Project Sign soon followed as the proponents were reassigned and only opponents who thought saucers were nothing but a nuisance manned the new project, assigned the ominous name of Project Grudge. The tone matched the title as members explained away reports by any means necessary without an investigation or study. Lasting only about a year, Grudge lapsed into inactivity by the end of 1949.[20]

Meanwhile, the saucers reappeared to annoy their doubters. Continued reports led to a revival of Air Force investigations under the more benign name of Project Blue Book, and an entity under this title would last until 1969. The new director was Capt. Edward J. Ruppelt, and he made a gallant effort to find out what the saucers really were, even during the chaos of the mammoth 1952 wave. Yet lack of support and outright hindrance from his superiors stymied his effort and left him to wonder if they even wanted an investigation.[21] In January 1953 a CIA-sponsored group of scientists known as the Robertson Panel concluded that flying saucers probably did not represent any form of foreign technology and posed no threat to national security. The only danger could be the public response if, for example, large numbers of people jammed official communications channels with saucer reports in a time of genuine emergency. A decision to "strip [UFOs] of . . . the aura of mystery they have unfortunately acquired" followed the Robertson report, and orders went into effect to restrict reports by military personnel to military channels.[22] As a lid of official secrecy closed over UFOs, the official line remained that the military had nothing to hide, and this transparent lie led to a prolonged climate of distrust. Ruppelt left Blue Book in 1953, and it remained nothing more than a public relations front throughout its subsequent history.

No sooner did the saucers appear than the media began to associate them with Martians and spaceships. In its July 21, 1947, issue, *Life* magazine ran a cartoon of alien creatures bombarding the planets of the solar system with various forms of crockery, earth being the recipient of saucers.[23] If the spaceship idea enjoyed wide circulation, the prospect gained little credence with the public in those early years. The spaceship option did not register at all in a Gallup poll from late July 1947. Saucers were hoaxes, illusions, or imaginary, said 39 percent of people queried, while 15 percent opted for U.S. secret weapons and most others said they did not know. By May 1950, 29 percent favored American secret weapons or a new kind of aircraft and 3 percent thought the saucers were Soviet. Another 16 percent chose illusion or hoax and 5 percent said "comets, shooting stars, something from another planet."[24] Flying saucers became synonymous with alien spaceships in the popular culture of the 1950s, featured in jokes, political cartoons, advertisements, rock and roll songs, and in an entire subgenre of science fiction movies.[25] The movies introduced a dichotomy of opinions that persists today, on one side the hostile aliens portrayed in *The Thing from Another World* (1951), *Invaders from Mars* (1953), and *Earth Versus the Flying Saucers* (1956), on the other side the noble alien of *This Island Earth* (1955) and the benign ambassador of *The Day the Earth Stood Still* (1951).

A small welcoming committee already anticipated visitors from space. Occult groups like the Theosophists and the "I AM" movement included communication with extraterrestrials as part of their mythology,[26] while science-fiction magazines sometimes speculated about alien intervention in historical events. A back-cover illustration for the April 1948 issue of *Amazing Stories* shows the population of the now-deserted Cambodian city of Angkor Wat streaming aboard spaceships waiting to depart from earth, a what-if speculation that posed an alien cause for mysteries of the ancient past. Desmond Leslie, H. T. Wilkins, and M. K. Jessup wrote various books in the early days of the saucer era to link myths, medieval wonders, disappearing ships, and astronomical observations of alleged changes on the moon with flying saucers, advocating any curiosity, however far-fetched, as evidence for an alien role in human history.[27] This belief in alien influences on ancient civilizations hardened into a popular tenet of the UFO creed.

The extraterrestrial hypothesis found its most enthusiastic champion in a retired Marine Corps aviator and aviation writer, Major Donald E. Keyhoe. In an article for *True* magazine in 1949, he laid out the case he would promote throughout the 1950s, arguing that the government knew flying saucers were advanced vehicles from another planet but hid this fact from the public to prevent mass panic. Keyhoe was convinced and convincing. His network of military and government contacts leaked impressive sightings and behind-the-scenes rumors to him, making him the best-connected spokesman for flying saucers during this decade. He wrote with a flair that dramatized stale facts and events into an ongoing detective story in four best-selling books—*The Flying Saucers Are Real* (1950), *The Flying Saucers from Outer Space* (1953), *The Flying Saucer Conspiracy* (1955), and *Flying Saucers: Top Secret* (1960). The titles stated his foremost concerns, the texts crackled with tense expectation that the secrecy campaign verged on collapse and the hidden truth would soon spill out that visitors from space swarmed our skies. On April 17, 1952, Keyhoe picked up an influential ally when *Life* magazine published "Have We Visitors from Space?" an article sympathetic to the extraterrestrial hypothesis.[28]

Even as Keyhoe built a case that saucers were too strange to be earthly aircraft, some earthlings insisted that not only was he right, but they knew all about it straight from the aliens themselves. From 1952 onward a growing list of "contactees" claimed that they met "Space Brothers" from Venus, Mars, Saturn, or the unknown planet Clarion and even hitched a ride aboard the saucers for tours of outer space. George Van Tassel, George Adamski, Truman Bethurum, Daniel Fry, George Hunt Williamson, Orfeo Angelucci, Laura Mundo, Howard Menger, Gloria Lee, Buck Nelson, Reinhold Schmidt, and a host of others communicated with extraterrestrials by radio, telepathy, or good colloquial English, and enthusiastic followers paid to hear lectures or flocked to the California desert to attend Van Tassel's annual Giant Rock convention. Ernest and Ruth Norman founded Unarius, and George King founded the Aetherius Society, contactee organizations that continue today even after the founders' deaths. Long on interplanetary goodwill and short on evidence, the contactees spread insipid spiritual teachings to the faithful, yet the mix of feel-good philosophy and salvation from the skies struck an appealing note for 1950s seekers troubled by the nuclear threat and dissatisfied with conventional religion.[29]

Keyhoe and other serious ufologists deplored the contactee movement as nothing more than flimsy tales of make believe pieced together out of religious sentiments, New Age metaphysics, and trappings of science fiction. Worse still, contactees discredited the entire saucer phenomenon. Who could take it seriously when its most visible advocates were charlatans spreading wild and unsubstantiated claims in an effort to cash in on popular interest? A great divide opened between the two camps, with contactees appealing to spiritual seekers with an alternative religious movement while ufologists began a struggle for scientific respectability and official recognition that continues today.

When scientific indifference and government secrecy frustrated the curiosity that saucers inspired, amateur enthusiasts filled the void by forming a scattered folk community to search for answers. A local sighting might lead interested persons to form a club that disbanded once interest waned. Few saucer clubs lasted more than two years, but their mimeographed newsletters kept interest alive during intervals when the national press ignored the subject.[30] While most 1950s saucer organizations were ephemeral and ineffectual, a few earned a reputation for integrity and discipline, among them Civilian Saucer Intelligence of New York and Civilian Saucer Investigation in Los Angeles; Leonard Stringfield's Civilian Research, Interplanetary Flying Objects (CRIFO) in Cincinnati; and the Aerial Phenomena Research Organization (APRO), founded by Coral and Jim Lorenzen in 1952 and lasting until 1988. A fledgling and foundering organization based in Washington, D.C., the National Investigations Committee on Aerial Phenomena (NICAP) appointed Donald Keyhoe as director in 1957, and he set about transforming the committee into the preeminent UFO organization of its time. His name conferred instant recognition and respect while he filled the board of directors with scientists, academics, and retired military officers. With NICAP as the standard-bearer for serious ufology, thousands of people joined and some set up local subcommittees to link national headquarters with a valuable network of information and investigation. NICAP toed a conservative line by favoring reports from pilots, police, the military, and other presumably reliable sources while rejecting sensational and most close-encounter claims. Keyhoe set his sights on congressional hearings as the surest way to blow the lid off the Air Force cover-up. He trusted that the accumulation of sober evidence would convince enough leaders of Congress to act and end the secrecy once and for all.[31]

A lurid throng of rumors, claims, controversies, and speculations always scurried beneath the feet of respectable ufology. Occultist Meade Layne called the saucers "ether ships" from other planes of existence, while Kenneth Arnold and others suggested that the saucers were animals native to the upper atmosphere.[32] Ray Palmer, editor of *Amazing Stories* in 1947, took an early interest in Arnold's sighting and promoted saucers in *Fate*, a magazine he cofounded in 1948. Later he edited *Flying Saucers*, the only regular newsstand magazine devoted to saucers in the late 1950s and 1960s. Always colorful and opinionated, Palmer quarreled with NICAP and rejected the extraterrestrial hypothesis in favor of a civilization living inside the earth as the source of the saucers.[33] An early mystery-within-a-mystery began in late 1953 when Albert K. Bender suddenly shut down the International Flying Saucer Bureau, a thriving club he had started the previous year. Not only did his abrupt termination of the club puzzle his friends, but Bender fled any further contact with UFOs and left no explanation except to hint, with manifest fear and trembling, that three men dressed in black suits had visited him. This clue inspired Gray Barker to write a speculative investigation of the Bender case and strange behavior among other ufologists, *They Knew Too Much about Flying Saucers* (1956). The Three Men in Black entered UFO lore as its resident bogeymen, perhaps sinister government agents frightening into silence anyone who learned inconvenient secrets, perhaps the aliens themselves policing the overly inquisitive. When Bender told his story in a 1962 book, he revealed that the men were indeed threatening aliens with glowing eyes and a demonic sulfurous smell, but they recently had returned to their home planet and left him free to speak.[34]

Something of a trickster figure in ufology, Barker published an irregular and irreverent magazine between 1953 and 1962, first entitled the *Saucerian* and later *Saucerian Bulletin*. The "Wild Rumors" column was a prominent feature where Barker reveled in tales of landings, aliens, crashes, and contacts largely ignored by serious ufologists but evidence for an underground current of beliefs within the UFO community. Another ufologist with a sense of humor was James W. Moseley, editor of *Saucer News*. Like many magazines of the era, *Saucer News* printed sightings and legitimate news of the field when there was anything available to print, but in times of information drought the pages filled with gossip, opinion, and attacks on other UFO publications or organizations. Barker and Moseley carried on a famous feud for years, though it was all in fun and the two men were actually good friends. With other players in the saucer field these feuds could degenerate into mean-spirited name-calling. A "letter to the editor" published in *The UFO Reporter* in 1964 exemplifies the tenor of such less cordial discourse: "UFO research needs you bums like it needs a hole in the head. Why don't you do everyone a favor and leave Ufology to competent, mature adults? The worthwhile organizations such as NICAP have to spend more time undoing the harm done by pinheads like you than on constructive, original research."[35]

Adrift in the Doldrums.—Boom times favored UFOs until 1958, but the next half dozen years proved a bust. The saucers still put on a good show—for example, in 1959 three large luminous spheres paced an airliner flying over Pennsylvania as passengers and crew watched, while in New Guinea an Anglican missionary, Father William Gill, and thirty-seven of his parishioners watched a UFO for four hours as it hovered a few hundred feet away and figures like men came and went on the top of the craft. The next night, June 27, the UFO returned. Gill and about a dozen others waved at the figures, and they waved back.[36] As good sightings remained sporadic, press attention as well as public interest in UFOs began to wither. Never financially secure despite its sizable membership, NICAP felt the pinch and appeals for donations filled the mails more frequently than issues of its publication, the *UFO Investigator*. The hope for congressional investigations slipped away as the saucers slipped out of the public spotlight. Another casualty was a sense that the mystery headed toward some climactic resolution, perhaps because of a break in government secrecy, perhaps through dramatic actions of the aliens; but in any case a conviction had prevailed throughout the 1950s that a definitive event was impending, and it would change the world. When the big event failed to materialize, the earlier excitement and momentum ran down as the faithful wearied of a lack of direction in the phenomenon. The saucer clubs squabbled and theorists speculated, but the drive toward a conclusion had come to a standstill.

More and more the Air Force and the skeptics seemed to win the upper hand. Edward J. Ruppelt first published his experiences with Project Blue Book in 1956 as *The Report on Unidentified Flying Objects*. In the original edition he acknowledged that the Air Force found no explanation for a number of puzzling cases, but an expanded edition issued in 1959 reversed his earlier position and denied that any significant number of cases eluded conventional resolution.[37] Ruppelt may have undergone a genuine change of mind, but Keyhoe and other ufologists believed the military had pressured him to recant, and his death in 1960 foreclosed any elaboration or explication he might have offered.[38] Harvard astronomer Donald H. Menzel emerged as the foremost scientific critic in his 1953 book, *Flying Saucers*, where he explained many saucer sightings as mirages and atmospheric phenomena. He struck again with *The World of Flying Saucers* in 1963, where he repeated that atmospheric and astronomical phenomena accounted for most UFO reports and heaped ridicule on the subject as a myth of the space age. Menzel's blast underscored—for anyone not already well aware—that ufology was a movement in retreat. This crisis might have proven fatal had not a resurgence of UFO activity intervened.

The Era of High Strangeness, 1964–1974

A Time of Waves Heaped on Waves.—It began near Socorro, New Mexico, in the late afternoon of April 24, 1964. Police officer Lonnie Zamora was pursuing a speeding car along a desert road when he heard an explosion and broke off to investigate, bouncing along a gravel side road toward a cone of flame rising from behind a hill. By the time he reached the top of the hill, all was quiet and he saw no flame, but an object like an overturned white car sat in a ravine while two figures the size of boys, dressed in white overalls, stood nearby. He radioed a report of a possible accident to headquarters, but when he looked toward the scene again, the figures were gone and the "car" started to spout smokeless flames as it rose in the air. The oval object roared close overhead while he took cover behind his car, fearing the object would explode. An examination of the landing site found burnt bushes and four indentations such as landing gear might leave. Critics charged that the story was a hoax and the landing traces required nothing more sophisticated than a spade and a can of lighter fluid, but the police, the Air Force, and the media flocked to the scene, and UFOs entered the news for front-page attention once again.[39]

Publicity surrounding this Socorro landing heralded a new wave and a new era. Over the next ten years UFOs enacted the most dramatic episode in their saga, a time of soaring expectations, dashed hopes, and a remarkable recovery. More than ever before or since, UFOs left little breathing room from sighting to sighting, wave to wave, as a worldwide pandemic raged from 1964 to 1968. Not only did UFOs return for an unprecedented concentration of activity, but they came back bolder than ever. Their pilots seemed willing to land, to show themselves, to take a purposeful and sometimes frightening interest in humans. Close-up sightings revealed structural details of the craft and reinforced the identity of UFOs as physical vehicles, but a paradox asserted itself when the more witnesses saw, the less material UFOs appeared to be. Surreal accounts entered the record of UFOs that appeared and disappeared like ghosts, changed shape, played tricks with time, and bent or twisted light like a solid substance. A new term—"high strangeness"—entered the ufological vocabulary and became the new frontier and new focus of investigation.

UFOs of the 1960s looked and acted like UFOs of the 1950s but went about their business on a larger scale in shorter time. Some areas like the Uintah Basin of Utah seemed to open a "window" for frequent UFO visitation, while the English town of Warminster became a UFO watchers' Mecca for nearly a decade.[40] National, regional, and local waves visited Canada, Mexico, Australia, Chile, Argentina, Spain, Romania, and the Soviet Union between 1965 and 1968; even meteorologists at remote Antarctic stations witnessed UFO displays in 1965. Domestic outbreaks in July and August 1964; July, August, September, November, and December 1965; spring 1966; and February, March, and April 1967 kept the home fires of interest ablaze, but quality as well as quantity thrust UFO reports into the news.[41] The Exeter classic of 1965 remains intriguing. Another celebrated case began in the predawn hours of April 17, 1966, in

Portage County, Ohio, when Deputy Sheriff Dale Spaur heard several reports of a
UFO in the area during his late-shift patrol. About 5 A.M. he saw a light in the trees.
It rose into clear view, an oval object so brilliant his eyes watered to look at it, and
began to move away. Spaur and his partner Barney Neff pursued the UFO in their
cruiser in a high-speed chase that carried them eighty-five miles from Ohio into Pennsylvania. Other law enforcement officers learned of the chase by radio and spotted the
object. The skeptics blamed Venus, but the news media gave the incident extensive
coverage.[42]

High Tide of Acceptance.—A newfound sense of purpose took shape within ufology at the best possible time. Just at the onset of the 1964 UFO revival, NICAP published a book by assistant director Richard Hall, *The UFO Evidence*, and gave copies
to members of Congress as the organization continued to push for hearings. What
distinguished *The UFO Evidence* as an important research document was a comparative study of patterns in the best reports, and with this quiet, systematic march of evidence Hall marshaled a more convincing case for UFOs as unearthly physical vehicles
than the whole parade of 1950s anecdotal literature. In 1965 Jacques Vallee, a graduate
student in astrophysics and computer science at Northwestern University, published
Anatomy of a Phenomenon, a lucid preamble to the scientific study of UFOs that highlighted the evidence and how to approach it. James McDonald, an atmospheric physicist at the University of Arizona, maintained an interest in UFOs since he sighted one
in the 1950s. When he went public as an investigator in 1966, UFOs gained their most
vigorous and outspoken scientific advocate of the late 1960s.[43]

A change in tone among the press and public accompanied the increasing quality
of sightings. Where reporters once treated the subject as good only for a laugh, they
covered UFO stories as legitimate, even important news by 1965, and one editorialist
after another spoke up for the need to investigate a mystery that grew more and more
mysterious.[44] *Saturday Review* columnist John Fuller went to New Hampshire for a
journalistic investigation into the recurrent sightings around Exeter in the fall of 1965.
The more witnesses he interviewed, the deeper his conviction became that they saw
something real and inexplicable. Fuller wrote of his experiences in *Incident at Exeter*,
where he concluded that UFOs were probably extraterrestrial spaceships and called
for the government to "reveal what it knows, or to order a scientific investigation on a
major scale."[45] By the time this book appeared in mid-1966, a breath of swamp gas had
blown down the skeptics' house and set in motion that very investigation.

The turning point followed a rash of sightings in Michigan during March 1966. A
rural family in Dexter watched a red glowing disk land in a swampy area on the twentieth. The police saw a bright light in the woods when they arrived, and a red-lighted

object followed the car when they departed. The following night at Hillsdale, a town some sixty miles away, eighty to ninety college students watched from their dorm windows as lights flew low to the ground.[46] These incidents garnered attention in every newspaper from the *New York Times* to the local daily, and *Life* magazine featured the Michigan sightings as part of a seven-page spread on UFOs in the April 1 issue.[47] The furor reached such a pitch that the head of Blue Book sent J. Allen Hynek to investigate. He was not much impressed by the famous sightings or the UFO hysteria he found. At a press conference a few days later, Hynek pointed out that many Michigan sightings resolved into planets or stars with a little investigation, and he suggested that the lights seen in marshy locations around Dexter and Hillsdale might have originated with swamp gas.[48]

Hynek's remarks raised a howl of derision heard around the world. An exasperated Hillsdale civil defense director complained that the UFO appeared in a park, not a swamp,[49] and citizens outraged at the insult to their intelligence wrote their congressmen. Press and public reacted with unprecedented indignation as they lampooned the swamp gas explanation as an idea that "smells" and berated the Air Force for refusing to level with the public. Several influential voices—*Time*, the *New York Times*, and Walter Cronkite in a CBS News special that aired in early May among them—still seconded the Air Force line, but the skeptics fought a losing defense against public opinion that had swung hard in favor of UFOs.[50] A Gallup poll taken in mid-April found that 96 percent of the population had heard about flying saucers, 46 percent thought they were real, and 5 percent had seen one.[51] A more threatening vote of no confidence in Air Force handling of the subject took shape in Washington as two Michigan representatives, one of them Gerald Ford, the influential House Republican minority leader, responded to the public outcry and called for formal congressional hearings. Three Air Force representatives testified before the House Armed Services Committee on April 5; one was Hynek, and he favored an independent scientific investigation. The Air Force agreed and began to search for a major university to host the study. After several candidates shied away, the University of Colorado signed a contract with the Air Force in October, with noted physicist Edward U. Condon to head the investigation.[52]

The project, eventually funded at more than half a million dollars, included a staff of astronomers, physicists, psychologists, and other specialists. Their investigations began in earnest early in 1967 and ended in the spring of 1968, with the remainder of the year spent in writing up a massive study report of case investigations and supplementary material on such topics as radar and the psychology of human perception. Condon contributed a long introduction stating the official conclusions of the project. Long before he signed his name to the final draft and released it to the press during the first week of 1969, a bitter controversy had embroiled the study and demolished any pretenses of an unbiased inquiry.[53]

A spirit of goodwill greeted this effort as the scientific study UFOs had always needed. Donald Keyhoe feared the Air Force still pulled the strings, but Condon had a reputation for independence and Keyhoe pledged the cooperation of NICAP to make certain that investigators confronted the best reports. Hynek, Jacques Vallee, Keyhoe, and Richard Hall briefed the project personnel, and prospects seemed bright for a fair and aboveboard hearing, yet the honeymoon ended soon after it began. In January 1967 an Air Force representative suggested an anti-extraterrestrial conclusion as a way to help the Air Force get out of the UFO business. Condon had never thought very highly of the subject and seemed glad to oblige. By the end of the month he declared in a public speech that he thought there was nothing to UFOs—"but I'm not supposed to reach that conclusion for another year." Condon spent little time on the project and showed interest only in crackpot cases, while his continued flippant public remarks strained relationships with cooperating groups like NICAP and APRO. Internal tensions divided the project workers as well. Robert J. Low, assistant dean of the graduate school, served as project coordinator and sided with Condon, while many working members of the project, led by University of Colorado psychologist David R. Saunders, rankled at administrative bias and contemplated a minority report.[54]

The most damning evidence of that bias surfaced in July 1967. In a memo dated August 9, 1966, to other university administrators, at a time when acceptance of the UFO project was uncertain, Low stated, "Our study would be conducted almost exclusively by nonbelievers who . . . could and probably would add an impressive body of evidence that there is no reality to the observations. The trick would be . . . to describe the project so that, to the public, it would appear a totally objective study but, to the scientific community, would present the image of a group of nonbelievers trying their best to be objective but having almost a zero expectation of finding a saucer."[55] This cynical approach expressed Low's desire to win project funding for the university and belied his initial open-minded approach to UFO research, but project members already concerned about the drift of the study read a confirmation of their worst fears. Condon's disdain for the subject and lack of rapport with the staff combined with Low's support for Condon and loyalty to the university's bottom line to widen a growing divide between administrators and investigators. Low's "trick" message poisoned the waters beyond any hope of recovery. Saunders circulated the memo to other project members; it soon reached Keyhoe and James McDonald, who recycled it back to the author. Low and Condon felt betrayed and made a bad situation worse. Condon fired Saunders and another investigator on February 8, 1968, while an assistant administrator resigned in protest three weeks later. As the committee disintegrated as a cooperative team, McDonald publicly denounced the project, NICAP withdrew its cooperation, and John Fuller blasted the study in a May 14 *Look* magazine article titled "Flying Saucer Fiasco."[56] Saunders told his story of good evidence ignored and politics triumphant over science in *UFOs? Yes! Where the Condon Committee Went Wrong* (with R. Roger Harkins, 1968).[57]

Disaster and Recovery.—Ufologists resigned themselves to rejection, but when it arrived the bleak and absolute dismissal stung with bitter disappointment. Condon pronounced that the project uncovered nothing to justify further study of UFOs, and the reports added nothing new to scientific knowledge.[58] Readers who ventured into the cavernous interior of the study objected that the conclusion seemed written in a vacuum, disconnected from the study proper and even at odds with the investigative reports. How could UFOs hold no interests when over one-fourth of the cases remained unexplained, including many of the most detailed, provocative examples?[59] How could science fail to gain when some of the explanations raised more questions than they answered, like one case evaluated as a "natural phenomenon, which is so rare that it has apparently never been reported before or since"?[60] Despite criticisms, controversies, and inadequacies, the National Academy of Sciences and the *New York Times* rubber-stamped the study with instant approval while the Air Force welcomed this pretext to shut down Project Blue Book as unnecessary. Everyone heard the verdict; no one listened to the appeal. A once sympathetic press and believing public wrote off UFOs as a serious matter. The Condon experience began with the euphoric faith that a fair hearing would convince everyone but ended with a conviction that the subject would never get a fair shake from official science. This betrayal set in concrete an "us-versus-them" mentality among ufologists as they came to distrust whatever official science and government had to say about UFOs.

The immediate consequences of the Condon report were catastrophic for ufology. Domestic sightings had declined after mid-1967, and by early 1969 the UFOs themselves contributed nothing to cushion the shock. The tide of public interest had turned from spaceships to metaphysical preoccupations in the interim. Extraterrestrial themes continued to flourish only in connection with the Bermuda Triangle and ancient astronauts, as Erich von Däniken's *Chariots of the Gods?* (1970) set off a flurry of speculative books about alien visits in the distant past. By December 1969 membership in NICAP plunged below 5,000 after a peak of 14,000 in 1966. The Board of Governors fired Keyhoe to save the financially strapped organization, but this radical surgery killed the patient as a meaningful agent in UFO research, and NICAP lingered on as a ghostly vestige until disbanding in 1980.[61] APRO suffered but survived; other landmarks, like James Moseley's *Saucer News*, disappeared in the lean years from 1969 to 1973.

Out of this wreckage a new ufology began to rise. If the public ear had fallen deaf, a hard core of serious supporters rallied to rebuild a civilian investigative capability. Begun in May 1969, the Midwest UFO Network soon expanded nationwide to become the Mutual UFO Network. MUFON delegated investigative responsibilities to statewide and local-level subgroups, initiated an education program for field investigators, published a magazine (now monthly and titled the *MUFON UFO Journal*), and sponsored an annual symposium to create the largest and most active UFO organization in the country.[62] Stirrings of mainstream scientific curiosity not only survived the Colorado project but gathered force over the next several years. The American Institute of Aeronautics and Astronautics established a subcommittee on UFOs, while the House Committee on Science and Astronautics held a hearing on July 29, 1968, and the American Association for the Advancement of Science (AAAS) sponsored a UFO symposium on December 26–27, 1969. In the House hearings and the AAAS symposium James McDonald and other proponents argued a strong defense against skeptical astronomers Donald Menzel and Carl Sagan.[63]

At both meetings McDonald found an unlikely ally at his side—J. Allen Hynek, the longtime astronomy consultant to the Air Force. Hynek's conversion from doubter to proponent progressed over the years until even as he spoke of swamp gas he already regarded UFOs as an intriguing scientific problem.[64] Slow to go public with his convictions, the urging of his former student Jacques Vallee and pressure from McDonald combined with the events of 1966 to convince him that the time was right to say UFOs merited serious study in a letter to *Science*, published on October 21.[65] Hynek laid out strong cases and a framework for study in his 1972 book, *The UFO Experience*. He classified reports in a descriptive scheme that included daylight disks, nocturnal lights, radar-visual sightings, and close encounters of the first, second, and third kinds (defined as UFOs viewed within a few hundred feet; physical effects from a UFO; and occupants associated with a UFO). These close-encounter designations entered popular usage, with *Close Encounters of the Third Kind* becoming the title of a famous Steven Spielberg movie in 1977. Hynek was impressed that UFOs presented a limited range of appearances and actions that set UFOs apart as an independent phenomenon. He avoided speculation about the nature of UFOs but concluded that beyond misperceptions there remains "a stubborn, unyielding residue of 'incredible reports from credible people.'"[66]

Hynek emerged as the undisputed scientific spokesman for UFOs after McDonald's death in 1971. He stood out as the iconic leader of the movement, a thoughtful, cautious, eloquent figure who inspired confidence and lured other interested scientists into an "invisible college" of experts, bringing hope that UFO study would progress outside the channels of official science. In late 1973 Hynek lent his name and reputation to a new organization when he joined with some of his hitherto invisible colleagues to form the Center for UFO Studies (CUFOS), intending it to represent the flagship of scholarly excellence for the field. The center would publish case histories, research monographs, and a refereed journal, functions that along with the MUFON symposia and research grants awarded from 1979 onward by the Fund for UFO Research (FUFOR) decked out ufology with the regalia of a quasi-academic discipline.[67]

A skeptical front challenged the new sophistication of ufology with the organization of the Committee for the Scientific Investigation of Claims of the Paranormal (CSICOP) in 1976. Its magazine, *Skeptical Inquirer,* has become the forum in a crusade against UFOs, creationism, astrology, "alternative" medicine, and other supposedly pseudoscientific or irrational beliefs.[68] Aviation editor Philip J. Klass emerged as the most outspoken UFO skeptic from the 1970s to the 1990s. He found conventional explanations for seemingly inexplicable cases and argued that all UFO evidence broke down into hoax, error, belief, and self-delusion on close examination. Other CSICOP skeptics, among them writer Robert Sheaffer, former police investigator Joe Nickell, former NASA mission controller James E. Oberg, and University of Kentucky psychology professor Robert A. Baker, joined Klass to harry the credulous—or muddy the waters with half-truths, flimsy theories, and ad hominem invective, as ufologists often see it.

Curiouser and Curiouser.—Ufologists of the 1950s listened for the clank of metallic craft with advanced but clearly technological characteristics and filtered out any contradictory or overly bizarre reports as instances of hoax, exaggeration, or error. From the mid-1960s onward this restrictive attitude turned around as ufologists not only accepted but even sought out the strangest claims as the most revealing face of the phenomenon.

The British magazine *Flying Saucer Review (FSR)* became the leading forum for close-encounter and high-strangeness reports in the 1960s. An example is the case of Maurice Masse, a respected farmer of Valensole, France. Early in the morning of July 1, 1965, as he worked in his lavender field, he heard a whistling sound and walked around a hillock to find an egg-shaped object the size of a car perched on four legs, like a giant spider. Near it stood two humanoid beings the size of children, with enormous hairless heads and mouths like lipless holes. One being pointed a tubelike device at Masse, and he was suddenly unable to move. The beings entered their craft and it took off with great speed but did not recede into the distance; rather it climbed some twenty meters then vanished in an instant. Masse's immobility wore off after twenty minutes, and a few days later he experienced a prolonged need to sleep. Indentations on the ground and damaged plants marked the landing site.[69] Here was *FSR* at its best, documenting the physical effects and baffling actions of a close encounter of the third kind with interviews and field investigations by leading French ufologist Aimé Michel. Readers could also find reports of UFO-related physical injury and healing, unusual animal reactions, bending beams of light, and teleportations, tales of motorists suddenly finding themselves hundreds of miles from the spot where they encountered a UFO. *FSR* did not play the advocate and insist all accounts were true, rather it portrayed the UFO phenomenon as wider and stranger than nuts-and-bolts ufologists admitted.

One case stood out from all others as the most arresting close encounter of the era. Barney and Betty Hill drove home to Portsmouth through the mountains of New Hampshire on the night of September 19, 1961. The road was deserted and the landscape lonely as the Hills watched a distant light seem to pace the car for a number of miles then turn and draw gradually nearer, growing over time into a huge object the shape of a pancake with two rows of lighted windows hovering ahead of the car. Barney stopped to look at the object with binoculars and saw several beings inside the craft; one of them looked back at him and he sped off in panic. A series of beeps sounded, followed by a second series, and suddenly the UFO was gone. The Hills felt groggy and surprised when a road sign located them thirty miles from the place where they had been seemingly minutes before. They reached home about sunrise feeling unclean and anxious. Ten days later Betty experienced vivid and recurrent nightmares of strange beings taking her aboard the UFO. She described the sighting in a letter to Donald Keyhoe, and several NICAP investigators interviewed the Hills beginning in October. In reviewing the sequence of events the Hills became aware that they arrived home some two hours later than they should have.[70]

Over the following months Barney sought medical attention for blood pressure and ulcers, but his problems seemed rooted in psychological rather than physical causes. He became a patient of Boston psychiatrist Benjamin Simon, who identified the UFO experience as an apparent source of anxiety and carried out hypnosis sessions with both the Hills from February till June 1964. Under hypnosis a mental block seemed to crumble, and they filled in the missing hours of their journey with the story of a UFO encounter of the closest and most astounding kind.

In this story the Hills drove onto a side road after the first beeps and stopped when a party of humanoids barred their way. About five feet tall and with elongated eyes that wrapped around the sides of their large hairless heads, these beings had faces that were otherwise nearly featureless, with the ears and nose vestigial and the mouth a lipless slit. The Hills lost all will to resist and accompanied the beings to a clearing in the woods where the UFO had landed. Both the Hills underwent a medical examination, with the examiner taking samples of Betty's hair and skin and scanning her with a lenslike device. As she lay naked on a table, the examiner inserted a large needle into her abdomen for a "pregnancy test," causing her to cry out with pain until the leader relieved it in an instant by waving his hand in front of her eyes. Barney remained more docile and kept his eyes closed throughout much of his examination, but he recalled that the beings extracted a sperm sample and inserted a device into his rectum.[71] After Betty's examination she conversed with the leader by telepathy, answering questions about foods, colors, time, and other common concepts that seemed to puzzle these beings. The leader showed her a star map and promised her a book as a souvenir but withdrew the offer when the crewmen objected. He also suggested that she not remember what happened this night. The Hills walked back to the car to watch the craft take off then drove away, going some miles before the beeping sounds repeated. At that point their conscious memories returned, and they began to talk about the UFO sighting earlier in the night, but by the time they arrived at home all memories of their two hours of captivity had disappeared except for indistinct feelings.[72]

John Fuller learned about the case while he investigated UFOs in New Hampshire and prepared a book with cooperation of the Hills and Dr. Simon. Published as *The Interrupted Journey* and serialized in *Look* magazine in October 1966, the Hill abduction became perhaps the most talked about encounter in a year crowded with spectacular UFO stories. For once the account was full, detailed, and documented. For once two witnesses confirmed the experience and both were respected members of their community. Dr. Simon believed the abduction was a fantasy nurtured by the frightening UFO sighting and Betty's nightmares. After considering these explanations Barney rejected them, saying that the abduction memories felt as real to him as any other memories and he had to accept them as such.[73] An Ohio school teacher, Marjorie Fish, constructed a model of the local star system and compared it with the star diagram Betty Hill drew under hypnosis. The pattern matched a view of the Zeta Reticuli star system. An ensuing debate appeared in *Astronomy* magazine in 1974, with Carl Sagan arguing that the match was a matter of chance, while some ufologists continue to point out that the more we learn about Zeta Reticuli, the better it suits the criteria for a habitable star system.[74] Despite the potential importance of the Hill case for understanding UFOs, ufologists did not know quite what to make of it and were slow to factor it into their thinking. It remained a gray eminence, isolated from the rest of ufology until abductions took center stage during the next decade.

Strange as it was, abduction represented high strangeness of a comprehensible sort. If aliens studied the earth with scientific curiosity, sooner or later they would have to take an interest in the most plentiful large mammals and give humans a once-over in the lab. Other UFO-related activity appeared to have more in common with hauntings than with extraterrestrial visitation, and none more so than a series of weird events around Point Pleasant, West Virginia, in late 1966 and 1967. Sightings were commonplace in this window area, and a favorite rendezvous for UFO-watching was a large desolate reserve that had served for explosives storage during World War II. Two couples drove through the grounds one night in November 1966 when a tall figure loomed up ahead of them, humanlike until it unfolded batlike wings and stared at the startled witnesses with red glowing eyes. The young couples fled, but the "Mothman" flew after them even at speeds up to 100 miles per hour. Hundreds of people combed the explosives site the next day; over the next year more than a hundred adults would see Mothman.[75]

John A. Keel, a veteran writer on strange phenomena, joined the investigation and interviewed witnesses throughout 1967. He recounted his experiences in *The Mothman Prophecies* (1975), a book interwoven with one weird incident after another, not only UFOs and the monster but strange sounds and TV interference, a thirty-foot circle burned into a farmer's field, and animals that disappeared or died in mysterious ways, sometimes with the blood drained as if attacked by a vampire. Time and again Keel encountered the Men in Black—odd looking, oddly dressed individuals speaking in peculiar ways, seemingly too otherworldly to understand the need to wear a coat in subfreezing weather, yet somehow aware of Keel's activities down to secret details. The last Mothman sighting occurred on November 15, 1967; one month later the Silver Bridge between Point Pleasant and Ohio collapsed, resulting in over forty deaths. Many people came to regard the strange events of the past year as a premonition of this disaster.[76] A tolerance for strangeness had not grown robust enough in the 1950s to accept shadowy figures and eerie phone calls as interlocking pieces of the puzzle, but by the late 1960s a growing number of ufologists perceived every strange event as part of a pattern no matter how vast, tenuous, and outlandish it grew.

With rising acceptance for strangeness came adventurous attempts to explain it. Jacques Vallee nailed a series of radical theses to the door of established ufology, starting with *Passport to Magonia* in 1969. There he sought "to build a bridge between two clusters of rumors, observations, and reports," one the claims of UFO encounters, the other an unlikely company of fairy legends and demonological traditions. Stripped down to basic events, UFO accounts and fairy folklore revealed enough likenesses to suggest a unitary phenomenon.[77] UFOs, he said, existed at a juncture between the

material and mental, where they manifested both physical and nonphysical properties. The intelligence behind UFOs was inherently elusive and misleading, but the very
absurdity of anomalous "encounter" events constituted their logic, since they operated
like a schedule of reinforcement to break old conceptual habits and rearrange our
mythological structures. The goal of this conditioning was unclear. Did it nudge us toward cosmic consciousness or portend a new religion? In any case, UFOs were just one
facet of a mystery that encompassed all paranormal phenomena.[78] John Keel proposed
an ultraterrestrial intelligence that perpetrated an Operation Trojan Horse on humanity, with aliens, angels, and poltergeists some of the various disguises assumed by this
intelligence as it spread deception and nonsense to disorient conventional thought and
lead some recipients toward enlightenment, others toward madness and ruin.[79]

These mind-stretching theories invigorated the staid conceptual framework of
ufology but divided its intellectual strategy. As ufologists with a scientific bent tried
to groom the mystery for official favor, "paraufologists" rejected science as inadequate
and buried the extraterrestrial hypothesis as a science-fiction caricature. The truth no
longer depended on hard evidence or even discrimination of hoaxes from sincere experiential claims. Every piece belonged to the puzzle, if only the theorists could make the
puzzle big enough. An idea that vast mysterious forces united all things strange into a
coherent whole began well before this time, so did a willingness to engage in speculative associations and to explain one mystery with another mystery. The "New Ufology"
simply sanctioned this visionary openness and its methodological liabilities with intellectual respectability, bequeathing a heritage that shapes ufology to the present day.[80]

The UFOs themselves reaffirmed the vitality of the mystery when a wave of sightings swept northward from the Gulf Coast to inundate the entire country in October
1973.[81] Notable among hundreds of reports was a case from Pascagoula, Mississippi,
where Charles Hickson and Calvin Parker went fishing on the night of October 11
when a glowing blue disk landed nearby. Three short mummylike creatures with crab-
claw hands seized the men and floated them into the craft. Parker fainted while a large
eyelike device examined Hickson.[82] On the eighteenth the crew of an Army Reserve
helicopter flying over Ohio noticed a light approaching at high speed on a collision
course. Capt. Larry Coyne dived to escape the object, but it hovered in front of the helicopter, a cigar-shaped craft that filled the forward window and beamed a bright green
light into the cockpit. A few seconds later the UFO flew off, and Coyne found that the
helicopter had ascended some 3,000 feet in that brief time.[83] Critics dismissed Pascagoula as a hoax and Coyne as a combination of errors, with the helicopter actually
climbing when the pilot thought it descended, but Hickson and Parker seemed genuinely frightened, and extensive investigations of the Coyne case affirm the presence of

an unknown object against all criticisms.[84] Such impressive UFO activity won national news coverage even in competition with the Yom Kippur War and resignation of Vice President Spiro Agnew as the Watergate scandal began to surface. The public opinion scorecard for a Gallup poll taken in early November found that 95 percent had heard of UFOs, 54 percent thought they were real, and 11 percent said they had sighted one.[85]

Chasing the Next Big Thing, 1975–1990

The 1973 wave rekindled public interest for the rest of the decade, and ufology emerged stronger than ever after the Condon setback. Attention shifted from pursuit of ephemeral objects in the sky toward new classes of evidence offered by abductions and Roswell—evidence that promised not only concrete proof of UFO reality, but also unprecedented insight into the nature and purpose of UFOs. Ufology seemed poised at last to steer UFOs into the scientific mainstream, yet changes were afoot that, while not fully realized until years later, fostered a corrosive specialization and popularization to create a sense of motion without much sense of direction. A shift of interest from the phenomenon to its implications, a growth of UFOs as a cultural presence rather than a scientific subject, have abetted development of the UFO myth.

Prospects for the scientific study of UFOs looked bright in the late 1970s and early 1980s, when domestic organizations enjoyed a new level of quality and an international problem inspired international response. The French space agency, equivalent to NASA, opened an official UFO investigation in 1977, the Groupe d'Etudes des Phénomènes Aérospatiaux non Identifiés (GEPAN). Between 1979 and 1983, GEPAN received over 1,000 reports and carried out eighteen detailed field studies to conclude that some impressive cases left evidence that did not square readily with conventional solutions.[86] The British UFO Research Organization (BUFORA) matured into a leading voice for UFO research in Britain, while quality research organizations arose in Australia, Italy, Spain, Belgium, and Scandinavia. The United Nations in 1978 and the British House of Lords in 1979 held talks on UFOs to confirm that the subject was coming of age as a topic for serious discussion.[87]

Spectacular UFO sightings justified a revitalized inquiry. Between 1977 and 1979 Wales and the British Midlands hosted visits, landings, and high-strangeness events.[88] Off the Adriatic Coast of Italy in 1978, UFOs dived into the water or burst out from beneath the sea with such frequency that fishermen feared to sail.[89] China experienced a major wave in 1980, and northeastern Brazil served as the setting for some of the strangest UFO reports on record from 1977 till 1980. Night hunters reported that luminous rectangular objects pursued them into the jungle and tried to kidnap them or fired a beam of light that resulted in the victim's death within a few hours or days. Others reported UFOs that sucked blood from humans and animals, for which reason the objects were called *chupa-chupas* ("suckers"). At times people went hungry because they felt too threatened to hunt or fish, and Brazilian military authorities responded to the near panic with an investigation.[90] Two 1978 incidents in a Southern Hemisphere wave made international news, once when an airline crew filmed UFOs near Kaikoura, New Zealand, on December 21, and earlier on October 21, when pilot Fred Valentich disappeared while flying across the Bass Strait from Moorabben, Australia. In a radio exchange with the air traffic controller, Valentich reported an aircraft with four lights, a huge object that darted around him at high speed, then "orbited" overhead. No further messages followed from Valentich, only a loud metallic sound. Extensive searches found no trace of plane or pilot.[91] A localized wave of luminous phenomena began at Hessdalen, Norway, in 1981 and continued for several years, attracting an investigation that captured photographs and recorded instrumental data.[92]

A UFO wave covered the Soviet Union during much of 1989. The most sensational report came from Voronezh on September 27, when several teenagers playing in a park late that afternoon saw a spherical object land. A hatch opened and forty adults watched a giant robot creature exit and walk about, causing the paralysis or disappearance of several witnesses before the robot and craft also disappeared—high strangeness played out before a large audience.[93] For critics the only thing giant about the Voronezh story was the audacity of the lie, while its publication simply proved that the Russians had discovered the pleasures of tabloid journalism as the Soviet Union began to crumble and Communist control over the press loosened. Numerous reports of triangular aircraft over Belgium from late 1989 through 1990 were harder to dismiss. Photographs and videotapes provided ample documentation for some unfamiliar aircraft bearing bright lights, while authorities denied that military maneuvers were responsible for the sightings.[94]

If lively waves played out in other parts of the world, it was a different story in the United States. Occasional local waves continued, such as a concentration of sightings centered on Belleville, Wisconsin, in January to March of 1987, or Fyffe, Alabama, in February 1989.[95] The Yakima Indian Reservation in Washington State became a site for numerous observations of luminous objects during 1975–1976, and sporadic sightings of triangular objects near Corydon, Indiana, occurred throughout the 1980s and 1990s.[96] A spectacular series of multiwitness reports described lighted, V-shaped objects over the Hudson Valley in 1983–1984, and these "Westchester Wing" sightings even attracted considerable media attention.[97] But in a major departure from the older pattern of UFO activity, after 1973 no massive, nationwide surge excited the entire country and captivated media interest.

The quality of reports worldwide did not suffer despite a dearth of press coverage, and candidates for the honor roll would surely include these noteworthy examples:

- On September 19, 1976, an Iranian Air Force jet sent to intercept a brilliant object near Tehran lost all guidance and communications capabilities as it approached the UFO. A second interceptor locked radar on the object but lost targeting and communications when the pilot tried to fire a missile.[98]

- Fourteen children at a Welsh school reported a UFO landing and occupant sighting in 1977, while some sixty children at the Ariel School in Zimbabwe had a similar experience in 1994.[99]

- On the night of December 29, 1980, Betty Cash was driving along a Texas road with Vickie Landrum and Landrum's young grandson when they saw a huge diamond-shaped object hovering ahead, jetting flames from its underside. The two women left the car to see the object better, but Landrum soon returned to comfort the frightened boy. A feeling of heat emanated from the object, and the car became hot to touch despite the chilly evening. After some minutes the object rose in a blast of flame and two dozen large helicopters joined it as it flew slowly away. The witnesses drove on but began to feel sick by the time they reached home, with their symptoms proportional in severity to the duration of direct exposure to the object. Betty Cash entered the hospital with peeling skin and patches of hair falling out, remaining there for a total of nearly four weeks. Vickie Landrum suffered sickness and damaged eyesight; neither fully recovered. The boy remained in the car and experienced only minor, temporary illness.[100]

- A farmer in Trans-en-Provence, France, on the afternoon of January 8, 1981, saw an object like two saucers upside down land in his alfalfa field and then take off after a few minutes. An extensive GEPAN investigation on the damaged plants and indentations in the ground revealed effects consistent with some sort of radiation and an object weighing four to five tons. These findings remain controversial, but few other landing cases have had the benefit of such a prompt and thorough investigation.[101]

- A Japan Airlines plane flying over Alaska on November 17, 1986, encountered a Saturn-shaped object described as twice the size of an aircraft carrier. Several smaller objects accompanied the larger one, and the pilot reported feeling heat from the large object when it drew close. Radar from the ground also tracked the UFO.[102]

- Four adult members of the Knowles family were driving near Mundrabilla, Western Australia, at 4 A.M. on January 20, 1988, when a light approached the car. The light proved to be an egg-shaped object that pursued and dived at the vehicle for a while, then chased a car passing in the opposite direction. The object returned and swooped over the Knowleses' car, lifting it into the air then dropping it and rupturing one of the tires. Several other witnesses in the area reported an egg-shaped luminous object.[103]

Reaching for the Jackpot.—A certain malaise afflicted the field despite its renewed prospects. By 1977 the UFO mystery was no longer a youngster. It had reached the ripe old age of thirty, with tens of thousands of reports on record and numerous investigations carried out, but what did it all prove? In 1976 CUFOS could afford a full-time investigator and Allan Hendry took on the job. A recent college graduate with a degree in astronomy, he investigated 1,307 reports by 1979 and failed to identify only 113 cases (8.6 percent) as conventional objects. For him the impasse of ufology resulted not from inherent elusiveness of the phenomenon but from the limitations of human witnesses spreading confusion through the data. With growing pessimism he bemoaned the naïveté of UFO investigations and concluded *The UFO Handbook* (1979) with a prophetic assessment: "Unless we develop *drastically* new ideas and methodologies for the study of the baffling UFO cases and the human context in which they occur, we will watch the next thirty years of UFO report gathering simply mirror the futility and frustration of the last thirty years."[104]

The sighting report remained the basic unit of UFO study, but even when combed and examined with microscopic closeness, an account of an object in the sky was still relatively information starved. Descriptions of ordinary sightings had reached their level, and a thousand more of the same would add nothing new. The field needed a breakthrough, and ufologists reached for the compelling, potentially definitive evidence of abductions and Roswell to prove the reality of UFOs once and for all. This reorientation changed the popular face of UFOs from vessels in the sky to spaceships on the ground and added unprecedented complexity to the UFO story.

By 1975 abductions remained rarities on the periphery of UFO inquiry, but a shift toward the center began late that year. As a crew of seven loggers drove home near Heber, Arizona, on the evening of November 5, they stopped the truck to look at a disk with luminous panels hovering just off the road at treetop level. Travis Walton ran from the truck toward the object until a beam of light from the UFO knocked him backward. His companions fled in panic. When they drove back to the scene a few minutes later, the men found no trace of Walton or the disk. For five days police searched for the missing man, until about midnight on the tenth, when he telephoned relatives and told the few events he remembered from his captivity. He said he awakened in a room surrounded by several short gray beings with large heads and eyes. He threatened them and fled to another room, where he sat in a chair and manipulated a sort of star map. A tall human man with blond hair then escorted Walton outside the craft into a vast hangarlike area. They entered a room where others who looked like clones of the guide waited, and one of them, a woman, placed a device like an oxygen mask over his face and he blacked out. He next found himself lying on the ground beside a highway, looking up at a disk as it receded into the sky.[105]

Walton's story captured national attention and rekindled public interest in abductions, but skeptics cried hoax. Phil Klass proposed that the woodcutters fell behind schedule on a logging job and concocted a tall tale based on *The UFO Incident*, an NBC TV movie about the Hill abduction that aired on October 20, as a way to escape their contract.[106] Yet counter to Benjamin Franklin's dictum that three people can keep a secret if two of them are dead, none of the other witnesses has recanted or attempted to spoil the modest fame that Walton has enjoyed. Abductions also appealed to a newcomer, noted New York artist Budd Hopkins. After he published a UFO article in the *Village Voice* in 1976, people began to contact him with vague misgivings that resonated with possible UFO phenomena. One such individual was Steven Kilburn, a young man who told Hopkins, "There's probably nothing to it ... but something may have happened to me when I was in college. I can't remember anything specific, but something has always bothered me about a certain stretch of road."[107] Hypnosis unfolded a full abduction experience as the substance behind that formless dread. In *Missing Time* (1981) Hopkins introduced a series of similar cases as evidence that experiences with conscious clues amounted to the tip of an iceberg, while the true extent of the abduction problem remained out of sight and unfathomed, marked in the everyday lives of most abductees by no more than a surface ripple of anxiety.

The trickle of cases grew into a torrent with some three hundred in the literature by 1985 and thousands more in the files of investigators. International in scope, abduction reports came from Africa, Australia, Europe, South America, and proliferated in former Soviet territories and in China.[108] The most newsworthy claimant to step forward has been popular horror novelist Whitley Strieber. He sought out Hopkins in 1986 to cope with a baffling experience, and hypnotic investigation soon uncovered memories of aliens removing him from his bedroom for examination aboard a UFO. This experience became the basis of his best-selling book, *Communion* (1987), bearing a cover illustration of an alien face that became a popular icon.[109] That same year Hopkins published his second book, *Intruders*, telling the story of a young Indianapolis woman with a lifelong history of abductions. What made the story of "Kathie Davis" (Debbie Tomey) especially striking was her recollection that the aliens impregnated her, removed the fetus, and years later introduced her to a frail child with a combination of human and alien features.[110]

Abductions lit up the UFO scene with a fresh burst of excitement. The stories were incredible yet surprisingly consistent, and the narrators were sincere people from all walks of life, qualities that won over initial doubters like Temple University history professor David Jacobs and Harvard psychiatrist John Mack, who became vigorous and convinced investigators. Such accounts kept getting better—for instance, when four campers along the Allagash River related similar accounts of capture and examination, or a hovering UFO removed a woman from her New York apartment while security guards and an alleged world leader looked on.[111] Promise of some definitive proof seemed almost within grasp, whether in documentation for a missing fetus, recovery of an alien implant, or videotape of a bedroom intrusion. Abductions dominated the 1987 MUFON Symposium and became the subject of a conference held on the campus of MIT in 1992, where abductees, ufologists, and scholars in multiple disciplines met to consider the phenomenon.[112]

Another emerging body of assertions—that UFOs have crashed and the government retrieved the wreckage—served even better than abductions to stir public and ufological adrenalin. The story began as a small footnote to the 1947 wave: On July 8 the wire services sent out news that the military had captured a fallen disk near Roswell, New Mexico. Rancher Mac Brazel first spotted the wreckage, and an intelligence officer, Maj. Jesse Marcel, took charge of collecting the debris and flew it to Eighth Air Force headquarters in Fort Worth. The next day headlines in the *Roswell Daily Herald* read "Gen. Ramey Empties Roswell Saucer," and photos showed Marcel holding flimsy wreckage of a balloon and radar reflectors.[113] This sudden anticlimax ended the Roswell saga for thirty years without a hint of future glory.

When Marcel told his story in 1978, he stated that the sticks and tinfoil spread on the floor for newspaper photographers was unrelated to the crash and the real debris did not come from this earth. Witnesses began to step forward, such as a man claiming that he flew the wreckage out of Roswell, and acquaintances of Barney Barnett, a deceased civil engineer said to have reported a second crash site on the Plains of San Agustin, 150 miles west of the Brazel site. Barnett went on to describe a saucer-shaped craft that had plowed into the ground and short, large-headed aliens who were found dead near the wreck. He also mentioned some archaeologists who witnessed the scene before soldiers arrived and swore everyone to secrecy. By 1980, when William Moore and Charles Berlitz publicized the crash in *The Roswell Incident*, investigators had interviewed some sixty direct or indirect witnesses. The number increased to over two hundred by the early 1990s.[114]

The story as it first emerged during the 1980s built up a compelling case that the military quickly cordoned off a mysterious crash site and cleared the area of debris. Witness after witness confirmed having seen the material, participated in the cleanup, or transported the debris. Marcel and others described fragments that were sticklike and almost weightless yet too strong to bend or break, while other pieces resembled shards of tinfoil. No flame or attempt at cutting had any effect on these shards, and if folded they soon resumed their original shape. Hieroglyphic figures covered some of the fragments. The more sensational story of aliens also found willing collaborators, one being Glenn Dennis, a Roswell undertaker who claimed that he delivered four child-sized coffins to the air base in Roswell and that he heard a nurse stationed there describe the dead aliens. Investigators striving to reconcile the various parts into a coherent whole could draw up time lines and plausible accounts of a credible event.[115]

This credibility began to suffer when testimony did not stop with corroboration or filling in the gaps but proliferated into rival, often incompatible scenarios. Crash sites multiplied as Jim Ragsdale claimed in 1993 that he and a now-deceased girlfriend saw a UFO fall during a thunderstorm at a place thirty miles south of the Brazel site. Frank Kaufmann, who claimed to be an intelligence official, located the alien bodies about thirty miles southeast of Brazel's find and transferred the archaeologists to this site in a later revision of the story. Kaufmann also revealed that the craft was not disk shaped but elongated like a modern stealth aircraft. In 1990 Gerald Anderson reported that his family and a party of archaeologists had stumbled onto the scene at San Agustin just after the crash, where they saw an alien survivor walking near the wreckage. Before Anderson's yarn collapsed as a hoax, several other witnesses had stepped forward to confirm one or more live aliens and the claim took root as an established element of the story. Additions, changes in testimony, contradictory claims, and flexible hypotheses lost the thread of history in a Roswell labyrinth bewildering in its twists and turns.[116]

If the story confused ufologists, it fascinated the public and made Roswell a household name. Widespread interest led New Mexico Representative Steven Schiff to initiate a General Accounting Office investigation in 1994. Meanwhile, the Air Force rushed its own investigation and concluded that the wreckage belonged to a Project Mogul balloon array that had disappeared in June 1947. Project Mogul was an effort to detect anticipated Soviet nuclear tests and was top secret at the time—thus explaining the secrecy and care taken to gather all scraps of wreckage.[117] The GAO report appeared in July 1995 and satisfied skeptics by finding no evidence for a crashed spaceship, but the investigation also reaffirmed suspicions of a cover-up by revealing that a great many documents from the era had been lost or destroyed.[118] A 1997 Gallup poll revealed that 31 percent of respondents believed that a spaceship had crashed and 64 percent doubted that balloons were responsible for the Roswell story.[119]

In a larger sense official reports and learned disputes ceased to carry any weight because the cultural reality of the Roswell crash overshadowed its historical reality. Roswell has entrenched itself so deeply in the popular mind that audiences for the blockbuster movie *Independence Day* (1996) took in stride a captive saucer kept so secret not even the president knew of it. Movies based on the Roswell incident and a TV series about teenage aliens in the local high school have further promoted this belief. The UFO Museum in Roswell is one of the major tourist attractions in New Mexico, while the annual Roswell Days has drawn tens of thousands of visitors, especially during the fiftieth anniversary celebration in 1997.[120] The Roswell mythology continues to flourish and evolve as claimants continue to come forward with accounts of seeing wreckage or working with unearthly technology. An alien autopsy film showing the supposed dissection of a dead Roswell alien surfaced in 1995 and caused a brief sensation, though most investigators regarded the film as a transparent hoax.[121]

A suspicion that the government hides the truth about visiting spaceships runs the entire length of modern UFO history, but nothing reinforced this notion like Roswell. An opportunity to find out what the government really knew opened in 1974 as the Freedom of Information Act invited a plague of ufologists to descend on the Air Force, FBI, CIA, and National Security Agency in search of UFO-related documents. Thousands of recovered pages exposed exciting case materials like the multiple air base intrusions of 1975, as well as intriguing tidbits like NORAD tracking some ten million uncorrelated targets between the 1960s and the early 1980s to answer, at least to ufologists' satisfaction, the question of how UFOs could be real but never detected by sophisticated defense radar.[122] These inquiries also indicated that the authorities were more troubled about UFO activity than they admitted. In some instances the documents trapped their agency of origin in an outright lie. For example, in its responses to initial FOIA requests the CIA claimed that its UFO involvement ended with the Robertson Panel in 1953, only to face proof of continuing interest from the earliest years to the present once a court battle wrested the telltale files from the agency.[123]

These discoveries nailed down proof that the government knew much, cared much, and hid much about UFOs while telling the public just the opposite, but the findings were also important for what they did not show. No smoking gun confirmed Roswell, and years of government interest betrayed a lack of answers, not the certainty and direction that ought to follow from having a UFO in custody since 1947. One solution for this dearth of favorable evidence escalated the scope of conspiracy so that not the Air

Force or even the CIA had the real answers, only agencies above the law and separate from day-to-day government operations knew the truth. Hints about the identity of those ultimate guardians of UFO secrecy soon began to leak out. One rumor destined for a stellar career in UFO mythology alleged that President Truman established "Majestic 12" or MJ-12, a group of high-ranking military and scientific figures to oversee all UFO-related matters. An associate of William Moore, Jaime Shandera, found a roll of microfilm in his mailbox during December 1984. This film contained a purported presidential briefing document from MJ-12 with the now-familiar scoop on crashed saucers and captive aliens. Various ufologists have continued to find or receive other mysterious documents referring to MJ-12 and its clandestine work.[124]

Weaving in and out among abductions, Roswell, and conspiracies, other sensations have taken briefer turns in the limelight as promising new hopes for a ufological breakthrough.

Cattle Mutilations.—During the mid-1970s farmers and ranchers began to find seemingly healthy cattle suddenly dead without any sign of struggle. Blood seemed drained from the carcass, and genitals, eyes, and ears were removed with apparent surgical precision. The blame first fell on Satanists, but rumors that the killers traveled aboard mysterious helicopters soon implicated UFOs as more likely agents. The cattle mutilation theme entered abduction stories and became a staple in conspiracy tales with grisly details to convict the aliens of hostile intentions.[125] An investigation headed by former FBI agent Kenneth Rommel Jr. during 1979–1980 concluded that the cattle deaths were due to natural causes, the supposed surgical removals the typical work of scavengers. The deaths appeared out of the ordinary only under the influence of expectations aroused by publicity.[126] Some veterinarians dissented that the incisions had the character of laser burns, while Linda Howe and other ufologists still maintain that mutilations are too mysterious for conventional answers to explain. The deaths have continued here and there over the years, with a major epidemic in Argentina beginning in the late 1990s.[127]

The Face on Mars.—The Viking Mars Orbiter sent back a startling image from the Cydonia region in 1976. This photograph showed a remarkably human face of gigantic size gazing up from the surface, an image soon to serve as Exhibit A in an argument that an advanced ancient civilization once lived on the planet. Further exhibits came to light as proponents pored over photographs to identify pyramids and citylike structures near the face. NASA bowed to public interest and targeted the area with the Mars Global Surveyor in 1998, gathering images with tenfold better resolution that broke down the facial features into a natural pile of rubble. Proponents undaunted by this disappointment and determined to save Face have accused NASA of doctoring the photographs, even sabotaging two subsequent Mars probes to hide the truth about ruins and monuments on the planet.[128]

The Rendlesham Landing.—Something baffling happened in the early morning of December 27, 1980, in the Rendlesham Forest, on the east coast of England near two air bases leased to the U.S. Air Force under a NATO agreement. A memorandum from the deputy base commander, Lt. Col. Charles Halt, stated that guards investigating a possible plane crash came across a triangular, tent-shaped object near the ground that illuminated the forest. The next day a patrol found indentations and traces of radiation where the object touched down. That night a pulsing red light moved among the trees, broke into several white objects, and disappeared before Colonel Halt and other witnesses. If this official version was not remarkable enough, many rank-and-file servicemen had a story to tell. In the elaborated versions the original three guards lost consciousness when the UFO flashed a light on them, while on the second night parties of troops saw the shadowy figures of occupants inside a translucent UFO, or in yet another version, the UFO landed and aliens emerged to communicate with a general. Three British researchers introduced the case in a 1984 book, while Larry Warren, a serviceman on duty at the time, became a spokesman for some of the more sensational claims. An inquiry in Parliament in 1996 ended with the Ministry of Defence stating that the incident had no defense significance. Efforts to explain the UFOs as beams from a nearby lighthouse have not proved very convincing in a case that continues to confuse even as it still attracts attention.[129]

Gulf Breeze.—One of the most divisive events in UFO history began in the Florida town of Gulf Breeze in November 1987, when several vivid UFO photographs appeared in the local newspaper. Ed Walters, head of a construction company, said he snapped several shots of a lighted object as it hovered near his home. He added that the object struck him with a beam of blue light and lifted him into the air, while a series of contact and abduction claims followed, as well as more clear photographs of structured craft.[130] UFO watches on the beach became commonplace. Gulf Breeze surged to the forefront of interest as some ufologists defended Walters, arguing that he stood to gain little from a hoax and the photos defied explanation as fakes. The opponents responded that when a UFO photo looks too good to be true, it probably is not, and a book contract provided Walters with several hundred thousand dollars of incentive. Discovery of a model UFO in a house formerly owned by Walters provided damaging evidence, reinforced when local teenagers said that he had entertained them by creating double-exposure photographs before the UFO business began.[131] MUFON held its

1990 symposium in Pensacola with Walters and the local sightings as central attractions, but in a field where strident controversy is the norm, Gulf Breeze pumped up the volume to exceptional levels during its few years on the UFO scene.

Crop Circles.—Mysterious circles began to appear in the wheat fields of southern England during the summer of 1980. These circles started out as lone swirls of flattened plants but graduated in complexity season by season to a main circle with smaller satellites and to vast and intricate works of art by the 1990s. Despite little reason for a UFO connection, crop circles filtered into the UFO literature, and by the 1990s they became staple topics at UFO conventions. The mystery seemed about to blow away in 1991 when two retired men, Doug Bower and Dave Chorley, demonstrated how to construct circles by simple means, but proponents refused to let go and dismissed the "Doug and Dave" hoax solution as inadequate to explain how intricate forms could appear overnight without any disturbance to arouse the neighbors. The undeniable beauty of the formations continues to inspire wonder and a mystical turn where some people read alien messages in crop circles and link them with transformation of consciousness.[132]

By the late 1980s most thoughtful ufologists had given up exotic theories and returned to the extraterrestrial hypothesis (ETH). Abductions suggested it, Roswell demanded it—the foremost influences on the field thus lent a powerful incentive to reconsider the ETH. Jacques Vallee reemphasized the physical aspects of UFO phenomena even as he continued to theorize about a control system, and Jerome Clark renounced his speculations from *The Unidentified* to reembrace the ETH as the best solution available.[133] "Best" in this case came with reservations. An awareness of complexity and strangeness, of interactions with psychology and social processes, replaced the simplistic science-fiction image with a sense that any alien presence was more subtle, more deeply entangled with human history than heretofore imagined.

The 1990s and Beyond: Uforia without UFOs

A quality of paradox has marked the last decade of the twentieth century and the first decade of the twenty-first. An alien invasion swept through modern culture even as news coverage of sightings dwindled, UFOs thrived in popular acceptance yet organized ufology fell on hard times, the Internet democratized UFO communication but undercut rational study, and UFO politics replaced scientific, evidence-based inquiry as the center of attention. Gallup polls in 1990, 1996, and 2001 reflect a slight erosion of interest in a physical phenomenon offset by hints that UFOs have grown as a social issue. Most people still say they have heard or read about UFOs, though percentages declined to 87 percent in 1996, as opposed to 96 percent in 1966 and 95 percent in 1973. Nearly half the samples believe UFOs are real, 47 percent in 1990 and 48 percent in 1996, down slightly from a peak of 57 percent in 1978. On the other hand, believers that extraterrestrials have visited some time in the past have increased from 27 percent to 33 percent between 1990 and 2001, while percentages of people who think they have seen a UFO hold almost steady at 14 percent in 1990 and 12 percent in 1996, higher than at any time in the history of these polls. Asked in 1996 if they think the government knows more than it tells about UFOs, a whopping 71 percent of respondents said yes.[134]

Opinion polls tell only a bare-bones story of a decade when UFOs shed much of their folk status to shine with pop-culture glitter. Helped by the fiftieth anniversary of Kenneth Arnold and Roswell in 1997, boosted by media promotion of the end of the millennium as an occasion of paranormal significance, UFOs became newsworthy even in the absence of immediate UFO activity. Movie versions of the Walton and Strieber abductions and a TV miniseries based on *Intruders* introduced important UFO stories to anyone still unfamiliar with them.[135] Steven Spielberg created the miniseries *Taken* for the SciFi Channel in 2002 with a dramatized retelling of UFO history from World War II to the present, full of Roswell, evil government, and hybrid children. *The Mothman Prophecies* (2001) created a creepy cinematic version of John Keel's book, while filmmaker M. Night Shyamalan burst the New Age bubble on crop circles in *Signs* (2002), where they spelled out the message that a hostile alien invasion was coming. Countless TV documentaries and late-night radio programs have enabled the curious to tune in a UFO discussion any night of the week. Respected TV journalist Larry King interviewed ufologists with Area 51 as a backdrop; ABC News anchor Peter Jennings hosted an often favorable documentary, *UFOs—Seeing Is Believing*, in 2005; and Web sites concerned with UFOs have multiplied into the tens of thousands.[136] UFO books surfeited the market in the late 1990s as publishers rushed to cash in on the fashionableness of UFOs. Many of the efforts were derivative and slipshod, but such works as Jerome Clark's *The UFO Encyclopedia* (1998) and Richard Hall's *The UFO Evidence II* (2001) set the gold standard for quality scholarship. The *X-Files* TV series captivated audiences with a phrase that has entered both public and ufological common currency—"The truth is out there." The truth remains elusive, but the idea of UFOs flourishes as a cultural reality.

Scientific and scholarly engagement with UFOs continued to make headway. In 1997 Laurance Rockefeller sponsored a conference for ufologists to present radar, photographic, and other "hard" evidence to a party of skeptical scientists. The scientific panelists saw insufficient reason to accept UFOs as extraterrestrial machines but acknowledged that the reports did not resolve readily into familiar categories and that scientific knowledge stood to gain from further investigation.[137] Two years later a study of outstanding cases by French scientists and military officers attempted to assess defense implications of UFOs. This COMETA (Comité d'Études Approfondies) group concluded that UFOs were likely vehicles under intelligent extraterrestrial control, and the semiofficial status of the group meant that they spoke at least informally for the French government.[138] The United Kingdom Ministry of Defense sponsored a UFO study between 1996 and 2000, and the secret document of nearly five hundred pages became public in 2006. Project Condign concluded that unidentified aerial phenomena over UK airspace held no defense significance and accounted for sightings as military "black projects" and atmospheric plasmas, but the author accepted a physical basis for reports and acknowledged that the causes were sufficiently unknown to warrant further study.[139] The formation of standing groups of experts, like the National Aviation Reporting Center on Anomalous Phenomena (NARCAP), the National Institute for Discovery Science (NIDS), the Sign Historical Group, and Budd Hopkins's Intruders Foundation, reflected an ongoing commitment to explore the scientific potential of UFOs.

In contrast to the rosy cultural complexion of the subject, the current state of organized ufology looks wan and haggard. The major U.S. and British organizations saw a steady membership decline in the 1990s, first as glossy newsstand magazines and then later the Internet usurped the informative role once exclusive to these groups. Paying members stopped paying and helped themselves to the rich, if not always nutritious diet of alternative sources while organizations starved in the midst of plenty. The current robust state of disorganized ufology owes much to the Internet, with its instant gratification and a chance to monitor news, developments, rumors, and opinions on a day-by-day, hour-by-hour basis. Quality Web sites often remain known only to veterans, while the uninitiated find themselves awash in sites that borrow content from elsewhere, errors and all, or retail personal opinion with little regard for objectivity.[140]

Crash-Retrievals, Disclosure, and Exopolitics.—New research initiatives perpetuated an assumption that the business of ufology was to take a scientific approach to a scientific problem, but in the wake of Roswell a departure from this long-dominant model rewrote the ufological master narrative into a political thriller. Many people interested in UFOs now listen to the insider and whistleblower rather than to the eyewitness and experiencer as the most valuable sources. Meanwhile, the ufological quest has transformed from a question for science to answer into a prize to pry loose from its jealous governmental guardians.

Release of the MJ-12 papers in 1987 whipped up a frenzy of dark-side beliefs that would dominate ufology for several years. An intelligence agent told William Moore that extraterrestrials had manipulated human DNA over thousands of years and military efforts were under way to back-engineer a spacecraft from extraterrestrial models. This latter claim received confirmation from Robert Lazar, who enjoyed a brief period of celebrity with vivid accounts of his work with alien technology at Area 51, though his credentials as a physicist proved as elusive as his alien hardware.[141] Especially influential was a statement issued in December 1987 by pilot and former CIA operative John Lear. Shadowy informants spun a story to him about multiple UFO crashes and government attempts to fly captured UFOs in 1962. The sites for these experiments included Area 51 in Nevada and an underground facility near Dulce, New Mexico. Later in the 1960s an agency so secret even the president was not privy to its actions made a treaty with the aliens to exchange technology for a limited abduction program. The aliens soon reneged on their part of the bargain, withholding technological information while kidnapping thousands of people, implanting them with control devices, using humans for food, and creating an android race by genetic manipulation. After attempts to stop the aliens by military force met with disaster, these informants said, President Reagan initiated the Star Wars program, not to defend against Soviet missiles but to develop advanced weapons that could expel the aliens from their underground hideaways.[142]

The surreal world of dark-side visions crumbled in 1989, but their followers, left sadder but little wiser, have reassembled some of the same scenarios piece by piece.[143] A conviction remains unshaken that the government holds one or more crashed UFOs and that the secrecy surrounding them is deep and dark. A saucer in hand holds more consequences than a saucer in the sky. If the government recovered a disk in 1947, the implications seem inescapable that UFOs were never unknowns but tangible proof of alien visitation and left authorities with reduced incentive to investigate mere sightings. Those in the know must have adapted their thinking to an alien presence, and every act of government, every course of scientific inquiry from the moment of recovery onward adjusted to this reality. The blissful ignorance of the public regarding these stupendous events meant that powerful and undemocratic organizations manipulated information from the shadows and kept the truth about UFOs a secret. This reasoning flows smoothly from the Roswell premise and reinterprets government actions in a way that reinforces the same premise. Roswell has become a baseline truth in much of the UFO literature over the past two decades, and the widely read books of such writers as Timothy Good, Nick Redfern, Jim Marrs, and Richard M. Dolan cast the history of the second half of the twentieth century as an aftereffect of that event.

Dolan rose to the status of favored historian in the field with publication of *UFOs and the National Security State, 1941–1973* in 2000. In this 500-page book he amasses an abundance of cases to demonstrate military interest in UFOs as well as apparent UFO interest in sensitive sites like defense installations and nuclear facilities. He emphasizes that the importance of the reports carries over to an earthly issue, the growth of an "invisible government" that went hand in hand with management of UFO information. A world-changing secret stayed hidden to prevent panic and social breakdown, or to protect corporate profits and the status quo, by means of black budgets, disinformation, and control of the media. UFOs brought visits by multiple alien races, crashed saucers, recovered technology, and a relationship between earthly powers and the aliens, but these secrets represent only part of the whole. The full secret encompasses behind-the-scenes social changes as a transnational elite replaced democratic states, and an understanding of UFOs provides a key to how this power elite controls the world.[144]

Such an argument takes for granted that UFOs have had a profound effect on human history but at the same time demotes them from the stars of their own show to bit players in a larger drama. One pillar of evidence to support this unconventional history comes from the accumulating documents recovered by FOIA requests. Perhaps the largest public archive of these findings is *The Black Vault*, a Web site founded in 1996 by researcher John Greenewald Jr. when he was a high-school student. Among the thousands of pages he has collected from military and intelligence agencies, he finds confirmation that the CIA, NSA, and others maintain interest in a subject that is supposed to hold no defense or scientific significance, as well as clues that secretive government projects draw on exotic technology related to UFOs.[145]

This ufological revision depicts an unfamiliar world where alien contact and a secret government determine the real course of history while the public goes about life as usual in complacent ignorance. A sharper contrast between apparent reality and genuine reality could hardly be imagined, yet the Dolan version is far more conservative than the assertions of informants bearing even more staggering secrets. Just in time for the fiftieth anniversary Roswell celebration, a retired Army colonel, Philip J. Corso, declared in *The Day after Roswell* (1997) that he assumed leadership of a secret research and development project in 1961 to carry out reverse engineering on the wreckage. From this work came lasers, integrated circuits, image intensifiers, fiber optics, particle beams, and Kevlar bullet-proof material. In fact, most of the technological advances since 1947 began with aliens, according to Corso, and many of those developments transferred from his research group to industry.[146] The book amalgamated so many UFO-related claims and rumors that Roswell investigator Karl Pflock dubbed it "a veritable unified field theory of practically everything ufological and ufoological,"[147] but despite its errors and implausible claims, despite its round condemnation as a hoax by serious UFO researchers, Corso's tale has settled into the literature to be cited and quoted again and again as undisputed gospel.[148]

Corso lent a face to his story, but nameless shadows serve as sources for many exotic claims. One example that pumped up excitement on the Internet in 2005–2006 was Project Serpo, a repetition of earlier claims that an alien survived the Roswell crash and cooperative contacts between the government and the aliens followed, but with the new wrinkle that military personnel returned with the aliens to their home planet Serpo. The movie *Close Encounters of the Third Kind* embeds information leaked about this project, according to Mr. Anonymous, though most members abide by security oaths taken years ago.[149] Even stranger is the evidence from remote viewers, psychics trained by intelligence agencies to visualize distant scenes. These spies contact aliens or view other planets in stories that combine exotic government projects with confirmation of standard notions like multiple alien races and future catastrophes on earth.[150]

A vigorous synthesis of UFO-related ideas and assimilation of new associations have continued with unabated fervor ever since the dark-side era. While abduction researchers debate whether the aliens are helpful or exploitative, anonymous informants, mysterious documents, and remote viewers repeat stories of treaties allowing aliens to abduct humans and refugees from a dying planet attempting to settle on the earth, with hybridization the favorite method and cattle mutilations part of a gruesome plan to modify earthly DNA for alien purposes. Messages to abductees that a cataclysm or time of tribulation is near have raised questions of whether the aliens mean to warn or to deceive, while discussions of crop circles have treated them as goodwill tokens or alien-to-alien communications.[151] Though apocalyptic preoccupations have cooled since the turn of the millennium, a supposed prophecy associated with the year 2012 in the Mayan calendar has emerged as a new focus of speculations about UFOs and the end of the world.[152]

Recent ufological thinking has grown ever more adept at enmeshing current and historical events in a net of UFO rumors. When John Lear returned to the UFO scene in 2003, he asserted that President Eisenhower had ordered "In God We Trust" added to coins and paper currency to reaffirm faith after the aliens declared God did not exist; that Americans and Soviets faked the cold war to distract public attention from the alien presence; and that Venus is an earthlike and inhabited planet but portrayed as hellishly hot and lifeless to lead the public astray.[153] Several researchers have explained unusual numbers of airplane crashes during the 1950s as the result of hostile UFO activity, probably in response to military aircraft opening fire on UFOs.[154] So far aliens have not received blame for the 9/11 terrorist attacks of 2001, but accusations that government agents carried out the attacks using demolition explosives have circulated widely, and some of the same conspiracy theorists who assert that the government hides the truth about UFOs also propose that attacks staged to look like the work of terrorists now provide a pretext to undermine civil liberties and further establish the New World Order.[155]

Aliens have dominated the speculations of ufologists, and the alien idea has served as an imperialistic principle throughout the history of ufology, absorbing assorted mysteries and taking over various events until UFOs become an all-purpose answer to every question. Some recent proposals have challenged this UFO-centric preeminence and subordinated UFOs to other people's agendas. UFO sightings, especially the ones involving big triangular objects, are really secret aircraft like the Blackbird or Aurora undergoing tests, according to some theorists, though these ideas sometimes take another turn to become products of alien technology recovered from Roswell and developed at Area 51.[156] The claims that military personnel participate in abductions finds one explanation in the deceptive illusions of aliens, another in a notion that the military kidnaps abductees to find out what they learn from the aliens, while a third answer replaces aliens altogether to designate these experiences as MILABs, or military abductions, with mind-control experimentation as their real purpose.[157] A new twist on Roswell purges it of aliens to allege that an experimental atomic-powered aircraft crashed and the supposed aliens were Asian former POWs of the Japanese, deformed by germ-warfare experiments and then victimized again to test how the human body withstood radiation. The source of these charges is the usual crop of secretive informants.[158]

These developments represent only a fraction of the ideas currently found on Web sites and in the literature—there are not enough hours in the day to keep up with all of them. Few people appear to accept any one or another of the more exotic proposals, and they do not count as the consensus opinion of the field. What they attest to is the profuseness of speculations and rapid circulation of rumors with little check or critical review, as well as a general readiness to credit an abundance of rumors as reason enough to believe that some of them must be true. A consistent collective drift becomes apparent in these claims: The quantity as well as the content of UFO discussions reflects a change of direction from the days of McDonald and Hynek, when the science of UFOs was central, toward an unmistakable preoccupation with political activism as the way to solve the UFO mystery. This reorientation is implicit in the importance afforded government secrecy in current ufological thinking, explicit in the aims and actions of perhaps the most vociferous branch of ufology today, the disclosure and exopolitics movement.

In 1993 a physician, Steven M. Greer, began to gather testimonies of military and government officials who had witnessed UFO activity or cover-ups. His aim was a humanized assault on UFO secrecy, and the first strike came in 1997 when some of these witnesses met in Washington to brief congressional and Pentagon officials in an attempt to force congressional hearings.[159] Stephen Bassett, a business consultant turned lobbyist for UFO disclosure, founded the Paradigm Research Group in 1996 and the Extraterrestrial Phenomena Political Action Committee in 1999, then sponsored a press conference in 2001 with some seventy-five witnesses and nearly annual "X-Conferences" since 2004 to keep up pressure on Congress. He ran unsuccessfully for a Maryland congressional seat in 2002 on a platform of disclosure but has continued to seek political attention through questions to presidential candidates in the 2008 primaries and thousands of faxes to the new Obama administration.[160] Exopolitics goes arm in arm with disclosure as its theoretical background and ultimate goal. Lawyer and futurist Alfred Lambremont Webre and professor of international affairs Michael E. Salla contend that aliens have visited the earth throughout history, but clandestine, increasingly powerful organizations use disinformation, intimidation, and ridicule to hide the truth while they exploit ancient, recovered, or shared alien technology. A planetary quarantine, perhaps the result of some violation of cosmic law in ancient times, is responsible for lack of open contact, and the task for exopolitical awareness is to accept the larger context of the earth, reform the unacceptable conditions like war and poverty that sustain the quarantine, and reconnect with other civilizations in the universe.[161]

The disclosure/exopolitics movement assumes that the alien presence is incontrovertible and a secret government hides the truth. Solidifying these hypotheses into facts replaces hesitancy with direction and purpose as the struggle becomes a conflict between good and evil, the right of free citizens to know the most monumental truth of the ages versus paternalistic authorities that withhold the secret to serve their selfish purposes. A sense of hope surrounds the movement as Greer sees disclosure as the beginning of an era when alien technology relieves the energy crisis and reverses global warming.[162] Bassett recognizes the enormity of the "Secret Empire," with its black budgets, media puppets, and undemocratic power, but has confidence that a grassroots effort can force out the truth as well as restore the constitutional republic that Americans have lost. A motto on one of his Web sites reads, "It's not about lights in the sky, it's about lies on the ground."[163] These few words sum up a fashionable conviction that UFOs suffer from lack of openness rather than lack of evidence, and that the persuasiveness of human testimony exerts better leverage than the cold facts of science to break what Bassett calls the "truth embargo."

At its best the disclosure program can etch sharp impressions even outside ufo-logical circles. On November 12, 2007, documentary producer James Fox and journalist Leslie Kean sponsored a press conference in Washington to call for UFO investigation. The fourteen witnesses included a former governor of Arizona and a retired Iranian general who, as a pilot in 1976, attempted to intercept a UFO over Tehran. These participants presented responsible testimony and received a respectful hearing.[164] When other gatherings undercut their own credibility by mixing dubious claims with sound testimony, the press responded with laughter. Even noteworthy supporters have proved disappointing—for example, Paul Hellyer, who served as Canadian defense minister and deputy prime minister but whose UFO opinions derived from reading Colonel Corso's book rather than from official knowledge.[165] Ample evidence attests to censorship, stonewalling, and lies from various agencies about UFOs, but some highly visible figures in ufology take a giant step beyond established fact when they speak of a vast and sinister secret government as proven truth or alien visitation as the key to every facet of modern history. The prevailing ufological explanation builds an imposing edifice from such shaky materials as inference, speculation, hearsay, and questionable evidence, held together by one supposition supporting another. The structure stands if most of the parts are true, but falls flat if too many parts are false. Demanding so much and demonstrating so little, the current strategy of persuasion largely fails to convince anyone not already convinced.

The Phenomenon Goes On.—UFOs have continued to mark the sky with their mysterious hieroglyphs even at a time when magazine articles, books, and conventions have favored human treatments of UFOs over observations. Peter Davenport has directed the National UFO Reporting Center since 1994, and it is probably the best-known clearinghouse for sightings, with a Web form available for anyone to submit a report. His posted totals from 2002 to 2007 average about 4,000 reports a year—impressive numbers in themselves but even more striking when compared with Project Blue Book figures of only 1,501 reports during the great wave of 1952 or 1,060 in 1966.[166] Newspaper coverage of UFOs diminished during the 1990s, but people still see UFOs and report them under the right circumstances, with the success of Davenport's Web site a testimony that the Internet has reoriented behavior.

Now as always, nothing restores the raw sense of wonder in UFOs like a spectacular new sighting. On March 8, 1994, police and several dozen other witnesses watched lights in the sky over Holland, Michigan, between 9:15 and 11:00 P.M. National Weather Service radar also tracked several objects of enormous apparent size for twenty to thirty minutes.[167] A V-shaped formation of lights passed over Phoenix, Arizona, on the night of March 13, 1997, and a second formation appeared two hours later. Distant flares used in military maneuvers may have been responsible for the second observations, but witnesses to the first passage, including then-governor Fife Symington III, insist that the "Phoenix Lights" belonged to a large dark object that blotted out the stars.[168] A similar formation or formations of red-orange lights attracted many witnesses over Carteret, New Jersey, and Staten Island about midnight on July 14–15, 2001, in an area where heavy population and commercial air traffic made usage of flares irresponsible.[169] UFOs again favored heavily populated areas on August 21 and October 31, 2004, when hundreds of witnesses in the Chicago suburbs of Tinley Park and Orland Park watched the passage of multiple lights on an apparent triangular object, the events recorded in numerous photographs and videos.[170] The crowded skies hosted a surprise on the afternoon of August 9, 1997, when a white cylindrical object flew past a Swissair jetliner on a near-collision course as the plane flew out from New York. The FAA explained the object as a weather balloon, though the pilot denied this answer and no known weather balloon was in the area.[171] A report from Siberia on January 26, 2001, claimed that a UFO hovered over an airport for ninety minutes. One air crew refused to take off and a second diverted to another landing field while the UFO was present.[172]

An impressive report for any decade began at 4 A.M. on January 5, 2000, when a man in Highland, Illinois, spotted a bright star moving toward him. As it neared he saw that the light was attached to a rectangular object he described as the size of a football field, with two rows of windows along the side and red lights on the bottom. Rows of lights similar to the windows also covered the rear of the object. The witness notified the Highland police, and an officer in the nearby town of Lebanon heard the dispatch around 4:15 A.M. The Lebanon officer soon sighted the UFO, a massive triangular object with a large white light at each corner, silent and blotting out the stars as it passed. He watched the object change direction as if it pivoted in mid-air, and he saw a band of light across the rear of the craft. Eight miles to the southwest, an officer in the town of Shiloh spotted the object just after it left Lebanon. He described it as arrowhead-shaped, with three bright lights and red and green lights along the back side. At 4:29 an officer in Millstadt reported a triangular object with three bright lights and a luminous rear side. He photographed the object with a Polaroid camera, but the morning cold hampered his efforts, and he obtained only one photo of poor quality before the object flew out of sight. An officer in Dupo also saw lights high in the sky just after the Millstadt sighting, but whether he observed the same object is questionable. Local Air Force radar was not operating at the time, but the air base reported no military traffic. The fact that Venus was at its brightest raises suspicions that the planet teamed with imagination to create another spectacular but erroneous UFO, though

Venus did not clear the horizon until just after 4 A.M. and remained too low to explain the sightings. The photograph also showed that the object was not a point source but multiple lights extended in space.[173]

Still the beat goes on. The crew of a Mexican Air Force plane on drug surveillance patrol picked up radar returns on the afternoon of March 5, 2004. Nothing was visible to the naked eye, but the excited crewmen watched as their infrared equipment recorded formations of bright objects flying in and out of the clouds. The spectacular videos made international news, and physicist Bruce Maccabee analyzed the footage at the behest of the Mexican government, presenting his preliminary findings at the 2004 MUFON Symposium in Denver. He found that the "object" sightings aligned with offshore oil fields where flares burning off natural gas could provide intense infrared sources, while the appearance of moving objects was the "racing moon" illusion, with the stationary infrared sources appearing to speed through the intervening clouds because of the motion of the aircraft. The radar contacts might have detected nothing more mysterious than a truck on the highway.[174] In this case the UFO turned out to be conventional. A year after the O'Hare UFO, media attention converged on Stephenville, Texas, after some fifty people reported a huge, silent triangular object with multiple lights and flying sometimes at high speed, sometimes slowly, on the night of January 8, 2008. Several witnesses reported that fighter jets chased the object. What followed was a pattern as familiar as a worn-out comedy routine when the Air Force first denied that any military aircraft were active in the area, then reversed themselves and explained the sightings as the result of ten F-16s on a training mission, despite the fact that this training would bring the aircraft perilously close to the closed airspace around President Bush's ranch at Crawford. Adding further to ufologists' suspicions was the sudden firing of Angelina Joiner, a reporter for the *Stephenville Empire-Tribune* who first reported the sightings in the area. She lost her job for the alleged reason that she actually did her job, covering a real news story to the offense of prominent people who did not like the international publicity their town was receiving and pressured the editor to terminate her.[175]

A Mythological Checklist

The history of sixty-plus years of UFOs is the biography of a living, evolving system of ideas with a growing stock of motifs, plots, characters, and themes. An outline summary of the basic, recurrent elements of the UFO story includes the following.

Something mysterious is flying around in the sky. Thousands of people have observed disks, triangles, or other shapes flying at extraordinary speeds and performing
impossible maneuvers. UFOs sometimes leave traces on the ground or have effects on
humans, animals, and machinery. The ability of radar to track these objects or a camera
to record them further attests to a physical presence.

UFOs are extraordinary aircraft and probably extraterrestrial spaceships. They
appear mechanical yet exhibit shapes and performances that rule out earthly origin,
leading to widespread supposition that UFOs are the craft of superior alien visitors.
In some descriptions UFOs behave more like ghosts than machines, and magical
alien technology is the usual explanation, though an alternative theory attributes the
strangeness of UFOs to some sort of paranormal manifestation. The skeptical perspective reduces all UFOs to conventional terms, with misidentifications, errors, and
hoaxes sufficient to explain all reports.

Humanoid occupants man the craft. Recurrent reports of iconic humanoids with
short stature, large heads, and elongated eyes further confirm an unearthly origin for
UFOs, though the occupants may also appear human, reptilian, insectlike, robotic, or
monstrous.

UFO occupants abduct humans. One of the most prominent UFO experience stories tells of people taken aboard a craft for a medical examination and the creation of
hybrid human-alien children. Messages and teachings may also be part of the experience, and abductees may undergo life-changing alterations of consciousness as a result
of the encounters.

The UFO occupants intend help or harm to humans. Early notions that aliens
came to earth as explorers or invaders have given way to more nuanced scenarios. The
contactees described Space Brothers coming to rescue humanity from nuclear war;
later claims indicate that the aliens may heal humans or lead them toward an expanded
consciousness that will save mankind from ecological catastrophe and the evils of materialism. Many abductees describe an exploitative relationship as the aliens create a
hybrid stock to serve their own purposes and treat humans as mere guinea pigs. An
underlying implication is that danger threatens the earth, and heavenly outsiders serve
as either the cause or the solution of this planetary crisis.

UFOs sometimes crash. The ultimate physical evidence for UFOs is the wreckage
from accidents such as the one supposed to have occurred at Roswell in 1947. According to this story military authorities collected the wreckage and learned about alien
visitation from an early date.

The government maintains secrecy about UFOs. The early evidence that military authorities censored UFO information has grown into elaborate claims that the government clamped strict security on the Roswell findings and a powerful organization, MJ-12, controls information about the alien presence.

The history of the world since 1947 is in fact a hidden UFO history. In this view the government has held the public in ignorance of treaties and interactions with aliens, while most modern technology derives from captured alien models. The real power structure on earth is a totalitarian, international cabal working with the aliens or using their technology to dominate the world.

UFOs have visited the earth for millennia and have taken part in the development of mankind. Ancient astronauts brought the seeds of civilization, either as benevolent teachers or as masters using humans as slaves. The aliens leave traces of their presence in the monuments and literature of the ancient past and in artifacts on Mars and the moon.

Many mysterious events have their origin in alien activity. Rather than just flying around, alien visitors interfere in earthly affairs and are responsible for Men in Black, cattle mutilations, crop circles, power blackouts, and the disappearance of ships and airplanes. Or, considered another way, UFOs are simply one manifestation of a larger field of paranormal occurrences that have always mystified humanity.

Part a matter of observation and experience, part theory and speculation, part inference and association, the cultural understanding of UFOs builds up a vigorous story from these constituent motifs, plots, and themes. The list is not exhaustive, neither does it do justice to the ready blending of the themes nor the eclectic syncretism of external ideas into the UFO framework, but it touches on the most prominent elements. Taken together they comprise the UFO myth, a popular image of what these objects are and how they relate to the human world. The extent and popularity of the stories attest to their appeal and apparent psychological function. The thematic affinities of UFO stories with older traditions like otherworld visitation and fantastic others or apocalypse and salvation reestablish age-old notions, but give them a chance to shake off the dust of ages and return in the shiny chrome of futuristic technology, the guise updated but the underlying form intact. This resulting image may be true or false but most likely blends fact and fiction into a distorted, misleading whole that nevertheless has some basis in reality.

CHAPTER THREE

UFOs of the Past

> Ezekiel saw de wheel,
> Way up in the middle ob de air . . .
> An' de little wheel run by faith,
> An' de big wheel run by de grace ob God,
> 'Tis a wheel in a wheel,
> Way in de middle ob de air.
> —Old Spiritual[1]

> [Science's] seeming approximation to consistency, stability, system
> positiveness or realness—is sustained by damning the irreconcilable or
> the unassimilable—
> All would be well.
> All would be heavenly—
> If the damned would only stay damned.
> —Charles Fort, *The Books of Charles Fort*[2]

Kenneth Arnold discovered flying saucers, but the first UFO did not suddenly swoop down out of the blue one summer day in 1947. Witnesses before him had watched mysterious objects in the sky for thousands of years, objects as provocative of wonder, speculation, and dread as UFOs today, though not necessarily the circular, metallic aircraft of modern times. Historical UFOs refer to whatever sightings people have considered strange. These historical reports lend a valuable comparative dimension, a perspective to demonstrate that, whether yesterday or yesteryear, ideas about what UFOs are supposed to be intervene between the observation and the report. The results set a straightforward example that expectations lay a heavy hand on UFO narratives and mask any observational reality with a mythic visage.

Three distinctive explanatory frameworks and their associated descriptions illustrate the close relationship between conceptions and reports of aerial mysteries over the course of history. The earliest understanding attributed them to supernatural intervention, either messages from the gods or glimpses of a parallel otherworld. With the advent of a scientific worldview in the eighteenth century, an unusual manifestation of standard natural events became the prevailing solution for anomalies. A third conceptual berth opened as the potential for human flight evolved during the nineteenth century, when expectation for things extraordinary in the sky shifted to man-made flying machines or extraterrestrial spaceships. Along with the explanation go distinctive patterns of content and associations to underscore the considerable, often sobering debt that observation owes to the human factor in reports of experience.[3]

The Heavens Are Telling: An Age of Signs and Wonders

The Prodigy Tradition.—Historical literature of ancient, medieval, and Reformation times attributed anything strange in the sky, anything remarkable on land or sea, to a divine message for mankind. The Romans' broadest term for such events was "prodigy." It covered extraordinary appearances indicative of a disturbance in the relationship between the human and divine realms. Portents and signs were public appearances directed at the state, while omens applied to individuals.[4] When the gods phoned, they seldom made small talk. Prodigious events foretold important, often catastrophic happenings or lodged a complaint; but if the message inspired fear, it was not reason for despair. Warnings allowed measures like sacrifice to avert the consequences of divine displeasure. As the most visible and spectacular breaches in the normal course of events, celestial prodigies held the highest importance and interest.

Examples of noteworthy atmospheric or astronomical phenomena are almost universal, appearing in European, Arabic, Babylonian, Assyrian, Hebrew, Chinese, Japanese, and Mesoamerican historical records. Perhaps the earliest case comes from the reign of Pharaoh Thutmose III (1504–1450 B.C.), in an inscription that tells of a star shooting toward an enemy camp and killing the men of the night watch. Their horses bolted in terror, and the king took advantage of the confusion to rout his enemies.[5] Though this "miracle of the star" offers few details and might have resulted from some natural meteoric or electrical phenomenon, the entry shows Egyptians ready to interpret an anomalous event as proof that the gods favored Pharaoh. Similar favorable religious meanings surround biblical stories of the pillar of cloud and pillar of fire that guided the Children of Israel out of Egypt, the fiery chariot that carried Elijah to heaven, Ezekiel's Wheel, or the Star of Bethlehem.[6]

A concern for prodigies thrived in Rome as a cornerstone of the state religion. Pliny the Elder included prodigies in his natural history, and historians like Livy and Dio Cassius recorded them as integral elements of the historical record. Julius Obsequens, an obscure writer of the fourth century A.D., collected the wonders from Livy's history into a separate book, *Prodigiorum liber*, which suggests that independent interest attached to such accounts.[7] Like UFOs today, prodigies also met with skepticism from learned quarters. Plutarch wrote that a stone fell by the Chersonesus River in Greece just before the Peloponnesian War ended. A writer named Damachus added that for seventy-five days before the stone dropped, a large body of fire like an inflamed cloud moved this way and that in the sky with a broken motion. "It is plain that Damachus must have very indulgent readers," was Plutarch's dry comment, "if this account of his gains credit."[8] Cicero mounted the most systematic attack against signs and portents to survive from antiquity in *De divinatione*. He discounted the idea that crowing roosters foretold victory on the grounds that roosters crow all the time, and who could believe that Jupiter stooped to passing his messages through poultry? After reducing traditional beliefs to absurdity, he made clear his opinion that prodigies held only the significance an interpreter read into them.[9]

A prodigy accompanied the beginning of the Middle Ages when the emperor Constantine saw a cross in the sky and a message—"In this sign, conquer." He kept his pledge to convert to Christianity when he won a battle in A.D. 312.[10] Little changed in the form or interpretation of strange sights in the sky between ancient and medieval times. The Roman belief that prodigies foretold deaths and calamities lived on—for example, in a passage from Gregory of Tours in 584: "A great beacon traversed the heavens, lighting up the land far and wide some time before the day dawned. Rays of light shone in the sky, and in the north a column of fire was seen to hang from on high for a space of two hours, with an immense star perched on top of it. . . . In my opinion this all announced the coming death of [the Pretender] Gundovald."[11]

Early Christian writers came to frown on wonder stories as a liability in the effort to build a logical theology and maintain orthodox doctrine. The miraculous could not be denied, but some arguments relegated it to an earlier dispensation; others incorporated prodigies into demonology.[12] If marvels troubled the intellectuals of the Church, such stories found enduring favor with the common folk and added to the popularity of the hagiography literature.[13] Typical of these heroic biographies of saints and martyrs are the stock supernatural motifs scattered throughout the life of Saint Columba, who lived from 520 to 597 and converted Scotland: A passing priest saw a brilliant light within a house and entered to find a ball of fire hovering over the sleeping infant Columba. Once he was unjustly excommunicated, but a "brilliant pillar wreathed with fiery tresses" went before him. White-robed angels swooped down from heaven to gather around the saint as he prayed, and once when he celebrated mass, "a ball of fire like a comet" burned on his head and rose up like a column. At his death, some fishermen noticed a sudden brightness at midnight as a great pillar of fire rose into heaven from the spot where he died.[14]

Medieval chroniclers duly included unusual events alongside battles, crusades, disasters, and the acts of kings as matters worthy of record. A love of the marvelous led to collections of curiosities like the *Otia imperialia* of Gervase of Tilbury, the *King's Mirror*, and *De nugis curialium* of Walter Map. Sometimes the writer added a touch of personal experience, like this demonic bedroom intrusion from the twelfth-century monk Rodolfus Glaber:

> One night . . . a manikin-like being of terrible aspect appeared before me from the direction of the foot of the bed. As far as I could judge he was of middling stature with a thin neck, skinny face, jet-black eyes, and a lined and wrinkled forehead; his nostrils were pinched and he had a wide mouth and blubbery lips; his goat-like beard covered a receding and pointed chin, while his ears were shaggy and pointed; his hair was a disordered mop and he had dog-like fangs; he had a pointed head, a swollen chest, a hunchback, and mobile haunches; clad in dirty clothes, his whole body seemed to quiver with effort as he leant forward, seized the head of the bed, gave it a mighty blow, and said: "You will not remain longer in this place." I woke in terror. . . . Then I leapt out of bed, ran into the church, and cast myself down before the altar.[15]

The social and intellectual upheavals of the sixteenth and seventeenth century ushered in a golden age of prodigies. Religious revolution, social unrest, and widespread armed conflict in Europe fostered millenarian and apocalyptic expectations, while the advent of printing made mass communication possible for the first time.[16] Conrad Lycosthenes, a Basel theologian and humanist scholar, undertook a grandiose project to cull prodigies from every available historical source and list every strange event from the creation of the world to the present as evidence that the Second Coming was truly nigh. Published in 1557 as the *Prodigiorum ac ostentorum chronicon*, his collection filled hundreds of pages with monstrosities, earthquakes, fabulous animals, and aerial wonders. An English cleric, Stephen Bateman, or Batman, translated Lycosthenes into English in 1581, under a more fearsome title of *The Doome Warning All Men to the Judgemente*. Bateman also entered into the spirit of the project by updating the chronicle and interpolating prodigies from English sources unavailable to the Swiss collector. A host of others before and after Lycosthenes compiled prodigy books, but readier sources for the masses were innumerable pamphlets and broadsides proclaiming "Strange News" or "Look Up and See Wonders."[17]

Most prodigy collectors let the cumulative mass of cases speak for itself and wasted little time on theory. A common rationale held that God relied on peculiar natural events to call the attention of people to their sins or sent signs to terrify sinners into contrition.[18] Martin Luther and most other Reformation theologians accepted prodigies as signs of the Second Coming, but these leaders also deplored popular preoccupation with wonders. John Calvin stressed that too much interest was tantamount to doubting divine providence. Miracles happen every day, he cautioned, and people should not distract themselves from contemplation of God out of concern for worldly events.[19] While Calvin meant to downplay interest in prodigies, some collectors set out to prove the literal truth of his dictum. The anonymous author of *Mirabilis annus*, an English collection of strange events issued in three parts between 1660 and 1662, did not reach the goal of confirming a miracle a day, but he took satisfaction in finding about two per week.[20]

By the time *Mirabilis annus* was published, the gleam had begun to fade from the golden age of prodigies. Their authority suffered when the finger of God began to favor political factions in the English Civil War, and Restoration authorities sought without success to apprehend the writer of *Mirabilis annus* for using fake reports as Puritan propaganda.[21] Intellectual critics like Polydore Vergil and John Spencer followed the path of Cicero and demolished the rationale of prodigies.[22] They continued to flourish in popular culture and survived as matters of intellectual concern in Puritan enclaves until the early eighteenth century, with both Increase and Cotton Mather collecting "illustrious providences" in New England.[23]

A supernatural conception for unusual aerial events faded but never entirely dissipated, as occasional revivals still accompany a time of crisis or religious excitement. Months after the British army retreated from Mons in 1914, a rumor spread that Saint George, angels, or a troop of fifteenth-century archers had protected the troops or even joined the battle. The "Angels of Mons" became so entrenched that many soldiers averred that they had seen the angels—or at least a nurse or fellow soldier claimed to hear the story from a witness.[24] A series of Marian apparitions at Fátima, Portugal, in 1917 reached its climax on October 13 when 50,000 people watched the sun turn pale, spin on its axis, and seem to tumble out of the sky. Prophecies given to three children and kept secret by the Vatican became the stuff of legend for the apocalyptically inclined, and the vision of the spinning sun entangled Fátima with UFO beliefs.[25]

The aerial sights worthy of note in ancient, medieval, and Reformation literature include comets, eclipses, meteors, auroras, and atmospheric phenomena like mock suns and halos. In many cases the nature of the phenomenon is apparent from the description, in contradiction of the usual low expectations for human observers in general or premodern observers in particular. One example from the twelfth-century *Chronicle of John of Worcester* says that in February of 1130 or 1131, two priests and two clerks were leaving church in the middle of the night when they saw a light in the sky. "The object from which the bright light came was covered with a white cloud. For short periods it would emerge from the cloud as though it was moving upwards, and then after a short interval it would reenter the cloud. . . . In shape and size it was like a small pyramid, broad at the bottom and narrow at the top." The color of the object was a blend of full moon and blazing flames, and an appearance like a plank stretched upward a long way from the cloud where the brilliant object had been. The frightened and amazed witnesses cried out for others to come and see, though by the time other people arrived, "all that light was completely blotted out except for the faintest trace which could barely be seen on its north side." Watchmen and shepherds also witnessed this spectacle and John drew his account from eyewitness reports.[26]

A short duration and circumstantial description reveal the typical phenomenology of a large meteor as it leaves a trail and illuminates clouds or creates one of its own. Even without a conceptual framework for meteors, the witnesses provide a creditable account without any evident contamination from prior expectations or beliefs. Side by side with these accurate reports, other prodigy accounts manifest extreme reliance on stereotypical imagery and cultural meanings. Popular and official Church ideas of demonology echo through Rodolfus Glaber's bedroom visitation, while the scarcity of crosses in the sky before the rise of Christianity and their subsequent frequency attest to the influence of belief. So too does the symbolic elaboration apparent in a case that Roger de Hoveden describes from Dunstable in 1188: "The heavens opened, and, in the sight of many . . . a cross appeared, very long and of wonderful magnitude; and it appeared as though Jesus Christ was fastened thereon with nails, and crowned with thorns; His hands also were stretched out on the cross . . . and His blood was flowing down, but did not fall upon the earth. This appearance lasted from the ninth hour of the day till twilight."[27]

Even more fanciful tableaux, composed of ships in the sky, battles being fought in the air, or combinations of dramatic and symbolic events, are scattered through prodigy accounts. The Reformation theologian Joachim Camerarius summarized a series of marvels seen widely in Germany at the end of 1560. In the hours after midnight a great red fire broken by white furrows or streaks stretched across the northern sky, seeming to move from place to place until near dawn, when the fire gathered together in the form of a tower and slowly vanished. One witness added that beams of light rose from the earth, and when a burning cloud passed before the beams, lights like shooting stars fell from it. Drawing together diverse sources, Camerarius found descriptions of aerial spears and crosses, a claim that a host of men fought in the air, an account that a sound like a boiling pot descended into a hill and later issued from underground, and a report that there appeared in a field a fiery globe containing a bear and a lion engaged in combat. In one place a globe of fire flew so near the rooftops that villagers were afraid their houses would catch fire, and in many areas the residents turned out to fight a supposed conflagration. Camerarius read allegorical meanings into each event so that a red fire betokened war and bloodshed, but the end of the prodigy at sunrise promised that the tribulations would not last long. He considered the larger picture wherein prodigies portended the end of the world, but for all the fear and dread they inspired, they also promised salvation.[28]

In historical hindsight this example illuminates the interaction of observation and belief with exceptional clarity. Modern understanding recognizes in the bright streaks, burning clouds, and shifting beams a terminology for the aurora borealis that is still current today. References to fires collecting into a tower, spears and crosses, even armies fighting in the sky, reflect stereotypical images for auroral displays in premodern accounts. Fireballs threatening houses and fears of a great fire express the apprehensions of unsuspecting people confronted with a rare and unaccustomed event. They also highlight the likelihood that these accounts are grounded in real observation of a widespread and spectacular aurora. The claims that mysterious sounds descended from the sky or spheres with lions and bears landed in a field steer the accounts into fantastic territory, and they also parallel similar escalations of extraordinary claims during modern UFO waves. A real and recognizable event occurred that night in 1560, but the choices of Camerarius both preserve and distort the record. He accepted all sources without apparent critical reservations and paid little attention to the natural side of the events. The human significance of war and calamity or God's punishment and mercy held far more interest for him than the natural mechanisms that inflamed the sky. In his selection of data, descriptive terminology, and strategy of interpretation, he stands at the normative center of his historical setting, expressing the same belief system, the same amalgam of religious and natural mythology common among learned people in his time. He speaks nothing more or less than the accepted truth of his era, but a truth that riddles the observational record with cultural distortions.

Aerial Oddities in Folk Tradition.—Chroniclers preserved anomalous events of interest to the learned elite, but a broader spectrum of oddities excited the common people, and traces of folk beliefs appear in contemporary writings as well as in collections of oral traditions from the nineteenth century. Folklore has its version of elaborate aerial scenes in the Wild Hunt or Furious Host, a troop of spirits flying through the air accompanied by dogs with fiery eyes. Said to be the lost souls of pagans and sometimes led by Wotan or Thor, this host may swoop down to kidnap a passerby to join the troop. This captive then disappears forever or reappears some distance away, often demented and with a finger cut off. When the headlight of a phantom airship made news in 1897, immigrants in Iowa recalled sightings of the "Devil's Army" in the 1850s over western Germany. This army, another version of the Wild Hunt, also included a bright light at the forefront, and astronomers blamed the planet Venus in this case, as well as with the airships.[29]

Ghostly apparitions often involve strange luminous appearances. The Brown Mountain lights of North Carolina appear over the crest of the mountain and float down it, with local teenagers alleging that they park on remote roads to watch tiny balls of light bounce and scatter like sparks while yardwide globes from the mountaintop hiss and roll as they swoop low overhead.[30] In Texas the Marfa Lights dart close to the ground and inspire their own lurid teenage legends of cars that are incinerated when they pursue too closely.[31] The will-o'-the-wisp or jack-o'-lantern appears in remote or marshy areas and leads travelers astray, while the Min-Min light of Australia and the Dragon Lantern of Japan and China are other small, darting lights with supernatural attributes.[32] Death omens maintain an enduring presence in folk belief, such as the corpse candles of Wales, small lights floating above the ground that foretell a death some few days before it occurs.[33] An informant from Illinois said that "just at sunset I was out in the yard and I saw a big ball of fire in the heaven and a little ball of fire drop from it. I knew someone was going to die. And my sister took sick and died in two days after that, and her baby died a month after that."[34]

Some strange appearances seem to serve only as reminders that mysterious things still happen. A Tennessee fugitive hiding in an orchard saw a big wheel of fire roll by. It lit up the surroundings and made a crunching sound like footsteps in snow. A Pennsylvania informant said that while driving along a road one rainy day in 1923 a golden red fireball four feet in diameter floated to the ground then rose back into the air. Some folklore accounts parallel the electromagnetic effects and physical injuries reported by UFO witnesses. A West Virginia ghost story tells that as a rider passed the spot where a murdered man was buried, his horse seemed suddenly burdened with a heavy weight, and he looked around to see a headless body sitting behind him. It disappeared once the horse struggled past the grave, whereupon the horse galloped home and shied away from that stretch of road ever after. Another man suffered paralysis after he struck a ghostly light with his stick, and his mouth remained twisted to one side for a long time.[35]

Procession of the Damned: Aerial Anomalies in a
Scientific Age

A supernatural conception did not commit ancient and medieval interpreters to wild or irrational beliefs. The intellectual elite understood celestial events in largely naturalistic terms, yet they preserved a notion of dual causation that allowed comets to belong to nature even as they harbingered war or the death of kings. Even this limited partnership unraveled as rationalism and science drove an absolute divide between nature and the supernatural. Edmund Halley established comets as predictable orbital bodies, Isaac Newton laid out the physical laws governing motion, and Pierre-Simon de Laplace formulated a self-stabilizing celestial mechanics that led to a supposed conversation when Napoleon asked where God was in the equations and Laplace answered that he had no need for that hypothesis. Astronomy and physics—later organic chemistry and evolutionary biology, and still later psychoanalysis and existential philosophy—would clip away link by link the notions that all things interrelated in a Great Chain of Being.[36] Scientific thinking declared independence for natural events so that they ran their course isolated from human affairs, moral values, or divine intervention, free of any dual causation and without any prophetic tie to the future.

In a scientific framework, aerial sights became meteoric, auroral, or weather related, with no cranny or corner left over for miracles and prodigies. This rigid view demanded exclusive natural causation or nothing, with any claim to the contrary due to human error, "vulgar superstition," or an unfamiliar aspect of nature waiting to be cataloged and classified. Yet a curious thing happened on the way to a world free of mysteries. Even as science swept away all supernatural appearances, it began to shape a new class of natural anomalies out of the odds and ends of scientific observation itself. The duty to observe and record natural events included attention to anything out of the ordinary, so that newspapers and scientific magazines became repositories for anecdotal accounts of noteworthy oddities. Nature refused to obey its own laws all the time and presented reliable witnesses with the occasional baffling, seemingly unnatural event, like the meteor that flew up instead of down in unconscionable defiance of proper meteoric behavior.

Most scientists gladly ignored these challenges to the standard version of scientific reality, but such leftovers attracted the interest of the American author Charles Fort (1874–1932). He spent most of his adult life searching journals and newspapers for accounts of black snows, rains of frogs, spontaneous human combustion, and strange lights cruising in the night, events that came to be known as "Fortean phenomena" in his honor. His four books, *The Book of the Damned* (1919), *New Lands* (1923), *Lo!*

(1931), and *Wild Talents* (1932), revel in the accumulated evidence that the world is not as neatly circumscribed as scientific dogma alleges and skewer with fine wit the exclusionary habits of scientists as they sacrifice the phenomena to save the theories. "A procession of the damned," he wrote to introduce his subject. "By the damned, I mean the excluded. We shall have a procession of data that Science has excluded. . . . The power that has said to all these things that they are damned, is Dogmatic science. But they'll march."[37]

Fort offered his own theories, sometimes more than one for the same events. He was ambivalent about extraterrestrial visitation, sometimes defending it, sometimes arguing that he could sooner believe a grasshopper could jump on a shooting cannonball than accept interplanetary travel.[38] As an alternative he proposed that outer space held vast islands floating in a cosmic "Super-Sargasso Sea," now and then visible to astronomers, here and there dropping chunks of ice or fish to fall from the sky as otherworldly flotsam and jetsam washed up on the earthly shore.[39] Fort valued the chance to needle orthodoxy more than the solution. His friend Tiffany Thayer turned attacks on orthodoxy into a lifelong crusade. Thayer founded the Fortean Society in 1931, and Fort, the true iconoclast, refused to join; but members included such literary lights as Theodore Dreiser and Booth Tarkington. The society persisted until Thayer's death in 1959, issuing *Doubt*, an irregular journal that printed accounts of Fortean events and expositions of unconventional theories. A cover illustration that sums up the offbeat creed of the society depicts a cherub urinating on mathematical equations. When the saucers began to fly in 1947, *Doubt* carried extensive coverage, but also Thayer's characteristic rejection of orthodoxy, even a freshly minted one, when he complained that since the saucer business started, no one bothered to see peculiar meteors any more.[40]

The sort of reports that attracted Fort included strange meteoric appearances—for example, a stream of luminous bodies that rose from the horizon a little before sunrise on March 22, 1880, at Kattenau, Germany, and traveled from east to west like a string of beads shining with a brilliant light.[41] In an example from an evening in 1868, several witnesses in Oxford, England, noticed "a fine white cloud about five degrees in length and one degree in breadth" (the full moon occupies one-half of one degree of arc).

> As the observer was pointing out its comet-like appearance . . . it appeared to start into motion, taking a course directly west . . . and leaving a train behind. . . . When it approached Leo it deviated from the straight line which it had previously taken, and turned somewhat towards the south . . . and then bent northwards again. The time that it was visible must have been nearly four minutes. Its appearance . . . was

very like that of the flame and smoke combined which sometimes issue from a railway engine.[42]

Phenomena attributed to atmospheric electricity or ball lightning sometimes suggested something else to Fort: As a thunderstorm threatened Burlington, Vermont, at noon on July 2, 1907, a sharp explosion knocked a horse to the ground and several citizens reported that a ball of fire had exploded as it fell from the sky. Three men startled by the explosion looked up to see "a torpedo-shaped body some three hundred feet away, stationary in appearance and . . . about fifty feet above the tops of the buildings. In size it was about six feet long by eight inches in diameter, the shell or cover having a dark appearance, with here and there tongues of fire issuing from spots on the surface resembling red-hot unburnished copper." As the object began to fly away, bright red flames spurted out as the cover seemed to rupture. Though the writer did not say how the torpedo disappeared, he had some credentials for honesty, since he was a Methodist bishop and was conversing at a street corner with a former governor of the state.[43]

Some observations fitted no ready-made category and simply pointed toward more strangeness than conventional science allowed. One account that Fort took for support of his "islands in space" theory came from a Swiss astronomer who saw a spindle-shaped body obscure part of the sun on August 9, 1762. The object might have been an elongated sunspot except it moved so slowly that its transit required a month. Another observer some distance away also watched the progress of the object, but it crossed a different segment of the solar disk while Paris observers did not see the object at all, indicating relative closeness to earth.[44] For sheer weirdness few accounts can rival the aerial monster of Crawfordsville, Indiana. As two icemen hitched their team at 2 A.M. on September 5, 1891, "a strange sensation of awe and dread" swept over them. A headless apparition, 20 feet long by 8 feet wide and seemingly 100 feet overhead, flew by means of several pairs of fins. The men fled into the barn and watched the object circle. Corroboration came from a Methodist minister who stepped outside and saw something similar to floating drapery squirm like a serpent as it rose and descended over his church. Other residents reported that the birds chirped all night as if in distress, and that clue convinced two skeptics that the town's recently installed electric lights had disturbed a flock of killdeer into flying about in confusion. Yet one witness also attributed a single red glowing eye to the creature—similar to the light soon destined to become a standard feature in phantom airship reports. The unfortunate minister became recipient of unsolicited advice to take the Keeley cure for alcoholism, foreshadowing the ridicule later to descend on UFO witnesses.[45]

Loose in an Airship: Aerial Anomalies
Become Technological

Humans have long envied the birds and dreamed of flight. Legendry and literature include flying chariots of the Indian epic *Ramayana,* and Icarus, whose wings of wax and feathers melted when he soared too near the sun.[46] Nothing came of such airy visions until the Mongolfier brothers sent their first balloon aloft in 1783. Controlled flight seemed just around the corner; however, this optimism hid a festering truth that although balloons could rise into the air, the balloons remained at the mercy of the winds, and no practical heavier-than-air craft succeeded during the nineteenth century. While steamships and locomotives, telegraph and telephone, electric lights and motors, phonographs and X-rays sprang unheralded from workshops to surprise the public and change the world, the long-awaited flying machine remained elusive. Inventors both serious and crackpot worked on the problem in seemingly every town, but too many trials ended in pratfalls and established flying machines as a proverbial folly. Yet failures never dashed a faith that aerial navigation would come to pass, and newspaper writers even proclaimed that it would serve as the crowning achievement of the nineteenth century. As time ran out and expectations went unfulfilled, hope took over from reality as people began to report wonders in technological form.

Some accounts imagined the real possibility of lost or innovative balloons. In January 1886 New Yorkers gathered nightly to watch a brilliant light, and a rumor circulated that a balloon sent up from Thomas Edison's Menlo Park laboratory in New Jersey lifted an arc light several miles high. Sightings of the "Edison Star" became yearly affairs for a while, and even as late as 1910 Edison continued to receive letters asking him to explain his invention or begging him to settle a bet. When he answered at all, the response was a terse note that the star was nothing but Venus.[47] An expedition to reach the North Pole by balloon left Sweden in the summer of 1897, and repeated sightings from both Canada and Siberia of a pear-shaped body carrying a light raised hopes that Salomon Andrée had succeeded in his quest. In fact, he was never seen alive again, and only in 1930 were the remains of the balloon and its crew found on an island well short of the pole, after a flight that never reached Canada or Siberia.[48]

Magazines like *Scientific American* and illustrated newspapers had planted the image of an oval gas bag with an undercarriage and propeller as the aircraft design most likely to succeed. By the 1890s reports aired that such a machine was actually flying. Dispatches from Russian Poland in 1892 claimed nightly visits of a lighted cigar-shaped dirigible from Germany that flew deep into Russian territory on espionage missions. On the night of March 23, "the people of Warsaw were startled by an intensely bright light in the sky. All eyes were turned upward, but nothing could be seen save a path of light that ended in a small focus. Suddenly the ray of light swept in another direction, and, when their eyes accustomed to the darkness that followed, the people could see, far up in the sky, a balloon." Such feats of control and long-distance flight so far surpassed the acknowledged aeronautical capabilities of the day that the *New York Times* labeled the report "a fishy story that comes from Russian sources," but a similar supposed intrusion over the forts at Kovno resulted in the garrison opening fire to drive off the invader.[49]

The Great Airship Wave of 1896–1897.—Of all the strange stories to titillate readers of American newspapers, few can surpass a report in the Sacramento, California, *Evening Bee* for November 18, 1896. "Voices in the Sky," the headline read. "People Declare They Heard Them and Saw a Light. Aerial Ship, Ghost Story, or Meteor—As You Like." The reporter's mock-heroic style could not conceal a breathless hope that some inventor had solved the problem of aerial navigation before the end of the century after all:

> Last evening between the hours of 6 and 7 o'clock, in the year of our Lord eighteen hundred and ninety-six, a most startling exhibition was seen. . . . People standing on the sidewalks . . . saw coming through the sky over the housetops, what appeared to them to be merely an electric arc lamp propelled by some mysterious force. It came out of the east and sailed unevenly toward the southwest, dropping now nearer to the earth, and now suddenly rising into the air again as if the force that was whirling it through space was sensible of the dangers of collision with objects upon the earth.

Hundreds of people saw the light, a few saw a dark balloon shape above the light and a wheel driving the object, and some heard a voice calling, "Lift her up quick! You are making directly for that steeple!"[50]

Reports spread up and down the state over the next three weeks while newspapers buzzed with attempts to explain the apparition. Some speculators asked if a New York inventor fulfilled his boast to fly to San Francisco, others blamed the light on a lantern attached to a kite or toy balloon. One answer for the more elaborate stories turned to a "car barn conspiracy" of city streetcar drivers enjoying a good hoax. The *San Francisco Call* played up the story with headlines and illustrations of the ship as an egg-shaped body with a gondola beneath, four vast propellers along the sides, and a brilliant light attached. A rival newspaper, William Randolph Hearst's *Examiner*, played the skeptic and ridiculed the *Call* for credulity.[51]

At the end of January 1897 sightings of a bright flying light resumed in Nebraska

and Kansas. The reports remained local news until appearances in Omaha beginning in mid-March attracted national attention. Some two hundred Topeka residents
watched a square red light on the twenty-seventh, among them Governor Leedy and a
crowd on the statehouse steps. "I don't know what it is," he said, "but I hope it will solve
the railroad problem." On April 1 the ship appeared at Kansas City, and over the next
six weeks the airship put on an exhibition that would far surpass the California display
in number of reports and geographical scope.[52]

The airship reached its high tide of credibility on April 9–12 as the vessel spent a
weekend touring the largest cities of the Midwest. Crowds observed the ship from the
rooftops of Chicago on Friday night, the ninth, and hundreds of Evanston people saw
a brilliant light swing back and forth like a searchlight. An astronomer explained the
light as Alpha Orionis (Betelgeuse), but many witnesses scoffed at this explanation
since the searchlight was much brighter than any star. Crowds in St. Louis watched
a floating light for half an hour on Saturday night, while a square reddish light half
the size of the moon dimmed and flashed over Minneapolis that same night, then returned before thousands of witnesses on Sunday.[53] Milwaukee had its turn on Sunday
night when thousands saw the lighted object. "It travelled toward the southwest until
it reached a point directly over the City Hall, where it stopped for a quarter of an
hour. Then the excitement in the downtown districts became intense. It was reported
that attempts were being made to anchor the ship."[54] On Monday it returned to Saint
Louis, where great crowds saw the searchlight sweep the ground.[55] For the moment,
newspaper writers declared that "within the last three days the evidence that something unusual is moving midst the clouds has become so conclusive and has so much
corroboration that wiseacres have ceased to jibe, and while wondering what the mystery can be, they are doing their utmost to solve it."[56]

Some newsmen proposed that a secretive inventor headed for Washington and
intended to patent his invention there.[57] They mapped an eastward progression from
Illinois to Indiana, Ohio, and West Virginia, but by midmonth any semblance of consistent movement collapsed when reports fanned out across the country. As airships
appeared in places hundreds of miles apart at the same hour and minute, once-favor-
able commentators reversed their views. A proliferation of hoaxes and fantastic tales
further eroded the credibility of the claims. One airship crashed in Missouri, another
blew up in midair over Michigan. The anchor snagged an Iowa man's trousers, leading
to a headline that read "Farmer's Garments and Veracity Badly Strained."[58] Stories of
landings began to multiply during mid-April when two Illinois farmhands talked with
crewmen as they worked to repair the electrical apparatus.[59] If this account was well
behaved enough to sound plausible, another was harder to swallow, since the lighter-

than-air craft stopped at Linton, Indiana, to take on three tons of coal.[60] Newspapers, such as the *Detroit Evening News* on April 16, ridiculed both the subject and the witnesses as the airship grew increasingly implausible:

> Shelby.—Airship seen. Looked like big balloon with two lights. Temperance town, too.
> Grand Rapids.—Naughty boys fooled a copper into believing he saw the airship. Toy balloons.
> Lansing.—About 200 Lansing people, most of them sober, claim they saw the airship last night. It's believed they saw a paper balloon.[61]

Three of the most elaborate tales featured Martians. A Missouri hiker came across an airship on the ground and saw a man and woman as naked as Adam and Eve standing nearby. Though unable to communicate in English, the strangers pointed to the sky and seemed to indicate that Mars was their home.[62] At Aurora, Texas, an airship crashed into a windmill and exploded, scattering fiery fragments and leaving the disfigured remains of the pilot for burial in the local cemetery. This man "was not an inhabitant of this world" and presumably a Martian, according to the *Dallas Morning News* of April 19.[63] A few days later a sensational yarn arrived from Le Roy, Kansas, where commotion among the livestock wakened farmer Alexander Hamilton, who rushed outside with his son and hired man to behold an airship three hundred feet long over his cow lot. Strange beings scanned the area with a searchlight and raised the ship when the men approached, but the beings had roped a heifer and its head was caught in a fence. Hamilton cut the fence and the airship departed with the heifer, but another farmer found the remains of a butchered cow the next day and puzzled over an absence of footprints in the soft soil. A who's who of the county's prominent citizens vouched for Hamilton's trustworthiness in a signed affidavit.[64]

The great airship wave of 1896–1897 makes a striking impression on anyone who reads the newspaper reports as they unfold from day to day, but a disappointment lurks beneath the surface: not one of the thousand or so reports seems to describe a genuine UFO. Most accounts say nothing more than "the airship was seen last night," while sightings reported at greater depth resolve into accurate observations of conventional phenomena or spectacular appearances due to hoaxes. A respected editor of a Troy, Kansas, newspaper wrote an honest and straightforward account of a sighting:

> We have read a great deal ... about a mysterious air ship, and supposed it was some trick or sensational story. But last Sunday night ... our citizens had a sight of it. It was directly over town, and somewhat resembled the headlight of a locomotive.

After slowly moving westward, maneuvering as it went, it sank below the horizon. Whether there is a trick in this matter or not, there is something mysterious about it.[65]

Honest and straightforward but in a sense insipid, the description easily applies to the planet Venus, then brilliant in the west. The slow movement befits a heavenly body as it sets, and the maneuvering suggests autokinesis, an illusion of motion in a point source of light when watched against a dark background.

In other cases where people saw multiple lights or structural features, a fire balloon or a kite bearing a paper lantern was the likely culprit. Paper hot-air balloons with candles or alcohol lamps to provide lift and illumination were a popular form of Fourth of July fireworks. When two Iowa reporters from the *Burlington Hawk-Eye* sent up several of these balloons, dozens of witnesses described full-blown airships with headlights, machinery, and aerial voices. Many local papers concluded an airship story with the names of the citizens who sent up the balloon as a joke on their neighbors, while in some cases a balloon left its burnt-out carcass in some farmer's field or became a fire hazard, setting a haystack on fire or causing minor damage to a rooftop.[66]

Modern standards of journalistic integrity did not prevail in the 1890s, and newspaper hoaxes were a popular form of entertainment. When news ran scarce, the "snake editor" concocted a yarn about giant snakes or other sorts of "nature fakes," and airships fitted perfectly into this tradition. With correspondents paid for their submissions by the column inch, they had incentive to produce printable news even if they had to imagine it. Local rivalries led one newspaper to attribute an airship—and insobriety— to another community as a form of practical joke, while civic pride dictated that every town should have its visit, a feeling expressed in an Illinois newspaper: "Durand is determined not to be outdone by any of her one-horse neighboring towns, and is bound to keep in touch with everything that is going the rounds."[67] Courting couples discovered yet another reason to see the airship—they could excuse themselves for staying out late at night. The Aurora crash appears to be a fabrication since local historians found no evidence for it, and residents had a motive for telling the story since the town had been struggling after the railroad bypassed it a few years earlier and a hoax might draw attention.[68] Hamilton confessed his calf-napping hoax in response to a newspaper editor's inquiry, and subsequent research made clear that Hamilton belonged to the same Saturday-afternoon liar's club as the prominent people who signed the affidavit attesting to his truthful character. In a time when interactions were face to face and people knew the honesty of their neighbors, documents meant little and a joke did no harm to a man's reputation.[69]

Strong circumstantial accounts remain that have no obvious paper balloon hanging over them or any charms of Venus. A case in point comes from a Texas lawyer riding on the night of April 15:

> I was astonished by a brilliant flash from an electric search light. . . . My horse was . . . frightened and came near over turning the buggy. . . . Fortunately the light rested on us scarcely a second, but glided along over the fields and the country till it was suddenly turned upward. . . . I beheld, about 1000 feet above me . . . , a huge black monster, from which the light emanated. It was in shape something like a cigar, but underneath there appeared to be a body similar to the body of a ship. . . . The search light was presently shut off and a number of incandescent lights flashed around the lower edge. . . . The lights were soon extinguished and it glided like a small black cloud in the air.[70]

An argument for a genuine flying object could stand on this sort of testimony, but while the description is strong the testimonial value must rate as weak. Only one witness affirms the sighting, and other cases make plain that even reputable individuals can be guilty of tale-telling. With questions overshadowing this remainder of quality reports, the authenticity of even one phantom airship seems doubtful.

The Advent of Aviation and the Airship Pandemic of 1908–1917.—The crowning achievement of the nineteenth century had to await the onset of the twentieth, when Count Ferdinand von Zeppelin flew his first successful dirigible airship in 1900. For once reality outstripped imagination as the sleek and enormous Zeppelins overawed crowds of admiring onlookers. The Wright Brothers tested the first successful heavier-than-air craft in 1903, but their efforts left little deeper public impression than attempts by a host of other would-be aviators until 1908, when the U.S. Army invited the Wrights to demonstrate their flier and the airplane suddenly emerged from its cocoon of wooly rumors as a practical reality at last.[71] The world then went on a glorious binge of air craziness for several years to come.

Where supernatural and naturalistic anomalies changed little over time, descriptions of mysterious aircraft kept pace with the rapid development of genuine aviation technology—or rather, stayed one step ahead of the game. These reports offer transparent glimpses of expectation shaping the description and interpretation of strange sights in the sky, starting in the latter half of the nineteenth century and leading up to the advent of flying saucers in 1947. The phantom doubles of airships and airplanes appeared almost constantly from 1908 through the First World War, in a global pandemic of sightings that unfolded to a mood initially giddy with excitement over the new wonder of aviation, later turning somber in tone as aerial attack became a threat and then a reality. The design of phantom aircraft in 1897 left much to the imagination as claimants fantasized chimerical combinations of gas bags, propellers, and bird wings in aerodynamically impossible configurations.[72] Air-conscious witnesses of the great pandemic constrained themselves to see the same airworthy designs that real pilots flew, though the hallmark searchlight persisted despite its implausibility, given that the weight of such an apparatus challenged even the great Zeppelins.

The airship season of 1909 opened in March when a patrolling British constable heard an engine and looked up to see a powerful light attached to a narrow, oblong body outlined against the stars. By May airship sightings became a daily affair and the source of conflicting rumors about inventors, advertising schemes, and toy balloons, but a growing suspicion took hold that a German craft had arrived on a spying mission. Seeming confirmation came when a Mr. Lethbridge reported a tube-shaped machine on the ground and overheard two men in fur coats speak a foreign language.[73] If the British preferred a dirigible shape, the claims of Massachusetts inventor Wallace E. Tillinghast that he flew an airplane to New York and back set the pattern for sightings across New England in December, when crowds in Boston saw a brilliant headlight and residents of Revere watched two lights reflected on huge wings. Experienced sky watchers complained that Christmas shoppers grew excited over Venus rather than Tillinghast's airplane.[74]

When the light of an "unknown aircraft over Dover" flew in from the sea on January 4, 1913, the British immediately suspected the Germans. They replied that a round trip to Britain would strain the capabilities of a Zeppelin and that flights simply attracted too much attention to remain secret, while the German press ridiculed airship nervousness with a cartoon of the British lion spooked by a paper lantern tied to its tail.[75] Unease over foreign aircraft afflicted much of Europe, with southwestern Russia invaded by alleged Austrian airplanes carrying brilliant headlights while Rumanian troops fired on a supposed Russian plane. One fantastic story claimed that Austrian fliers kidnapped the mayor of a Polish town, tied him to the wing of their plane, and flew him a distance of sixty miles.[76] Reports multiplied with the outbreak of the war— an airplane with a bright searchlight troubled South Africa in 1914; airplanes, Zeppelins, and moving lights crossed Norwegian and Swedish skies throughout the war; and reports that airplanes from the American side of the border headed toward Ottawa on February 14, 1915, prompted a blackout of the Canadian Parliament building.[77] Similar wartime fears over air raids and sabotage reached the United States in 1916 with reports that a lighted airplane circled the Du Pont gunpowder mills in Delaware and shadowy biplanes haunted prime targets like loading docks and rail lines in Minnesota and Wisconsin.[78]

Ghosts of the Skies.—By war's end familiarity had dulled the amazement that airplanes once inspired, but they gained a new hold on human interest when a series of "ghost flier" reports from Sweden and Norway aroused suspicions that liquor smugglers had updated their delivery methods. Starting in late 1933 and reappearing for several years to come, accounts from witnesses described the flier as a large airplane with a searchlight. Some witnesses said they heard an engine noise as the plane flew even in the worst blizzard conditions.[79] Mystery airplanes also appeared at this time over English locations, first to suspicions of criminal activity, then to worries over Nazi espionage.[80] A new round of mysterious aircraft for a new World War included several round objects that flew over Los Angeles in the early hours of February 25, 1942, only weeks after Pearl Harbor. Anti-aircraft batteries fired 1,430 rounds at the intruders, and a news photograph shows an apparent round object or objects caught in crisscrossing searchlight beams while shells burst nearby, though to no apparent effect.[81] By late 1944 air crews reported that balls of fire paced bombers and night fighters flying missions over Germany. The mystery lights were called "foo fighters" by the Americans and "buckets of blood" by the British. Many airmen feared a secret enemy weapon, but the only harm done was to their peace of mind.[82]

The postwar years marked another era of mercurial development in aviation as jets and rockets crossed over from science fiction to reality, as new experimental designs and speed records proliferated. A dark object carrying a bright light had prevailed for fifty years as the standard appearance for technological aerial anomalies, but something new was in the air. During the summer of 1946 the Swedish military received nearly a thousand reports of luminous trails and wingless cigar-shaped bodies that came to be known as "ghost rockets." An astronomer reported a torpedo-shaped body ninety feet long and glistening like metal on August 12. This object exploded with a silent but blinding flash. Swedish critics noted that sightings rose as the Perseid meteor shower peaked in August, but reports that the rockets flew at low altitude, reversed direction, and made a buzzing sound led to fears that the Soviets were testing German rocket designs. Similar strange objects flashed through the skies of Greece, Hungary, France, Italy, Austria, and Germany.[83] San Diego newspapers reported that a big airplane-like object, equipped with two lights or a surrounding glow, maneuvered and flapped its wings over the city on October 9, 1946. A medium picked up communications from the occupants saying they were from space and that the name of the ship was *Kareeta*. If editorialists treated the *Kareeta* as a joke, the U.S. military had already collected reports of unknown oval, silvery, or self-luminous flying objects, and by the summer of 1947 Kenneth Arnold's nine objects skipping like saucers over Mount Rainier simply added one more case to the list.[84]

The Ufological Uses of the Past

A clear sense of purpose motivated Lycosthenes, the Mathers, and the author of *Mirabilis annus* to collect aerial prodigies. Religious doctrine gave meaning to these sights as signs from God and joined them with prodigious wonders of all sorts as examples of divine providence. The conceptual framework lent importance, even urgency to one scattered, stereotypical, and often overblown account after another. Natural anomalies had a place in the scientific scheme of understanding but little significance or meaning. They remained fringe occurrences that observers were obliged to record but seldom to reckon with as challenges to prevailing theory. Phantom airships and their successors excited great temporary interest but never acquired a continuity of awareness. They remained manifestations of the expectations of their time, of concern to law enforcement, national defense, or public curiosity, but they were too well "known" to qualify as anomalies. No one wondered what they were, only who invented or piloted them. Without some overriding concern even the 1897 wave quickly passed from memory, and only one or two newspapers printed vague references to the earlier furor during the renewed excitement in 1909. Each airship wave seemingly flared up as an isolated event and never caught fire with a sense of past or larger purpose.

Charles Fort introduced a new conceptual framework that brought back coherence to strange sights in the sky. He looked beyond preoccupation with secretive inventors to propose an unearthly origin for unknown lights and aerial objects, whether they belonged to space-faring Martians or visitors sailing the Super-Sargasso Sea. His explanation reached out to embrace rains of fish, black snows, and a host of other weird happenings ignored by science, so that this orphan phenomena acquired a new conceptual family as meaningful events in a Fortean cosmology distinct from the prevailing scientific worldview. Ufology promoted a less imaginative but more immediately appealing framework. It borrowed the conventional scientific universe and an extraterrestrial hypothesis where aliens do little more than earthly astronauts, only with more advanced technology. Yet like Fort's vision, the concepts of ufology provided for a flexible reconstruction of the past and bettered him as a way to adapt present events. So versatile is the understanding of ufology that it does not so much descend from Fort as absorb him, uniting strange phenomena, past history, and current events into the mythology of alien visitation. The "big picture" of Reformation prodigies enlarges into a "theory of everything" in ufology.

Historical reports have held a continuing place in ufological thought and argument as key evidence for extraterrestrial visits. No 1950s saucer book was complete without a nod to historical cases. Donald Keyhoe filled several pages of *The Flying Saucers Are Real* (1950) with accounts of airships and other Fortean reports. H. T. Wilkins extended the ufological past to Roman and medieval times in *Flying Saucers on the Attack* (1954), while Desmond Leslie reached back to cite the *vimanas* from Hindu epics as advanced aircraft of an ancient nuclear war in *Flying Saucers Have Landed* (1953). Astronomer M. K. Jessup reread biblical chariots and fiery clouds as spaceships in *UFO and the Bible* (1956), and Fort's rains of fish and changes on the moon as examples of alien activity in *The Case for the UFO* (1955) and *The Expanding Case for the UFO* (1957). These early pro-UFO treatments established the ideas of an age-old lineage for flying saucers, while opponent Donald Menzel began an enduring critical trend in *Flying Saucers* (1953) when he cited airships and prodigies as examples of natural causes mistaken for wonderful occurrences and concluded that the same confusion continues today.[85]

Erich von Däniken's *Chariots of the Gods* fascinated readers in 1970 with wild claims that ancient astronauts had visited earth and intervened in human affairs. Ufologists responded to his unsubstantiated assertions with less enthusiasm, but he only repeated ideas that had accumulated quietly in the literature since the 1950s. These speculations hold an inherent attractiveness. Once pointed out, the similarity of a carving on a Mayan sarcophagus to an astronaut in a rocket ship is hard to forget, while the conventional interpretation of a man suspended between this world and the next amid symbolic religious figures seems bland and unimaginative by comparison. Another memorable souvenir of the ancient astronaut era is *The Spaceships of Ezekiel* (1974), wherein a technological facelift by NASA engineer Josef Blumrich turns the biblical vision into jet exhausts and whirling propellers on an alien spacecraft.[86] Plausible or not, such connections related UFOs to the romance of ruins and lost civilizations and promoted aliens from mere tourists to vital participants in human history. The writers who looted archaeological sources and religious texts for evidence of ancient astronauts did much to enlarge the mythic dimensions of UFOs.

Ufologists expand the UFO myth by adding various historical puzzles. The disappearance of the Norfolk Regiment at Gallipoli was a genuine unsolved mystery of World War I, but the matter veered into UFO territory in the 1960s when several old soldiers came forward with a startling claim. They said that they watched men of the regiment march into a well-defined cloud or fog bank on the ground. Hundreds of men went in, but none came out; after a while the cloud lifted into the sky and took its place among other clouds.[87] A question posed in a 1960 issue of *FSR* asked how an alien visitor might act on earth, and a response drew the enigmatic figure of Spring-heeled Jack into UFO lore. He was a tall, gaunt man dressed in glistening clothing and a metallic helmet who terrorized London for several months in 1837–1838 by bounding out of the darkness and attacking people with clawlike hands. Claims that his eyes glowed and his mouth spewed blue fire joined with his superhuman leaping abilities to transport Jack into the realm of the supernatural. He returned several times during the nineteenth century, and similar figures like the 1944 "Mad Gasser of Mattoon" (Illinois) have attracted ufologists' attention as parallels to Springheeled Jack, whose long career has cast him as ghost, devil, aristocrat, villain, and, finally, honorary alien.[88]

NICAP and other visible collection centers attracted reminiscences of people relieved to find, after years of silence, someone to listen to their strange experiences. One example came from two young male professors at DePauw University who were driving east of Indianapolis in 1923 when they saw an enormous saucer glide across the road and cast a brilliant red light all around. The revolving saucer gave off no sound and vanished suddenly after it moved off to the southwest. An apparent abduction attempt came to light in 1988 when a seventy-eight-year-old Louisiana woman revealed that while riding with another teenager one night in 1926 they drove into a garage to escape an approaching object like the full moon. It gave off the sound of a running motor, followed by a hiss, as the object sprayed a liquid on top of the building. Unable to breathe, the two girls ran for the house, but the narrator received some of the cold, numbing spray on one arm before she reached the door. The object hovered for a while and the witnesses heard voices, then the object flew off westward. A burning sensation set in the next day when sunlight struck the narrator's arm, and the roof of the garage caught fire where the spray had fallen.[89]

UFO prehistory came into its own as a topic of serious research in the 1960s when Jerome Clark, Lucius Farish, and other investigators began systematic exploration of original sources. Newspaper searches revealed the enormity of the phantom airship episodes and discoveries of one sighting, one wave after another suggested a vigorous UFO presence before 1947. Jacques Vallee introduced the Hamilton calf-napping incident in *Anatomy of a Phenomenon* (1965), and this tale seemed like the smoking gun to prove that old reports dealt with alien spacecraft. When Gordon I. R. Lore and Harold H. Deneault Jr. opened NICAP's file of pre-1947 reports in *Mysteries in the Skies: UFOs in Perspective* (1968), these cases hinted at a grassroots reservoir of personal experiences with far greater depth than the published accounts in newspapers and magazines. In the mid-1970s ufologists even descended on the Texas town of

Aurora to dig up the body from the 1897 airship crash. These resurrectionists neglected to inform local residents and soon confronted irate, gun-toting citizens who took a dim view of strangers digging up their cemetery. Rumors abounded in the ensuing circus, with mysterious persons said to have robbed the alien grave and an elderly man blaming UFO radioactivity for his rheumatism. No support for the story turned up, but the effort attested to the value that old reports had acquired.[90]

Under critical examination even the most promising treasures of the past usually pan out as fool's gold. Pliny wrote that "a burning shield darted across at sunset from west to east, throwing out sparks," in 100 B.C.,[91] while the *Royal Frankish Annals* recorded that in A.D. 776 , when the pagan Saxons stormed a Christian castle, God sent the likeness of two shields, "red with flame wheeling over the church," and the Saxons fled in terror.[92] In 1926 Nicholas Roerich, an explorer, artist, and mystic, was mountain climbing in the Himalayas when his party saw "something big and shiny reflecting the sun, like a huge oval moving at great speed. Crossing our camp this thing changed in its direction from south to southeast. . . . We even had time to take our field glasses and saw quite distinctly the oval form with a shiny surface, one side of which was brilliant from the sun."[93] Though saucerlike in description, meteors probably explain the Roman and Frankish examples. The Roerich party may have sighted a weather balloon released by another expedition in the Himalayas at the same time.[94] Holinshed's *Chronicles* record a fiery appearance seen in many parts of England during the fall of 1361: "To some it appeared in the likeness of a turning wheel burning; to othersome round in the likeness of a barrel, flashing out flames of fire at the head; to othersome in the likeness of a long burning lance." When travelers walked alone at night this object would accompany them and stop when they stopped, but it stayed far off when people traveled in groups.[95] According to Naima's *Annals of the Turkish Empire* for 1617, a black circular cloud dropped a rain of blood and manifested fiery crosses. Smoke issued from the cloud and then there was a thunderclap of such loudness that cattle in the fields fell to their knees and fled in all directions.[96] In spite of some coincidental similarities to modern UFOs, the English case has aspects in common with the will-o'-the-wisp, while an unusual storm probably explains the Turkish case. And so it goes, with conventional solutions seldom hard to find.

The severest disappointments have accumulated around the airship waves. Ufologists warmed to them because they prefigured modern UFO activity at a time when no earthly technology cluttered the skies to confuse witnesses. A striking continuity became apparent—the moving lights, structured craft, sightings surges, alien associations, animal reactions, ground traces, landings, crashes, and wreckage prefigured modern UFO phenomenology with uncanny prescience. Yet increasing knowledge proved too much of a good thing. Nationwide surveys of the U.S. 1897 and British 1913 waves saw the great airship hope implode into a great letdown of hoaxes and errors.[97] The adjustability of the objects proved even more disillusioning. Airships fitted the technological expectations of their era, but gas bags, gondolas, and flapping wings had little in common with UFOs today. Year by year descriptions evolved from airships to airplanes to secret weapons and ghost rockets, but a good flying saucer was hard to find. Only a scant few published reports break the time barrier; they tell of bat-winged dirigibles or ghost fliers, not flying saucers. By contrast, saucers are common in personal recollections from long ago, but these "post facto" accounts are equivocal. The witnesses may have said nothing because saucer-shaped craft made no sense at the time; then again, modern influences may have rewritten memory or planted the suggestion for a saucer tale.

If so many witnesses could be wrong about airships, a shadow of a doubt necessarily falls over all other UFOs. So many saucers after 1947 in contrast with so few before are embarrassing as well; so is the responsiveness of descriptions to the prevailing ideas of the time. These facts argue not for a coherent phenomenon that bridges the ages from ancient Egypt to the morning's news, but for a creation of the social imagination that owes its content to long-term human interests and its form to current imagery. Jerome Clark recognized the difficulties implied by airships as early as the mid-1960s and attempted to save the mystery by including technology as one manifestation of a broader paranormal phenomenon, but hostile critics seized on airships as straightforward examples of a cultural image mirrored in witness reports.[98] The airship has stood as a cornerstone of psychosocial opposition to UFOs ever since.

The ufological history lesson affirms that human interests dominate the aerial mystery narrative. Not unearthly vehicles but mistaken identities or imaginative exaggerations tied to expectations, beliefs, and stereotypes explain most historical accounts. But history teaches another lesson worth remembering—humans can be quite accurate observers, sometimes delivering raw phenomenology without intervention of belief, like John of Worcester's meteor—more often distorting the phenomenon yet leaving enough of it to identify, like the aurora of Camerarius or Venus in accounts of the Edison Star. And even if hundreds of chronicles and thousands of old newspapers yield few instances of aerial phenomena that look or act like modern UFOs, the cupboard is not entirely bare.

In some historical accounts a similarity in appearance or activity justifies comparison with current UFOs. Unnatural motions characterize a red meteor that moved to and fro three times over the camp of a Chinese general in A.D. 235.[99] Obsequens says that in 91 B.C. a golden fireball rolled to the earth, then increased in size and lifted from the ground and grew large enough to blot out the sun.[100] According to Lycosthenes, two suns appeared over Erdford, Germany, in 1520, then a burning in the sky fell to the ground and destroyed many places before returning to the air and taking on a round form.[101] Too little information undercuts the value of these accounts, but the recurrent appearance of a mysterious Chinese "pearl" offers both detail and one of the most UFO-like claims as the early records have to offer. At some time between 1056 and 1063, wrote the eleventh-century scholar Shen Kua in a book entitled *Brush Talks from Dream Brook*, a large luminous object began to appear at night in the vicinity of a lake. "The trees cast shadows, exactly as when the sun has just come up. In the distance you saw only a sky reddened as if by a forest fire. All of a sudden it went far off, moving as if in flight, floating over the waves, shining like the sun." A friend of the author said that the pearl came near one night and opened its door slightly, and from the opening shot a golden ray of light. When fully opened, the door revealed the interior bright with a silvery light, so bright the witness could not look at it directly. For ten years the pearl was a popular tourist attraction, then it was seen no more.[102]

A noteworthy case of anomalous meteors occurred at sea off San Francisco just before sunrise on February 28, 1904. Three crewmen aboard the USS *Supply* sighted three egg-shaped objects near the horizon and below the clouds. The leader appeared as large as six suns, the second as large as two, and the third the size of one. These bright red objects headed toward the ship in echelon formation then soared up above the clouds, rising out of sight after two minutes of observation. The objects were large, the witnesses reliable, and of course no one knew what to expect of UFOs in 1904. A recent critical reexamination proposed that the objects only seemed to fly below the clouds, that in fact three meteors were distant enough to appear low on the horizon, visible in open sky beyond the cloud deck or through breaks in the scattered clouds. Bruce Maccabee consulted the log of the *Supply* in the National Archives and found that the sky was 90 percent covered by stratus clouds. In his analysis he concludes that the objects flew in front of the clouds at an altitude of less than a mile, traveled at speeds too slow for meteors but characteristic of some UFOs, and maneuvered in unmeteoric fashion by actually pulling up into the cloud layer. These "meteors" well deserve their designation as "remarkable."[103]

Under the title of "Curious Phenomenon in Venezuela," *Scientific American* published a letter from a member of the American consulate describing an event of October 24, 1885. The night was stormy when a family of nine persons sleeping in a hut

were awakened by a loud humming noise and a vivid, dazzling light, which brilliantly illuminated the interior of the house. The occupants, completely terror

stricken ... threw themselves on their knees and commenced to pray, but their
devotions were almost immediately interrupted by violent vomitings and extensive swellings ... particularly noticeable about the face and lips. The next morning
the swellings had subsided, leaving upon the face and body large black blotches.
No special pain was felt until the ninth day, when the skin peeled off, and these
blotches were transformed into virulent raw sores.

> The hair of the head fell off upon the side which happened to be underneath
> when the phenomenon occurred, the same side of the body being, in all nine cases,
> the more seriously injured.

No damage befell the house, but trees around it withered suddenly on the same ninth
day when the human victims developed sores. The writer said that he had visited the
victims in a hospital and the injuries were severe. He attributed them to some sort of
electrical phenomenon, while the similarity to supposed UFO-induced injuries in the
Cash-Landrum case and others of recent times is striking.[104]

Perhaps no other premodern UFO leaves an impression as convincing as the
"Robozero Marvel" of August 15, 1663. The Russian town of Robozero lies about thirty
miles southwest of Belozersk, in Vologda Province, beside a small lake a mile and a
half long by two-thirds of a mile wide. Many people had gathered for the Feast of the
Assumption of the Virgin when a loud noise drew them out of church to see what was
the matter.

> At noon, a large ball of fire came down over Robozero, arriving from the clearest
> part of the cloudless heavens. It came from the direction whence winter comes
> (north), and it moved toward midday (south) along the lake, passing over the wa-
> ter's surface. The ball of fire measured some 140 feet from one edge to the other,
> with blue smoke on its side, and over the same distance (140 feet), ahead of it, two
> ardent rays extended.

The object disappeared but returned less than an hour later, this time moving from the
south to the west. A short time later the object returned a third time.

> The same fire ball appeared more terrific in width, and disappeared having moved
> to the west, and it had remained over Robozero, over water, for an hour and a half.
> ... As the ball of fire was coming over water, peasants who were in their boat on
> the lake, followed it, and the fire burned them by the heat not allowing them to
> get closer. The waters of the lake were illuminated to their greatest depth of 30
> feet and the fish swam away to the shore. And where the fire ball came the water
> seemed to be covered with rust under the reddish light; it was then scattered by the
> wind and the water became clean again.

The writer of this account, Ivachko Rievskoi, had interviewed a farmer who witnessed the event and contacted some priests who also confirmed it. Rievskoi sent the account to his clerical superiors, and his letter still survives. It was published in 1842 by the St. Petersburg Archaeographic Commission. Here we know the report actually exists—a basic consideration but not a matter to take for granted where the UFO literature is concerned. No contamination by current UFO belief is possible because no one would hear of flying saucers for more than a century. The case is remarkable for a number of reasons: The luminous object was enormous, its diameter the height of a twelve-story building; and even allowing for exaggeration, the fact that the object was visible for a long time and people could approach it in a boat reduce the scope of error. In any case, the object seems to have been huge. An effort to explain the event as three meteors passing in succession makes the mistake of selecting the suitable elements of the account while ignoring the rest, such as the changing directions and the fact that the earth keeps turning and meteors in a train would not pass the same spot on the surface over a period of two or more hours. A meteor might glow like a fireball, smoke, and make noise, but it would not hover close over the surface of the lake for an hour and a half; neither would ball lightning, though it would not form on a clear day, in any case. The apparent beams of light projecting forward from the object and the burning sensation felt by the boatmen sound like modern UFO traits, while circumstantial details such as the fish fleeing the object and its ruddy light on the water add to the realism of the description. Almost free of theory and interpretation, devoid of commonplace stereotyping, distinctive from any other report of its era, this account would do credit to UFO reporting in any age as a straightforward narrative of a remarkable event.[105]

CHAPTER FOUR

From the Otherworld to Other Worlds

> [God], who through vast immensity can pierce,
> See worlds on worlds compose one universe,
> Observe how system into system runs,
> What other planets circle other suns,
> What varied Beings people every star,
> May tell why Heaven has made us as we are.
> —Alexander Pope, *Essay on Man*

> Heav'n is for thee too high
> To know what passes there; be lowly wise:
> Think only what concerns thee and thy being;
> Dream not of other Worlds, what Creatures there
> Live, in what state, condition or degree. . . .
> —Milton, *Paradise Lost*

> We are not alone.
> —Walter Sullivan[1]

> Where are they?
> —Enrico Fermi[2]

No attribute attaches more closely to UFOs than their extraterrestrial origin. "UFO" and "alien spaceship" go together like bread and butter or coffee and cream, the little green man with his flying saucer an inseparable combination in 1950s popular imagery and the big-eyed humanoid in a UFO equally familiar today. This marriage of representations might have been made in heaven, but it was not inevitable. Other identities might work just as well and certainly did for centuries when signs, natural anomalies, and airships accounted for strange sights in the sky. Alternate explanations for recent UFOs have included secret weapons, space animals, paranormal manifestations, electric plasmas, earth lights, leftover Nazis, angels or demons, visitors from the future, holograms from space, and aircraft piloted by inhabitants of the hollow earth or lost continents. These contestants lack nothing for imaginativeness, but they rank as distant also-rans at best. In fact, there is really no contest. In popular ideas and in the preponderance of ufological thinking, UFOs are alien spaceships. End of story.

Since the early 1950s the extraterrestrial hypothesis has held much the same position in ufology as evolution theory in biology. It is the indispensable connecting thread that makes sense of everything. Popular understanding takes this central idea for granted, and it underlies most cultural representations related to UFOs, but so much unanimity brings its own hazards. No one comes to the subject as a blank slate; no one is innocent of how UFOs are supposed to look and act. This prior knowledge imposes order and imagery on conception, expression, and interpretation, so even when witness evidence joins reasonable inference to support the extraterrestrial hypothesis, its very pervasiveness raises questions of whether the alien attributes are, after all, more mythical than natural and inevitable.

Historical perspectives raise another reason to doubt. Nothing appears more modern—or rather, futuristic—than notions of other inhabited worlds and space-faring aliens, but this appearance is mistaken. Jacques Vallee has cautioned repeatedly against isolating UFO accounts:

> There is ... [a] very important aspect to the entire abduction problem that has never been considered seriously by American ufology. ... What I am referring to is the simple fact that abduction stories are not specific to the UFO phenomenon and certainly did not begin with Betty and Barney Hill in 1961. I pointed out ... that the structure of abduction stories was identical to that of occult initiation rituals ... that contact with ufonauts was only a modern extension of the age-old tradition of contact with nonhuman consciousness in the form of angels, demons, elves, and sylphs.[3]

These warnings name abductions but apply equally well to the rest of UFO narratives, and especially so to interpretations like the extraterrestrial hypothesis. It channels a storied heritage of themes about otherworld visitation and marvelous beings from afar into modern UFO thinking, and most features now attributed to extraterrestrials have antecedents or close parallels in other contexts. Three strands of tradition with beginnings in antiquity deserve close attention—early cosmologies, travelers' tales, and the doctrine of the plurality of worlds. Mythic ideas about the nature of the cosmos, the inhabitants of faraway places, and journeys to the otherworld have set a course for imagination through the ages, while extraterrestrial concepts, now all but inseparable from UFOs, have not strayed far from the same map.

Somewhere Next to Dragon Land:
The Supernatural Otherworld

"The eternal silence of these infinite spaces frightens me,"[4] said the philosopher Pascal, in what could stand as an epigraph for the entire history of human relationships with the universe. If nature abhors a vacuum, so does human thought. Modern scientific concepts scatter space with galaxies, solar systems, and habitable planets; but premodern peoples also envisioned themselves surrounded by a crowded cosmic neighborhood of many tenements and no vacancies. The premodern cosmos represents an all-important reserve of order created and maintained for man in the midst of chaos, but sharing in this creation are multiple races of supernatural beings, some physical and some immaterial, some great in power and others small, some benign toward humans and some indifferent, unfriendly, even hostile. Flesh and spirit, the living and the dead, the seen and the unseen cohabit the cosmos in their own proper spheres and interact with one another in an intricate network of obligations and possibilities. The result is an extended community of humans and nonhumans never far apart or long out of contact with one another.

The Floor Plan of the Cosmos.—A child's Sunday school lesson sets God in heaven and the devil underground. As elementary as this spiritual geography may sound, a three-story arrangement of heaven, earth, and hell or the underworld summarizes a cosmographic plan characteristic of the most familiar mythologies. The Greek gods inhabit Mount Olympus, while Hades, the home of the dead, is a recess in the earth; Norse myth divides the cosmos into Asgard as home of the gods, Midgard as the earth of mortal humans, and Hel as the underground realm of the dead.[5] In one version of ancient Egyptian cosmology, the solar barge of Ra sails the celestial Nile by day and the subterranean Nile by night. In another version, the sky goddess bends over the earth, and Osiris, enthroned beneath it, presides over the dead.[6] Various subdivisions of the tripartite scheme multiply the number of otherworlds a cosmos can hold. The Aztecs prescribed twelve heavenly and nine underworld levels, while Babylonians and Hebrews favored seven, derived perhaps from the sun, moon, and five visible planets. Buddhist cosmology elaborates an already complex Hindu structure with innovations like systems of hot hells side by side with cold hells, and minor hells sprouting out from the major levels.[7] Horizontal space introduces another otherworldly dimension. Babylonian belief populated deserts, ruins, and mountains with demons;[8] Greek mythology described the Fortunate Isles and the Elysian fields; and Celtic literature spoke of the Land of the Living and the Land of the Young, distant islands of paradisiacal beauty and eternal bliss somewhere to the west.[9]

A picture emerges of the supernatural cosmos with every niche filled, of human imagination that lets no potential habitat go to waste. Norse mythology squeezes the frost giants into Jötunheim, at the edge of the world, and assigns the dwarfs to mountains and caverns.[10] A readiness to fill every possible corner of the cosmos with otherworlds often proceeds to the point of overcrowding. Some African religions recognize visible and invisible worlds side by side, with physical objects and their spiritual complements always nearby or even overlapping.[11] In Europe the fairies lived just under the earth, so close that humans had to take care that their wastewater did not offend them.[12] Eclectic folk cosmographies pack jumbled conceptual attics and basements full of realms and entities with little respect for place or hierarchy. When interviewed about his cosmological conceptions, Hungarian master tale-teller Lajos Ámi described the earth as a flat disk with water above and below and the sky closing on the edges like a tent, while separate suns shone on an upper world and a lower world. Deriving his cosmos from the worldview of folktales, Ámi assumed that a land of dragons belonged to the underworld and found room for hell down there as well, "some place next to Dragon Land."[13]

The Topography of the Otherworld.—Cosmic architecture typically resists isolation of the tiers and facilitates access between them. The waters around the earth, Jacob's Ladder in the Bible, and the rainbow bridge to Asgard link the worlds; a hole in the sky allows passage between heaven and earth in Star Husband tales among American Indians. Familiarity with the folktale cosmos convinced Lajos Ámi that a fabled hole in the ground somewhere in Russia permitted descent to the world below.[14] The celebrated Irish cave of St. Patrick's Purgatory and Lake Avernus among the Romans join with countless local beliefs that some cavern, pit, fissure, or other natural landmark serves as an entranceway to the underworld.[15]

A widespread cosmological concept holds that all realms meet at the axis mundi, the center of the world and a nexus for travel between worlds. Sometimes imagined as a pillar or pole that holds up the sky, this center often takes the form of a tall mountain. The Hindu and Buddhist Mount Meru (or Sumeru) stands at the center of the earth, and the heavenly bodies orbit above. Babylonian ziggurats copied the structure of the world mountain and served as stairways to heaven, with a literalness mocked in the biblical story of the Tower of Babel. The axis may also take the form of a tree, like Yggdrasill in Norse mythology. The world tree may grow out of the earth, while its branches reach into heaven and its roots probe the underworld to tie the cosmos together with a continuous arboreal passageway from realm to realm.[16]

The otherworld landscape typically reflects good and bad extremes. Happy otherworlds embody widely shared mainstays of beauty and pleasure: heaven has streets paved with gold and bright mansions with all unhappiness refined away; Olympus is a place of soft, perpetual light where no rain or chill disturbs the peace of the gods; and the Elysian fields offer cool, luminous meadows where the blessed sing and dance. A medieval Irish literary tale, *The Voyage of Bran*, pictures the Celtic otherworld as a land full of beautiful women, fruit-bearing trees, musical birds, and crystalline buildings.[17] In folk tradition fairies inhabit a verdant subterranean kingdom of unsurpassed beauty where no sun shines and a uniform twilight prevails, but in most cases the underworld inverts the qualities of paradise to present a gloomy, dank recess inextricably bound up with death and decay. A typical netherworld appears in the Akkadian story of Ishtar's decent into the house of the dead, where inhabitants are deprived of light and where "dust is their food, clay their bread."[18] When Odysseus sails into the underworld, the spirits rustle like dry leaves, shadowy figures devoid of memory or will until they taste the blood of a sacrifice. Then their torpor lifts for a time and the shades lament that even the lowliest life on earth surpasses their afterlife existence.[19]

Visions of the otherworld pull out all the stops whenever the afterlife acquires a moral dimension. Zoroastrians meet their good and evil deeds face to face as beautiful or hideous personages, and they accompany these escorts to a blissful paradise or ugly hell.[20] Chinese and Japanese Buddhists have developed colorful versions of hell where fierce demons hammer sinners flat with a huge mallet, drive them into a snake-infested river, or stir them in a pool of fire.[21] Medieval Christian theology metes out reward and punishment according to a meticulous system wherein the worthy rise close to God, the wicked funnel downward, and the worst keep company with Satan.[22] Renaissance artists portray scenes of the last judgment where demons hang, boil, and prod sinners in lurid fire-lit alcoves amid the craggy rocks of underworld caverns.[23]

The Personnel of the Otherworld.—The physical appearance of supernatural entities may be anthropomorphic (humanlike), humanoid (humanlike but with differences), theriomorphic (animallike), chimerical (combinations of several forms), monstrous (grotesque and terrifying), or apparitional (immaterial or shape-shifting). The major gods typically look human, perhaps because visible kinship offers reassurance that the most influential powers are on our side; but human imagination is too restless to settle for monotonous anthropomorphism. Some Egyptian gods combine animal features with human bodies to give Thoth the head of an ibis; Horus, a falcon; and Anubis, a jackal. The Phoenicians picture Dagon as fishlike, and the Mesoamerican Quetzal-coatl appears both as a human and as a feathered serpent. Hindu deities include the elephant-headed Ganesh and Hanuman, the monkey god, while Shiva waves multiple arms attached to a purely human figure and sometimes presents multiple faces. Wings add exotic appendages to angels, Mesopotamian deities, and the harpies of Greek mythology.[24]

Just as good looks go with good behavior among gods, a frightening appearance often marks evil or dangerous spirits. Babylonian demons mix parts of lions, scorpions, and birds of prey to create chimerical monsters. Netherworld inhabitants reflect the dread this region inspires, with Pluto, Persephone, and the Hindu Yama portrayed as gloomy and imposing, while Mictlantecuhtli, the Mesoamerican lord of the dead, displays a terrifying skull-like visage.[25] Some of the most familiar portrayals of otherworld denizens originate with artists of the Italian Renaissance, who assigned their devils animal characteristics, especially bat or moth wings, in addition to the horns and cloven hooves inherited from the satyrs of antiquity. Botticelli amplified the wrongness of his devils by making them hairy and hermaphroditic, some with tails, pig snouts, and tusks, and some with talons for feet, and pigs' or asses' ears.[26] Northern European artists delved even deeper into the fantastic. Albrecht Dürer, Friedrich and Michael Pacher, Matthias Grünewald, and Pieter Bruegel depicted a riotous menagerie of monkeylike imps and strange bird creatures mingled with other forms based on insects or seafood. This tradition of fantastic images reaches its summit in the feverish visions of Hieronymus Bosch, whose countless devils combine human, animal, and inanimate parts into forms of dizzying weirdness. One example out of many from *The Last Judgment* shows a red-eyed creature with a batlike face, clawed hands and feet, a tail, and a hot stove for a belly.[27]

Traditions of fairylike creatures range over a variety of forms, with the Celtic fairy realm hosting tall, beautiful heroic races like the Tuatha de Dannan, shorter trooping and solitary fairies, and tiny nature spirits dear to Victorian painters. The selkies appear as seals when at sea but assume human form on land. Less human are the rough and hairy, but hardworking and helpful, brownies and the pixies, with their pointed ears and homely faces. Still other types are mischievous or even dangerous, such as the poltergeistlike bogies, boggles, and pucks. More distant relatives include shape-shifters like the kelpies, which take on the form of a horse to carry their riders to their death in the water, and monsters like the Nuckelavee, a Scottish sea creature with the mouth of a whale and one red eye, which ravages the land whenever it comes ashore.[28]

The most nearly universal entities in world traditions are giants and dwarfs, though preferences seem to favor beings at the short end of the scale. One Christian concept of

the soul casts it as a small, childlike homunculus without sexual identity.[29] The Norse
dwarfs lived underground, while on the other side of the world, a Tzotzil Indian from
southern Mexico expressed a similar view that just under the earth and above the realm
of the dead was a land of dwarfs.[30] Short supernatural beings thrive in folk tradition,
like the dwarfish trolls of Scandinavia and the Japanese *kappa*, a small, scrawny water
spirit resembling a cross between a human and a turtle. An indigenous race of dwarfs
goes by the name of *Menehune* in Hawaii and *Mmoetia* in western Africa, while a researcher found traditions of diminutive land, water, or subterranean beings among 85
percent of 380 native ethnic groups in North and South America.[31]

Otherworld beings typically have superhuman powers and skills. Gods create the
cosmos and preside over the forces of nature as well as all things important to humans—feast and famine, seasons and fertility, sickness and health, love and war, birth
and death. Malicious entities are responsible for the evil in the world, and trickster
figures like the Norse Loki and Coyote of the American Indians cause discord. Angels
and demons serve as agents of higher powers, while fairies may cause sickness and
injury or threaten children and livestock. These same beings are capable of invisibil-
ity, flight, and deceptive illusion. Where giants are builders, especially on a large scale,
dwarfs often act as blacksmiths and have a reputation as skilled craftsmen.[32]

The Otherworld Journey.—Isolation is seldom an option in the supernatural cosmos. Its distances are modest, as the sky hangs as close as the treetops and the underworld begins no deeper than a well. Gods and angels fly to earth with wings or arrive
by magic; others favor vehicles like Thor, who drives a chariot drawn by two goats amid
the storm clouds, or Rama, who can ride aerial chariots or the bird-god Garuda. A
stubborn faith endures that spirits of the dead escape their graves to pursue unfinished
business on earth, and the old Roman custom of opening tombs on special days to
release these spirits finds a parallel in the welcome extended to souls returning to their
former homes on the Mexican Day of the Dead.[33]

The boundaries between worlds are permeable and invite trespass, so that meetings with unearthly entities may happen literally just around the corner. Fairies share
this world yet appear in it as strangers. They belong to the otherworld and breathe its
eerie chill into encounters like that of a young Irishman walking home from work with
a friend one night early in the twentieth century: As they reached a crossroads, there
stood three figures in a close group, facing one another in a circle or triangle. These
figures were tall and dressed in deep black robes, with their arms hanging down at
their sides and their heads bent as if in profoundest sorrow. The men gave wide berth
to these unnerving figures, and one man soon went his way, leaving the narrator to

continue homeward alone. Now faraway from where he had first seen the three figures, he stopped in terror to see them again on the road ahead, as still, silent, and dark as before.[34]

Though otherworld beings often visit earth, the traffic runs both ways. Humans seldom make a grand entry. Their transportation is usually nothing more remarkable than a ladder, a boat, a dream, or their own two feet, while reasons for the trip may be heroic quests, initiatory ordeals to gain supernatural power, or just plain chance. An almost universal tradition recognizes entry into the afterlife as an otherworld journey that everyone must take. A common belief holds that the deceased must cross some sort of barrier, perhaps a body of water, such as the river Styx, where the ferryman Charon accepts only passengers able to pay the fare, or a gate guarded by a monstrous dog like the Greek Cerberus or the Norse Garmr.[35] Both Zoroastrians and Christians envisioned a bridge narrow at the center, where the righteous passed easily but the wicked slipped and fell as demons snatched at their heels.[36] In one Aztec tradition the soul wandered for four years through perilous regions along difficult paths before reaching its final abode. The nature of a man's death rather than the moral tenor of his life determined where he spent his hereafter, but typical of travel between worlds, he faced obstacles in reaching even this predetermined destination.[37]

In another widespread belief, the dead confront a test to determine what quality of afterlife they have earned. The Christian image of a last judgment, where Christ sends the saved to heaven and the damned streaming into hell, represents the most familiar version of a moral reckoning, but the concept is also central in Zoroastrian, Islamic, and Buddhist belief. No culture elaborated the judgment theme in richer detail than the ancient Egyptians. They envisioned the path of the dead to the otherworld as a complex series of gates with gods or demonic guardians, each requiring the deceased to recite proper ritual texts and to have received the necessary offerings from mourners. This passage climaxed with a weighing of the soul in a balance before Osiris to determine if the soul deserved paradise or destruction.[38]

An extensive Judeo-Christian literature previews the afterlife in visionary journeys to heaven and hell. In a pseudepigraphic elaboration of the passage in Genesis (5:24) that God took Enoch away to heaven, he ascends through various heavens to see the storerooms of the stars and winds, to learn the various ranks of angels, and to meet with God. His angelic guide shows him the torments of the rebel angels, the abode of the dead, and a prevision of the last judgment.[39] In the Islamic tradition of Mohammed's Night Journey, the angel Gabriel leads the prophet from Mecca to Jerusalem and then to heaven and hell. Mohammed meets with Jesus, Moses, Noah, and Abraham before entering the presence of Allah to learn God's laws and his status as God's cho-sen prophet. Revealed as well are the delights of paradise for the blessed and the miser-ies of the wicked in hell.[40]

Tours of heaven and hell flourished in the Middle Ages as a form of conversion lit-erature, an effort to reform sinners by use of divine scare tactics. The *Visions of Tondal* tells of a fast-living young knight far along the road to perdition when paralysis seized him at a dinner and he fell down as if dead. His naked soul separated from his body, and his guardian angel escorted him to witness sinners tortured in fires and dark pits at the hands of horrific demons. The tour climaxed with a glimpse of Satan lying on his back and waving multiple legs like some gigantic cockroach at the bottom of hell. Thoroughly frightened by what he saw, Tondal then observed the tribulations of souls serving a term of penance in Purgatory and finally beheld the joys of the righteous in heaven, after which he reentered his body and came back to life a changed man, dedicated for the rest of his days to the well-being of his soul. Tondal's vision follows a popular literary pattern that culminates with Dante's *Divine Comedy*.[41]

The process of initiation often includes an otherworld journey, sometimes in the form of symbolic death and rebirth, sometimes in visionary travels to acquire sha-manic powers. Nearly all cultures mark important transitions with rites of passage, rituals that lend social meaning to major changes of status or condition such as birth, adulthood, marriage, death, or becoming a healer. According to the classic study of anthropologist Arnold van Gennep, these ceremonies "enable the individual to pass from one defined position to another which is equally well defined" through a process of separation, transition, and incorporation.[42] In Greco-Roman mystery religions the participants descended into a cave then reemerged into the light, mimicking the soul's descent from heaven at birth, and return there when released from the body at death.[43] In other cases initiation is involuntary, beginning with a life-changing supernatural encounter but continuing the ritual pattern. When nine years old and sick with a fever, the Sioux holy man Black Elk saw two men descend from the clouds and summon him to heaven. A small cloud lifted him, and supernatural horses carried him to the teepee of the six Grandfathers, who taught him sacred truths and gave him powers. His spirit returned to his body, and this vision guided him in his adult role as a man able to heal, combat drought, assure a successful hunt, and maintain spiritual harmony between humans and nature.[44] The Asian shaman travels between this world and the other in an ecstatic trance, first to gain necessary powers, then to escort souls, appease the spir-its of sickness, and communicate with the dead.[45]

Mortals visit the upper or lower world by their own initiative in the quest story. In the famous example of Orpheus, he descends into the underworld to rescue his dead wife, Eurydice, persuades the lord of the dead to release her, then loses her again when he violates an interdiction against looking at her before they leave Hades.[46] Another example of the type is the Babylonian epic of Gilgamesh, where the hero's efforts to rescue his friend Enkidu from death take him on a journey to the end of the earth, across the waters of death, and finally to the immortal sage Utnapishtim, the Babylonian Noah; but Gilgamesh gains and loses the gift of immortality twice, once because he fails a test to stay awake for seven nights and again when a serpent steals the gift while he bathes.[47] Other visits to the otherworld result from kidnap, allurement, invitation, or even accident. An Ojibwa Star Husband tale begins with two girls pointing to the stars they wished to marry before they went to sleep. When the girls awoke, they found themselves in the sky world, where they married the star-men of their wishes and later escaped to earth through a hole in the sky.[48] The medieval story of a boy named Elidurus relates that he was playing hooky from school when he chanced upon an opening in a riverbank and entered to find the fairy kingdom. He came and went daily without the usual negative consequences of contact with fairies. He enjoyed a game played with a golden ball until one day he tried to steal the ball. Once the fairies recovered their property, they sealed the hole and left Elidurus to the displeasure of his schoolmaster.[49]

Making UFO-Sense of the Traditional Past

The enduring appeal of myths challenges narrators to keep their stories up to date, and UFO mythology is no exception. Ancient-astronaut proponents are responsible for perhaps the most conscious effort when they read early cosmologies and cosmogonies as allegories of alien activity. Several mythic themes provide the raw material for rewriting history. One is withdrawal of the gods from earth, a story that contrasts the present blighted state of humanity with a primordial age of bliss when gods and humans lived side by side in paradise. Through some error or transgression, man fell from grace and the gods abandoned mankind to suffering, hardship, and mortality. A little imagination translates this scenario into a time of close contact with an extraterrestrial civilization, when technology provided abundance until some rupture caused the aliens to depart and leave mankind to fend for itself. Wars among the gods suggest the earth as a battleground for interplanetary powers with advanced weaponry. A related theme avers that the act of creation sets off an epic conflict between chaos and cosmos. Myths like Noah's Flood tell that a great catastrophe nearly obliterated mankind and embody an ageless fear that destructive outside powers threaten to overwhelm the world, but speculations may replace gods with aliens as the agents of this crisis. In many ancient narratives the gods meddle in human affairs to help or deceive, save or destroy. An important form of divine intervention is the arrival of the culture hero to teach primitive humanity the skills of civilization. Ancient-astronaut writing is an exercise in euhemerism, in which theorists recast the gods of mythological texts as aliens and treat the fanciful events as literal histories of extraterrestrial intervention.

Some myths are almost too suggestive to ignore. In an Egyptian withdrawal story, the sun god Ra once lived on earth and ruled over humans until they began to blaspheme, calling him old and impotent and setting up an ambush to kill him as he sailed along the Nile. His son Horus learned of this plot and attacked the conspirators in the form of a flying disk, dazzling the rebels so that they killed one another. Ra refrained from destroying all humans, but he deserted the earth to sail only the celestial Nile, while the image of a winged solar disk commemorated this event ever after in Egyptian art.[50] The Mesoamerican god Quetzalcoatl brought agriculture, building, sculpture, astronomy, and a religion of peace. This mysterious culture-bearer presents an especially intriguing résumé. In one tradition or another he came from heaven; was associated with the planet Venus; had a long beard, unlike native Mesoamericans; and departed after conflict with an evil sorcerer but promised to return.[51] If other mythic narratives are less transparent, they still tempt interpreters with rousing accounts and rich detail easy to recast in extraterrestrial terms.

An early revision of history based on UFO visitation originated with contactee George Hunt Williamson in the 1950s. He proposed that Venusians introduced advanced civilization to inhabitants of the lost continents Atlantis and Lemuria. As these cultures grew corrupt and their destruction drew nigh, the visitors ferried away the remnant of good earthlings while a few higher beings volunteered to reincarnate as wise teachers and to rehabilitate mankind. Among them was a Venusian leader named Merk, whose spirit returned as pharaoh Tutankhamen; biblical figures Aaron, Ezekiel, and Mark; and the Inca Atahualpa. In a second historical fantasy Williamson introduced migrants arriving from Sirius and settling into the bodies of apes. These visitors created chimerical animals like centaurs and unicorns, but mixing matter and spirit proved destructive and necessitated a flood to cleanse the earth of these abominations. A second group of aliens, the Wanderers, came to earth and entered the reincarnation cycle to elevate the spiritual consciousness of mankind over time.[52]

Another speculative writer, Brinsley le Poer Trench (later Lord Clancarty), based his prehistory on biblical mythology in *The Sky People* (1960). The extraterrestrial Elohim came to earth, and one group among them, the Jehovah, created humans to be their servants and hid this illicit creation in the Garden of Eden, located on Mars. The

Serpent People discovered the innocent humans and taught them secrets, and as a consequence the humans became independent-minded, while the Jehovah became angry. Flown back to earth aboard Noah's Ark, the humans interbred with the Serpent People but retained the bestial human as part of their nature. When humans attempted to reconstruct their former paradise on Atlantis, conflict arose between agrarian and technological factions, and warfare between them led to the climactic disaster of the Deluge. Kept since in a state of quarantine, the former extraterrestrial masters of mankind have intervened to help the noble elements of human nature triumph over the base, with the modern visitation of flying saucers being the latest episode.[53]

In Greek mythology the Titan Kronos (Saturn) castrated his father, the sky god Ouranos (Uranus), and became the chief deity. He swallowed his children so they could not supplant him, but the mother of Zeus (Jupiter) saved him, and he grew up to chain his father and rule as king of the gods. Zeus then fought the monster Typhaeus (or Typhon) and a race of giants, striking them down with thunderbolts when they piled mountain upon mountain in an assault on heaven.[54] An interpreter with a classical orientation, W. Raymond Drake recapitulated this mythological history as successive waves of visitors from different planets. First the Uranids brought a Golden Age, then came the Saturnians to conquer the Uranids. The Titans descended from the Uranids and battled the Jovians when they invaded, with the Titan Prometheus raiding the planet Jupiter to steal nuclear fire. Prometheus civilized the surviving populations on earth, but an invading comet or wandering moon called Typhaeus brought natural disaster throughout the solar system and ended interplanetary visitation. Wars and disasters reduced earth to a primitive state, and recovery has taken thousands of years.[55]

Those destructive comets and wayward planets appeared as solutions for mythic calamities in the writings of Ignatius Donnelly in the 1880s and Immanuel Velikovsky in the 1950s, so that ancient astronaut writers simply picked up an established revisionist tradition.[56] It develops further in the books of Zechariah Sitchin, the foremost proponent of ancient-astronaut theories today. In a Babylonian creation myth the indolent old gods had their rest disturbed by the celebrations of their offspring. Tiamat, in the form of a great dragon or sea monster, rose up to destroy the young gods until Marduk killed her and created the earth from pieces of her body. Sitchen's interpretation turns the god Marduk into a stray planet and explains the earth and the asteroid belt as results of a near collision with the planet Tiamat. Marduk swung out of the solar system on an eccentric orbit but returned every 3,600 years. The inhabitants of Marduk, the Nefilim, none the worse for spending thousands of years in the outer darkness, arrived in rocket ships 450,000 years ago to colonize and mine the earth. The leaders were the great gods, and the lesser gods, the Annunaki, performed menial labor until a rebellion spurred the leadership to create a hybrid race of humans to serve as slave laborers. In an event that became known as the Fall, humans discovered that they could procreate and live a life independent of their creators. In fact, humans proved so good at procreation that they multiplied and attracted the Nefilim, but interbreeding roused the leadership to cleanse the earth with a great flood, though humans survived because Utnapishtim heeded a warning to build an ark. The gods were appalled at the scale of the devastation and taught the arts of civilization to the survivors, but conflicts arose as humans strove for forbidden knowledge. In Sitchen's tale the Tower of Babel actually describes human effort to duplicate the rockets of the gods until divine intervention overthrows the project.[57]

The Otherworld Journey of UFO Abductees

The idea of extraterrestrial visitation connects UFOs with the otherworld journey in a superficial sense. In abduction accounts the relationship deepens as multiple elements of the story correspond to elements recited throughout history in the traditional otherworld journey—and with much of the strangeness intact. Whether reality resembles tradition or tradition informs fiction, or symbiosis of experience and tradition shapes narrative, two sets of texts, one about UFO abduction and one about the supernatural otherworld, share sometimes striking parallels.[58]

Entity types differ little between the two sets of texts, with the Space Brothers and tall, blond, blue-eyed Nordics of some abductee accounts similar in kind to the beautiful gods and noble fairies of the past. Short humanoid aliens predominate in UFO encounters, just as diminutive supernatural beings dominate the fairy population. Sometimes the resemblance amounts to more than looks. The distinction between UFO occupants and fairies stretches thin in abductee Betty Andreasson's account of a walk in the woods when she was a young girl. A short being like the aliens she would meet later in life rose out of the ground, dressed not in the sleek uniform of a space traveler but in the greenish, barklike attire of an earth spirit.[59] The apparitional creatures of folklore have a penchant for household invasion. Demons waken sleeping monks, and evil spirits burst into Eskimo dwellings, just as humanoid aliens enter bedrooms in the dead of night.[60] Aliens converge with traditional deathbed spirits in an informant's report that a figure descended the stairs from his mother's bedroom moments after she died in 1937. He and two other terrified witnesses had never seen a being like this one before, but he recognized its face again fifty years later in the alien staring out at him from the cover of Whitley Strieber's *Communion*.[61]

Not only the actors but the plot of the story closely parallels traditional antecedents. Eight potential episodes characterize most abduction reports in the literature—capture, examination, conference, tour, journey, theophany, return, and aftermath. Few reports include all eight possibilities, but those episodes that appear follow this order with surprising consistency. Events within individual episodes, especially capture and examination, also unfold according to a complex and recurrent pattern.[62] Expressed in general terms the abduction story repeats the initiatory pattern of separation from this world to an alien environment, where the subject undergoes an ordeal and teachings, then returns a changed person with special knowledge and powers. A table of comparisons reveals the correspondence of abduction plot and incidents with accounts of shamanic initiation, tours of hell, judgment of the dead, and visits to fairyland.

The appearance of a UFO, a light, or strange beings in the bedroom marks the onset of abduction. An estrangement of the environment or "Oz Factor" accompanies this stage as crickets and night noises fall silent or normal traffic seems to cease, as if the abduction takes place in a vacuum. Mental and physical alterations steal over the abductees as they drive off the highway for no good reason. Bedroom abductees hear hypnotic drones or musical sounds and report a creeping numbness that leaves them paralyzed. Once the aliens appear, they are always in total charge. The abductee feels dreamlike, groggy, with a sense of euphoria alternating with fear, no longer able to resist. Aliens escort, carry, or levitate—sometimes in the literal sense of floating or flying in a beam of light—the captive to a UFO.

Many otherworld journeys also start with alterations of consciousness. Tondal passed out and remained in a deathlike coma while his soul toured hell. The shamanic candidate often begins initiation during a feverish delirium, and some altered state of consciousness—trance, sleep, sickness, or spell—typically opens the doorway to another world. An angel, fairy, divine guide, or helpful spirit accompanies the traveler through the otherworld environment, fulfilling a role so widespread it has acquired the technical name of "psychopomp," one who conducts souls to the otherworld. The commonplace motif of supernatural flight manifests when a dreamlike lightness of body allows the shaman to fly, when a human captive sweeps through the air with trooping fairies, or when witches ride their broomsticks to the Sabbat.

Aboard the UFO, abductees enter a domed, luminescent room and lie naked on a slablike table or bed as the examination begins. This episode is the most vivid and common onboard experience. It is an ordeal fraught with pain, humiliation, and terror as

Table 4.1
Comparison of UFO Abductions and Traditional Otherworld Journeys

UFO Abduction Events	Comparative Events (Type)
I. Capture	
Premonition, droning, or musical sound	Candidate sick, delirious with fever (A)
UFO or alien beings appear	Encounter with fairies (D)
Witness paralyzed	
Witness has no will to resist	
Time lapse begins	Loss of consciousness (A, C); death (B)
Beings escort witness	Spirit (A); god (B); angel (C); fairy escort (D)
Floating or sense of flotation	Walk or fly to the underworld
Enter UFO	
Rise in beam of light, ramp made of light	
No memory of entering ship	
II. Examination	
Captive passes through hallway	Through tunnels (A, C, D), hallways (B)
Enters smooth, rounded examination room	Enter cave/judgment room/hell/fairyland
Lighting fluorescent, from no one source	No sun but uniform twilight (D)
Room cool, moist, air hard to breathe	
Captive lies on slablike table	Demons dismember candidate (A)
Being stares into eyes of captive	Demons torture sinners with pitchforks (C)
Manual and instrumental examinations	Soul weighed in balance (B)
Scanning device descends from ceiling	
Removal of sperm/egg sample or fetus	Theft of baby (D)
Implant inserted into captive's body	Reassemble with magic crystals in head (A)
Mental and emotional tests, illusions	Ordeals (A); fright over fate of wicked dead (C)
III. Conference	
Enters comfortable room or auditorium	In another cave (A); in Purgatory (C)
Leader or sage communicates with captive	Tutelary spirits teach candidate (A); angel explains fate of wicked, less wicked (B); gods welcome soul of deceased (C); fairies entertain guest (D)
Warning or images of coming catastrophe	Learns fate of sinner on Judgment Day (B)
Education for future helpful role	Candidate learns magic of shaman (C)

Table **4.1** (*continued*)

UFO Abduction Events	Comparative Events (Type)
IV. Tour	
Sees inside of ship, engine room	Sees Satan at bottom of hell (C)
Visits incubatorium, sees fetuses in tanks	
Meets hybrid child	Human baby replaced with changeling (D)
V. Otherworldly Journey	Deceased enters otherworld paradise (B)
Fly to other planet or strange place	Visits several magical environments (A)
Enters enclosure like giant aircraft hangar	
Planet looks barren, desolate	
Lush environment, but subterranean	Fairyland underground (D)
Beautiful cities, buildings of crystal	Visits heaven (C); fairy buildings crystalline (D)
VI. Theophany (encounter with seemingly divine being)	Encounter with sacred spirits/gods/angels and the blessed (A, B, C)
VII. Return	
Aliens allow or say it is time to return	Shaman acquires drum, magical objects (A)
Captive tries but fails to take souvenir	Object stolen from fairyland turns into ordure, dry leaves (D)
Farewells	
Back to former environment, resume activities	Fever breaks (A); regains consciousness (C)
Memory of abduction fades	Discovers supernatural lapse of time (D)
VIII. Aftermath	
Immediate aftereffects (mostly physical: thirst; sense of being dirty, nausea, sunburn, eye irritation, nosebleed, scars)	Partial paralysis, blindness in one eye (D)
Intermediate aftereffects (mental: sleep disturbances, nightmares, anxiety, panic reaction in doctor's office, preoccupation with site of mysterious encounter)	Regret, pines away (D)
Long-term aftereffects (change of habits, lifestyle, values, more concern for spiritual matters, sense of mission)	Assumes role as healer, diviner, escort of souls, protector and destroyer (A); leaves off sinning for life of holiness (C)

Note: A = shamanic initiation; B = Egyptian judgment of the dead; C = tour of hell (Tondal);
D = visit to fairyland.

impersonal alien examiners apply handheld instruments and scan the captive with an eyelike device. Some procedures are gruesome, like the insertion of a tiny implant into the brain or spine, a long needle into a woman's abdomen, or a probe into the anus. The beings may collect samples, most often sperm or eggs. Sometimes the beings replace something in a woman's uterus, and she soon manifests signs of pregnancy. Before the fetus comes to term, the aliens return and remove it. The aliens show an interest in human behavior and emotions that is second only to their interest in reproduction. A huge-eyed alien stares into the abductee's eyes at very close range, seeming to scan the captive's mind and perhaps to read thoughts or insert new ones. Mental or emotional tests and staging procedures may follow, in which the aliens create illusions in an apparent study of human response to scenes ranging from everyday family relationships to situations of extreme danger.[63]

An ordeal comprises a key episode in shamanic initiations as unfriendly demons dismember the candidate. Friendly spirits then reassemble the torn body according to a different plan, with magical powers built into the bones and organs or magical objects like rock crystals inserted into the head or other parts of the body.[64] Tondal does not suffer the physical tortures of the damned, but tourists in hell suffer vicariously as they witness enthusiastic devils inflict torments on imprisoned sinners. The Egyptian weighing of the soul scenario casts the deceased as an anxious onlooker closely watched by a monstrous creature who devours any soul that fails the test.[65] Instruments are as much a part of the otherworld ordeal as they are part of UFO examination procedures. The shaman's demons use knives, while devils in hell favor crude prods and piercing instruments. The Egyptian balance for weighing souls is more sophisticated; it appears as well in Renaissance Christian art, where angels determine who is saved and who is damned, but once again a mechanical device serves as a central prop for examination of human subjects.[66] Alien interest in reproduction and breeding of hybrids has wide parallels in beliefs about the otherworld—for example, fairies also need human help to give birth, interbreed with humans, and replace human children with changelings. The penis of the devil is said to be sharp and cold, again anticipating the metallic devices of aliens as they extract semen and perform artificial insemination procedures.[67]

Abductions serve as learning experiences when the staring procedure instills knowledge, or when a discussion, formal conference, or presentation of images follows the examination. The aliens warn against harmful human practices and prophesy catastrophes. They also sometimes charge abductees to help avoid or mitigate the catastrophe or to assist in a rescue operation, though they will recall the details of this mission only "when the time is right." Often confusing and apparently secondary to the examination, this episode is tainted with suspicions that the aliens are deceitful, their teachings manipulative, and their prophecies false; but a growing number of abductees view knowledge imparted by their captors as the true heart and soul of the encounter.

In traditional otherworld journeys the balance leans toward education as central to the traveler's transition from old state to new. The shamanic candidate is physically reborn or remade, but much preparation for his career as a practitioner of sacred arts comes from instruction by tutelary spirits. They teach him the skills and spells he will need to carry out his magical duties, though he too may have to await maturity before he can practice what he has learned.[68] The tour of hell is foremost a learning experience, a reminder of God's laws and the fate of those who disobey. The transformational experience underlying shamanic initiations, exemplary journeys, and judgment of the dead centers around an encounter with the self, a revelatory epiphany as subjects gain awareness of themselves and their place in the divine scheme of things. In these cases the learning occurs within a sacred context; the rarity of overtly sacred teachings in abduction reports conforms to the modern secular spirit and the technological setting of the encounter, but the convergence of all these experiences on a transcendental lesson is unmistakable.

The double-dealing of aliens has ample antecedents, with Satan's stint as the subtle serpent of Eden serving as the prototype of devils as deceivers. Demons try to intimidate or mislead otherworld travelers, but a guide protects the human, just as the alien leader serves as an intermediary between the abductee and the unfeeling crewmembers. Fairy magic often depends on glamour, an ability to create illusions such as gold coins from dry leaves or a rich banquet from dirt and ordure. Shape-shifting is a common practice among demons and some tribes of fairies, while aliens use alleged mind-control techniques to assume human or other appearances in staging procedures and emotional tests. The major trickster figures of mythology overturn social norms and bring creative change to the cosmos. If aliens operate on a more modest scale, their subtle deceptions, mind tricks, and apparent "haunting" of abductees nevertheless mark extraterrestrials as improper guests similar in spirit to tricksters. Much folklore reaches the verdict that otherworld beings are not trustworthy.[69]

Three less common episodes of tour, journey, and theophany may follow the abductee's conference. Sometimes the tour is a sightseeing trip to the engine room or a look at a star map. In other cases abductees visit an incubatorium, a room with tanks containing tiny fetuses floating in liquid. Women may meet a hybrid child, half human and half humanoid alien, and learn that this child grew from her stolen fetus.[70] Most abduction events occur inside a UFO, but sometimes the aliens fly their captive on a brief trip to some otherworldly location. Little flight time elapses before arrival at a devastated, desert planetary surface with a feeble sun and sparse, sickly vegetation or a lush and beautiful environment, sometimes enclosed or subterranean, with a well-lighted sky but no visible sun. Beautiful cities or geometric structures occupy the landscape, and crystal often serves as building material. On rare occasions the abductee witnesses some kind of sacred ritual among the aliens or has a religious experience during the abduction. A British family saw an aged alien holding a glowing sphere called the "seed of life" and felt the life ebb from it, learning that a similar disaster had befallen the aliens' home world. Betty Andreasson witnessed a giant phoenix consumed by fire in the alien subterranean otherworld and heard a voice she took to be the voice of God.[71]

The tour and journey episodes revive the most wonderful sights of traditional otherworld journeys. Shamanic initiation requires travels underground, across the surface of the earth, and into the sky, while the deceased Egyptian passes through numerous gates before reaching the subterranean hall of judgment. Tondal sees Satan in the lowest chamber of hell—in effect the engine room of the infernal regions—then visits purgatory and heaven. The uniform lighting of the UFO examination room reappears on a larger scale in the bright but sunless alien underworld, while similar conditions characterize the luminous cave where the shaman learns magical secrets, the divine light of Tondal's heaven, or the twilit sky of fairyland and the Elysian fields. The beautiful crystalline architecture of the Celtic otherworld returns in Betty Andreasson's descriptions of alien glasslike towers and a forest made of crystal.[72]

By the time the abductee departs from the UFO a bond may have grown with the alien leader, and abductees sometimes express sadness that the experience is over. A few abductees attempt to bring home a souvenir, but the aliens remain too vigilant ever to have lost an artifact. After farewells, hints to forget, and a promise to return, the aliens escort the abductee back to bed or car, and the UFO flies off while the abductee drifts off to sleep or resumes driving. Drivers may go on for miles before becoming aware of their surroundings, and by then the "missing time" phenomenon has set in as all memories back to the early stage of the abduction fade away to leave only an uneasy sense that something happened and an unaccountable loss of two hours or so.

The time lapse motif stands out as a striking element in both abduction and traditional lore, though the "supernatural lapse of time" in fairyland bears only a remote analogy to the "missing time" of abductees. Visitors to fairyland suffer no loss of memory but return to earth, where tens or hundreds of years have passed in a day or a year of fairy time. A break in the continuous and universal flow of time characterizes both situations, but they diverge on the nature and consequences of that break. A closer parallel appears in a legend of a Welsh witch stealing a church bell when a waterman sees her rowing away. She said to him, "You will speak of it when you think of it," and he forgot the theft. Years later when church bells tolled for the funeral of another witch, the memory returned to him.[73]

How noteworthy the similarities can be between fairy and UFO encounters stand out in a Welsh account published in 1896, taken from the mother of a minister. She described that as a young woman she walked home one evening with her servant, David Williams, better known as Big David. He carried a side of bacon and fell behind, but she was surprised when three hours passed before he arrived. He was equally surprised that he was more than three minutes behind her, but had a reason:

> He observed ... a brilliant meteor passing through the air, which was followed by a ring or hoop of fire, and within the hoop stood a man and woman of small size, handsomely dressed. ... When the hoop reached the earth these two beings jumped out of it, and immediately proceeded to make a circle on the ground. As soon as this was done, a large number of men and women instantly appeared, and to the sweetest music that ear ever heard commenced dancing round and round the circle. ... The ground all around was lit up by a kind of subdued light, and he observed every movement of these beings. By and bye the meteor ... appeared again, and then the fiery hoop came into view, and when it reached the spot where the dancing was, the lady and gentleman ... jumped into the hoop, and disappeared in the same manner in which they had reached the place. Immediately after their departure the Fairies vanished from sight, and the man found himself alone in darkness.[74]

Though Big David went his way thinking he had watched the scene for no more than a few minutes, three hours of earthly time had slipped by.

The immediate aftermath of abduction is largely physical and transitory. Abductees describe thirst, sunburn, nosebleed, scars, eye irritation, gastrointestinal upset, a missing pregnancy, and a sense of being dirty or contaminated. Intermediate effects of a psychological nature set in days or weeks later as general anxiety, hypervigilance, vivid recurrent nightmares, and an obsessive desire to return to the site of a UFO sighting may afflict the abductee. Certain suggestive settings like a doctor's office or sights like an alien face may result in disproportionate panic reactions. A nagging sense that something happened or the experience of specific but fragmentary flashbacks spurs many abductees to seek eventual hypnosis from abduction investigators. The most noteworthy aftereffects take shape in the long term, months or years later when abductees give up smoking or discover artistic talent, become more spiritual and open-minded, perhaps seek out jobs that allow creative expression or helping other people, with all these changes in values, habits, and lifestyle seeming to stem from an abduction experience. Abductees often report increased psychic abilities and further paranormal experiences involving apparitions, poltergeist activity, or Men in Black. Though a single abduction may qualify as the adventure of a lifetime, many abductees experience a whole lifetime of abductions starting in childhood and lasting into old age, while abduction may run in the family, with several generations reporting encounters.

Supernatural otherworld journeys also end with transformational consequences. Abductees may return fearful and troubled, and the strain has led to mental breakdown or suicide in a few cases. Negative consequences may afflict the otherworld traveler as well. A captive brought back from fairyland may pine away for the beauty of the place, and victims taken and returned by the Wild Hunt are often demented. Encounters with the supernatural often result in injury. A glimpse of La Llorona may cause fainting and sickness, and striking a ghostly light can result in a paralyzed arm. Among the Navajo a healing ritual is necessary for recovery from ghost sickness, an affliction of fainting, delirium, nightmares, and terrors in the night that follows the sight of a ghost.[75] In modern culture hypnosis helps relieve the anxiety of abductees. For all the hardship along the way, traditional otherworld journeys end in successful transformation when the candidate becomes a practicing shaman, Tondal reforms his sinful ways, or the dead reach paradise. Many abductees share a similar positive prognosis as they report changes for the better, not a turn toward conventional or even New Age religion but toward a humanistic spiritual awareness of global—or cosmic—responsibility, duty to others, and rejection of materialistic obsessions. Some interpreters relate abduction to initiation and see abductees as reborn into the next generation of consciousness, the new shamans to heal the psychic crisis of modern times and lead all mankind to spiritual awareness.[76]

Such breathtaking visions pull emotions along even as they leave evidence behind, but they recognize the religious overtones of otherworld contact in both its past and present forms. To dismiss UFO abductions on the grounds that they are like traditional otherworld journeys goes too far, but without a doubt the old and new versions share much in common.

The Charm of Distance

Alongside the supernatural tradition of otherworlds in antiquity, a secular tradition of marvelous lands with exotic inhabitants grew up in the form of travelers' tales.[77] Travelers arrived by conventional means and faced barriers of hardship and distance rather than magic; but if the stories fashioned faraway places to a human scale and confined them to earthly space, the descriptions suffered no impoverishment in wonder. Ranking as the prototypical traveler's tale, Homer's *Odyssey* recounts the years Odysseus spent wandering among mysterious lands and strange beings as he tried to sail home after the Trojan War. He meets the Lotus Eaters, people whose diet leaves them in a blissful stupor; the Sirens, mermaids whose song lures sailors to destruction; the Cyclopes, one-eyed giants without laws or manners and hungry for human flesh; and Circe, a witch who turns Odysseus's crew into swine.[78] Odysseus encounters extremes of strangeness in places, beings, customs, and powers once he leaves behind the known world, and this sense that anything goes, that the world beyond the bounds of the familiar must be fraught with wonders and dangers, has continued to set standards for concepts of the alien throughout history.

Travel tales specialize in escape from both the physically and the conceptually ordinary. Distance works its charm by casting travelers into unfamiliar space where possibilities of difference run riot. Remoteness warrants strangeness, and the farther travelers range from their cultural center, the more outlandish the tale can be. The quest of Gilgamesh takes him to the scorpion men who guard the portal where the morning sun emerges, to an earthly paradise full of gemstones and fruit trees, and to the waters of death and the source of eternal life. The Phoenician admiral Hanno sails beyond the Pillars of Hercules and piles up a list of weird phenomena as he passes along the African coast—phantom music, a flaming river, sea monsters, and hairy men—until too much weirdness unnerves his crew and he has to turn back.[79] The premise of venturing into unknown territory enables authors around the world to stage one amazing encounter after another. A popular form of Eskimo folktale follows the wanderings of a traveler from one village after another where something is strange about the inhabitants—here they are all left-handed, there they are cannibals, farther along they each have one long and one short leg. Such stories can go on and on as the narrator strings episodes together to hold his listeners with a continuing parade of exotic encounters.[80] If more sophisticated in form, adventure tales from Jason and the Argonauts and Sinbad the Sailor to *Star Trek* also rely on a succession of wonders to refresh the interest of the audience.

The well-traveled ancient Greeks stocked their literature with exotic news about distant lands. Herodotus fills the remotest regions of the earth with one-eyed people, bald people, goat-footed people, and griffins guarding treasures of gold.[81] The expedition to India of Alexander the Great discovered a parade of wonderful races like the Cynocephali, hairy dog-headed people who lived in the mountains and communicated by barking; the Panotii, who could wrap themselves in their enormous ears or even use them to fly; and the Sciopoda, who lay on their backs and shaded themselves by raising their huge feet like a parasol.[82] The Roman writer Pliny the Elder devoted a chapter of his encyclopedic *Natural History* to monstrous inhabitants of faraway geographic regions, among them the Ethiopian Troglodytes (cave dwellers) and the Libyan Blemmyae, headless people with faces on their chests.[83]

Plinian monsters reappeared as requisite figures in medieval travel literature whether or not a traveler actually visited the lands he claimed. Marco Polo describes a genuine journey through the vast empire of Kublai Khan between 1271 and 1295, and if most of the marvels are natural ones, the savage dog-headed people and cannibals also return.[84] Sir John Mandeville wrote his *Travels* in 1356, and the book became one of the most popular of the Middle Ages, though the author never seems to have strayed from the comfort of his writing desk. Borrowing from one source after another, Mandeville retailed familiar fabulous accounts of monsters, wealth, and beauty.[85] When European explorers reached the New World, they found abundant natural wonders but also colonized the new lands with the usual cannibals and Amazons and sought traditional otherworldly treasures in El Dorado and the Seven Cities of Cibola. The efforts of Ponce de Leon to find the Fountain of Youth simply extended the search for a stock feature of the earthly paradise from the Old World to the New.[86] Exotic peoples relocated northward when Olaus Magnus wrote about Pygmies in Greenland, where in another remote corner of the world they battled flocks of cranes, just as their kindred did in Libya and India.[87] The Chinese *Classic of Mountains and Seas,* some parts of it written as early as the third century B.C., catalogs a menagerie of monstrous races inhabiting regions beyond the bounds of Chinese culture. The little people, one-eyed people, hairy people, three-handed people, bird-headed people, and one-armed people of the Chinese collection demonstrate its writers pursuing similar paths of the imagination as European authors.[88]

The otherness of a distant place enhances its desirability but offsets the appeal with awareness that the physical and social landscapes are alien, so that the traveler stands naked and vulnerable before the unknown. An otherworld may be a place of beauty and marvels but never a paradise free for the taking. Monsters of story and imagination guard faraway places and threaten any interlopers. These inhabitants are nonhuman, often bizarre, probably dangerous. Travelers' tales caution that "they" are not like "us" but alien in customs, manners, and appearance, so that whether visiting the cannibal or being visited by spacemen in science fiction, the lesson persists that humans have something to fear when they meet the alien "Other."

Even as late as 1933 the movie *King Kong* invoked an unknown island where dinosaurs and monsters survived, but "lost world" fantasies already belonged to the realm of nostalgia. The earth had grown too small for aliens; its secret places were all used up. The future of monsters seemed to belong in the inner psyche as Jack the Ripper and Hitler replaced the uncharted with the unhinged, though many people found the jetsam of this inner tide unsatisfying and continued to yearn for a literal and external Other, finding homes for all sorts of Bug-Eyed Monsters in the endless distances of outer space. If habitats and modes of travel have changed and expanded outward beyond the earth, the power of distance to loosen restraints and harbor exemplary otherness thrives in popular depictions of extraterrestrials, though the principles have not changed much for envisioning otherworldly places and their occupants.

Beyond the Earth

The Plurality of Worlds.—A third ancient tradition was a belief that the celestial bodies were not just planets, moons, and stars, but worlds, complete habitats suitable for life like the earth. This doctrine of the plurality of worlds insisted that every body in the universe was populated, and the idea flourished as late as the mid-nineteenth century.[89] Pluralism was philosophical rather than observational and depended on a line of reasoning such as the Epicureans proposed: They argued that all matter consists of atoms and atoms are infinite in number. With infinite atoms come infinite possibilities for atoms to combine and build larger bodies until the universe fills with a multitude of worlds, some like and some unlike our own, inhabited by creatures like and unlike ourselves. Central to the case for habitation was the concept of plenitude. It holds that every possibility of being will necessarily be fulfilled, that the existing universe will reflect all possibilities for existence, and that the universe grows better as the abundance of existing things increases. A universe full of inhabited worlds follows as the consequence of this principle.

Philosophers also pondered the moral and mental attributes of otherworld inhabitants. Gottfried Wilhelm Leibniz argued that God had created the best of all possible universes and that its goodness included the existence of all beings that could possibly exist. Whether earth was the best of all possible worlds was doubtful, since it is possible to imagine worlds where the inhabitants have never sinned. Earth could be the worst world in the best possible universe, and neighbors nearer to perfection than ourselves might surround us. In his lighthearted *Entretiens sur la pluralité des mondes* (1686), Bernard de Fontenelle mixed scientific and philosophical speculations to imagine that a planet as hot and rapidly orbiting as Mercury obliged its people to move with great haste and have no time for deep thinking. The people of Saturn were just the opposite—slow, thoughtful, serious, and without humor.[90] Less whimsical was *Cosmotheoros* (1698) by Christian Huygens, a leading astronomer of his day, whose reasoning combined philosophy and theology with ideas that have shaped discussions of otherworld beings down to the present. According to Huygens, other planets must have rational beings to appreciate creation and adore the Creator. Like humans, these beings would need senses, fire, and tools, hands to build, an upright posture, and the curiosity to study nature. This study would lead them to astronomy, mathematics, and writing. And since the laws of mathematics and music are everywhere the same, these arts are alike on every world. A covering of wool or feathers might protect aliens in their native climate, and they might be larger than humans but not so tiny that they lacked the strength to work. The inhabitants of other planets need not look like us, and might be ugly by our standards, yet still seek truth, practice virtue, and possess a rational soul.[91]

Pluralism entered as standard intellectual furniture for eighteenth- and nineteenth-century thinkers. It shaped the expectations of leading astronomers like William Herschel, who discovered the planet Uranus in 1781 and concluded from observations of the melting polar caps on Mars that the inhabitants "probably enjoy a situation in many respects similar to ours." He even argued that beings lived on the surface of the sun, shielded from the heat of its luminous atmosphere by an insulating layer of opaque clouds. In 1824 Franz von Paula Gruithuisen published a description of roads, walls, and cities on the moon, and he explained the ashen light of Venus, a faint glow seen in telescopes from time to time on the unlighted portion of the planet's disk, as the result of large-scale forest fires set to celebrate the coronation of a new king. Methods of communicating with the inhabitants of the moon or Mars and attributed to the mathematician Carl Friedrich Gauss appeared in print as early as the 1820s. In these schemes a triangle with Pythagorean squares laid out on a vast scale in the forests of Siberia, or dug into the Saharan sands and lighted with kerosene fires, would speak to alien astronomers in the universal language of mathematics.[92]

Many nineteenth-century astronomers continued to advance pluralism in their writings. Thomas Dick, a Scottish divine and amateur astronomer, estimated that the moon had 4.2 billion inhabitants and that 8 trillion beings populated the rings of Saturn.[93] Richard Anthony Proctor popularized astronomy in the 1870s and 1880s with books like *Other Worlds Than Ours*, where he declared that the other planets of the solar system were certain to harbor life at some time in their history. The earth had reached a proper cosmic and geologic age, the moon's time had passed, and Jupiter and Saturn were young planets still warm from contraction, but their turn would come once they cooled.[94] The French astronomer Camille Flammarion remained a tireless advocate of pluralism from his first publications in the 1860s until his death in 1925. He was not satisfied with the anthropomorphic tendencies of many pluralists and spoke out for aliens that might assume truly indescribable forms.[95]

Storytellers through the ages have taken advantage of the opportunities suggested by pluralism. The astronomer Johann Kepler's *Somnium* of 1608 describes a dream journey to the moon, where monstrous creatures shelter from the long cold nights and equally long hot days in caves or the lunar seas. One of the most celebrated newspaper hoaxes in American history appeared in the *New York Sun* in 1835, when a series of reports described increasingly sensational observations of lunar life. Attributed to the famous astronomer John Hershel (the son of William), who was conveniently stationed in remote South Africa at the time, the dispatches claimed that a remarkable new telescope allowed him to see various strange animals, constructions, and ultimately human beings with batlike wings flitting about the lunar landscape. The perpetrator, R. A. Locke, may have intended a satire on pluralist excesses, but it backfired because readers swallowed the story as credible.[96] In 1900 George Griffith, an early writer of science fiction, adopted Proctor's theories for stories about a British couple touring the solar system on their honeymoon. The travelers found the ruins and bones of a civilization that died when the moon lost its atmosphere and a primordial water-world on Saturn.[97]

Science Reconstructs the Universe.—Scientific discoveries wrought vast changes in ancient cosmologies, displacing the earth from the center of the universe and quantifying celestial mechanics. Many tenets of pluralism found confirmation in the process. Galileo's telescope revealed mountains on the moon and moons around other planets. Later the spectroscope demonstrated that stars consisted of the same elements found on earth. Perhaps the most humbling discovery of astronomy, from the days of the earliest telescopes to the Hubble Space Telescope today, has been the enormity of the universe. Where philosophers postulated infinity, instruments allowed observers to gaze on something like it, no longer an abstract idea but a visible vastness of stars without number and without end. The likelihood for a plurality of worlds grew with the sheer number of places that could be worlds.

Pluralism enjoyed an easy ride deep into the scientific age, popular with the public, largely immune to critical challenge from philosophers, and free from obligations of evidence levied against other claims about the natural world by increasingly rigorous scientists. A reversal of fortune began in the mid-nineteenth century and the accepted scope of life in the universe contracted for the next hundred years in scientific thought. Astronomers learned that most stars belonged to binary or multiple systems and seemed to lack the gravitational stability that allowed planets to form and persist. Extremes of heat and cold, gravity too strong or too weak, and atmospheres composed of poisonous gases disqualified most of the known planets for life. Around 1900 a long-standing theory that planets formed alongside stars in a condensing cloud of dust gave way to an alternative planetesimal theory, wherein a wayward star passing close to the sun pulled out materials later to cool into planets. Catastrophe theories prevailed for several decades and imposed sharp limits on the plurality of worlds, since these events would be rare and planets necessarily scarce.[98]

A series of theological, philosophical, and scientific attacks began around 1850 and soon cost old truisms like plenitude and divine providence their persuasiveness.[99] Alfred Russel Wallace, who independently of Darwin proposed the theory of evolution by natural selection, brought a biologist's concern for the requirements of living organisms to his book, *Man's Place in the Universe* (1903). He drew a portrait of the fortunate earth, a planet rare if not unique in its ideal balance of conditions suited to the evolution and maintenance of life. Carbon-based organic molecules require a limited range of temperatures such as a planet too near or too far from the sun will not maintain. A suitable planet needs an earthlike mass and thickness of atmosphere, a similar distribution of land and seas, and a comparable axial inclination to provide seasons and day-night variations. The Pacific basin is important in preserving the ideal arrangement of land and sea, but this feature formed when the moon broke away from the early earth. No other moon in the solar system appears to originate in a similar way, further adding to the improbable string of happy accidents that prepared earth for life. Evolution of intelligent beings requires a planet to enjoy stable conditions over millions of years, but the life span of the sun as Wallace understood it just suited the earth but would not last long enough for Jupiter and Saturn to become habitable. The astronomy of the day located the solar system near the center of the stellar universe, where gaseous matter falling inward fed the sun and maintained its steady temperature over the eons. Wallace concluded that few other stars hold such favorable positions and little chance remains that their planets fulfill the additional requirements for life, leaving the earth alone in the universe as the one unlikely success story, the sole home of intelligent life.[100]

The Great Mars Romance.—An all-encompassing pluralism at the onset of the nineteenth century had diminished by the end to earth and other bodies within the temperate "habitable zone" of the solar system—the moon, Venus, and Mars. The airless moon presented a poor prospect. Venus was appealing as the twin sister of earth in size, but the enshrouding clouds of the planet left it a beautiful blank. Only the Red Planet presented a discernible surface to the telescope and was as forthright with clues of habitability as Venus was secretive, revealing a riddle of dark and light spots on the ruddy globe to intrigue observers. A sense that Mars was both earthlike and home for intelligent life passed from pluralist faith to observational inference with discovery of the Martian "canals." They established plurality in the case of Mars with such convincing finality that the question of life elsewhere in the universe scarcely mattered any longer. Those spidery lines across the Martian surface netted the imagination of a generation and outlined the archetypal image of an alien planet still prevalent today.

A gradual image of a kindred world had built up since telescopic observations first began. Every two years when Mars was in opposition, astronomers puzzled out the faint markings and by the mid-nineteenth century regarded the planet as a duplicate earth with seasons, continents, seas, polar snows, and clouds. The close opposition of 1877 brought two exciting discoveries—one was a pair of tiny moons, named Deimos and Phobos; the other was the famous Martian canals. In Milan the respected Italian astronomer Giovanni Schiaparelli undertook a careful study of Mars and drew a detailed map of the planet. Where previous maps had attached the names of astronomers to the features, Schiaparelli chose names from classical and biblical geography so that land areas became Hellas, Moab, Lybia, and Eden; the waters became Mare Tyrrhenum, Sinus Sabaeus, Solis Lacus, and Syrtis Major. In the process he transformed more than mere names. Mars had ceased to be just a light in the sky once it presented a face for observers to map, but by fitting the poetic names of antiquity to the Martian features, Schiaparelli shrouded Mars with the fanciful allure of the earthly past to create a world faraway and exotic, yet not a stranger.[101]

Something new besides nomenclature stood out on Schiaparelli's map. Where his predecessors pictured the Martian continents as blank spaces, Schiaparelli crossed them with some three dozen narrow linear features. These lines bent and curved like natural waterways, and he named them for rivers—Nilus, Indus, Ganges, Phison, Euphrates, and Hiddekel—though they never began in the midst of a continent like an earthly river but always connected sea to sea or merged with another line. When the planet returned in 1879 he continued his observations and added more of the linear features, now longer, thinner, and straighter, though still appearing more or less natural. The term he used to describe the lines was *canali*, an innocent Italian word for channels but suggestive in English of canals, implying artificial construction and, in the era of the Suez Canal, construction of heroic dimensions.[102] Astronomers were willing enough to take these channels as simply the next step in resolution of the Martian surface, but Schiaparelli's next startling discovery would soon replace channels with canals in concept as well as in name.

The definitive break with naturalism came in the opposition of 1881–1882 as the Martian spring progressed. Schiaparelli watched one canal after another undergo "gemination," or doubling, whereby a second canal appeared alongside the first at a distance of 200 to 400 miles and paralleled the length of the original with the mathematical precision of railroad tracks over hundreds or even thousands of miles. This process might take days or only hours. It began when the initial canal became broad and indistinct and ended when both canals emerged as clear as lines drawn with a ruler. Schiaparelli admitted that nothing on earth resembled this doubling process, and while he was uncertain about the nature of these appearances, he felt absolutely certain of his observations.[103] No one doubted the ability or integrity of Schiaparelli, but no other observer saw more than one or two streaks here or there, while he mapped about sixty canals in 1881–1882 and added still more in 1884–1885. Confirmation came in 1886 when several observers spotted the lines, both single and double, and thereafter he would have plenty of companionship in redrawing a planet that seemed to appear ever more artificial with each opposition.

Little about these canals looked natural any longer. They appeared like straight and purposeful connections following the shortest routes from the southern to the northern seas via round "lakes" amid the continents. A genuine puzzle had arisen and set imaginations racing. In 1882 Proctor wrote the *London Times* to say, "we might . . . infer that engineering works on a much greater scale than any which exist on our globe have been carried on upon the surface of Mars."[104] He added that "it would be rash . . . at present to speculate in this way," but the rash were already busy speculating that we should expect great engineering feats from the Martians because the lesser gravity would allow them to grow fourteen feet tall and possess enormous strength.[105] Recurrent rumors of signals from Mars further inflamed public excitement. Astronomers sometimes saw bright clouds over the surface of the planet or standing out along the rim, but newspapers reported these observations as flashes of light from the Martians as they attempted to communicate.[106] Schiaparelli remained largely aloof from the question of intelligent inhabitants, saying, "I am very careful not to combat this supposition, which includes nothing impossible."[107] He usually expressed faith in natural causes without being able to specify what they might be, though at times he allowed himself to speculate how an artificial canal system might operate.

In 1894 a newcomer jumped headlong into the controversy to become champion of Martians and spokesman for an enduring vision of life on other worlds.[108] Percival Lowell, a wealthy Boston aristocrat by birth, was the nephew of poet James Russell Lowell. His sister Amy was another famous poet, and his brother was a president of Harvard. Percival founded the Lowell Observatory under the clear skies of Arizona and began a feverish study of Mars. He observed an abundance of canals and saw in them the master key to understanding the planet. In three popular books—*Mars* (1895), *Mars and Its Canals* (1906), and *Mars as the Abode of Life* (1908)—in numerous articles, and in standing-room-only lectures in America and Europe, Lowell transformed Schiaparelli's continents and seas into reddish deserts and dark tracts of vegetation. As a smaller body farther from the sun, Lowell argued, Mars solidified earlier than earth, and life there evolved sooner. The lesser gravity of Mars allowed its atmosphere to escape over the ages, its water to seep into the interior, and its oxygen to bond with iron in the crust and produce the rust-red Martian surface. "We have before us the spectacle of a world relatively well on in years, a world much older than the Earth. . . . Advancing planetary years have left their mark legible there. His continents are all smoothed down; his oceans have all dried up. . . . If once he had a chaotic youth, it has long since passed away."[109]

Lowell's Mars was not only an aging planet, it was a dying one. No water remained except that locked in the polar caps, and their springtime melting released the precious moisture to revitalize plant life in a wave of greening that crossed the planet from pole to equator, but the process was not entirely natural. The canals pumped water across the deserts, where the polar runoff could not reach, not in broad open channels but in narrow ditches or piping systems made visible from earth by tracts of irrigated vegetation along the sides. These spidery lines intersected at small dark spots in the desert, not lakes, as Schiaparelli called them, but oases, perhaps the ancient Martian cities left stranded by the retreating seas and now maintained by a lifeline of canals. At first, single canals carried the runoff; later, a second parallel canal handled the overflow at the peak of the melting season.[110]

Lowell accepted that the Martians might grow into giants and have the capacity for prodigious work but warned that intelligent life did not mean humans and that some reptilian strand of evolution might just as well occupy the planet.[111] Yet whatever form the Martians might take, their existence and intelligence were undeniable.

> A mind of no mean order would seem to preside over the system we see. . . . Party politics . . . have had no part in them; for the system is planet wide. Quite possibly, such Martian folk are possessed of inventions of which we have not dreamed, and with them electrophones and kinetoscopes are things of a bygone past, preserved with veneration in museums as relics of the clumsy contrivances of the simple childhood of the race. Certainly what we see hints at the existence of beings who are in advance of, not behind us, in the journey of life.[112]

United for the common good and armed with technology far surpassing our own, the Martians were winning their struggle to survive for the moment, but there was no happy ending to this story. The course of planetary evolution predestined the outcome, and the long history of Martian civilization approached a foreseeable conclusion.

To our eventual descendants life on Mars will no longer be something to scan and interpret. It will have lapsed beyond the hope of study or recall. Thus to us it takes on an added glamour from the fact that it has not long to last. For the process that brought it to its present pass must go on to the bitter end, until the last spark of Martian life goes out. The drying up of the planet is certain to proceed until its surface can support no life at all. Slowly but surely time will snuff it out. When the last ember is thus extinguished, the planet will roll a dead world through space, its evolutionary career forever ended.[113]

Ideas of a plurality of worlds had soothed generations with the assurance that beings lived in outer space, too far away to crowd us but credible enough to prevent any sense of cosmic loneliness. This faith remained familiar but unexciting before Mars infused a newfound immediacy. Once our next-door neighbor yielded visible evidence of earthlike conditions and signs of intelligent life, even high civilization, an alien presence hove into sight here and now. Lowell's vision added one thing more, an emotional appeal missing from all earlier pluralistic speculations. As his Martians struggled to survive on an imperiled planet, the people of earth became spectators in a great tragedy. It played out on a geological time scale, but Lowell instilled such a sense of urgency that the Martian catastrophe appeared to unfold in historical time, before the eyes of the helpless audience, and gained the emotional voltage of dramatic unity by this compression of time. He created a race at once heroic and romantic, godlike in superiority yet doomed to fail. In the process he humanized his aliens. Popular writers echoed Lowell's vision as they cheered the Martians' engineering triumphs and pinpointed their cities, found human motives among these faraway beings, and forgot that they might be frightful and repulsive. The Martians transformed from vague and colorless abstractions into thrilling flesh-and-blood realities, kindred spirits if not kindred forms bound up in human sympathetic concern—a bond that has informed ideas of aliens down to the present.

If always controversial among astronomers, the canals excited the public like few other scientific issues. Among the popular literature was "The Things That Live on Mars," an article published in *Century* magazine in 1908, where H. G. Wells reasoned that intelligent beings capable of engineering feats would have upright bodies, large brains, and free forelimbs for work. The thin air of the planet required large lung capacity and a covering of fur or feathers to help inhabitants endure the chill Martian nights. The illustrator of the article pictured Martians as large headed, large-eyed humanoids with wings and antennae. These beings rode unicycles along giddy elevated roadways in towering cities and used solar energy to power the great water pumps of the canals.[114] In 1891 the Prix Pierre Guzman established an award of 100,000 francs to anyone who contacted another planet and received a response—any planet, that is, except Mars, since it was too easy a target. A conference held in France in 1899 considered huge mirrors to reflect sunlight and flash coded messages to Mars, while the electrical inventors Nikola Tesla and Guglielmo Marconi thought they picked up mysterious signals from Mars. Interest in radio contact peaked in 1924 when military and civilian stations ceased transmissions for several hours when the planet was closest. Listeners reported strange signals, and the most optimistic concluded that we had heard from the Martians.[115]

Lowell championed the canals and the Martians until his death in 1916. Energetic, eloquent, and persuasive, he captivated the public with his theories, but he infuriated many astronomers as they questioned both his observations and his inferences. No one could take his drawings at face value and doubt that the canals belonged to an artificial system. By the same token, much of the case for intelligent Martians depended on the accuracy of his observations, and over this point many astronomers begged to differ. One alternative explanation identified the canals as illusions resulting from the tendency of the eye to connect faint, irregular details into straight lines. A French observer, E. M. Antoniadi, saw canals through small telescopes but came to doubt their reality. Then, during the prime opposition of 1909, he had an opportunity to observe the planet through the largest refractor in Europe.

> The first glance cast on the planet at Meudon ... was a revelation. ... [I] did not believe that our present means could ever yield us such images of Mars. The planet appeared covered with a vast and incredible amount of detail held steadily, all natural and logical, irregular and chequered, from which geometry was conspicuous by its complete absence. ... *Mare Tyrrhenum* [appeared] like a leopard skin!. ... A maze of complex markings covered the S. part of *Syrtis Major*, and although these were held quite steadily, no trace whatever of "canals" in the dark regions could be detected.[116]

In retrospect, Antoniadi resolved the controversy in 1909, though the canals continued to keep astronomers awake at night for another twenty years before realization that he "saw true" finally sank in. Even as scientists left Lowell's Mars behind, popular faith in Martians held firm, and ufologists of the 1950s kept an ear close to the ground, listening—selectively—for any news that pointed to Mars as the home of flying saucers. Even without canals the planet had surprises to spring. Recurrent "W"-shaped clouds, now known to form over the giant volcanoes of the Tharsis region, revived rumors of messages from the Martians. In 1954 a new dark area the size of France suddenly appeared—had plant life blossomed in the desert by natural or artificial means? A bright starlike flare erupted on the planet in 1951 and lasted about five minutes, followed by the formation of a small, dense cloud. Had a volcano erupted or a nuclear bomb exploded?[117] Though sidelined throughout the canal controversy, the two Martian moons enjoyed an inning of space-age glory in 1959 when Soviet astronomer I. S. Shklovskii proposed that their peculiar motions could be explained if they were, in fact, gigantic Sputniks launched millions of years ago by a long-dead Martian civilization. There was always something new out of Russia in those days, and another speculation built on this theory to propose that no one discovered the moons in the 1860s, despite searches with adequate instrumentation, because the Martians did not launch their satellites until shortly before 1877.[118] All these mysteries drew close attention in the UFO literature.

According to a hypothetical scenario proposed in early Air Force saucer studies and repeated by Donald Keyhoe in 1950, Martian spaceships had patrolled the earth infrequently for hundreds or thousands of years. The upheaval of the Second World War attracted them in greater numbers, but the onset of nuclear tests threw the Martians into a panic. They had not expected the backward, primitive earthlings to develop both atomic and rocket technology at the same time, so the saucer onslaught of 1947 resulted from the Martians flocking to earth in unprecedented numbers to take a closer look. A pattern seemed to emerge as years with oppositions of Mars—1950, 1952, and 1954—also hosted major waves of saucer sightings. Moreover, the nearer the planet approached, the larger the wave grew. With 1956 the year of a prime opposition, ufological bets favored the biggest wave of all, perhaps even some climactic event like a landing or invasion. In fact, nothing exceptional happened in 1956, but efforts to salvage the correlation between UFO waves and the close approach of Mars continued long after. Mars figured in many contactee yarns, but the Martian of choice for ufologists and the public alike was not the friendly Space Brother, rather a hostile creature in the market for new real estate with one or multiple eyes set on the earth.[119]

Mars was dying step by step in scientific opinion even as ufologists adopted it as home of the saucers. Most astronomers still accepted vegetation as responsible for the dark areas until theories of inorganic processes caused support even for primitive plants to wither. When *Mariner IV* returned the first photographs in 1965, the disappointment was almost audible. Mars presented a cold, barren, cratered, and bone-dry planet too inhospitable to support any sort of life. Subsequent probes rekindled interest in the planet as they discovered a geological wonderland of enormous volcanoes and yawning canyons, but tests of the surface soil dug up no evidence for organic molecules, and the dark areas proved to be nothing more than darker areas of rock after all. Yet signs of water, perhaps even standing seas and torrential floods, have raised the possibility that a Martian environment favorable for life existed for brief periods in the distant past.[120] A potato-sized Martian meteorite recovered from Antarctica made news in 1996 for containing microscopic formations suggestive of fossil bacteria.[121] The Face on Mars rekindled some interest within ufology, and life on Mars seems to quicken the pulse whether the evidence is scientific or fanciful, as if people of earth are determined to keep an old friend alive by any means necessary.

The Fictional Life of Martians.—Martians have enjoyed an enduring life in mass and popular culture, subjects of hoaxes during the 1896–1897 airship wave, advertisements and sheet music at the turn of the twentieth century, and imaginative fiction most of all.[122] One story type is the fantastic voyage, a travelogue where the hero visits Mars and describes a succession of unearthly scenes. In Stories of Other Worlds (1900), George Griffith's honeymooning couple found an advanced but unfriendly civilization on Mars, defeated a fleet of Martian airships, and fought off crowds of nine-foot-tall beings in a city.[123] Le Docteur Oméga: Adventures fantastiques de trois Français dans la planète Mars (1905), by Arnold Galopin, includes encounters with humanoid "nains" (dwarfs), spindly large-headed Martians scarcely one foot tall. The space opera genre devotes even more attention to action. Most famous for his Tarzan adventures, Edgar Rice Burroughs also earned popularity for his John Carter of Mars series written between 1911 and 1941. Carter fought hostile monsters, befriended exotic natives, and romanced a Martian princess in one swashbuckling adventure after another. Barsoom was part Lowell's dying planet of deserts, canals, and advanced technology, part feudal kingdoms and ancient empires with opportunities for sword fights and escapes by airship around every corner. Burroughs spread Lowell's ideas to an audience unacquainted with the scientific controversy and popularized other worlds as a backdrop for heroic action, a tradition that has thrived from Buck Rogers and Flash Gordon to the Star Wars saga today.[124]

A third type of Mars fiction, the invasion story, is perhaps the kind most readily associated with the planet. Two notable examples appeared in 1897. In Auf Zwei Planeten the German author Kurd Lasswitz told of explorers discovering a Martian base at the North Pole manned by friendly Martians. Their planet was aged but technology prevented it from dying, and they came to earth on a mission of contact rather than conquest. The superior Martians exercised a benevolent control that soon tightened until a rebellion broke out. Helped along by the human appearance of the Martians, the two worlds made peace and earth headed toward a utopian future.[125] The most famous of all invasion-from-Mars stories began serialization in Pearson's magazine just as the phantom airship wave drew to an end. H. G. Wells depicted the Martians of *The War of the Worlds* as anything but human or benevolent.

> No one would have believed in the last years of the nineteenth century that this world was being watched keenly and closely by intelligences greater than man's and yet as mortal as his own. . . . Yet across the gulf of space, minds that are to our minds as ours are to those of the beasts that perish, intellects vast and cool and unsympathetic, regarded this earth with envious eyes, and slowly and surely drew their plans against us.[126]

Wells borrowed Lowell's theories of an old and dying planet with evolutionally advanced and technologically adept inhabitants. Lowell's imagination was considerable but limited. He condemned his Martians to die a slow death confined to their planet, but Wells saw in the Martians' superiority a resourcefulness to overcome their planetary doom.

> The immediate pressure of necessity has brightened their intellects, enlarged their powers, and hardened their hearts. And looking across space with instruments and intelligences such as we have scarcely dreamed of, they see . . . a morning star of hope, our own warmer planet, green with vegetation and grey with water, with a cloudy atmosphere eloquent of fertility.[127]

Well versed in evolution theory, Wells recognized that the imperatives of survival drove the Martians to an undertaking as bold as their technology was advanced.

> The intellectual side of man already admits that life is an incessant struggle for existence, and it would seem that this too is the belief of the minds upon Mars. Their world is far gone in its cooling and this world is still crowded with life, but crowded only with what they regard as inferior animals. To carry warfare sunward is, indeed, their only escape from the destruction that generation after generation creeps upon them.[128]

Cylinders fired from a space cannon fall upon the earth and the Martians crawl out, octopuslike creatures the size of bears with great eyes and beaklike mouths. Though similar to humans in the distant past, evolution has turned the Martians into the humans of the future, all head and hands, gigantic brains and thrashing tentacles. The digestive system has atrophied, and the Martians draw their nutrients directly from inferior animals by sucking blood from them, a purpose for which humans prove useful. With little body to rest, the Martians need no sleep, and they reproduce by budding, thereby escaping the emotional turmoil of sexual relations.[129] When curious humans approach them, the Martians burn the intruders with a heat ray, then with the help of machinery to overcome the oppressive gravity of the earth, the invaders build towering three-legged fighting machines to march across country at express-train speed, incinerating cities with their heat rays and exterminating populations with clouds of poison gas. Yet the Martians have no immunity to earthly bacteria, and these natural biological agents soon exterminate the alien invaders.

This combination of Lowell, evolutionary theory, and Western imperialism visited upon the West left an indelible impression on perceptions of Mars, but also on expectations of alien life ever after. The sinister planet of war reasserted itself as the saintly sages and heroic engineers of other worlds gave way to ruthless monsters dedicated to conquest, and superiority of technical prowess meant only more efficient destruction of primitive earthlings. The first reaction to aliens would henceforth be suspicion. When Orson Welles wanted a Halloween scare for his Mercury Theater audience in 1938, he adapted *The War of the Worlds* by changing the setting to New Jersey and interrupting seemingly normal radio programming with news flashes announcing the descent of the Martian cylinders and the onset of the war. So realistic did the broadcast seem that many people took the invasion for real and panic ensued. Mars still held enough plausibility as a home of intelligent life for many people to accept the alien invasion as a reality.[130]

The movies have favored invasion plots as the most explosive way for humans and Martians to meet. George Pal's *The War of the Worlds* (1953) relocated the invasion to southern California. With their fighting machines protected by a force field against artillery, aerial bombardment, and even the atomic bomb, the Martians devastate Los Angeles before bacterial infection fells them. *Invaders from Mars* (1953) introduced a clandestine invasion as a flying saucer plunges underground. Commanded by a Martian brain housed inside a glass globe, biological robots pull humans into subterranean chambers where a device implanted in the back of the neck turns captives into puppets and they commit sabotage for the Martian masters. In perhaps the best of all Mars movies, *Five Million Years to Earth* (1968), life on Mars is now extinct, but millions of years ago, as a way of surviving by proxy, the grasshopperlike inhabitants genetically manipulate ancestral humans to share the hive mind of the Martians. A space capsule dug up in a London subway reactivates this alien mentality and sends mobs on a destructive spree to purge the population of anyone capable of independent thought.

Remakes of Mars movies have distanced the aliens from earth. *Independence Day* (1996) updates *The War of the Worlds* with the aliens as space scavengers traveling from solar system to solar system aboard a gigantic space station. This time a computer virus rather than bacteria foils the aliens before they destroy the earth. Steven Spielberg's

2005 *War of the Worlds* has the fighting machines rise from underground, where they have awaited activation by the aliens for millennia, in an emergence of chthonic de-structive forces that befits a time when terrorists lurk close to home. Even as fictitious aliens have rocketed outward to the stars, memories of the Red Planet persist. The dying planet idea motivates alien invaders in *Killers from Space* (1954), *Earth Versus the Flying Saucers* (1956), and *The Arrival* (1996), while the kind and benevolent Martians of Kurd Lasswitz reappear in Klaatu, the Christlike emissary of peace in *The Day the Earth Stood Still* (1951), in the childlike innocence of *E.T. the Extra-Terrestrial* (1982), and in Superman, a refugee from a destroyed planet who uses his powers to fight for truth, justice, and the American way. If the aliens from current fiction gather in some cantina of a galaxy far, far away, chances are good that they received their elementary education in how to be alien from Martian teachers.

The Search for Life Goes On.—Even as prospects for a habitable Mars faded away, scientific opinion swung back in favor of life beyond the solar system. When a sophisti-cated reworking returned the nebular hypothesis to favor in the 1940s, planets became inevitable consequences of star formation once again. Efforts to detect unseen planets by measuring the perturbations and light fluctuations of stars have paid off since the 1990s with detection of over three hundred probable examples.[131] Biological discover-ies broadened conceptions of the versatility of life from a familiar regime of photo-synthesizing plants and oxygen-respiring animals to include anaerobic organisms that derive energy from sulfur compounds. Bacteria of this type thrive in hot springs de-spite seemingly intolerable heat, while large, complex organisms live without sunlight or oxygen around deep-sea volcanic vents. The possibility of liquid oceans under the icy crust of Jupiter's moon Europa has raised hopes that life, not as we know it but based on some anoxic regimen, may flourish in these sunless seas.[132] By the 1950s many astronomers took intelligent life in the universe seriously enough to suggest listening for alien broadcasts by radio telescope. The first attempt, Project Ozma in 1960, led to the Search for Extraterrestrial Intelligence (SETI), sponsored both by government and private funding over the past twenty-five years.[133]

The new plurality of worlds enjoyed a golden age of confidence during the years of the space race, but accumulating doubts were already pushing the pendulum the other way. In an offhand lunchtime remark in 1950, nuclear physicist Enrico Fermi asked that if intelligent beings were so commonplace in the universe, where were they? If even one technological civilization evolved in the galaxy and began to spread outward star by star, that one civilization should be able to occupy every available planet within a few million years. No implausible travel beyond the speed of light would be necessary, only relatively low-speed migrations of self-sustaining colonies looking for a suitable planet to occupy. In time, each successful colony would then send out its own colonizing expedition, and on and on until the galaxy filled up. Multiple civilizations would ideally accelerate the process, yet we find no visitors at our doorstep.[134]

This troublesome Fermi Paradox has inspired scores of solutions. Some assert aliens are here after all; others assert that aliens exist, but we have not found the evidence; and still others argue that no evidence means there are no aliens. Recent reconsiderations of the needs for a habitable planet have battered the permissive views of a few decades ago and returned to Wallace's "Goldilocks" planet, where conditions strike a fine—perhaps a razor-fine—balance between too much of this or too little of that and create a world that is just right for life. One problem is that while stars may be many, suitable stars may be few. Stars a little larger than our sun give out too much radiation and burn out too quickly for intelligent life to evolve. Stars smaller than the sun often expel violent flares harmful to living things. Many stars are variable at some point in their life cycle and for that reason are unfavorable for life. All in all, a reliable sun is hard to find.[135] A habitable planet seems to need its neighbors' help, such as giant planets in the outer solar system to vacuum up destructive comets as they head sunward and an unusually large moon to stabilize axial tilt, keep the iron core churning, and maintain tectonic activity. Such "double planets" as the earth-moon system may be the rare result of a chance collision early in planetary formation; but without such a partnership, the earth might have frozen into a ball of ice or gone the way of Venus, hardened into geologic inertness and heated into an inferno by a runaway greenhouse effect.[136]

Even if life gains a foothold, intelligent life in some recognizable form does not follow with predestined inevitability. Such notable evolutionary biologists as Ernst Mayr, George Gaylord Simpson, and Stephen Jay Gould agree that human existence owes so much to environmental circumstances and historical flukes that were the tape of evolution replayed with any changes along the way, we would most likely be conspicuous by our absence. Mayr highlights the long odds with a sobering observation that some one billion species have evolved on earth but only one has evolved intelligence. On the other hand, Simon Conway Morris allows that convergent evolution could lead to adaptations that meet similar environmental challenges in similar biological ways. Humanoid beings with problem-solving abilities like our own may be a recurrent consequence of evolution, though planets suitable for such beings would be relatively few. Yet even the evolution of intelligent life does not assure the rise of technological civilizations. Porpoises might develop high intelligence but never achieve space travel, since they would not master fire underwater or manipulate their environment without hands. A civilization may develop technology but not survive it for long, with nuclear war, self-poisoning by pollution, or social refutation ending the possibility of contact with earth. Few living things may have a voice to answer the galactic roll-call.[137]

To expect a crowded universe may be overly optimistic, but the utter silence that frightened Pascal three hundred years ago continues to lend a somber counterpoint to the pluralistic hope today—so does the absence of visible feats by super-civilizations working on an appropriately grandiose scale, like the stars of an entire galaxy rearranged in an artificial configuration. Proposals serious and humorous have attempted to account for the apparent absence of aliens: they have set aside the earth as a national park; they are so truly alien that we would not recognize one even if we stepped on it; and, they have moved ahead to such advanced technologies that by tuning in to radio frequencies we are in effect listening for talking drums.[138] The pluralistic faith has on its side the principle of mediocrity, the oft-confirmed view that the earth is average, one planet among many, with odds stacked against the possibility that just this once the exclusivist view has it right and intelligent life really is unique to earth. But for now the universe keeps silent.

UFOs and the Otherworld Theme

For ufologists and in much popular thinking, wherever UFOs are accepted, the answer to Fermi's question is self-evident: alien life does not languish in a far corner of the galaxy but flies over hearth and home on any given night. The extraterrestrial hypothesis has dominated ufological thinking not merely because this idea is exciting, but because it is the most viable solution for the mystery as ufologists construct it. This understanding is so familiar that it seems natural and so modern that it seems new, but the extraterrestrial hypothesis grafts UFOs onto the stock of otherworld traditions outlined here so that an established pattern defines and confines understanding of the subject.

Some relationships with tradition are too conspicuous to belabor any further. Otherworlds have modernized into planets and visitation between worlds into space travel, but the basic understanding of a cosmos full of inhabited niches and inhabitants that travel to and fro remains intact. Godlike saviors from the sky transfer from mythology to the contactee literature with only superficial changes, travelers' tales of monstrous and threatening creatures echo through fears of flying saucer invasions and alien abductions. The development of Martian mythology popularized technologically

superior aliens driven by need to escape their dying planet, and early ufologists borrowed this template largely intact as they constructed ufological theory. If Mars can no
longer satisfy the requirements of an alien home, the search carries similar ideas deeper
into the universe as otherworld traditions continue to leave their mark.

Other influences from the past are less obvious and bear more subtle consequences.
One archaic idea that persists in opposition to modern understanding is the ease of
travel between worlds. In early traditions the otherworld was close at hand and distance a minor impediment, with a spell, a trance, or pluck and luck the only ticket a
traveler needed. Today scientists warn that limitations apply. Matter cannot accelerate
faster than the speed of light, so lay aside the fond hope of rocket ships commuting
to the stars and returning home in time for dinner. The discovery of cosmic distance
counts as a cornerstone of modern cosmology, one of the great ideas of the ages and
a basic tool of reasoning to understand the universe. Skeptics often cite insuperable
distance as reason to doubt that UFOs could be interstellar visitors; in popular ufology
such distances seldom pose a problem. Reading far and wide in the ufological literature
turns up some interest in scientific speculations about cosmic wormholes and other
exotic forms of travel, the occasional nod to colony ships such as Fermi proposed, bases
on the moon and Mars, and rationalizations like the warp drive of *Star Trek*; but for
most people interested in UFOs, no high-noon showdown confronts the implications
of physical theory for the extraterrestrial faith. The term "light-year" has entered into
general usage, but the implications do not sink into popular thinking inside or outside
of ufology, a situation apparent when movies continue to exploit the adventuresome
possibilities of rapid interstellar travel and disregard its problems. The universe of both
popular ufology and moviemakers reflects not the daunting yardstick of science but the
intimate and accessible cosmos of tradition.

A further continuity of thinking results when ufologists borrow scientific theory
that itself only modifies older tradition. They have some exotic alternatives, but the
most popular strand of ufological thinking favors the extraterrestrial hypothesis. It
sides with the scientific opinion that intelligent life exists in the universe and adopts
the scientific universe of stars and planets, in an orthodoxy that sounds right and has
astronomical theory for support yet forecloses other imaginable directions of thought.
René Descartes envisioned a universe where vortices of motion create space and differ-
entiate matter into bodies. Charles Fort imagined wandering bodies of planetary size
and currents in an interplanetary Super-Sargasso Sea. Modern cosmological theorists
posit multiple dimensions and interconnected universes. By comparison, the ETH
cosmology is unimaginative and staid. It accommodates rather than innovates, echo-
ing the extraterrestrial concepts of normative astronomy as befits a field that craves

acceptance by official science. That same science has blown the roof off the world as a close-fitting sky becomes the infinite universe, shattered the crystalline celestial spheres to tether the heavenly bodies with a mysterious force of gravity, and replaced the three-tiered cosmos with innumerable solar systems; but these revolutions build on old foundations rather than start from scratch. Ufologists hardly deserve condemnation for sharing common ground with science, but the result is a body of theory that conserves the traditional cosmological blueprint in general plan if not in every detail.

One consequence of extraterrestrial premises is a narrowing influence. They resist a conventional explanation even when one seems possible or probable, and they oppose alternate theories like paraphysical phenomena, even if such solutions hold explanatory advantages for certain aspects of UFO activity. When recognized at all, high-strangeness phenomena, like reports of aliens passing through solid walls or emerging from a ball of light, often become technologized. In one recent interpretation, aliens travel by a space-time shift in a luminous bubble that startles witnesses as it suddenly opens into this world.[139] The scientific tone of this explanation appeals to technological enthusiasts even while the science itself remains vague. Concepts of UFOs as alien spaceships lead an editing process of additions or subtractions in descriptions to meet the obligations of an ideal image. The ambiguous lights of observation may sharpen into something more distinctive with retelling. During the *Zond* reentry of 1968, burning debris gained nuts and bolts and the physical structure of windows for a few observers, and the distant military flares responsible for some of the Phoenix Lights reports of 1997 became lights of a disk-shaped craft supposedly larger than a football stadium.[140] Such conceptual reworking of the visible facts channels the UFO of observation toward the UFO of expectation.

This process of conceptual leading may begin with the witness but often escalates in the verbal and visual representations of ufological publications to reinforce a clearer construct than observations warrant. The graphic images of a UFO have an especially persuasive power to stereotype a case. One depiction of the Exeter UFO in a widely circulated Time-Life book, *The UFO Phenomenon*, shows a thick disk tipped to one side while panels of red lights flash around the rim. This version stays close to verbal reports but still takes liberties by solidifying the body when the witnesses saw nothing so definite behind the bright lights, and of interpreting the flashing lights as surrounding the circumference even though the reports do not support this understanding. A more fanciful illustration portrays a structured metallic flying saucer with portholes and fins, in willful defiance of the observational record.[141] Both pictures are based on witness descriptions but present an imagined version of the Exeter sightings. By the time a case reaches the literature, an image straight from UFO mythology often supplants the ambiguities of observation and the fumbling of description so typical of actual reports to become the new "fact" of the matter. The verbal and visual rhetoric of this transformation addresses the audience with a persuasive but perhaps misleading argument that witnesses saw a mechanical spacecraft.

Much about ufological theory and popular representation suggests cultural borrowing, but this fault does not necessarily carry over to the UFOs themselves. Yet experiential accounts also embed apparent traces of otherworld traditions even when the source of influence remains obscure. The pattern of shamanic initiations—altered state of consciousness, visit to a strange environment, ordeal at the hands of unearthly beings, acquisition of knowledge and power—also applies to abductions. The fact that parallels exist is too evident to doubt and suggests a causal relationship rather than mere chance hits. Whatever the ultimate causes may be, an intermediate cause seems clear—key points of UFO conception and interpretation simply continue old habits of thought, adapted to modern situations with alterations in detail but faithful to the thematic patterns of traditions tracing back to ancient times. In this view, much thinking about UFOs takes shape from preexisting templates, and the result is a mythic version that mixes the underlying reality with abundant cultural influences.

Sixty years of interest in UFOs have resulted in an extensive international literature. Author photo.

A woodcut from the 1589 edition of the *Prodigiorum Liber* by the Roman author Julius Obsequens (Lugduni [Lyons]: Joann Tornasius, publisher) illustrates two aerial prodigies from the year 98 B.C.: a "burning torch" that fell from the sky, and an object like a round shield that flew from west to east.

A terrible sign like a column appeared in 384 A.D. according to Lycosthenes. The depiction, stereotypical for its time, comes from *Die Wunder Gottes in der Natur,* a 1744 reprint of sixteenth-century illustrations from the German edition of his collection of prodigies (Franckfurth [Frankfort]: unnamed publisher).

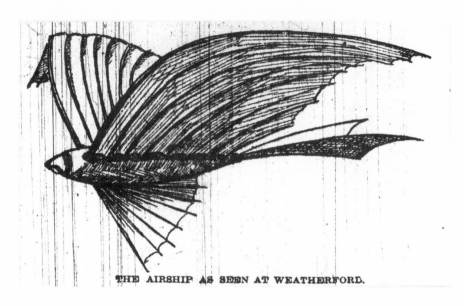

THE AIRSHIP AS SEEN AT WEATHERFORD.

Extravagant and aerodynamically implausible designs characterized conceptions of the 1897 phantom airship. *Right*: This image appeared in the *Minneapolis Times* on April 13 and shows headlights mounted on top. *Above*: This image, from the *Dallas Morning News* of April 16, illustrates a report from Weatherford, Texas, of an airship with a swallow tail and enormous wings.

Visual mythology: Kenneth Arnold's flying saucers (*left*) are unmistakably metallic and mechanical on the cover of the spring 1948 issue of *Fate* magazine. But one of Arnold's own sketches (*below*), drawn on the back of an envelope, shows less definite forms. Popular representations of UFOs have often stereotyped them as machinelike whether or not the actual reports warrant it. Magazine cover courtesy of *Fate* magazine; Arnold's sketches courtesy of CUFOS.

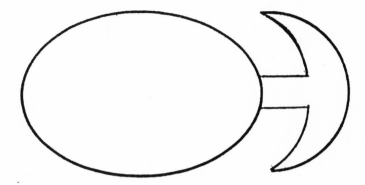

Above: A B-52 flew over a landed UFO that glowed like lava or molten metal near Minot Air Force Base on the night of October 24, 1968. This illustration is a redrawing of the sketch that copilot Bradford Runyon, Jr., provided in a report to CUFOS. Courtesy of CUFOS.

Right: A lighted, triangular object passed over several towns in southern Illinois before dawn on January 5, 2000. The upper illustration is a redrawing of a sketch by Shiloh police officer Thomas Barton; the lower illustrations, from Millstadt officer Craig Stevens, show the underside and the structure of lights at the rear of the object. These sketches reveal similarities of shape and distribution of lights in the two independent observations.

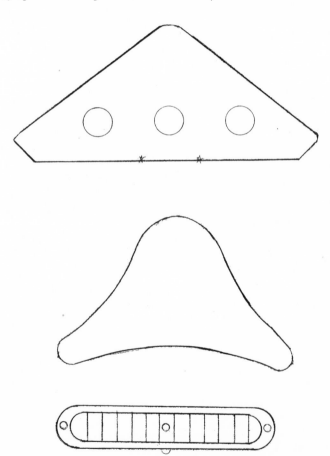

Near Exeter, New Hampshire, Norman Muscarello and two police officers observed a UFO with flashing lights on the morning of September 3, 1965. J. Allen Hynek presented a slide showing this illustration of the Exeter sighting at many of his lectures. Courtesy of CUFOS.

Most of the thousands of alleged UFO photographs fall under suspicion as hoaxes or conventional phenomena. One exception came from Costa Rica, where an aerial mapping crew photographed an unidentified disk below them and over a lake on September 4, 1971. An analysis, published by Richard F. Haines and Jacques Vallee in the *Journal of Scientific Exploration* ("Photo Analysis of an Aerial Disk over Costa Rica," 3, no. 2 [1989]: 113–131, and "Photo Analysis of an Aerial Disk over Costa Rica: New Evidence," 4, no. 1 [1990]: 71–74), uncovered no conventional identity for this apparently large object. Photo courtesy of Dr. Richard F. Haines.

Diminutive humanoids took hold as the predominant form of UFO occupants in numerous reports from Europe and South America in 1954. On the morning of November 28, two men near Caracas came upon a spherical object on the ground and scuffled with several hairy dwarfs having large heads and glowing eyes. The illustration comes from an unknown Venezuelan newspaper. Courtesy of CUFOS.

Opposite page: Short, hairless humanoids with large heads and eyes became the standard occupants in abduction reports from their beginnings in the 1960s onward. Three early examples include a case from Idaho in 1977 (*APRO Bulletin*, November 1977), Casey County, Kentucky, in 1976, and Oregon in 1975 (*MUFON UFO Journal*, January 1977, November 1979; courtesy of MUFON).

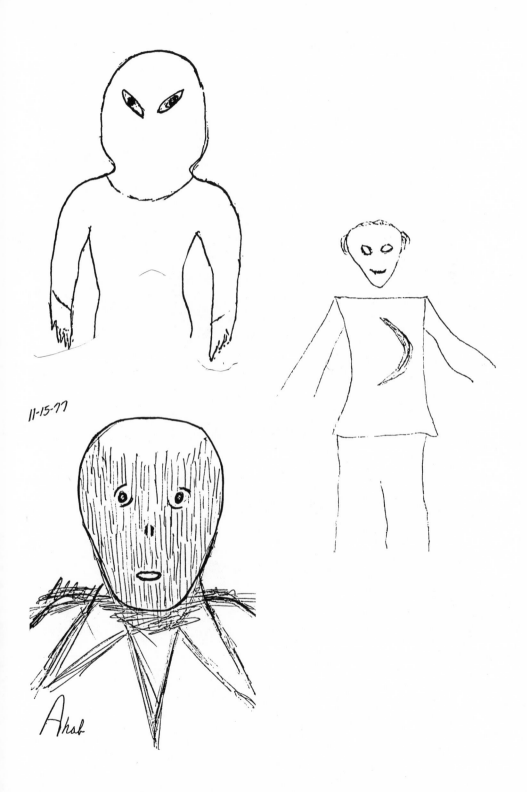

11-15-77

Ahab

Top: Another photograph analyzed and investigated by Richard F. Haines was taken by a young woman on vacation with her family in Vancouver, British Columbia, on October 8, 1981. She did not see the disk over the mountain until she viewed the developed photograph, but the witness appeared to be of high reliability, and no common hoax like a flying Frisbee seems possible. *Above:* Detail. Photo courtesy of the Fortean Picture Library.

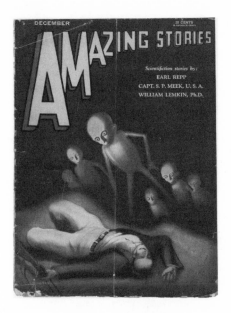

Science fiction literature has portrayed a vast variety of alien forms, but thin, diminutive beings with large hairless heads and staring eyes have a recurrent history. This example, by artist Leo Mora, appeared on the cover of *Amazing Stories* for December 1930.

In an 1893 article entitled "The Man of the Year Million," H. G. Wells foresaw evolution leading to future humans with large heads and frail bodies. In "1,000,000 A. D.", published November 25, 1893, the British magazine *Punch* gave humorous treatment to this idea.

Speculations about how Martians would look grew popular in the late nineteenth and early twentieth centuries. The idea that Martians would need larger heads to accommodate their superior intelligence became a fixture in most depictions, whether based on evolutionary theory, as with the invaders in *The War of the Worlds*, or, in this example from the *St. Louis Republic* of February 13, 1916, whimsical elflike beings.

CHAPTER FIVE

The Space Children:
A Case Example

If I hadn't believed it, I wouldn't have seen it.
—Attributed to Yogi Berra

The real is as imagined as the imaginary.
—Clifford Geertz, *Negara: The Theatre State in Nineteenth-Century Bali*[1]

Where the last chapter pursued alien visitation, one of the large themes of ufology, this chapter applies a similar approach on a smaller scale. Numerous minor themes have a rich cultural and historical background of their own, but this in-depth case study will have to serve as a representative example of others too numerous to explore. The overall message remains the same: mystery, uncertainty, human interest, and emotional concern. These qualities of UFOs offer reason for treatments to pull away from the strict line of objectivity and lean on human preferences in representation. Both large and small themes demonstrate that observation and experience build content in the UFO literature, but so do rumors, half-truths, wishes, beliefs, speculations, and cultural borrowings.

The subject will be the role of children in UFO accounts. Children occupy a small corner of UFO literature, their active involvement limited mostly to abduction reports or interpretations of this experience; but the accounts cast children in sufficiently recurrent parts to establish coherent themes. An underlying principle for this study is the functionalist assumption that cultural representations reflect the psychological makeup of a society. To identify an important axis of thought, look for signs of things feared and things hoped for wherever imagination has freedom—in religious enthusiasm, escapist entertainment, moral panics, prejudices, and bogeymen. Especially revealing is anything regarded as abnormal, unknown, remarkable, or extraordinary. Children enter often into human hopes and fears, both the realistic and the fantastic, so asking how children in UFO narratives relate to children in other cultural representations poses a meaningful question. The study method will be comparison. Its initial task is to identify robust thematic domains within the material, subtopics treated in many narratives and around which numerous motifs cluster. The data for study will be texts drawn from the UFO literature, while the comparative materials will be texts from contemporary and historical sources that deal with social concerns about children. The goal of this comparison will be to find how far the UFO-related texts reflect the imaginary roles of children in texts from cultural sources with no UFO content.

A comparative study of this sort allows only limited conclusions. Few similarities will indicate little connection between the UFO experience and mundane concerns about children; however, many similarities will suggest that similar avenues of thought and patterns of expression exist within the UFO literature and elsewhere. Why such similarities exist—whether they reflect common psychology, borrowed ideas, or co-incidental similarities between two realities—remains outside the scope of this case study. The most that can be said is that if close parallels recur in diverse contexts, the theme in question reflects human concerns that transcend particulars of content or situation. Even when real events underlie the texts, recurrent themes and their recurrent treatments caution that similar avenues of thought and patterns of expression may reconfigure the facts into a mythic version more or less removed from historical truth.

Children assume three general roles in the UFO literature—victims, hybrids, and harbingers of the future, sometimes as threats and sometimes as saviors. These stories contain their own distinctive and recurrent story elements, but no element exists in a vacuum. Each one has noteworthy parallels in such independent contexts as fairy lore, witchcraft beliefs, science fiction literature, and various social panics like the 1980s excitement over child abuse. To give away the secret at the start, comparison will reveal patterns of thematic isomorphism between the UFO literature and established cultural ideas.

In the mid-1960s UFO abduction reports introduced a story of captives hauled aboard a UFO for medical examination by extraterrestrial beings.[2] Abductions appeared opportunistic at first, as if alien scientists bagged and tagged available specimens on a one-time, chance-only basis. Any involvement of children seemed to be an accident of circumstance. Such was the case for Patty Roach, a divorced mother in Utah who awoke one night in 1973 with the children screaming that they saw a skeleton and with feelings of her own that an intruder had entered the house. She and several children later recalled examinations aboard a spaceship.[3] A year later, John Day and his wife and three children were abducted as they drove near Aveley, England. Two of the children held no apparent interest for the aliens and remained asleep in the backseat of the car.[4] The abduction experience even took a beneficial turn in a few circumstances. Mrs. Roach's seven-year-old daughter and the child of Texas motorist Megan Elliott no longer suffered from chronic illnesses after receiving treatment from aliens.[5]

By the beginning of the 1980s a deepening awareness of the abduction phenomenon challenged the notion that children were nothing more than collateral targets. More and more abductees described recurrent encounters in a lifelong history of abductions. Pioneering abduction investigator Budd Hopkins recounted the story of Virginia Horton, who was six years old when she found a mysterious cut on her leg. Years later, under hypnosis, she recalled that she spent some hours inside a UFO, conversing with a friendly, grandfatherly alien who eventually took a blood sample from her leg. Ten years later she met the aliens again, and they took another blood sample as a follow-up to their previous research.[6] Investigating a 1967 abduction of Massachusetts housewife Betty Andreasson led ufologist Raymond E. Fowler to uncover memories of encounters when she was seven and twelve, while an elaborate abduction with examinations, messages, and an otherworld journey occurred when she was thirteen.[7] Reports that abduction begins in childhood are the norm among cases now available.

Not only did abductees report multiple encounters, but a life-cycle pattern began to emerge. For young children the experience was often friendly or even playful, as the aliens simply kept watch on their new acquaintances with occasional meetings. The aliens might perform some medical procedures or impart some teachings, but stresses on the young abductee were typically minimal. This easygoing relationship took a dramatic turn with the onset of puberty: The aliens increased the frequency of their visits, and examination procedures came to dominate each encounter. Cold, businesslike efficiency replaced the former friendliness. From this time through young adulthood and prime maturity, the alien procedures focused unmistakably on the reproductive system. Men reported technological extraction of semen, and women described a needle-in-the-abdomen procedure that suggested the harvest of eggs. The abductors left further clues about their purpose when they turned loose elderly or infertile captives as unsuitable.[8]

What interested the aliens was clear; why they were interested remained in the dark. Hopkins revealed a startling answer in 1987 with publication of *Intruders*, an account of the experiences of a young Indianapolis woman. She related a series of abductions beginning with removal of eggs, the implantation of what turned out to be an embryo, her subsequent pregnancy, and the disappearance of the fetus immediately after another encounter. Several years later the aliens introduced her to a small, frail child, human but with wispy hair, large eyes, and a large head—a hybrid mix of human

and humanoid alien traits.[9] Hopkins and Temple University history professor David
Jacobs discovered a number of women who experienced a mysterious onset and end of
pregnancy amid a series of abductions and who later met their hybrid children. These
investigators also discovered men who had served as sperm donors. Some abductees
toured an incubatorium aboard the ship where tiny fetuses floated in tanks of liquid.
The aliens scheduled meetings for abductees to touch and nurture the weak, listless
hybrid children in an apparent attempt to invigorate them with human emotions.[10]

Discovery of this hybridization program provided a motive but no reason for
the industrial scale of abductions. In time an ominous answer took shape. The aliens
dropped hints that they belonged to a dying race, sometimes by saying outright that
they could no longer reproduce, sometimes by showing scenes of a devastated or barren alien planet.[11] Jacobs gathered even more suggestive clues in the testimonies of his
abductees—that hybrids were growing steadily in number, that some of them became
more human with each generation and now mingled with the human population. A
time called "The Change" was approaching when hybrids and humans would coexist
openly in an idyllic world. If the promise was a peaceable kingdom, the reality looked
all too much like a new world dominated by hybrids as they supplanted humanity with
a population human in appearance but alien in mind.[12]

Though many clues seemed to point toward doom and gloom, some abductees
and researchers read an ultimate positive message in the experience. The aliens were
not always indifferent. Sometimes they promised to help in a time of future tribulation or they prepared abductees for a future mission. Some people returned from
their encounters transformed in thinking and enhanced in abilities. Whitley Strieber
acknowledged the harrowing side of abductions but found a transformative purpose
behind the pain and fear. The experience suggested a communion of the earthly and
everyday with something mysterious and wonderful to lead humanity toward a rebirth
or new awareness.[13] John Mack emphasized the shock value of abduction to break old
assumptions and redirect human consciousness from its current materialistic, rationalistic preoccupations toward oneness with nature and acceptance of an enlarged reality
beyond ourselves. In this light, hybridization becomes "an awkward joining of two species . . . for a purpose that serves both of our goals with difficulties for each."[14] These
contrary views of abduction reversed it from exploitative to helpful and redefined the
role of children from victims of a self-serving alien agenda to the vanguard of world
salvation, taught by alien masters and changed in consciousness to lead humanity toward a future of higher awareness and cosmic citizenship.

A more personal attachment emerges when some abductees recognize one alien as
a familiar, recurrent figure throughout their abduction career. Such recognition may

extend prior to birth and encompass an apparent former existence on another planet as an alien. This sense of dual reference, of being on earth but belonging elsewhere, evokes feelings of sadness, abandonment, alienation, and longing to return home.[15] For abductees the sense of being torn between two worlds is all the more wrenching because, however joyful a reunion with the aliens may be, it is also fraught with pain and terror and consequently a source of unhappiness in both worlds.

An allegiance with an extraterrestrial home connects abductees with an observation that received news media attention in 1996: children's IQ test scores have risen dramatically during the twentieth century, not just in one country but in many.[16] Have the tests dumbed down, have social influences like video games skewed the tests by improving specific skills like spatial relations, or are children today literally a world apart from what children used to be? Many New Age followers prefer the latter view. Called the New Children, Millennium Children, Indigo Children, or Star Children, these offspring born since about 1980 are alleged to be exceptionally intelligent, psychic, and spiritual. They remember past lives or manifest matter-of-fact familiarity with paradise-like places and seemingly divine beings. These children are sometimes diagnosed with attention deficit disorder, but they are not sick, only bored by a confining educational system.[17] The New Age faithful hail these special children as bearers of a transformation of consciousness and explain them sometimes as the results of an evolutionary leap, sometimes as missionary visitors from sacred realms, other dimensions, or other planets.[18] It comes as little surprise that these alleged Star Children fulfill the expectations of some UFO proponents for alien-human hybrids.[19]

Perhaps the most obvious and pervasive theme involving children in UFO abduction stories is endangerment by a nonhuman Other. The very premise is involuntary capture by powerful unearthly beings for mysterious alien purposes, and like conventional kidnap, UFO abduction threatens children with physical, emotional, and sexual harm. Whitley Strieber became distraught when the aliens showed him a vision of his young son in the land of the dead.[20] Judy Doraty, a Texas woman abducted with her teenage daughter, saw a calf lifted into a UFO at the same time that their examination began. She watched the aliens perform a gruesome dissection of the calf and feared for the safety of her daughter, saying, "I thought they were going to harm her. That they were going to do to her what they did to the animal."[21] Abductees sometimes bring home a lingering trauma; at a bare minimum, the experience is one of helplessness and lack of control. The abductors subject children to frightening procedures and parents must stand by unable to offer protection, the emotions of fear and outrage multiplied for women who find themselves artificially inseminated and then deprived of the fetuses by the unfeeling, uncomprehending technicians. Such an encounter is always a mixed blessing, even when ultimately beneficial, since the means are inevitably harrowing and uncongenial.

An almost equally prominent but more ambiguous theme is that of metamorphosis. The abduction experience changes captives, either in their thinking or in their genetic line. With hybrids the aliens attempt to become part of our world by becoming part of us. This union operates through our children, and human concern for their safety goes without saying. They are the future of humanity, the continuation of all that we hold dear, protected by universal bonds like marriage and kinship but always fragile and vulnerable. Any tampering with this most personal and closely guarded aspect of life is serious business, bound to provoke strong feelings and play out in polarized expressions of hope and fear. The possibility of hybridization lends itself to interpretation as a conspiracy of evil, nonhuman forces to wrest the earth from us by changing humans into aliens, the process made all the more repellent because it depends on unstoppable, techno-magical kidnap and rape. Such subversion raises xenophobic fears of an outside race hostile to the good, aliens so subtle they go almost undetected even while they work on a grand scale to destroy the human lineage and essential integrity of the species.

For interpreters who look beyond the unpleasant methods and suspect motives of the abductors, the Star Children invite a positive spin on abductions. Any physical changes are subordinate to mental changes intended to improve mankind and make a better future for all children. The Star Children come (indirectly) from the sky as saviors to break the impasse of materialism, greed, and violence that threatens the world, here to teach and lead, even to simply replace the bad and broken lot of humanity with pure and perfect successors. This altruistic potential of UFO encounters introduces the theme of the divine child, an advanced or better spirit born into the world and destined to bring about a rebirth of humanity into a genuine New Age. The child becomes the hope of the world and the terrifying encounter with aliens an initiatory experience preparing the young hero for a sacred career. No abductee has risen to fulfill this promise, and the few UFO-based messiahs have succeeded only as bland sectarian leaders or dangerous cultists, not as world transformers or archetypal protagonists in a vital movement. Nevertheless, the thematic raw materials are abundant in narratives of human interaction with UFOs.

Whether harmful or ultimately helpful, UFO abduction is a disturbing proposition. Abduction nullifies free will and exposes adults to vulnerability they rarely experience in everyday life, a combination of fear, pain, shame, helplessness, uncertainty, and loss of personhood. The anguish multiplies when children become the victims, because they face potential danger and no protective measure can keep them safe. At the same time, little about abduction sounds very alien. The scenario of unearthly strangers coming by night to harm innocent victims reactivates the primal dread at the heart of the supernatural legend, the fear that assault by some mysterious power will overturn the illusion that the world is safe, predictable, and just. Themes of supernatural kidnap, metamorphosis for good or evil, cosmic conspiracies against mankind, child saviors from the sky, and sexual endangerment of the innocent have abundant parallels in religion, mythology, folklore, literature, and social concerns. So many expressions in varied contexts betray the continuity of interest in these themes and increase the likelihood that they stand out for human reasons rather than for causes inherent in the phenomenon.

The folktale of Hansel and Gretel has grown perhaps too familiar to evoke much sense of horror, but the story is horrific to the core: Two children abandoned in a forest find the gingerbread house of a witch and become her prisoners, held in cages until they have fattened up enough for the witch to cook and eat. The children trick the witch and burn her in her own oven, but this happy outcome was not the fate of predecessors lured to the same house. A similar basic plot of children imperiled by otherworldly danger plays out with a varied cast of supernatural assailants in folk belief. The witch and the sorcerer are humans with magical powers; demons and fairies belong to separate supernatural races; vampires are revenants; and cannibal ogres are brutish subhumans. Like UFO aliens, these entities pose a threat to children and share noteworthy parallels in the way they threaten.

A basic model for supernatural attack on children derives from behaviors of the primordial night witch.[22] One of the truly terrifying creations of the human imagination, this creature is a shape-shifter sometimes taken to be primarily human but able to assume the form of an animal, such as an owl or wolf, and sometimes regarded as an animal capable of taking on human form. This malevolent entity prowls the night, often flying from house to house and rendering the inhabitants helpless while she steals their blood, body fat, or life force, resulting in sickness and death. Children are favored victims, sometimes killed by the night witch and sometimes kidnapped for food or for parts to use in potions or spells.

The night witch or a child-killing entity with similar practices has almost universal distribution.[23] In ancient Rome the common people feared the *strix*, a woman who carried out her depredations in the form of an owl.[24] Ovid tells of *striges*—"big is their head, goggle their eyes . . . their feathers blotched with grey"—flying into the bed chamber of a five-day-old prince where they scratched him with their claws and "sucked his infant breast with greedy tongues" to leave him drained of color. The prophylactic rituals of a nymph staved off further attacks, and the boy recovered his health.[25]

The eighth-century writer John of Damascus sums up several traditional properties of *striges*, saying "that they are to be seen at night passing through the air, and that when they happen to come to a house . . . make their way in and throttle infants. Others say that the Strix devours the liver and all the internal organs of the children. . . . And they stoutly declare . . . that they have seen . . . the Strix entering houses, though the doors were locked, either in bodily form or as a spirit only."[26]

The Greek witch Medea murdered her children when her husband, Jason, left her, but she remained a literary figure, whereas the child-killing demons Mormo, Gello, and Lamia had wide popular circulation, at least as bugbears, to frighten children. These women became enemies of children due to the loss of their own. Adults also had reason to fear these beings, since they caused miscarriages, slaughtered pregnant women to steal their unborn children, and assumed an attractive form to seduce and murder men.[27] Mesopotamian demonology filled the streets and countryside with evil beings prowling the night in search of homes to invade. Traditions that trace back to Sumerian civilization refer to the *Lil*, spirits of dust storms that later became associated with blood-sucking night demons. The Babylonian *Lilitu* was the female version of a class of lascivious demons, and a relief pictures her accompanied by a pair of owls and with talons for feet, like a bird of prey. Her milk was poisonous, and she sought to feed it to nursing children.[28] This demon entered Hebrew mythology as Lilith, the first wife of Adam, who flew away from him after a quarrel, ever after seducing men and killing children because she could not bear any of her own.[29]

Traditions of night witches can be found among Germanic peoples in early medieval times, and many popular Russian folktales about Baba Yaga describe the witch kidnapping children to cook and eat.[30] Similar evil beings and threatening practices are commonplace outside of Europe. Widespread African beliefs recognize hereditary witches that fly at night with owls or ride hyenas, ant bears, or crocodiles on missions to cause sickness, death, impotence, barrenness, and miscarriage.[31] The Dinka of the Sudan suspect witches of spreading the blood of dead cobras about a victim's house, so that the entire family suffers sickness or death from contact with the poison.[32] Many criminal cases arising from witchcraft accusations among the Shona of Zimbabwe indicate that children are favored victims and that the night witches are cannibals who eat the psychic as well as the physical substance of victims.[33]

Quite similar ideas pervade Asian cultures. According to anthropologist Bronislaw Malinowski, the Trobriand Islanders tell of a type of witch that sends out her spirit double, the *mulukwausi*, in the form of a bird, bat, firefly, or shooting star to find corpses to eat or shipwrecked sailors to kill. Invisible gatherings of these *mulukwausi* feed on the dead from the inside out and attack the living in the same way. Those people whose internal organs are consumed will sicken and die within a few days.[34] Philippine folk tradition contains several viscera-sucking demons, such as the *aswang*, usually described as a beautiful young woman who detaches the upper part of her body from the lower to go out on forays at night. She assumes the form of a bird and perches on the roof of a house. Her long tongue seeks out the anus of a sleeping boy or girl and sucks out the entrails. The victim dies as a result. These viscera suckers attack sick adults, but above all favor the hearts and livers of infants and children, and the fetuses of pregnant women.[35] Chinese historical records note recurrent outbreaks of mass hysteria based on activities akin to night-witch depredations.[36] One example is the "soul-stealing" epidemic of 1768, when accusations spread through multiple provinces that sorcerers were clipping the tips of queues and collecting names, mostly of male children, in order to steal the victims' souls. A powder blown into the victim's face stupefied him long enough for the attacker to do his work and sickness or death followed.[37] A gruesome testimonial to night-witch ideas in Japanese tradition can be found in an 1885 Ukiyo-e print by Yoshitoshi, lurid even by his standards, that shows a pregnant woman bound and hung head-down from the ceiling, her distended belly exposed to a hag sharpening a knife to cut out the fetus. The Noh play that was the basis for this image explained that the hag relished the blood of the unborn child.[38]

In the New World, the Navajo skinwalker assumes animal form and joins in cannibalistic feasts with other witches. These skinwalkers climb to the top of hogans in the night and drop a powder made from the bones of children down the smoke hole to bring sickness, misfortune, or death to the sleeping inhabitants.[39] In the Andes the *kharisiri* or *nakaq* ("slaughterer") attacks travelers at night and breaks into houses, inducing helplessness or a deep sleep by use of a powder made of human bone. This being may be supernatural but is usually described as human and often looks like a white man. He extracts blood or body fat through small puncture wounds, and the victim dies of anemia within a few days.[40] Among the people of rural Tlaxcala, Mexico, the *tlahuelpuchi* is a witch, usually female, that must suck human blood or die. This thirst is inborn and first manifests with puberty, whereupon she transforms into an animal, often a turkey, and seeks sleeping infants, children, and adults for victims. Informants describe the witch traveling in animal form as luminous or in the shape of a fireball, and say that when she invades a house, she releases a glowing mist that causes the inhabitants to fall into a deep sleep. The victim's body shows bruises and purple marks, the survivors suffer from headaches, nausea, nightmares, and fear. Single cases and occasional epidemics of child deaths attributed to these witches occurred even as late as the 1960s.[41]

A distinctive thematic pattern takes shape in many traditional societies of the night witch as a terrifying attacker of children, born and unborn, and secondarily as a threat to reproduction by interfering with pregnancy, fertility, and sexual behavior. Many characteristics do not parallel descriptions of UFO aliens—children are not destroyed by aliens, most notably—but the list of similarities is striking. Like night witches, aliens are associated with lights traveling through the air, enter houses at night, mysteriously disable human abilities to resist, and steal biological materials from children as well as genetic materials from adults. If aliens manifest one adaptation of the night-witch idea, it has proved versatile enough to find still other homes in modern belief. In Peru the "slaughterer" has urbanized into an entrepreneur who peddles body fat to IBM for computer lubricant and children's dismembered body parts to upscale Lima restaurants. Rumors spread in 1988 that uniformed gringos attacked a school and tore out the eyes of children to sell abroad or sought children to mutilate for their organs.[42] One of the best-known figures of current Hispanic folklore in the American Southwest is La Llorona, often identified as the mistress of Hernando Cortez, who killed their children when he returned to Spain and thereafter wandered as a weeping, wailing phantom. She sometimes appears as a ball of fire or an owl, sometimes as a robed figure, and sometimes as an alluring woman who turns to reveal a terrifying face to any young man that accosts her. Her appearance may sicken or kill anyone who sees her, though some narratives cast her as a moral agent who shocks lecherous men into reforming. Her relationship with children is equally ambivalent. She may lure them away or drown them, but she may also admonish careless mothers to watch their children more closely. She embodies many motifs of the night witch but assumes added responsibilities in popular belief as a supernatural agent of justice and morality.[43]

Fifty years ago social scientists took for granted that modernization would spell the end of witchcraft beliefs in Africa.[44] Just the opposite happened. Witchcraft found new footing in urban settings and gained fresh importance in the countryside. Newfound affluence of some Africans amid the continued poverty of their neighbors and the conspicuous, self-serving corruption of some government officials reinforced traditional attributes of the sorcerer as selfish and greedy.[45] Rumors and urban legends have proliferated with the message that people have become commodities, community has collapsed, and the urban environment brings dangers to anyone who pursues its allurements—a message that often embodies old patterns associated with supernatural exploitation of the young. The Mawri of Niger emigrate into Nigeria to work but tell stories of husbands selling their wives and children to Igbo people as food for cannibal feasts, or youths seeking jobs across the border only to fall victim to cannibals and headhunters.[46] In Cameroon wealthy businessmen and government officials acquire a supernatural aura in a recurrent accusation that they turn themselves into boa constrictors and swallow innocent young women.[47] In Sierra Leone politicians supposedly acquire supernatural appeal through potions made from the reproductive organs of children and young women.[48]

The AIDS crisis has driven many Africans to fall back on old answers in the face of a new and overwhelming problem. A wasting disease like AIDS fits the traditional stereotype of supernaturally induced illness. AIDS also strikes the young and vigorous, leaving parents to care for the sick and mourn the dead in fulfillment of expectations that malevolent enemies prey on children. Multiple responses to AIDS have emerged in Zimbabwe: Some people follow traditional belief and accuse marginal people of practicing sorcery, but here too suspicions take a modern turn and point to the successful and affluent.[49] Another traditional belief carried over into a modern setting is the servant-being, a sorcerer's familiar that is sexually promiscuous and favors young, unmarried women. The victims are not fully conscious during the encounter but find evidence for it in the form of body fluids in the morning and nightmares thereafter. These servant-beings collect wealth for their master and spread disease out of innate malevolence.[50] Another understanding of the epidemic blames white Africans for trying to commit genocide so they can take over land and natural resources. AIDS becomes a creation of CIA biological weapons laboratories, an accusation supported by the reluctance of America to provide affordable drugs for treatment.[51] A widespread image has crystallized of greedy, malicious persons with esoteric knowledge who contaminate water and condoms or infect innocent individuals in the guise of providing medical treatment. Even as these conspiracy theories secularize the crisis, they also preserve traditional concepts of evil, demonstrating once again that whether the actors are witches or aliens, their means magical or technological, similar fears and their means of expression underlie the representations.

The history of witchcraft in Europe exemplifies how conceptions of supernatural endangerment of children evolve into new forms yet conserve old patterns. Throughout most of the Middle Ages witchcraft remained individual acts subject to local control.[52] In the fifteenth century various traditions and doctrines coalesced into a conviction that witches posed a vast and urgent threat. The emergent image of the witch portrayed an apostate that willfully rejected Christ and allied with Satan; a practitioner of *maleficium*, or harm done to person or property by supernatural means; an agent of evil with extraordinary powers, such as the ability to fly by night or enter locked houses; and a member of a community that gathered for periodic sabbats to worship the devil, plot future evildoing, engage in orgiastic celebrations, and feast on murdered

children.[53] In this process witchcraft escalated from a limited problem to a cosmic conspiracy, from scattered individual activity to a militant, hierarchical heresy bent on the
destruction of all Christendom.

Parts and pieces of existing traditions united in the conceptions underlying the
great witch hunt of the sixteenth and seventeenth centuries. Traditional supernaturalism already included the night witch; practitioners of *maleficium,* who caused death,
sickness, impotence, or loss of livestock; and Frau Holle, a fertility goddess who flew
on night journeys with a retinue of beautiful women.[54] The nightmarish practices of
witches and a key element of the sabbat fantasy were already common knowledge before the Church assimilated these elements into ecclesiastical demonology. Two further traditions joining in this convergence highlighted witchcraft as a conspiracy and,
incidentally, thrust peril to children into the forefront. One was the Blood Libel, a
claim that Jews kidnapped Christian children and murdered them in religious rituals.
In England the deaths of William of Norwich in 1144 and Hugh of Lincoln in 1255
provoked riots when rumors spread that Jews had tortured and crucified the boys
to mock Christ's passion.[55] The medieval Catholic Church found itself forever beset
by heresies, and their description also came to rely on stereotypical calumnies. In the
second century A.D. rumors circulated that Christians participated in incestuous or-
gies and served up babies cooked in dough. These distortions of the love-feast and
Eucharist were rampant enough to oblige refutations from Tertullian and other early
apologists. Similar rumors had attached to celebrants of Dionysus in pagan Rome and
continued little changed into the Middle Ages. For example, in one account twelfth-
century French Manichaeans supposedly met in secret to have sexual relations with
anyone at hand. A child born from these promiscuous unions was tossed back and
forth through a fire until dead and then burned to ashes. The ashes were mixed in
bread for a blasphemous sacrament.[56]

By the fifteenth century witchcraft had become the ultimate heresy, its reality and
fantastic attributes accepted by the Inquisition and civil authorities. A growing literature systematized the theory and procedure of prosecutions, most famously the "Hammer of Witches," the *Malleus Maleficarum* (1486) of the Dominican monks Henricus
Institoris and Jacob Sprenger. This witch-hunter's manual helped assure that questioning of suspects would confirm the prescribed pattern. What marked witches as worthy
of destruction was their direct opposition to all human goodness. They rejected Christ
for Satan, desecrated sacraments, and harmed neighbors, with the enormity of this
moral inversion explicit in the relationship of witches to sexuality, reproduction, and
children. According to the *Malleus,* where the proper purpose of sex was procreation,

devils snared despondent or lustful individuals with sexual temptations. Demons perverted natural reproduction when the succubus stole semen from men and the incubus impregnated women with the stolen seed. By this breeding program the devil enhanced long-term opportunities to swell his ranks. Witches serving as midwives committed newborns to Satan before baptism, and children became vital ingredients in magical salves and potions—an idea commemorated in the witches of *Macbeth*, who needed a "finger of birth-strangled babe" for their cauldron.[57] The compendium of horrors that comprised the sabbat climaxed as witches cooked and feasted on children, in a ritual that turned the hopefulness of a child's new life into an offering to death, damnation, and evil. By these perversions witches declared their separation from humanity and loyalty to an inimical alien order. Again the current portrayal of aliens does not present anything like a complete inversion of the good, but witchlike characteristics persist of a clandestine secret society menacing mankind, a xenophobic fear of an alien Other, and a superhuman threat to the well-being of children.

Though most current treatments of alien hybrids emphasize the potential danger they might pose, many ancient traditions cultivated a more positive image of supernatural beings creating a hybrid race. Greek mythology recounts the philandering of Zeus as he sires a series of children by human women. Like father like sons, the divine children of Zeus practice similar habits, and this uninhibited behavior sifts downward to the nymphs, satyrs, and other lowlier creatures of the Greek mythological cosmos.[58] The offspring of divine unions are destined to be exceptional. Genesis says that "the sons of God saw the daughters of men that they were fair," and "when the sons of God came in unto the daughters of men, and they bare children unto them, the same became mighty men which were of old, men of renown" (6:1–4). The offspring of Zeus include the superlatively beautiful Helen of Troy and the famous heroes Herakles, Achilles, and Alexander the Great. When the messianic prophecies of Isaiah (11:6) promise that the wolf and the lamb will dwell together "and a little child shall lead them," his image of the son of God as Christ child establishes the innocence of children as the model of salvation for Christian tradition.

Though these children achieve great things on earth, ambivalence surrounds their fate as they incur the enmity of gods and men to meet—or bring—misfortune. Christ is crucified, the Greek demigod heroes must perform labors and die young. Helen's face launches a thousand ships, a long and brutal war, and forces that destroy most of its participants. The mighty men of Genesis are giants in the earth but regarded in a negative light as Nephelim, or "fallen ones," neither human nor angels but the monstrous offspring of illicit unions and destroyed in the Flood. An elaboration of this episode in the apocryphal *Book of Enoch* identifies the fallen angels with the Watchers, those sons of God who violated their trust when they mated with humans and God cast them out of heaven for disobedience.[59]

While liaisons with the gods belonged largely to high literary culture, the common people faced the prospect of less exalted commingling. In widespread traditions humans share the earth with fairylike beings whose actions are sometimes benevolent but often dangerous. Fairies seduce mortals, but the consequences of yielding to temptation are always dire and usually fatal. Mermaids and sirens lure sailors to their doom. The Danish Hulle maiden entrances young men with her beauty and then dances them to death, while the Ganconer, or love-talker, allures young women with his enchanting talk but reveals his evil nature by vanishing when she makes the sign of the cross. Her death soon follows. Even well-intentioned encounters with fairies often end in tragedy as a human returned or rescued from fairyland pines away and dies on account of lost happiness.[60]

Fairies share with aliens a striking lack of reproductive self-sufficiency. To maintain their race, the fairies lure men and women into fairyland, and while the marriage may be a happy one, it becomes permanent because mortals can no longer return to earth once they eat fairy food. Many captives are unwilling victims stolen from their homes and families by raiding fairies.[61] Fairy women cannot easily give birth but require human assistance in a common folk legend known as "Midwife to the Fairies." In one version, a dark man summons the midwife late one night and they seem to fly through the air until they reach a splendid castle. She delivers the baby and rubs it with a salve as instructed but accidentally touches the ointment to her eye, whereupon the castle resolves into a cave, its drapes and trappings nothing more than rags and leaves, and the noble fairies themselves scrawny, ugly creatures.[62] Abduction accounts also describe illusory scenes that dissolve when alien mind control techniques wear off.[63]

A second strategy for replenishing their stock leads fairies to kidnap human infants and carry them off to fairyland. The raiders may hide their theft by leaving behind an animated stock, a stick of wood that gives the illusion of a live infant for several days but soon withers and dies. Another replacement is the changeling, an elderly or sickly fairy left behind so that mortal parents will care for its demanding hunger, perpetual crying, and malevolent mischief.[64] Intermarriage does not entail residence in fairyland when a mortal captures a fairy bride; for instance, if a man hides the feathers of a swan maiden or the sealskin of a selkie, she must remain in human form and usually marries to raise a family.[65] The offspring of these unions are often beautiful, heroic warriors, talented in music and poetry and possessed of magical powers like the ability to read minds or foresee the future. A fairy heritage is not always beneficial, since children born of fairies may be restless and unruly, while at worst they can be monstrous, like the deformed and corrupt sons of Melusine, a fairy version of the lamia, cursed to turn into a snake when exposed to water.[66]

Children serve as victims of witchcraft and as prizes or pawns in fairy traditions, but they reverse these passive roles to become heroes in other contexts. Heaven mounted a counterstrike against the advancing armies of Satan in apparitions of the Virgin Mary, whose frequent choice of children as the primary witnesses and messengers began in the Middle Ages and continued onward to Lourdes in 1858, Fátima in 1917, and Medjugorje in the 1980s. The adolescent Joan of Arc, burned at the stake in 1431 and reviled as a witch in *Henry the Sixth, Part 1* when Shakespeare repeated the English prejudice against her a century and a half after the fact, was revered by the common French people as a divinely inspired savior of her country and fulfillment of the prophecy that a maid of Lorraine would drive out the English invaders.[67] These hopeful roles magnified the renewal inherent in children from personal to cosmic scope and parallel current hopes for supposed Star Children.

Representations of the endangered child, the hybrid child, and the messenger or savior child have endured far beyond their ancient and medieval roots to continue a thriving existence in the modern era, sometimes adapting with little change to different times and places. Nothing seems as inimical to the modern spirit as witch hunts, yet an unsettling facsimile unfolded as recently as the 1980s in a nationwide panic over child sexual abuse and satanic ritual abuse. Several prongs of social concern united in a remarkable example of old threats made new. Incest and child molestation had occupied a back corner of public awareness as unfortunate realities, though expert opinion rated them as thankfully rare. By the early 1980s an academic interest in these crimes began to grow when some clinicians suspected post-traumatic stress disorder (PTSD) as the reason for certain childhood misbehaviors and sexual abuse as the underlying cause.[68] The police took newfound interest in sexual molestation of children and raised public expectations that pedophiles might be active in the community, but these suspicions reached panic proportion once they coalesced into rumors that abuse took place in day care facilities—where else were the children vulnerable?—and a cycle of suspicion and confirmation gained momentum. As abuse became headline news, an epidemic of accusations soon outraged the country from California to North Carolina when parents became alarmed and intensive questioning of youngsters by social worker "experts" confirmed all the worst fears. The horror of each story surpassed its predecessor as seemingly traumatized preschoolers told secrets they had been too scared to reveal and unmasked child care in America as an ongoing nightmare of sexual perversion.

With an aroused public demanding action, cases went to court and dozens of day care workers went to jail.[69]

The day care scandal reinforced a conviction among feminists that sexual abuse was a grossly underestimated social problem. How many women suffered rape, incest, or molestation at some time of life? Official statistics said few, personal experience said many, with the difference attributed to a screen of silence and decorum hiding the truth that all was not right with suburbia. An evolving self-help movement brought women together to discuss their experiences. In this supportive environment many women remembered their abuse quite vividly, but an unexpected second group began to emerge—women with no memory of abuse in their past suddenly experienced flashbacks of traumatic incidents piercing through the facade of a seemingly normal, happy childhood.[70] The notion solidified that many psychological problems of women resulted from girlhood sexual abuse perpetrated mostly by fathers and condoned by mothers. A recovery movement grew out of its self-help predecessors and its bible was *The Courage to Heal*, a best-selling book that guided the reader through a series of steps to discover and overcome this legacy of abuse. In a bid for relief, empowerment, and closure, many adult women went to court accusing bewildered, often elderly parents of molestation, rape, and even murder, revealed with the help of a new cadre of therapists specializing in the retrieval of repressed memories.[71] An academic and polemical literature built a theoretical framework that betrayal by primary caregivers caused girls to dissociate and repress traumatic memories as a necessary adaptation for survival.[72] The publicity of TV talk shows and testimonies of celebrities like actress Roseanne Barr and a former Miss America furthered popular acceptance for recovered memories of childhood sexual abuse.[73]

The conventional crimes of child abusers were heinous enough, but the horror escalated into unconventional and increasingly improbable territory with the discovery of satanic ritual abuse. In 1980 *Michelle Remembers* introduced the public to extraordinary memories recovered by Michelle Smith during therapy with psychiatrist Lawrence Pazder. Michelle told a story of growing up in a secret satanic cult whose membership led ordinary, respectable lives by day but turned into monsters of evil by night as they tortured children like Michelle by imprisonment in a cage full of snakes and rounds of sexual abuse. The Satanists held obscene rituals that included human sacrifice of babies and cannibalism. Her initiation climaxed in a "Feast of the Beast," attended by Satan himself, but she defied him and the cult expelled Michelle and her mother.[74] Too fantastic to gain much credence in 1980, her claims attracted attention of evangelical Christians and eventually the recovered-memory movement. Investigators of day care accusations soon reported similar claims of satanic rituals, and repressed memory therapists heard lurid tales of sadism, murder, and perversion from scores of ritual abuse survivors.[75] Another fear played out between 1982 and 1992 as rumors swept through dozens of communities in the United States and Canada that Satanists intended to kidnap a blond, blue-eyed virgin for human sacrifice. Termed "satanic panic" by sociologist Jeffrey Victor, these outbreaks led to intense local scares as families kept their children indoors and vigilante groups targeted teenagers suspected of practicing witchcraft or Satanism.[76]

In the end this ado was all about nothing. The alleged incidents of day care abuse owed everything to tendentious questioning of impressionable children by alarmed parents and overzealous social workers. The recovered memories of abuse amounted to false memories created by expectations and faulty therapeutic techniques. The tales of satanic rituals turned out to be hoaxes, delusions, and more false memories, with no physical evidence uncovered in spite of diligent searches for bones, secret tunnels, and other artifacts at the reported sites. When they had any basis at all, the satanic panics grew out of innocuous adolescent play without any serious satanic intent. Like the witch hunts of old, the recent abuse panic required the support of authorities to bestow the semblance of credible reality, with therapists, social worker "experts," "cult cops," academic theorists, and ideologically motivated activists replacing inquisitors as the driving force behind the movement. Citizens sufficiently alarmed by expectations of evil no longer noticed the flimsiness of evidence or the patent absurdity of many claims.[77]

Even more striking than the similarity of mechanisms behind the witch hunt and the abuse panic was the similarity of content. The abuse panic seldom adopted overtly supernatural beliefs, but it revived and accepted ideas of an antihuman conspiracy operating in the everyday world yet invisible to all eyes, hidden by repression or masked by the smiling faces of neighbors, trusted caregivers, and even seemingly loving parents. The conspirators were malevolent, numerous, well organized, and given to ritualistic activity. They inverted social norms by engaging in perverted sexual acts with children and confirmed their alien morality by abominable practices like cannibalism or torture of children.[78] A secularizing process recast witches and demons as perverts and cultists, but the roles remained the same. The idiom modernized, but thematic expressions familiar since ancient times, repeated the fear of inhuman monsters who threaten society with subversion and children with kidnap, physical harm, and loss of purity. The similarities to accounts of alien abductions are obvious, and many psychologists dismiss abductions as nothing more than another example of false memories created by leading questions and hypnosis, another case of emotional panic with an imaginary origin.

The recent abuse panic offers an exemplary case of old themes renewed in modern guise, but other, less complete instances demonstrate that the tendency to imagine some events in terms of traditional evil is continual rather than haphazard, even without recourse to extraterrestrials. Representations of kidnapping have readily absorbed notions of conspiracy and monstrous inversion of behavior. In 1750 mobs in Paris attacked police officers on the suspicion that they kidnapped children to sell for labor in the colonies, but further accusations that the king bathed in the blood of murdered children returned this panic to the older realm of satanic practices.[79] The press quickly implicated organized crime in the kidnap and death of Charles A. Lindbergh's son in 1932. Wonder over how the kidnapper could enter the house and steal the child while the parents and servants were at home introduced an almost magical element into the story, but apprehension of a German immigrant as the culprit aligned the crime with down-to-earth prejudices of the time and reinforced images of some foreigners as inhuman aliens. Eight years earlier, Nathan Leopold and Richard Loeb, two wealthy, brilliant, well-educated young men, kidnapped and murdered a fourteen-year-old boy for no apparent reason other than to see if they could get away with it. As the plot unraveled, it reimaged kidnapping as a senseless and random crime that could strike at anyone. It portrayed the perpetrators as cold, emotionless, and insane and introduced sexual perversion as attendant behavior.[80]

An alarm over "alien" invasions as threats to racial and cultural purity echoes through much of American history. Martin Scorsese's film *The Gangs of New York* (2002) depicts violent conflict between immigrants and "American-born" groups prior to the Civil War. Despite no European American being long off the boat, supporters of a powerful nativist movement resisted Irish newcomers in the 1830s and 1840s as rumors abounded that the Catholic Church conspired to overthrow the American government.[81] Accusations reminiscent of the witchcraft era revived in scurrilous publications like *The Awful Disclosures of Maria Monk* (1836), the purported confession of a young escapee from a Montreal nunnery who fed prejudicial hatreds with tales that priests tortured and sexually abused the captive nuns then murdered the resulting babies in blasphemous rituals.[82] New waves of immigration inflamed fears that Italians, Jews, and Eastern Europeans were "not the stuff of which Americans can be made" and diluted or corrupted the virtue of Anglo-Saxon stock.[83] A recurrent pattern of racial stereotypes cast significant "Others" as both physical and sexual dangers—in portrayals of Indians as implacable enemies and savage abusers of captive white women; in pulp fictions treating the "Yellow Peril" of Asian temptresses, invasions from the East, and super-villains like Sax Rohmer's Fu Manchu; and in racist configurations of African American men as barbarous in slave rebellions or riots and ever lustful for white women, so that only the vigilance of a chivalrous order like the Ku Klux Klan stood between the white race and destruction. Laws against miscegenation have persisted until recent decades, and the image of African American men as criminal and violent still thrives in popular entertainment.[84]

Misgivings about foreign aliens reunited with subversion and innocence imperiled in the moral panic over white slavery. The subject excited the social conscience in Britain and America during the late nineteenth and early twentieth centuries, a time when prostitution was rampant and most of the women involved were immigrants or the poor; but their plight roused far less public indignation than allegations that criminals lured American-born teenage girls from farms and small towns to the brothels of large cities. A stereotypical story developed of a dapper city man who strikes up an acquaintance with an innocent girl, overwhelms her with his charm, and then concludes the whirlwind romance with a proposal of marriage. Once she elopes with him to the city, the man drugs her with knockout drops or opium, and she wakens to find herself a fallen woman, raped and sold into a house where she is forced to work with little hope of escape and destined to die of disease in a few years. The emotional tone intensified by identification of the girls as respectable Anglo-Saxons, while the procurers were foreigners—Jewish, French, or Italian.[85]

White slavery looks in retrospect like a quaint melodrama of its time. Genuine cases existed, but the confessions that fed literature, early movies, and reform crusades owed more to myth than to reality. At the same time it was an effective myth, one that piled imaginative excess onto sordid reality to enhance shock value. Much of the story pattern is familiar territory. The hidden conspiracy became an early instance of organized crime, with a supposed interstate network of traffickers procuring thousands of girls a year with such efficiency that the public was none the wiser. Narcotics replaced magical spells as the means to overcome free will and·moral judgment. The girls were always pure and helpless victims, the villains alien in origin and values, the authorities often complicit in the crimes. Conflict between urban and rural values, tension between newcomers and old-stock Americans, risks of newfound mobility versus the security of a closed community sustained concerns that white slavery posed a real and imminent danger.

The theme of young people in sexual danger holds an important though secondary place in witchcraft beliefs, but shifts to the heart of modern fears. Recurrent alarms have clamored over teenage runaways or immigrants from Asia, Eastern Europe, and Latin America coerced into prostitution. Accusations that religious cults brainwash vulnerable youths into a life of sexual slavery arise time and again. Urban legends, always close·to the pulse of societal fears, warn that in this world of senseless violence, Halloween apples contain razor blades, date-rape drugs have the same effects as the white slaver's knockout drops, and boys risk castration if they enter a public toilet alone. The mutilations occur as an initiation rite for black or Hispanic gang members, while the victims are white and store owners conspire with law enforcement to suppress negative publicity from these atrocities.[86] Here we find sexual endangerment and destruction of children, conflict of "us" versus a villainous "them," and a conspiracy to hide the truth, all condensed into a single miniature narrative.

Young minds as well as young bodies risk victimization in the historical cavalcade of fears. First in 1919–1920, then again in the early 1950s, a Red Scare shook America with alarms that this alien ideology inimical to individualism and economic success had infiltrated the country. Workers might convert out of misconceived self-interest, but young people, especially students and intellectuals, were particularly vulnerable to deceptive Communist indoctrination. It supposedly twisted the mind with subtle lies and almost magically alluring propaganda to transform the victim from a free-thinking citizen into the robotic slave of a foreign enemy.[87] Science fiction movies of the 1950s echoed fears of Communist mind control, most vividly *Invasion of the Body Snatchers* (1956), where seeds from space replace one person after another with crafty, soulless imitations bent on taking over the world. In one chilling scene, a family now human only in appearance takes a pod to place in the baby's cradle. "No more crying, no more tears," says the emotionless voice; but without emotion, love, or individuality, the result is no more humanity.

A no less heartfelt struggle over "traditional values" targets mass entertainment as responsible for the erosion of morals, manners, and faith among the young. One of the more implausible censorship crusades took aim at comic books. They became the reading material of choice for children, teenagers, and young servicemen during the late 1940s and early 1950s, at the same time juvenile delinquency grew as a social concern. Assumptions of a causal connection soon followed. The chief crusader was psychiatrist Fredric Wertham, whose studies on the negative effects of segregation were influential in the celebrated 1954 desegregation decision of the Supreme Court. He campaigned for legislation to impose stringent standards on the content of comics and authored a book with the revealing title of *Seduction of the Innocent* (1954), where he implicated comics in juvenile crime, disrespect for authority, sexual deviance, and habits of deception, since children exchanged and read undesirable comics in secret.[88] Others blamed comics for the susceptibility of American POWs in Korea to Communist brainwashing and for a coming generation of illiteracy, since even comics unobjectionable in content were bad reading that forced out the good.[89] An undeniably lurid segment of the industry emphasized crime, violence, bondage, and gory horror; but the subtler offense of comics lay in their providing a nascent youth culture with alternatives to the obedient mores and triumphant, all's-fine-with-America spirit of the times. Critics pointed to this contrariness as reason to fear that comics threatened nothing less than the downfall of the nation. Who would have imagined that the fifth Horseman of the Apocalypse was Donald Duck?

Closer in spirit to fears associated with UFOs is a perception that technology threatens children. A popular movement attributes increases in children's autism, asthma, birth defects, and cancer to contamination of food, water, and air by industry and government. The culprits are aware of the danger but conceal the truth to protect profits, paralleling the conspiracy theories so prominent in ufology. When scientific evidence fails to support the assertions of the movement, its members question the motives of the scientists to demonstrate that above all else, distrust is epidemic.[90] Whether the provocation is Dr. Frankenstein's experiments or eugenics, the misgivings that surround artificial intervention into life and reproduction usually lead authors to portray the worst. In *Alraune* (1911), a decadent novel by the Austrian Hanns Heinz Ewers, an amoral scientist inseminates a prostitute with semen from an executed criminal. The scientist raises the baby girl into a beautiful but (literally) soulless young woman who destroys every man close to her. Heredity is destiny in this novel, and the artificial circumstances of the girl's begetting assure evil results.[91] In vitro fertilization led to outcries as unnatural, unethical, and sure to do harm, and though it has now entered standard medical procedure, the battle lines have re-formed around human cloning and fears that genetic manipulation will lead to "designer babies" with, once again, predictions of ominous consequences for individual and social well-being.[92]

The space children find an especially inviting playground in science fiction. Alien hybrids become a source of horror in H. P. Lovecraft's "The Shadow over Innsmouth" (1936), a story of the strange inhabitants of a Massachusetts town that turn out to be loathsome amphibious descendants of humans and an aquatic elder race seeking to regain dominance of the earth. In the movie *I Married a Monster from Outer Space* (1958), refugees from a destroyed planet need human women to replenish their species and take over the bodies of human men. When an alien's wife learns the truth, she asks, "But what kind of children?" "Our kind," her husband answers, though heroic humans destroy the invaders before their plot succeeds. An extraterrestrial energy field causes everyone in the *Village of the Damned* (1960) to fall unconscious for several hours. Soon after this "time out," every woman of child-bearing age in the village discovers that she is pregnant, and the children are born similar, blond and blue-eyed and possessed of extraordinary powers. The children can read and control minds and use this power to punish or kill any human that threatens them. Emotionless and prone to walk in lockstep, they are nearly ready to disperse and take over the world when their teacher blows them up.

In fiction not all hybrids are sinister, and children assume a favorable role as intermediaries between earthlings and extraterrestrials. A short novel by H. G. Wells, *Star-Begotten* (1937), includes almost every element that would reappear in recent Star Children speculations. While a man awaited the birth of his first child, he noted that more children were born exceptional and gifted than in the past. A conversation led him to imagine that Martians bombarded the earth with cosmic rays intended to induce genetic mutations in humans, not just random change but progressively controlled alterations that "Martianized" humanity. In time Martian mind would be the dominant mind on earth. But were these invaders evil, ugly creatures bent on destroying the human essence? His attitude changed for the better when he saw that his son was normal and beautiful. If these star-begotten children were arriving in increasing numbers, they would surely sense some kinship and work together, not as agents of malevolence but with reason and goodness of heart. They would occupy skilled and educated positions in society and use those opportunities to further the common good, perhaps by sabotaging weapons or making certain that surgery on a dictator failed; but quietly, gradually, they would supplant the negative actions and inclinations of mankind with superior Martianized qualities and bring a Golden Age.[93]

Though the list of comparisons is long, some established cultural portrayals of children are rare or absent from the UFO literature. For example, aliens do not kill, dismember, eat, or retain their young captives forever. The accusing child so prominent in the Salem witch trials of 1692 and the recent day care furor has no equivalent. Neither do abduction accounts cultivate a concept of the evil child, so popular in movies like *Rosemary's Baby* (1968) and *The Omen* (1976), where offspring of the devil are destined to become the Antichrist, or *The Ring* (2002) and *The Grudge* (2004), where the supernatural threat is the malevolent ghost of a child. Little in the accounts of human encounters with aliens suggests demonic possession, a long belief tradition that finds modern expression in *The Exorcist* (1973), where an evil spirit invades a twelve-year-old girl. UFO accounts have not picked up on the idea of child heroes with supernatural powers, now popular thanks to Harry Potter and his fellow students of wizardry or to Buffy the Vampire Slayer, one of a series of Chosen Ones who discovers at age fifteen that her destiny is to defend the world from evil beings. Whether these possibilities have not yet appealed to fantasy or the UFO experience offers them no opportunity to take root, their omission demonstrates that UFO narratives are not comprehensive copies of cultural models but maintain some degree of independence.

Nevertheless, a comparative study musters enough likenesses to sustain two general conclusions: (1) The themes of child as victim endangered by an alien power, child as an ambiguous blend of this world and some otherworld, and child as heavenly herald

or agent of a better future persist from age to age; and (2) similar means to express
these themes recur despite intervening historical and cultural changes. The similarity
is often partial or diffuse, strong but one-dimensional in the case of a vast conspiracy
behind both satanic witchcraft and modern-day sicknesses of children, no more than
a faint echo in parallels between the supernatural means of night witches and the remarkable subtlety attributed to real-life kidnappers. On the other hand, a new representation may re-create the past in close detail, like the striking parallels between the
child abuse/satanic ritual abuse panic of the 1980s–1990s and the witch hunts of the
Reformation era. The quality and vigor of a representation appears independent of its
ontological status. The ritual abuse panic achieved thematic richness, yet the episode
was complete make-believe, a perfect storm of ideology, promotion, belief, credulity,
and error with tragic consequences but no evidence for any basis in reality beyond a
few peripheral instances of teenagers playing at devil worship or trying to organize an
orgy. At the same time, sexual predators are all too real. News reports of kidnappers
and mothers who murder their children leave the public aghast with wonder if there is
any limit to inhuman behavior. Truth as well as fantasy can provide a foundation for
the growth of stereotypical narratives.

A third conclusion is that UFO narratives channel into these same currents of thematic tradition. Comparison of UFO abduction accounts with witchcraft, fairy, child
abuse, and the other types of cultural texts discussed above reveals an unmistakable
pattern of broad similarities in the roles of children:

Witches belong to the realm of hell, fairies to the otherworld, child molesters to practices beyond the human pale. White slavers are foreigners.	UFO occupants are nonhuman beings from another planet.
Witches and fairies have supernatural powers.	Aliens have "magical" technology.
Witches and Satanists steal children; fairies kidnap children.	Aliens abduct children.
Witches kill and eat children; ritual abusers torture, molest, and sacrifice children.	Aliens examine children with strange machinery.
Witches blight reproduction; fairies are unable to reproduce.	Aliens come from a dying planet and have lost the power to reproduce.
Satanists and abusers sexually molest children.	Aliens examine genitalia at puberty or before.
Demons steal semen and breed children for Satan; fairies replenish the race with stolen human children and interbreed with mortals.	Aliens extract eggs and sperm to create hybrids.
Demon-bred children are prone to evil; clones are soulless.	Hybrids are ultimately alien in mind.

Fairy hybrids and offspring of gods have special powers.	Star Children have psychic and spiritual powers; abductees return with enhanced sensitivities.
The Virgin Mary gives children messages to save the world.	Abductees and Star Children receive messages and have altered consciousness.
Witches and Satanists comprise a secret society; fairies belong to a "secret commonwealth"; white slaving is a form of organized crime.	Aliens operate in secret on a vast scale and act in an orderly, purposeful, and efficient manner.
Witches conspire against human well-being; Satanists and slavers deliberately transgress the human moral order; fairies are often harmful; and scientists are amoral or cold-blooded.	Aliens serve their own purposes without regard for mankind and treat captives like guinea pigs.
Witches help Satan dominate the world; moneyed interests and politicians collude to control the world without regard for human welfare.	Hybridization program aims at world dominion?

In addition to these larger thematic parallels, the various stories share some specific motifs as well:

Witches and fairy troops fly by night and carry off children through the air.	UFO abductions often occur at night. Aliens fly in UFOs and float or levitate captives.
Witches and fairies enter houses magically.	Aliens enter houses through closed doors.
Witches' spells and powders, fairies' glamours, white slavers' drugs, and Satanists' tricks create illusions and control the minds of victims; abuse causes traumatic repression of memory.	Aliens block memories, control thoughts, show illusory scenes.
Witches appear as ball of light; fairies are luminous.	Light from UFO may precede abduction.
Witches take on the form of an owl.	Owls serve as screen memory for alien.
Bruises or marks show where a witch has attacked.	Cut or scoop marks show where aliens have taken a blood or skin sample.
Headaches, nausea, nightmares, and fear follow witch attack and ritual abuse.	Abductees return with nosebleeds, thirst, nausea, anxiety, nightmares, and PTSD.

Even if the match falls short of a perfect fit, treatments of children in UFO accounts revisit an impressive array of themes and motifs common in traditional narratives of otherworldly contact. Old forms give way to new circumstances and concepts, but the changes are superficial because the substitutes serve as close functional equivalents. UFO aliens step in for night witches, fairies, demons, foreigners, Communists, and satanic day care workers, the latest actors to endanger or elevate, mislead or save children in roles that differ in little more than adaptation to the prevailing historical context. Aliens serve as supernatural beings for an age when ghosts and fairies have gone out of fashion. Alien super-science replaces magic with results that are equally astounding and inexplicable. The costumes and names may modernize, but audiences hear the same thematic refrains whenever children meet otherworldly beings.

This case study shows that themes and motifs concerning children in UFO narratives do not need UFOs to exist. These widespread story elements have more to do with the way humans think than with any physical reality that they think about. In this narrow sense, the psychosocial proponents are right, but cultural and psychological contributions may help explain a story yet say little about its underlying experiences. No winner takes all in this dispute because there is no winner. The literalists must accept that the Space Children have playmates with obvious cultural affinities; psychosocial proponents must acknowledge that the stories sometimes have a reality or two behind them. The likeness of UFO representations to cultural sources proves nothing for or against a UFO phenomenon, only that whether the theme is large or small, cultural models provide meanings for an experience and ways to communicate it to others. A full understanding requires consideration of the cooperative interplay of both culture and experience.

CHAPTER SIX

Secret Worlds and Promised Lands

And I saw a new heaven and a new earth; for the first heaven and the
first earth were passed away; and there was no more sea.... And God
shall wipe away all tears from their eyes; and there shall be no more
death, neither sorrow, nor crying, neither shall there be any more pain:
for the former things are passed away.
—Revelation 21:1–4

There shall not be left here one stone upon another, that shall not be
thrown down.... For nation shall rise against nation ... and there
shall be famines, and pestilences, and earthquakes, in divers places.
... Immediately after the tribulation of those days shall the sun be
darkened, and the moon shall not give her light, and the stars shall fall
from heaven, and the powers of the heavens shall be shaken.
—Matthew 24:2, 7, 29

It's the end of the world as we know it (and I feel fine).
—R.E.M.

Dickens characterized the extraordinary era of the French Revolution as the best
of times and the worst of times. Even in ordinary times every uncertain prospect or
changing situation seems to undergo a trial by hope and fear, as though no possibility passes through human thinking without stretching to the imaginary extremes of
promise and peril. UFOs have a predictable rendezvous with this exploratory urge. On
the one hand, they are a bad dream come true, threatening a war of the worlds or malevolent takeover of our minds and genes, clues to a world of dark secrets and sinister
conspiracies. On the other hand, they answer our prayers, bringing Space Brothers to

save us from ourselves or sages to guide us from materialism to cosmic consciousness. At the very least UFOs represent an unknown quantity. They arouse concern with the possibility that the larger universe has shouldered in to make a difference for better or worse in our earthly condition, and where concerns lie, imagination is bound to follow. Where imagination heads does not remain a matter of chance. Mythic patterns have received UFOs, lent them form and expression, and connected them with networks of human meaning. This connection relates UFOs to other threats and promises throughout history so that a measure of familiarity replaces the mystery of UFOs, though once again the price of understanding through the myth is a loss of individuality for the phenomenon.

Traditions of Hope and Fear

Whether as memories of a lost past, judgments of the present situation, or previews of the future, visions of optimistic and pessimistic possibilities stand out for sheer variety in worldwide traditions of folklore, religion, and mythology. These established patterns facilitate a quick rewrite of new events in mythic terms, and some of the prominent examples deserve a quick review.

Heaven and Hell.—The fate of the dead embodies the most familiar opposition between best and worst. In tomb paintings of the heavenly Nile the Egyptian dead carry on with commonplace agricultural activities, but even where little dichotomy separates life from afterlife, abundance and recreation prevail over toil.[1] The ancient Greeks contrasted the beauty of Elysium with the dank underworld of Hades, while conditions of the future life reach their extremes when rewards or punishments for the dead balance the books for injustices in earthly life. The blessed Christian spends eternity rapt in adoration, and the Buddhist achieves the nothingness of nirvana, though popular religion favors more human, less otherworldly rewards, like blissful existence in countless Buddha-lands, the attendance of Houris in the Muslim afterlife, or the caricature of harp-strumming angels in Christian heaven. If superlatives of happiness await the righteous, the sinner faces superlatives of everlasting misery as troops of demons, like overzealous recreation directors on a hellish cruise ship, smother their guest with unwelcome attention. Sacred traditions of heaven and hell oppose bliss and misery with the starkest possible contrast.

Paradise and Wilderness.—A place on earth reflects heaven in the earthly paradise of Eden or the Hesperides, both gardenlike scenes of beauty where inhabitants live without effort or hardship in innocent harmony with nature and God. Paradise may be a time as well as a place, an idyllic Golden Age when sickness and death are unknown until some human error or transgression ends the good life. Forced into the "real" world, fallen humans enter a rough, barren wilderness full of wild animals and eke out a living by the sweat of their brows from recalcitrant soil. Death, sickness, and pain become the new realities, hunger, privation, and sorrow the new constant companions of the human condition. An understandable yearning to recover paradise occupies the folk legends of fairyland, like Tir Nan Og, the Land of the Living in Irish folklore, where the landscape is always fruitful, dancing and merrymaking fill the hours, and no one ever ages. Medieval travelers sought paradise in faraway places, and early explorers of the New World thought they had found it—Columbus claimed to discover one of the four rivers of Eden, while his successors pursued treasures in an enduring quest to escape the hardship and finitude of everyday human existence.[2]

Dreams of ideal happiness adapt to the wishes of the dreamers in medieval visions of the Land of Cockaigne, a poor man's paradise of effortless abundance. Here pastries shingle the houses and pigs and geese walk around already cooked, with knives stuck in their flesh so that idle inhabitants can cut off a slice without having to stir from the shady spot where they doze.[3] What made Cockaigne paradisiacal was its imaginary release from want at a time when hunger was a recurrent reality. In an age when local success for the agricultural season determined feast or famine, the possibility that a well-fed man today could be a hungry man tomorrow never slipped far out of mind. The Four Horsemen of the Apocalypse—war, famine, pestilence, and death—haunted the imagination as ever-present threats to human happiness.

Similar ideas of effortless plenty regroup in the song of "The Big Rock-Candy Mountain," where hobos go boating in a lake of stew, cigarettes grow on trees, and jails are made of tin. Here is no dream of fabulous wealth, just a comic turnaround of realities so that nature provides for simple pleasures while threats of labor and the law dissolve into harmless caricatures.[4] America has embodied opportunity for generations of immigrants, a promised land of beginnings and possibilities where gold once was free for the taking and boundless acres were available at little or no cost. A song from the 1850s called on immigrants to flock in: "Our lands they are broad enough, don't be alarmed, For Uncle Sam is rich enough to give us all a farm." To own land was wealth in itself for many Europeans, and America promised them an attainable paradise, one they could literally help carve out of the wilderness.[5]

Utopia and Dystopia.—Too restless to wait for heaven, too homebound to comb the globe for paradise, humans try time and again to reinvent their own society from the bottom up according to some model of the ideal. When Thomas More imagined a perfect society with all property held in common and everyone equal under the law in his 1516 book, *Utopia,* he planted the seed of a literary genre destined to sprout branches in philosophy, political science, and fiction, especially science fiction.[6]

The utopian society is achievable, at least in principle. It does not require super-natural abundance from nature but cooperation of humans for the common good, an advance of wisdom, beneficence, and justice to ameliorate natural and man-made hard-ships.[7] One feature typical of most utopias is a sense of deliberate break with the past to pursue a new adventure in society building. The early Christians held goods in com-mon and cared for one another as fellows in a community of faith, and the patriots of the American Revolution sought to create a "new order for the ages" wherein liberty and the will of the people prevailed.[8] Efforts to establish utopian societies flourished in the nineteenth century. Some were based on Charles Fourier's efforts to reinvent social relationships along rational lines; others were founded on religion, such as the commu-nal sect of the Shakers. Robert Owen began New Harmony, an experimental society where workers were partners rather than laborers as a practical demonstration that the dehumanizing tendencies of industrialization were not inevitable.[9]

With its literal meaning of "no place," "utopia" hints that human cooperativeness is perhaps as elusive as the obliging indulgence of nature. The closely associated term "eutopia"—"good place"—has an unsettling way of squaring off against its opposite, "dystopia," or "bad place," in literature and history.[10] The French Revolution began with high ideals to overthrow the old regime and replace it with an Enlightenment republic, but the guillotine cut short such idealism. Karl Marx envisioned a revolution in society to abolish both wealth and poverty, with all property shared and production dedicated to the satisfaction of human needs. In time the political state and class divisions would dissolve and human consciousness itself would transform so that everyone would work for the common good as a natural goal. The Russian Revolution opened the way for the great Communist experiment, but its realization required force-fitting all people into a single predetermined mold. Not only did the experiment fail to reach Marx's ideal as people showed little enthusiasm to work without personal reward, but efforts to confine human diversity to the requirements of the plan led with almost tragic fatal-ism to a brutal totalitarian nightmare.[11]

The road to utopia sometimes takes an inner route when thinkers map a course of individual and cultural change. The perfectibility of man has endured as a philosophi-cal theme,[12] and this idea that innate potential for moral goodness and rational thought can eventually win out against baser human nature persists in the New Age hope for a better world through revolution in consciousness. A counterbalance for such plans meets them with fears of brainwashing, thought control, and regimentation, such as George Orwell depicted in *1984,* where Big Brother is always watching, the thought police enforce conformity, and government control is so absolute it oppresses the human spirit almost to extinction.

Millennium and Doomsday.—Wouldn't it be wonderful if a miraculous hand swept away the miseries of the world and righted all its wrongs? Rational debate centers on what kind of tomorrow human effort can invent, but a more heartfelt speculation imagines a sudden, total, supernatural reinvention of the world. The most familiar example is the millennium, a prophetic promise in the Book of Revelation that Christ will return to reign on earth for a thousand years. During this time Satan will languish bound in hell while all martyred Christians return to life and earth is a righteous paradise. Countless millenarian movements have opposed chaotic realities with expectations of a paradisiacal future. The cargo cults of Melanesia gave natives a mythic explanation for why they lacked the marvelous material goods brought by foreigners and a way to correct this injustice by ritual magic. Natives destroyed their own material goods to oblige the gods to provide Western products in the "Vailala Madness" episodes of the 1920s, then built landing fields to lure airplanes from heaven laden with the desired cargo after World War II. Expectations often extended to an inversion of reality. Dead ancestors returned to life, yams sprouted on trees, and coconuts grew underground.[13] The Ghost Dance of the Plains Indians lasted from 1870 until 1890 as traditional nomadic, hunting culture broke down under pressure from whites migrating westward and ceremonial dancing became the focus of hope for renewal. This ritual promised to protect warriors from soldiers' bullets, to bring back the buffalo and resurrect the dead—in short, to restore a way of life that had vanished within the lifetime of the dancers.[14] Even before Europeans arrived in Brazil, the natives repeatedly followed prophets on a migratory journey to find the Land-without-Evil. As many as 60,000 people at a time abandoned their homes to pursue this moral and physical paradise, and the trek could cover thousands of miles from the Atlantic coast to the Amazon headwaters in Peru. Few stayed the course, fewer survived the ordeal, but the hope endured.[15]

The Judeo-Christian form of millennial prophecy has roots dating back to about 1500 B.C., when the Iranian prophet Zoroaster was born into a world considered static and changeless from its creation but beset by demonic forces and human evil. Zoroaster's solution envisioned a dynamic cosmos headed toward a great battle, when the present world would end, but good would triumph over evil and a perfected cosmos would abide forever.[16] The end of the world has secularized in recent times and laid more emphasis on fear than hope. Camille Flammarion portrayed the astronomer's chosen scenarios—the aging earth could dry up and lose its atmosphere, like Mars; it could be exposed to creeping cold as the sun burns out; it could be incinerated by an explosion of the sun; or it could be destroyed by impact with a comet or an asteroid.[17] The favored with-a-bang-not-a-whimper finale in the 1950s was nuclear holocaust. Nevil Shute's novel, *On the Beach* (filmed in 1958), treats human extinction by nuclear war as the drifting fatal cloud of radiation from the northern hemisphere gradually covers the last human enclaves in Australia. The final scenes of wind-swept, lifeless streets and a tattered banner reading, "There's still time, brother," close the movie with indelible chilling images.

Apocalyptophilia Now!

Far from relics of the past, millenarian expectations maintain an ongoing vitality as they lend meaning to events and purpose to actions. An effort to understand the cross-cultural appearance of millennialism comes from anthropologist Anthony F. C. Wallace, who argues that when extraordinary stresses overwhelm established cultural coping techniques, a revitalization movement may arise to create a new collective un-derstanding of how all the cultural parts fit together. This adaptation reshapes the cul-ture into a way of life once again able to satisfy individual needs.[18] The effort may or may not appeal to supernatural agents and miraculous events, but inversions of present reality, yearning for a new world of eternal perfection, and a corollary fear that the pres-ent world will end in cataclysm often figure into the vision. A sense that things have fallen apart and that worse is yet to come is hardly rare; common too is recourse to established symbolic meanings of millennial mythology for a response. One instance of falling back on traditional patterns is the contemporary interest in apocalyptic proph-ecy, a movement that qualifies as one of the most significant religious trends in the United States since World War II.[19] In another example, Tolstoy opens *War and Peace* with a salon-room conversation that identifies Napoleon with the Antichrist. Later generations bestowed the same epithet on Hitler and Soviet leaders, even Mikhail Gorbachev, in testimony to the persistence of a stock apocalyptic idea even when the attribution is more inept than apt.[20]

Millenarian ideas provide templates of meaning and purpose for nations as well as individuals. The Nazis drew a deliberate parallel with the millennial myth by designat-ing their regime the "Thousand-Year Reich," and Hitler served as a messiah in every-thing but name as the one leader able to restore order to a chaotic Germany. To save the Aryan race and ensure the triumph of German culture, he pursued an apocalyptic war and Holocaust to cleanse the world of evil enemies like Jews and Bolsheviks. Enough people bought into the millenarian ideals of Nazism to devote themselves to bringing about its promise whatever the cost.[21] For their part, Soviet Communists acted with a sense of messianic mission to spread their revolution worldwide and bring about a proletarian millennium.[22]

Biblical millennialism is woven deep into the fabric of American history according to Pepperdine University professor of religion Richard T. Hughes, who delineates a series of national myths with religious roots that shape an American sense of identity and purpose. The Puritans conceived of America as a chosen nation holding a special covenant with God; the second Great Awakening affirmed America as a Christian nation, where the people lived in accordance with Christ's teaching and received divine blessing for their righteousness. The Enlightenment spirit of the Revolution emphasized America as nature's nation, where human rights derived from natural law and the land itself provided for a pure and Edenlike new beginning. A combination of these myths, that Americans were chosen and righteous and born in natural truth, gave rise to the idea of America as the millennial nation, whose mission was to spread liberty and democracy and redeem a fallen world. One famous offshoot of this sense of mission was Manifest Destiny, a doctrine that white Americans had both a right and duty to occupy the continent. These same myths converged to reinforce capitalism by equating economic success with divine approval, and this national mythology continues, he argues, in an ongoing faith in America as the innocent nation, its actions always aimed toward the ultimate benefit of mankind and deserving the love of all peoples for this benevolence.[23]

Two divergent interpretations of the Christian millennium have influenced both thought and action in American history. A postmillennialist tradition foresees gradual improvement through human efforts at moral and social betterment, leading to a perfected world that Christ then returns to rule. This optimistic view with a role for human action has motivated reformers and progressives to strive for social uplift through good works and legislation. The opposing view is premillennialism, a pessimistic view that the human condition can only worsen until Christ intervenes to clean up the mess with fire and thunder. In this thoroughly fatalistic version appealing to biblical literalists, no human effort can alter the preordained course spelled out in biblical prophecy, and the only hope of salvation lies in God's grace. Hal Lindsey plotted the milestones on the road to Armageddon in his best-selling book, *The Late Great Planet Earth* (1970), and its successors, replacing the symbolic language of apocalyptic prophecy with corresponding current events so that the birth of Israel as a Jewish state, invention of nuclear weapons, and formation of the European Common Market mark significant stages in the countdown to the end. Fundamentalist leaders Pat Robertson and Jerry Falwell identified the 9/11 terrorist attacks as examples of Old Testament punishment, part of an expected pattern of God's retribution for a once-righteous nation that sinks deeper into sin as the apocalypse approaches.[24] Evangelicals continue to round up social trends, rumors, and urban legends to confirm that the world stays its course for biblical calamity.[25]

Millennial and apocalyptic patterns of thought have spread beyond religious frontiers by adapting to secular issues in outer specifics while holding true to the inner form. Participants in the ecology movement share the fear of a coming ecocatastrophe but divide their strategies in a manner suggestive of the premillennial/postmillennial conflict. Mainstream environmentalists participate in a rationalist social movement by relying on scientific evidence and consensus building to seek gradual reform through established channels of protest or political and legal action. These people trust that the future has yet to be written and human effort can avert disaster. Extreme environmentalists shun reform as doomed to fail and look forward to the advent of a primitive paradise after civilization collapses. Martin W. Lewis, professor at the Duke University School of the Environment, sums up the vigorous millenarian urge of radical environmentalism, or "deep ecology," to transform earth and humanity into a utopian ideal:

> Radical environmentalists would have us abandon urban, industrial, capitalist civilization and return to the earth. Here our modern social maladies will be healed as we find true harmony between land and life. The call is for a simpler existence and a more direct relationship between humanity and nature, one in which natural landscapes are transformed by human agency as little as possible. People must never be so arrogant as to "manage" nature; rather, nature should always be allowed to exemplify its own essential harmonies.[26]

The focus for much millenarian attention since World War II has been the government, and changing popular attitudes toward it are particularly relevant for the development of thinking about UFOs. During the cold war years the standoff between the United States and the Soviet Union assumed proportions of a Manichaean conflict between the good and the wholly evil, with a real prospect of nuclear apocalypse as the outcome and danger that the enemy would subvert the nation through propaganda or brainwashing. In this big issue the government was on our side. However clumsy or misguided it may have been at times, government still served the best interests of its citizens. Reflecting this attitude was the favorable representation of authority figures in 1950s science-fiction movies, where the military mounted heroic defense, scientists worked for the common good, and industry joined with government to defeat the alien invaders, themselves transparent proxies for a real-world Communist enemy.[27]

A great disillusionment set in as Vietnam, Watergate, and the environmental movement undercut trust in government and the other figures of authority. They had now turned against us, dedicated to their own interests, in collusion to deceive the public while they increased their own profits and power. This emerging internal enemy has also tended toward the form of a familiar devil. When President George H. W. Bush described the 1991 war with Iraq as part of an effort to build a "new world order," he intended a hopeful image of peace and democracy without aggressive dictators, but suspicious listeners heard a very different message. For them this "order" meant our national leaders had betrayed America to some foreign, or more properly, some ultranational power, sold out freedom for socialism and Christianity for secular humanism.[28] This idea repeats an age-old belief that unseen worlds coexist with our own, whether they are the secret commonwealth of fairies or the hidden community of witches, the armies of Antichrist or the invisible empire of the Ku Klux Klan, Jewish bankers or the international Communist conspiracy. The imagination has re-created a powerful and malevolent secret society over and over as a threat to cherished values. The plots of the clandestine powers today enter the realm of the improbable, as did their ancestors, with rumors that the government plans mass thought control by inserting microchips into everyone, or with assertions that the United Nations has thousands of foreign troops stationed around the country.[29]

The most popular understanding of how these shadowy cabals exercise control takes the form of conspiracy theories. A recent survey of conspiracies with the largest and most persistent followings includes the 9/11 terrorist attacks (were they carried out by domestic government agents?), the John F. Kennedy assassination (another inside job, or the work of organized crime?), the moon landings (a NASA hoax?), the death of Princess Diana (was she murdered to prevent her marriage to a Muslim?), and the AIDS epidemic (was the virus created in a laboratory?).[30] The examples share a common thread that some powerful agency manipulates the truth to deceive the public and further a hidden agenda. Michael Barkun, professor of political science at Syracuse University, delineates three major postulates in the logic of conspiracy belief: Nothing happens by accident, all seeming happenstances are really under control of some intentional agency; nothing is as it seems, since that same agency conceals the truth and the observer sees only deceptions and half-truths; and everything is connected, as a pattern underlies seemingly unrelated events and its secret awaits anyone who can piece the pattern together.[31] The result is a coherent answer for who is responsible for what is wrong with the world, how they get away with it, and why resistance is futile.

At the same time, this understanding is a dark one that blames deliberate actions of malign villains with almost supernatural powers for every misfortune and injustice. It is the premillennial vision all over again.

Whether they take the form of conspiracy theory, radical environmentalism, or end-time prophecy, millenarian beliefs share a similar goal. All of them participate in a quest for meaning, an attempt to make sense out of the misery, frustration, confusion, and anger provoked by social stresses. When hopes run up against a brick wall of disappointment, answers like accident, bad luck, or personal failure trivialize the pain. Such understandings are simply not good enough. Bad things must happen to good people for a reason; history "ought to go someplace."[32] A more satisfying solution is a mythic cosmos where good clashes with evil in epic combat, and the enemy—Antichrist, government, big business—is not an abstraction but a force with identity and personality. Defeat of the ultimate bad makes way for the ultimate good. Says University of Oregon professor of English and folklore Daniel Wojcik:

> Directly countering feelings of helplessness, despair, and uncontrollability, apocalyptic belief systems promise the annihilation and regeneration of contemporary civilization through radical supernatural transformation, a promise that brings to individuals a sense of control, meaning, and self-esteem. Apocalyptic traditions offer comprehensive meaning systems that explain current crises as well as personal turmoil, bestow individual salvation upon believers, and fulfill the universal yearning for an ideal, harmonious world free from suffering, sorrow, and injustice. Faith in imminent worldly destruction is accompanied by optimism about and confidence in a divine fate, in the form of God's plan, that is moral and benevolent.[33]

Present millennial currents represent more a tendency of thought than a call to action. Survivalists prepare for impending collapse and antigovernment militias train for a showdown, but these overt responses belong to the fringe. The people who embrace traditional values and participate in conservative politics pursue a mainstream outlet for their dissatisfaction. Others sense the tension of the times. The recent economic decline and job loss have left many Americans feeling like they are going the way of the horse when the automobile took over; increasing social diversity dissolves old patterns of dominance and morality, and spreads confusion over life's fundamental questions of right, wrong, and proper social roles, but many citizens stand by as inactive spectators. They see a conspiring government where their ancestors saw secret societies and domestic subversives cast in a similar role with a similar script. For those who dare to hope, the New Age, technotopia, and ecoparadise repeat the ideal bliss already envisioned in Eden, the Golden Age, and Shangri-la. Current millennial expectations rely so much on traditional images that the future looks not so much unimagined as un-imaginative. At least the methods have evolved. Barkun identifies improvisation as the most common form of millennial thinking today, a style that throws off the restraints of established traditions and allows participants freedom to borrow ideas from here, there, and everywhere.[34] As Jodi Dean points out, the rise of the Internet and the ero-sion of authority level the field so that anyone can promote a theory and reach an audi-ence.[35] The result is a multiplication of proposals assembling facts and pseudo-facts into a mythic bricolage to explain the way things are and why the world is out of kilter. Religion, politics, rumors, beliefs, and hopes fit equally well into this crazy quilt, and the process readily catches up UFOs as something new to stitch into the old-fashioned pattern. After all, everything is connected.

A Helping Hand from Outer Space

Flying saucers arrived almost side by side with the cold war, and concerns surround-ing the two kept close company throughout the 1950s. No one needed a reminder that atomic bombs could fall any day, but some people in need of a savior looked elsewhere rather than to conventional religion when they turned to the skies. Beginning around 1952 the contactees preached an upbeat faith that saucers brought friendly space people to rescue the earth from its impasse of Free World versus Communist Bloc, and an uncritical following embraced these naive tales, so attractive in their simplicity and so transparently a response to earthly hopes and fears.[36]

It was hard not to like the contactees' aliens. They were always human and beauti-ful with no monsters allowed. George Adamski described Orthon of Venus as a man with long blond hair, and Truman Bethurum was clearly smitten with Aura Rhanes, the female captain of the craft he encountered.[37] More than one contactee spun roman-tic yarns around his or her favorite visitor, while Howard Menger and Marla Baxter married after discovering that they had been in love in a former life when he was a Saturnian and she a Venusian.[38] The space people lived for centuries without sickness or the ravages of age, and death was not an end since reincarnation or entry into some higher spiritual plane followed. In personality these visitors were benevolent, gentle, loving, wise, unpretentious, patient, and caring. They were the Space Brothers, older brothers here to help their younger siblings find the way or even parental figures who had come to teach and guide their stumbling children.[39] Adamski stated plainly what the beauty and spiritual refinement of these Brothers implied when he identified them as angels with technological wings.[40]

The Space Brothers dropped by for more than a friendly chat or romantic tryst. They confirmed fears that nuclear bomb tests poisoned the atmosphere, altered the weather, caused earthquakes, and might knock the earth's axis out of alignment. The aliens pointed to the asteroid belt as the ruins of a planet destroyed when its inhabitants misused nuclear energy as humans were now misusing it.[41] Some messages sounded grimly prophetic. George Hunt Williamson learned that "if you knew how soon destruction could come to Saras [earth] you would go screaming through the streets!"[42] Orfeo Angelucci's aliens spoke sadly of "The Great Accident," an impending Armageddon to be fought by the nations of earth.[43] At the same time some Space Brothers promised assistance in preventing nuclear war and others to ferry refugees from the earth before cataclysm struck.[44] Ashtar, first channeled by George Van Tassel and the breakaway favorite alien entity among various contactees, perhaps appealed to a broad following because he commanded vast fleets of spaceships and offered physical rescue for a certain elect.[45]

Most aliens concerned themselves less with the crisis than with its root cause, usually diagnosed as an imbalance between overheated scientific progress and the backwardness of human social and spiritual wisdom.[46] When they warned of the future the aliens meant probabilities rather than certainties; disaster was not inevitable, because humans had free will to choose their course.[47] Though constrained by a policy of noninterference, the Space Brothers encouraged submission to the universal law that governed all worlds. What this law might be needed few elaborations, since its truths underlie all religions and philosophies and even children know it intuitively—love one another, serve others first, make peace, do no harm.[48] These simple truths had gotten lost in the egotism and selfishness of earthlings; but if the nature of man was the problem, the solution also lay inside.

> Your planet will be destroyed of its own self if you continue to live in the old ways. Understand these Truths and you can master self. This is the secret to change your world—*change yourselves.*[49]

> Our only remedy for saving ourselves is to turn from hate and national enmity to love and a realization of the Fatherhood of God, the Motherhood of Nature, and the Brotherhood of Man.[50]

Saving the earth meant a revolution of consciousness, and in this effort the Space Brothers could lend a hand. Their spaceships arrived to provoke curiosity, to stimulate humans to think of the greater universe beyond their earthbound problems. A growing number of aliens contacted people. They were not the famous or powerful, but individuals with some glimmer of spiritual enlightenment who would spread the teachings of cosmic truth by word and example. They would face incredulity and ridicule from a resistant audience while feeling secure in the importance of their mission. Little by little, a spiritual awakening would then sweep the world, and all conflicts and hatreds, evils and errors of the present would vanish like a bad dream.[51] With this transition would come the New Age, the Golden Age, the era of cosmic consciousness; and the contactees envisioned it in ecstatic, millenarian terms:

> The time shall be when your planet will be the brightest star in our solar system. When this takes place, the rest of the solar system will be so joyous. The music of the spheres will be with us all. Indeed, this one inharmonious note that emanates from your planet will then be in tune with the song of the whole system.[52]

> It will be a new world where work and worth go hand in hand, where men's lips are rich with love and truth. A race will exist without disease of flesh or brain, for health will come to all as a divine heritage. And above it all will be the Eternal Father.[53]

> For the rainbow of eternal promise is now in the heavens. The shining hosts of the great brotherhood of the spiritual federation of the universe are waiting to receive us into their midst and to let us know them as they really are. The highest flights of our imagination and our wildest dreams cannot compare with the wonderful world of reality that lies ahead in Time for us.[54]

Abduction accounts introduce a sinister alternative to pleasant encounters with Space Brothers. The typical contactee story focuses on the message. Any other interaction with the aliens is peripheral and serves only to legitimate the message as the word from above. Abductions are quite different. They are all about what happens in frightening encounters with nonhuman aliens fixated on their own agenda. Yet even this bleak UFO story genre has adapted to an optimistic rewriting in some cases. A conference, conversation, or lecture may follow the examination and hint that the aliens take interest in humanity as well as human tissue after all. The abductee message resembles the basic contactee message: A time of tribulation is at hand because human folly and rapaciousness threaten the ability of the earth to sustain life.[55] Cataclysms will cleanse the earth unless a shift in human behavior ends materialism and greed.[56] Images rather than words may drive home the point, like the vision Whitley Strieber saw of the earth exploding and of his young son in the land of the dead; other abductees see a dark cloud blotting out life, environmental deterioration unfolding before their eyes, or apocalyptic scenes of devastation.[57]

The life transformations that follow in some abduction accounts resemble transformations found in religious conversion and sainthood. Abductees may adopt a healthier lifestyle; change jobs to pursue helping, teaching, or creative expression; and take newfound interest in art, education, and spirituality. Their concern for the environment, peace, and the well-being of others replaces preoccupation with money and worldly advancement. Some abductees report an onset of psychic abilities, paranormal experiences, and sensitivities to unconventional realities, also a mission to teach others or assist in some way to save humanity when apocalyptic times arrive.[58] Most transformations remain personal, but in one exception from 1989 three aliens floated Linda Cortile, a Manhattan housewife living near the Brooklyn Bridge, from her apartment to a hovering UFO that then dived into the river. Two witnesses later surfaced who claimed to be security guards escorting a high-ranking United Nations official when the abduction occurred. This official witnessed the event as if the aliens had staged a public appearance, in contrast to their usual secretiveness, leading to speculations that perhaps the aliens sought to begin a new phase of open contact.[59]

The most coherent voice for an optimistic future depends on interpretations of the abduction experience rather than on overt claims. John Mack admitted the traumatic aspects of abduction but cast them in a broader context as necessary to an experience that "seems almost like an outreach program from the cosmos to the spiritually impaired." He saw the frightening and unpleasant events creating "ontological shock," experiences disturbing at every level because they overturn the sense of human control and shatter the comfortable boundaries of familiar reality. When no bridge to the past remains unburned, abductees are forced to head into unknown territory. This confrontation with the unknown compels transformative growth as they leave behind the fragmented psyche and find oneness with nature, mankind, and the spiritual creative power known as God or Source.[60]

> What the abduction phenomenon has led me ... to see is that we participate in a universe or universes that are filled with intelligences from which we have cut ourselves off. ... It has become clear to me that our restricted worldview or paradigm lies behind most of the major destructive patterns that threaten the human future.[61]

> Each of the principal elements of the phenomenon—the traumatic intrusions; the reality-shattering encounters; the energetic intensity; the apocalyptic ecological confrontations; the reconnection with Source; and the forging of new relationships across a dimensional divide—contributes to ... the great ego death, that is marking the end of the materialistic business-as-usual paradigm that has lost its compatibility with life in the world as we now know it.[62]

Other students of the phenomenon, among them psychologists Leo Sprinkle and Kenneth Ring and writer-abductee Whitley Strieber, concur that transformation of consciousness is the real business of abduction. Beyond the trauma and messages, the bottom line is that abduction leaves the experiencers different people. They outgrow a parochial planetary awareness for the broader perspective of cosmic citizenship, relate with aliens and hybrids in a communion of opposites to create a new unity, break through materialistic consciousness to access other realms of awareness.[63] The abductee discovers new worlds of spirituality and a relationship—physical, symbolic, and spiritual—with Others, whether extraterrestrial or something else. These changes have touched a few pioneers but soon will spread throughout all of humanity to replace current ways of thinking and realize an impending millennium that will not be so much a physical Eden or New Jerusalem as an inner paradise.

Contact stories are explicit, while abduction accounts are partial and enigmatic in their promises of a millennial future. Neither type of story belittles a sense of crisis, yet the long-term prognosis seems comic rather than tragic. An optimism prevails that the transition from present troubles to the New Age will be largely painless, a rebirth without a death. In any case, the New Age unfolds in human terms. It does not whirl off into futuristic visions of space travel and exotic technology despite the relationship with otherworld visitors. Instead, the envisioned UFO millennium reclaims a mythic sense of cyclical time, the notion that a primordial state of authentic human truth and wholeness was the best while the subsequent fragmentations brought on by rationality and modernity represent a decline. Yet rituals of transformation can, so to speak, rewind the clock and bring mankind back to the ideal state of innocence when the lion truly lies down with the lamb.[64]

Danger from the Stars

UFOs can ferry an enemy from space as easily as saviors from the stars, and many interpretations elaborate the prospect for hostile encounters. The earliest of these fears was earthbound. Both the saucers and the ghost rocket epidemic of 1946 raised concerns that German rocket technology had fallen into Soviet hands, and provoked anxiety that our cold war enemy flaunted its superiority for purposes of propaganda and intimidation.[65] Any official worries abated in 1953, when the Robertson Panel concluded that saucers posed no threat to national security, and further dissipated two years later when statistical studies reported in Project Blue Book Special Report no. 14 found no patterns consistent enough for superior aeronautical technology.[66] Failure of the Soviets to take advantage of their wonder-weapon proved once and for all that the sky was not falling, at least not on account of foreign-made UFOs.

Biblical end-time expectations keep some evangelical Christians expecting the worst from UFOs. The appearance of strange objects in the sky fulfills the prophecy for signs and wonders. Reinterpretations in the UFO literature—of Ezekiel's Wheel or the Star of Bethlehem as spaceships, channeled messages that link Jesus and Satan with the Ashtar Command, Billy Meier's claim that the spirit of Jesus entered him, assertions of The Two that they would be killed and then rise from the dead—make perfect sense to the Christian as examples of Satan and Antichrist acting as deceivers and manipulators, spreading false hopes and violating the integrity of Scripture. Aliens manifest a perverted interest in sex, harm their captives, and claim equality with God. Men in Black terrify people, and the Heaven's Gate cult lured its followers to commit suicide. Such efforts betray the classic tactics of demons as they confuse and mislead their victims to win their souls for hell. For evangelicals, UFOs are real and a serious matter because they are the old demonic enemy hiding behind an extraterrestrial mask.[67] As recently as 1997, and about 400 years too late (let us hope), evangelist Pat Robertson called for abductees to be stoned as agents of the devil.[68]

So much science-fiction literature typecast aliens as monstrous villains that space visitors suffered a serious image problem before they ever stepped off the ship. The movies of the 1950s reinforced this negative stereotype, as did early UFO writers when they presented various UFO events in terms appropriate for minor Gothic horror. The Mantell crash of 1948 served as the first exhibit, abetted by rumors that the pilot's body disappeared and a magnetic or radioactive ray disintegrated the aircraft.[69] H. T. Wilkins and M. K. Jessup filled several books in the 1950s with suggestions that UFOs were responsible for some mysterious plane crashes and disasters at sea. An airliner en route to Santiago, Chile, vanished over the Andes on August 2, 1947. After the last contact with ground control, the radio operator picked up a strange code word, "Stendec," repeated several times. Did a UFO snatch the airliner out of the sky? This story became an early staple in the literature, and it was only a few years ago that the wreckage was found on a mountainside.[70] Another classic concerned the ship *Ourang Madan* in the Malacca Straits on February 4, 1948. The ship sent out an SOS and when rescuers arrived, everyone aboard was dead, even the ship's dog, and the corpses on deck all stared skyward with horrific grimaces on their faces. Before rescuers could explore any further, the engine room exploded and the ship sank a few minutes later. This story poses a fine mystery indeed. It includes no UFOs, but a little imagination is enough to envision marauding aliens raking the ship with a death ray, and the possibility passed into UFO lore as a quasi-fact. Later suggestions implicate an accident with war-surplus poison gas as the cause of the disaster.[71]

A widespread fear of the early era anticipated that aliens arrived as invaders and carried out surveillance before an outright attack. As an Annapolis-trained Marine officer and a cold warrior who published articles about military danger from the Soviets, Donald Keyhoe extended those concerns to flying saucers. He did not want to believe they were hostile, but he found motive in the possibility that the aliens inhabited a dying planet and in the alarm that our simultaneous development of atomic energy and space travel might inspire in nearby worlds. With an eye for strategy he worried that the saucers showed interest in key targets like aircraft, military bases, industrial centers, and atomic energy facilities, until enough evidence piled up to say, "It looks as though they're measuring us for a knockout."[72] The disappearance of an F-89 while attempting to intercept an unknown object over the Soo Locks of Michigan on November 23, 1953, also troubled Keyhoe. Radar controllers at Kinross Air Force Base vectored the jet across Lake Superior and watched the two blips draw closer, then suddenly seem to merge. The larger UFO blip quickly rose out of radar range. No further radio contact indicated the jet was still in the air, and search parties never found a trace of the plane or its two crewmen.[73] Today in the Louisiana hometown of the pilot, Lt. Felix Eugene Moncla, stands a memorial with an inscription stating that he disappeared while pursuing a UFO. Keyhoe led his readers to suspect that a giant spaceship had swallowed the jet and carried it away.[74]

Concerns about alien invasion faded as the years went by and still no armada of spaceships hove into sight, but the high-strangeness era of the 1960s and 1970s replaced outright aggressiveness with more subtle dangers. Jacques Vallee theorized that the UFO experience altered perceived realities and ultimately worldviews through a process of "subliminal seduction." He saw an unwelcome purpose behind this manipulation, since the rising UFO counterculture promoted public distrust of science, irrational faith in extraterrestrial intervention, doubt in human mastery over our own destiny, and preference for a totalitarian, racist, and antidemocratic social order.[75] John Keel arrived at a similar conclusion but cast it in even more pessimistic light. He argued that the phenomenon, or the intelligence behind it, sowed confusion and nonsense on a worldwide scale and had the potential to destroy the sanity of believers. A better world might be coming but so might another Dark Age.[76] "Suppose the plan is to process millions of people and then at some future date trigger all of those minds at one time? Would we suddenly have a world of saints? Or would we have a world of armed maniacs shooting at one another from bell towers?"[77]

Hostilities opened on a broad new front with the advent of abduction. It introduced UFO danger on a personal level and left no one safe, not even at home in bed, as aliens claimed defenseless captives without so much as a please or thank-you. Many abductees compared themselves to guinea pigs.[78] At least the aliens were not deliberately cruel or sadistic, just businesslike and indifferent; but the apparent nature of the aliens' business steered abductions back toward apprehensiveness. Their preoccupation with genetic materials to create hybrids explained the purpose of the examination, while a purpose behind the abduction project peeped out in hints that the aliens faced some threat to their survival and scavenged their salvation from human bodies.[79] What David Jacobs heard from his informants convinced him that the multiplying hybrids improved their adaptation to life on earth and were already human enough to mingle unnoticed with the general population. The aliens promised a transition to come, a time of bliss and peace called "The Change"; but undercurrents suggested that the reality would bring not equality and coexistence but a world with the human element replaced by the alien in a subtle takeover of the earth without firing a shot.[80] The prospect of The Change is ambiguous, promising the beauty and harmony of the millennium but at the same time threatening destruction through an undesirable alteration of the human essence.

A careful reading of abductees' responses stacked further evidence against any apparent willing acceptance of the experience. Some abductees who report rapturous feelings, a sadness to depart, and longing to return to the company of the aliens then belie their own claims by dreading the next encounter and living in fear that the aliens will return. Budd Hopkins tells the story of a young man who no sooner rejoices over the birth of his first child than he undergoes a vasectomy to prevent the fathering of any more hybrid children from his sperm, even though he wanted to cooperate with the aliens when in their presence.[81] Such ambivalence of feeling discredits the hopeful image of aliens as harsh but benevolent teachers and implicates them in trickery, manipulation, or thought control.

The Enemy from Earth.—A growing trend in popular ufology replaces villainous aliens with villainous earthlings as the proper center of concern. Some versions of UFO conspiracy theories lead away from extraterrestrial origins, but the most imaginative tradition synthesizes government machinations and alien contact into elaborate yarns that stretch from the Roswell crash to clandestine pacts with aliens and earthly cabals seeking control of the world. This miasma of evil spawns a secular demonology well suited to the UFO myth, and the idea that a conspiracy hides the greatest secret of modern times has entrenched itself as an axiomatic assumption with broad explanatory powers.

Donald Keyhoe distrusted the government as early as 1950 after he encountered official behavior that was almost as puzzling as the saucers themselves. The Air Force pronounced all sightings solved, but the specific solutions often amounted to unworkable, even absurd conventional explanations, as if someone tossed out answers without the slightest investigation. The simple conclusion might be that the authorities wasted no time on a nonexistent phenomenon, but Keyhoe knew better. He saw the kind of impressive cases the Air Force received because military sources working off the record passed such reports along to him. His reporter's instincts convinced him that "the biggest story since the birth of Christ" lumbered behind these contradictions, and the only fitting answer also happened to fit his personal conviction: the military authorities were hiding the truth about visitors from space.[82]

Rejection of UFO reality became standing policy, and this policy acquired teeth as the Air Force began to censor UFO reports. Despite official denials of censorship in any form, Keyhoe ended his 1955 book with reproductions of two orders of several years' standing that required military personnel and commercial pilots to restrict UFO reports to military channels, with legal penalties for failure to comply.[83] Keyhoe envisioned a tug-of-war within the Air Force between the disclosure group and the silence group as they wrestled for control of UFO information. "In revealing this censorship, I am not attacking the Air Force as a whole," he said. "Most of the officers and officials I have encountered are simply obeying orders. Nor do I attribute unpatriotic motives to the 'silence group' members who originate these orders. Undoubtedly they are actuated by a high motive—the need, as they see it, to protect the public from possible hysteria."[84] The paternalism of this policy of secrecy might be wrongheaded, but it had the common good at heart and served as the standard rationale for official behavior throughout the 1950s. This attractive explanation replaced the unacceptable possibility that the denials were true with the exciting prospect that the saucers were all too true, a matter of such import that authorities feared it and kept it secret to defend the status quo.[85]

The supposition that UFOs held the utmost significance comforted believers but foundered on the facts. In 1953 the Robertson Panel dismissed UFOs as a mere nuisance; Project Blue Book always remained an agency of little consequence; and prejudice seemed to trump science in the Condon Committee report of 1969. Nothing about the visible treatment of the subject suggested a deep-seated concern, and the assumption of secrecy to avoid panic wore thin over the years, in part because the idea of alien visitors acquired cultural familiarity, in part because the stopper remained firmly in place on a mystery supposedly too big to stay bottled up for long. The inconsistency between so important a problem and so listless an official response was simply unfathomable at face value and obliged believers to posit that something more, some vital pieces of the puzzle, remained off the table.

Rescue from this crisis of credibility came by a process that would serve the UFO myth well over its career—by an escalation of assumptions to enlarge the size and scope of the conspiracy. Keyhoe had started to look higher up the ladder by 1973, breaking his fixation on the Air Force to admit that it was not the master but the puppet, and the CIA had pulled the strings all along.[86] After Vietnam and Watergate, the public grew receptive to ever more extreme accusations. The cattle mutilation panic of the 1970s implicated malevolent aliens but also fed on suspicions that secret military tests or maneuvers were responsible, a prospect made all the more plausible after 6,000 sheep died in 1968 after release of nerve gas at a Utah proving ground went wrong.[87] Thousands of pages of documents recovered by FOIA requests confirmed UFO interest within the military and intelligence agencies. Startling old secrets came to light, like an interview of missile scientist Robert Sarbacher by Canadian scientist Wilbert B. Smith in 1950, when Sarbacher asserted that the subject of flying saucers "is classified two points higher even than the H-bomb. In fact it is the most highly classified subject in the US Government at the present time."[88] This avalanche of documents unearthed no absolute proof that UFOs were real, but it piled up a tangible vindication for Keyhoe and others who had suspected a conspiracy of silence all along.

The secrecy was real but lacked a motive equal to its imagined magnitude. Without a compelling reason such as the panic argument had lent the 1950s, suspicions in the 1970s remained too fragmentary to coalesce into a convincing conspiracy theory. The 1980s began with the unification of scattered beliefs and a spectacular rewriting of UFO history under the influence of a new rationale, a conspiracist's messiah that ushered in two feverish decades of creative paranoia—and the savior's name was Roswell.

All Roads Lead to Roswell.—How much did the government know about UFOs? Keyhoe took for granted that their interplanetary origin was accepted at the highest levels, but he also assumed that this knowledge derived from inference and accumulation of evidence. What the authorities had not learned perhaps mattered more than anything they knew, since uncertainty about the visitors' intentions and unfamiliarity with their technical capabilities would limit the military to a defensive stance toward the saucers and an evasive stance toward the public. But what if the authorities knew a great deal about UFOs and knew it from the start? Under this supposition a radically different picture would take shape with some agency in full control as it manipulated public attitudes with purposeful direction and a close-knit plan. Everything ufologists thought they understood about the relationship between UFOs and the government would amount to a gross underestimate of the situation.

Rumors of a crashed saucer and all it might reveal had drifted through ufology since the 1950s without ever taking hold, until 1978 when the possibility suddenly acquired the appearance of a certainty. Nuclear physicist-turned-ufologist Stanton Friedman was lecturing in Louisiana when he learned of a local man with a UFO crash story to tell. Friedman hit the jackpot when he met Maj. Jesse Marcel, who related a convincing account of investigating debris from a crashed aircraft while an intelligence officer at Roswell in 1947, and of a hush-hush operation to clear the field of unearthly wreckage. He also charged that military authorities moved to quell public interest by staging newspaper photographs of him with shards of a radar target balloon.[89] Over the next several years as investigators discovered dozens of witnesses to confirm the mysterious crash, a hidden history gradually came to light, startling in its implications yet largely unspoken for thirty years. Evidence of secrecy pervaded the story. Abrupt retraction of the initial press release, military and civilian participants sworn to silence, and a claim that Mac Brazel, the rancher who first discovered the debris, was held in custody for a week and then suddenly had the money to buy a new truck all added clues that an organized effort had stifled news of the crash. The elite status of the Roswell Army Air Field lent credibility to both a resort to secrecy and cooperation of everyone involved. This base was the home of the 509th Bomb Group, in mid-1947 the world's only strike force trained to deliver atomic bombs. A special sense of mission and a serious attitude toward security naturally followed, and if military authorities had reason to keep a secret, residents of Roswell were ready to go along.[90]

The Roswell story spiraled outward into exotic claims of more to hide than debris, like hearsay accounts of servicemen recovering bodies or guards glimpsing dead aliens under a tarpaulin, but always too fearful of the consequences to speak of the matter. Secrecy oaths reentered when a party of archaeologists alleged to have stumbled onto the crash scene and observed the bodies was intercepted by the military and ordered to keep quiet about the find.[91] The Roswell mortician Glenn Dennis told of being physically removed from the base hospital by military police and warned by a nurse acquaintance that his life was in danger if authorities thought that he knew of alien bodies brought into the hospital.[92] Even more fanciful accounts alleged that a live alien was in custody and had a liking for strawberry ice cream.

Roswell handed the faithful a secret as big as they had always wanted. Still missing was the identity of who kept the secret, but the answer surfaced with the MJ-12 (or Majestic 12 or Majic) papers in 1984. This alleged group included a who's who of important military and scientific figures, among them at one time or another were Secretary of Defense James Forrestal; Air Force Gen. Hoyt Vandenberg; CIA chief Adm. Roscoe Hillenkoetter; National Research Council chief Detlev Bronk; presidential science adviser Vannevar Bush; and, most ironically, the astrophysicist who was the longtime nemesis of UFOs, Donald H. Menzel. The papers contained a briefing document for president-elect Eisenhower and reported the discovery of wreckage near Roswell from a craft without any conventional means of propulsion or identifiable electronic parts, while the bodies of four "Extra-terrestrial Biological Entities" (EBEs) lay with an escape pod about two miles away.[93]

MJ-12 filled in the motivational blank and promised secrecy on a properly enormous scale. The government not only knew UFOs were extraterrestrial but knew it a week after Kenneth Arnold's sighting. Nothing about UFOs happened without full understanding of the authorities, and nothing reached the public without leave of an all-knowing, super-secretive agency invisible to most elected officials and independent of democratic oversight. Roswell marked the onset of what Friedman called the "Cosmic Watergate," a conspiracy to hide the greatest secret of all time. This secret made sense of Air Force indifference and the Condon rejection. It was not that UFOs were insignificant; rather they were too important for the military to handle. Years of suffering and ridicule now paid off with resounding triumph as Roswell proved to be everything believers could hope for, a pivotal event that restructured government, redirected the history of the world since 1947, and continued to guide the future with consequences yet to unfold.

The release of MJ-12 papers and John Lear's statement in 1987 primed readers of UFO literature and conference audiences to accept even more extreme claims. Milton William Cooper thrust himself onto the scene about the same time. He claimed that as an enlisted man in the Navy during the early 1970s he had seen documents confirming Lear and a great deal else. MJ-12 and the CIA began as groups to handle the alien presence, he said, while the hidden governments of other nations formed the Bilderberg group to maintain international UFO secrecy. Eisenhower concluded a treaty with a delegation of aliens and then funneled vast amounts of money into developing alien technology without knowledge of Congress. By 1955, when the aliens had broken the treaty, development of weapons to stop the otherworld enemy began. Another threat emerged with the realization that overpopulation would destroy the earth by 2000. The secret government plotted to dispose of undesirable surplus populations by creating new diseases like AIDS and by promotion of drug addiction, while crash programs applied alien technology to save some people from the apocalypse by sending them to the moon and Mars. When John Kennedy learned about these secrets and threatened to expose the truth, the higher governmental powers had him killed. Since then the real rulers of the world, the Illuminati, have prepared concentration camps for patriots and clandestine forces to take over America when they are ready to establish their new order in the open.[94]

In Cooper's sprawling tale all bad things truly interconnect. He joined UFOs with New World Order conspiracy to make a large and virulent theory still larger, ramping up MJ-12 and alien contact into cornerstones of what Michael Barkun calls a super-conspiracy, a "theory of everything" that explains the world in terms of an interrelated hierarchy of conspiracies with, in this instance, the UFO secret at the apex of the pyramid.[95] Equally grandiose speculations came from John Grace, a prolific theorizer in books under the pseudonym of "Valdamar Valerian" and editor of a periodical outlet for conspiracy rumors and speculations, *The Leading Edge*. He emphasized that conspiracies piled one on top of the other until even the wariest defender of freedom scarcely knew friend from foe: "The degree to which the EBEs have interpenetrated our civilization is massive. They maintain bases all over the world ... and control virtually every aspect of our society at the root level. At the superficial power domination level, the Illuminati-related groups control areas that interface directly with terrestrial humans. What humans view as 'conspiracy' is only a superficial perception of a deeper, multi-level problem."[96]

The rising tower of conspiracy theories held the UFO world agog until the whole structure came tumbling down at the 1989 MUFON Symposium. Much of the disillusionment followed a confession of ufologist William L. Moore at the Saturday night banquet. Paul Bennewitz, an inventor and electronics executive, believed he had intercepted communications from UFOs and contacted an Albuquerque intelligence operative in 1980. Encouraged by the operative, Bennewitz continued to pass along progressively more frightening messages until his increasingly paranoid behavior landed him in a mental hospital. Moore revealed that Bennewitz had indeed picked up mysterious signals, but his equipment had inadvertently tapped into secret Air Force communications rather than alien chatter. To protect military secrets, intelligence agents fed Bennewitz ever more fantastic disinformation that was certain to discredit any public announcements he might make. These same agents recruited Moore to keep tabs on UFO groups to see if the ploy succeeded. These admissions left the audience in an uproar, and in deference to future digestive peace the MUFON custom of combining dinner with a talk came to an end.[97]

The fatal implications of Moore's confession sank in before long. A real conspiracy existed, but it belonged to the imaginations of low-level intelligence personnel and deceptions by one of ufology's own, not to vast machinations of aliens and secret societies. Whatever their sources, whatever connections they postulated, Lear, Cooper and the rest simply elaborated on the Bennewitz story, and their claims collapsed along with it. Cooper was ambivalent all along about whether aliens or Illuminati ran the show and sometimes argued that "if extraterrestrials are not visiting earth, then it would make sense to invent them in order to convince opposing forces to unite against the threat."[98] During the 1990s he dispensed with literal aliens and pronounced them a ruse devised as an imaginary enemy to justify seizure of power by the secret government, underscoring that his commitment lay all along with the idea of a plot to create a New World Order rather than with the idea of UFOs.[99]

A divorce of ufology from the superconspiracy theories of Cooper and Grace derives not just from exposure but also from backlash against an uncongenial brand of conspiracism. Both conspiracists and "dark-side" UFO proponents cultivate an elaborate theory of how evil operates in the world. The two faiths overlap, but they are ultimately incompatible, since the core belief of one depends on a vast and sinister plot by a powerful cabal to enslave the world, while the other concentrates on alien visitation. UFOs serve conspiracists by confirming elaborate government efforts at secrecy and providing a secret worth keeping. Conspiracy theories serve UFO believers by convicting the government of hiding the truth about aliens. The two beliefs can work together. Their merger serves both agendas by inflating the size and importance of the conspiracy, but the transition from New World Order to New Otherworld Order throws both beliefs off center. Aliens are simply too Neverland for conspiracists. They are passionate and driven to action, convinced that a few brave souls stumble onto the truth and undertake the mission of some modern Paul Reveres—or Cassandras—as they spread the word to open the eyes of others. These conspiracists need a human villain, some immensely powerful, secret, and malign but ultimately flesh-and-blood Illuminati pulling the strings of world control, just as witch hunters pursued human subversives rather than the devils that instigated and empowered the practitioners of *maleficium*. UFO believers are passive, concerned enough to understand but not to take a stand, and conspiracy matters to them only insofar as it explains government behavior toward UFOs. One side could not accept the subservience that the other imposed on its core beliefs, and a parting of the ways was as inevitable as the once-fervent union.

In any case, "divorce" is too strong a word. Ufology stays wedded to its conspiracies, with claims milder only by degree from those of the "dark-side" era still a thriving part of UFO mythology. The motif of recovered technology revived during the 1990s in Colonel Corso's claim that he back-engineered the Roswell wreckage and in supposed tests of alien-derived aircraft at the mysterious Area 51.[100] Vestiges of the dark side return in Michael E. Salla's book, *Exopolitics* (2004), when he rewrites Eisenhower's famous warning against the military-industrial complex as a veiled confession that a secret coup had shifted real power from elected officials to clandestine groups that control both extraterrestrial policy and national governance.[101] Conspiracy writer Jim Marrs has taken up the old theory that Nazis invented flying saucers, adding claims about a bell-shaped antigravity device and the secret rise of a Fourth Reich plotting to take over the world.[102] MILAB (military abduction) theories explain occasional abductee reports of military personnel working with aliens, while conspiracy writer David Icke relates "reptilian" aliens to ancient contacts with a reptile species that still manipulates human society from the shadows.[103] When a drunk driver killed John Mack in September 2004, conspiracist Web sites transformed a tragic accident into proof that his abduction research brought him too close to the secret for the powers that be to tolerate.[104] The conspiratorial imagination remains as tireless as it is predictable.

Conspiracies that promise the end of the world as we know it circle only the fringes of UFO belief for the moment, but secrecy continues as a mainstay of current ufological thinking. On the Internet, in the literature, and at the conventions most participants take for granted that UFOs are a big issue for government, and a hidden world of bureaucracy suppresses that fact. The popularity of Richard Dolan's books attests to the factual status that such beliefs have acquired within ufology. Confirmation of sorts came from moon-walking astronaut Edgar Mitchell during a radio interview in July 2008, when he declared that "we have been visited on this planet and the UFO phenomenon is real, though it's been covered up by governments for the last 60 years or so." His statements caused a hubbub in the UFO community and attracted the attention of the news media, though his convictions depended on secondhand testimony rather than firsthand experience.[105] The goal of the disclosure movement is to break official secrecy, and in the aftermath of the 2008 election Stephen Bassett's "Million Fax on Washington" program urged citizens to bombard president-elect Obama with requests to release all hidden UFO information.[106] A suspicion that the government hides something about UFOs spreads beyond ufology to opinion polls, and to the place of Roswell as the third most popular conspiracy, after 9/11 and the Kennedy assassination.[107]

UFOs and the Millenarian Theme

For anyone persuaded that UFOs are real spaceships, the next and all-important question concerns why they are here. Discussion arrives at diverse answers, but they converge toward the same few conclusions. The proposals anticipate positive and negative possibilities typically expressed as extremes—extraterrestrial saviors to rescue us from

ourselves, or invaders to conquer, exploit, or subvert humanity. Few proposals fall anywhere in between. A preoccupation with best and worst outcomes has antecedents
whenever people contemplate an uncertain future or the world as it ought to be, with
similar images logged time and again in opposing visions of the afterlife, the earthly
paradise, or the ideal society.

One conceptual template that encompasses both the best and worst in a single
narrative is the millenarian myth, a pattern with a proven track record of broad historical and cross-cultural appeal. A prophet or messiah arises with a plan to set things
right when the world falls into chaos. A time of tribulation and destruction intervenes;
heroes combat enemies and save the faithful for rebirth into an ideal new world. This
myth is satisfying because it explains how things are and previews events to come, and
it is even more attractive because of its inherent drama, with good versus evil and apocalyptic terror relieved by the promise of a perfect future. All these events unfold with
concentrated unity as if they belong together, and the result is a ready-made story able
to bring meaningful form to varied content.

Millenarian ideas shape both positive and negative viewpoints on UFO visitation.
The contactee movement responded to anxiety over the state of the world by casting
extraterrestrials as angelic saviors. A later sense of ecological irresponsibility provided
the background for reimagining aliens as agents of a new consciousness. In both cases
the conflict is not against Satan or some other external agent of evil but man against
man, humanity against its own foolishness; and instead of supernatural inversion of
the physical world, human nature reverses from warlike to peaceful or materialistic to
altruistic. This transformation fulfills the millenarian pattern by envisioning the chaotic, destructive aspects of humanity replaced with its better, idealized potentials, with
dangers, hardship, maybe even physical cataclysm possible in the transition, but with
the apocalyptic threat largely kept at a distance. Even the harrowing experiences of
abductees are mild by apocalyptic standards, and the UFO millennium arrives with a
soft landing.

On the negative side, the invader theme portrays destruction by direct attack or
genetic subversion but cannot qualify in itself as a distinctly millenarian idea. The conspiracy theme fills in some missing parts by joining the external threat of otherworldly
enemies with the inner threat of a government that hides important truths from the
people, or betrays its citizens for power and control, or, worst of all, serves some shadowy secret society that really runs the show. These rulers embody greed, deceit, secrecy,
and ambition to create adversaries that are untouchable, unreachable, and powerful to
the point of being magical. They are in fact indistinguishable in their inhumanity from

alien invaders and provoke the same sense of helpless rage from people who feel small, impotent, and trapped before an incomprehensible, unassailable foe.

UFO conspiracy theory shares the dark vision of apocalypse, a sense that the world is sliding toward catastrophe and ruin. The situation in any conspiracy theory is always dire, and this sameness hints that the picture owes more to theory than to its factual background. Even when the conspiracy starts with UFOs, the true center of attention remains human, and the theory expresses concern over not the end of the physical world but the demise of moral integrity. Evil forces subvert the goodness we cherish and seek to replace freedom, independence, even humanity itself with a totalitarian New World Order. Whether the villain is the Illuminati or aliens makes little difference because the results are the same—real power, the autonomy to choose one's own life, passes from the people to the clandestine elite. Conspirators go about their business with inexorable purpose and cunning to undermine life as we know it and would have it be. Yet with awareness comes the possibility to rise up and defeat the creeping tyranny before it strangles freedom entirely. Though the odds are long, hope is alive and victory is still possible.

Parallels with the millenarian myth stand out in ufology's preoccupation with apocalyptic fears, New Age hopes, behind-the-scenes powers, and forbidden secrets. At the same time, the similarities remain scattered elements. UFO thinking leaves the millenarian pattern incomplete, without a messiah, without a ritual or struggle to transform the world. Contactees look ahead to a better world but await it passively, trusting the Space Brothers to do most of the work and to prevent any apocalyptic inconvenience. Conspiracists trumpet their fears of apocalypse but make few plans to stop it, and the best they hope for is a return to basic American liberties rather than a future paradise. Ufologists seek understanding rather than reform, and this narrow commitment limits their fulfillment of the millenarian pattern.

The rudiments of a true millenarian movement appear most distinctly in the evolving vision of exopolitics. This movement embraces the conspiratorial notions of secret governmental or other powerful interests in charge of the world and in possession of the truth about alien visitation, but looks forward to salvation through disclosure. UFOs now belong to the realm of stigmatized knowledge, but disclosure will normalize it, wresting it from its keepers in a classic struggle of good against evil. Once the truth is out, it will free us from the stranglehold of the secret cabals and transform human consciousness with realization of the true scope of our cosmic context, while alien technology will then belong to the people and revolutionize our material world to bring about a futuristic utopia.[108] Here at last the millenarian story begins to fill out to its traditional proportions, where we find, as of course we should, the villains clandestine, the struggle titanic, the peril known only to the faithful, and the outcome transcendent.

Millenarian ideas have become central fixtures in ufological thinking. They serve as such important load-bearing structures in mainstream theory that without them UFO understanding would collapse or at least be left desolate of content. The relationship is not reciprocal; the millenarian myth has gotten along for many years without UFOs, and they are largely superfluous to it. What UFOs provide is a pretext to translate supernatural terms into technology and aliens, an opportunity to draw on the emotional energy from current distrust of government and uncertainty about the future, an occasion to take control of current problems by fitting them into a timeless myth with desirable solutions to offer. The preoccupation with human agents over UFOs is an unmistakable oddity of ufology, but no great surprise. In the UFO millennium, aliens blend with government villains to keep suspicions grounded in human concerns and urgent with outrage against realistic adversaries while the story outline remains old and familiar. This earthward slant serves as a reminder that the millenarian myth enters into ufology because it attends to human needs, not because it adds to an objective understanding of the phenomenon of UFOs.

CHAPTER SEVEN

Other than Ourselves

These are the voyages of the Starship *Enterprise:* Its five year
mission—to explore strange new worlds, to seek out new life and new
civilizations, to boldly go where no man has gone before.
—*Star Trek*

The truth is out there.
I want to believe.
Trust no one.
Fight the Future.
—*The X-Files*

The idea that flying saucers brought space visitors captured the popular imagination
in the 1950s, and this extraterrestrial association has continued to guarantee UFOs a
long, fruitful lease on life. Just as the canals of Mars stirred excitement at the beginning
of the twentieth century, UFOs have benefited from curiosity about otherworld beings, all the more so because anyone can see a UFO, and it might land even in one's own
backyard. In the understanding that popular ufology has created, extraterrestrial visitation is not simply important but the central truth of history, the axis around which
politics, policy, science, and military strategy turn, the determinant from which the
future of the world unfolds.

In another sense the outer space connection is superficial and misleading. The human portrayal of aliens seldom looks very alien at all, certainly not the Renaissance angels whose outer beauty mirrors their inner perfection to portray a human ideal. Devils
are just the opposite, all wrong as they mingle human and animal, male and female, one
species and another in grotesque, loathsome, and disturbing combinations. Though

ostensibly depicting denizens of unearthly realms, the artist first and foremost represents the abstracts of good and evil as concrete visuals. This preoccupation with moral concepts betrays an origin in human concerns, and so it goes with UFO aliens. Their characterization in the literature suggests that the real fascination of extraterrestrials lies not in their exotic address but in their reflection of human interest in otherness. Extraterrestrials succeed today, like distance and the supernatural in bygone times, as a blank page of possibilities, a premise to excuse any amount of strangeness, any defiance of natural law or logical contradiction. These aliens are different and advanced: with them all things are possible, and the human imagination takes over from there.

Despite an apparent free hand, UFO aliens never enjoy the versatility of aliens in fiction. UFO reports show limitation in possibilities, a narrowness that results from observations of reality, according to ufologists, but also could result if psychological functions configure mythic beings. In ufology the aliens abduct and invade, but in thematic terms their job lies elsewhere. They work hard not on Zeta Reticulan business but on being exemplars of contrasting relationships between the human and the not-human, ideals of what humans should and should not be, and as embodiments of technology and progress. They warn against what the future might hold. Whatever UFO aliens really are, the meanings assigned to them enliven issues in ongoing cultural disputes and update traditions of encounters with beings unlike ourselves.

The Face in the Mirror

Gods and monsters, fairies and devils, wild men and extraterrestrials hold little of appearance or habit in common, but all share the quality of alienness. They may be like us in vital ways, but they are not us, not human as we are human. These entities may be more than human or subhuman, a perversion of the human form or the opposite of the moral norm, but in any case they are different. They are the outsiders to our familiar personal, social, and cultural inside yet close at hand with necessary but unsettling reflection and commentary. They are the Others to remind us of who we are by exemplifying what we are not—or hope we are not. "Monsters are in the world but not of the world," says Case Western Reserve University professor of biblical literature Timothy K. Beal. "They are paradoxical personifications of *otherness within sameness*. That is, they are threatening figures of anomaly within the well-established and accepted order of things. They represent the outside that has gotten inside, the beyond-the-pale that, much to our horror, has gotten into the pale."[1]

If we take stock of what is alien about Others, recurrent themes soon grow insistent.

Aliens belong to the distance yet refuse to stay there. Actual mileage separates extra-terrestrials and the monsters of travelers' tales from the familiar environment, while fairies and wild men live close by yet inhabit a world apart, the barrier between the worlds metaphysical rather than substantive but divisive all the same. Distance casts its estranging spell. Aliens are free to be grotesque in form and manners, even obli-gated to strangeness and wonder. They practice inhumane and antisocial behaviors or, alternately, embody ideals for beings free of human faults and limitations. These aliens grow in superiority until they surpass humans in power and knowledge, able to carry out every great good or heinous evil that mortals can only imagine.

So many characteristics carried to extremes load aliens with an explosive mixture of traits. It gives reason to be in awe of them and to fear them at the same time. This side of the alien brings to mind Rudolf Otto's classic description of the holy as *myste-rium tremendum et fascinans*, the wholly other that overwhelms the subject with a sense of awe, mystery, power, and fascination.[2] Otto designated the mental state inspired by these qualities as the numinous, and while he reserved it as unique to sacred experi-ence, the idea invites extension to kindred responses before any manifestation of the Other. Insofar as aliens are strange enough to strip away the handholds of familiar understanding and send us tumbling into the unknown, the resultant vertigo and hair-raising terror surround these beings with a sense of the numinous. The alien thus taps into some of the profoundest and most disturbing of human emotions.

The trouble with UFO aliens is not so much that some voltage of this numinous charge attaches to them, but that they confront us with it in the everyday world. As long as they keep a safe distance we can think fondly of anomalous beings, but aliens simply will not keep their place. Inherent intrusiveness thrusts them into our attention even when we would prefer to ignore them. The traveler bumps into Plinian races at the end of a long journey, but extraterrestrials usurp the travelers' role and insist on making house calls. In the end, distance counts for nothing. It allows an extravagance of strangeness but not an ounce of protection. Aliens are always close at hand. Their eerie faces press close to the windowpane at night, and they are worse than the wolf at the door, because not even the strongest lock can keep them out.

Such ease in crossing the boundaries between worlds suggests that aliens rely on more than technology. A Copernican revolution seems necessary to account for their origin, one that renders them not just physically external but also a part of us, inherent in the mythic identity we create for them. An inner identity for the Other has appealed to psychoanalysts as an example of early experiences creating monstrous consequences for later life. In this view the child's experience of adults prefigures later ideas of mon-sters as beings of overwhelming size, strength, and power. Freud explained the uncanny quality of otherness as the "return of the repressed," the reemergence in adulthood of anxieties so troubling that the child shut them out of consciousness, now reasserting themselves as alienated, objectified, and grown large.[3] No wonder aliens know our deepest fears and rattle us to the bone. The aliens of our imagination spring from the very fears we have tried hardest to forget, personified out of the unconscious recesses of human nature. If these psychological musings seem too speculative, the importance of the human intermediary is inescapable. Whether UFO aliens are visitors from outside or are an inside job, ideas about them match the contours of countless myth-based preconceptions of what the Other should be.

Making Monsters.—No separation of "us" from "them" is more immediate than bizarre physical appearance, and from Pliny to Hollywood to the UFO literature, aliens often reveal their difference at first sight. Behavioral and cultural differences are less apparent at a glance but measure otherness better than skin-deep traits. The Greeks accepted that barbarians could possess civilized attributes like language, clothing, customs, religion, and governmental organization, but barbarian culture always remained inferior because it never achieved Greek ideals of wisdom, courage, restraint, and justice. Greeks viewed the Persians as cruel and cowardly, willing to fight in large armies but not man to man. Even less to their credit, the Persians had a luxury-loving, servile nature and obeyed a despotic king whose pride and impiety, in the case of Xerxes, drove him to flog the Hellespont in a fit of rage.[4] The remoteness of Scythians allowed Herodotus to draw their differences in even bolder strokes as contrary to everything Greek. Where the city was the heart of Greek social life, the Scythians were nomads with no fixed home. They were pastoralists rather than farmers, raiders rather than warriors, and ruled by a king rather than by the people. Scythians had no architecture, art, or other intellectual refinement, but they were guilty of many repellent practices—they were inhospitable to strangers, drank blood out of skulls, and even ate their dead.[5]

A still more radical separation becomes possible with Plinian races. Not only are they monstrous in appearance and located farther afield than the barbarians, but their acts and culture assume an idealized opposition to the good, not a mere falling short but a pure inversion of civilized norms. Descriptions of Plinian races often include absence of language or clothing, sleeping in caves, eating raw food, and living off the land without agriculture, industry, arts, or crafts. Monsters are primitive in their lack of all the materials and customs of civilization, but also savages since their cannibalism, bad manners, lack of hospitality, and irreverence for the gods oppose civilized norms.[6] Travelers' tales divide alien monsters from civilized humanity by the starkest possible contrasts.

Traditions of the European wild man forge perhaps the clearest case of the Other unfettered with observation and left wholly for the imagination to shape into an exemplary opposite. Where vast and brooding medieval forests bordered the precarious habitations of humans, he joined the host of natural and supernatural dangers residing there and embodied every wilderness quality that the simple farmer or shepherd had to fear, dreaded all the more because he was both man and beast, more than animal but a perversion of humanity. Though there were wild women as well as wild men, they lived apart without forming family units. Hairy, strong, lawless, and libidinous, the wild man inhabited the wilderness without fire or shelter, a companion to wild animals and an enemy to man. He represented everything the medieval mind abhorred, having no place in the social hierarchy, no religion, name, reason, or soul. Devoid of control over his natural self, the wild man acted as an aggressive brute ruled by instinct and driven by emotions to satisfy his appetites. He kidnapped human women and held them as slaves to his lust until some knight came to the rescue, though only the strongest knight could overcome the wild man, and the lustfulness of the wild woman sometimes turned even the would-be rescuer into a victim.[7]

In this purely negative image of the wild man lies the germ of a continuing conflict between self and other in Western civilization. Time and again the idea of a base savage or enemy of mankind has arisen to threaten civilization and justify drastic measures to stamp out the supposed evil.[8] The European witch hunts enacted an archetypal crusade for social purification against a cabal of enemies. Witches reversed all that was sacred and right by rejecting God to worship the devil, murdering rather than protecting children, and practicing cannibalism and sexual perversity. Witches were neighbors but subversive since they violated normal social relationships and betrayed the bonds of community to attack crops, livestock, and health by supernatural means. The anti-Semitic propaganda of the Nazis harnessed similar themes of a malevolent and destructive conspiracy eating at the heart of society, secularized into graphic images like packs of rats swarming up from sewers to drive home the message that Jews were vile contaminants threatening Aryan civilization. In both holocausts a demonized, bestialized image of the Other lifted the constraints of reason and moderation to invite the mass extermination of imagined enemies.[9] A similar tactic dehumanized Native Americans as so cruel that the only good Indian was a dead Indian,[10] and African Americans as lazy, dirty, oversexed, and violent.[11] The Irish, Jews, Italians, Chinese, and many other ethnic immigrants faced accusations that they brought disease, crime, anarchy, promiscuity, economic ruin, or un-American religions and values.[12] In wartime the portrayal of enemies often focuses on atrocities, wanton cruelty, and rejection of the rules of civilized conduct.[13] Godless Communists, drug-crazed hippies, and greedy corporate executives have since replaced the barbarous German Hun, serving their turns in the trenches as stereotypical opponents in the war between good and evil.

Aliens from space take up where monsters of the past left off. Science fiction has passed far beyond the simplistic alien to create nonhuman characters of depth and nuance, but the most popular view still favors a shallow conception where aliens step or slither into the role of two-dimensional villains. In the pulp literature, comic books, and 1950s movies, aliens are typically frightful to behold and are threatening in behavior. The movie *Independence Day* (1996) casts aliens as heirs to the savage nomads, a violent and merciless horde devoid of any human qualities, any redeeming hint of a soul, that wanders from planet to planet to strip it bare of resources and leave only devastation behind.

Unmaking Monsters.—A good myth comes full circle. Rather than allow indefinite headway to one trend of thought, such a myth pulls back the other way to strike something of a balance. The myth of the Other has served civilized values long and well by providing the ideal foil, but a great deal of ambivalence also surrounds aliens in the human imagination. Faraway races and wild men near at hand appear in purely negative terms for certain historical moments, until countercurrents of longing, admiration, and envy come along to mix favorable meanings into the relationship. At times the pendulum swings so far that the Other has its day of glory as quite the positive ideal. More often civilization coexists with its savages and monsters in a state of confused suspension as multiple, often contradictory attitudes load the alien with mystery and possibility for mythical cultivation.

Ancient defenders of civilized superiority could accent the negative side of the Other only by silencing a contradictory nostalgia for the uncivilized state long entrenched in their mythology. Like most peoples, the Greeks envisioned a Golden Age replaced with the present era of evil and suffering. Weighed against the former perfection, civilization marked not improvement but a feeble recovery after catastrophic loss. Once upon a time no one needed the amenities of civilization. Clothing was useless because the weather was clement and shame was unknown, laws and government were superfluous because everyone was honest and peaceable, religion was unnecessary because gods and men lived side by side. Even as the Greeks vaunted the quality of their culture, the possibility nagged them that remote Others might still enjoy this former purity and innocence. Thinking to impress the Ethiopians with manufactures, artistry, and agriculture of the civilized world, the Persians sent gifts only to have the Ethiopian king reject them one after another as shams. To him a dyed robe was fakery, gold a metal inferior in strength, and bread made from wheat grown in manured fields the proof that Persians ate dung. Ethiopians continued to live in the state of nature, receiving their food miraculously without toil—and already cooked—from a magical Table of the Sun.[14] The Persians succeeded only in revealing the poverty of civilization, and Herodotus by telling this story reminded his readers how poorly civilization substituted for paradise lost.

Over time the Other evolved positive connotations to supplant or supplement earlier negative attributes. Monsters represented a pure form of villainy in the era of heroic demigods and austere values. Herakles killed monsters to make way for civilization, and they served as unambiguous opponents certain to put up a good fight and die a good death as they reaffirmed the hero's prowess.[15] Later the refined cultures of Athens and Rome polished the monster's image, taming the old wild crew into residents of a peaceful Arcadia, where they posed as characters for art and comedy. The medieval wild man exemplified the anti-Christian, antihuman tendencies of nature, but the desert wilderness was not simply a lair for owls and jackals but also a solitude for contemplation and trial, where Moses, Elijah, and Jesus prepared for their prophetic roles. In the early Christian tradition of desert saints, individuals seeking purity and atonement retreated into the desert to become solitary, ragged, hairy figures as beastlike as the wild man.[16] A similarly ambiguous relationship linked him with madness. The biblical King Nebuchadnezzar went mad and turned into a hairy beast of the fields, while medieval sinners copied this example when crime, guilt, depravity, or divine wrath drove them insane and exiled them to the wilderness, cut off from God, civilization, and reason.[17] This moral harshness mellowed in time as the madman's wilderness evolved into a place of healing. Living in close proximity to nature brought the sinner closer to God, resulting in eventual redemption and saintliness. By the late Middle Ages, the once-forbidding wilderness transformed into an idyllic garden where the wild man joined the wild woman to live in family happiness, and humans went to sample a foretaste of paradise.[18]

The Other has continued to personify the conflict between nature and culture. New World "savages" repelled civilized sensibilities with human sacrifice and cannibalism, yet won admiration because they drew native wisdom from their closeness to nature and lived free of the deceit, cynicism, and artificiality of civilization. Montaigne asked whether the cannibal custom to eat a dead man was worse than the civilized habit to torture, tyrannize, and betray a live one.[19] In this comparison civilized man had nothing to boast about, no reason to feel superior. Civilized mores were as rude and barbarous as the worst practices of the savage but without the compensating nobility. Rousseau saw the savage as more happy and fortunate than civilized man because he was not troubled with good or evil and had no needs but those that nature readily fulfilled. Only with civilization came inequalities, oppression, and discontent.[20]

Ambivalence toward civilization complicated the understanding of Self and Other even before science, technology, and industry ratcheted up the conflict to a whole new level.

Fear of the Machine

The tension between nature and culture held more intellectual than practical interest prior to the nineteenth century, but since then a radical separation from the natural world has become the everyday norm. Most people in developed countries inhabit a world that exists by, of, and for human purposes and is concerned with business, law, politics, manufacturing, information, and customer relations. We live vaccinated, globally wired, and abundantly fed in a built environment insulated from heat and cold and spared the inconvenience of distance by cars, airplanes, and cell phones, approaching no nearer to the source of our food than a can or a menu. Civilization has liberated us to pursue our desires and ambitions, to live in luxury no pharaoh could imagine, to improve on the gods for wonder-working, to spend our days in a better paradise than imagination could contrive. For all these boons our gratitude has been mixed. We gladly applaud the material benefits of civilization yet never escape a nagging worry, expressed everywhere, from philosophy and high literature to popular culture and folk belief, that the gains also bring physical, intellectual, and spiritual losses; that the power, freedom, and safety of the man of our own making leaves him sadder, diminished, and less wise compared with the man that nature made.

The most optimistic advocates of civilization saw little good in natural man. The nineteenth-century positivist philosopher Auguste Comte proposed that mankind began in savagery but progressed over time to barbarism and finally civilization.[21] All but inseparable from this theory of cultural evolution was belief in progress, the idea that the present is better than the past and the future will be better than the present, with each stage marked, in the words of pioneer anthropologist E. B. Tylor, by "the general improvement of mankind by higher organization of the individual and society, to the end of promoting at once man's goodness, power, and happiness."[22] According to the positivist view of history, as rationalism replaced magical thinking, education overcame ignorance, and inhumane social orders beneficial to the few yielded to liberal institutions protective of everyone, the history of mankind would proceed through a long course of trials and errors, fits and starts, toward a paradise of human making.

Technology does not define civilization, but technology often serves as the yardstick to measure how far the present has left the past behind. A confident optimism toward human ability to build a better future with our own hands flourished during the Victorian era and the first half of the twentieth century. Americans idolized Thomas Edison as the most spectacular example of an untutored genius inventing the world of tomorrow.[23] They also admired his colleagues, who tinkered with flying machines and mechanical devices in barnyards and workshops around the country. Similar sentiments celebrated builders of railroads and canals, as well as explorers of jungles, deserts, and ice caps, as heroes who extended human control over untamed, unattainable, and unknown elements of nature. Schoolbooks held up Christopher Columbus as an exemplary culture hero, the man who dared big and won big when he challenged the accepted truths of his day and sailed west, not to fall off the edge of the earth but to discover a whole new world.

Challenging nature and testing the limits made for a high-risk occupation with many casualties along the way, from polar explorer Robert Falcon Scott to the *Challenger* and *Columbia* astronauts. What was certain to an earlier generation was the worthiness of the sacrifice. Why take the risk, why bother at all? The answer was frivolous on the surface but profound as an index of cultural ethos: Climb Mount Everest because it is there, said George Leigh Mallory, who then died in the attempt. Our species found motive enough for its restlessness in the mere existence of anything outside of human control. Nothing was fixed and immovable simply because it was natural or traditional.

Little by little, piece by piece, we would reengineer the universe in our own image. Nature was nothing to get sentimental about, no friend or haven. At worst it was the medieval wilderness, a destructive force in need of control; at best it was a valuable commodity to exploit and turn to human uses. In America, where the historical past was shallow, conquest of the wilderness became the national epic, with a narrative emphasis laid more often on acts like the western migration or building the transcontinental railroad than on individuals as heroic ideals.[24] If rivers were unruly, dam them; if wolves became a nuisance, wipe them out; if the climate was too dry, irrigate. Tame, harness, cultivate, conquer, subdue—these terms attested to the vision of human dominance over nature, a goal rooted in religious and secular belief that the state of nature was imperfect and realized its innate potential only with the help of human improvements. To strive outward, to combat nature as an enemy forever inimical to human welfare and forge a destiny in human terms whatever the cost—this course seemed to be not just worthy and good, but also the essence of human spirit. H. G. Wells said it best in his script for *Things to Come* (1936), when two fathers, one a proponent of the progressive urge and the other against it, watch the space capsule bearing their children as it streaked across the sky.

I feel that what we've done is monstrous.
What they've done is magnificent. . . .
And what if they don't come back?. . . .
Then presently others will go.

Oh God, is there never to be any age of happiness? Is there never to be any rest?
Rest enough for the individual man. Too much and too soon, and we call it death.
But for Man no rest and no ending. He must go on. Conquest beyond conquest. . . .
And when he has conquered all the deeps of space and all the mysteries of time—
still he will be beginning. It is this or that. All the universe or nothingness. Which
shall it be?[25]

The preeminence of technology in shaping human life over the past two centuries has popularized efforts to imagine what the technological future will be like. A
lighthearted series of illustrations from 1900 foresaw the year 2000 as a time of flying
machines gridlocked in traffic jams and education made easy by grinding books in a
hopper and passing the contents into the heads of pupils through electrified helmets.[26]
If this extrapolation foresaw only the same old world with a few gadgets added, science-fiction writer Arthur C. Clarke filled *Profiles of the Future* (1962) with anticipated
advancements that would be fundamental enough to change the world forever. Space
travel and global communication have arrived already; permanent space outposts are
still pending but attainable. Some of the more spectacular achievements of progress—
versatile robots, energy from nuclear fusion, easy transmutation of elements, true artificial intelligence, and immortality—remain somewhere in the distance yet nascent
in ongoing research. Clarke looked ahead only to the year 2100 and foresaw an unprecedented technotopia as human ingenuity provided abundant energy, endless raw
materials, machines to perform all labor, and human life free of disease or death.[27]
Predictions of dazzling possibilities founded on scientific fact continue to issue from
futurologists like Freeman Dyson or inventor Ray Kurzweil, who sees the next step of
human evolution in the union of human biology and computer technology to create a
cyborg species.[28]

Science fiction continues as the most exuberant oracle of a technotopic future with
human powers multiplied to godlike proportions. Isaac Asimov carried progress to an
imaginative ultimate conclusion in his 1956 short story "The Last Question." Humans
asked a series of progressively more advanced automated computers (ACs) if entropy,
the natural running down of the universe to a state of disorder, was a reversible process, and the computer always answered that it had insufficient data. Over the eons this
computer intelligence grew from planetary to galactic to cosmic scope and exchanged

electronic for molecular, and at last subatomic, working parts. Meanwhile, the universe aged, the stars burned out, and the AC absorbed all human intelligence. The process of entropy brought the universe to a cold, dead finish, but at last AC had an answer to the old question.

> The consciousness of AC encompassed all of what had once been a Universe and brooded over what was now Chaos. . . .
>   And AC said, "LET THERE BE LIGHT!"
>   And there was light—[29]

The positivist combination of evolution with progress laid out a pathway to paradise that applied not just to this world but also to any technological culture. Advancement to civilization, and civilization to a perfected state, was assumed to be universal, the innate destiny of intelligent minds wherever they resided. If aliens surpassed us in their science and technology, we glimpsed not the unique accomplishments of an Other but our future selves, the better state we could expect to attain in good time. Lowell's idea of Mars as an older world where the Martians cooperated on a planetwide scale to build their canal system for the common good was, in the years when nationalistic divisiveness dragged Europe toward the Great War, an enviable testimony that progress had bettered the moral as well as the material quality of Martian life.

For now progress rolls on despite dogging questions. Some critics replace the ladder pointed ever upward with self-limitation or cycles of rise and fall in civilizations,[30] though the question of *will* progress continue attracts far less interest and passion than the question of *should* it continue. One major cultural dispute distinguishes the quality of human existence from technological or any other material measures. Ambivalence over progress pervades modern society in misgivings that our life-sustaining environment, our human values, and our integrity as meaningful persons are at risk—that for the sake of ease and convenience we have sold our souls for thirty pieces of Chicken McNuggets. No one doubts that science has and will allow us to do more, only now the murmurs grow louder with objections that by doing more we only make things worse—that man raised to godhood has risen beyond his competence.

The splendid strivings of civilization have always clashed with much of the wisdom of the ages. A source as old as the Gilgamesh epic teaches that it is better to savor a finite life than to pursue a futile quest for immortality.[31] No one in the ancient world enjoyed greater adulation than Alexander the Great, but he also demonstrated overweening ambition as a leader ready to drive his troops beyond the bounds of the known world. The Roman philosopher Seneca mingled fascination over expeditions to seek the source of the Nile with concerns that Roman expansion grew too audacious.

He worried that striving for distant lands upset the order of nature, angered the gods, and speeded moral decline by promotion of greed. To find distant peoples bore a dangerous double edge. Not only would they learn of the explorers' existence, they could prove ambitious and powerful enough to conquer them.[32] This criticism applies to modern efforts to broadcast messages to distant stars. If we send out our calling card today, an enemy may knock at our door some distant tomorrow.

If empire-building stirs misgivings, efforts to cross established intellectual boundaries bring on seizures of alarm. Seneca's cautions and God's anger that builders of the Tower of Babel tried to reach heaven condemn human efforts to transcend natural limits as hubris or blasphemy, the respective worst offenses of Greco-Roman and biblical cultures. Alexander Pope pleaded the Great Chain of Being as reason for all things to keep their place, since a break anywhere along the chain would disorder the entire universe. The wisdom of that unity was divine in origin and evident to any rational mind, but ambition was blind to the static perfection of things ("whatever is, is right") and rationalized upsetting the natural order.

> In Pride, in reasoning Pride, our error lies;
> All quit their sphere, and rush into the skies.
> Pride still is aiming at the blest abodes,
> Men would be Angels, Angels would be Gods.[33]

The greatest and the humblest thinkers have concurred that too much seeking is wrong. As a UFO witness reflected, "I think God didn't mean for us to understand everything. He doesn't want us to know everything. Man might want to know everything. I think there's some things out there that He doesn't want us to figure out and know what they are."[34]

An equation of civilization with moral advancement and technology with greater human happiness has never balanced for many people. In 1725 the philosopher Giambattista Vico proposed that the savage was a natural poet, gifted with creative imagination that allowed him to impose forms on the chaos of perceptions and thereby begin the creation of order. This poetic capability decayed as order grew into the stifling sophistication of civilization and required cyclical renewal, a throwing off of decadence for a return to simpler unfettered and creative barbarism.[35] In this view the growth of rational thought and accompanying technical mastery of nature brought not an increase in human capabilities but a second fall from Eden. C. G. Jung borrowed the same tradition when he argued that flying saucers appear as symbolic agents to liberate the creative forces of the unconscious from the modern domination of reason.

Continuing this suspicion of rational, materialistic thought, the romantic movement of the nineteenth century frowned on the Industrial Revolution and the rising stock of scientific understanding. William Blake condemned "dark Satanic mills," and William Wordsworth advised that "our meddling intellect Mis-shapes the beauteous forms of things:—We murder to dissect." Alfred Lord Tennyson shrank from the evolutionary view of "nature red in tooth and claw," while Walt Whitman grew ill listening to the "learned astronomer" but healed under the beauty and wonder of the starry sky.[36] Romantic writers expressed their objection to human tampering with nature in antiheroes like Faust and Victor Frankenstein, one who sold his soul to the devil for knowledge and power, one who usurped the prerogative of God by creating life. Despite some ambivalence in the treatment of these characters, the message unfolds with the harshness of a medieval morality tale. Humans are clever enough to manipulate the natural order for their purposes but not wise enough to foresee the consequences. As a result, they are doomed to suffer tragic punishments when the consequences recoil, as they inevitably must, on their presumptuous instigators.

Many fictional meditations have weighed the siren-song attractions of technology against the challenges to human well-being that such progress might bring. Famous writers of the nineteenth century used railroads readily but loved them little. Hawthorne and Thoreau looked askance at the train as an intruder bringing business, noise, and hurry into the pastoral landscape. Tolstoy cast the engine as a devouring monster that mangled the body of Anna Karenina. Dickens did not lose his considerable enthusiasm for rail travel after a fearsome wreck in 1865 left him with post-traumatic stress disorder for the remaining five years of his life, yet even Dickens felt misgivings as he watched railroads destroy the peaceful ways and bucolic landscape of preindustrial England.[37] H. G. Wells countered the shining technotopia of *Things to Come* with the sinister vision of *The Time Machine*, where in the far future the working classes mutate into underground cannibals, the Morlocks, while the ruling classes degenerate into the effete Eloi, who serve no purpose but to provide Morlocks with dinner entrees. A recurrent suspicion casts technology not as a tool of freedom but as the lock and key of slavery. Aldous Huxley's *Brave New World* portrays a glittering future of satisfaction and pleasure, yet little that is truly human remains since people are bred in bottles, with their intelligence and social roles predetermined by technology, while even the intellectual elite live as Lotus Eaters amid a static perfection that they cannot upset. Much literature of dystopia sounds a fear that science gains us the world but costs us our souls.

Even while the moon landing crowned the outward impulse with its greatest triumph, an inward swing of sentiment reversed the value ascribed to any sort of adventurous heroism and technological striving.[38] The counterculture movement of the 1960s became as vehement with cultural self-loathing as the preceding generation had been smug with self-satisfaction, stripping industrialists, the military, government officials, and scientists of the heroic status they had previously enjoyed as masters of nature and condemned them for the same reason. These new villains exemplified spiritually bankrupt materialism and a determination to corrupt everything natural and right into something utilitarian and profitable, no matter who or what gets hurt. Postmodernists recast Columbus from discoverer to destroyer of worlds and cursed him as a colonialist and imperialist.[39] Another voice against the Faustian drive has come from the ecology movement. At its dawn Barry Commoner laid blame for the crisis on new industrial and agricultural technology.[40] A study by the Club of Rome warned that indefinite economic and population growth was not sustainable and that limitations would be necessary to attain equilibrium.[41] When this report, *The Limits to Growth*, appeared in 1972, the idea of finite environmental capacity as a check on human progress seemed absurd, but the principle attracted almost a consensus in the case of global warming.

This reversal of values has spilled into the mainstream. Ordinary citizens no longer trust the experts to know best, and they insist on a say in where the collective future is headed. The shadow of Frankenstein stretches over stem cell research and cloning, and creationists wrangle with state legislatures to bring "intelligent design" into the schoolroom.[42] Questions reach into the previously sacrosanct area of biomedical research as the quest to cure disease, relieve suffering, and prolong life no longer stands as an absolute good. An observation by ethicist Leon Kass that "victory over mortality is the unstated but implicit goal of modern medical science" is most remarkable for the fact that anyone felt a need to state it.[43] Long taken for granted as an obvious goal, Kass and other critics ask if medical advances in prolonging life cost too much in terms of its intangibles—in our sense of humanity, in moral values and meaning, and in the integrity of our place in nature.[44] Some doubters have sat in high places, such as the President's Council on Bioethics, and their call for bans on certain lines of research carries clout. A few voices even favor human extinction over any effort to divert an approaching asteroid or comet, arguing that catastrophic impacts are ultimately beneficial since they set the course of life off in a whole new direction.[45] Our end becomes as inevitable as the demise of Lowell's Martians, but it is something more—an outcome that happens for the best. Missing is the old sense that such a threat, enormous as it might be, poses just another challenge for human ingenuity to overcome. Missing as well is the inviolable sense of our own importance. We are no longer special but a disposable part of nature resigned to say the last goodnight with stoic equanimity.

Few arenas for dispute over cultural direction have proved as contentious as the space program. Many a child growing up in the 1950s and 1960s looked forward to space travel as the great adventure, a job for heroes and a true "giant leap for mankind."[46] Landing on the moon inspired national pride and became an instant milestone of human history, but some critics called going to the moon a wasteful stunt, the last lap in a space race with the Soviets diverting resources from earthly needs. For postmodernists the space race was political theater to demonstrate the superiority of capitalist democracy over Communism and an example of male hubris spreading the colonialist impulse to other planets.[47] Even fanciful proposals to mine the lunar surface or terraform Mars have met with resistance on the grounds that mining operations would deface the beauty of the moon and that we owe Mars the moral right to its own destiny.[48] The fact that any disruption visible from earth would have to be enormous, and that a dead world has no ecology to disrupt, simply unmasks the complaints as objections not to a particular project but to taking any action at all. An impulse to press outward against physical frontiers clashes once again with a conviction that the proper business of humans lies inward within themselves. The *Star Trek* mission to "boldly go where no man has gone before" sets the mood for an optimistic time, now mutated into fear and doubt in the shadowy *X-Files* landscape of secrecy and conspiracy where the proper attitude is "fight the future."

Aliens in the Technophobic Mirror

Nothing on earth rivals the potential for otherness inherent in aliens from space. Not of this planet, not products of its evolutionary history, not restricted by its biology or bound to its natural or social laws, aliens can outdo the monstrousness of any earthly creature or reflect every physical and mental shape human thought projects onto them. Fiction and tradition take full advantage of these potentials; UFO descriptions do not. Most UFO personnel split between the human and the humanoid. They are either like the Space Brothers, who act as angelic as they look, or like the dwarfish Grays, who attend to their duties with emotions and compassion stunted like their bodies. A few Reptilians and Insectoids bring a touch of the Hollywood monster to UFO abductions, and hybrids blend human with alien physical features and join personality traits of the two species in an imperfect union. Abductees sometimes report tall Nordics, blond, blue-eyed, and bewitching humans much like the Space Brothers, though less clearly benevolent in intentions, as well as human civilian and military accomplices of the gray humanoids. Sinister and comical at the same time, the Men in Black know impossible secrets about people they visit but little about how to dress or speak correctly.

Why UFO-related entities in experiential reports manifest such limited variety poses an intriguing question. Less mystery surrounds how interpretive discussions characterize aliens and their purposes. Ufologists of all stripes, from the most rigorous to the most speculative, portray aliens according to readings of the reports, but those readings settle into stereotypical thematic patterns. As presented in the literature and discussions, Space Brothers parallel traditional idealizations of the good Other, while Grays often represent the bad Other. The interpreter builds a case that the evidence presents a coherent image, or else imposes a chosen image on the given facts. Either way, the entities become actors in a narrative and are subject to treatment as characters in a literary text. If the nature of the entities in reports remains unknown, the entities in the interpreter's text act in ways that echo human concerns. Portrayal of the gray entities provides one prominent example of the UFO text conveying this sort of message. In going about their business and simply being themselves, they express enough thematic terms of an earthbound love-hate relationship with technology to say that, at least from the standpoint of characterization, space aliens serve purposes that are very human after all.

A hallmark of otherness is difference sufficiently marked to separate "them" from "us." Freedom from sin allows angels to be perfect in form and character; an excess of pride turns Lucifer and the fallen angels into devils. Fairies are missing some essential human part. They may have hollow backs as a disturbing physical difference or, more important, lack a soul or virtues such as honesty and reluctance to do harm. An unmistakable superiority differentiates UFO aliens from humans. The Space Brothers look ordinary enough to walk down the street and mingle with the crowd, but they are not ordinary and are not likely to become beer buddies or carry out the trash for Monday morning pickup. The contactees emphasize that these aliens are better than human, exalted by their purpose and spiritual advancement into a pure and positive ideal. The Grays are visibly nonhuman and easily recognized as alien. They are nevertheless human enough to accept as fellow rational creatures and to expect that our two species can share common ground, until they spoil this prospect by abducting humans and stealing their genetic materials. These beings are superior in power and intellect but deficient in humanity, a combination that casts a negative polarity on their superiority and places them in company with traditional monsters from afar.

What sets UFO aliens apart from supernaturals, Plinian monsters, and wild men is the uniquely modern concept of superiority through technology. Exotic creatures of the past might possess magical or superhuman abilities, but these powers were asides, whereas overwhelming technology is the central, immediately recognizable quality of aliens in both fiction and the UFO literature. UFO aliens arrive as inevitably advanced beings. The fact that they can arrive at all attests to the advancement of their space-faring machinery. They have surpassed the earthly level of material civilization and left human technology behind as primitive by comparison, so that we cannot think of extraterrestrials unless we reckon with knowledge and capabilities greater than our own. Where our thoughts go from here depends on what the aliens do with their superiority and on human attitudes toward technology.

Ideas about flying saucers in the 1950s expressed the best and worst expectations for technological advancement. The Space Brothers reflected a positivist vision where the material development of a civilization progressed apace with increasing enlightenment of mind and benevolence of heart. Just as a gradual realization on earth that all people were equal in worth and legal standing led to abolition of slavery, surely the broader scope of alien understanding must encompass the struggling inhabitants of backward planets in a greater sphere of compassion. An enlarged humanity must compel the aliens to extend their caring to practical action beyond any principle of noninterference or scrupulous respect for the cultural free will of other species. Real brothers do not stand by and watch. They take an active part in guiding their juniors on other worlds along a path of universal morality and truth. Such was the contactees' hope, and it repeated the goals of progressive politics, religious uplift, and social action on earth.

The manipulation of the Space Brothers to suit human ideals and desires is explicit at every turn. These visitors are simply too good to be true. They appear angelically beautiful, speak colloquial English, and act so down-to-earth that nothing at all seems alien about them. They may have lives of their own back home on Venus, but on earth they are nothing but saviors, paragons to perform stereotypical hero roles with no ulterior motives, no other purpose than to fulfill the hopes of mankind. Such aliens portray humans grown perfect, the way we want to become once we advance beyond war, cruelty, injustice, intolerance, and poverty. In contactee stories the aliens wear their godlike power lightly as they employ technology only in the cause of good. Heart and soul dominate over intellect while machinery simply enables them to spread their innate goodwill across interplanetary space. In abduction stories the same stubborn hopes sometimes arise in a sterile environment of examination rooms and strange machinery with aliens that are not human or brotherly or kind. Despite suffering terror and pain, some captives return to assert that these aliens, like strict unsmiling schoolmarms of a bygone age, hold human welfare at heart and employ harsh methods only to knock some sense into our materialistic heads.

Though the alien classroom is gentle in one case and rough in the other, both images oppose the secular view of an impersonal universe with what is, ultimately, a religious outlook. Simply by affirming the existence of universal values the Space Brothers satisfy a timeless longing for absolutes of right and wrong. By partaking in a program of transformation, the Grays confirm that the human race is worth saving. The broader message behind these accounts of extraterrestrial intervention fulfills the hope that earth is not isolated, accidental, or inconsequential in the vastness of space. Once again the earth and its inhabitants matter, and once again they become the center of attention as some wise, powerful, and ultimately compassionate Other leads us in the right direction. Perhaps no human hopes have a longer, more insistent history than these: that human existence is meaningful in the cosmic scheme of things and the powers of the cosmos care about us. The varied expressions stay on theme in various religions and philosophies and continue to do so in this recent entry to the record, where the means of travel is technological and the heavenly visitors are extraterrestrial, yet still they bear a welcome, familiar, and very human reassurance.

A rosy image of the savior has not fared as well in either ufological or popular representation as an image of the sinister or threatening alien. The progressive hope that soul and intellect, moral scope and technical capability increased in tandem had a precarious basis from the start because the driving force of evolution was natural selection—a competitive, winner-take-all process characterized by selfishness rather than altruism. Lowell condemned his Martians to a slow death on a dying planet, but H. G. Wells rescued them with the can-do spirit of his age as he sent them off to colonize the earth. Martians confronted with a threat to their survival chose self-interest over sacrifice and turned their technological prowess toward destruction. The possibility that UFO aliens also eye this world as a new home cuts through the history of ufological thinking as the dying planet motif appears in 1950s theories and again in abduction imagery. Whether as the straightforward invaders of Keyhoe and moviemakers, or as surreptitious subversives infiltrating the populace one hybrid at a time, or as participants in a nefarious collaboration with the government, aliens often assume the role of invading monsters bent on conquering the world and enslaving, destroying, or cannibalizing humanity. While no one welcomes a hostile takeover, the motive is all too familiar in human behavior and human fears of how our fellows will behave. Suspicion of similar action allows us to recognize UFO aliens, in a perverse and distasteful way, as our kind of people.

Reports of alien abduction provide the most detailed close-ups of UFO occupants, and the picture is largely a chilling one. The aliens most often encountered in both experiential and interpretational UFO literature are the Grays, entities that oppose human values in an almost exemplary demonstration of civilization gone wrong. What they do is technical, efficient, and focused; how they do it is businesslike, cold, and frightening. The superior intellect of the Grays is evidenced by their bulging heads and powerful eyes, their otherworldly equipment and proficiency in using it, their well-planned agenda and emotionless commitment to duty. Vast intellect frees the Grays from human limitation and prepares them to work wonders, but superhuman ability also empowers them to do great harm. The Grays seem oblivious to any basic human restraint like moral conscience or the social contract. They permit no possibility of dialogue or choice on equal terms. Diplomacy, negotiation, compromise, and empathy have no place in dealings of their kind with our kind, leading to a one-sided relationship of masters to captives treated without any standing as persons. With their manifest attitude of aloof disregard the aliens share no information and care nothing for human culture or knowledge. Humans are subjects or victims and nothing more.

A large cranium and a small, frail body bestow on the Grays a physical appearance that intercepts some familiar prophecies of how humans will evolve. The idea that evolution would augment the brain, eyes, and manual dexterity at the expense of the rest of the body traces back at least to 1893, when H. G. Wells published an article entitled "The Man of the Year Million." As he described these men, "Great hands they have, enormous brains, and liquid, soulful eyes. Their whole muscular system, their legs, their abdomens, are shriveled to nothing, a dangling, degraded pendant to their minds." These beings hop on their hands into pools of liquid to absorb nutrients, since their digestive system has disappeared. Gone too are the animals and plants of the earth as irrelevant—"In the last days man will be alone on the earth, and his food will be won by the chemist from the dead rocks and the sunlight." Machinery does the work that muscle can no longer accomplish, and human society becomes a paragon of order and calm, since "the irrational fellowship of man will give place to an intellectual co-operation, and emotion fall within the scheme of reason."[49] Many subsequent science-fiction stories have exploited this evolutionary premise, often in dystopic visions of a future without cherished human qualities or physical vigor, just an existence of cerebration and dependence on machinery.[50] A similar image of "eggheads" and "nerds" has entrenched in general culture and meets scathing disapproval in "Gonzo" journalist Hunter S. Thompson's description of materialistic people today: "Huge brains, small necks, weak muscles and fat wallets—these are the dominant physical characteristics of the '80s . . . The Generation of Swine."[51]

Though extraterrestrial in origin, the Grays embody our own misgivings about where civilization and progress are taking us. With such flimsy bodies they are nothing without their machinery. It is the source of their power, not any individual or cultural virtue. The machine reaches to the aliens themselves so that they become its extensions, robotlike automatons of pure science and cold reason without imagination, suited for ships having austere and steely interiors devoid of amenities like art, comfort, or beauty. The Grays suffer not from a lack of civilization but from too much of it. They have not so much fallen short of humanity as they have cast it off as a worthless encumbrance, choosing materialism over moral development and committing to the inhumane potential of civilization. Technological superiority at the expense of love, freedom, and goodwill sides them with barbarians and wild men, with Nazis and Communists, or with social insects as a parallel in nature. Replacing a human soul with a utilitarian drive makes monsters out of both the humans who have rejected their humanity and of aliens who have failed to cultivate its possibility. The alien planet fares no better. Abductees describe a barren or blasted landscape, a dying or subterranean world as visible testimony that the alien civilization has wrought havoc on nature.

The Grays are disturbing not just for reasons of xenophobia but because they foreshadow an alienated human future. They have reached where we will someday arrive to bring a warning that if we advance too much, we too may lose our humanity. In personal UFO accounts the Grays are striking for their blandness. For all their intellect, they lack identity or personality. This one may serve as leader, and that one may perform a specialized task, but these distinctions resemble differences in insect castes rather than indicate individuality. The vast alien eyes bespeak power and yet they remain blank, mirrors not of a soul but of an empty void, while the rest of the alien face is rudimentary and destitute of character. Colorless and sunless with funguslike skin, aliens manifest the grayness we commonly associate with drab institutional places and dull boring people. These entities are sickly dwarfs without gender or musculature, names or personalities, without any life or purpose aside from the work they do. Technology has denatured them, so much so that they do not seem to eat, and even a basic function like reproduction is lost to them as they depend on human surrogates. The aliens of abduction reflect human nature destroyed by human civilization, a version of the modern condition carried to monitory extremes. With very little imagination we can step into the mirror and see ourselves become the Other, shriveled and gray and dehumanized as we work with mechanical intensity like mindless insects, ground down and homogenized, alien from any self we value or life with meaning. Literary monsters retain an air of heroic and individualized being, but UFO aliens are too much like ourselves to stand out from the anonymous crowd and make good monsters. Such aliens bring to life a future Self we abhor.

Abductions and conspiracies add a UFO-inflected voice to quarrels already strident in society over threatening trends in technology and modern civilization. UFO abductions revitalize in technological form a persistent anxiousness over genetic integrity, with extraterrestrial hybrid-makers replacing the undesirable foreigners that were once the focus of concern and sharing with Satanists the recent fears of supernaturally powerful and secretive child molesters. A woman's place in the clutches of the wild man or King Kong or the Creature from the Black Lagoon was both helpless victim and irresistible object, reaffirming a faith that humans are special, desirable, and always in peril from monstrous Others. Science-fiction movies continue to portray women as victims of technologically overpowering aliens and so do abductions, though the procedures have grown more repellent. Her captors circumvent the human element of reproduction as they harvest eggs, implant embryos, and steal the developing fetus in a clinical, utterly mechanical process of technological rape. The woman serves as biological equipment and the fetus becomes a commodity stacked and stored in the tanks of alien baby farms, completely depersonalized by alien technology. Quality of life falls under assault as government secrecy withholds the truth about UFO visitation and free energy that alien technology could provide.[52] What part aliens play in this conspiracy varies from one theory to another, but every version portrays the government itself as grown monstrous and antihuman, an alien force of great power ready to betray its own kind by collaborating with the Grays and to manipulate the population with technologies like personal barcodes, surveillance, and thought control. A tightening net of machinations hastens the day when a full-blown dictatorship locks the chains of slavery on all mankind.

The characterization of aliens in the UFO literature may or may not correspond to the character of any actual alien, living or dead. Like characterization in a novel or biography, the result depends on how the author combines fact and fiction, observation and inference to present an audience with a meaningful but not necessarily accurate text. The "authorship" of witnesses is typically limited to reports of raw experiences, sensations, and reactions; ufologists become the go-betweens to interpret alien character, selecting what to keep and what to ignore, introducing theories, agendas, concerns, and expectations to fill in the gaps when curiosity overreaches evidence and to construct meaningful portraits from a mass of details. One trend apparent in ufologists' characterization of aliens is gravitation toward exemplary types like saviors, exploiters, or conspirators. The Space Brothers are easy to understand as products of imagination that model an image of perfection on angels and messiahs. The Grays present an image of villainy, though an imperfect one. They are bad but imagination could make them worse. Some limitation—perhaps in reported characteristics or in willingness of interpreters to imagine the worst—fetters the characterization of Grays so that they fall short of becoming pure opposites of the good. Ambivalence also riddles these aliens as some interpreters find only self-serving behaviors; others dig clues of benevolence from the rocky ground of abduction testimony. Such fluidity of image suggests that UFO occupants as we understand them owe more to interpreters' predispositions than to hard facts about aliens.

Another trend in characterization is the tendency for representations to repeat, emphasize, and develop possibilities that resonate with ongoing earthly concerns. A myth often distills the experience of scattered individuals into symbols meaningful to all. Fritz Lang's *Metropolis* symbolized the factory as a latter-day Moloch consuming workers as human sacrifices, while *Modern Times* captured the essence of industrial dehumanization as assembly line production ran Charlie Chaplin through the cogs and gears. An abductee who has no say-so or control, who serves as a lab rat to be manipulated, processed, and discarded without courtesy or consideration repeats the fate of the modern Everyman who is nothing more than a number, consumer, and human resource, and who is dispensable whenever economic winds change direction. The abductee probably does not intend to describe anything other than a personal experience, and the ufologist cares about UFOs rather than the human condition, but whether by chance or some convergence of thought, the Grays occupy roles very similar to impersonal corporate exploiters on earth. Even if Grays literally abduct humans, the take-home message is not really about an isolated encounter or the strange things that extraterrestrials do. In literary perspective, abductions gain their most identifiable dimension of meaning when they cease to tell an individual's story and sum up widespread human experiences.

The literal sight of a big-headed alien does not carry an inherent meaning. The meaning comes from outside, in the attributions of interpreters, who may understand the physiology and behavior of this strange being by connecting it with ideas about the man of the future. A correspondence between the Grays and earthly matters happens not by happenstance but because mere facts, even about aliens, hold limited significance. More compelling meanings take shape when the story aligns with current beliefs, interests, and concerns, when it parallels established networks of thought. No one rhapsodizes over the Grays' work ethic or the utilitarian efficiency of their examination rooms. In another time the technological adeptness of these entities might meet with admiration, in the same one-sided manner that epic movies from the 1920s to the 1950s cast builders of the Union Pacific railroad as heroes and Plains Indians as one-dimensional enemies of progress. Fashions have reversed to sympathize with the Indians and reduce the builders to greedy invaders; our aliens too emerge as embodiments of hopes and fears active in our time and cultural environment. The correspondences that tie alien characterization to human interest may not be intended or even important to any witness, but they stand out because those points of intersection bear prior meaning and transfer that meaning to the aliens, turning a story of unique and unknown events into representative actions of earthly significance. These points provide interpreters with issues to focus on and develop into characterizations, perhaps to the detriment of understanding extraterrestrials, but to the betterment of expressing human relationships with an Other that has, all along, mirrored and commented on ourselves.

CHAPTER EIGHT

Explaining UFOs:
An Inward Look

—'Tis strange, my Theseus, what these lovers speak of.
— More strange than true; I never may believe
These antique fables, nor these fairy toys. . . .
—But all the story of the night told over,
And all their minds transfigured so together,
More witnesseth than fancy's images,
And grows to something of great constancy.
    —Shakespeare, *A Midsummer Night's Dream*

We are such stuff as dreams are made on.
    —Shakespeare, *The Tempest*

When Dorothy and her friends have an audience with the Wizard of Oz, his blazing, roaring figure transfixes them until her dog Toto snatches away a curtain to expose Oz the Great and Terrible as nothing but illusion and humbug, the work of a man pulling levers as he puts on a show. UFOs amount to considerably more than deception, but the man behind the curtain remains on the job. He is not malicious or even aware that he participates in a show. He is nothing more sinister than our collective self, searching for understanding with good intentions but with limited means at his disposal. His understanding applies less to the phenomenal UFO than to the mythical UFO, the sum and system of ideas that he associates with the subject. The myth often replaces incomplete, obscure, confusing facts with an appealing substitute rich in meaning but not necessarily true to the phenomenon. Much as ufologists wish it otherwise, much as they want beliefs on one side and facts on the other, interpretations over here and ob-servations over there, the myth leaps all fences to assemble a coherent image of reality out of scattered parts. This myth has become an inseparable piece of modern culture and as important to understanding UFOs as the UFOs themselves.

Two opposing sides vie over interpretation of the UFO myth. Uncritical ufologists see no myth at all but a representation synonymous with the truth—that is, the assembly of alleged facts and the system of meanings to organize those facts render an accurate account of ongoing unconventional phenomena usually taken to be extraterrestrial visits to earth. The skeptics see nothing more than a myth in the narrowest sense, a hodgepodge of errors and beliefs wherein everything unconventional is illusory. Once satisfied with a snicker or a rant, opponents now respect the social fact of UFOs sufficiently to propose conventional solutions that are nuanced and plausible. Few critics still rely on a single unconditional answer. One size cannot fit all in a mystery of such diverse parts, so old favorites like hoax, mirage, or mass delusion explain a little but not a lot, and surely not everything.

The most creditable conventional solution combines psychological, sociological, and cultural causes to explain UFOs in a strategy covered by the term "psychosocial." This designation applies to certain criticisms aimed specifically at UFOs, to psychological theories of anomalous experiences like multiple personalities and alien abductions, and to a growing body of scholarship that addresses origins of the supernatural in religion, mythology, and folklore. In a succinct description of psychosocial premises applied to UFOs, David Sivier, writing for the British journal *Magonia*, says that

> the UFO phenomenon is merely the modern variant of a range of paranormal encounters and visitations by supernatural others. Despite their technological trappings, modern UFO sightings are merely the scientistic expression of deep religious and mystical impulses from within the human psyche, impulses which have given rise to previous ages' myths of encounters with angels, demons, elves and ghosts. Far from being encounters with objectively real, nuts and bolts extraterrestrial spacecraft, UFO visitations, and much of the culture surrounding them, is a twentieth century technological religious experience.[1]

Psychosocial explanations permit an experiential basis for UFO narratives, though the observation behind a sighting is an airplane or Venus, the frightening sensations associated with abductions are due to sleep paralysis, and the crash at Roswell was real but only a Mogul balloon. Ambiguous in itself or made so by expectations, the experience acquires its strangeness through a transfusion of cultural beliefs about UFOs. Conscious or unconscious borrowings from books, movies, tradition, and current social issues provide the raw materials; the encouragement of people open to belief and the influence of fellow believers provide a reinforcing social setting. The imagination constructs a distinctive UFO experience out of these parts, translating or adapting ser-viceable ideas according to the cultural model of how UFOs should look and behave. Though the emphasis may vary from psychological to social to cultural causes, some version of psychosocial theory provides the economical solution of choice for orthodox critics.

The critics unmask a psychosocial cause for just about every aspect of UFOs. Mass delusions egged on by the media account for the 1896–1897 airships, according to soci-ologist Robert E. Bartholomew, and also for the British "scareship" waves of 1909 and 1913, according to Nigel Watson writing in *Magonia*.[2] Expectations continue to bind unrelated ordinary events into a Roswell mystery or turn jet fighters into the enormous triangles reported at Stephenville, Texas, in 2008.[3] Abductions serve as the favorite exhibit for cultural influences building a fictitious story. Alvin Lawson, an English pro-fessor at California State University at Long Beach, finds precedents in science fic-tion, cartoons, and similar accessible sources for every alien type in abduction reports.[4] Ufologist Kevin D. Randle, documentary filmmaker Russ Estes, and clinical psycholo-gist William P. Cone trace the story content of abductions to prior accounts or ficti-tious portrayals and the course of events to a "cultural consciousness" established in the media.[5] Skeptic Martin Kottmeyer argues that the order of abduction accounts reflects nothing more remarkable than a culturally preferred "right way to tell a story."[6] French researchers Bertrand Méheust and Michel Meurger have uncovered numerous ante-cedents of UFO belief in science fiction and folk narrative.[7] Peter Rogerson cites many key abduction motifs in a book published in 1967, just as alien kidnap first entered public awareness. As he writes in *Magonia*, "Let's get this straight: a work of fiction had introduced the 'enchantment' or 'Oz factor,' the supernatural cold, the doorway amne-sia, the alien in disguise, the whole drama of disinterested scientists experimenting on us like guinea pigs."[8] How seriously, the Magonians ask, can we take the possibility of literal UFOs when their every aspect has close antecedents in fiction and folklore?

In one sense the psychosocial critics are indisputably right and UFO literalists wrong. Too many parallels exist between UFOs and other cultural materials to doubt the general thesis that human rather than alien causes underlie much of what is told and thought about UFOs. An understanding of UFOs cannot take observation for granted or trust the printed word as fact, and psychosocial theory rightly obliges reck-oning with personal, collective, and cultural influences on the UFO story. The stron-ger conclusion—that shared themes in culture and UFO narratives mean the former cause the latter with nothing left over—appeals to many psychosocial proponents but is problematic. Two potential truths may contribute to a UFO story. One is historical, the events that really happened; the other is human, the events as they should have happened, and both join with seamless unity in the narrative text. A contrast between observation and interpretation, phenomenon and constructions of meaning, remains a crucial distinction to keep in mind. This chapter considers whether psychological, social, and cultural causes have the answer for all things ufological or if that answer calls for thinking outside the myth.

Sources of UFO Belief, Theory, and Argumentation

The Psychology of UFO Believers.—An unusual subject like UFOs often raises suspicions that UFO witnesses and proponents possess unusual psychological qualities. As long ago as the airship waves, popular humor derided witnesses as crazy or drunk, and this tenacious stigma persists in a recent declaration, from no less a source than *Science* magazine, that "calling in all the people who have seen strange things just gets you a roomful of strange people."[9] The question of psychological normalcy among UFO witnesses invites scientific research, and here, for once, quite a few studies address the issue. The most sweeping attempts by professional psychologists reduce seeing UFOs to perceptual and conceptual errors, and believing in UFOs to a reaction against stress through magical thinking, delusions, and hallucinations.[10] A sociological solution identifies UFO believers as status inconsistent—they work at low-paying jobs despite a high level of education or do not enjoy a degree of respect commensurate with their social rank. Such discrepancy leads to a sense of marginality and attraction to fringe ideas as an expression of rebellion against mainstream thinking.[11]

Abductees draw the keenest scrutiny on the expectation that their mental profile will match the strangeness of their claims. An abiding psychological explanation casts abductees as fantasy-prone or boundary-deficit, members of a fraction of the population that is unable to separate truth from fiction and quick to mistake imaginary incidents for reality.[12] The use of hypnosis to recover abduction memories has raised suspicions that abductees might be especially susceptible to suggestion, as well as unduly subjected to it by aggressive UFO investigators, while experiments with hypnotized nonabductees found evidence that cultural exposure enabled anyone to tell a creditable abduction story.[13] Two psychologists have explained the gruesome, sexually charged claims of abductees as masochistic fantasies of individuals as they attempt to escape ordinary self-awareness.[14] Laurentian University psychologist Michael Persinger traces close encounters and other paranormal experiences to abnormalities of the temporal lobe of the brain. If the hemispheres of the brain fall out of synchronicity, one side may detect the other as an external presence, while aberrant temporal lobe activity creates sounds, smells, false pregnancies, and sexual stimulation closely resembling the descriptions of abductees.[15]

Psychologists have learned that remembering seemingly bizarre events does not require the participation of bizarre people. Memories, far from written in stone, are vulnerable to modification by subsequent information, personal expectations, and the influence of others. Experiments by memory expert Elizabeth Loftus, professor of psychology at the University of California at Irvine, demonstrate that not only is eyewitness testimony prone to reworking, but a seed of suggestion nurtured by social reinforcement can grow a false memory as vivid as real life and upheld by the same convincing "feel."[16] The 1980s child abuse panic provided shocking examples of how readily ordinary people could confabulate grotesque recollections of events that never happened. Paul Ingram, a respected deputy sheriff in Tacoma, responded to groundless accusations by his teenage daughters with ever more elaborate confessions of satanic and abusive practices. Given a suggestion and a few hours to mull it over, he returned with a thorough horror story confessed with sincere conviction, even when the claim was as improbable as that the dogs of the police K-9 unit raped his wife.[17]

Further evidence from sociocognitive psychologists confirms the surprising malleability of both memory and behavior. From this perspective hypnosis is not a specific trance state but a socially scripted drama, wherein the subject brings expectations of how to play the part of a hypnotized subject and responds to cues and suggestions that the hypnotist provides. Both participants strive toward a shared goal in the hypnosis context, and their give-and-take succeeds if the subject acts like a hypnotized person according to their mutual understanding of hypnotic behavior.[18] Multiple personality disorder, where one body houses sometimes scores of distinctive personalities, each with its own voice and memories, results not from a traumatized mind fragmented into independent compartments but from role-playing enactments. Subjects are, according to Carlton University psychologist Nicolas P. Spanos, "actively involved in using available information to create a social impression that is congruent with their perception of social demands, with the self-understandings they have learned to adopt, and with the interpersonal goals they are attempting to achieve."[19] This act is not a deliberate hoax but an unconscious effort to fulfill the demands of a social context that nevertheless results in false claims.

In this view the UFO abduction experience exists only as a fantasy enacted by a suggestible subject to please an overzealous ufologist and fulfill the socially defined role of abductee. Like multiple personality disorder, abduction was a rare condition that suddenly proliferated once it received media attention and investigator interest. Both sexual abuse and abduction scenarios lead to role-playing opportunities and suggestive, high-demand questioning, just the sort of fertile environment where false memories flourish. People as normal as you or I invent these "believed-in imaginings," but they are no more than fictitious reminders of how far astray even memories of personal experience can lead us.[20]

Little of the appeal to abnormal psychology survives head-on collision with the facts. Actual studies counter armchair theories with findings that UFO observers and abductees are free of psychopathology or temporal lobe disturbance, neither are they marginal, maladjusted, or inclined to reject mainstream culture.[21] People reporting UFOs are even high achievers, and in a psychological study led by Spanos (an important study because the investigators were unfriendly to UFO claims), tests revealed that abductees actually outstripped control subjects on measures of mental health.[22]

If UFO experience and belief have no link to psychopathology, their relationship to compromising mental processes is also unclear. Experiments with hypnosis end with mixed results—abductees take up some suggestions that an investigator plants but just as readily leave other suggestions behind. How important hypnosis is to the recovery of abduction memories becomes doubtful when considering an experiment with eleven abductees that uncovered new episodes in only two subjects, while two others remembered nothing new under hypnosis and seven simply elaborated on episodes consciously remembered.[23] Not all results are similarly negative. Recent experiments by Harvard psychologists Susan A. Clancy, Richard J. McNally, and their associates uncover heightened propensity for false recognition and false recall, as well as higher scores on perceptual aberration and magical ideation tests, which lead the investigators to conclude that alien abduction claimants are prone to false memories, though five other tests of abductees for fantasy proneness have failed to find it.[24] Subsequent failure to confirm susceptibility to false memories by University of London psychologist Christopher C. French, though he began with a similar hypothesis and applied similar tests, casts further doubt on the Harvard solution as a final answer to the genesis of abduction memories.[25]

At the same time, abductees drop a hint that something is different about them. They tend to be creative, original, and have a rich inner life. They are often unconventional, independent, and willing to acknowledge unusual attitudes, ideas, and feelings. An increased frequency of paranormal encounters, ESP, out-of-body experiences, and other oddities leads University of Connecticut psychologist Kenneth Ring to describe abductees as having "experience-prone personalities."[26] Spanos found no increase in paranormal experience among high-strangeness claimants but noted heightened acceptance among UFO believers, as they embraced not only aliens but New Age ideas and past lives.[27] Another study found that abductees favor feeling over thinking and accept

a broad spectrum of spiritual ideas, from conventional religion to witchcraft.[28] Abductees also present a weak sense of identity, sensitivity, vulnerability, and defensiveness,
even a mild paranoid tendency in their suspicion and guardedness, as well as schizoid
tendencies in their eccentricity and creativity.[29] A final characteristic of abductees and
other people with intensive UFO experiences is a tendency toward unhappiness, a sort
of "close encounter social dissatisfaction cluster." It includes anxiety, a history of childhood abuse or unhappiness, job and family problems, suicidal thoughts, and a sense
that no place is safe.[30] The most extreme findings along these lines appear in a study
where the subjects were rife with poor self-esteem, impaired interpersonal relationships, and sexual dysfunction.[31]

To keep these distinctions in perspective, they are usually slight tendencies among
normal people rather than flashing neon lights of acute peculiarity. Investigators faced
with nothing very striking about their samples sometimes stress even rather marginal
findings just for the sake of having something to say. These characteristics also lend
themselves to opposing interpretations. A skeptic like Spanos concludes that UFO
witnesses "are predisposed toward esoteric beliefs in general and alien beliefs in particular and . . . interpret unusual sensory and imaginal experiences in terms of the alien
hypothesis."[32] Skeptics have cited the fact that Betty Hill read one of Donald Keyhoe's
books and promptly wrote him a letter describing her 1961 close encounter as proof
that she was already a believer, but this argument entangles itself in a catch-22. Had
she not contacted NICAP, her story would have died in the limbo of weird but un-
spoken experiences, while reading one UFO book hardly boosts her interest to the
level of an obsession. Proponents see curiosity about unusual phenomena as a natural
response to an unusual experience, a consequence rather than a cause. They also read
abductees' nightmares and reactions to an alien face or doctor's office as the aftershocks
of an extraordinary encounter, the post-traumatic outbursts that fall into place as clues
to a hidden abduction experience. As Budd Hopkins expresses it, "though conventional
psychological theory cannot explain UFO abduction experiences, UFO abduction experiences *can* explain unconventional psychological behavior in the abductee."[33]

Even if abductees ultimately prove to share a psychological profile, the fact remains
that close-encounter witnesses represent only a fraction of UFO claimants. They are
legion, and chances seem remote that millions of UFO observers share any meaning-
fully distinctive psychology. As a collective, these people comprise a heterogeneous
group united more by what they see than by any predispositions to see it. Even when
the experiences are bizarre, the psychological evidence adds up that the experiencers
are not. What joins them, and the one thing they have in common, seems to be the
experience itself.

The Psychology of UFO Belief.—Though abnormal psychology falls short, the psychosocial school invests considerable interest in the normative psychology of ufologists as a potentially revealing approach. In this view, UFO proponents comprise a community with a culture of its own. Members of this community share distinctive ways of seeing and doing things as well as assumptions that structure beliefs and ways of thinking. One characteristic that emerges out of the rhetoric of UFO argument and refrains of the literature is a tendency toward paranoia. Another pervasive style of thinking ingrained in UFO culture is an undisciplined independence that resembles a pioneering or frontier mentality. A third frequent habit of ufological thinking calls on fallacious forms of reasoning to arrive at desired conclusions.

Individuals can practice paranoid thinking without being paranoid in a clinical sense. In her classic anthropological study, *Patterns of Culture*, Ruth Benedict recognized that a dominant mode of thinking may characterize entire societies, with restraint and reason the traits of an Apollonian culture, while outbursts of emotion and irrationality mark Dionysian cultures. She described the Dogu of New Guinea as a paranoid culture because suspicion and treachery are cultural norms. Trust is in short supply since malevolent witches surround everyone, their hostile actions responsible for every unfavorable event, from bad weather to sickness. The Dogu live in fear of poisoning and regard death itself as the unnatural consequence of some conspiring enemy, often one's own spouse.[34] Paranoid thinking can dominate complex modern cultures as well, as in the cases of the European witch hunts, Nazi Germany, and the Stalinist era in the Soviet Union. Historian Richard Hofstadter's essay on "The Paranoid Style in American Politics" identifies a virulent strand of paranoid thinking in American political thought, from anti-Masonic and anti-Catholic campaigns in the nineteenth century to anticommunism in the twentieth. He defines the paranoid's world as coherent to a minute degree. Accident and error play no part. Everything happens for a premeditated reason, and good and evil are as absolute as black and white. A malevolent conspiracy of almost supernatural powers endangers the righteous way of life and represents the driving force of history. In the exaggerated view of paranoids the conspiracy is always vast, urgent, and apocalyptic, compelling opponents to document the threats in an indiscriminate mix of plausible and implausible claims.[35]

From invasions and Men in Black to conspiracy theories and disclosure proclamations, UFO ideas express the same sense of threat, secrecy, and grandiosity that characterizes paranoia. Martin Kottmeyer finds UFO thinking shot through with such typical paranoid themes as "apocalypses, amnesia, persecutions, chases, influencing machines, and conspiracies." Surveillance is a longstanding rationale for UFO visitation, with much anxiety expended over alien spying on military bases and atomic

energy facilities, or with the internalized monitor of implants in abductees. A preoccupation with contamination surfaced with 1950s concerns over exposure to radiation
from UFOs and again in Barney Hill's feeling of dirtiness after his abduction. These
concerns, along with theft of genetic materials and fetuses, link UFO experiencers to
the hypochondria common among paranoids. Another locus of paranoid fear is some
external control manipulating the thoughts and actions of people against their will.
Much of the abduction story concerns involuntary intrusion, loss of volition, temporary paralysis, thoughts stolen or implanted, and deprivation of memory. An obsession
with sexual perversion characterizes outbreaks of social paranoia, like the witch hunts,
the anti-Catholic movement, and recent furor over satanic ritual abuse, while the geni-
tal interests of alien examiners catches abductions in the same tradition.[36]

Kottmeyer further contends that the developmental course of paranoia through
the lifetime of individuals recapitulates in the thoughts and actions of UFO believers. Landmarks of evolving paranoia include growing social sensitivity and difficulty
in relationships, fear and suspicion, hypochondria and concern with external control,
imagining grandiose delusional threats and a personal role in overcoming them. These
stages map a course through ufological history as proponents squabble in jealous turf
wars and fear the aliens, first as invaders and later as manipulators of human minds.
The importance of the UFO mystery has escalated from scientific visitation to manipulation of the human gene line and radical revision of the entire human future. Abductees have morphed from victims into the vanguard of a new cosmic consciousness
with a vital mission in some imminent apocalypse, while government perfidy has enlarged from withholding information to betraying humanity to the aliens. This parallel
unfolding of UFO history and personal psychohistory convinces Kottmeyer that UFO
belief develops as a paranoid system.[37]

Another pattern characteristic of thinking about UFOs might be called frontier
mentality. The historian Frederick Jackson Turner proposed in his "frontier thesis" that
pioneer values and American values were largely synonymous.[38] Having no deep history of their own, no King Arthur or Robin Hood to look back on, Americans seized
on a romanticized version of the pioneer experience to express a distinctive national
character. Several keynotes of the American experience set the tone for a rough and
ready way of thinking that carries forward into ufology today. America as we know it
began with exploration. To explore meant an adventurous willingness to plunge into
the unknown, a readiness to accept mystery and danger as next-door neighbors. The
newness of the New World has captured the American imagination with the idea that
a pioneer could redeem failure or dissatisfaction by moving to the frontier, where obligations and rules did not exist and life became a blank slate again. This footloose

detachment from the past fostered a forward-looking, future-oriented readiness to favor fresh solutions and to forget the lessons of history, to prefer practical results over theory and absolutes of right and wrong over nuances.[39] A central image of pioneer life casts individuals alone with only their own resources to fall back on, and while pioneers typically relied on communal cooperation and mutual assistance, Americans continue to prize ideals of independence and self-sufficiency.[40] Above all other gifts and achievements, Americans value their freedom. Wide-open spaces fostered it, individualism nurtured it, and the Revolution enshrined it as a defining national trait. Thanks to this same creed Americans expect to have a problem with authority, whether civil or intellectual, and take pride in resisting officialdom. Hand in hand with freedom goes the companion value of equality in matters of knowledge or understanding, manifested in distrust of expertise and a long American history of anti-intellectualism. One opinion counts as much as another, and Americans trust their own untutored judgments, even in this complex technological age.[41]

This summary is a loose description of tendencies rather than a scientifically precise analysis, but UFOs invited a frontier association from the start. They came from outer space at a time when space was the new frontier and shared the allure of unexplored mysteries.[42] In a society where the physical frontier belonged to nostalgia, where suburbia, restrictions, and conformity replaced unfettered individuality, UFOs reawakened the explorer spirit in people who saw themselves as trailblazers on the frontiers of knowledge. If space travel was a government-controlled spectator sport, ufology offered a grassroots quest with hands-on roles for everyone. The authorities abandoned UFOs by denying their existence. This neglect opened a void for amateurs to fill, and they crowded in, needing no formal training or preparation to investigate, gather information, and read and write about the subject. They were able to leap straight out of humdrum lives into hot pursuit of an exciting, cutting-edge mystery. The UFO frontier remained unorganized territory, not yet stifled by too many rules or overrun by bureaucrats, still open as a genuine meritocracy where self-taught participants earned esteem through ability and contributions rather than through the tedious acquisition of college degrees. One energizing self-image of ufologists portrays a necessary band of heroes with wagons circled in a prolonged fight against scientists who question eyewitness testimony and a government that knows everything about UFOs but tells nothing. This black-and-white vision of good versus evil sets up a standoff between ufologists as egalitarian populists against arrogant experts and as righteous truth-seekers against mendacious officials.

Ufology has drawn some of its most respected defenders from among trained and credentialed scientists who adhere to rigorous standards of thought, but popular ufology has often depended on widely accepted though faulty lines of reasoning to build its case.[43] In popular thinking, where there's smoke, there's fire; in ufological argument, too many people have reported too many UFOs for everyone to be wrong. This appeal to sheer numbers belongs to the "bundle of sticks" fallacy in terms of scientific logic. One thousand or ten thousand reports do not add plausibility to UFOs in the way that more sticks add to the strength of a bundle. The case for UFO existence is only as strong as the strongest individual case, but without corroboration of the crashed saucers, unambiguous photographs, and undeniable implants so abundant in rumor but so scarce in hand, multiplying reports only proves that many people believe they have seen UFOs, not that UFOs exist. Another sign of unscientific thought is a readiness to see rejection of UFOs in terms of human rather than evidential weakness. The rhetoric of popular ufological argument blames critics for arrogance, prejudice, stupidity, or duplicity in ad hominem attacks that ignore the possibility that doubters just may not find enough reason to accept UFOs.

The scientific ideal requires an even hand for weighing both favorable and unfavorable evidence. Popular ufologists typically welcome claims that confirm a chosen belief and reject or ignore even the strongest negative evidence, turning scientific procedure on its head by subordinating facts to the needs of theory. Ample research into the 1897 airship wave has uncovered thousands of reports across nearly the entire country, but a recent book revives an implausible theory that a secret society of aviation pioneers built an airship and flew it that year. How the ship could be seen in so many places on the same night ceases to be a problem through the author's choice to emphasize only Texas reports—and only the fraction of them that conform to the alleged flight paths of the mysterious inventor.[44] Tendentious selection of data allows the construction of a desired image of reality, just not a very likely one.

An overextended inclusiveness of ufological theory contrasts with the scientific goal to identify a limited and well-defined domain of phenomena. The extraterrestrial hypothesis applies one and the same solution to every problem, so for all questions, from the statues of Easter Island to gaps in human memory, aliens, aliens, and more aliens are the answer. Such breadth of explanatory power draws in matters that have no apparent tie to UFOs. Crop circles began as an unrelated mystery but soon shared the same pages with discussions of UFOs, until it came to seem only natural that aliens would write their symbolic messages in wheat fields. A relationship blossomed in belief that did not exist in fact. Such scattered evidence allows proponents to sidestep any hard test of one claim by shifting their attention to another, so that confirmation never fails and refutation never stands a chance.

The Science and Pseudoscience of Ufology

The advocacy practices of ufologists open a revealing window on their collective self-conceptions and aspirations. Skeptical outsiders see only credulous persons hopelessly awash in error and unreason as they satisfy personal needs with exotic fantasies. Insiders reject any notion that they are mere true believers and insist that they are committed to rigorous study of a genuine phenomenon. Most UFO proponents revere science or at least the appearance of science and crave its approval as the final word. Titles of MUFON Symposium proceedings like "The Emergence of a New Science," "A Scientific Paradigm," "A Scientific Enigma," and "Connecting with the Scientific Community" reveal a chronic infection of science envy and the unrequited wish of ufologists for acceptance by their harshest critics.[45] The honored place that science occupies in the thought world of ufology and the widespread desire for official science to investigate UFOs comes tempered with disappointment over a sorry history of scientists ignoring, mishandling, or ridiculing the subject. Against this dereliction Hynek, Vallee, and other of the best practitioners of ufology have attempted to raise the standards of the field to a scientific level. But the truth remains that ufology is a creature of many parts, and approaches to the "ology" of its name so varied that they range from the strictly rational to the mystical, from reliance on fact-based evidence to wishes and fantasies. On the whole, ufological practice, especially in its popular manifestations, has fallen well short of the scientific goal.

The argument for UFO reality begins with observations of something apparently out of the ordinary. UFO believers seek a foot in the scientific door when they identify UFOs as anomalous, a term defined in a psychological treatise as "an uncommon experience ... or one that, although it may be experienced by a substantial amount of the population ..., is believed to deviate from ordinary experience or from the usually accepted explanations of reality."[46] Taken in this sense, an anomaly requires no commitment to an explanation, only recognition that something odd is going on and more investigation is warranted. Straightforward reports of anomalous experience seem innocuous in themselves and a good place for science to begin. In fact, these irregularities are doubly damned—first, because they challenge the established norm with a prospect of upheaval, though they seldom carry enough evidential leverage to provide good reason, and, second, because anomalies often bear the burden of a prior explanatory agenda. At once exalted and despised, they are important because a few of them break established paradigms and create revolutions in scientific thinking, as Thomas Kuhn has argued. But they are mostly anomalies that languish as rare, transient events recorded only in anecdotal testimony, where questions surround not just the nature of the occurrence but even its factuality. UFOs, monsters, ghosts, and ESP belong to a motley band of misfits encamped outside the gates of science, begging for admittance that never comes.

UFO proponents clash with scientific gatekeepers from the start over the value of eyewitness testimony. Most evidence for anomalies is of this sort and ufologists prize it as direct and reliable, but philosopher David Hume cautioned that "no testimony is sufficient to establish a miracle, unless the testimony be of such a kind, that its falsehood would be more miraculous, than the fact, which it endeavors to establish."[47] Such a stringent rule essentially forecloses the possibility of a miracle and warns that experiential testimony is insufficient to establish a scientific truth. Skeptics continue to honor Hume's high standard with the almost equally rigorous demand that "extraordinary claims require extraordinary proofs." Occam's razor, the principle that the preferred explanation does not multiply terms unnecessarily, provides another working rule in favor of rejection. The simplest and therefore best explanation for anomalies usually sides with convention. When observation runs afoul of everything we know of physical reality, the verdict comes down without benefit of trial—the observations must be wrong. A third criterion usually opposed to anomalies is philosopher Karl Popper's rule that a scientific proposition must be subject to falsification. An untestable proposition cannot be scientific, and by this standard Freudian theory fails to pass muster, while most anomalies remain, at best, historical events without possibility of falsification.[48] Anomalies offer low prospect for reward relative to effort invested, and methodological defenses arm scientists with formal criteria to judge and reject such claims without even a close look. This approach is a form of gambling, but the game plan is sound—summary rejection will be right most of the time.

Ufologists cling to the faith that they are backing a rare exception to the rule. They reinforce this conviction by collecting examples of official deceit or dogmatic denial, such as a 1961 incident when Jacques Vallee witnessed anomalous objects while working as a satellite observer at the Paris Observatory.

> I saw a satellite brighter than second magnitude. I had time to log a few data points. On another occasion several of us recorded no less than eleven points. The next morning Muller, who behaves like a petty Army officer, simply confiscated the tape and destroyed it, although a similar object had just been tracked by other astronomers....
>
> "Why don't we send the data to the Americans?" I asked him. Muller just shrugged. "The Americans would laugh at us."[49]

For proponents, an official "no" never means simply "no." It shows at a minimum that authorities do not want to know the truth or, more probably, that a conspiracy of silence hides a truth of utmost importance.

Another frequent refrain calls on the adventure inherent in a seminal discovery to cast UFO study as a vital and courageous intellectual enterprise. The prospect that UFOs represent an anomaly so major that it will revolutionize the world as we know it appeals to ufologists, and they are seldom modest in proclaiming the exceptional quality of their subject. At a 1968 congressional hearing, James McDonald blamed neglect of UFOs on an unimaginative scientific response to a challenging phenomenon:

> The UFO problem is so unconventional, involves such improbable events, such inexplicable phenomenology, so defies ready explanation in terms of present-day scientific knowledge, has such a curiously elusive quality in many respects, that it is not surprising ... that scientists have not taken it very seriously. We scientists are ... not too well-oriented towards taking up problems that lie, not just on the frontiers of our scientific knowledge, but far across some gulf whose very breadth cannot be properly estimated.[50]

The hidebound reluctance of science to consider anything new is a common accusation in ufological argument. J. Allen Hynek set this negligence in historical perspective with an implication that the lessons of the past have gone to waste on scientists today. The view was that UFOs could not exist, therefore they did not exist. "This, of course, is a violation of scientific principles, but the history of science is filled with such instances. Some scientists refused to look through Galileo's telescope at sunspots, explaining that 'since the sun was perfect, it couldn't have spots, and therefore it was no use looking for them.' Other scientists refused to believe in the existence of meteorites."[51] Their example recurs in the literature as a promise of future vindication: How could reports of stones falling from the sky be true when stones simply cannot fall from the sky? Better to reject the observational claims of impressionable peasants than upset an entire established understanding of the world. In this case the observations of peasants overturned scientific norms and the impossible became possible. Hynek was fond of reminding his audience that the science of today does not have all the answers. "I have begun to feel that there is a tendency in 20th-century science to forget that there will be a 21st-century science, and indeed, a 30th-century science, from which vantage points our knowledge of the universe may appear quite different. We suffer, perhaps, from temporal provincialism, a form of arrogance that has always irritated posterity."[52]

These arguments cite the occasional anomaly that has made good with scientific acceptance, but the same defenses can also apply to crank claims and failed theories. A faith that orthodoxy is always wrong and that a seemingly inexplicable event has no conventional explanation represent commonplace fallacies of pseudoscientific thinking.[53] Despite scientific trappings and aspirations, popular ufology lands in the camp of pseudoscience for a number of procedural reasons. Scientific knowledge grows as a process of self-correction weeds out the false and builds on the true; pseudoscience on the other hand is people friendly—it preserves a desired belief by selecting favorable evidence and rationalizing failures. The debates and evidence-gathering go on indefinitely, but a firm resolution never settles the issue, because the proponents' case always falls short of proof. Hynek chided scientists for judging UFOs by the tautological maxim, "It can't be: therefore it isn't," but popular ufology deserves equal blame for a guiding principle that seems to read, "It might be: therefore it is." The result is a field riddled with uncritical, self-confirming, and fallacious reasoning. Dependence on anecdotal evidence, commitment to a tenet like alien visitation or government conspiracy not as hypothesis but as unquestionable fact, and readiness to see patterns linking all sorts of events to UFOs without consideration of alternatives underscore the contrast between conventional science and ufology. One tests propositions and challenges theory, the other asks too few questions of evidence as long as it protects the accepted mythology from embarrassing confrontations.

An example of the scientific and pseudoscientific countercurrents of ufology played out when the June 1997 issue of the *MUFON UFO Journal* published a scathing critique by Kent Jeffrey, an airline pilot who had spent a great deal of his own time and money investigating Roswell.[54] Starting as a believer, Jeffrey finished a doubter and concluded that no spaceship crashed. The fact that a UFO researcher changed his mind based on original research and that a UFO journal published negative results speaks well for a spirit of open inquiry, and so does subsequent praise of the article by readers and others who challenged it on evidential grounds. A less tolerant attitude surfaced in a subsequent flurry of indignation as the Internet crackled with accusations that Jeffrey was a government disinformation agent, while one letter to the journal complained of the "awkward and complete dominance of an entire issue by an anti-UFO article." Another letter writer railed, "you seem to lean over backwards to discredit the crash of an alien space craft" and "attempt to put down the claims of eyewitnesses and UFO researchers," and then recommended Art Bell's radio talk show as an "undisputed source of accurate and objective news reporting," where "you would . . . hear about the true facts involved in the massive UFO cover-up by our federal bureaucracy."[55]

Here a reliance on rationalizations bares itself in complaints that negative evidence is pointless since the crash is a proven fact, and in attacks on the critic as a spreader of deceit. Some answers have become so axiomatic that they no longer raise a question; for instance, the reason any likely Roswell witness fails to confirm the accepted story is that he continues to honor a security oath sworn to sixty years ago.[56] During a space shuttle mission on March 13, 1989, an amateur radio operator monitoring flight communications picked up this message: "Houston, this is *Discovery*. We still have the alien spacecraft under observance." A brief flurry of excitement soon ended when both ufologists and skeptics determined that the transmission was a hoax, but the tale never entirely died out. It continues to float around in the literature as an alien encounter backed by the coveted authority of astronauts yet little known because, as usual, the government hid the truth.[57] Not all rationalizations are stock responses. UFOs sometimes appear as solid, metallic craft, sometimes as amorphous, seemingly immaterial blobs of light; and a recent Internet posting tackles this troublesome duality with an innovative solution. The government supposedly has carried out studies on the Roswell debris and learned that "ET must have . . . mastered the ability to manipulate states of matter and energy so that they become interchangeable. . . . They can change solid matter into a variety of other states at will."[58] The difference between a rationalization and a scientific hypothesis may sometimes grow thin, but most efforts to account for apparent immaterial properties of UFOs seek to save the observations rather than question them. This defensiveness, especially when it calls on speculation rather than evidence, characterizes both pseudoscience and mythic thinking.

Few practices blow the whistle on pseudoscience like the uncritical readiness of popular ufologists to read almost any anomalous claim into the record. Attempts like Richard Hall's *The UFO Evidence* to sort out reliable cases are rarities and bear little influence on the prevailing current of ufological discourse, where strong reports have to contend with weak testimonies, speculations, and even hoaxes on a more or less equal footing. Instead of a solid foundation of facts, much of the UFO database is top heavy with nothing better than rumor, the following example being no more egregious than countless others:

Back around 1968, during a four-week period, there were said to have been at least 36 sightings of UFOs disappearing into the depths of this sacred lake [Titicaca], all reported officially by the Peruvian Navy. In the midst of all this, . . . undersea explorer Jacques-Ives Cousteau appeared on the scene with . . . two miniature submarines to (it was reported) prepare a TV documentary about the lake. Some speculated that the real reason was to look for traces of underwater UFO activity. In fact, it was reported that a scientist . . . had been appointed by Peru's Naval

Ministry to ... act as an observer ... and to promptly report anything unusual to the Peruvian Navy.[59]

This exuberant collage of assertions mixes fact, fiction, and speculation without even a source citation for support. With few UFO believers actually engaged in UFO research, their overwhelming appeal is to the authority of the printed word—"if I read it in a book, it must be true." Once enshrined in the literature, a claim acquires the status of a fact. Instead of winnowing out the doubtful, contradictory, and discredited claims, the UFO literature too often makes room for them all. As a result, this literature does not increase in reliability and substance with time, with the critical give and take of test and review characteristic of scientific knowledge: this literature increases only in size.

Mythic "facts" then lay down the foundation for a whole new round of belief construction. A manifesto for the Disclosure Project proclaims that there is "contact between humans and extraterrestrial beings" and an "extraterrestrial component of American national security policy," and that there are "domestic actions by government to impede, undermine, and obfuscate the study of extraterrestrial phenomena" and "government derived decisions to release or sequester certain extraterrestrial technologies."[60] Though disclosure supporters defend these sweeping assertions as factual, the most glaring fact is that each claim is largely hearsay and depends on background claims of little or no sturdier substance. Many believers have listened to one another for so long that they take such ideas as beyond doubt and see no need to waste more time on evidence or proof. Where science grows brick by brick out of demonstrable, tested, and confirmed propositions, pseudoscience builds castles in the air out of loud and confident but insubstantial assertions.

Not all the blame lies with UFO proponents since skeptics may be equally pseudoscientific. They rely on authority to argue that no aliens can get here from there and set up a straw man easy to knock down by misstating a case or addressing only an explainable selection of facts.[61] Skeptics often settle for any flimsy or ill-fitting explanation as long as it is conventional. A barrage of implausible solutions aimed at the Mexican Air Force case of 2004 included a new type of stealth aircraft (so stealthy it was invisible in daylight), a meteor procession (in sight half an hour), ball lightning (without storm clouds), balloons (moving as fast as an airplane), and equipment malfunction (possible but unsupported). In all fairness, some skeptics proposed the oil-field flares at an early date, but the overall course of response suggests a skeptics' board game with explanations chosen by a toss of the dice or the spin of a wheel.[62]

Efforts to duplicate the ways of science lend a distinctive shape—though not necessarily much credit—to arguments on both sides of the UFO debate. The ufological community may share similar interests, but it fragments into incompatible camps over how to take a scientific approach to UFOs. McDonald and Hynek advocated orthodox methods, and NARCAP pursues some of the most objective studies today; but popular approaches often favor a ufology with the science no more than skin deep, an afterthought to gain credibility and respect for UFOs but not the essential tool to understand them. The anthropologist Bronislaw Malinowski said that "science is founded on the conviction that experience, effort, and reason are valid; magic on the belief that hope cannot fail nor desire deceive."[63] Ufology often hides a subjective soul behind a scientific facade, so that the magical thinking of myth replaces rigor with a comforting solicitude for hope and accommodation for belief.

Psychosocial Answers to UFO Problems

One strength of a psychosocial explanation for UFOs lies in recognition of multiple causes. Personal or collective psychology, styles of thought, may predispose people to associate aliens with unusual experiences or to accept favorable lines of reasoning, but these influences are insufficient in themselves. They explain aspects of how UFO proponents think but cannot explain the substance of that thought or the appeal of such ideas. Answers have to come from somewhere else, and psychosocial theory excels in locating cultural sources for UFO narratives as well as human motives for UFO belief.

Perhaps the basic and most successful insight of the psychosocial approach is that *UFOs conform to cultural antecedents.* Why UFO representations resemble traditions and current concerns is debatable, but the similarities themselves are too plain to ignore. Evidence for human over alien sources includes changes in the attributed nature of strange sights in the sky from supernatural to natural to technological as historical expectations evolve. Popular images of how a flying machine should look shaped newspaper stories of how the phantom airship of 1897 really looked, and the "flying disk" version of Kenneth Arnold's sighting in 1947 imposed a saucer shape on thousands of subsequent newspaper reports. Three chapters of this book have argued that ideas about the origin of UFOs derive from traditions of the otherworld and extraterrestrial life; that the purpose of UFOs derives from traditions of salvation and apocalypse; and that the character of UFO occupants derives from traditions of response to technology and progress. These three themes resound through the literature in almost every effort to explain UFOs and their interactions with humanity. Even a minor story element like the "space children" parallels multiple thematic antecedents.

Story types such as the life of the Magus and the epic of defeat recur century after century to lend a particular shape to folk, popular, literary, journalistic, and political versions of history. A subject as strange and uncertain as UFOs seems especially vulnerable to becoming mythic history in the same way, and suggestive instances are easy to find. Distance continues to license expectations of the marvelous and extreme, and dwarfish aliens repeat actions once attributed to diminutive supernatural beings. UFO narratives repeat traditional specifics like the crystalline beauty of the otherworld, its luminescence without sunlight, and the supernatural lapse of time in fairyland. These means have served to describe gods and fairies, heaven and hell, initiation rituals and travels to the ends of the earth; they have proved flexible enough to adapt to human-oids, spaceships, and other planets with little strain and even with little change. The terms become technological and extraterrestrial and thoroughly modern, but the patterns remain ancient, their substance the magic and supernaturalism of old, their course the ordeal, the otherworld journey, the savior, the perilous encounter, just as before. A trade of magic for technology, fairies for aliens, looks drastic when it is in fact superficial. The psychosocial argument scores for its recognition that UFO storytelling is quite this-worldly insofar as it reflects continuing themes and patterns of human thought.

Psychosocial critics further object that *UFOs represent human ideas rather than alien realities*. The geneticist J. B. S. Haldane reminded us that "the universe is not only queerer than we imagine, it is queerer than we *can* imagine. . . . I suspect that there are more things in heaven and earth than are dreamed of, or can be dreamed of, in any philosophy."[64] By contrast, little about UFOs is strange in a convincingly extraterrestrial way. As Martin Kottmeyer says, "UFOs never melt cars into radioactive puddles, snatch up football stadiums, invert amino acid handedness in victims, or leave behind slabs of multiquark strong force adaptors when they crash. In short, there is nothing that requires an extramundane explanation."[65] In this view science fiction serves as the model for sleek metallic spaceships and big-headed aliens, the cold war as motivation for UFOs spying on military and nuclear installations, and preconceptions of human space exploration as the reason aliens collect soil samples or human specimens. The flying saucer represents an advanced vehicle design, but like the airships of the 1890s and the ghost rockets of 1946, each of these UFOs exceeds the technological capabilities of its day by a step, but only by a step. What seemed like credible spacecraft in the 1950s now looks antiquated, more at home in a museum of cold war relics than in the sky as evidence of alien visits.

Equally hard to credit is sixty years of stagnation in UFO technology. The tech-nology of the one civilization we know—our own—changes so rapidly that the 1953 movie version of *The War of the Worlds* could not repeat the original 1890s scenario but had to equip the Martians with electromagnetic protective shields against earthly military advances, or else the war would have ended before the audience finished its popcorn. Yet supposedly far-advanced UFO aliens have made few improvements or model changes in their craft since 1947. Aliens that breathe the earthly atmosphere without harm, function well enough in earthly gravity despite their frail bodies, and overcome the communication problem by telepathy wave another red flag of implausibility. Far from being beyond our ken, the reported behaviors of UFO aliens repeat 1950s science-fiction conventions that gather considerable rust today.

A hybrid-making program as the reason for abductions raises questions about how two species can evolve worlds apart and still be genetically compatible. Popular wisdom sets aside this objection by accepting that alien techno-magic can hybridize anything with the push of a button. Yet this argument self-destructs because of the same superiority. If aliens are advanced enough to unite any genes, they should be too advanced to practice hybridization at all. Real aliens would need a kitchen rather than an examination room, since they could simply create life to their specifications from raw materials up.[66] Let us make no mistake about the status of reproductive motifs. They belong to the abduction story all the way back to its beginnings and not, as some critics insist, only since Budd Hopkins and David Jacobs "created" the issue. Apparent genetic sample-taking, clonelike entities, and containers with fetal or unfinished beings precede any attempt to bundle these motifs into a unitary theme. Reproductive concerns are not just asides but embedded in the story. With the aliens focused on their dying planet and inability to reproduce, they are voracious for humans in their reproductive prime and quick to reject the aged or sterile.[67] A hybridization solution draws together a cluster of narrative facts under a theory meaningful according to what abduction reports say about alien needs and motives. This theory nevertheless clashes with reasonable expectations for the scientific capabilities of advanced aliens, so that the solution makes meanings without making proper sense. In psychosocial terms, ufologists strain to save their construction of the phenomenon by committing the aliens to implausibly cumbersome practices.

What purposes do UFOs serve? The question—applied to human rather than alien interests—leads to anthropological functionalism for an answer that *UFOs accommodate human needs*. Literary critics from Aristotle onward have recognized the simple but oft-forgotten fact that tales of the unusual carry entertainment value. Ufology as a pursuit inspires curiosity, emotion, and commitment within a community that shares these feelings. A sense of mission may appeal to proponents as they participate in adventures of discovery as well as David-and-Goliath conflicts of grassroots opinion against government and the scientific elite, while skeptics can enlist in a crusade against irrationalism. In a world too well lit with realism, UFOs restore shadowy corners of mystery to comfort those people who wish to find that human knowledge is limited and that greater powers hold sway in the universe. Psychosocial commentators have long recognized the symbolic and expressive potential of UFOs. They provide a sort of living Rorschach test as people project their concerns onto the pliant contents of the subject, reshaping aliens as proxies for human preoccupations or as puppets to act out the inner life of believers.

UFO stories repeat the timeless shudder of every legendary encounter with the otherworld, but they also voice a serious message about dangers here and now. A few decades ago urban legends like "The Hook" and "The Boyfriend's Death" expressed an established moral code. Death and dismemberment befell the teenage victims, but these stories reserved horrible happenings for unwary couples when they parked in remote places for illicit sexual activity. The moral of the story was an old one—punishment follows sin, safety lies in obedience to social rules. In later urban legends the perils creep closer to home as murderers lurk in the backseat, the Doberman chokes on fingers torn off a burglar hiding under the bed, and the crazy killer phones the babysitter from upstairs after he has murdered the children.[68] Gone is the semblance of moral cause and effect. The elemental atmosphere of the legend returns now that assailants attack without rhyme or reason, inscrutable nightmares in the dark hours of the night to bring doubt that we have any control over the world we live in. Aliens echo this cultural trend as they invade bedrooms and render captives helpless or conspire with governments to suppress the truth and strangle liberty.

An important exhibit in the psychosocial case draws parallels between changing social concerns and the intentions attributed to UFOs. In the 1950s aliens reflected the hope that some power would sort out our differences in time to save us from nuclear war and from the dread that flying saucers threatened the same sneak attack that our Soviet enemies might mount.[69] When Hollywood cast extraterrestrials as body snatchers and thought controllers, substitution of super-technology for brainwashing reallocated a popular image of villainy from Communists to aliens.[70] Rejection of materialism and technology in the counterculture years of the 1960s corresponded with UFOs growing phantomlike and occupants assuming trickster or fairylike roles. Aliens continue as spokesmen for current cultural themes when they warn of environmental disaster and prophesy apocalypse at the new millennium or in 2012. After trust between government and public eroded with Vietnam and Watergate, Roswell and Area 51 entered the popular vocabulary as bywords for official double-dealing. Suspicions no longer fester only within the UFO community. The same climate, if not the specific beliefs, has spread through the public at large to leave scarcely any visible line between perceptions of literal fact and *X-Files* plots.

One function of UFOs has been to provide an explanatory master code for otherwise inexplicable events. In 1954, when hundreds of people in Seattle reported that small pits appeared overnight in automobile windshields, blame for the epidemic fell on hydrogen bomb tests in the Pacific. The H-bomb was the odds-on favorite cause for anything out of the ordinary at the time, but Donald Keyhoe staked a claim on this incident as perhaps a case of aliens bombarding the earth as a warning against hostile actions toward flying saucers.[71] UFOs and creationism made strange bedfellows in a 2005 editorial from *UFO Magazine*, where the gleeful writer welcomed a comment from the president in favor of schools teaching intelligent design as an alternative to evolution, on the grounds that this assault on scientific orthodoxy could also benefit acceptance of UFOs.[72] If the editorial was tongue-in-cheek, it nevertheless followed a UFO-centric strategy to reduce the complexity of the world by converting every problem into a UFO-relevant matter. Whether as explanatory tools or symbolic expressions, UFOs possess the versatility to serve a broad range of beliefs, fantasies, hopes, fears, resentments, and suspicions. Though the stories tell of alien visitation, they are really all about us, our eternally favorite theme.

While UFOs seldom sustain a full-blown religion, personal responses indicate that UFOs may contribute to spiritual satisfaction. Susan Clancy's informants identified abduction as the most traumatic yet most positive experience of a lifetime, one that terrified but also transformed them with a sense of awe and realization of a greater universe. Abduction belief knitted together the scattered threads of life into a meaningful fabric, not merely to explain or relieve personal problems but to change the believer, heighten awareness, and instill confidence and hope for the future, so that life without the encounter seemed flat and empty.[73] Religious scholar Brenda Denzler too finds UFO experience serving, in the words of one abductee, as "the catalyst that woke me up to my spirituality." UFOs draw believers over the edge of conventional reality to explore larger concepts of self and cosmos. UFO belief "has crystallized within itself the language and praxis of a scientific modernity along with the myths and symbols of [a] ... human quest that first found a home in religion."[74] If the language is scientific, the message is religious and resonates beyond mere curiosity through a broad register of human concerns—and these concerns sound out human rather than interplanetary origins for UFOs, according to psychosocial interpretations.

A case for cultural origins settles down to a fundamental question: Shouldn't we expect UFO aliens to be more alien? The protest that we cannot know how aliens think carries little force when too little about them seems otherworldly and too much expresses human attitudes or earthly concerns. If aliens say we must give peace a chance, give up greed and materialism, or live in harmony with the earth and one another, they simply tell us what we already know. Psychosocial critics see that aliens inhabit this world too comfortably to act like they come from anywhere outside it and infer that instead of real aliens sharing our concerns, our concerns create imaginary aliens to speak as an externalized conscience, savior, menace, or whatever other role human needs contrive. Whether or not a particular description in the UFO literature traces to a current image or a traditional pattern, the result is the same: UFO ideas are not original, not inherent in some external mystery, but issue from ourselves.

Observation and Cultural Influences

Accepting that cultural models shape understanding, speculation, and debate comes easier than allowing that culture influences observation itself. The reality is one of the most sobering lessons UFOs can teach—observers sometimes create UFO reports without participation of any real UFOs, and the mistakes can be spectacular. In 1967 a witness reported a UFO that appeared evening after evening for several months. Described as greenish and as large as a two-story building, the UFO was sometimes round, sometimes oblong, and binoculars showed it domed with two rows of windows. The object often landed several miles from the observer, with jets spewing from the lower side and lighting up the snowy landscape.[75] Condon Committee investigators easily identified the object as Venus setting in the west. The account accurately described the planet distorted by thick atmospheric layers near the horizon and the effects of scintillation magnified through binoculars. Here the veil of confusion was thin as UFO preconceptions translated observational realities into fictitious features. Interpretation constructed standard structures of a spaceship out of natural phenomena and sustained a believer's convictions.

From simple misconception to a complex error involving multiple witnesses, a similar process can build a UFO of impressive credibility out of parts connected only in the human mind. A Spanish airliner carrying 109 passengers approached Valencia at 11 P.M. on November 11, 1979, when two red lights rushed toward the plane with alarming speed. The lights seemed attached to the extremities of an object the size of a jumbo jet and performed impossible maneuvers around the aircraft as if playing with it. This UFO stayed within half a mile of the witnesses for about eight minutes before the captain broke from his course to avoid a possible collision and made an emergency landing at Manises airport a little before midnight. Several witnesses on the ground reported one or more red lights over the airport, but military radar did not detect any unknown targets. About an hour later a Spanish Air Force jet arrived to investigate. The pilot chased several unknown lights for over an hour, never reaching any of them but experiencing apparent disturbances in his communications and weapons systems during the pursuit.

The Manises incident entered UFO literature as an immediate classic. It enjoyed the advantages of qualified observers in the air and on the ground, apparent confirmation by a military pilot, mysterious electromagnetic interference, and the newsworthy fact that a UFO caused a commercial airliner to make an emergency landing. All the elements of this complex encounter converged together in support of a genuine extraordinary event.

After twenty years as an exemplary unknown, the Manises incident fell apart piece by piece under close reexamination by Spanish engineer Juan Antonio Fernández Peris. He identified the two red lights as gas burn-off flares from a nearby oil refinery that were distorted by a temperature inversion layer in place that night. The lights seen by the grounds crew at the Manises airport traced to stars and planets, converted into anomalies after many recent UFO reports prepared the witnesses to see any light in the sky as unusual. Some family problems of the airliner pilot predisposed him to overanxious reaction when confronted with seemingly anomalous lights and the failure of Barcelona air control to provide a conventional solution. The electromagnetic interference reported by the fighter pilot resulted from the electronic countermeasures of a U.S. Navy ship nearby in the Mediterranean, operating under a heightened state of alert as the Iranian hostage crisis developed. On its surface the Manises case seemed airtight and convincing, yet when examined in depth, the UFO dissolved into conventional events held together by preexisting beliefs.[76]

A specific incident of cause-and-effect influence of culture on UFO testimony appears in the abduction case of Barney and Betty Hill. When Barney underwent hypnosis in February 1964 to explore the missing time associated with their close 1961 UFO encounter, he described an entity that stared at him from the window of the UFO as having elongated or "wraparound" eyes. These eyes also seemed to speak to him in his head. Martin Kottmeyer discovered years later that less than two weeks before the hypnosis session, a TV series, *The Outer Limits*, aired an episode entitled "The Bellero Shield." It featured an alien with elongated eyes, and this alien explained that he "spoke" through his eyes in a form of telepathic communication.[77] Influence rather than coincidence seems like the best explanation for how a TV show anticipated two striking features of Barney Hill's alien.

Ufologists have disputed this challenge at considerable length. When it arose,

Barney was no longer alive to answer questions, but Betty stated that they never watched *The Outer Limits*.[78] Her response is unequivocal enough, but it cannot settle the issue, since while the answer may confirm that the Hills were not regular or intentional viewers, it cannot foreclose the chance of accidental exposure. Barney might have caught a few minutes of the show while flipping channels or while in a store, diner, or lounge, and remembered a fleeting glimpse or a few words overheard even though he paid little attention. Such casual exposures may stick as cryptomnesic memories, wherein the gist persists without conscious awareness and shorn of source or context.[79] A subject may then incorporate these deceptive contents into a different but inappropriate context, mixing them with genuine recollections to form a partially false memory. This case also meets two archaeologists' rules of thumb for culture contact: the traits in question are too complex for independent invention to explain readily, and the timing is coincidental enough to make borrowing plausible. We can never be certain one way or another. Neither can we escape the possibility that a cultural source contaminated his memory. The potential influence is there, the mechanism of memory is well known, and enough supporting evidence converges to render borrowing a persuasive possibility.

At the same time, the skeptics should not make too much of this discovery. Abductees' memories are no more perfect than anyone else's, and the struggle to understand a confusing experience would naturally leave them vulnerable to some inaccuracies in recall. Kottmeyer's argument applies only to two discrete elements of a complex story, while the prolonged emotional upset associated with the Hills's UFO experience, which for Barney amounted to traumalike symptoms, stands as a reminder that this case remains remarkable and inadequately explained in conventional terms.

The Psychosocial Alternative to Literal UFOs

Some aspects of the psychosocial thesis are too commonsensical to raise many objections. Few ufologists question that everyone picks up bits and pieces of UFO-related cultural themes and story types as part of a general cultural education. Certain instances of cultural influence appear quite straightforward, such as the prospect that expectations transformed the *Zond* reentry of 1968 into a spaceship at treetop level for a few witnesses, or that cryptomnesic memories of the mythological phoenix returned to Betty Andreasson in her abduction account of a giant bird consumed by flames and then reborn. UFO stories echo unmistakable leitmotifs of the great mythological themes: culture-bearers and saviors from the sky, supernatural enemies and the end of the world, visits to and from the otherworld, rituals of initiation and transformation, interbreeding with otherworld entities, magical events and trickster figures like Men in Black. The initiatory journey of the shaman echoes through the examinations, conferences, and otherworld visits of abductees, apocalyptic configurations through UFO conspiracy theories. Whether these similarities are borrowed or coincidental may serve as a subject of contention, but at least a psychosocial position that they depend on cultural influence—for their form if not their substance—has defensible grounds.

The influence of culture is not a question of whether but of how much, and it is over this issue that the fights break out. Ufologists predictably resist the reduction of their subject to a psychosocial fiction, with perhaps the most cogent counterargument expressed in *The UFO Encyclopedia* by Jerome Clark, himself a former advocate of psychosocial theory.[80] One objection blames such solutions for undermining the uniqueness of the UFO phenomenon with unfair comparisons. In this view the pursuit of cultural parallels is an armchair literary exercise that treats the UFO narrative as the whole story, without paying due attention to the experiential basis, in a search that can never fail since somewhere in the vast body of human creative output a similarity for anything and everything is bound to lurk. The promotion of scattershot analogies without an established genetic pedigree, selection of convenient fragments of a tradition while ignoring the rest, and comparisons of terms abstracted to a level that makes similarities all but meaningless add to the complaint that psychosocial criticism contributes nothing worthwhile to understanding UFOs. Ufologists also fume over the improbability and unclear mechanism of some supposed influences when they probably have influenced no one. Though some science-fiction stories from the 1920s describe alien kidnap, how many modern abductees are likely to have chanced across these publications and borrowed their plot? Such remote prospects serve as reason for justifiable doubt that many ufologists have gladly extended to psychosocial explanations in general.

If psychosocial proponents discredit their cause with an overzealous readiness to find influences, ufologists can be equally impractical in their criticisms. I have argued the role of the "Bellero Shield" in the Hill abduction account with several ufologists whose judgment I respect and whose familiarity with the case is deep. I accept that a transfer of imagery occurred, they do not. Our positions are reasoned but differ on a point of how to deal with inevitable uncertainty about what really happened. The experience was a historical event, the evidence anecdotal, the truth not decided with the definitiveness that physical evidence or laboratory test might assure. No omniscient observer exists to settle the issue, and decisions have to depend on the inference of truth from imperfect human testimony. I stress that availability of the TV show, close similarity of content, and timing legitimate an inference of exposure and borrowing, as near as we can ever know. My opponents insist on a full chain of evidence that Barney Hill actually saw the episode and repeated its contents in his account. Since no proof solidifies that chain, the facts that he had an extraordinary UFO experience and selected the strange eyes out of all the other images he might have borrowed make reasonable, to my friends, an inference that he actually observed the eyes he described. The controversy reaches an "is so/is not" stalemate and calls for added weight as the only way for either side to raise the probability of its case above fifty-fifty.

An issue of procedural fairness favors the psychosocial approach against the stringent demand of full proof. What really happened to the Hills or any other witness is unknown to both sides, and judgment must fall back on incomplete and uncertain evidence. Knowing whether or not the witness was a regular viewer of *The Outer Limits* is important but does not resolve the core question of whether he saw the "Bellero Shield" alien. A person-by-person study of abductees to learn if they were ever exposed to *Killers from Space* or fairy folklore would be desirable from the standpoint of thoroughness, but again the results would leave too many holes for a definitive answer. After all, in the case of cryptomnesia the memories most dangerous for contaminating a story are the very ones lost to conscious recall. What subjects say under direct inquiry cannot tell everything they know; only their behavior offers observable evidence of whether influence has occurred. When stories and beliefs copy current concerns or traditional mythic patterns and particulars, those expressions reveal the speaker's sources as most likely cultural in origin. The conclusion is probable rather than certain, a matter of backward inference from testimony. Fact may truly mimic fiction, but when UFO stories parallel a cultural source in meaningful ways and contact is at least possible, as in the case of Barney Hill and the "Bellero Shield," benefit of the doubt must go to the psychosocial inference that similarities are due to influence as the more likely of the two uncertainties. This resort to a methodological tiebreaker may sound too glib and unsatisfactory when we all agree that something extraordinary happened to the Hills, but such a course must win out as the safest when we are all equally lost in the dark. True or not, the borrowing hypothesis makes the better argument.

Also problematic in ufological criticism of psychosocial solutions is a narrow understanding of the mechanism of cultural influence. An insistence on direct borrowing overlooks indirect causes that may achieve the same result, so, for example, instead of an obscure science-fiction story influencing subsequent abduction accounts, a diffuse milieu of ideas prefigured both the fiction and UFO abduction. The near-death experience (NDE) illustrates a possible way that one source writes the "cultural script" for multiple narratives. NDE scholarship has recognized that otherworld journeys such as the visions of Tondal unfold according to a pattern like the near-death pattern, and its imagery compares with medieval descriptions of heaven.[81] Some scholars argue that NDEs serve as basis and reinforcement for widespread primary ideas about the other-world.[82] If a recurrent experiential source establishes the basic image, religious vision-aries can incorporate these expectations into their own experiences, and oral accounts of fairyland adopt the same ideas. Popular views of heaven can standardize from these accounts, and literary treatments can then develop and disseminate the ideas in deriva-tions increasingly distant from the source. Even if visits to the otherworld began with experience, they have continued as cultural ideas and have evolved into multiple ver-sions that reach potential narrators through multiple channels, perpetuating the influ-ence of the NDE by indirect means.

The suggestion that abductions resemble NDEs in some aspects has provoked a response that the comparison is not very fruitful. The critics are right to point out that abductees do not die, and the NDE specifics (out-of-body rush through a tunnel to a place of light and beauty, conversation with beings, and a decision to return to life followed by a change of consciousness) do not correspond very closely to abduction experiences. Though any direct relationship between abduction accounts and NDE accounts seems tenuous, the psychosocial proposition may yet find a measure of vin-dication through the concept of secondary influences. Accepting that NDE ideas have suffused into the "collective consciousness" in various versions from differing sources licenses the inclusion of suspected derivatives, such as the judgment of the dead, into the comparison, where the resemblances are closer and more familiar and more likely to have influenced the thinking of real narrators. This vindication is limited. It must acknowledge only roundabout influence of the NDE itself. All a narrator may borrow is the means to describe genuine experiences rather than the means to imagine events that never happened.

Once the principle of indirect influence gains acceptance, it replaces unduly restric-tive notions of how culture can participate in UFO stories with a more comprehen-sive—and realistic—understanding. In this inclusive vision science-fiction treatments of alien invaders and bug-eyed extraterrestrials join other sources in mass and popular culture to not only suggest particular content but also set guidelines for the imagi-nation, even when no specific borrowing is apparent. With such guidelines in place, creativity, far from acting as a free agent, stays within established bounds, so that a sort of convergent evolution assures that different individuals compose similar stories, even in the absence of similar experiences. UFO narrators may adopt a general story pat-tern as well as content. The abduction account chronology of capture and examination, conference, and return becomes, in this view, not the course of a real experience but the formal sequence of ascending action, dramatic climax, and resolution that characterizes a standard form of storytelling.[83] Underlying traditions of fear not specific to one context or phenomenon can transpose into concurrent social issues such as conspiracies and satanic ritual abuse, as well as UFOs. These mechanisms of cultural influence permit psychosocial sources to have ancient roots and little visible relationship with alien encounters, yet still act as templates to shape modern UFO narratives.

An appeal to cultural learning explains many UFO-related ideas but not all striking parallels of UFOs with religion, mythology, and folklore. Some of the most fascinating stories of strange encounters count as universals, or at least as cross-cultural and widespread. The night witch, diminutive supernatural beings, and the patterns of initiation and otherworld journey exemplify complex thematic clusters that recur more or less intact across many cultures. These same themes reappear with only superficial modifications as important elements of the UFO story, often down to small details, and display greater fidelity than random or even culturally structured borrowing seems able to explain. Jung's archetypes of the collective unconscious and Freud's stages of psychological development once provided appealing explanations for universals. These notions of innate content or processes common to all mankind have fallen out of favor, but more scientifically sophisticated notions of inherent source have taken their place.

Cognitive psychologists have discovered that a complex grasp of the physical and social realms develops at an early age and develops independently of learning. Children find out that zebras have stripes through a picture book or a trip to the zoo, but they know a great deal more about zebras without experience or instruction. Even the very young understand that zebras eat and sleep, that they are not made of metal or in need of repair. No teacher may specify such facts, but innate assumptions about ontological categories fill in these essential qualities. An intuitive understanding of certain domains, such as animate and inanimate objects, physical causation, and social relationships, has a universality based in evolution and genetics. This innate cognitive background shapes the cultural representations of those domains and is responsible for the similarities of thought and action observed across cultures. Experimentally verified operations of thought exert selective pressure on the full range of possible ideas. This pressure restricts choices so that statistical preferences emerge—universal ways of thinking guide choices in belief and practice so that the ideas of all peoples converge toward certain similarities.[84]

Pascal Boyer, an anthropologist at Cambridge University, explains the recurrence of religious representations as the action of selective behavior guided by cognitive universals. Religious beliefs are full of extraordinary entities that violate intuitive expectations—gods and ghosts are invisible, eternal, and able to fly or to know un-spoken human intentions. Many cultures share similar ideas, and Boyer proposes that cognitive similarities lead to independent invention. The unnatural features of religious representations are quite limited, in the sense that ghosts are strange but never incom-prehensible. They act in a supernatural manner, but they are typically quite ordinary in their psychology. They are subject to anger and appeasement, wants and needs, just like ordinary mortals. A ghost that acts on human motives behaves in natural ways, ac-cording to a narrow range of possibilities many cultures might reinvent. The religious representations most likely to succeed strike an optimal balance between the odd and the ordinary, where familiar properties draw a rich intuitive base into the representa-tion and make it friendly to human comprehension, while counterintuitive properties provide the spice that keeps an idea interesting. The representations most likely to recur are not the ones supported by observation or instruction, but the ones that fit best into human predispositions of thought, even if those predispositions are contrary to reality in its everyday or scientific sense.[85]

The prospect of inherent cognitive domains offers a tempting explanation for why themes of the UFO myth often have a long and varied ancestry. Today's alien hybrid updates the offspring of Zeus, fairy children, and the *Star-Begotten* musings of H. G. Wells to maintain a thread of ideas persistent throughout history and adaptable to the beliefs of different eras. Even if gods begetting children with mortals is a familiar story, something more than a free-floating tradition seems necessary to account for the many and elaborate reincarnations of the idea. Here the notion of a ready-made category or preferential tendency of imaginative thinking comes in handy to explain why aliens act like gods and fairies. UFO aliens bring a measure of strangeness from the stars yet manifest enough earthly motivations and purposes to keep one foot on this planet and one on another. Whether or not a particular cognitive theory explains cross-cultural ideas, the prospect that some patterns may be innate or some predispositions favored at a biological level adds another reason to credit a psychosocial approach with the true answer for UFO origins.

Once the UFO myth assimilates traditional ideas and patterns, the myth itself becomes the primary mechanism of cultural influence. UFO ideas seldom stand by themselves. They interconnect in a structure of facts, beliefs, and meanings to form a self-referencing mythic world, improbable to outsiders but credible and convincing from within. UFO thinking is prone to enclose itself within its own circle, to base the credibility of UFOs not on empirical test and revision of theory but on the coherence of an inner relationship of tenets and justifications. Observations diminish in importance as the system grows in size. The larger and more integrated the UFO belief system becomes, the more genuine it appears, the more necessary its internal logic seems, and the stronger its imitation of reality stands against criticism or doubt. In the end, belief lifts off from the solid ground of observation and hovers in independent isolation, a world to recognize as mythic not because it is false but because it is self-contained and self-sufficient as it answers only to itself.

As a result of this mythical world, thinking about UFOs is anything but haphazard or muddled. Arguments often follow clear lines of reasoning—for instance, proponents may deduce from assumptions about a UFO crash and government cover-up in 1947 that secrecy explains why the crash is not universally accepted and the official response to subsequent UFO activity is negative. This explanatory train answers many questions and does so with deductive formal properties, so that thinking about UFOs becomes a logical process, even if the facts are wrong and beliefs mistaken. When ideas join in a systematic whole, each supports the other in a coherent structure. Psychosocial theorists have paid little attention to UFO belief as a rational system and thereby neglect one of its important sources of persuasive power.

Though mythmaking inspires romantic visions of artistic, even poetic work, in popular ufology little is imaginative about the UFO myth. Its creative battles are over, the core beliefs have solidified into a well-organized body of truisms, and few, usually only peripheral ideas, are still under negotiation. This myth serves the same function for ufologists as Thomas Kuhn's theoretical paradigms for scientists. A paradigmatic theory provides adherents with their prevailing conceptual model of reality, prescribes the goals for research, and controls scientific inquiry by prescribing which observations are allowable and what meaning they can have. Working within the paradigm constitutes "normal science," an effort to explore the implications and confirm the predictions of the theory. If anomalies appear, they can be explained in available theoretical terms or explained away to avoid precipitating a revolutionary shift of paradigms.[86]

Popular ufology is an exercise similar to normal science within the extraterrestrial paradigm. Many complementary claims converge in support of the prescribed extraterrestrial hypothesis, with sightings, abductions, Roswell, government denials, ancient astronauts, and crop circles interlocking in belief, if not in fact, to build a coherent understanding of alien visitation to earth. This system of ideas defines for its supporters what UFOs and ufology are all about. It is a continual work in progress, but most of its efforts simply add more of the same as practitioners busy themselves to collect accounts, order them according to accepted categories, and read off the accepted interpretations. The day-to-day business of the UFO myth, like any other, is essentially a maintenance chore. Proponents build and preserve the communal understanding, spread it to the uninformed, defend it against attacks from nonbelievers, and enforce orthodoxy within the ranks. The paradigm, the mythic image of UFOs, continues to make sense of the world and settles in as a matter-of-fact truth too normal and normative to doubt. Followers demonstrate their commitment to the paradigm when they accept only aliens and spaceships, allowing observers to see nothing else, the literature and databases to record nothing else, and respectable ufological discourse to discuss nothing else. See no evil, hear no evil, speak no evil serves popular ufological orthodoxy, so that anyone who submits alternative theories or insufficiently mechanistic reports risks feeling the sudden frostbite of a communal cold shoulder.

A consequence of the systematic nature of UFO ideas is that UFO thinking has little need for experience, only the illusion of it. The myth covers all the important bases—who or what is here, where UFOs come from, why they are immensely important, and how this vital truth remains on the fringe. With the necessary answers already in place, questioning becomes selective, not a matter of asking whether alleged events are real but how they fit into the accepted framework. Assertions that a giant UFO scrambled the codes of nuclear missiles at Malmstrom Air Force Base in 1975 enjoy a hardy resilience as established facts in the UFO literature, seldom questioned and impervious to efforts to set the record straight. This version improves on the facts to create the history that should have happened. Ufologists have incentive to uphold this version as true because it fulfills their wishes, but also because it confirms expectations backed by the weight of a whole system of supporting ideas. A corrupted version of real events replaces the original as a plausible truth, but from a psychosocial perspective, belief becomes evidence for belief as the UFO myth distances itself from real-world experiences to provide both its own source of facts and the basis for judging them.

Beyond question or doubt, the psychosocial challenge mounts a formidable opposition to literalist views of UFOs. According to its conclusions, nothing within the whole range of UFO-talk, from experiential reports to interpretations and explanations, escapes a conventional explanation. Human solutions settle all accounts. Too many themes, motifs, plots, characters, story patterns, and meanings point toward human concerns, expressive stereotypes, and cultural traditions to deny that preexisting patterns, not independent phenomena, lend most of the shape to UFO narratives. Understanding something new always requires associating it with something old, fitting aspects of the strange into categories of the familiar. These approximations begin to make the unknown knowable but come at the price of eroding the uniqueness of the subject. Such a tradeoff is inevitable as critics strip away the raw strangeness of UFOs and recognize the human contribution, but the psychosocial proposition in its triumphal form declares that human factors explain everything, absolutely everything, and no unconventional phenomenal truth remains.

Psychosocial theory is powerful but not airtight. Enough alternative solutions and unmet expectations exist to ask if all the answers are really in hand. A TV show likely explains one bit of the Hill testimony, but dismissal of the entire story as a grab bag of cultural borrowings would overstep the evidence. A man struggling to understand a strange experience might well grasp some of the unconnected images floating around in his memory as pieces of the puzzle. The result is confusion of facts, not the authoring of fiction. Adaptability of UFO stories to influential cultural trends serves as an important psychosocial argument, but lack of adaptability in UFO stories is sometimes the more telling response. Overpopulation loomed as a major ecological concern two and three decades ago, and movies catered to this trend in the bleak urban landscape of *Blade Runner* (1982), the recourse to humans for food in *Soylent Green* (1973), and authoritarian control of women's bodies in *The Handmaid's Tale* (1990); but an overpopulation theme never infiltrated the abduction story. In keeping with the readiness of belief to connect UFOs with just about anything, a few efforts to attribute AIDS to malicious alien intervention have appeared, though current fears of global epidemics so far have not carried over to UFO reports.[87] Abductions maintain their own integrity, compromised now and then by cultural bleed-through like the prospects for ecocatastrophe, but refractory to many popular and mass media influences. These few examples must sow at least a small seed of doubt that the relationship between culture and UFOs is entirely garbage in, garbage out.

The psychosocial approach aims primarily at texts, the verbal records of what people see as UFOs and what they think about them. These texts are undeniably human creations and cultural products, not immediate perceptions of the physical world. Cultural influences shape the texts, imagination contributes to them, and the outcome is in some respects fictitious. Every UFO story belongs to a mythic world that informs the narrator what UFOs and stories about them should be like. Given these truths, psychosocial proponents ask why they should take any UFO story as true; but this question has another side—if UFOs are real, why not assume that cultural influences will distort the representation? Venus emerges from the cocoon of expectations as an alien spaceship, in a transformation repeated throughout UFO history. It seems only reasonable to imagine that this process is reversible and works equally well on any genuine spaceship, so that cultural influences force the right perceptual givens into the wrong conceptual framework, and the result is a description closer to expectations than to reality. The similarities between UFO stories and cultural ideas apply to human expressions and not necessarily to any underlying phenomenon. Psychosocial critics mistake these similarities for a verdict when they are only diagnostic tools, not the last word but reminders that continuities of human interests and means of expressing them will intrude on UFOs. Whether all UFO reports describe a myth or some fraction distort a real phenomenon depends not on arguments and possibilities but on whatever evidence there might be for a genuine unconventional phenomenon.

CHAPTER NINE

Explaining UFOs:
Something Yet Remains

Some people have experiences that are so strange, they attribute them
to alien intervention of some kind. . . . I had one of those experiences
myself. To say it was aliens is to assume a lot. But to say it was weird
is to understate it. It was extraordinarily weird. . . . I wouldn't try to
publish a scientific paper about these things, because I can't do any
experiments. I can't make glowing raccoons appear. I can't buy them
from a scientific supply house to study. I can't cause myself to be lost
again for several hours. But I don't deny what happened. It's what
science calls anecdotal, because it only happened in a way that you
can't reproduce. But it happened.
—Kary Mullis, *Dancing Naked in the Mind Field*[1]

If that thing landed in my back yard, I wouldn't tell a soul.
—Police Officer Barney Neff[2]

Company executive John Timmerman served as treasurer and board member of the
Center for UFO Studies for twenty-five years. Among his many services to ufology, he
organized a UFO photo exhibit for display at shopping malls, universities, and conferences, setting up the exhibit for over fifteen years across several states from his Lima,
Ohio, home. Many people who browsed the photographs also had personal UFO stories to tell, and Timmerman was there to record hundreds of them.[3] In 1990 one informant gave him an account of a sighting from a June night fifteen years before, when
the informant and two other young men had parked their truck on a ridge and released
their beagles to chase rabbits. The ridge was an open pasture with woods on one side
and a hollow on the other. Across the hollow was a pond with a security light nearby,
and 300 yards farther away were two houses on a hilltop, each with a security light.

A light moving behind the trees caught the men's attention. The light soon entered the clearing at the far end of the pasture, 600–800 hundred yards away, and meandered above the opposite hill, waving back and forth a little as it approached the houses. When the object was closest, the witness saw that it had the shape of a domed saucer with white lights around the perimeter. Meanwhile, the dogs ran back to the truck and jumped into their box as if frightened—except for one, noted for his stubbornness. The object continued to approach the houses at slow speed, traveling 50 to 75 yards before it stopped to rock back and forth for a short while, then moved onward again. When it reached one of the security lights, the object hovered about 100 feet overhead, and the security light seemed to dim. The object eased over to the next light, and it too dimmed. Anxious to get a camera, the men shouted for the missing dog but were startled when the object seemed to respond and head toward them. They were ready to flee when the object halted over the security light by the pond. The light dimmed, and the missing dog arrived as the object receded over the hill where the houses were. The men drove to the hilltop and watched the object pass over the bottomlands, still pausing now and then over one farm or another. About a mile away, the object stopped and the white light turned a faint red, then over a few seconds the faint red grew bright red like a tail light and suddenly disappeared. The men saw no more of the object.[4]

Nothing about this account is notably spectacular. It describes no aliens, no dazzling maneuvers, no extraordinary effects in violation of physical principles. The evidential value of such a report cannot count for much when it depends on the testimony of a single witness and offers no photograph or physical evidence for support. What this case exemplifies is a good middle-of-the-road UFO account, better than a light in the sky but less informative than an abduction, less formidable than multiwitness, instrumented observations. If you or I sighted a UFO at moderately close range, this sort of detailed but indeterminate account is the story we might have to tell. Thousands, perhaps even millions of people have comparable personal experiences, though few will ever reveal them outside a circle of acquaintances. This story would have remained one of the lost had John Timmerman not been there to record it.

As a "story" this account lacks drama and goose bumps. It does not cry out for listeners to attend or approve. It is not a vehicle for art or structured to entertain, lacking formal traits like a surprise or punch line, or even a satisfying structure of complication, climax, and resolution. In fact, the account dangles unresolved, and for that reason resembles many narratives of the paranormal or mysterious encounter. If the story has a message, it is limited to a demonstration by example that we really do not know the world we think we know. The witness is not a participant in any sense other than observer and recorder and comes away with no consequences but puzzlement. His role is simply to bear witness that unexpected strangeness broke into the day-to-day stream of events, and to lend the face of a real person to the account. Whatever entertainment value the story possesses derives from the events themselves. The result of their recitation is a collection of minor marvels, a little eerie, a little curious, given to the listener to take or leave at face value. Our narrator has done his job simply by reporting the facts as he claims them to be.

The narrator classifies his experience as a UFO sighting by the fact that he reports it to a UFO investigator. Beyond that, he leaves matters of interpretation or explanation up to the listener. His account is full of recurrent UFO motifs—the saucer-shaped object, its seemingly purposeful wanderings, its swaying motions while it hovers, its changing colors when it disappears. The account includes some classic effects of UFOs—the object frightens the dogs, apparently responds to human voices, and causes electromagnetic interference by dimming the lights, even though the appearance may amount to nothing more than contrast with the luminosity of the object. By intention, accident, or observation, the narrator has described a UFO incident with the same circumstantial details of many other well-reported incidents.

At the high end of UFO weirdness is the abduction story, and the case of Kary Mullis nearly tops the scale. Stripped of interpretation and without the usual UFO crew or examination room, the account of his experiences still delivers a remarkable narrative. Who is Kary Mullis? He may not be a household name, but he won the 1993 Nobel Prize in Chemistry for invention of the polymerase chain reaction (PCR), a process that allows large-scale duplication of DNA from minute samples. Viewers of *Jurassic Park* may remember the reconstruction of a dinosaur out of DNA recovered from amber. Though dinosaur-making is fanciful, the movie rightly depicts use of PCR as a step necessary to produce working quantities of DNA, while in the real world of genetic engineering Mullis's discovery is as indispensable as the wheel. More outspoken than most Nobelists about unusual experiences in his life, Mullis describes a strange incident from 1985 in his autobiographical book, *Dancing Naked in the Mind Field* (1998).

He owned a cabin in a wooded area of northern California, a rather primitive place with electricity provided at night only by the batteries of a solar generator and toilet facilities by an outhouse some fifty feet away. He arrived about midnight after having "passed the functional sobriety test" of driving successfully through the mountains. Once he turned on the lights and left sacks of groceries on the floor, he lighted his path to the outhouse with a flashlight. On the way, he saw something glowing under a fir tree. Shining the flashlight on this glow, it seemed to be a raccoon with little black eyes. The raccoon spoke, saying, "Good evening, doctor," and he replied with a hello.

His next awareness came in early morning some six hours later. He walked a road uphill from the cabin with no memory of how he got there, his clothes clean and dry despite the heavy dew of the night. The cabin lights had dimmed from staying on several hours and he retraced his path to the outhouse in search of the raccoon and his flashlight, but he found neither. After several hours of sleep, he went about his business and decided to clean out a pipe, aware that the incidents of the night before did not disturb him as much as they should. The pipe was in the woods some 200 yards from the cabin, but no sooner did he enter those woods than he panicked and fled, no longer able to approach the area, even though the spot was his favorite. Considering where he was walking when he regained his awareness, he decided that whatever happened to him had happened in those woods. Six months later, he was able to walk there with his two sons, but the spot still troubled him some two years after the incident. One night he took a semiautomatic rifle and shot up the site, yelling for whatever was there to get out of his woods. This bout of frontier psychotherapy served its purpose and exorcised his fears, if not the woods themselves.

A little later he ran across Whitley Strieber's *Communion* in a bookstore and immediately began to read the account. His daughter called to tell him about the book, since it aroused in her the same vague recognition that he felt. She too had experienced missing time at the cabin when she disappeared for three hours while her fiancé called and searched for her. She found herself walking the same road uphill from the cabin with no memory of where she had been. In conversations with Mullis, Australian ufologist Bill Chalker learned that other odd events have clustered around the cabin. In 1993, during several days of partying to celebrate the Nobel, a guest spotted the glowing raccoon, though he knew nothing of the earlier incident. As he fled back to the cabin, he was further unnerved when a small glowing man enlarged into a full-sized man and promised to see him tomorrow. The following night, the apparitional man met him and again he fled the ongoing party, later telling his story to Mullis. The frightening figure turned out to be a neighbor, encountered in the flesh on the second night but not present to account for the apparition.[5]

Here is a story of surpassing weirdness describing an intensely personal experience. Mullis does not think he was abducted by aliens, and he did not see a UFO or a typical alien. He is well aware of the idea of abduction and draws parallels between his experience and those described by Whitley Strieber, but he circumscribes this interpretation with his own critical concern that aliens would have the biochemical savvy to make any genetic material they needed without having to steal it from human captives. As we might expect for a Nobel laureate, he takes charge of his own mystery and looks for a more original answer than aliens. He wonders if the raccoon was some sort of holographic projection and speculates that multidimensional physics on a macroscopic scale may be responsible. If Mullis remains uncertain about the nature of the experience, he is adamant that the events really happened. He is also aware of the awkward status of his experience. His story floats in the gray area of anecdote without prospect of duplication or lab work, the event as unquestionable to him as it is impossible to prove by scientific means. Lost in this limbo, he shares the loneliness of many other people who have encountered the paranormal.

Once Mullis revealed his account, it ceased to be his personal property, and a battle for the soul of the story began among interpreters. Ufologists read his account with a knowing nod. They have heard the likes many times before. Even the absurdity of a glowing raccoon with a friendly greeting raises no eyebrows in the context of UFO abduction reports. Those accounts may begin in an encounter with an animal, often an owl or deer, but usually an animal with large, dark, or luminous eyes. A period of missing time follows, and subjects return to their senses confused about where they are and how they got there. Mullis found himself mysteriously dry amid the dewy night, other people waken in bed to find their feet wet or muddy. Though haunted by a sense that something happened, they go about mundane business on automatic pilot. A compulsion to return to the scene often leads to an emotional explosion of terror. The fears and anxieties linger sometimes for years, and relatives and friends may report similar experiences.

The emotional responses and odd behaviors, so out of proportion to any apparent provocation, hint of hidden depths. Something more than meets the eye seems to have happened during that forgotten span of time. Hypnosis or spontaneous return of memory may break down an apparent mental barrier and the secret tumbles out. The secret is a coherent but surpassingly strange story of alien kidnap, and however impossible the memories seem, they fill in the blanks with uncanny perfection. The confusion dissipates, the oddities and terrors fall into place as meaningful consequences of the hidden experience. In various accounts the animals in conscious recollection resolve into short humanoid aliens with big eyes, as if a screen memory had concealed the truth from the witness. For some people the alien illustration on the cover of *Communion* has acted as a catalyst to loosen the hidden memories. Mullis felt only a vague attraction to the picture and found no flashbacks of aliens, no evidence that any such experiences might fill in his lost hours. He leaves his experience a mystery, yet ufologists see too many parallels with classic abduction reports to draw a distinction. His account fits their expected template despite some gaps and, just as tellingly, fails to fit the psychosocial alternative. Without benefit of sleep paralysis or a wish for alien contact, without hypnosis or leading questions from an investigator, Mullis describes

important parts of the same extraordinary experience that hundreds of UFO abductees describe, as if the phenomenology obeyed some inner necessity and refused to
climb meekly into the explanatory boxes prepared for it.

In contrast to the solo nature of many extranormal encounters, UFO experiences
are often communal affairs. Such a story bristling with witnesses unfolded on the night
of October 24, 1968, at Minot Air Force Base in North Dakota. About half past midnight maintenance crews began to report starlike objects, and by 3 A.M. a large reddish-
orange object flew over Minuteman missile sites with ground patrols in pursuit. At
some point the security alarm sounded for one of the sites. Weather radar picked up
the object before it seemed to land and its light went out. While these actions were
under way ground control contacted an approaching B-52 at about 3:30 A.M. and asked
the crew to be on the lookout for anything unusual in a certain direction, telling the
men that they would know it if they saw it. About 4 A.M. the radar navigator picked up
an object approaching from behind at an apparent speed of 3,000 miles per hour on a
collision course. The men prepared to eject, but the object stopped abruptly off the tail,
not visible in the heavy haze but recorded on radar with a blip size larger than a tanker.
At the same time, both radio systems aboard the bomber went dead until the B-52 was
ten miles from the landing field and the object fell away as the plane descended for a
landing. As soon as radio contact resumed, the crew received a request to turn around
and fly over the object, which by this time had landed. Flying at 1,000 feet, the B-52
passed near the object then circled back by it. The pilot and copilot saw an object below
them, on or near the ground and of considerable angular size, estimated at several hundred feet long. The object was oval and glowing red-orange like molten steel or lava,
while a crescent-shaped structure projected from one end of the main object like an
automobile bumper, connected by means of a single short tube. Blue, green, and orange
lights played within the inner side of the crescent. The plane landed about 4:20 A.M.

Rumors of tampering with missile facilities accompany this incident and may owe
more to confusion than fact, but the factual elements are impressive enough. Fourteen
people in various locations on the ground saw some sort of aerial object or objects,
and so did the pilot and copilot of the B-52. Weather radar on the ground picked up
returns, and so did the B-52 radar, and photographs of the screen confirmed a robust
return of exceptional size. This object appeared to travel at great speed then suddenly
slow to pace the plane, and during its approach an unusual double failure of communications systems occurred. The object landed, and the B-52 observers saw it from above
as a large structured object on the ground.

Project Blue Book responded to this incident by not bothering to send anyone to
investigate but found answers for everything after reading some written reports and

making a few phone calls. The people on the ground mistook the star Sirius and the B-52 for UFOs, and the airmen thought the star Vega, then low on the horizon, was a barn-sized glowing object on the ground. Ball lightning or some sort of plasma fooled the radar, disrupted communications, and contributed to visual sightings. Throw in a temperature inversion to increase visual and radar distortion, and the result is a classic Blue Book recipe for a tossed salad of explanations, with pieces thrown at every part of the reports in hopes that enough would stick to hide the mystery. Interviews of fifteen witnesses by documentary filmmaker Thomas Tulien, James Klotz (of the Computer UFO Network), and others reveal a hectic night that may have included some mistaken identities, but also very strange happenings that do not readily resolve into conventional terms.[6]

Multiple voices tell the Minot story, or rather each voice tells a personal story of eyewitness events, and an interpreter assembles the accounts, rightly or wrongly, into an overarching whole. For Blue Book, the meaning was a comedy of errors as people in the grip of UFO excitement confused stars and weather phenomena for aerial craft; for ufologists, the real story is a mystery with a cast of trained, experienced personnel witnessing an impressive unconventional object from various perspectives, with sophisticated instrumentation indicating the object in a certain place and visual observers confirming the presence. Interpretation takes away the stories of observers for interpreters to use. It reveals a larger truth but risks distorting the facts by aligning and enlarging on them to fill a hypothetical meaning. In both versions the reports reaffirm prior convictions—that UFOs are only mistaken identities and that UFOs are physical objects of unknown origin and government response is inadequate or disingenuous.

These three cases present remarkable incidents from credible witnesses. The stories demand an answer to the mystery they describe even without any certainties in sight. Another quality these cases share may go overlooked but deserves the closest examination—they are not remote histories but direct accounts of personal experience. Experience alone cannot settle whether the source of the observation was conventional or unconventional, internal or external; but an experiential encounter with UFOs moves the inquiry away from purely mythic territory toward questions of observational data and into scientific considerations of how and why such experiences occur.

"Seeing Things" or Seeing "Things"?

A story expressing an understanding of UFOs differs from a story of UFO experience. The one relies on expectations and theories to make sense of the facts, the other sticks to the facts whether they make sense or not. One is rich with human meaning, the established mythology of UFOs; the other describes a perceived phenomenon, the story that UFOs tell about themselves. Accounts of experiences call attention back to basics, back to sightings and encounters as fundamental units of the mystery. Is an encounter with UFOs relevant for their cultural image? Does UFO belief even need UFOs? In many respects the answer is clearly no, since the mythic UFO has such a robust reality in thought and so many connections with society and culture that the phenomenal UFO may fade into insignificance by comparison. On the other hand, examples like the three above reiterate a basic truth that people not disposed to see UFOs nevertheless see them. Legions of people insist that they are witnesses, not tale-- tellers, tradition-bearers, or purveyors of hearsay but reporters of firsthand news about real-world events.

Firsthand testimony goes to the heart of credibility in its everyday sense. The sight I see with my own eyes is thoroughly convincing to me, and the word of a reliable witness sounds persuasive to most hearers. A report of experience exchanges an ab- stract text for the sensations and conceptions of a real person who becomes a proxy for ourselves, describing not a remote event through an impersonal record but reliv- ing the occurrence for us as if we had shared in witnessing it. Testimonial evidence carries real-world authenticity to prove, on a human level, that something more than fantasy keeps the fires of interest and commitment burning. Trust in witnesses is not enough for scientists. They require extensive corroboration for testimonies, however potent their human force. The track record for backing UFO reports with hard evi- dence has been a disappointment. Tantalizing photographs, fragments, and ground traces have come forward, but never anything as unequivocal as a crashed saucer on the nightly news or the proverbial landing on the White House lawn. Without sup- port even the finest eyewitness reports do not measure up to the stringent standards of science.

No amount of argument can compensate for the lack of solid proof, but neither do empty hands resolve the issue in favor of a skeptical conclusion. Most observational accounts of anomalies are individualistic. The claim remains no more than a claim, and little else can be said about it, yet with UFO observations the testimonial texts may of- fer something more. When the encounter is experiential rather than hearsay, the expe- rience transpersonal rather than individualistic, the descriptions recurrent rather than devoid of pattern, and the contents unexpected rather than true to cultural anteced- ents, then the accounts present significant characteristics of objectivity. This evidence for a physical phenomenon is inferential, and the appearance of reality can unfold into illusions after various twists and turns; but in a less than perfect world, where the

primary evidence is testimonial, these considerations lend at least a soft form of supporting evidence for a phenomenal reality independent of the myth.

The Puzzle of Recurrence.—Anomalies may not form enough of a pattern to attract scientific interest, yet they amount to more than random oddities. Not just UFOs
but also the reports of many types of strange occurrences persist throughout history
and cross cultural boundaries with a noteworthy inertia in descriptions of action and
content. Accounts of ESP, near-death experiences, apparitions of the dead, diminutive supernatural beings, and appearances in the sky repeat in diverse contexts and
frameworks of interpretation but maintain phenomenological likeness impervious to
cultural fashion and authoritative criticism. Some claims yield to commonsense solutions—for example, seeing departed loved ones suggests nothing more mysterious
than a universal longing to overcome the barrier of death. On the other hand, the bizarre antics of the poltergeist seem to persist as an invariant core, whether the reports
come from ancient Rome, Dark Ages Germany, England two hundred years ago, or
America today, in a mingling of apparent objectivity with uncertainty that traps such
anomalies halfway between the scientific community that refuses to accept them and
the public that refuses to renounce them.[7] "All argument is against it; but all belief is for
it," Samuel Johnson said of the appearance of ghosts, though the statement can stand
for anomalies in general.[8]

This matter of recurrence has proved a provocative oddity in many sorts of anomalous experience, while a favorite supportive argument for UFOs relies on consistency
of description in their reports. Saucer-shaped craft and short humanoids dominate
throughout the modern UFO era, missing time and a consistent sequence of events accompanies abductions. These repetitions are widely known but less familiar traits, such
as electrical failures in the presence of UFOs; objects that descend with a wobbling,
falling-leaf motion; or a vehement emotional response that follows a close encounter. These traits have less widespread exposure, yet similar accounts recur worldwide.
J. Allen Hynek stressed the peculiar confinement of variation in UFO reports. "The
'strangeness spread' . . . is quite limited. We do not, for instance, receive reports of dinosaurs seen flying upside down, Unidentified Sailing Objects, or strange objects that
burrow into the ground. If UFOs are indeed figments of the imagination, it is strange
that the imaginations of those who report UFOs from all over the world should be so
restricted."[9] Although boomerang craft and Nordic aliens appear side by side with saucers and humanoids, even these differences join the pattern of regularity by occurring
in more or less steady proportions. To hear similar reports from different individuals
practically defines objectivity in everyday thinking. Even though the matter is never

so direct with UFOs, an explanation passes the minimum test for adequacy only if it answers for the apparent patterns of recurrence.

Not everyone agrees that any significant consistency exists. From the analysts of Project Blue Book Special Report no. 14 in 1955 to some psychosocial critics today, one argument against UFOs cites too little evidence for a truly coherent phenomenon.[10] Even Allan Hendry, a sympathetic investigator for CUFOS who spent a year investigating over a thousand reports, found little pattern among them.[11] The complaint distinguishes between similarities that are true but trivial, like the saucer shape, too readily the result of media-induced expectations, and a scarcity of meaningful repetitions that observations of similar objects should produce. UFO descriptions scatter into such varied forms and actions that truly good cases never seem to happen twice. For example, the celebrated 1959 sighting of Father Gill had occupants waving from atop the UFO, but this instance of a UFO with a deck on top appears unique. Hynek in *The UFO Experience* and Richard Hall in *The UFO Evidence* argue for the defense. Once they separate the best cases from the raw sample, similarities zoom into focus for classification in limited categories and for tabulation as examples of recurrent descriptions. The recurrence is not robust enough to convince critics or superficial enough to discourage proponents, but UFO researchers have identified enough consistency among quality cases to call for a considered explanation.

An alternative solution that relies on human causes in place of observational similarities identifies recurrence as a property of narratives. Anthropologists and folklorists have marveled at the likeness in myths and tales from widely separated localities and explained it in terms of transmission—that similarities happen because narrators borrow from one another—or polygenesis—that comparable stories arise independently out of the psychic unity of mankind; that is, stories grow from the needs, mental capacities, and life situations common to everyone. Innate ideas, universal processes, or cognitive predispositions may explain universals like diminutive supernatural beings and ghosts, but theories of polygenesis work more credibly for larger issues of consistency than for the small details. The ability of wandering peoples to carry plots and motifs far and wide explains why the war of the gods or Cinderella appears in Asia, Europe, and the New World, according to transmission theory, while the Internet spreads urban legends around the world overnight. A search for where most UFO ideas come from needs to canvass no further than cultural borrowing, as psychosocial critics so often argue. Traditional and current influences join to build a cultural script, and one UFO story then resembles another because all narrators read off the same script.

Folklorists concentrate not on what anomalies are but on their verbal treatment.

The formulation of a story follows rules of narration that serve human satisfaction first and accurate history second, often a remote second, but impose a consistency all their own. The raw material of folk belief is less often an abstract declaration of faith than a concrete observation or encounter. In other words, belief starts, at least in theory, with a firsthand account or *memorate*. It is ideally a description of a purely personal experience and thereby nontraditional, but most of the time such accounts relate an instance of some recognized belief, like a ghost, and consequently inherit established traditions about ghosts. The hypothetical future of the initial report is successive re-telling by others until it becomes a third-person, friend-of-a-friend legend, or *fabulate*, removed from the actual observers and impersonal in configuration but still at heart an assertion that a witness saw something happen at a given time and place. In practice, this straightforward lineage grows tangled as narrators appropriate the third-person story and recast it as a first-person experience, at once restoring immediacy of interest to the account and muddling its history.[12]

When they repeat a story, narrators seldom rely on rote memory, as if they recited the Gettysburg Address in front of a classroom. Retelling means loss and gain, stream-lining and reshaping with each repetition. In the 1920s Cambridge psychologist Fred-eric C. Bartlett experimented with the transmission of American Indian narratives and found that his European subjects shortened and simplified the story, rationalized and stereotyped the plot according to European norms, and eliminated or revised any part culturally alien to the hearers. Bartlett proposed that subjects altered the text to suit their established schemata of understanding in a sacrifice of accuracy to gain coher-ence and meaning.[13] Sociological studies of rumor discovered that repeated transmis-sion led to leveling, the concentration of accounts into more concise form; sharpening, a selective emphasis on limited details; and assimilation, the shaping of the message into a form consistent with the presuppositions of the tellers.[14] In the transition from *memorate* to *fabulate* a similar process plays out as narratives exchange individuality for stereotypical generality.[15] They crystallize into expressions consistent with belief, ex-pectation, and social norms so that the dynamics of narrative transmission contribute to an appearance of consistency that may belie the original truth.

A claim of extraordinary experience is more than a matter of idle curiosity. Such events are inherently worth talking about and communicating to others; such claims are also controversial. Folk legends are strongholds of extranormal claims and oppose the official viewpoint so sharply that folklorists once defined the legend in terms of false or unscientific content. The controversy also spills over from a dichotomy of folk versus rationalistic belief into conflicts among various factions of folk belief. Indiana

University folklorist Linda Dégh describes legend transmission as a self-organizing system based on a process of natural selection. Many people listen to a story. Some listeners accept the story as told and repeat it to other listeners; some of those listeners will find the initial version congenial and pass it along in turn. A conduit of believers takes shape as people preserve and transmit the believers' version over time and space. Some hearers will disagree and spin a skeptical version. It too will find listeners of the same opinion and grow a conduit for skeptics. Other listeners will accept the initial story all or in part but frame it in a different interpretation, as some people prefer a religious or government conspiracy notion of UFOs to the extraterrestrial hypothesis. These people with alternative beliefs will vary the story to reflect their views, and the proponents of each version will present it to listeners. Some will let it die, while others will approve and take it up to channel yet another conduit of advocates through the social matrix.[16]

Since these conduits concern a related claim, they seldom diverge far from one another and often intersect as participants defend the same content according to their respective beliefs. Such confrontations stake out social boundaries between "us" and "them" and promote solidarity within the opposing factions. No side is likely to win, no resolution is likely to emerge, but disputation enlivens a claim from dry text or static creed to an active communal question about truth.[17] Dégh argues that the discussion plays out in a dialectic process of pro and con, one interpretation versus another, in a circle of assertion and refutation by citation of concrete incidents as well as abstract argument. Uncertainty provides the necessary medium for stories of extranormal experience, a state of intellectual disequilibrium that assures controversy as long as people continue to disagree over a claim. Each conduit of believers, each defending faction constitutes a folk group united by their shared claims. The group conserves a version that suits the members' beliefs and becomes an agent of continuity.[18] Applying this view to UFOs, similarities appear because people repeat stories and argue positions that express shared beliefs. The appearance of consistency depends on tradition—on ideas learned and passed along—but needs not owe anything to real-world similarities.

The Answers Fall Short.—Traditional patterns, borrowed contents, and shared beliefs can explain some recurrences in UFO narratives but still leave important questions unanswered. Why would stories that depend on cultural sources and fantasy without a factual anchor nevertheless display the inhibition apparent in UFO reports? A tale-teller faces opportunities for creative freedom, not the ball and chain of obligatory compliance. Reasonable usage of psychosocial theory predicts that narrators bombarded with Hollywood representations of aliens ought to reciprocate with equally diverse feats of monster-making, yet even before publicity lent favor to short humanoids, they served as the aliens of choice in close encounters.[19] Abductees insist on an invariant sequence of events, though the story remains equally meaningful whether examination or conference comes first. With a whole universe of imaginative possibilities available and a suggestive premise such as visitors from space inviting creative elaboration into space opera, heroic adventure, and interplanetary romance, why are abductees so reticent to elaborate along these lines?

The example of urban legends predicts a very different outcome. One of the most embarrassing habits for a narrative alleging to tell the truth is the inability of fictitious claims to stick to just one story. Legend is the loose-lipped drunkard of folk narratives. Around its core idea reels a swarm of variants, each a part of the legend and no one of them any more the "true" version than any other.[20] Like memory itself, the legend-making process constructs a story from parts. Even with plots so tightly structured that every piece counts and any change threatens to shatter the meaning of the entire story, urban legends stay true to their nature but not to their model as they fragment and reassemble in kaleidoscopic variation. The same hook-handed killer stalks teenagers in multiple plots, here on Lovers' Lane, there in the backseat of a car, or lurking upstairs where the babysitter's charges sleep. Then again, a basic plot of thieves getting their comeuppance plays out with varied content when they steal a shopping bag containing a dead cat, a beer bottle that holds a urine sample, or a car with a corpse tied on top. Imagination finds a way to vary every aspect so that the legend reveals itself not as a specific text but what Bill Ellis, Pennsylvania State University professor of English and American Studies, calls "a social impetus to create new narratives in the shape of the old."[21] Even the stability of a variant in its conduit amounts to one trickle amid a torrent of diversity as the thrust of creativity realizes the possibilities, evident and not so evident, serially or simultaneously, of the constituent ideas.

A notion of cultural script is misleading, since it implies that a story is written down for actors to read verbatim. The performers are more likely to ad lib their lines with more attention to personal preference and creative license than fidelity to an ideal version. Ample evidence points to recent claims of satanic ritual abuse as creations of imagination. Nothing more unites them than a few obvious motifs like candles, chanting, and hooded figures, or well-known allegations like human sacrifice and cannibalism. The personal accounts often share a premise that the protagonist was chosen and raised from childhood to become a high priest or priestess. What narrators do with these loose similarities is quite idiosyncratic. No common plot emerges as the claimants go their separate ways to relate very different autobiographies. Where one climaxes with a "Feast of the Beast" attended by Satan himself, another depends on allusions to Voodoo, and another is a sham with the rituals nothing more than a pretext for an orgy.[22] The garrulous nature of legends, their socially motivated and inevitable multiplicity, heaps doubt on the truthfulness of their truth claims and confirms variation as so characteristic of their kind that unless a truth-claiming narrative varies, it probably is not folklore.

In contrast to accounts of satanic ritual abuse, abduction reports repeat one another to the point of monotony. Details may vary, but the plot lines and main descriptive features read as pretty much alike from one account to another, including many little-known and unpublicized elements. The devil inspires an individualistic relationship, whereas encounters with aliens are impersonal and rigid, surely reason enough to question any explanation that assigns an ontological sameness to both types of story. If cultural influences chart the course of abduction reports, the movie *Close Encounters of the Third Kind* in 1977 and the 1987 books of Whitley Strieber and Budd Hopkins should serve as turning points in the development of the story. Comparative study of abductions shows that the reports fail to develop very much at all. The descriptions of aliens changed little in response to the movie and have changed little over the years. More instances of stolen fetuses came to light after 1987, but the increase owes more to greater recognition of existing tendencies, probably as a result of the Hopkins book, than to any actual innovations because of it.[23] Hopkins raises the point that the often-seen alien illustration on the cover of *Communion* actually misrepresents the entities reported by Strieber—that, in fact, they had a much more bulbous head. Yet as misleading as this single most familiar image of a UFO alien ought to be, few abductees have copied its error. This prominent cultural icon has failed to alter the preference for big heads in actual reports.[24] When multiple narrators adhere to a supposed script down to the obscure details, that same invariance is a clue that they cling to firmer ground than cultural ideas can provide. In their unimaginative similarities, the sober reports do not fulfill their potential as products of imagination but act like what they claim to be, descriptions of independent events.

From Cultural Source to Experience.—The UFO myth can explain much of what is said *about* UFOs and the expectations that lead many observers into error, but this same system of ideas that influences thought and even observation is not always a convincing answer. Cultural sources are insufficient to account for Kary Mullis's interrupted journey to the outhouse. A UFO story that does not manifest the creative freedom of a fictitious narrative or fulfill the expectations of its supposed cultural source hints that another ingredient enters into the mix. For some UFO reports, it is not the idiosyncrasy of personal fantasy but the substantive record of experience that seems responsible for their peculiar form.

First-person claims of extranormal experience have bedeviled scholars of religion, psychology, parapsychology, sociology, anthropology, and folklore. Finnish folklorist Lauri Honko voiced the standard response of his field when he attributed experiential claims to a subjective combination of psychology and tradition.[25] Say I walk by a graveyard at midnight. The initial conditions are right to imagine a paranormal experience, because in the back of my mind I know graveyards are the wrong place to be on a dark and lonely night. Though neither timid nor a believer in ghosts, I add to my receptiveness by feeling uneasy and thinking about them, so that the primary stimuli for an imagined encounter are all in place. A releasing stimulus appears when I see a shapeless pale form over a tombstone. At this stage, the form lacks interpretation, identity, even a definite appearance and can be called a numen; but in keeping with things numinous, the appearance is fraught with mystery, fear, and awe. I try to make sense of this uncanny appearance, and the traditional interpretation of a ghost intrudes because what I see looks like the graveyard ghosts I have heard about in legends and folk beliefs. All the parts fall together in a meaningful fit. I go my way, probably in a hurry, maybe not a believer in ghosts but without an emotionally convincing alternative. I tell the story and hearers retell this personal account so that it reinforces collective ideas of ghost encounters, its example an influence on current and future audiences so that they too expect a ghost in dark cemeteries. What did I see? Maybe it was nothing more than a moonbeam on a wisp of fog, but the nature of the stimulus no longer matters once social and psychological causes elaborate this trifle into an encounter vivid with emotion and specific with cultural meaning.

This cultural-source hypothesis long passed the academic verdict on extranormal experiences until David Hufford, professor of behavioral science at the Pennsylvania State University College of Medicine, published *The Terror That Comes in the Night* in 1982. While living in Newfoundland Hufford had investigated a living tradition of the region, an experience of awakening in the night overwhelmed by fear but unable to move while a shadowy form entered the room. A frightening and tangible presence, the intruder choked or pressed on the victim until, by an effort of will, the movement of a finger or toe broke the nightmarish spell. Suddenly the entity was gone and the paralysis too. Locals identified the attacker as the Old Hag, a witch figure in Newfoundland folklore and suited to the standard notion that vague feelings and stimuli, real enough in themselves, gelled into an illusory supernatural experience only when traditional ideas provided a catalyst. When he returned to Pennsylvania, Hufford described the

Old Hag experience to his classes, and students stepped forward to say that the same thing had happened to them. Finding the Old Hag so far from home turned from mild surprise into astonishment when he learned that most of these students had never lived in Newfoundland and knew nothing of the Old Hag tradition. They described the phenomenology but knew nothing of the cultural expectations. Few of the students had ever confided their experience to anyone because they did not even have a name for it.[26]

Further research uncovered that experiences like the Old Hag were widespread both in geography and history. As much as one-fourth of the population may undergo the experience at least once in a lifetime. Interpretations like "hag-riding," ghosts, or vampires vary widely from culture to culture, but the basic experience persists, familiar enough and old enough that the original sense of "nightmare" embodies the characteristic oppression by a supernatural agent. Hufford generalized supernatural assault accounts under the term of "Mara attack" and recognized that the experience, with its consistency of phenomenology and independence from tradition, posed a head-on challenge to the prevailing academic consensus on anomalistic encounters.[27] The evidence made a compelling case that tradition does not always give rise to experience; rather experience sometimes returns the favor and gives rise to tradition. For Hufford, "a fundamental reason that spiritual beliefs have been able to resist the enormous social pressures toward secularization is that they are, in part, rationally founded on experience (that is, empirically grounded)."[28] He broke with folklorists' accepted emphasis on cultural acquisition and proposed an experience-centered approach to understand experiential claims from the standpoint of the claimants.[29]

A similar quandary troubles religious studies when rational understanding batters claims like miracles, otherworld journeys, mysticism, conversions, and speaking in tongues, yet these claims continue to prosper at the grassroots level. As William James argued in 1902, volumes of theological reasoning or abstract understanding of natural order does little to create religious faith; rather it grows from the bottom up out of individual religious experiences and their resultant feelings and intuitions.[30] Pennsylvania State University College of Medicine professor James McClenon has researched anomalous experiences around the world and found considerable cross-cultural similarity in their reported phenomenology. He designated as "wondrous events" certain recurrent happenings like encounters with apparitional beings, spiritual healing, extrasensory perception, out-of-body experiences, and near-death experiences. These occurrences, he proposed, inspire and reinforce religious tenets such as beliefs in other worlds, higher powers, souls and spirits, life after death, miracles, and providence. Whether NDEs owe their apparent universality to a visit to heaven or to physiological properties of the dying brain makes no difference; the experience is influential as a sociological fact, whatever its nature. Little leap of faith is necessary to imagine an important role for wondrous events or rumors of them in the origin and maintenance of religious belief.[31]

However large and self-sustaining the UFO myth grows, observations of UFOs have shaped the history of the subject and allow widespread personal participation. The persuasiveness of experience offers a straightforward answer for why witnesses believe, why others believe them, and why UFOs inspire emotional commitment and a lifelong quest. What the witnesses saw, what happened to them—these questions crowd into mind—but what witnesses saw is secondary to the fact that they saw something. Tens of thousands of people have reported in good faith what they took for UFOs, and these observations qualify the observers as more than secondhand believers. Their experiences provide a potential missing link to understanding how UFOs sometimes put on the appearance of a recurrent and independent phenomenon.

A Glimpse behind the Myth

From Experience to Event.—The value of an experience-centered approach to anomalous encounters lies in its calling attention to observable phenomena, to the descriptions, emotions, and responses of the experiencer. Beyond any reasonable doubt not everyone who reports a UFO hallucinates or perpetrates a hoax; rather, some claimants actually see something, encounter something, have the same sensations that accompany the observation of an external, transpersonal event. The fact of an experience is one point on which the contenders in UFO discussions can usually reach an agreement, however grudgingly, and this recognition nudges the discussion away from the observer toward the observed, where ufologists usually want to go.

With an avowed purpose to understand UFOs, ufologists typically hasten past phenomena of human behavior in pursuit of a physical cause. Proponents of UFOs or any other anomaly may claim that experience happens as a straightforward consequence of an underlying physical event and thereby cite the experience as proof of an external reality, but the critics can counter that seeing "something" does not mean seeing something unconventional. Jumping to a conclusion that experience equates with reality ignores alternatives, such as internal origin or a combination of internal and external sources for experiential accounts, and the prospect that a mistake can inspire the same awe and excitement as a real encounter with the unknown. Hufford takes an agnostic view on the origin of Mara attacks. He finds the physical and sensory effects consistent with phenomena of sleep paralysis, but the experiential account is richer than this explanation can encompass.

> What has been gained has been a description of physiological events that seem to account for the production of the state . . . during which a complex and frightening experience may take place. The specific contents of the experience, however, have not been explained. They seem if anything more odd than they did before. If they are related to ordinary dreams . . . , why is their content so consistently the same without apparent regard for culture?[32]

Hufford's statement recognizes that anomalous experience does not reduce to a single identifiable cause. Once cut loose from the cultural thread that bound the similarities to a learned source, the possibility opens that they depend on some unknown properties of the experience itself. Hufford does not take the extra step of assuming that similarities result from recurrent observation of the same real-world events; rather, a subjective experience might also possess fixed properties. He simply urges scholars to follow the lead of their subjects and realize that an explanation for traditional belief must at least consider going as far as they are willing to go, even to an event as the possible cause. In this spirit scholars have built strong cases that memories of a volcanic explosion on the island of Thera are responsible for the legend of Atlantis, various motifs of vampire legends originate in the phenomena of bodily decay, and finds of fossil bones in ancient times account for some mythical monsters.[33] Even as absurd a subject of folk humor and tall tales as the Jackalope (a jackrabbit with the antlers of an antelope) has an unfamiliar basis in reality after all, since infections with *Shope lapine papilloma* virus cause hornlike growths on the heads of rabbits and hares.[34]

Hufford's experience-centered approach has turned around the academic study of anomalies and restored respectability to experiential claims, but to the tune of considerable dissent from adherents who defend the cultural-source hypothesis. Academics already leery of an experiential basis for anomalies are even more reluctant to dig down another layer and consider underlying events. When they pursue real-world correlates, humanists or social and behavioral scientists overstep their expertise and lose themselves in a labyrinth of issues extraneous to their legitimate disciplinary concerns, according to some well-considered warnings.[35] Yet the people these scholars try to understand have no such misgiving; they have experiences instead, and any effort to grasp the human condition must reckon with culture, experience, and event as parts of an indivisible package. For UFOs the question is not whether to study the contribution of potential events, but how.

The Limitations of Experience.—Experience occupies a central but equivocal position in the chain of UFO arguments. An experiential report stakes a potent claim of firsthand knowledge, yet experience remains a human process with human limitations, not an open window on real-world events. Thousands of cases in the annual crop of UFO reports turn out to be false alarms. Even multiple-witness sightings can implode as bubbles of mistaken identity. The influence of expectations on a few extreme reports of the *Zond* reentry, Allen Hynek's anecdote of riding a police car in hot pursuit of a UFO that he recognized as the star Arcturus,[36] and Allan Hendry's repeated cases of unwary witnesses confused and excited by the moon:[37] these examples teach that perhaps the bitterest lesson ufologists can face, if they face it, is the fallibility of the human observer as a source of information. In broader perspective, people also report seeing angels and ghosts as legitimate experiences. The ufologist may ask what such claims have to do with UFOs, but processes of human error can just as well carry over from one type of experience to another. Either ufologists accept one anomalous encounter and reject another by arbitrary choice, or they must admit that blind faith in eyewitness testimony is unjustified even when the eyewitness is sincere and honest to a fault.

The findings of experience-centered research underscore how stubbornly indeterminate the relationship between experience and event can be. A scholarly program to construct reliable history from the statements of nonliterate peoples made the confident assumption that as long as accounts corroborated one another, they likely provided accurate accounts. Careful methodology could, according to the theory of oral history, extract historical truth from the distortions of tradition.[38] Quite a bit more pessimism followed from investigations in eastern Africa, where accounts of encounters with vampires have flourished since the 1920s. Widespread rumors of firemen, policemen, and game wardens capturing hapless individuals and draining their blood, perhaps for use by Europeans, and of prostitutes maintaining a chamber for blood-taking beneath their place of business, has formed an oral tradition that many narrators borrow. One man gave an account of being attacked by bloodsuckers while using a public latrine, but his improbable account of heroic escape hinted that his story had less to do with a real encounter than with portraying himself in a socially favorable light. Though often expressed as personal experiences, these vampire accounts draw on collective beliefs and appear to corroborate one another only because they echo stereotypical ideas. The narrators talk about vampires, but the accounts serve as a means to talk about other things, diverging from the unlikely phenomenal subject to express a richness of human meanings.[39]

A popular source of information in the UFO literature and Internet discussions is the "insider" whose personal experiences support exceptional claims. In the late 1980s when Bill Cooper issued one fantastic assertion after another about alien contacts with the U.S. government, one of his revelations claimed that the military held in custody an ice cream–loving alien named "O. H. Krill," who was described in some of the top-secret papers that Cooper always seemed to chance upon during his duty in the Navy. The presence of Krill in official papers from years before came as a surprise to two other dark-side advocates, John Lear and John Grace, since they had recently fabricated Krill as a joke.[40] Despite the likelihood that Cooper saw nothing more secretive than the papers of two colleagues, his claims took root as facts in some discussions, and papers appeared under Krill's name detailing alien technology and purposes. Some insiders may reveal genuine secrets, but in this case Cooper assimilated false information and presented it as truth, supported by his alleged personal reading of official documents. In this case the voice of experience turned out to be recycled fiction and serves as a reminder that even firsthand testimony remains a slippery guide to real-world events.

The Value of Strange Experiences.—Encounters with the Old Hag and the UFO share a dual nature. On the one hand, they both belong to cultural categories and conform to popular images of how such encounters are supposed to play out. Narratives often reflect appropriate traditions and fulfill expectations of appearance and behavior. On the other hand, people describing their experiences sometimes see more than expectations prepare them to see. The apparent independence of an experience may reveal itself only in perspective, as the Old Hag escapes the shadow of local tradition in comparison with examples from other parts of the world, while UFOs drop a hint whenever unfamiliar descriptions recur or elements of strangeness intrude into the story without a good cultural reason. How the flashing lights of the 1965 Exeter UFO presented a constant angle remains hard to understand, whether they hung on the rim of a spaceship or the line of a kite. Kary Mullis describes many key elements of the abduction story, but a glowing raccoon is an unlikely substitute for the standard alien. The bumperlike projection on the UFO as the Minot B-52 pilots looked down at it was neither necessary nor expected, just there. In all three cases the narrators make poor choices if they are simply telling tales and want to persuade an audience. Better to keep the listeners happy with a familiar UFO than baffle them with a description that is odd or hard to comprehend, better to dazzle them with a crackerjack tale than disappoint them with narratives that are tentative and inartistic; but the record is full of accounts that seem to cling to the strangeness and confusion of an experience over a story crafted to please the crowd. In these tidbits of gratuitous strangeness, perhaps something more than myth and cultural image steps into view.

Though skeptics scarcely question that the experiential basis for UFO abductions is sleep paralysis, it leaves much to be desired as an explanation. The more cases that begin in the bedroom, the more phenomenology associated with sleep paralysis we should expect to find, like descriptions of immobility, ringing sounds, and floating sensations. Bedroom intrusions have supplanted highway encounters as the primary setting for abduction, but while bedroom reports increased from less than 20 percent prior to 1977 to nearly 60 percent after 1987, the reported occurrence of paralysis, odd sounds, and flotation has maintained largely the same proportion over the years. The descriptions of witnesses contradict the predictions of theory if sleep paralysis is responsible for abduction claims. A total of 54 percent out of 437 reports from the beginning until 1996 involve highway or outdoor encounters, including cases like those of the Hills and Kary Mullis that are rich with abduction phenomenology but do not involve sleep.[41] Sleep paralysis fares poorly as an explanatory panacea when it figures into less than half of the cases.

The *Zond IV* reentry, described in chapter 1, tells a horror story of conceptual errors, and its wildest deviations arm critics with a forceful counter to any UFO claim. Less appreciated is the overall accuracy of most accounts of this event submitted to authorities. The descriptions reflect reality, and explanations often identify the correct nature of the event. Errors less often represent conceptions distorted by UFO beliefs than loose terminology or mistakes not specific to a UFO context, like inaccurate estimates of altitude and speed. Such faults add error but not much of consequence for descriptions of the object itself. The usual conservatism tied to observational facts reassures us that most people are good observers, but still some are not. Witnesses who identified the burning *Zond* as space debris felt less motivated to report the incident than individuals who mistook the reentry for a UFO event.[42] Those few mistaken accounts may become selectively influential if they enter the record as evidence for a distinctive UFO phenomenon. A false mixture of aerial apples and oranges with no inherent relatedness could, when taken together, concentrate the errors into a coherent body of claims. It would give the appearance of a mysterious phenomenon where in fact the only strangeness was imaginary.

Skeptics follow up their attack on observation with a reminder that an unidentified report is not necessarily unidentifiable. Extensive investigation resolves some intriguing UFO cases but not all. Still the doubt lingers—could another investigation, another perspective, or more facts in hand crack the unknowns? The kind of observational error responsible for the best UFO cases might not be an ordinary one but the consequence of some extraordinary circumstance, like the witness seeing a bright meteor head-on. Such an occasion would leave an inexplicable image and a very shaken observer. Certainly in the distribution curve of conventional phenomena some instances must fall at the trailing ends where a normal appearance becomes an abnormal rarity, while as the Manises case demonstrates, mistaken combinations of ordinary events might sum up to an extraordinary and baffling experience. Failure to identify a UFO can owe more to social or situational factors than to the mysterious qualities of a spaceship.

The inherent weirdness of some UFO reports, even when they are of high quality, introduces a dimension of strangeness that does more to confuse than affirm the independence of the mystery. A UFO seen in the Yukon Territory on December 11, 1996, seemingly had the right stuff to topple the dominoes of current understanding. At least thirty-one witnesses along two hundred miles of highway described a dark circular object bearing more lights than a Christmas tree and rows of rectangular windows, illuminating the landscape as it hovered and drifted through the sky at speeds too slow for meteors or space debris. Triangulation established the object as somewhere between half a mile and a full mile in diameter, with a thickness almost as great.[43] Consistent descriptions from independent witnesses support the presence of an immense object inexplicable as an astronomical phenomenon or earthly aircraft traversing the countryside for several hours, and such impressive testimony would stand up well enough in court to hang many a defendant; yet the exclusive gates of science remain closed because the case stumbles on a point of physical reasoning. What happened to the enormous volume of air this object should displace? Not a hurricane, not even a breeze accompanied the passage of this giant; yet even aliens advanced enough to joyride in a flying football stadium have to accommodate the substantial air if they travel in a substantial craft.

At issue is not a matter of government chicanery or learned arrogance but a contradiction so clear-cut even a child can comprehend it. An affront to reality as we know it clashes with the coherent testimony of the Yukon eyewitnesses. We can save the testimony if alien technology bends the otherwise inflexible rule that solid objects displace air, or if the supposedly solid object is not solid after all but a collection of independent lights. Each solution settles uneasy on the mind, one because it multiplies hypotheses about the magical power of aliens, the other because anything goes once the object ceases to be solid. A less tortured alternative questions not the fact that the witnesses observed something but the literal accuracy of their testimony, with observational error or conceptual construction responsible for building the image of a colossal, solid UFO out of less remarkable stimuli. Yet even this alternative requires an uncomfortable tampering with the eyewitness testimony.

Here is a case impressive for its strangeness, only the strangeness is too difficult to assimilate. The testimony is consistent and reliable, but the result fails to make proper sense and leads to a dead end. To accept the experience of the witnesses at face value obliges a sacrifice of reason that ufologists, but few others, will be willing to make. Certainly scientists are unlikely to share in this leap,[44] so this UFO lands along with many others in the gray shadow of uncertain identity. Whether plagued by breaks in the chain of evidence, the vagaries of human observation, or inherent strangeness so implausible it defeats their credibility, even the best UFO cases begin and end in mystery. Norman Muscarello and the police officers of Exeter described an unmistakably mysterious object that all conventional solutions have failed to explain. The reports divulge enough to tantalize our curiosity but reveal too little to tell us what the witnesses saw. Evidence at once so striking and insufficient needs something more to tip the balance, but no UFO case has weighed in with enough proof to set aside all objections. Kary Mullis acknowledged as much when he asserted the reality of his experience yet confessed that he could not replicate or test or write scientific papers about it. The indeterminate nature of these experiences allows believers to uphold them as spaceships and skeptics to favor an uncertain though unremarkable solution, but skeptics hold the advantage. An audacious assertion that overturns the prevailing reality paradigm requires commensurate evidence. Without it, the default solution appeals to the identity that least rocks the boat. This resolution does not address the mystery of the observation but neutralizes it, leaving it without official recognition or interest to march as a forlorn ghost in the ranks of Charles Fort's damned and excluded.

A Case for Objectivity.—This state of exile is a poor place to leave UFOs. The problem with high-quality reports is a strangeness that cries out for explanation, not a flimsiness that poses no challenge. They are undeniably difficult, dependent as they are on anecdotal evidence and on-the-fly observation, yet some small fraction of the thousands of UFOs presents not just strangeness but defensible strangeness. That is, these cases offer enough evidence to criticize yet resist every effort to explain them away and leave no more holes in the argument than any other claim where testimonial evidence is decisive. Such cases bring forward enough substance to resist attack and throw the question of their nature back on the attackers, so that the critics bear the burden of proof and must put up or shut up. Though the available evidence for objectivity will not earn a judgment beyond the shadow of a doubt, that same evidence meets the lower preponderance-of-evidence standard and surely deserves a hearing on those grounds alone. These are the cases that pass the following tests:

1. The alleged event fulfills basic authenticity requirements. Reports originate in real incidents and are not hoaxes, rumors, or literary constructions; documents and interviews confirm the alleged events. Testimonies derive first-person from specific individuals and not through hearsay from a friend of a friend. The mixture of truth and

fiction in the Malmstrom incursion of 1975 warns that facts in a UFO case can be elusive, but not every one strays from its factual basis as investigations into the 1968 Minot sightings and the Cash-Landrum physical injury show, where the emerging story does credit both to the perseverance of the investigators and to the incidents themselves as evidence for extraordinary events.

2. Quality testimonial and instrumental evidence supports an anomalous event. Some anecdotal UFO evidence is better than others. Transpersonal testimony is not foolproof, but several witnesses are better than one, since more people dilute the possibility of hoax or idiosyncratic errors and provide different perspectives of observation. Timeliness in the presentation of testimony is important because with the passage of time distortions of memory increase from fantasy, reinterpretation, subsequent information, and influence of others. Instrumental evidence like photographs or radar returns enhances the statements of witnesses when it supports their testimony. Cases like Exeter, Minot, and the southern Illinois police sightings of 2000 gain in credibility because they have the support of multiple witnesses going on record soon after the event. Even though the one police photograph from Illinois is of poor quality, it still shows an extended object with multiple lights and counters identification of the UFO as the planet Venus. Physical effects like the Cash-Landrum injuries add a new dimension of evidence and possibility for investigation.

3. The strange quality of the alleged event lies not in the vagueness of inadequate description but in the unusual character of well-specified incidents. Too much evidence to deny, rather than too little to work with has long served as an argument that the best UFO cases result from genuine anomalous phenomena. One of the most intriguing aspects of the 2006 "saucer" over O'Hare Airport is the "cookie cutter" hole in the cloud deck, an unprecedented sight to all the witnesses who independently noticed it. No known natural phenomenon, no everyday man-made effect creates such a hole. Here then is an observation that remains anecdotal yet invites investigators to do some science and determine the considerable concentration of energy necessary for such an effect while challenging skeptics to explain the unknown source of energy or some other conventional mechanism that could account for the observation.

4. A coherent account emerges from reports of an anomalous event. An understandable confusion surrounds many UFO reports when different people view from different vantage points and excitement replaces dispassionate observation, but the results are all the more impressive where forgiveness of human and situational variables is unnecessary. Such is the case in Illinois, where one police officer after another described a triangular UFO, or at Minot, where the air and ground observations

corroborated one another. Since causes like the influence of one witness on another might account for this consistency, it by no means proves real-world events; but lack of it would offer reason to doubt them.

5. The alleged event bears some similarities to other accounts. If UFOs belong to a unified phenomenon, independent reports should reflect that unity even after allowing leeway for idiosyncrasies in perception, conception, interpretation, and communication. Hynek's reminder that UFO reports manifest a limited range of variation seems confirmed in the widespread recurrence of disks, delta-shapes, and a few other forms. This evidence rates as no better than ambivalent since similarity could derive from cultural expectations as well as observations, leaving a pattern of consistent forms as necessary but far from sufficient to establish that people see similar objects.

6. The alleged event differs in some respects from expectations. With the heavy hand of belief always ready to stretch a report toward conformity, the report gains credit as evidence if some signs of independence defy the cultural norms. The Robozero Marvel crisscrossed the town and hovered over the lake to make clear on many counts that this giant object differed from the typical prodigies of 1663, but it far better compares to some of the UFOs that appeared three centuries later. The constant angle of the Exeter UFO and the diamond shape of the Cash-Landrum object do not fall outside the pale of the UFO record, but these descriptions are rare within it. The insistence of the witnesses on these descriptive peculiarities suggests a conviction based on observation rather than reliance on a cultural default. Historical accounts like the meteor in John of Worchester's chronicle demonstrate a precedent for accuracy, since when an observation is sufficiently unique and awe inspiring, it can blow away both mythological interpretation and the temptation to make personal use of the event to leave behind an unadorned description of the event itself.

7. The report of an alleged event has undergone strenuous critical examination but survives alternative explanations with the anomalousness of the event intact. An unchallenged report carries little persuasive power, but a report that defies explanations for good cause has taken an important step toward establishing an anomalous event. Attempts to explain the Exeter UFO as an advertising airplane, Air Force refueling operation, or flashing lights on the kite string of a hoaxer have failed to hold up under cross-examination. Explanations of Father Gill's UFO with waving aliens from 1959 have included Venus and bad eyesight, as well as a fishing boat viewed under distorting atmospheric conditions, but the facts of the case—Father Gill recognized Venus and wore his glasses, the mystery object was over land and not out at sea—foil these solutions. A solution for the O'Hare sighting blames idling jets on the runway for sending up bubbles of heated gases, but even a layman can wonder how a situation as common

at airports as idling jets and low ceilings has never before produced reports of holes burned in the clouds.[45] After several laps around the explanatory track, these cases return to the starting line more baffling than ever. Some forthcoming answer may dispel the mystery, but to the best of current knowledge these cases have no conventional solution and lend tentative grounds for a conclusion that witnesses observed unknown events.

These rules of thumb are far from airtight, and ufologists like Jacques Vallee have proposed more rigorous systems to classify the strangeness in UFO claims,[46] but the purpose here is no more than to draw a bottom line, a threshold of credibility. By these standards a small but nonnegligible body of reports gathers impressive eyewitness testimony and instrumental corroboration for an anomalous and seemingly unconventional phenomenon. Investigators of current and historical UFO reports have sifted out cases with sufficient credible evidence to qualify as defensible. These cases suggest that the character of UFO narratives depends in some part on the character of UFO events, and those events owe their character to a source independent of UFO mythology. Even allowing for human fallibility and self-deception, a genuine mystery seems to be left over.

Leaving aside the ultimate nature of UFOs, their study illuminates the success of a modern myth to turn the idea of alien visitation into a means of explanation and expression with widespread human uses. Simple UFO sightings reaffirm that strange things happen every day and the world is not nailed down as tightly as the authorities insist. The abduction story addresses extremes of fear and hope, in one version voicing the outrage of victims of technological abuse, in another the testimonials of individuals touched, however roughly, by incomparable wonder. Equally at home with millennial visions or conspiratorial apocalypses, UFOs serve as flexible symbols to take up where supernatural traditions leave off, adapting otherwise obsolete ideas about the otherworld and Others to a new life amid secular sensibilities. The human dimension of UFOs is unmistakable, and the subject repays study with insights into the constants and currents of human concerns. So much can be said about UFOs without considering what UFOs really are that the reality comes to seem superfluous. If the only investigation worth undertaking adheres to a strictly human framework, and if a text, report, or belief counts as the issue to explain, and social or psychological processes count as the final answer, then man becomes truly the measure of all things ufological.

Such a one-sided conclusion recognizes that the UFO myth builds understandings, expressions, and even to some extent the observations of UFOs to suit cultural images, but it overlooks the equally likely possibility that the same construction disguises a phenomenal UFO with cultural camouflage. The human imagination is eclectic enough to spin stories out of fact as well as fiction. However distorted and altered the facts may become to satisfy the needs of fiction, enough evidence suggests that the UFO experience amounts to more than an unbroken round of human causes. Something from outside the human circle breaks in with elements independent of cultural prescriptions. In any case, no inquiry that ignores the event dimension is likely to succeed entirely in explaining the experiential, psychological, textual, or cultural dimensions. The explanation will be partial, a caricature that ultimately fails in its mission to account for human behavior as it really works.

What the nature of the events may be is uncertain, but this blank on the sheet of understanding hardly matters at present. Acceptance of a potentially interesting phenomenon does not require acceptance of a particular explanation for the phenomenon. The UFO myth succeeds as a cultural force—or mischief-maker—in its wedding of UFOs and alien spaceships as inseparable ideas, but researchers can take UFOs as a serious subject of study without the troublesome baggage that the extraterrestrial hypothesis imposes. Hynek wisely avoided the question of origins in *The UFO Experience* and sought only to build a case step by step for the existence of a phenomenon of scientific interest. Aliens may prove inevitable, but first things first. Their place in the process of understanding belongs somewhere back in line. It is a matter to consider only after research has established that UFOs represent consistent experiences, an unconventional phenomenon, and events with no plausible earthly origins.

As social facts and cultural phenomena, UFOs deserve a prominent place in academic inquiry. Intriguing claims in quality reports rate UFOs as worth their hire for scientific research as well. The Condon study was a failure of science yet still tallied an impressive list of unknowns; the French UFO studies have turned up clues that a new phenomenon may exist; and the British "Condign" report finds reason to accept the phenomenology, if not the interpretation, of UFO reports. A little science has gone a long way toward uncovering a worthy subject to investigate. Kary Mullis presents an incredible assertion from one of science's own, and even if no aliens are responsible, sleep paralysis cannot explain his experience, and it hints that at the very least some unsuspected psychological or physiological mechanism is responsible. UFOs pose enough interest that the hunting horns should be sounding and investigators tearing off to the chase, but only silence prevails. Scientists do themselves no credit when they sweep the subject into the dustbin of things that cannot be. Grade-school biographies portrayed Galileo opposing the rigid dogmas of Church authorities; now history has come full circle as scientists have traded in their heroic status of explorers and rebels for the role of priests, too confident in their authority, too prejudiced in the rightness of their knowledge, to look before they condemn. Such loaded treatment of the subject acts as a self-fulfilling prophecy when people withhold their testimony because they fear rejection and ridicule. An Ohio police officer who swore he would not report a UFO if it landed in his backyard is anything but a rare exception. Observations open the possibility of new knowledge. To greet them by deriding the observers is both poor human relations and a poor way to do science.

No one would choose to study UFOs for their ease of handling, but the throng of unruly reports stakes an observational claim to reality that is in its own way as deserving of attention as SETI's (Search for Extraterrestrial Intelligence) theoretical postulate of extraterrestrial communication. UFOs are rare birds that will not fly into the laboratory for experimental study, but the proper science for them may be a natural history approach rather than the experimental model. With a willingness to meet the mystery on its own terms, scientists can observe and learn about UFOs in field studies that will take time and lack the decisiveness of experimental proof, yet still compile a gradual understanding of whatever comprises the mystery. A justification to do so can simply borrow from the SETI manifesto published by Giuseppi Cocconi and Philip Morrison in 1959: "The reader may seek to consign these speculations wholly to the domain of science-fiction. We submit . . . that the presence of interstellar signals is entirely consistent with all we now know, and that if signals are present the means of detecting them is now at hand. . . . The probability of success is difficult to estimate; but if we never search, the chance of success is zero."[47]

A plea for serious scientific attention is nothing new. McDonald, Hynek, Vallee, and others raised the same call earlier and better, but the need to reiterate it more than thirty years later demonstrates that the old stalemate between the popular "what if?" and the scientific "so what?" remains firmly in place. The UFO myth grows and prospers. It may amount to nothing more than gaudy entertainment, but it also has social consequences since it reinforces a disturbing medley of paranoid beliefs and irrational ways of thinking. Official treatments have not solved the UFO problem so much as added to it. An uninformed and self-satisfied rejection affronts the observers and cements a breach with scientific authority when puzzled laymen feel convinced that their rightful concerns cannot receive a fair hearing. Unofficial authorities become the chosen arbiters of truth, and while some are worthy, others only lead their followers deeper into the mythic fog. As things now stand, the appealing myth and the unsettling experience of UFOs continue to trouble the mind's eye and the physical eye alike.

Appendix:
UFO-Related Web Sites

The Internet has become the inescapable and flourishing center of UFO belief. No responsible treatment of the subject can escape reference to Internet resources or fail to offer guidance where the options are so many and the quality so variable. The following list presents some of the important sites. It is in no sense complete. Exclusion does not imply that a site lacks value, and inclusion is no imprimatur of quality. This list simply provides a starting point from which the pilgrim will find authoritative or at least interesting information and discussion.

All established UFO organizations have Web sites, and some of them offer considerable depth of content. In addition to the national MUFON site, many state affiliates have sites of their own, including California, Colorado, Georgia, Illinois, Indiana, Kentucky, Maine, Massachusetts, Michigan, Minnesota, Nebraska, New Hampshire, Ohio, Rhode Island, South Carolina, and Texas, while Los Angeles and Dallas/Fort Worth affiliates also maintain sites. Most of the excellent foreign organizations listed here include some content in English.

UFO reporting sites like Peter Davenport's National UFO Reporting Center and George Filer's "Filer's Files" offer the latest and best in grassroots reports. The research sites are active centers of sorting the good reports from the bad and manifest some of ufology's most rigorous work, often applied to historical accounts. Larry Hatch's U*UFO Database offers worldwide maps of sightings, and Bruce Maccabee posts extensive research papers on various cases, such as the Kenneth Arnold sighting. UFO photographs are the subject of some sites and undergo considerable critical evaluation in the Fotocat maintained by Juan-Vicente Ballester Olmos.

For running discussions of UFOs, often with the participation of the best ufologists, see UFO UpDates, while James Moseley's Saucer Smear site is full of gossip and humor as well as serious discussion. UFOs as cultural phenomena dominate the sites dedicated to such matters as UFO-like representations in art or spaceships in comic books and pulp magazines.

Abductions have their own dedicated Web sites, with those of Budd Hopkins, David Jacobs, and the John E. Mack Institute being among the most important. Whitley Strieber and Linda Howe explore a range of strange phenomena beyond UFOs in their Web sites, while some sites concentrate on allegations of governmental cover-up, among them John Greenewald's "The Black Vault," with thousands of documents wrested from governmental files. The skeptics have their dedicated Web sites as well, with CSICOP attacking all sorts of paranormal claims and writers associated with the British magazine *Magonia* applying a psychosocial approach to UFOs and other strange beliefs.

In addition to the inherent value of these sites, many of them also include links to further sites, so the journey into cyberspace need never end.

Table A1
A Selection of UFO Web Sites

U. S. organizations	
Center for UFO Studies (CUFOS)	http://www.cufos.org
Fund for UFO Research (FUFOR)	http://www.fufor.com
Mutual UFO Network (MUFON)	http://www.mufon.com
(see also MUFON affiliates, e.g., California,	
Georgia, Indiana, Michigan, Texas,	
Los Angeles)	
Organizations, other countries	
Australian Centre for UFO Studies	http://www.acufos.asn.au/index.html
Brazil (Revista Brasileira de Ufologia)	http://www.ufo.com.br
Canada—British Columbia (UFO*BC)	http://www.ufobc.ca
Denmark (Scandinavian UFO Information)	http://www.sufoi.dk
France (CNES/GEIPAN)	http://www.cnes-geipan.fr
Germany (MUFON Central European Section)	http://www.mufon-ces.org
Italy—Centro Italiano Studi Ufologici	http://www.cisu.org
UFO Datanet	http://www.ufodatanet.org
Centro Ufologico Nazionale	http://www.cun-italia.net
UFO.it	http://www.ufo.it
Spain—Fundación Anomalía	http://www.anomalia.org
Centro de Estudios Interplanetarios	http://www.ctv.es/USERS/netcei
Sweden—Archives for UFO Research	http://www.afu.info
United Kingdom—British UFO Research	http://www.bufora.org.uk
Association	

Ufologie.net	http://ufologie.net/
Inexplicata: Journal of Hispanic Ufology	http://inexplicata.blogspot.com/
Sightings Reports	
National UFO Reporting Center (Peter Davenport)	http://www.ufocenter.com
Filer's Files (George Filer)	http://www.nationalufocenter.com
Research Sites	
Computer UFO Network (James Klotz)	http://www.cufon.org
National Aviation Reporting Center on Anomalous Phenomena	http://www.narcap.org
National Investigations Committee on Aerial Phenomena (Francis Ridge)	http://www.nicap.org
Project Blue Book Archive	http://www.bluebookarchive.org
Project 1947 (Jan Aldrich)	http://www.project1947.com
Sign Historical Group	http://www.project1947.com/shg/
Water UFO Research Site (Carl Feindt)	http://www.waterufo.net
Personal Research Sites	
Bill Chalker	http://www.theozfiles.com
Stanton Friedman	http://www.stantonfriedman.com
Bernard Haish	http://www.ufoskeptic.org
Bruce Maccabee	http://brumac.8k.com
Kevin Randle	http://kevinrandle.blogspot.com
UFO Photographs	
Fotocat (Anomaly Foundation)	http://www.fotocat.blogspot.com
UFO Casebook	http://www.ufocasebook.com
UFO Evidence	http://www.ufoevidence.org
Discussion and Gossip	
Saucer Smear (James Moseley)	http://www.martiansgohome.com/smear
UFO UpDates	http://www.virtuallystrange.net
UFOs and Popular Culture	
Flying Saucers in Popular Culture	http://www.ufopop.org
UFO Folklore	http://www.qtm.net/~geibdan/framemst.html
UFOs [Ancient Artwork]	http://www.scribd.com/doc/7596326/Ancient-UFO-Artwork
Abductions	
International Center for Abduction Research (David Jacobs)	http://www.ufoabduction.com
Intruders Foundation (Budd Hopkins)	http://www.intrudersfoundation.org
John Mack Institute	http://www.johnmackinstitute.com

Strange News (UFO and More)	
Earthfiles (Linda Howe)	http://www.earthfiles.com
Fortean Times	http://www.forteantimes.com
Whitley Strieber's Unknown Country	http://www.unknowncountry.com
Disclosure, Government Coverup	
The Black Vault (John Greenewald)	http://www.bvalphaserver.com
The Disclosure Project (Steven Greer)	http://www.disclosureproject.org
The Majestic Documents (Robert and Ryan Wood)	http://www.majesticdocuments.com
Paradigm Research Group (Stephen Bassett)	http://www.paradigmresearchgroup.org
Skeptics	
Committee for Skeptical Inquiry	http://www.csicop.org
The Skeptic Tank	http://www.skeptictank.org
Magonia	http://magonia.haaan.com
Magonia Supplement	http://www.users.waitrose.com/ ~magonia/index.htm
Robert Sheaffer	http://www.debunker.com
UFO Links	
UFOINFO	http://www.ufoinfo.com

Notes

Introduction

1. John Hilkevitch, "In the Sky! A Bird? A Plane? A ... UFO?" *Chicago Tribune*, January 1, 2007, http://www.chicagotribune.com/news/local/chi-0701010141jan01,1,3957154. column?coll=chi-news-hed&ctrack=1&cset=true. "They're Here! (Or So We'd Like to Think.)," *Chicago Tribune*, January 7, 2007; "Greetings from Planet Earth," *Chicago Tribune*, January 10, 2007. See http://infoweb.newsbank.com/iw-search/we/InfoWeb/?p_action=print &p_docid=116836F.

2. Douglas Curran traces the penetration of UFOs into folk and popular culture in his book *In Advance of the Landing: Folk Concepts of Outer Space* (New York: Abbeville Press, 1985). Influences on popular and mass culture fill Eric Nesheim and Leif Nesheim, *Saucer Attack!* (Los Angeles: Kitchen Sink Press, 1997). The response of artists to UFOs was the subject of an exhibition curated by Barry Blinderman and Bill Conger and a book, *The UFO Show* (Normal: University Galleries, Illinois State University, 2000). For a chronological listing and summary of movies, see David Hardy, *The Encyclopedia of Science Fiction Movies* (Minneapolis: Woodbury Press, 1984).

3. "Flying Saucers," *The Gallup Poll: Public Opinion 1935–1971* (New York: Random House, 1972), 2004; "Name Awareness," September 25, 1977, *The Gallup Poll: Public Opinion 1972–1977* (Wilmington, DE: Scholarly Resources, 1978), 1197.

4. Peter Davenport operates the National UFO Reporting Center and lists monthly totals at http://www.nuforc.org/webreports/ndxevent.html.

5. "Large Majority Thinks Government Conceals Information about UFOs," *Gallup Poll Monthly*, no. 372 (September 1996): 23–28.

6. Stuart Appelle, "The Abduction Experience: A Critical Evaluation of Theory and Evidence," *Journal of UFO Studies*, n.s. 6 (1995–1996), 44–47.

7. Donald H. Menzel, *Flying Saucers* (Cambridge, MA: Harvard University Press, 1953), vii. Carl Sagan, *The Demon-Haunted World* (New York: Random House, 1995), 63–77.

8. Sagan, *The Demon-Haunted World*, 37–39. Robert Sheaffer, *The UFO Verdict: Examining the Evidence* (Buffalo, NY: Prometheus Books, 1981), 235–238.

9. "Peter Jennings Reports: UFOs—Seeing Is Believing," ABC, February 24, 2005; "Cheers and Jeers," *TV Guide*, March 20, 2005, 22.

10. Sagan, *The Demon-Haunted World*, 193–194, 198.

11. Bruce Maccabee, "Still in Default," in *MUFON 1986 UFO Symposium Proceedings*, ed. Walter H. Andrus Jr. and Richard Hall (Seguin, TX: Mutual UFO Network, 1986), 130–160; updated version at Maccabee's Web site, http://brumac.8k.com.

12. Jerome Clark, *The UFO Encyclopedia*, 2nd ed. (Detroit: Omnigraphics, 1998), 2:731–732.

13. Edward U. Condon, "Conclusions and Recommendations," in *Scientific Study of Unidentified Flying Objects*, ed. Daniel S. Gillmor (New York: Bantam Books, 1969), 1.

14. J. Allen Hynek, *The UFO Experience* (New York: Ballantine Books, 1972), 217.

15. For example, see the case investigations in Philip J. Klass, *UFOs: The Public Deceived* (Buffalo, NY: Prometheus Books, 1983), and Robert Sheaffer, *The UFO Verdict: Examining the Evidence* (Buffalo, NY: Prometheus Books, 1981).

16. J. Allen Hynek defends UFOs in *The UFO Experience*, and James E. McDonald in "Science in Default: Twenty-Two Years of Inadequate UFO Investigations," in *UFOs: A Scientific Debate*, ed. Carl Sagan and Thornton Page (Ithaca, NY: Cornell University Press, 1972), 52–122.

17. Sagan, *The Demon-Haunted World*, 100.

18. David J. Hufford, "Traditions of Disbelief," *New York Folklore* 8 (1982): 47–55.

19. For a critical overview of the psychosocial hypothesis, see Clark, *The UFO Encyclopedia*, 2:749–759.

20. Gillmor, *Scientific Study of Unidentified Flying Objects*, 9.

21. Hynek, *The UFO Experience*, 12.

22. These types reflect Hynek's categories of nocturnal lights, daylight disks, radar-visual sightings, and close encounters of the first, second, and third kinds. See Hynek, *The UFO Experience*, 31–34.

23. Robert W. Balch and David Taylor, "Seekers and Saucers: The Role of the Cultic Milieu in Joining a UFO Cult," *American Behavioral Scientist* 20 (1977): 847–849.

24. Gillian Bennett, *Traditions of Belief* (London: Penguin Books, 1987), 26.

25. Hynek, *The UFO Experience*, 242.

Chapter 1. Who Goes There?

1. The most extensive treatment of the first flying saucer sighting is Bruce Maccabee's "Ultimate Arnold" Web site: "June 24, 1947: How It All Began," http://brumac.8k.com/KARNOLD/KARNOLD.html. See also Brad Steiger, ed., *Project Blue Book* (New York: Ballantine Books, 1976), 23–37, and Jerome Clark, *The UFO Encyclopedia* (Detroit: Omnigraphics, 1998), 1:139–143.

2. Interview of Bill Bequette by Pierre Lagrange, 1988, in "Note on Initial Press Interest and the Term Flying Saucer," in Maccabee's "Ultimate Arnold" site. See also Clark, *Encyclopedia*, 141.

3. Jan L. Aldrich, *Project 1947: A Preliminary Report* (N.p.: UFO Research Coalition, 1997), 1–8.

4. Ted Bloecher, *Report on the UFO Wave of 1947* (n.p.: Author, 1967), xiii.

5. Loren E. Gross, *UFOs: A History, 1947* (Fremont, CA: Author, 1988), 14.

6. Martin Kottmeyer, "The Saucer Error," *REALL News* 1, no. 4 (1993), http://www.debunker.com/texts/SaucerError.html.

7. For variety in shapes see Bloecher, sec. 5. For the North Carolina sighting, see Aldrich, *Project 1947*, 183–185.

8. "Is Hussein Owner of Crashed UFO?" http://english.pravda.ru/main/2003/01/ 31/42821 .html. Robert Sheaffer, "Special Forces Battle Giant Scorpions in Iraq," *Skeptical Inquirer* 27, no. 3 (2003): 20–21.

9. Michael A. Fletcher and Hamil R. Harris, "Farrakhan Builds Zeal for March at SE Church," *Washington Post*, September 18, 1995, D1, D3.

10. Karl Evanzz, *The Messenger: The Rise and Fall of Elijah Muhammad* (New York: Vintage Books, 2001), 95–96, 118–119. Florence Hamlish Levinsohn, *Looking for Farrakhan* (Chicago: Ivan R. Dee, 1997), 100–103.

11. Elijah Muhammad, *Message to the Blackman in America* (Chicago: Muhammad's Temple No. 2, 1965), 291.

12. Michael Lieb, *Children of Ezekiel: Aliens, UFOs, the Crisis of Race, and the Advent of End Times* (Durham, NC: Duke University Press, 1998), 138–142.

13. William K. Hartmann, "Processes of Perception, Conception, and Reporting," in *Scientific Study of Unidentified Flying Objects*, ed. Daniel S. Gillmor (New York: Bantam Books, 1969), 571–574.

14. Donald H. Menzel, "UFOs—The Modern Myth," in *UFOs—A Scientific Debate*, ed. Carl Sagan and Thornton Page (Ithaca, NY: Cornell University Press, 1972), 155–156.

15. Ibid., 160.

16. Cynthia Hind, *UFOs over Africa* (Madison, WI: Horus House Press, 1996), 16–20.

17. This version circulates widely in the literature and on the Internet; for instance, the Editors of Time-Life Books, *The UFO Phenomenon* (Alexandria, VA: Time-Life Books, 1987), 129–130. See also "Malmstrom AFB, Incident," *National Investigations Committee on Aerial Phenomena*, http://www.nicap.org/faded.htm; and "UFOs Intrude into SAC Base Weapons Area," *UFO Casebook*, http://www.ufocasebook.com/sacbaseweapons1975.html.

18. Lawrence Fawcett and Barry J. Greenwood, *Clear Intent: The Government Coverup of the UFO Experience* (Englewood Cliffs, NJ: Prentice-Hall, 1984), 16–56.

19. Roberta Donovan and Keith Wolverton, *Mystery Stalks the Prairie* (Raynesford, MT: THAR Institute, 1976), 42–52. Terry Hansen, *The Missing Times: News Media Complicity in the UFO Cover-up* (Bloomington, IN: X-Libris Corporation, 2000), 16–35.

20. Hansen, *The Missing Times*, 33–35. "C.I.A. Papers Detail U.F.O. Surveillance," *New York Times*, January 14, 1979, 23. Ward Sinclair and Art Harris, "What Were Those Mysterious Craft?" *Washington Post*, January 19, 1975, A1, A6. Patrick Huyghe, "U.F.O. Files: The Untold Story," *New York Times Magazine*, October 14, 1979, 107–111.

21. The Center for UFO Studies (CUFOS) compiled official Air Force documents describing UFO activity around Malmstrom in *Documents Describing UFO/Helicopter Overflights of U.S.A.F. Bases in 1975, Obtained by Citizens against UFO Secrecy* (Evanston, IL: CUFOS, n.d.).

22. Philip J. Klass, *UFOs: The Public Deceived* (Buffalo, NY: Prometheus Press, 1983), 100–105. Fawcett and Greenwood, *Clear Intent*, 31.

23. Linda Moulton Howe, *An Alien Harvest* (Littleton, CO: Linda Moulton Howe Productions, 1989), 23–24.

24. Linda Moulton Howe, *Glimpses of Other Realities*, vol. 2, *High Strangeness* (New Orleans:

Paper Chase Press, 1998), 78–87. Robert Salas and James Klotz, *Faded Giant: The 1967 Missile/ UFO Incidents* (North Charleston, SC: Booksurge Publishing, 2004), 16–23, 99, 108.

25. Fawcett and Greenwood, *Clear Intent*, 27–31. Richard H. Hall, *The UFO Evidence: A Thirty-Year Report* (Lanham, MD: Scarecrow Press, 2000), 2:90–91. Don Berliner, *UFO Briefing Document: The Best Available Evidence* (New York: Dell, 2000), 90.

26. The most detailed account is a report from Raymond E. Fowler of his field investigations, included in Committee on Armed Services of the House of Representatives, *Unidentified Flying Objects*, 89th Cong., 2nd sess., 1966 (Washington, DC: U.S. Government Printing Office, 1966), 6010–6042. He describes his investigation in his book, *Casebook of a UFO Investigator* (Englewood Cliffs, NJ: Prentice-Hall, 1981), 34–43. Fowler was unable to interview Muscarello before he left for boot camp, but Muscarello's statement and the Project Blue Book file are included in J. Allen Hynek, *The Hynek UFO Report* (New York: Dell, 1977), 154–165. John G. Fuller reports extensively on the case in *Incident at Exeter: Unidentified Flying Objects over America Now* (New York: G. P. Putnam's Sons, 1966), 11–17, 67–72, 79–82, but his polished reporting glosses over errors and confusions.

27. Fowler in *Unidentified Flying Objects*, 6015–6016; Hynek, *The Hynek UFO Report*, 160–165.

28. Philip J. Klass, *UFOs: Identified* (New York: Random House, 1968), 14–19, 276.

29. Robert Sheaffer, *The UFO Verdict: Examining the Evidence* (Buffalo, NY: Prometheus Books, 1981), 111–119.

30. Martin Kottmeyer, "The Exeter File: Part 1", *REALL*, http://www.reall.org/newsletter/v04/n09/exeter.html; "The Exeter File: Part 2", *REALL*, http://www.reall.org/newsletter/v04/n10/exeter2.html.

31. NASA's Glenn Research Center offers a Web site discussing the basic aerodynamics of kite flying (http://www.grc.nasa.gov/WWW/K-12/airplane/bgk.html), along with an "Interactive Kite Modeler" Web site (http://www.grc.nasa.gov/WWW/K-12/airplane/kiteprog.html), where users can try out variables of design and flying conditions to see the consequences for lift and stability. While the low wind velocity for the night of the Exeter sighting does not entirely preclude a kite of some sort getting off the ground, experimenting with various values makes clear that the conditions were marginal at best.

32. Kurt Ranke, "Einfache Formen," *Journal of the Folklore Institute* 4 (1967): 19.

33. Max Lüthi, "Aspects of the Märchen and the Legend," in *Folklore Genres*, ed. Dan Ben-Amos (Austin: University of Texas Press, 1981), 24.

34. For the multiple definitions and connotations of myth, see Lauri Honko, "The Problem of Defining Myth," in *Sacred Narrative: Readings in the Theory of Myth*, ed. Alan Dundes (Berkeley: University of California Press, 1984), 41–52. See also William G. Doty, *Mythography: The Study of Myth and Ritual* (Tuscaloosa: University of Alabama Press, 1986), esp. 9–11.

35. William Bascom, "The Forms of Folklore: Prose Narratives," in Dundes, *Sacred Narrative*, 9. Bronislaw Malinowski, *Magic, Science and Religion and Other Essays* (Garden City, NY: Anchor Books, 1954), 84, 144–146.

36. Rodney Needham, *Primordial Characters* (Charlottesville: University Press of Virginia, 1978), 59.

37. Edward B. Tylor, *Primitive Culture* (New York: Brentano's, 1924), 284–285.

38. Doty, *Mythography*, 133–136.

39. Claude Lévi-Strauss, "The Structural Study of Myth," in *Myth: A Symposium*, ed. Thomas A. Sebeok (Bloomington: Indiana University Press, 1971), 86–92, 106.

40. Tylor, *Primitive Culture*, 499–501.

41. David Bidney, *Theoretical Anthropology* (New York: Schocken Books, 1970), 388.

42. Claude Lévi-Strauss, *The Savage Mind* (Chicago: University of Chicago Press, 1966), 14–15, 22.

43. Jean-François Lyotard in Michael Drolet, ed., *The Postmodernism Reader* (New York: Routledge, 2004), 123–124, 137–138.

44. Doty, *Mythography*, 132–136.

45. Ibid., 148–152.

46. Northrop Frye, *The Anatomy of Criticism* (New York: Atheneum, 1966), 134–135, 158–160, 207–208.

47. Joseph Campbell, *The Hero with a Thousand Faces* (Princeton, NJ: Princeton University Press, 1971), 3–46.

48. Dundes, *Sacred Narrative*, 1.

49. Richard Howells, *The Myth of the Titanic* (New York: St. Martin's Press, 1999), 10–11.

50. Claude Lévi-Strauss, *The Savage Mind*, 16–22.

51. Stith Thompson, *Motif-Index of Folk Literature* (Bloomington: Indiana University Press, 1955); see Thompson's *The Folktale* (New York: Holt, Rinehart & Winston, 1946), 488–500, for a summary of motif categories. The most relevant motifs are A106, Opposition of Good and Evil Gods (War in Heaven); A541, Culture Hero Teaches Arts and Crafts; A561, Divinity's Departure for the West; A580, Culture Hero's Expected Return; F0–F199, Otherworld Journeys; F200, Fairies; F211.3, Fairies Live under the Earth; F320, Fairies Carry People Away to Fairyland; F377, Supernatural Lapse of Time in Fairyland.

52. John A. Saliba, "Religious Dimensions of UFO Phenomena," in *The Gods Have Landed*, ed. James R. Lewis (Albany: State University of New York, 1995), 32–55.

53. Jodi Dean, *Aliens in America: Conspiracy Cultures from Outerspace to Cyberspace* (Ithaca, NY: Cornell University Press, 1998), 7–21.

54. In Donald H. Menzel's book, *Flying Saucers* (Cambridge, MA: Harvard University Press, 1953), the subtitle *Myth-Truth-History* cued the reader that the truth and history of UFOs located them in the mythological category. In 1963 he subtitled *The World of Flying Saucers* (coauthored with Lyle G. Boyd, New York: Doubleday), *A Scientific Examination of a Major Myth of the Space Age*, and in 1972 he contributed a paper entitled "UFOs—The Modern Myth" to *UFOs: A Scientific Debate*, ed. Carl Sagan and Thornton Page (Ithaca, NY: Cornell University Press).

55. Curtis Peebles, *Watch the Skies! A Chronicle of the Flying Saucer Myth* (Washington, DC: Smithsonian Institution Press, 1994), ix–x.

56. Benson Saler, Charles A. Ziegler, and Charles B. Moore, *UFO Crash at Roswell: The Genesis of a Modern Myth* (Washington, DC: Smithsonian Institution Press, 1997), 4–7, 72–73, 149.

57. Terry Matheson, *Alien Abductions* (Amherst, NY: Prometheus Books, 1998), 34–39, 60–66, 297–303.

58. C. G. Jung, *Flying Saucers: A Modern Myth of Things Seen in the Skies* (New York: Harcourt, Brace & Co., 1959), xi–xiv, 8–11, 14–20, 151–152, 164–166.

59. Keith Thompson, *Angels and Aliens: UFOs and the Mythic Imagination* (Reading, MA: Addison-Wesley, 1991), 17–20, 36–41, 180–193, 228–236.

60. Michael Grosso, "UFOs and the Myth of the New Age," *ReVision* 11, no. 3 (Winter 1989): 11–13.

61. Whitley Strieber, *Communion* (New York: Beech Tree Books / William Morrow, 1987), 288–295. Kenneth Ring, *The Omega Project* (New York: William Morrow & Co., 1992), 168–172, 179–183, 190–193. R. Leo Sprinkle, "UFO Contactees: Captive Collaborators or Cosmic Citizens?" in *1980 MUFON UFO Symposium Proceedings*, ed. Walter H. Andrus and Dennis W. Stacy (Seguin, TX: Mutual UFO Network, 1980), 64–67. John E. Mack, *Abduction: Human Encounters with Aliens* (New York: Charles Scribner's Sons, 1994), 387–422; *Passport to the Cosmos: Human Transformation and Alien Encounters* (New York: Crown, 1999), 268–281.

62. Jacques Vallee, *Passport to Magonia: From Folklore to Flying Saucers* (Chicago: Henry Regnery Co., 1969), vii–viii, 148–160; Jacques Vallee, *The Invisible College* (New York: E. P. Dutton & Co., 1975), 1–2, 194–206.

63. John A. Keel, *UFOs: Operation Trojan Horse* (New York: G. P. Putnam's Sons, 1970), 57, 300–307.

64. Jerome Clark and Loren Coleman, *The Unidentified* (New York: Warner Books, 1975), 236–249.

65. In *America in Legend: Folklore from the Colonial Period to the Present* (New York: Pantheon Books, 1973), 1–9, folklorist Richard M. Dorson traced the themes and personifications prevalent in four distinctive American lifestyles from the early colonial era to the counterculture years of the 1960s, finding that the storytelling of each era reveals distinctive heroes and villains, approved and disapproved actions. The old assumption that human decisions depend solely on reason has yielded to recognition that moral, political, and even economic choices owe much to "foundation narratives," idealized stories based on biblical models or popular fictions like the immigrant success story. See Christopher Collins, *Homeland Mythology: Biblical Narratives in American Culture* (University Park: Pennsylvania State University Press, 2007), ix–x; Robert Wuthnow, *American Mythos* (Princeton, NJ: Princeton University Press, 2006), 1–5. For other examples of myth shaping ideals and expressions, see Raphael Samuel and Paul Thompson, eds., *The Myths We Live By* (New York: Routledge, 1990), 49–60, 216–224; Alan Davies, *The Crucified Nation: A Motif in Modern Nationalism* (Brighton: Sussex Academic Press, 2008), 1–4; John Shelton Lawrence and Robert Jewett, *The Myth of the American Superhero* (Grand Rapids: William B. Eerdmans, 2002), 1–8.

66. Bruce A. Rosenberg, *Custer and the Epic of Defeat* (University Park: Pennsylvania State University Press, 1974), 1–3, 49–84. John Hellman, *The Kennedy Obsession: The American Myth of JFK* (New York: Columbia University Press, 1997), ix–x, 88–90, 145–147; Rosenberg, *Custer and the Epic of Defeat*, 273–278. Carol Mason, *Killing for Life: The Apocalyptic Narrative of Pro-Life Politics* (Ithaca, NY: Cornell University Press, 2002), 1–4, 99–129; Celeste Michelle Condit, *Decoding Abortion Rhetoric: Communicating Social Change* (Urbana: University of Illinois Press, 1990), 25–28.

67. Jack Lule, *Daily News, Eternal Stories: The Mythological Role of Journalism* (New York: Guilford Press, 2001), 3–4, 15, 21–25.

68. Otto Rank, *The Myth of the Birth of the Hero* (New York: Vintage Books, 1964), 65–66.

Campbell, *The Hero with a Thousand Faces*, 30–36. Lord Raglan, "The Hero of Tradition," in *The Study of Folklore*, ed. Alan Dundes (Englewood Cliffs, NJ: Prentice-Hall, 1965), 144–157. Alan Dundes, "The Hero Pattern and the Life of Jesus," in *Interpreting Folklore* (Bloomington: Indiana University Press, 1980), 223–261. Stephen R. Haynes, *The Bonhoeffer Phenomenon: Portraits of a Protestant Saint* (Minneapolis: Fortress Press, 2004), xi–xii, 1–4, 133–143.

69. E. M. Butler, *The Myth of the Magus* (New York: Macmillan Co., 1948), 1–3, 160–172, 215–242, 261–263.

70. See Margaret Cheney and Robert Uth, *Tesla: Master of Lightning* (New York: Barnes & Noble Books, 1999).

71. Margaret Storm, *Return of the Dove* (Baltimore: A Margaret Storm Publication, 1959), 71. For connections of Tesla, aliens, and the Philadelphia Experiment, see Noel Huntley, "The Philadelphia Experiment," *Biblioteca Pleyades*, http://www.bibliotecapleyades.net/montauk/esp_filadelfia_1.htm; "The Philadelphia Experiment," Phil Cullen's Web site, http://www.phils.com.au/philadelphia.htm; "Philadelphia Experiment," *Crystalinks*, http://www.crystalinks.com/phila.html.

72. Sean Casteel, *Nikola Tesla Journey to Mars: Are We Already There?* (New Brunswick, NJ: Inner Light-Global Communications, 2002). For further discussion of Tesla as cult figure, see Marc J. Seifer, *Wizard: The Life and Times of Nikola Tesla* (Secaucus, NJ: Birch Lane Press, 1996), 467–470.

73. Richard VanDerBeets, *The Indian Captivity Narrative* (Lanham, MD: University Press of America, 1984), ix–x, 42–50. Kathryn Zabelle Derounian-Stodola and James Arthur Lavernier, *The Indian Captivity Narrative, 1550–1900* (New York: Twayne, 1993), 17–38. Gary E. Ebersole, *Captured by Texts: Puritan to Postmodern Images of Indian Captivity* (Charlottesville: University Press of Virginia, 1995), 1–14.

74. Catherine V. Scott, "Bound for Glory: The Hostage Crisis as Captivity Narrative in Iran," *International Studies Quarterly* 44 (2000): 177–188.

75. Michael Sturma, "Aliens and Indians: A Comparison of Abduction and Captivity Narratives," *Journal of Popular Culture* 36 (2002): 318–334. Andrew Panay, "From *Little Big Man* to Little Green Men: The Captivity Scenario in American Culture," *European Journal of American Culture* 23 (2004): 201–216.

Chapter 2. The Growth and Evolution of UFO Mythology

1. Charles Dickens, "Frauds on the Fairies," *Household Words* 8 (October 1, 1853): 97.

2. Donald E. Keyhoe, *Flying Saucers: Top Secret* (New York: G. P. Putnam's Sons, 1960), 283.

3. Whitley Strieber, *Transformation: The Breakthrough* (New York: William Morrow & Co., 1988), 11–12.

4. The best sources for the history of modern UFOs include Jerome Clark, *The UFO Encyclopedia: The Phenomenon from the Beginning*, 2nd ed., 2 vols. (Detroit: Omnigraphics, 1998); Ronald D. Story, ed., *The Encyclopedia of Extraterrestrial Encounters* (New York: New American Library, 2001); David M. Jacobs, *The UFO Controversy in America* (Bloomington: Indiana

University Press, 1975); and from 1947 to 1960, the numerous volumes of *UFOs: A History*, by Loren Gross (Fremont, CA: Author, 1982–2006).

5. Jan L. Aldrich, *Project 1947: A Preliminary Report* (N.p.: UFO Research Coalition, 1997), 28.

6. Gross, *UFOs: A History, 1948*, 2–8; Clark, *UFO Encyclopedia*, 603–607; "Flier Dies Chasing a 'Flying Saucer,'" *New York Times*, January 9, 1948, 11; H. T. Wilkins, *Flying Saucers on the Attack* (New York: Citadel Press, 1954), 89–92; Donald H. Menzel and Lyle G. Boyd, *The World of Flying Saucers: A Scientific Examination of a Major Myth of the Space Age* (Garden City, NY: Doubleday & Co., 1963), 33–39.

7. Wilkins, *Flying Saucers on the Attack*, 91–92.

8. Gross, *UFOs: A History, 1948*, 34–38; Clark, *UFO Encyclopedia*, 182–184.

9. Gross, *UFOs: A History, 1948*, 56–64; Clark, *UFO Encyclopedia*, 452–453; Menzel and Boyd, *The World of Flying Saucers*, 80–82, 111–114.

10. Clark, *UFO Encyclopedia*, 667; Thomas Tulien, "The 1952 Nash/Fortenberry Sighting Revisited," *IUR* 27, no. 1 (2002): 20–23, 27–28, http://www.nicap.org/nash-tulien.htm.

11. Thomas E. Bullard, "Waves," in Clark, *UFO Encyclopedia*, 1001–1023.

12. Clark, *UFO Encyclopedia*, 998–1004; Gross, *UFOs: A History, June–July 20, 1952*, 69–72, 75–84, and *UFOs: A History, July 21–31, 1952*, 20–31. See also Menzel and Boyd, *World of Flying Saucers*, 155–160.

13. Clark, *UFO Encyclopedia*, 581–582; Gross, *UFOs: A History, November 3–5, 1957*, 1–13. See also Menzel and Boyd, *World of Flying Saucers*, 174–176.

14. Clark, *UFO Encyclopedia*, 409–411. Gray Barker, "West Virginia 'Monster'—A Full Report," *Saucerian* 1, no. 1 (1953): 8–21. Joe Nickell, "The Flatwoods UFO Monster," *Skeptical Inquirer* 24, no. 6 (2000): 15–19.

15. Coral and Jim Lorenzen, *Encounters with UFO Occupants* (New York: Berkley Medallion Books, 1976), 116–118.

16. "Now They're in Italy," *Life*, November 29, 1954, 133.

17. Lorenzen, *Encounters with UFO Occupants*, 144–148.

18. Jerome Clark and Marcello Truzzi, *UFO Encounters: Sightings, Visitations, and Investigations* (Lincolnwood, IL: Publications International, 1992), 58.

19. Isabel Davis and Ted Bloecher, *Close Encounter at Kelly and Others of 1955* (Evanston, IL: CUFOS, 1978), 1–2, 23–38. Joe Nickell, "Siege of 'Little Green Men': The 1955 Kelly, Kentucky, Incident," *Skeptical Inquirer* 30, no. 6 (2006), http://www.csicop.org/si/show/siege_of_little_green_men.

20. Clark, *UFO Encyclopedia*, 360–361, 745–749.

21. Ibid., 730–731, 806. Edward J. Ruppelt, *The Report on Unidentified Flying Objects* (Garden City, NY: Doubleday & Co., 1956), 58.

22. Clark, *UFO Encyclopedia*, 802–804.

23. *Life*, July 21, 1947, 15.

24. George H. Gallup, *The Gallup Poll: Public Opinion 1935–1971* (New York: Random House, 1972), 666, 911.

25. For summaries of the 1950s movies, see Phil Hardy, *The Encyclopedia of Science Fiction Movies* (Minneapolis: Woodbury Press, 1986), 124–193. For a scholarly discussion of the genre,

see Patrick Lucanio, *Them or Us: Archetypal Interpretations of Fifties Alien Invasion Films* (Bloomington: Indiana University Press, 1987).

26. J. Gordon Melton, "The Contactees: A Survey," in *The Gods Have Landed*, ed. James R. Lewis (Albany: State University of New York Press, 1995), 1–2.

27. These connecting speculations filled such books as those of M. K. Jessup, *The Case for the UFO* and *The Expanding Case for the UFO* (New York: Citadel Press, 1955, 1957); H. T. Wilkins, *Flying Saucers on the Attack* and *Flying Saucers Uncensored* (New York: Citadel Press, 1954, 1955); and Desmond Leslie's part of Leslie and George Adamski, *The Flying Saucers Have Landed* (New York: British Book Centre, 1953).

28. H. B. Darrach Jr. and Robert Ginna, "Have We Visitors from Space?" *Life*, April 7, 1952, 80–96.

29. Clark, *UFO Encyclopedia*, 244–245.

30. Tom Lind's *Catalogue of UFO Periodicals* (Hobe Sound, FL: Author, 1982) lists over 1,100 serial UFO publications from English-language countries.

31. Clark, *UFO Encyclopedia*, 668–669. Keyhoe, *Flying Saucers: Top Secret*, 10.

32. Meade Layne, *The Ether-Ship Mystery and Its Solution* (San Diego: Borderland Sciences Research Foundation, 1950). Clark, *UFO Encyclopedia*, 142.

33. Clark, *UFO Encyclopedia*, 694–695.

34. Gray Barker, *They Knew Too Much About Flying Saucers* (New York: University Books, 1956). Albert K. Bender, *Flying Saucers and the Three Men* (Clarksburg, WV: Saucerian Books, 1962), 84–86, 90–91, 132–134, 138–139, 175.

35. *UFO Reporter* (Summer 1964): 30.

36. Keyhoe, *Flying Saucers: Top Secret*, 27–30; Willy Smith, "Over Pennsylvania: The Enigmatic Captain Killian Case, February 24, 1959," *IUR* 23, no. 1 (Spring 1998): 13–14, 29–30. N. G. Cruttwell, "Flying Saucers over Papua," *FSR Special Issue* (August 1971): 12–20.

37. Edward J. Ruppelt, *The Report on Unidentified Flying Objects* (New York: Doubleday, 1956).

38. Keyhoe, *Flying Saucers: Top Secret*, 258–260.

39. Clark, *UFO Encyclopedia*, 856–867. Philip J. Klass, *UFOs Explained* (New York: Random House, 1974), 105–114. Various explanations for the Socorro UFO have attributed it to a hoax to promote tourism for the town, a prank played by college students, and the test of a moon landing vehicle. Hynek felt that Lonnie Zamora was sincere. Zamora, who died on November 2, 2009, was a religious man but apparently went to his grave without confessing to participation in a hoax, thereby leaving a final testimony that he believed his story as he told it.

40. Frank B. Salisbury, *The Utah UFO Display* (Old Greenwich, CT: Devin-Adair, 1974), xx, 5–6. John and Ann Spencer, *Fifty Years of UFOs* (London: Boxtree, 1997), 55–60.

41. Bullard, "Waves," in Clark, *UFO Encyclopedia*, 1008.

42. Clark, *UFO Encyclopedia*, 719–728.

43. Ibid., 592–599.

44. David M. Jacobs, *The UFO Controversy in America* (Bloomington: Indiana University Press, 1975), 194–195. Richard H. Hall, *The UFO Evidence* (Latham, MD: Scarecrow Press, 2000), 2:4–5.

45. John G. Fuller, *Incident at Exeter* (New York: G. P. Putnam's Sons, 1966), 251.

46. Jacobs, *UFO Controversy in America*, 200–201. John C. Sherwood, *Flying Saucers Are Watching You* (Clarksburg, WV: Saucerian Publications, 1967), 21–37.

47. Paul O'Neil, "The Week of the Flying Saucers: A Well-Witnessed Invasion—By Something," *Life*, April 1, 1966, 24–31.

48. Clark, *UFO Encyclopedia*, 530–531.

49. William Van Horn, "Press Release" (Hillsdale, MI: Author, 1966), 7.

50. Hall, *UFO Evidence*, 2:7. Jacobs, *UFO Controversy in America*, 201–202.

51. "Flying Saucers" (1966), *The Gallup Poll 1935–1971*, 2004–2005.

52. Michael D. Swords, "The University of Colorado UFO Project: The 'Scientific Study of UFOs,'" *Journal of UFO Studies*, n.s., 6 (1995–1996): 149–153. J. Allen Hynek, *The UFO Experience* (Chicago: Henry Regnery, 1972), 196–197. Clark, *UFO Encyclopedia*, 946–947.

53. Swords, "University of Colorado UFO Project," 156. David R. Saunders and R. Roger Harkins, *UFOs? Yes! Where the Condon Committee Went Wrong* (New York: World, 1968), 21.

54. Swords, "University of Colorado UFO Project," 157–158. Clark, *UFO Encyclopedia*, 949–950.

55. Swords, "University of Colorado UFO Project," 168.

56. Ibid., 169–177.

57. Saunders and Harkins, *UFOs? Yes!*, 188–204.

58. Edward U. Condon in Daniel S. Gillmor, ed., *Scientific Study of Unidentified Flying Objects* (New York: Bantam Books, 1969), 1.

59. Clark, *UFO Encyclopedia*, 953–956. Hynek, *UFO Experience*, 192–195, 201–210.

60. Gillmor, *Scientific Study of Unidentified Flying Objects*, 140.

61. Clark, *UFO Encyclopedia*, 670.

62. John F. Schussler, "A Tribute to Walter H. Andrus, Jr., MUFON's International Director Extraordinaire," in *MUFON 2000 International UFO Symposium Proceedings*, ed. Walter H. Andrus Jr. and Irena Scott (Seguin, TX: MUFON, 2000), 21–24.

63. Committee on Science and Astronautics, *Symposium on Unidentified Flying Objects, Hearings before the Committee on Science and Astronautics*, 90th Cong., 2d sess., July 29, 1968, 18–85 (Washington, DC: U.S. Government Printing Office, 1968). Carl Sagan and Thornton Page, eds., *UFOs: A Scientific Debate* (Ithaca, NY: Cornell University Press, 1972).

64. Clark, *UFO Encyclopedia*, 530–531.

65. J. Allen Hynek, "UFOs Merit Scientific Study," *Science*, October 21, 1966, 329.

66. Hynek, *UFO Experience*, 23, 178.

67. Clark, *UFO Encyclopedia*, 538–539.

68. Kendrick Frazier, "From the Editor's Seat: 25 Years of Science and Skepticism," *Skeptical Inquirer* 25, no. 3 (2001), http://www.csicop.org/si/show/25_years_of_science_and_skepticism_--_part_1_of_2; Paul Kurtz, "A Quarter-Century of Skeptical Inquiry: My Personal Involvement," *Skeptical Inquirer* 25, no. 4 (2001), http://www.csicop.org/si/show/quarter_century_of_skeptical_inquiry_my_personal_involvement.

69. Aimé Michel, "The Valensole Affair," *FSR* 11, no. 6 (1965): 7–9.

70. John G. Fuller, *The Interrupted Journey* (New York: Berkley Medallion Books, 1974), 20–21, 25–35, 46–49, 64.

71. Fuller, *The Interrupted Journey*, 116–128, 146–157, 184–196. Walter N. Webb, "A Dramatic

UFO Encounter in the White Mountains, New Hampshire: The Hill Case—September 19–20, 1961," report to NICAP, September 1965, 11.

72. Fuller, *The Interrupted Journey*, 206–214.

73. Ibid., 319–320.

74. Terence Dickinson, *The Zeta Reticuli Incident* (Milwaukee: AstroMedia Corp., 1976). Clark, *UFO Encyclopedia*, 498–499.

75. John A. Keel, *The Mothman Prophecies* (New York: Signet Books, 1976), 52–53, 54, 61, 88–89.

76. Ibid., 11–12, 64, 76–80, 97, 99–100, 131, 207–209, 216–217.

77. Jaques Vallee, *Passport to Magonia: From Folklore to Flying Saucers* (Chicago: Henry Regnery, 1969), viii, 160–162.

78. Jacques Vallee, *The Invisible College* (New York: E. P. Dutton & Co., 1975), 28–30, 194–206, 208.

79. John A. Keel, *UFOs: Operation Trojan Horse* (New York: G. P. Putnam's Sons, 1970), 44, 47, 50–57, 168–169, 191–192, 247, 270, 274, 281, 290.

80. Clark treats paranormal theories in depth in *UFO Encyclopedia*, 696–713.

81. Hall, *UFO Evidence*, 2:340–346. Jacobs, *UFO Controversy in America*, 264–280.

82. Charles Hickson and William Mendez, *UFO Contact at Pascagoula* (Tucson: Wendelle C. Stevens, 1983), 9–15.

83. Jennie Zeidman, *A Helicopter-UFO Encounter over Ohio* (Evanston, IL: CUFOS, 1979), 1–5.

84. Philip J. Klass, *UFOs Explained*, 293–311; idem, *UFOs: The Public Deceived* (Buffalo, NY: Prometheus Books, 1983), 135–160.

85. "Unidentified Flying Objects (1973)," in George H. Gallup, *The Gallup Poll: Public Opinion 1972–1977* (Wilmington, DE: Scholarly Resources, 1978), 213–216.

86. Clark, *UFO Encyclopedia*, 461–463.

87. Ibid., 527–529, 945–946.

88. Randall Jones Pugh and F. W. Holiday, *The Dyfed Enigma* (London: Faber & Faber, 1979). Jenny Randles, *The Pennine UFO Mystery* (London: Granada, 1983), 56–85, 95–121.

89. Bullard, "Waves," in Clark, *UFO Encyclopedia*, 1005.

90. Wendelle C. Stevens and Paul Dong, *UFOs over Modern China* (Tucson: UFO Photo Archives, 1983), 146–203. Bob Pratt, *UFO Danger Zone* (Madison, WI: Horus House Press, 1996), xii–xiv, 177–183, 270–282.

91. Bill Startup and Neil Illingworth, *The Kaikoura UFOs* (Auckland: Hodder & Stoughton, 1980). Clark, *UFO Encyclopedia*, 964–968.

92. J. Allen Hynek, "Tracking the Hessdalen Lights," *IUR* 10, no. 2 (1985): 10–11. Hessdalen special issue, *MUFON UFO Journal*, no. 237 (January 1988): 3–16.

93. Jacques Vallee, *UFO Chronicles of the Soviet Union* (New York: Ballantine Books, 1992), 40–52.

94. Wim Van Utrecht, "The Belgian 1989–1990 UFO Wave," in *UFOs 1947–1997*, ed. Hilary Evans and Dennis Stacy (London: John Brown, 1997), 165–174.

95. Don Schmitt, "The Belleville Sightings," *IUR* 12, no. 6 (1987): 4–8; 13, no. 1 (1988): 17–19. Carey H. Baker, "The Fyffe, Alabama, Experience," in *MUFON 1990 International UFO*

Symposium Proceedings, ed. Walter H. Andrus Jr. (Seguin, TX: Mutual UFO Network, 1990), 86–91.

96. Greg Long, *Examining the Earthlight Theory: The Yakima UFO Microcosm* (Chicago: J. Allen Hynek Center for UFO Studies, 1990), 31–41. Francis L. Ridge, *Regional Encounters* (Evansville, IN: UFO Filter Center, 1994).

97. J. Allen Hynek, Philip J. Imbrogno, and Bob Pratt, *Night Siege: The Hudson Valley UFO Sightings* (New York: Ballantine Books, 1987), 14–15, 24–45, 71–113.

98. Hall, *UFO Evidence,* 2:94–95.

99. Randall Jones Pugh, "Broad Haven School Report," *FSR* 23, no. 1 (June 1977): 3–5. John E. Mack, *Passport to the Cosmos* (New York: Crown, 1999), 40–41.

100. John F. Schussler, *The Cash-Landrum UFO Incident* (LaPorte, TX: Geo Graphics Printing Co., 1998), 4–13, 17–28.

101. Clark, *UFO Encyclopedia,* 897–898. Eric Maillot and Jacques Scornaux, "Trans-en-Provence: When Science and Belief Go Hand in Hand," in Evans and Stacy, *UFOs 1947–1997,* 151–159.

102. Bruce Maccabee, "The Fantastic Flight of JAL 1628," *IUR* 12, no. 2 (1987): 4–21.

103. John Auchettl, *The Knowles Family Encounter* (Melbourne: Victorian UFO Research Society, 1989), 21.

104. Alan Hendry, *The UFO Handbook* (Garden City, NY: Doubleday & Co., 1979), 22, 285.

105. Travis Walton, *The Walton Experience* (New York: Berkley Medallion Books, 1978), 23–35, 77–80, 102–126.

106. Klass, *UFOs: The Public Deceived,* 161–189.

107. Budd Hopkins, *Missing Time: A Documented Study of UFO Abductions* (New York: Richard Marek, 1981), 52.

108. Thomas E. Bullard, "A Comparative Study of Abduction Reports Update," in *Alien Discussions,* ed. Andrea Pritchard, David E. Pritchard, John E. Mack, Pam Kasey, and Claudia Yapp (Cambridge, MA: North Cambridge Press, 1994), 45–46.

109. Whitley Strieber, *Communion* (New York: Beech Tree Books / William Morrow & Co., 1987), 20–30, 40–41, 62–73.

110. Budd Hopkins, *Intruders: The Incredible Visitations at Copley Woods* (New York: Random House, 1987), 108–122, 154–163.

111. Raymond E. Fowler, *The Allagash Abductions* (Tigard, OR: Wild Flower Press, 1993). Budd Hopkins, *Witnessed: The True Story of the Brooklyn Bridge UFO Abductions* (New York: Pocket Books, 1993), 3–21.

112. The conference proceedings appeared in 1994 as *Alien Discussions* (edited by Andrea Pritchard et al.), while reporter C.D.B. Bryan described the conference in the first six chapters of his book, *Close Encounters of the Fourth Kind: Alien Abductions, UFOs, and the Conference at M.I.T.* (New York: Alfred A. Knopf, 1995).

113. Kevin D. Randle and Donald R. Schmitt, *UFO Crash at Roswell* (New York: Avon Books, 1991), 21–22.

114. George M. Eberhart, ed., *The Roswell Report: A Historical Perspective* (Chicago: CUFOS, 1991), 45. Randle and Schmitt, *UFO Crash at Roswell,* 26–33; *The Truth About the UFO Crash at Roswell* (New York: Avon Books, 1994), 236–245.

115. Randle and Schmitt, *UFO Crash at Roswell*, 199–216.

116. Benson Saler, Charles A. Ziegler, and Charles B. Moore, *UFO Crash at Roswell* (Washington, DC: Smithsonian Institution Press, 1997), 2–29. Philip J. Klass, *The Real Roswell Crashed-Saucer Coverup* (Amherst, NY: Prometheus Books, 1997), 44, 74–75, 97–99, 105–109. John Carpenter, "Gerald Anderson: Disturbing Revelations—A Series of Hoaxes Casts Doubt on an 'Eyewitness' Crashed Saucer Account," in *MUFON UFO Journal* no. 299 (March 1993): 6–9.

117. Klass, *Real Roswell Crashed-Saucer Coverup*, 110–114, 123–129. Saler, Ziegler, and Moore, *UFO Crash at Roswell*, 74–76, 113.

118. Klass, *Real Roswell Crashed-Saucer Coverup*, 160–169.

119. "Gallup Short Subjects," *Gallup Poll Monthly* 382 (July 1997): 31.

120. In *Little Gray Men: Roswell and the Rise of a Popular Culture* (Albuquerque: University of New Mexico Press, 2000), author Toby Smith describes his experiences at the 1997 "Roswell Days" fiftieth anniversary celebration (see chapters 1 and 3). As early as 1980 the movie *Hangar 18* presented nascent Roswell mythology, while the Showtime movie *Roswell* (1994) portrayed the standard version of a saucer crash. *Roswell* the TV series, itself based on the *Roswell High* books for teenagers by Melinda Metz, appeared on the WB Network from 1999–2000 and on UPN for the 2001 season. "Little Green Men," an episode of *Star Trek: Deep Space Nine*, aired on November 6, 1995, with Ferengi aliens going back in time to 1947 and crashing in the desert outside Roswell.

121. Kent Jeffrey, "Santilli's Controversial Autopsy Movie: A Comprehensive Review," *MUFON UFO Journal* no. 335 (March 1996): 3–13.

122. Lawrence Fawcett and Barry J. Greenwood, *Clear Intent: The Government Coverup of the UFO Experience* (Englewood Cliffs, NJ: Prentice-Hall, 1984).

123. *Clear Intent*, xiii, 7, 112–113.

124. Clark, *UFO Encyclopedia*, 304–305, 310. Philip J. Klass, "The MJ-12 Crashed Saucer Documents," *Skeptical Inquirer* 12, no. 2 (1987–1988), 137–146, 279–289; "New Evidence of MJ-12 Hoax," *Skeptical Inquirer* 14, no. 2 (1989–1990): 135–140.

125. Bill Ellis, *Raising the Devil: Satanism, New Religions, and the Media* (Lexington: University Press of Kentucky, 2000), 240–278. Linda Moulton Howe, *Glimpses of Other Realities*, vol. 1, *Facts and Eyewitnesses* (Huntingdon Valley, PA: Linda Moulton Howe Publications, 1993), 209, 222.

126. Kenneth Rommel Jr., *Operation Animal Mutilation* (Albuquerque: Department of the District Attorney, First Judicial District, State of New Mexico, 1980), 207–224.

127. Linda Moulton Howe, "1994 Animal Mutilation Research Grant: Summary of Case Studies," in *MUFON 1995 International UFO Symposium*, ed. Walter H. Andrus Jr. and Irena Scott (Seguin, TX: Mutual UFO Network, 1995), 136–146. Colm A. Kelleher, "Research at the National Institute for Discovery Science," in Andrus and Scott, *MUFON 2000 International UFO Proceedings*, 161. Scott Corrales, "The Night Ravagers: Cattle Mutilations in Argentina," *Inexplicata* no. 11 (Spring 2003): 1–16, http://www.geocities.com/INEXPLICATA2000/issue11 .html. For more recent examples, see Scott Corrales, "New Cattle Mutilations in Argentina," *Rense.com* (2003), http://www.rense.com/general44/vis.htm; Corrales, "Argentina: More New Cattle Mutilations," *Rense.com* (2003), http://www.rense.com/general39/argcc.htm.

128. David Hatcher Childress, *Extraterrestrial Archaeology* (Stella, IL: Adventures Unlimited Press, 1994), 189–194. Mark Cashman, "Is Anyone Looking at Us? The Mars Face after Global Surveyor," *UFO Magazine* (U.S.), August 1998, 4–9. "Abducted: Mars Climate Orbiter," *UFO Magazine* (U.S.), December 1999, 9–12.

129. Brenda Butler, Dot Street, and Jenny Randles, *Sky Crash: A Cosmic Conspiracy* (Sudbury, Suffolk: Neville Spearman, 1984), esp. chaps. 1, 3, 11–15, 23. Larry Warren and Peter Robbins, *Left at East Gate* (New York: Marlowe & Co., 1997), 39–48. Georgina Bruni, *You Can't Tell the People: The Definitive Account of the Rendlesham Forest Mystery* (London: Sidgwick & Jackson, 2000), 269–272, 298–299, 303.

130. Ed and Frances Walters, *The Gulf Breeze Sightings* (New York: William Morrow & Co., 1990).

131. Richard Hall and Willy Smith, "Balancing the Scale: Unanswered Questions About Gulf Breeze," *MUFON UFO Journal* no. 248 (December 1988): 3–7. Bruce Maccabee, "The Scale Remains Unbalanced," *MUFON UFO Journal* no. 252 (April 1989): 3–24. Clark, *UFO Encyclopedia*, 463–466.

132. Montague Keen, "Doubt and Deviousness in the UK Crop Circle Scene," in *MUFON 1992 International UFO Symposium Proceedings*, ed. Walter H. Andrus Jr. (Sequin, TX: Mutual UFO Network, 1992), 38–52. Jenny Randles, *Alien Contact: The First Fifty Years* (New York: Sterling, 1997), 84–85, 118–119.

133. Jacques Vallee, *Confrontations: A Scientist's Search for Alien Contact* (New York: Ballantine Books, 1990), 16–23. Jerome Clark, "The Fall and Rise of the Extraterrestrial Hypothesis," in *MUFON 1988 International UFO Symposium Proceedings*, ed. Walter H. Andrus Jr. and Richard H. Hall (Seguin, TX: Mutual UFO Network, 1988), 59–72.

134. "Flying Saucers" (1966), *The Gallup Poll 1935–1971*, 2004. "Unidentified Flying Objects" (1973), *The Gallup Poll: Public Opinion 1972–1977*, 213. "Belief in Psychic and Paranormal Phenomena Widespread among Americans," *Gallup Poll Monthly*, no. 299 (August 1990): 40. "Large Majority Think Government Conceals Information About UFOs," *Gallup Poll Monthly*, no. 372 (September 1996): 26–27. "Americans' Belief in Psychic and Paranormal Phenomena Is Up over Last Decade," *Gallup Poll Monthly*, no. 429 (June 2001): 15.

135. The movie adaptation of *Communion* (1989) followed closely the events described in Whitley Strieber's book, while the CBS miniseries *Intruders* (1992) exercised considerable license in dramatizing the Budd Hopkins book of the same name. Travis Walton's aliens and onboard experiences underwent considerable metamorphosis in the movie, *Fire in the Sky* (1993).

136. See the appendix for a list of some important UFO-related Web sites.

137. Peter A. Surrock, *The UFO Enigma: A New Review of the Physical Evidence* (New York: Warner Books, 1999), 121–122.

138. Gildas Bourdais, "Quasi-Official French Document Looks at Defense Issues Related to UFOs," *MUFON UFO Journal*, no. 377 (September 1999): 10–13.

139. David Clarke and Gary Anthony, "The British MoD Study: Project Condign," *IUR* 30, no. 4 (August 2006): 3–13, 29–32. The entire Condign report is available at "The Real UFO Project: Condign: The Condign Report," *Flying Saucery Presents*, http://www.mod.uk/Defense Internet/FreedomOfInformation/PublicationScheme/SearchPublicationScheme/Unidentified AerialPhenomenaInTheUKAirDefenseRegion.htm.

140. See the appendix for respective Web site addresses.

141. Stanton T. Friedman, "Update on Operation Majestic-12," in *MUFON 1989 International UFO Symposium Proceedings*, ed. Walter H. Andrus (Seguin, TX: Mutual UFO Network, 1989), 82–84, 102–107. George Knapp, "Area 51, Robert Lazar, and Disinformation: A Reevaluation," in *MUFON 1993 International UFO Symposium Proceedings*, ed. Walter H. Andrus Jr. and Irena Scott (Seguin, TX: Mutual UFO Network, 1993), 231–238.

142. John Lear, "Statement," as posted on *Paranet*, December 29, 1987, http://www.ufomind.com/area51/people/lear/original.html.

143. For the story of the climax and collapse of the "Dark Side" melodrama, see chapter 6.

144. Richard M. Dolan, *UFOs and the National Security State: An Unclassified History, 1941–1973* (Rochester, NY: Keyhole, 2000), 1–6, 40, 159, 485–491 (vol. 2 appeared in 2009, covering 1973–1991); "The Extraterrestrial Presence on Earth: Why It Is Revolutionary," in *38th Annual International UFO Symposium Proceedings*, ed. James Carrion (Bellvue, CO: Mutual UFO Network, 2007), 49–67.

145. John Greenewald Jr., "Inside the Black Vault," in *MUFON 2000 International UFO Symposium Proceedings*, ed. Walter H. Andrus Jr. and Irena Scott (Seguin, TX: Mutual UFO Network, 2000), 234–246.

146. Philip J. Corso, *The Day After Roswell* (New York: Pocket Books, 1997). Chapters 12–14 discuss the integrated circuit chip, the laser, and antimissile defenses as spin-offs from alien technology.

147. Karl T. Pflock, *Roswell: Inconvenient Facts and the Will to Believe* (Amherst, NY: Prometheus Books, 2001), 204.

148. Corso's claims are prominent in the writings of the disclosure and exopolitics movements. See Steven M. Greer, *Disclosure: Military and Government Witnesses Reveal the Greatest Secrets in Modern History* (Crozet, VA: Crossing Point, 2001), 459–464. Michael E. Salla, *Exopolitics: Political Implications of the Extraterrestrial Presence* (Tempe, AZ: Dandelion Books, 2004), 8.

149. William J. Birnes, "Project Serpo: Truth or Dare?" *UFO Magazine* (U.S.), February–March 2006, 32, 34.

150. Jim Marrs, *Alien Agenda* (New York: HarperCollins, 1997), 301–332.

151. Marrs, *Alien Agenda*, 309, 332–347.

152. For some of the rumors associated with 2012, see "Secret Alien Communication Related to 2012?" *UFO Casebook*, http://www.ufocasebook.com/year2012.html; Ian O'Neill, "2012: No Planet X," *Universe Today*, http://www.universetoday.com/2008/05/25/2012-no-planet-x/. Whitley Strieber treated the year as a time of threatening UFO events in his novel *2012: The War for Souls* (New York: Tor Books, 2007).

153. "The Lear Briefing," *UFO Magazine* (U.S.), February–March 2004, 42–45.

154. Kenny Young, *June Jeopardies: Was There a Connection between UFO Sightings and Airplane Crashes in June 1951?* (Columbus: Mutual UFO Network of Ohio, 2007). Frank C. Feschino Jr., *Shoot Them Down! The Flying Saucer Air Wars of 1952* (Lulu Enterprises, 2007).

155. Jim Marrs, *Inside Job: Unmasking the 9/11 Conspiracies* (San Rafael, CA: Origin Press, 2004), 134–144.

156. Jim Wilson, "The CIA's Secret UFO Files," *UFO Evidence*, http://www.ufoevidence

.org/documents/doc2027.htm. "UFOs or Top Secret Spy Planes—the Aurora Mystery," *UFO Casebook*, http://www.ufocasebook.com/auroramystery.html.

157. See Helmut Lammer and Marion Lammer, *MILABs: Military Mind Control and Alien Abductions* (Lilburn, GA: IllumiNet Press, 1999).

158. Nick Redfern, *Body Snatchers in the Desert: The Horrible Truth at the Heart of the Roswell Story* (New York: Paraview Pocket Books, 2005), 207–208.

159. Steven M. Greer, *Disclosure: Military and Government Witnesses Reveal the Greatest Secrets in Modern History* (Crozet, VA: Crossing Point, 2001), 4.

160. Stephen Bassett, "Deception, Denial and Disclosure," in *35th Annual International UFO Symposium Proceedings*, ed. Barbra Maher (Morrison, CO: Mutual UFO Network, 2004), 33. Paradigm Research Group, "Open Letter to Senator Hillary Clinton, April 30, 2008," http://www.ufoevidence.org/documents/doc2027.htm. "Exopolitics and the 2008/2004 Presidential Campaigns," *Paradigm Research Group*, http://www.paradigmresearchgroup.org/main.html.

161. Alfred Lambremont Webre, *Exopolitics: Politics, Government, and Law in the Universe* (Vancouver: Universebooks, 2005), 45–47, 75–78. Michael E. Salla, *Exopolitics: Political Implications of the Extraterrestrial Presence* (Tempe, AZ: Dandelion Books, 2004), 2–6, 59–61.

162. "Announcing: The Orion Project," *The Disclosure Project*, http://www.disclosureproject.com/; "The Orion Project," *The Orion Project*, http://www.theorionproject.org/en/vision.html.

163. Steven Bassett, "Exopolitics: UFO RIP," December 2, 2006, http://www.paradigm researchgroup.

164. Sally Petersen, "International Press Conference on UFOs Held at National Press Club in Washington D.C.," *MUFON UFO Journal*, no. 476 (December 2007): 3–4.

165. Gord Heath, "Paul Hellyer and the Politics of Exopolitics," *UFO*BC*, November 5, 2005, http://www.ufobc.ca/Beyond/exopolitics.htm.

166. For monthly sightings totals, see Peter Davenport's National UFO Reporting Center Web site, http://www.nuforc.org/webreports/ndxevent.html. The Blue Book annual totals appear in Gillmor, *Scientific Study of Unidentified Flying Objects*, 514.

167. Michael D. Swords, "The Holland, Michigan, Radar-Visual Case, 1994," *IUR* 24, no. 3 (1999): 3–7.

168. William F. Hamilton, "Mass Sightings in Arizona," *MUFON UFO Journal*, no. 349 (May 1997): 3–6, 14. Bruce Maccabee, "Phoenix Lights Revisited," *MUFON UFO Journal*, no. 370 (February 1999): 3–8.

169. Dennis K. Anderson, "The Arthur Kill Sightings, July 14–15, 2001," *IUR* 28, no. 2 (2003): 3–6, 26–27. See also the Filer's Files Web site archives for 2001 at *UFO Information Center*, http://www.nationalufocenter.com/files/2001/FilersFiles30.shtml (also nos. 31, 32, 33, 34).

170. See the Tinley Park case at "Case Briefs and Past Highlights," *National UFO Reporting Center*, http://www.nuforc.org/CBIndex.html.

171. R. J. Durant, "Swissair Jet Has 'Near Miss' with UFO," *MUFON UFO Journal*, no. 377 (September 1999): 3–9.

172. "Global News Round-Up," *UFO Magazine* (UK), March–April 2001, 8.

173. Robert T. Leach, "The Illinois Arrowhead," *UFO Magazine* (U.S.), May 2000, 42–51.

David B. Marler, "Illinois Police Officers Track UFO Near Scott Air Force Base," *MUFON UFO Journal*, no. 393 (March 2000): 3–8.

174. Dwight Connelly, "Unique Mexican Encounter," *MUFON UFO Journal*, no. 434 (June 2004): 4–5. Bruce Maccabee, "The Mexican Air Force Encounter—and an Analysis of the Evidence," 2004, DVD of oral presentation at the 2004 Symposium, available from MUFON.

175. "Over 50 Witnesses Report UFO Sighting at Stephenville, TX," *MUFON UFO Journal*, no. 478 (February 2008): 3; Sally Petersen, "Update on Investigation of Stephenville, Texas Sightings," *MUFON UFO Journal*, no. 479 (March 2008): 3–5. Don Ledger, "Stephenville, Texas, UFOs," *Fate* 61, no. 3 (March 2008): 10–15.

Chapter 3. UFOs of the Past

1. R. Nathaniel Dett, *Religious Folk-Songs of the Negro* (Hampton, VA: Hampton Institute Press, 1927), 60–61.

2. Charles Fort, *The Books of Charles Fort* (New York: Henry Holt, 1959), 15.

3. For a discussion of supernatural anomalies, see Thomas E. Bullard, "Anomalous Aerial Phenomena before 1800," in *The UFO Encyclopedia*, 2nd ed., ed. Jerome Clark (Detroit: Omnigraphics, 1998), 121–138. As sources of anomalies treated as naturalistic, see Barry Hetherington, *A Chronicle of Pre-Telescopic Astronomy* (New York: John Wiley & Sons, 1996). See also collections of original sources by William R. Corliss, published in Glen Arm, Maryland, by the Sourcebook Project, especially *Strange Phenomena* (vols. G1 and G2, 1974); *Strange Universe* (A1, 1975, and A2, 1977); *Handbook of Unusual Natural Phenomena* (1977); *Mysterious Universe: A Handbook of Astronomical Anomalies* (1979); *Lightning, Auroras, Nocturnal Lights* (1982), and *Remarkable Luminous Phenomena in Nature* (2001).

4. Franklin Brunel Krauss, *An Interpretation of the Omens, Portents and Prodigies Recorded by Livy, Tacitus, and Suetonius* (Philadelphia: Author, 1930), 31–34. Lorraine Daston and Katherine Park, *Wonders and the Order of Nature 1150–1750* (New York: Zone Books, 1998), 50–51.

5. Barbara Cumming, trans., *Egyptian Historical Records of the Later Eighteenth Dynasty* (Westminster, UK: Aris & Phillips Ltd., 1982), fascicle 1, 4–5.

6. Exod. 13:21–22; 2 Kings 2:11; Ezek. 1–3; Matt. 2:1–10.

7. The manuscript of Julius Obsequens surfaced mysteriously around 1500 and disappeared again after publication in 1508. Many editions followed, with translations into Italian and French and with woodcut illustrations, one set by Bernard Salomon in 1553 and 1554, then with another set of illustrations in 1589. The most accessible modern edition is available as *A Book of Prodigies*, in *Summaries, Fragments, Obsequens*, vol. 14, Loeb Classical Library Livy (Cambridge, MA: Harvard University Press, 1959), 238–319.

8. Plutarch, *Lives* (Cincinnati: H. S. & J. Applegate, 1850), 297.

9. Cicero, *De senectute, de amicita, de divinatione* (Loeb Classical Library) (Cambridge, MA: Harvard University Press, 1964), 214–220, 435–437.

10. Eusebius, "Life of Constantine," in *The Essential Eusebius*, ed. Colin Luibheid (New York: New American Library, 1966), 184.

11. Gregory of Tours, *History of the Franks* (Baltimore: Penguin Books, 1977), 395.

12. G.H.W. Lampe, "Miracles and Early Christian Apologetic," in *Miracles*, ed. C.F.D. Moule (London: A. R. Mowbray & Co., 1965), 215. Augustine, *City of God* (New York: Fathers of the Church, 1950), 8:118–119, 359.

13. On the stereotypical supernatural motifs of saints' lives, see C. Grant Loomis, *White Magic* (Cambridge, MA: Mediaeval Academy of America, 1948).

14. *Life of St. Columba*, in *Historians of Scotland* (Edinburgh: Edmonston & Douglas, 1874), 6:79–80, 88–90, 93–99.

15. Rodolfus Glaber, *The Five Books of the Histories*, ed. and trans. John France (Oxford: Clarendon Press, 1989), 219.

16. Andrew Cunningham and Ole Peter Grell, *The Four Horsemen of the Apocalypse: Religion, War, Famine and Death in Reformation Europe* (New York: Cambridge University Press, 2000), 1–4.

17. Other authors of prodigy collections include Job Fincel, Marcus Frytschius (or Fritsche), Caspar Peucer, Pierre Boastuau, Simon Goulart, Johann Wolf, and Johann Praetorius. For scholarly discussions of this literature, see Lynn Thorndike, *A History of Magic and Experimental Science* (New York: Columbia University Press, 1941), 6:488–491; Bryan W. Ball, *A Great Expectation: Eschatological Thought in English Protestantism to 1660* (Leiden: E. J. Brill, 1975), 110–114; Robin Bruce Barnes, *Prophecy and Gnosis: Apocalypticism in the Wake of the Lutheran Reformation* (Stanford, CA: Stanford University Press, 1988), 88–93. Examples of broadsides treating strange aerial sights can be found in Dorothy Alexander, *The German Single-Leaf Woodcut 1600–1700*, 2 vols. (New York: Abaris Books, 1977), and Bruno Weber, *Wunderzeichen und Winkeldrucker* (Dietikon-Zürich: Urs Graf-Verlag, 1972). The Zentralbibliothek Zürich contains the Wikiana (or Wickiana) Collection of broadsides with many examples of aerial wonders—see Matthias Senn, *Die wickiana* (Küsnacht-Zürich: Raggi Verlag, 1975), and Bruno Weber, *Erschröckliche und warhafftige wunderzeichen 1543–1586* (Dietikon-Zürich: Urs Graf-Verlag, 1971).

18. For example, John Gadbury, "To the Reader," *Natura prodigiorum* (London: Printed for Fr. Cossinet, 1665).

19. Jean Calvin, *Institutes of the Christian Religion* (London: S.C.M. Press, 1960), 63, 200–201, 208–210.

20. *Eniautos Terastios: Mirabilis Annus, or the Year of Prodigies and Wonders* (London, 1661), i, iii–iv.

21. Keith Thomas, *Religion and the Decline of Magic* (New York: Charles Scribner's Sons, 1971), 95–96. C. E. Whiting, *Studies in English Puritanism* (New York: Society for Promoting Christian Knowledge, 1931), 546–551.

22. Denys Hay, *Polydore Vergil: Renaissance Historian and Man of Letters* (Oxford: Clarendon Press, 1952), 34–35. John Spencer, *A Discourse concerning Prodigies* (Cambridge: Printed by John Field, 1663).

23. Increase Mather published *An Essay for the Recording of Illustrious Providences* in 1684 and Cotton Mather the *Magnalia Christi Americana* in 1702. Like their predecessors, these collectors regarded providential occurrences to encompass a great deal more than aerial wonders, so that lightning striking a church steeple, an accident befalling a sinner, or a monstrous birth also held significance as an instance of divine intervention.

24. David Clarke, *The Angel of Mons: Phantom Soldiers and Ghostly Guardians* (Chichester, West Sussex: John Wiley & Sons, Ltd., 2004), 1–5.

25. William Walsh, *Our Lady of Fátima* (Garden City, NY: Doubleday, 1954), 137–150. For an attempt to link Fátima with UFOs, see Joaquim Fernandes and Fina D'Armada, *Heavenly Lights: The Apparition of Fátima and the UFO Phenomenon* (Victoria, BC: EcceNova Editions, 2005).

26. P. McGurk, ed. and trans., *The Chronicle of John of Worcester* (Oxford: Clarendon Press, 1998), 199.

27. Roger de Hoveden, *Annals* (London: H. G. Bohn, 1853), 2:98.

28. Joachim Camerarius, *The History of Strange Wonders, or The Epistle of One Friend to Another, of a Strange Fyre That Was Sene in the Aire both Longe and Brode almost through Al Germany* (London: Imprinted by Roulande Hall, 1561), 51.

29. Jacob Grimm, *Teutonic Mythology* (Gloucester, MA: Peter Smith, 1976), 3:918–950. "The Devil's Army," *Fort Dodge (IA) Semi-Weekly Chronicle*, April 17, 1897, 4. See also Hilda Ellis Davidson, "The Wild Hunt," in *Supernatural Enemies*, Davidson and Anna Chaudhri (Durham, NC: Carolina Academic Press, 2001), 163–176.

30. John Harden, *The Devil's Tramping Ground and Other North Carolina Mystery Stories* (Chapel Hill: University of North Carolina Press, 1949), 127–128. A former roommate described to me his visits to the base of the mountain, where local teenagers allegedly gathered for the weird spectacle of large lights swooping low overhead and smaller ones dancing on the car hood or bouncing near the ground.

31. Elton Miles, *Tales of the Big Bend* (College Station: Texas A&M University Press, 1976), 149–167.

32. Grimm, *Teutonic Mythology*, 3:916–918. Newbell Niles Puckett, *Folk Beliefs of the Southern Negro* (Chapel Hill: University of North Carolina Press, 1926), 135. Mark Moravec, "Strange Illuminations: 'Min-Min Lights'—Australian 'Ghost Light' Stories," *Fabula* 44 (2003): 2–24. M. W. de Visser, *The Dragon in China and Japan* (Amsterdam: Johannes Müller, 1913), 210. Further treatments of supernatural lights can be found in M. J. Walhouse, "Ghostly Lights," *Folk-Lore* 5 (1894): 293–299; R. C. MacLagan, "Ghost Lights of the Western Highlands," *Folk-Lore* 8 (1897): 203–256; William Wells Newell, "The Ignis Fatuus, Its Character and Legendary Origin," *Journal of American Folklore* 17 (1904): 39–60; Wayland D. Hand, "Will-o'-the Wisps, Jack-o'-Lanterns and Their Congeners," *Fabula* 18 (1977): 226–233.

33. John Aubrey, *Three Prose ·Works* (Fontwell, Sussex: Centaur Press, 1972), 104–105.

34. Harry M. Hyatt, *Folklore from Adams County, Illinois* (New York: Alma Egan Hyatt Foundation, 1935), 571 (item no. 9996).

35. William Lynwood Montell, *Ghosts along the Cumberland* (Knoxville: University of Tennessee Press, 1975), 143–144. Robert R. Lyman Sr., *Strange Events in the Black Forest* (Coudersport, PA: Potter Enterprise, 1973), 2:66. Ruth Ann Musick, *The Tell-Tale Lilac Bush* (Lexington: University of Kentucky Press, 1965), 59. H. F. Feilberg, "Ghostly Lights," *Folk-Lore* 6 (1895): 294.

36. Thomas, *Religion and the Decline of Magic*, 91–93. E.M.W. Tillyard, *The Elizabethan World Picture* (New York: Vintage Books, 1960), 25–36.

37. Fort, *Books*, 3. For Fort's life and work, see the biography by Damon Knight, *Charles Fort: Prophet of the Unexplained* (Garden City, NY: Doubleday & Co., 1970). See also Loren E. Gross,

Charles Fort, the Fortean Society, and Unidentified Flying Objects (Fremont, CA: Author, 1976). For a scathing critique of Fort's ideas see "Lo! The Poor Forteans," in Sam Moskowitz, *Strange Horizons: The Spectrum of Science Fiction* (New York: Charles Scribner's Sons, 1976), 218–248.

38. Fort, *Books*, 454. "Have Martians Visited Us?" letter to the *New York Times*, September 5, 1926, sec. 10, 14.

39. Fort, *Books*, 90–91, 98–99, 192–194.

40. Knight, *Charles Fort*, 180–181. *Doubt*, no. 17 (1947): cover. "In the Sky," *Doubt*, no. 48 (1955): 342.

41. *Nature* 22 (May 1880): 64.

42. *English Mechanic* 7 (July 10, 1868): 351; reprinted in Corliss, *Handbook of Unusual Natural Phenomena*, 112.

43. "Saw Ball of Fire," *Burlington (VT) Free Press*, July 3, 1907, 7; *Monthly Weather Review* 36 (1907): 310–311.

44. "An Account of a Very Singular Phenomenon Seen in the Disk of the Sun, in Different Parts of Europe, and Not in Others," *Annual Register* 9 (1766): 120–121.

45. "Was It a Case of 'Jag'?" *Indianapolis Journal*, September 6, 1891, 1; "Crawfordsville's Airy Spook," *Indianapolis Journal*, September 9, 1891, 1; "A Strange Phenomenon," *Crawfordsville (IN) Daily Journal*, September 5, 1891, 4; "Mr. Switzer Saw the Spook," *Crawfordsville (IN) Daily Journal*, September 7, 1891, 4; "The Spook Explained," *Crawfordsville (IN) Daily Journal*, September 8, 1891, 7, 9.

46. *Ramayana* (retold by William S. Buck) (New York: New American Library, 1978), 34, 173, 190, 278. Ovid, *Metamorphoses* (Baltimore: Penguin Books, 1971), 184–185. For other examples, see Berthold Laufer, *Prehistory of Aviation* (Chicago: Field Museum of Natural History, 1928), 20, 23–25, 59–60, 92.

47. Robert Conant, *A Streak of Luck* (New York: Seaview Books, 1979), 229. The Edison National Historical Site at Menlo Park, NJ, has an extensive Edison Star file.

48. J. Stadling, *Through Siberia* (Westminster: Archibald Constable & Co., 1901), 107–108. Newspaper reports of Andrée's balloon sightings can be found in "A Mysterious Balloon," *Morning Free Press* (Winnipeg, Manitoba), July 2, 1896, 4; "It Was No Dream," *Morning Free Press* (Winnipeg, Manitoba), August 13, 1896, 2; "Was Only a Cloud," *Morning Free Press* (Winnipeg, Manitoba), September 28, 1896 3; "Aerial Mystery," *Morning Free Press* (Winnipeg, Manitoba), July 20, 1897, 1; "Could It Be Andree?" *Morning Free Press* (Winnipeg, Manitoba), July 31, 1897, 1; "Big Balloon Story," *Morning Free Press* (Winnipeg, Manitoba), August 2, 1897, 1; "Was It Prof. Andree?" *Morning Free Press* (Winnipeg, Manitoba), September 18, 1897, 2; "Andree's Outlook," *Morning Free Press* (Winnipeg, Manitoba), September 22, 1897, 2; *Victoria Daily Colonist* (British Columbia), "What Is It?" July 20, 1897, 4; "Those Air Ships," *Daily Colonist* (British Columbia), July 31, 1897, 6; "That Morning Mystery," *Daily Colonist* (British Columbia), August 12, 1897, 6; "That Fiery Mystery," *Daily Colonist* (British Columbia), August 14, 1897, 7.

49. "Espionage by Balloon," *Guardian* (Manchester), March 26, 1892, 8, 31; "German Military Balloons," *Guardian* (Manchester), March 31, 1892, 8; "German Army Balloons in Active Use," *New York Tribune*, March 31, 1892, 1; "Balloons as German Spies," *New York Times*, March 26, 1892, 3.

50. "Voices in the Sky," *Sacramento (CA) Evening Bee*, November 18, 1896, 1.

51. "Have We Got 'Em Yet?" *Sacramento (CA) Evening Bee*, November 19, 23, 1896, 1; "Saw the Mystic Flying Light," *San Francisco Call*, November 22, 1896, 13; "A Winged Ship in the Sky," November 23, 1896, 1; "Queer Things You See When—," *San Francisco Examiner*, November 23, 1896, 12; "That Airship, It Won't Stay Put," December 4, 1896, 13.

52. "See an Airship at Hastings," *Omaha (NE) Daily Bee*, February 2, 1897, 7; "Visions of an Airship," March 16, 1897, 7; "Strange Light in the Sky," *Topeka (KS) Daily Capital*, March 28, 1897, 1; "The Air Ship," *Atchison (KS) Daily Globe*, April 2, 1897, 2.

53. "See Airship or a Star," *Chicago Tribune*, April 10; "California Airship on the Wing," *Chicago Tribune*, April 11, 1897, 1; "Aerial Wonder Seen in St. Louis," *St. Louis Post-Dispatch*, April 12, 1897, 1; "Genuine!" *Minneapolis Tribune*, April 11, 1897, 1.

54. "Say It Is an Airship and Not a Star," *Chicago Tribune*, April 12, 1897, 5; "Airship Is Seen Again," *Milwaukee Sentinel*, April 12, 1.

55. "Air Ship Seen," *St. Louis Post-Dispatch*, April 13, 1897, 1.

56. "Airship in the Heavens," *St. Louis Post-Dispatch*, April 10, 1897, 1.

57. "California Airship on the Wing," *Chicago Tribune*, April 11, 1897, 1.

58. "Airship Takes a Tumble," *Sedalia (MO) Evening Democrat*, April 8, 1897, 1; "High in the Air," *Detroit Evening News*, April 13, 1897, 4; "Farmer's Garments and Veracity Badly Strained," *Cedar Rapids Evening Gazette*, March 29, 1897, 1.

59. "A Springfield Story," *Decatur (IL) Daily Republican*, April 16, 1897, 1.

60. "Very Hard to Believe," *Indianapolis Sentinel*, April 21, 1897, 6.

61. "Odds and Ends," *Detroit Evening News*, April 16, 1897, 4.

62. "Golden Haired Girl Is in It," *St. Louis Post-Dispatch*, April 19, 1897, 1.

63. "The Great Aerial Wanderer," *Dallas Morning News*, April 19, 1897, 5.

64. "Airship Steals a Calf," *Kansas City Times*, April 27, 1897, 1.

65. "The Air Ship," *Weekly (Troy) Kansas Chief*, April 8, 1897, 3.

66. "The Air-Ship," *Burlington (IA) Hawk-Eye*, April 11, 1897, 1. Other cases of reported fire balloons are in "Blame the Airship," *Chicago Daily Inter Ocean*, April 13, 1897, 3; "The Airship Captured," *Salina (KS) Daily Republican*, April 19, 1897, 5; [no title], *Abilene (KS) Monitor*, April 22, 1897, 2; "All Saw the Airship," *Abilene (KS) Weekly Chronicle*, April 23, 1897, 5; "Near-By Neighbors: Hancock County," *Bushnell (IL) Record*, April 23, 1897, 8; "The Air Ship," *Cuba (IL) Journal*, May 6, 1897, 1; "The Air-ship," *Emporia (KS) Daily Republican*, May 7, 1897, 1.

67. "Heavens Full of 'Em," *Durand (IL) Clipper*, April 16, 1897, 1. Examples of hoaxes exposed appear in *Ellinwood (KS) Leader*, February 11, 1897, 1; "That Air Ship," *Everest (KS) Enterprise*, April 8, 1897, 1; "Airship," *Kansas City World*, April 24, 1897, 1.

68. Clark, *UFO Encyclopedia*, 261–263. Michael Simmons, "Once upon a Time in the West," *Magonia*, no. 20 (August 1985): 3–7.

69. Clark, *UFO Encyclopedia*, 59. "The Air-Ship in Kansas," *Rock Port (MO) Atchison County Mail*, May 7, 1897, 1.

70. "Flight of the Airship," *Dallas Morning News*, April 17, 1897, 8.

71. Gibbs-Smith, *Flight through the Ages*, 85, 90, 98, 108.

72. Illustrations of outlandish airship designs appeared during 1896 in the *San Francisco*

Call, November 19, 1; November 22, 13; November 23, 1; December 5, 1; *San Francisco Examiner*, December 2, 5. Examples for 1897 include *St. Louis Post-Dispatch*, April 14, 6; *St. Louis Republic*, April 29, 9; *Dallas Morning News*, April 16, 5; *Little Rock Arkansas Gazette*, April 22, 3.

73. "Quite a Sensation! What a Night Policeman Saw!" *Peterborough Advertiser* (UK), March 27, 1909, 7; "Who Owns the Airship?" *Daily Express* (London), May 15, 1909, 1; "Mystery of the Air," May 18, 1909, 1; "Mystery of the Air," May 20, 1909, 1. For discussion of British response to phantom airships, see Nigel Watson, *The Scareship Mystery: A Survey of Phantom Airship Scares 1909–1918* (Corby, Northamptonshire: Domra Publications, 2000).

74. "Tells of Flight 300 Miles in Air," *Boston Herald*, December 13, 1909; "Mysterious Air Craft Circles about Boston for Nearly Six Hours," December 24, 1909, 1; "Worcester Palpitating," *Boston Globe*, December 23, 1909; "Certain as the Stars," December 25, 1909, 1.

75. "Unknown Aircraft over Dover," *Times* (London), January 6, 1913, 6; "The English Phantom Airship," *Berliner Tageblatt*, February 25, 1913; "The Airship Psychosis in England," February 26, 1913.

76. "Aerial Kidnappers," *Daily Express* (London), February 5, 1913, 1; "Russian Aeroplane Scare in Roumania," *Guardian* (Manchester), January 31, 1913, 9; "Espionage in Russia," *Le Temps* (Paris), January 1, 1913, 6; "Venus et L'ignorance astronomique," *L'astronomie* 27 (1913): 133.

77. "Mysterious Aeroplane Flights," *Capetown Cape Times* (South Africa), August 15, 1914, 7; "Air Pilots in German Territory," *Capetown Cape Times* (South Africa), August 22, 1914, 7; "Aeroplane Sighted," *Capetown Cape Times* (South Africa), August 18, 1914, 5; "Aeroplane Reports," *Capetown Cape Times* (South Africa), August 20, 1914, 5; "Aeroplane Problem," *Capetown Cape Times* (South Africa), September 18, 1914, 5; "Airship Sighted to the North," *Morgenbladet* (Oslo), October 23, 1914, 4; "German Airship over Gotland," *Morgenbladet* (Oslo), November 17, 1914, 2; "A Light over the 'Seven Sisters,'" *Morgenbladet* (Oslo), November 19, 1914, 2; "Was an Airship Wrecked in Østre Slidre?" *Morgenbladet* (Oslo), July 16, 1915, 4; "The Night Visitor in the Air," *Morgenbladet* (Oslo), March 24, 1916, 4; "Yankees Sent Up Balloons Which Exploded at Brockville Causing Airship Raid Scare," *London Free Press* (Ontario), February 15, 1915, 1, 9.

78. "Mysterious Airship Hovering over Powder Plants," *Wilmington (DE) Every Evening*, February 3, 1916, 1; "Citizens Declare They Saw Airship," *Wilmington (DE) Every Evening*, February 14, 1916 1, 2; "Ashland Firemen Are Seein' Things," *Superior (WI) Telegram*, February 19, 1916, 3; "Airship Soars over Allouez Docks," *Superior (WI) Telegram*, February 26, 1916, 1; "Practical Jokers Get into Aeroplane Game," *Superior (WI) Telegram*, March 1, 1916, 4, 12; "Aeroplane Lands at Vermilion Lake," *Superior (WI) Telegram*, April 11, 1916, 8.

79. "Mystery Plane Is Hunted by Swedish Army Fliers," *New York Times*, January 1, 1934, 21; "Mystery Plane Reported Again," *New York Times*, January 10, 1934, 11; "Luminous Phenomenon Lurks," *Svenska Dagbladet* (Stockholm), December 13, 1933, 18; "All Lapland Has Observed a Flying Light," *Svenska Dagbladet* (Stockholm), December 30, 1933, 7; "'Ghost Flier' Opens the Season," *Svenska Dagbladet* (Stockholm), November 9, 1934, 26; "Firing at Russian Airplanes," *Svenska Dagbladet* (Stockholm), October 1, 1935, 7; "Ghost Flier Again in North Norway," *Svenska Dagbladet* (Stockholm), November 19, 1936, 9; "The Ghost Flier Seen by Military Men from Boden," *Svenska Dagbladet* (Stockholm), February 12, 1937, 5.

80. "Watch for Mysterious Aeroplane," *Times* (London), April 16, 1936, 9; "Mysterious Plane over Airport," *Daily Telegraph* (London), July 16, 1937, 6.

81. "Army Says Air Alarm Real," *Los Angeles Times*, February 26, 1942; February 27, 1942, 1. A case can be made that the "objects" were nothing more than puffs of smoke from exploding shells and the incident a result of overexcited reactions from inexperienced military personnel.

82. "Balls of Fire Stalk U.S. Fighters in Night Assaults over Germany," *New York Times*, December 14, 1944, 6; "Floating Mystery Ball Is New Nazi Air Weapon," January 2, 1945, 1, 4; Jeffrey A. Lindell, "Supernatural Belief Traditions: The Traditions of Belief and Disbelief and the Role of the Memorate in Illustrative Dialogue," folklore seminar paper, Indiana University, Bloomington.

83. "Swarm of Mysterious Rockets Is Seen over Capital of Sweden," *New York Times*, August 12, 1946, 1, 7; "Swedes Use Radar in Fight on Missiles," *New York Times*, August 13, 1946, 4; "Two Swedes Escape a 'Ghost Rocket,'" *New York Times*, August 14, 1946, 11; "Doolittle Consulted by Swedes on Bombs," *New York Times*, August 22, 1946, 2. "Swarms of Projectiles," *Svenska dagbladet* (Stockholm), July 11, 1946, 3, 9; "Rocket Bomb Falls in Mjösa," *Svenska dagbladet* (Stockholm), July 20, 1946, 9; "The Ghost Bombs Are V-2 Bombs, Believes a Specialist," *Svenska dagbladet* (Stockholm), August 2, 1946, 3; "A Shower of Space Rockets," *Svenska dagbladet* (Stockholm), August 13, 1946, 3; "Ghost Bomb over Austria," *Svenska dagbladet* (Stockholm), September 13, 1946, 14.

84. "Space Ship Flaps Wings over San Diego, 'Observers' Claim," *San Diego Union*, October 15, 1946, 1; Meade Layne, "Welcome, Kareeta!" *Round Robin* 2, no. 10 (1946): 3–7.

85. Donald E. Keyhoe, *The Flying Saucers Are Real* (New York: Fawcett Publications, 1950), 57–62; H. T. Wilkins, *Flying Saucers on the Attack* (New York: Citadel Press, 1954); Desmond Leslie and George Adamski, *The Flying Saucers Have Landed* (New York: British Book Centre, 1953), 22–36, 80–89; M. K. Jessup, *UFO and the Bible* (New York: Citadel Press, 1956); M. K. Jessup, *The Case for the UFO* (New York: Citadel Press, 1955); M. K. Jessup, *The Expanding Case for the UFO* (New York: Citadel Press, 1957); Donald H. Menzel, *Flying Saucers* (Cambridge, MA: Harvard University Press, 1953), 63–65, 106–123.

86. Clark, *UFO Encyclopedia*, 75–86; Thomas E. Bullard, "Ancient Astronauts," in *Encyclopedia of the Paranormal*, ed. Gordon Stein (Amherst, NY: Prometheus Books, 1996), 25–32; Josef F. Blumrich, *The Spaceships of Ezekiel* (New York: Bantam Books, 1974).

87. Jacques Vallee, *Passport to Magonia* (Chicago: Henry Regnery, 1969), 98–100; Melvin Harris, "The Nonmystery of the Disappearing Regiment," *Fate* 35, no. 1 (1982): 70–74.

88. J. Vyner, "The Mystery of Springheel Jack," *FSR* 7, no. 3 (1961): 3–6. Elliott O'Donnell, *Ghosts of London* (New York: E. P. Dutton & Co., 1933), 145–155; Mike Dash, "Springheeled Jack: To Victorian Bugaboo from Suburban Ghost," *Fortean Studies* 3 (1996): 7–125; Donald M. Johnson, "The 'Phantom Anesthetist' of Mattoon: A Field Study of Mass Hysteria," *Journal of Abnormal and Social Psychology* 40 (1945): 175–186.

89. Gordon I. R. Lore and Harold H. Deneault Jr., *Mysteries of the Skies: UFOs in Perspective* (Englewood Cliffs, NJ: Prentice-Hall, 1968), 106; "Belleville Senior Citizen Recalls 1926 UFO Sighting," *Brenham (TX) Banner Press*, September 29, 1988.

90. Clark, *UFO Encyclopedia*, 262–263. Simmons, "Once upon a Time in the West," 3–7; Hayden Hewes, "The UFO Crash of 1897—Aurora Astronaut Update," *Official UFO* 1, no. 5 (1976): 29–31.

91. Pliny, *Natural History* (London: Henry G. Bohn, 1855), 1:63.

92. Bernhard Walter Scholz, *Carolingan Chronicles* (Ann Arbor: University of Michigan Press, 1970), 53–55.

93. Nicholas Roerich, *Altai Himalaya* (New York: Frederick A. Stokes, 1929), 361–362.

94. Leon Davidson, "Pre-1947 UFOs," in *Flying Saucers: An Analysis of the Air Force Project Blue Book Special Report No. 14*, 3rd ed. (Ramsey, NJ: Ramsey-Wallace Corp., 1966). For the arguments of Brad Sparks against a weather balloon solution, see http://www.nicap .org/270805himalayasdir.htm.

95. Raphael Holinshed, *Holinshed's Chronicles of England, Scotland and Ireland* (London: Printed for J. Johnson, 1808), 2:829.

96. Mustafa Naima, *Annals of the Turkish Empire* (London: Oriental Translation Fund, 1832), 466.

97. Robert G. Neeley Jr., *UFOs of 1896/1897: The Airship Wave* (Mount Ranier, MD: Fund for UFO Research, 1985); Nigel Watson, Granville Oldroyd, and David Clarke, *The 1912–1913 British Phantom Airship Scare* (Mount Ranier, MD: Fund for UFO Research, 1987).

98. Jerome Clark and Loren Coleman, *The Unidentified* (New York: Warner Paperback Library, 1975), 159–163. Robert Bartholomew and Thomas Bullard, "A Real Nightmare, or a Flight of Fancy?" in *The Scareship Mystery: A Survey of Phantom Airship Scares 1909–1918*, ed. Nigel Watson, 143–151 (Corby, Northamptonshire: Domra Publications, 2000).

99. Peng-Yoke Ho, *Astronomical Chapters of the Chin Shu* (The Hague: Mouton, 1966), 245.

100. Obsequens, *A Book of Prodigies*, 291.

101. Stephen Bateman, *The Doome Warning All Men to the Judgemente* ([London]: Imprinted by Ralphe Nubery, 1581), 301.

102. Victor H. Mair, ed., *The Columbia Anthology of Traditional Chinese Literature* (New York: Columbia University Press, 1994), 593.

103. Frank R. Schofield, *Monthly Weather Review* 32 (1904): 115; Barry Greenwood, "The U.S.S. *Supply* Sighting of 1904," *UFO Historical Review*, no. 2 (September 1998): 2–7, also in "UFO Historical Review," *Computer UFO Network*, http://www.greenwoodufoarchive.com/ uhr/uhro2.pdf. Bruce Maccabee, "Even More Remarkable (UFOs in History: The U.S.S. *Supply* Sighting of Remarkable Meteors)," in *MUFON 2003 International UFO Symposium Proceedings*, ed. Barbra Maher (Morrison, CO: Mutual UFO Network, 2003), 55–70. See also "Meteors? Even More Remarkable," *Remarkable Meteors*, http://brumac.8k.com/RemarkableMeteors/ Remarkable.html.

104. Warner Cowgill, "Curious Phenomenon in Venezuela," *Scientific American* 55 (December 18, 1886): 389.

105. The Robozero account was published by the St. Petersburg Arkheograficheskaia Kommissiia in *Akty istoricheskie, sobranye i izdanye*, tome 4, 1645–1676 (1842), 331–332. Russian investigator Yury Roszius tracked down the original letter and published it in *Aura-Z* 1, no. 4 (1994): 10. Though extensively researched by Russian ufologists, the case first became widely known to American ufologists in *UFOs from Behind the Iron Curtain*, by Ion Hobana and Julien Weverbergh (New York: Bantam Books, 1975), 54–55. This translation, along with another in Paul Stonehill, *The Soviet UFO Files* (Godalming, Surrey: CLB International, 1998), 16–17, captures the facts of the case, as does "Robozero: The Ball of Fire," *WaterUFO*, http://www.waterufo .net/item.php?id=5. The translation used here is from professional translator Vladimir Rostov,

http://www.zt.ukrtel.net/russian/. For the meteoric explanation, see Hobana and Weverbergh, *UFOs from Behind the Iron Curtain*, 57–59.

Chapter 4. From the Otherworld to Other Worlds

1. The statement comes from the title of science writer Walter Sullivan's book, *We Are Not Alone: The Search for Intelligent Life on Other Worlds* (New York: McGraw-Hill, 1964).

2. The physicist Enrico Fermi asked the question, "Where are they?" or "Where is everybody?" in 1950 during a lunch conversation inspired by a newspaper cartoon of flying saucer occupants carrying off garbage cans to another planet. This question first expressed the Fermi Paradox—the universe is full of stars, and if they have the inhabited planets we expect, why haven't those inhabitants visited us? See Stephen Webb, *If the Universe Is Teeming with Aliens . . . Where Is Everybody? Fifty Solutions to the Fermi Paradox and the Problem of Extraterrestrial Life* (New York: Copernicus Books, 2002), 17–18.

3. Jacques Vallee, *Confrontations: A Scientist's Search for Alien Contact* (New York: Ballantine Books, 1990), 177.

4. Blaise Pascal, *Pensées* (Baltimore: Penguin Books, 1966), 95.

5. Hesiod's *Theogony*, lines 116–120, in *Hesiod and Theogonis*, trans. Dorothea Wender (New York: Penguin Books, 1973), 27. Brian Branston, *Gods of the North* (New York: Vanguard Press, 1957), 74–75.

6. E. A. Wallis Budge, *The Gods of the Egyptians* (New York: Dover, 1969), 1:170–171, 173, 323–324; 2:opposite 95.

7. Miguel León-Portilla, *Aztec Thought and Culture* (Norman: University of Oklahoma Press, 1963), 59. William Fairfield Warren, *The Earliest Cosmologies* (New York: Eaton & Mains, 1909), frontispiece, 46–48. Michael Hoskin, ed., *The Cambridge Illustrated History of Astronomy* (New York: Cambridge University Press, 1997), 78. Akira Sadakata, *Buddhist Cosmology: Philosophy and Origins* (Tokyo: Kōsei , 1997), 47–54.

8. Edward Langton, *Essentials of Demonology: A Study of Jewish and Christian Doctrine, Its Origin and Development* (London: Epworth Press, 1949), 21.

9. Franz Cumont, *After Life in Roman Paganism* (New York: Dover Publications, 1959), 80. Kuno Meyer, ed., *The Voyage of Bran, Son of Febal, to the Land of the Living* (London: David Nutt, 1895), 4–14.

10. Branston, *Gods of the North*, 59, 60.

11. John S. Mbiti, *Concepts of God in Africa* (London: SPCK, 1970), 257–258; Emefie Ikenga-Metuh, *Comparative Studies of African Traditional Religions* (Onitsha, Nigeria: IMICO, 1987), 263, 265–266.

12. Katharine Briggs, *The Vanishing People: Fairy Lore and Legends* (New York: Pantheon Books, 1978), 88.

13. Sándor Erdész, "The World Conception of Lajos Ámi, Storyteller," *Acta Ethnographica* 10 (1961): 332, 334.

14. Ronnie H. Terpening, *Charon and the Crossing: Ancient, Medieval, and Renaissance Transformations of a Myth* (Cranbury, NJ: Associated University Presses, 1985), 11–17. Snorri

Sturluson, *The Prose Edda* (Berkeley: University of California Press, 1964), 40. Stith Thompson, *Tales of the North American Indians* (Bloomington: Indiana University Press, 1968), 126–127. Erdész, "World Conception of Lajos Ámi," 333.

15. Eileen Gardiner, ed., *Visions of Heaven and Hell before Dante* (New York: Italica Press, 1989), 135–136. Cumont, *After Life in Roman Paganism*, 74.

16. Mircea Eliade, *Patterns in Comparative Religion* (Cleveland: Meridian Books, 1963), 99–100. Sadakata, *Buddhist Cosmology*, 26–30. Warren, *Earliest Cosmologies*, frontispiece, 36. Branston, *Gods of the North*, 73.

17. Howard Rollin Patch, *The Other World, According to Descriptions in Medieval Literature* (New York: Octagon Books, 1980), 3, 25–26. Rev. 20:18–21. Jean Delumeau, *History of Paradise: The Garden of Eden in Myth and Tradition* (New York: Continuum, 1995), 6–10. Alfred Nutt, "The Happy Otherworld in the Mythico-Romantic Literature of the Irish," in Kuno Meyer, *Voyage of Bran*, 1:142–143.

18. Alfred Jeremias, *The Babylonian Conception of Heaven and Hell* (London: David Nutt, 1902), 20–22. Alfred Jeremias, "The Descent of Ishtar to the Underworld," in *Myths from Mesopotamia: Creation, the Flood, Gilgamesh, and Others*, ed. Stephanie Dalley (New York: Oxford University Press, 1991), 155.

19. See Book 11 of the *Odyssey*.

20. Maneckji Nusservanji Dhalla, *Zoroastrian Theology* (New York: AMS Press, 1972), 176–177. Delumeau, *History of Paradise*, 6–10.

21. Richard Cavendish, *Visions of Heaven and Hell* (London: Orbis, 1977), 114–115.

22. The ultimate literary expression of heaven and hell as a system of circles where souls go according to their merits is Dante's *Divine Comedy*. The *Inferno* is memorable for sinners accommodated and punished according to their sins in the various layers, until in the ninth level of hell, Satan chews Judas Iscariot, Brutus, and Cassius in his three mouths as the worst of all sinners, those who betrayed their lord (see the Mark Musa translation [New York: Penguin Books, 1984], 88, 148, 379–381).

23. For depictions of hellish landscapes, see Francesca Flores D'Arcais, *Giotto* (New York: Abbeville, 1995), 200–201; John T. Spike, *Fra Angelico* (New York: Abbeville Press, 1997), 99; Kenneth Clark, *The Drawings by Sandro Botticelli for Dante's Divine Comedy* (New York: Harper & Row, 1976), *Inferno*, 27–85; Dirk De Vos, *Hans Memling: Complete Works* (Ghent: Ludion Press, 1994), 87.

24. For the animal-headed gods Thoth, Anubis, and Horus, see the judgment scene from the Papyrus of Ani in Budge, *Gods of the Egyptians*, back of volume 2. For Ganesh and Hanuman, see Heinz Mode, *Fabulous Beasts and Demons* (London: Phaidon Press, 1975), 61, 68, also 98 for harpies. For Shiva, see Alexander Eliot, *Myths* (New York: McGraw-Hill, 1976), 203. For winged Babylonian and Assyrian beings, see Annie Caubet and Marthe Bernus-Taylor, *The Louvre: Near Eastern Antiquities* (London: Scala Books, 1991), 32, 34; for sirens, see J. Michael Padgett, *The Centaur's Smile: The Human Animal in Early Greek Art* (Princeton, NJ: Princeton University Art Museum, 2003), 75, 77, 80.

25. For fearsome Babylonian demons, see Langston, *Essentials of Demonology*, frontispiece, 43, and Dalley, *Myths from Mesopotamia*, 316. A Greek vase portrays the court of Hades in a positive light as a realm of activity (Eliot, *Myths*, 282–283), but a medieval image reproduced in

Robert Hughes, *Heaven and Hell in Western Art* (New York: Stein and Day, 1968), 193, pictures a grim place with Pluto bestial and Persephone withered in appearance. Yama sometimes appears as a terrifying figure—see Royal Ontario Museum, *Homage to Heaven, Homage to Earth: Chinese Treasures of the Royal Ontario Museum* (Toronto: University of Toronto Press, 1992), 195—or as an imposing figure—see Anthony Christie, *Chinese Mythology* (Feltham, Middlesex: Newnes Books, 1983), 134. See images of Mictlantecuhtli in Irene Nicholson, *Mexican and Central American Mythology* (London: Paul Hamlyn, 1967), 26, 108.

26. Jonathan B. Riess, *Luca Signorelli: The San Brizio Chapel, Orvieto* (New York: George Braziller, 1995), 69, 72–73. Pierluigi De Vecchi, *Michelangelo: The Vatican Frescoes* (New York: Abbeville Press, 1996), 242–249. D'Arcais, *Giotto*, 200–201. Clark, *Drawings by Sandro Botticelli, Inferno XVIII*.

27. Peter Strieder, *Albrecht Dürer: Paintings, Prints, Drawings* (New York: Abaris Books, 1989), 179, 263. Nicolò Rasmo, *Michael Pacher* (London: Phaidon, 1971), 111. Ruth Mellinkoff, *The Devil at Isenheim: Reflections of Popular Belief in Grünewald's Altarpiece* (Berkeley: University of California Press, 1988), 51–52. Philippe and Françoise Roberts-Jones, *Pieter Bruegel* (New York: Harry N. Abrams, 2002), 105–113. Charles de Tolnay, *Hieronymus Bosch* (New York: Reynal & Co., 1966), 186. For more devils, see Lorenzo Lorenzi, *Devils in Art: Florence, from the Middle Ages to the Renaissance* (Florence: Centro Di, 1997), and Robert Muchembled, *Damned: An Illustrated History of the Devil* (San Francisco: Chronicle Books, 2004). For non-Western images of the demonic, see Stephen Addiss, ed., *Japanese Ghosts and Demons: Art of the Supernatural* (New York: George Braziller, 1985); Robert N. Linrothe and Jeff Watt, eds., *Demonic Divine: Himalayan Arts and Beyond* (New York: Rubin Museum of Art, 2004); Knud Rasmussen, *Myter og sagn fra Grønland*, 3 vols. (Kjøbenhavn: Gyldendal, 1921–1925); Janet Catherine Berlo, *Spirit Beings and Sun Dancers: Black Hawk's Vision of the Lakota World* (New York: George Braziller, 2001).

28. Katharine Briggs, *An Encyclopedia of Fairies* (New York: Pantheon Books, 1976), 30–33, 45–49, 98–102, 246, 311–313, 328–330, 336–338, 353–355, 412, 418.

29. Carol Zaleski, *Otherworld Journeys: Accounts of Near-Death Experiences in Medieval and Modern Times* (New York: Oxford University Press, 1987), 50–51.

30. Sturluson, *Prose Edda*, 41–42. C. Guiteras-Holmes, *Perils of the Soul: The World View of a Tzotzil Indian* (New York: Free Press of Glencoe, 1961), 285.

31. Briggs, *Vanishing People*, 51. Ishida Eiichiro, "The *Kappa* Legend," *Folklore Studies* (Tokyo) 9 (1950): 1–152. Katharine Luomala, "The Menehune of Polynesia and Other Mythical Little People of Oceania," Bulletin 203, Bernice P. Bishop Museum, Honolulu, 1951. Gabriel Bannerman-Richter, *Mmoetia: The Mysterious Little People* (N.p., Gabari , 1987). John E. Roth, *American Elves: An Encyclopedia of Little People from the Lore of 380 Ethnic Groups of the Western Hemisphere* (Jefferson, NC: McFarland & Co., 1997), vii.

32. George Hans Heide, "Dwarfs in German Folk Legends: An Inquiry into the Human Qualities of These Creatures" (Ph.D. diss., University of California at Los Angeles, 1976), 92–98.

33. For Thor, see Branston, *Gods of the North*, 120–121; for Rama's flying chariots, see William Buck, *Ramayana* (New York: New American Library, 1978), 190, 278; and for Garuda, see Mode, *Fabulous Beasts and Demons*, 45. Kay Turner and Pat Jasper, "Day of the Dead: The Tex-

Mex Tradition," in *Halloween and Other Festivals of Death and Life*, ed. Jack Santino (Knoxville: University of Tennessee Press, 1994), 139–140. R. C. Finucane, *Ghosts: Appearances of the Dead and Cultural Transformation* (Amherst, NY: Prometheus Books, 1996), 10–12.

34. Dermot Mac Manus, *The Middle Kingdom: The Faerie World of Ireland* (Gerrards Cross, Bucks: Colin Smythe, 1973), 43–44.

35. For international traditions of the ferryman of souls, see Terpening, *Charon and the Crossing*, 13–16, and 51, 120 for the motif of paying Charon a fare. On Cerberus as guardian of Hades, see Grimal, *Larousse World Mythology*, 137; and for a vase painting of the monster captured by Herakles, see Eliot, *Myths*, 151. For Garmr as guardian of Hel, see Branston, *Gods of the North*, 91.

36. Dhalla, *Zoroastrian Theology*, 57, 177–178, 273–274. Cavendish, *Visions of Heaven and Hell*, 52–53.

37. León-Portilla, *Aztec Thought and Culture*, 124–125, 127.

38. Scenes of the Last Judgment were popular among Renaissance painters, one example being Fra Angelico's balanced composition of the saved entering heaven on the right hand of Christ while to the left devils herd sinners into hell (Hughes, *Heaven and Hell in Western Art*, 206–207). For last judgments in Islamic, Zoroastrian, and Buddhist traditions, see S.G.F. Brandon, *The Judgment of the Dead: The Idea of Life after Death in the Major Religions* (New York: Charles Scribner's Sons, 1967), 139–142, 153–160, 174–176. The Egyptian Book of the Dead and tomb paintings detailed the ordeals that the soul would encounter in the underworld, among them the weighing of the soul before Osiris. See Budge, *Egyptian Heaven and Hell*, 158–161. For the depiction of this incident in the Papyrus of Ani, see Budge, *Egyptian Religion*, 137.

39. *1 Enoch* in H.F.D. Sparks, ed., *The Apocryphal Old Testament* (Oxford: Clarendon Press, 1984), 201–221, 231–236.

40. Marie Rose Séguy, *The Miraculous Journey of Mahomet* (New York: George Braziller, 1977), 9–17.

41. Thomas Kren and Roger S. Wieck, *The Visions of Tondal, from the Library of Margaret of York* (Malibu, CA: J. Paul Getty Museum, 1990), 37–59. For a collection of texts describing journeys to heaven and hell, see Gardiner, *Visions of Heaven and Hell Before Dante*.

42. Arnold van Gennep, *The Rites of Passage* (Chicago: University of Chicago Press, 1960), 3, 11.

43. Zaleski, *Otherworld Journeys*, 18.

44. John G. Neihardt, *Black Elk Speaks* (New York: Pocket Books, 1972), 18–39.

45. Mircea Eliade, *Shamanism: Archaic Techniques of Ecstasy* (Princeton, NJ: Princeton University Press, 1972), 31–32, 182, 215–217.

46. Michael Simpson, trans., *The Metamorphoses of Ovid* (Amherst: University of Massachusetts Press, 2001), 165–166.

47. *Epic of Gilgamesh* in Dalley, *Myths from Mesopotamia*, 95–119.

48. Thompson, *Tales of the North American Indians*, 126–127.

49. The story, from the medieval account of Giraldus Cambrensis, appears in Briggs, *Encyclopedia of Fairies*, 118–120.

50. E. A. Wallis Budge, *Egyptian Literature*, vol. 1, *Legends of the Gods* (London: Kegan Paul, Trench, Trübner & Co., 1912), xxxix, 57, 59.

51. Enrique Florescano, *The Myth of Quetzalcoatl* (Baltimore: Johns Hopkins University Press, 1999), 7–58, esp. 14–23, 36, 42–43, 56.

52. George Hunt Williamson, *Secret Places of the Lion* (London: Neville Spearman, 1958), 8, 13, 219. Williamson, *Other Tongues—Other Flesh* (Amherst, WI: Amherst Press, 1953), 194–246. Clark, *UFO Encyclopedia*, 76–78.

53. Brinsley Le Poer Trench, *The Sky People* (New York: Award Books, [1960]), 24–55. Clark, *UFO Encyclopedia*, 79–80.

54. Wender, *Hesiod and Theognis*, 28–29, 38–39, 43–47, 50–52; also Michael Simpson, trans., *The Metamorphoses of Ovid* (Amherst: University of Massachusetts Press, 2001), 12, 14–17.

55. W. Raymond Drake, *Gods or Spacemen?* (New York: Signet Books, 1976), 8–9. Clark, *UFO Encyclopedia*, 80–81.

56. In *Ragnarok: The Age of Fire and Gravel* (1883), Ignatius Donnelly explained mythological descriptions of catastrophe and the end of Atlantis as the consequence of a comet grazing the earth. Immanuel Velikovsky's *Worlds in Collision* (1950) repeated this claim, with the blame shifted to the planets Venus and Mars trading orbits. In both cases the events occurred only thousands of years ago; in both cases mainstream science roundly rejected the claims.

57. "The Epic of Creation," in Dalley, *Myths from Mesopotamia*, 233–255. Zecharia Sitchin, *The 12th Planet* (New York: Stein and Day, 1976), 182, 193–210, 226, 229, 256–259, 291–300, 305–317, 329–332, 351–359, 364, 372–373.

58. Most of the following descriptions of abduction reports and comparisons with other types of narratives are based on a study of 270 UFO abduction reports available in the literature to 1985, a second study based on a survey of thirteen abduction investigators having collective experience with about a thousand cases, and a third study based on 437 reports from the literature from the beginning to 1998. See Thomas E. Bullard's *UFO Abductions: The Measure of a Mystery*, 2 vols. (Mount Rainier, MD: Fund for UFO Research, 1987); *The Sympathetic Ear: Investigators as Variables in UFO Abduction Reports* (Mount Rainier, MD: Fund for UFO Research, 1995); and "What's New in UFO Abductions: Has the Story Changed in 30 Years?" in *MUFON 1999 International UFO Symposium Proceedings*, ed. Walter H. Andrus Jr. and Irena Scott (Seguin, TX: Mutual UFO Network, 1999), 170–199.

59. Raymond E. Fowler, *The Andreasson Affair, Phase Two: The Continuing Investigation of a Woman's Abduction by Alien Beings* (Englewood Cliffs, NJ: Prentice-Hall, 1982), 80–87.

60. Rasmussen, *Myter og sagn fra Grønland*, 1:opposite 72. For a case of aliens entering a house through the wood of a closed door, see Raymond E. Fowler, *The Andreasson Affair: The Documented Investigation of a Woman's Abduction aboard a UFO* (Englewood Cliffs, NJ: Prentice-Hall, 1979), 23–24.

61. Joseph Nyman, "The Familiar Entity and Dual Reference in the Latent Encounter," *MUFON UFO Journal*, no. 251 (March 1989): 12.

62. Bullard, *UFO Abductions: The Measure of a Mystery*, 1:48, 58–59, 61, 64, 82, 104–105, 113, 143.

63. David M. Jacobs introduced a detailed abduction itinerary from his own investigations in *Secret Life: Firsthand Accounts of UFO Abductions* (New York: Simon & Schuster, 1992). He identified Mindscan, or close staring by an alien with enormous eyes for apparent extraction and implantation of thoughts (96–99), and staging, illusory scenarios seemingly designed by the

aliens to test a captive's emotional responses (149–153), as central elements of the examination procedures. A rereading of older cases makes clear that these elements were part of the story even before Jacobs recognized them.

64. Eliade, *Shamanism*, 34, 39–42, 45–48, 52.

65. Kren, *Visions of Tondal*, 41–42, 50–51. The soul-weighing scene is graphic in the Papyrus of Ani, reproduced in Cavendish, *Visions of Heaven and Hell*, 18–19.

66. See Eliade, *Shamanism*, 36, 38, 41, 43, 46 for examples of supernatural death and dismemberment by knife, spear, arrow, and hook as part of the shamanic initiation. Examples of devils well equipped for torture appear in Hughes, *Heaven and Hell in Western Art*, 209, 210, 213, 214. For an example of the balance in the Renaissance iconography of the Last Judgment, see Dirk De Vos, *Rogier van der Weyden: The Complete Works* (New York: Harry N. Abrams, 1999), 255.

67. Walter Stephens, *Demon Lovers: Witchcraft, Sex, and the Crisis of Belief* (Chicago: University of Chicago Press, 2002), 19, 101.

68. See Eliade, *Shamanism*, 34, 39–42; Neihardt, *Black Elk Speaks*, 21–26, for examples of spirits giving gifts of power to the initiate.

69. Though Virgil guides and protects Dante in hell, a guardian angel more often leads Christians through the otherworld; see Kren, *Visions of Tondal*, 40, 42–46, 51. For fairy deceptions, glamours, and shape-shifting, see Briggs, *Vanishing People*, 21, 68, 77–78, 90, 95–96, 109–110, 122. On demonic shape-shifting, see Jacobus Sprenger and Heinrich Kramer, *Malleus Maleficarum* (London: Folio Society, 1968), 95–98. Jacobs, *Secret Life*, 149–150, discusses alien abilities to appear in various forms.

70. For alien incubation chambers and hybrid presentations see Budd Hopkins, *Intruders* (New York: Random House, 1987), 155–160; Jacobs, *Secret Life*, 121–122, 153–186; David M. Jacobs, *The Threat* (New York: Simon & Schuster, 1998), 128–160.

71. Andrew Collins, "The Aveley Abduction, pt. III," *FSR* 24, no. 1 (June 1978): 9. Fowler, *Andreasson Affair*, 73–86, 95–100.

72. One shaman's initiatory dreams included visits to various seas, mountains, caves, the sky, and the underworld; see Eliade, *Shamanism*, 39–42, for the luminous cave, see 41. The Book of Gates depicts the underworld journey of the sun as a series of tasks and trials; see Erik Hornung, *The Ancient Egyptian Books of the Afterlife* (Ithaca, NY: Cornell University Press, 1999), 59–77. Kren, *Visions of Tondal*, 52, 58–59. Fowler, *Andreasson Affair, Phase II*, 109–113, 122–130.

73. For the supernatural lapse of time in fairyland, see Edwin Sidney Hartland, *The Science of Fairy Tales: An Inquiry into Fairy Mythology* (London: Walter Scott, 1891), chaps. 7 and 8; Briggs, *Vanishing People*, 11–26; Meyer, *Voyage of Bran*, 32. For the witch's spell of forgetting, see Eric Maple, "The Witches of Canewdon," *Folklore* 71 (1960): 242.

74. Elias Owen, *Welsh Folk-Lore: A Collection of the Folk-Tales and Legends of North Wales* (1896; Norwood PA: Norwood Editions, 1973), 93–94.

75. Betty Leddy, "La Llorona in Southern Arizona," *Western Folklore* 7 (1948): 272–277. Norman Cohn, *Europe's Inner Demons* (New York: Basic Books, 1975), 206. For examples of paralysis or injury from encounters with ghosts or balls of fire, see Ray B. Browne, *"A Night with the Hants" and Other Alabama Folk Experiences* (Bowling Green, OH: Bowling Green University Popular Press, 1976), 204–205; H. F. Feilberg, "Ghostly Lights," *Folk-Lore* 6 (1895): 294. For

injury from passing among fairies, see Richard Bovet, *Pandaemonium* (1684; Totowa, NJ: Rowman and Littlefield, 1975), 124–125. An example of pining away after a fairy encounter is in Mary Julia MacCulloch, "Folk-Lore of the Isle of Skye," *Folk-Lore* 33 (1922): 203. For ghost sickness, see Leland C. Wyman, W. W. Hill, and Iva Osanai, "Navajo Eschatology," University of New Mexico Bulletin, Anthropological Series, vol. 4, no. 1 (Albuquerque: University of New Mexico Press, 1942), 30.

76. Kenneth Ring, *The Omega Project: Near-Death Experiences, UFO Encounters, and Mind at Large* (New York: William Morrow & Co., 1992), 156, 175–176, 190, 218–222, 239–243. Keith Thompson, "The Stages of UFO Initiations," *Magical Blend*, no. 18 (February–April 1988): 9–16.

77. For an overview of the travel-tale genre, see Mary B. Campbell, *The Witness and the Other World: Exotic European Travel Writing, 400–1600* (Ithaca, NY: Cornell University Press, 1988).

78. *Odyssey*, Bks. 9–12.

79. James S. Romm, *The Edges of the Earth in Ancient Thought: Geography, Exploration, and Fiction* (Princeton, NJ: Princeton University Press, 1992), 19–20.

80. Knud Rasmussen, *Eskimo Folk-Tales* (Copenhagen: Gyldendal, 1921), 90–92.

81. Herodotus, in Francis R. B. Godolphin, ed., *The Greek Historians*, vol. 1 (New York: Random House, 1942), 4.13, 4.23, 4.25, 4.191.

82. Romm, *Edges of the Earth in Ancient Thought*, 86–88. John Block Friedman, *The Monstrous Races in Medieval Art and Thought* (Cambridge, MA: Harvard University Press, 1981), 5–25.

83. Pliny the Elder, *The Natural History of Pliny* (London: Henry G. Bohn, 1855), 2:122–135.

84. Marco Polo, *The Travels of Marco Polo* (New York: Orion Press, n.d.), 3.18.

85. John Mandeville, *Travels of Sir John Mandeville* (New York: Penguin Books, 1987), 134, 137.

86. Campbell, *The Witness and the Other World*, 171, 174, 180, 213, 226–227, 247–248. Valerie I. J. Flint, *The Imaginative Landscape of Christopher Columbus* (Princeton, NJ: Princeton University Press, 1992), 138–144, 151–154.

87. Olaus Magnus, *Historia de Gentibus Septentrionalibus: Description of the Northern People* (London: Hakluyt Society, 1996), 1:105.

88. *Classic of the Mountains and Seas* (New York: Penguin Books, 1999), 159, 169, 177, 181, 185, 193. See also Richard E. Strassberg, ed., *A Chinese Bestiary: Strange Creatures from the Guideways through Mountains and Seas* (Berkeley: University of California Press, 2002).

89. Historians have served the plurality of worlds exceptionally well in Steven J. Dick, *Plurality of Worlds: The Origins of the Extraterrestrial Life Debate from Democrates to Kant* (New York: Cambridge University Press, 1982) and *The Biological Universe: The Twentieth Century Extraterrestrial Life Debate and the Limits of Science* (Cambridge University Press, 1996), and in Michael J. Crowe, *The Extraterrestrial Life Debate 1750–1900: The Idea of a Plurality of Worlds from Kant to Lowell* (Cambridge University Press, 1986).

90. Crowe, *The Extraterrestrial Life Debate*, 27–29. Bernard le Bovier de Fontenelle, *Conversations on the Plurality of Worlds* (Berkeley: University of California Press, 1990), 49, 60.

91. Christian Huygens, *The Celestial Worlds Discover'd* (London: Frank Cass & Co., 1968), 17, 20–24, 27, 37, 41, 50–51, 54, 60–64, 71–79.

92. Crowe, *The Extraterrestrial Life Debate*, 62–68, 203–207, 223–225, 236. William Herschel,

"On the Remarkable Appearances at the Polar Regions of the Planet Mars," *Philosophical Transactions of the Royal Society* 74 (1784): 273.

93. Thomas Dick, *Celestial Scenery* (Brookfield, MA: E. & L. Merriam, 1838), 280; see also Crowe, *The Extraterrestrial Life Debate*, 198–200.

94. Richard A. Proctor, *Other Worlds than Ours: The Plurality of Worlds Studied under the Light of Recent Scientific Researches* (New York: D. Appleton & Co., 1880), 152–158, 173–174, 187, 191–193.

95. Camille Flammarion, *Popular Astronomy* (London: Chatto & Windus, 1907), 469–470, 639, 673. Idem, *Urania* (Boston: Estes & Lauriat, 1890), 232–256.

96. John Lear, *Kepler's Dream* (Berkeley: University of California Press, 1965), 123–124, 150–158. David S. Evans, "The Great Moon Hoax," *Sky and Telescope* 62, no. 3 (1981): 196–198; no. 4 (1981): 308–311.

97. George Griffith, "Stories of Other Worlds," in *Science Fiction by the Rivals of H. G. Wells*, ed. Alan K. Russell (Secaucus, NJ: Castle Books, 1979), 117–188.

98. Hoskin, *Cambridge Illustrated History of Astronomy*, 287. Dick, *Biological Universe*, 167–170.

99. See Crowe, *The Extraterrestrial Life Debate*, 265–353.

100. Alfred Russel Wallace, *Man's Place in the Universe: A Study of the Results of Scientific Research in Relation to the Unity or Plurality of Worlds* (New York: McClure, Phillips & Co., 1903), 182, 195, 205–215, 229–239, 258–266, 304–305, 311–312.

101. Camille Flammarion's history of Mars observations, *La planète Mars et ses conditions d'habitabilité: Synthèse générale de toutes les observations* (Paris: Gauthier-Villars et Fils, 1892), covers the earliest observations to the first results from 1892 and profuse illustrations offer a striking display of the growth of astronomical knowledge as vague spots of the seventeenth century resolve into distinctive surface features by the nineteenth. A second volume published in 1909 covered subsequent work through the early years of the twentieth century. For an excellent modern treatment of the history of Mars study, see William Sheehan, *The Planet Mars: A History of Observation and Discovery* (Tucson: University of Arizona Press, 1996); see p. 74 for Schiaparelli's 1877 map.

102. See Sheehan, *The Planet Mars*, 71–77 for discovery of the canals, and Flammarion, *La planète Mars*, 332–333 for Schiaparelli's 1879 map.

103. Flammarion, *La planète Mars*, 353–356, 391–395, 472. See also Schiaparelli's series of seven memoirs covering each opposition from 1877 to 1890.

104. Richard Anthony Proctor, "Canals on the Planet Mars," *Knowledge* 14 (April 1882): 519.

105. "Life in Mars," *Chambers's Journal* 12 (June 12, 1886): 370.

106. Sheehan, *The Planet Mars*, 88.

107. "Schiaparelli's Latest Views Regarding Mars," in *Mars*, ed. William H. Pickering (Boston: Richard G. Badger, 1921), 92. First published in 1894 in *Astronomy and Astrophysics*, Pickering's translation of an article by Schiaparelli remained the primary direct source of his views available in English throughout the canal controversy.

108. Sheehan, *The Planet Mars*, 98–109.

109. Percival Lowell, *Mars* (Boston: Houghton, Mifflin & Co., 1895), 207–208.

110. Lowell, *Mars*, 200–212; idem, *Mars as the Abode of Life* (New York: Macmillan, 1908), 184–216, esp. 208–209, 214.

111. Lowell, *Mars*, 202–205, 211.

112. Ibid., 208–209.

113. Lowell, *Mars as the Abode of Life*, 216.

114. H. G. Wells, "The Things That Live on Mars," *Cosmopolitan*, March 1908, 334–342.

115. Frank H. Winter, "The Strange Case of Madame Guzman and the Mars Mystique," *Griffith Observer* 48, no. 2 (1984): 2–15. A. Mercier, *Communications avec Mars* (Orléans, France: Imprimerie Orléanaise, 1899), 13–17. Dick, *Biological Universe*, 401–402, 408. Jeffrey Sconce, *Haunted Media: Electronic Presence from Telegraphy to Television* (Durham, NC: Duke University Press, 2000), 95–103. Nikola Tesla, "Talking with the Planets," *Collier's Weekly*, February 19, 1901, 4–5.

116. E. M. Antoniadi, "Reports of the Observing Sections: Mars Section," *Journal of the British Astronomical Association* 20, no. 2 (1909): 79.

117. E. C. Slipher, *Mars: The Photographic Story* (Cambridge, MA: Sky, 1962), 116, 138. Tsuneo Saheki, "Martian Phenomena Suggesting Volcanic Activity," *Sky and Telescope* 14, no. 4 (1955): 144–146.

118. I. S. Shklovskii and Carl Sagan, *Intelligent Life in the Universe* (San Francisco: Holden-Day, 1966), 373–374. F. Zigel, "There IS Intelligent Life on Mars," *Space World* 1, no. 10 (1961): 20–21, 48–51. For ufologists' interpretations of the moons, W-clouds, and light flashes, see Donald E. Keyhoe, *The Flying Saucer Conspiracy* (New York: Henry Holt & Co., 1955), 122–130; Max B. Miller, *Flying Saucers: Fact or Fiction?* (Los Angeles: Trend Books, 1957), 52–61; Aimé Michel, "Do Flying Saucers Come from Mars?" *FSR* 6, no. 2 (1960): 13–15; W. R. Drake, "Is There Life on Mars?" *FSR* 6, no. 3 (1960), 27–29; Jacques Vallee and Janine Vallee, "Mars and the Flying Saucers," *FSR* 8, no. 5 (1962), 5–11.

119. Donald Keyhoe, *The Flying Saucers Are Real* (New York: Fawcett Publications, 1950), 129–131; Keyhoe, *Flying Saucer Conspiracy*, 122.

120. Sheehan, *The Planet Mars*, 149–151, 154–161, 165–166, 190–192, 201–203.

121. Robert Naeye, "Was There Life on Mars?" *Astronomy* 24, no. 11 (1996): 46–53. Vanessa Thomas, "Life on Mars Debate Heats Up," *Astronomy* 30, no. 11 (2002): 28.

122. For examples of "Martian" or extraterrestrial aircraft visiting the earth in the nineteenth and early twentieth century, see "A Celestial Visitor," *Lincoln (NE) Daily State Journal*, June 8, 1884, 5; "The Magical Meteor," *Lincoln (NE) Daily State Journal*, June 10, 1884, 4. "Three Strange Visitors," *Stockton (CA) Evening Mail*, November 27, 1896, 1. "The Great Aerial Wanderer," *Dallas Morning News*, April 19, 1897, 5. "Airship Steals a Calf," *Kansas City Times*, April 27, 1897, 1. "Golden Haired Girl Is in It," *St. Louis Post-Dispatch*, April 19, 1897, 1. "Airship of the Past," *Houston Post*, May 2, 1897, 4. "Is Mars Signalling Kent?" *Seattle Post-Intelligencer*, February 11, 1908, 2. "A Visit from Mars," *Wellington Evening Post* (New Zealand), July 30, 1909, 6. For Mars and Martians in advertising, entertainment, and comic strips around the turn of the twentieth century, see "The First Message from Mars," Pears Soap advertisement, 1901; Raymond Taylor, "A Signal from Mars: March and Two Step," arranged by E. T. Paull (New York: E. T. Paull Music Co., 1901); and Winsor McCay, *The Complete Little Nemo in Slumberland, 1910–1911* (Seattle: Fantagraphic Books, 1990), 4:26–42.

123. Griffith, "Stories of Other Worlds," in Russell, *Science Fiction by the Rivals of H. G. Wells*, 131–144.

124. John Flint Roy, comp., *A Guide to Barsoom* (New York: Ballantine Books, 1976), 1–4, 6–10.

125. Kurd Lasswitz, *Two Planets* (Carbondale: Southern Illinois University Press, 1971).

126. H. G. Wells, *A Critical Edition of The War of the Worlds: H. G. Wells's Scientific Romance*, introduction and notes by David Y. Hughes and Harry M. Geduld (Bloomington: Indiana University Press, 1993), 51.

127. Ibid., 52.

128. Ibid.

129. Ibid., 148–151.

130. Hadley Cantril, *The Invasion from Mars: A Study in the Psychology of Panic* (New York: Harper Torchbooks, 1966), 158–160. For an early identification of the Orson Welles broadcast panic as the reason for government secrecy about flying saucers, see Donald E. Keyhoe, *The Flying Saucers from Outer Space* (New York: Henry Holt & Co., 1953), 12.

131. Harold Spencer Jones, *Life on Other Worlds* (New York: Mentor Books, 1964), 149–154. Robert Zimmerman, "Seeking Other Earths," *Astronomy* 32, no. 8 (2004): 42–47. Ray Villard, "Lucifer's Planets," *Astronomy* 33, no. 1 (2005): 68–71.

132. Robert Pappalardo, "Jupiter's Water World," *Astronomy* 32, no. 7 (2004): 34–41.

133. Dick, *Biological Universe*, 414–431.

134. Webb, *If the Universe Is Teeming with Aliens*, 2, 17–18.

135. Ibid., 159. For an extended discussion of the many conditions necessary for a Goldilocks planet, see Peter D. Ward and Donald Brownlee, *Rare Earth: Why Complex Life Is Uncommon in the Universe* (New York: Copernicus Books, 2004), with a summary of required conditions on xxxi–xxxii, and "A Galaxy's Dead Zone," *Sky and Telescope* 116, no. 5 (2008): 20.

136. Webb, *If the Universe Is Teeming with Aliens*, 163, 184–189.

137. Ernst Mayr, *What Makes Biology Unique? Considerations on the Autonomy of a Scientific Discipline* (New York: Cambridge University Press, 2004), 209–217, esp. 214. Simon Conway Morris, *Life's Solution: Inevitable Humans in a Lonely Universe* (New York: Cambridge University Press, 2003), xiii–xvi, 87–105, 228, 329. See also George Gaylord Simpson, "The Nonprevalence of Humanoids," *This View of Life: The World of an Evolutionist* (New York: Harcourt, Brace & World, 1964), 253–271, esp. 265–269. Stephen Jay Gould, "SETI and the Wisdom of Casey Stengel," *The Flamingo's Smile: Reflections in Natural History* (New York: W. W. Norton & Co., 1985), 403–413.

138. Webb, *If the Universe Is Teeming with Aliens*, 46–51.

139. Robert Collins, "The UFO Propulsion System Is Not Nuclear," *Peregrine Communications*, http://www.ufoconspiracy.com/.

140. "The Phoenix Lights," *UFOs at Close Sight*, http://ufologie.net/htm/phoenix.htm.

141. *The UFO Phenomenon* (Alexandria, VA: Time-Life Books, 1987), 100–101. Hilary Evans, *UFOs: The Greatest Mystery* (London: Chartwell Books, 1979), 68–69.

Chapter 5. The Space Children

1. Clifford Geertz, *Negara: The Theatre State in Nineteenth-Century Bali* (Princeton, NJ: Princeton University Press, 1980), 136.

2. For an overview of abductions, see Thomas E. Bullard, "Abduction Phenomenon," in *The*

UFO Encyclopedia: The Phenomenon from the Beginning, 2nd ed., ed. Jerome Clark (Detroit: Omnigraphics, 1998), 1–26.

3. Jim Lorenzen and Coral Lorenzen, *Abducted!* (New York: Berkley, 1977), 9–24.

4. Andrew Collins, "The Aveley Abduction, pts. I–III," *FSR* 23, no. 6 (1978): 13–21, 21–25; 24, no. 1 (1978): 5–15.

5. Lew Willis, "Mother and Child Texas Abduction Case," *MUFON UFO Journal*, no. 167 (January 1982): 3–7.

6. Budd Hopkins, *Missing Time* (New York: Richard Marek, 1981), 128–153, 184–215.

7. Raymond E. Fowler, *The Andreasson Affair, Phase Two* (Englewood Cliffs, NJ: Prentice-Hall, 1982), 42–56, 79–93, 94–179, 183–186.

8. Budd Hopkins, *Intruders* (New York: Random House, 1987), 195–197. For examples of the character of childhood experiences, see Whitley Strieber and Anne Strieber, eds., *The Communion Letters* (New York: HarperPrism, 1997), 13–48. See also Thomas E. Bullard, *UFO Abductions: The Measure of a Mystery* (Mount Rainier, MD: Fund for UFO Research, 1987), 1:36, 263; idem, *The Sympathetic Ear: Investigators as Variables in UFO Abduction Reports* (Mount Rainier, MD: Fund for UFO Research, 1995), 60–64.

9. Hopkins, *Intruders*, 76–83, 121–122, 154–163.

10. Ibid., 164–173. David M. Jacobs, *Secret Life* (New York: Simon & Schuster, 1992), 107–131, 153–186.

11. Bullard, *UFO Abductions*, 1:106–107, 115; idem, "UFO Abductions," in Clark, *The UFO Encyclopedia*, 15. For examples of apocalyptic visions and scenes of devastation, see Strieber, *Communion*, 64–66; John E. Mack, *Abduction: Human Encounters with Aliens* (New York: Charles Scribner's Sons, 1994), 104, 323–324, 327, 395.

12. David M. Jacobs, *The Threat* (New York: Simon & Schuster, 1998), 127, 128–130, 161, 185–186, 226–253.

13. Strieber, *Communion*, 215, 283, 294–295; Strieber, *Transformation*, 242–243.

14. Mack, *Abduction*, 39–40, 415; John E. Mack, *Passport to the Cosmos* (New York: Crown, 1999), 207.

15. Joseph Nyman, "The Familiar Entity and Dual Reference in the Latent Encounter," *MUFON UFO Journal*, no. 251 (March 1989): 10–12. Mack, *Passport to the Cosmos*, 17, 278–279.

16. Sharon Begley, "The IQ Puzzle," *Newsweek*, May 6, 1996, 70–72.

17. Phoebe Lauren, *Star Children among Us* (West Palm Beach, FL: Garev Publishing International, 2004), 7–27. See also "Indigo Child," *The Skeptics Dictionary*, http://skepdic.com/indigo.html and *The Star Children*, http://www.reconnections.net/starchild.htm.

18. Lauren, *Star Children among Us*, 8, 32–34.

19. See case histories in Jenny Randles, *Star Children* (London: Robert Hale, 1994). See also Colin Wilson, *Alien Dawn: An Investigation into the Contact Experience* (London: Virgin, 1998), 309. Helen Littrell and Jean Bilodeux's *Raechel's Eyes* (Columbus, NC: Granite, 2005) alleges that Littrell's blind daughter had an unusual college roommate who might have been an alien hybrid living in everyday society.

20. Strieber, *Communion*, 65–66.

21. Linda Moulton Howe, *Glimpses of Other Realities*, vol. 1, *Facts and Eyewitnesses* (Huntingdon Valley, PA: LMH Productions, 1993), 209–210, 221.

22. See Norman Cohn, *Europe's Inner Demons* (New York: Basic Books, 1975), 206–224.

23. Needham, *Primordial Characters*, 41–42.

24. Cohn, *Europe's Inner Demons*, 206–210. For comparisons of Old and New World witches associated with owls, see Alex Scobie, "Strigiform Witches in Roman and Other Cultures," *Fabula* 19 (1978): 74–101.

25. Ovid, *Fasti*, trans. James George Frazer (Cambridge, MA: Harvard University Press, 1996; Loeb Classical Library, Ovid V), 327–331.

26. John Cuthbert Lawson, *Modern Greek Folklore and Ancient Greek Religion: A Study in Survivals* (New York: University Books, 1964), 181.

27. Sarah Iles Johnston, "Defining the Dreadful: Remarks on the Greek Child-Killing Demon," in *Ancient Magic and Ritual Power*, ed. Marvin Meyer and Paul Mirecki (Boston: Brill Academic, 2001), 365–380.

28. Edward Langton, *Essentials of Demonology* (London: Epworth Press, 1949), 15–16.

29. Raphael Patai, *The Hebrew Goddess* (Detroit: Wayne State University Press, 1990), 223–224, 233–237. For the goddess with talons and flanked by owls, see the British Museum Web site on the *Queen of the Night* relief, http://www.britishmuseum.org/explore/highlights/highlight_objects/me/t/the_queen_of_the_night_relief.aspx.

30. Cohn, *Europe's Inner Demons*, 209. Andreas Johns, *Baba Yaga: The Ambiguous Mother and Witch of the Russian Folktale* (New York: Peter Lang, 2004), 85–92.

31. E. E. Evans-Pritchard, *Witchcraft, Oracles and Magic among the Azande* (Oxford: Clarendon Press, 1937), 33–39. Lucy Mair, *Witchcraft* (New York: McGraw-Hill, 1969), 33–42. John Middleton and E. H. Winter, eds., *Witchcraft and Sorcery in East Africa* (London: Routledge & Kegan Paul, 1963), 62–67, 99–101, 196–197, 225–227, 262–263.

32. Godfrey Lienhardt, "Some Notions of Witchcraft among the Dinka," *Africa: Journal of the International African Institute* 21 (1951): 305–310.

33. J. R. Crawford, *Witchcraft and Sorcery in Rhodesia* (London: Oxford University Press, 1967), 112–122.

34. Bronislaw Malinowski, *Argonauts of the Western Pacific* (New York: E. P. Dutton & Co., 1961), 76, 237–244.

35. Maximo D. Ramos, *Creatures of Philippine Lower Mythology* (Manila: University of the Philippines Press, 1971), 12–15, 62–68, 106–110, 127–134, esp. 114–123.

36. Barend J. ter Haar, *Telling Stories: Witchcraft and Scapegoating in Chinese History* (Leiden: Brill, 2006), 1, 28–32, chap. 3.

37. Philip A. Kuhn, *Soulstealers: The Chinese Sorcery Scare of 1768* (Cambridge, MA: Harvard University Press, 1990), 1–29, esp. 26–27, 78.

38. Shinichi Segi, *Yoshitoshi: The Splendid Decadent* (Tokyo: Kodansha International, 1985), 81, 144.

39. Clyde Kluckhohn, *Navaho Witchcraft* (Boston: Beacon Press, 1944), 25–27. Margaret K. Brady, *"Some Kind of Power": Navajo Children's Skinwalker Narratives* (Salt Lake City: University of Utah Press, 1984), 19–21.

40. Nathan Wachtel, *Gods and Vampires* (Chicago: University of Chicago Press, 1994), 72–74.

41. Hugo G. Nutini and John M. Roberts, *Bloodsucking Witchcraft: An Epistemological Study of Anthropomorphic Supernaturalism in Rural Tlaxcala* (Tucson: University of Arizona Press, 1993), 54–60, 64–68, 132–153.

42. Wachtel, *Gods and Vampires*, 82–85.

43. Shirley L. Arora, "La Llorona: The Naturalization of a Legend," *Southwest Folklore* 5, no. 1 (1981): 23–40. Judith S. Beatty, ed., *La Llorona: Encounters with the Weeping Woman* (Santa Fe: Sunstone Press, 2004), xi–xii, 1–2.

44. Stephen Ellis, "Witching-Times: A Theme in the History of Africa and Europe," in *Imagining Evil: Witchcraft Beliefs and Accusations in Contemporary Africa*, ed. Gerrie ter Haar (Trenton, NJ: Africa World Press, 2007), 44–45.

45. Peter Geschiere, *The Modernity of Witchcraft: Politics and the Occult in Postcolonial Africa* (Charlottesville: University Press of Virginia, 1997), 3–10, 39–40, 69.

46. Adeline Masquelier, "Of Headhunters and Cannibals: Migrancy, Labor, and Consumption in the Mawri Imagination," *Cultural Anthropology* 15 (2000): 92–95.

47. Francis B. Nyamnjah, "Delusions of Development and the Enrichment of Witchcraft Discourses in Cameroon," in *Magical Interpretations, Material Realities: Modernity, Witchcraft and the Occult in Postcolonial Africa*, ed. Henrietta L. Moore and Todd Sanders (New York: Routledge, 2001), 33–34.

48. Rosalind Shaw, "Cannibal Transformations: Colonialism and Commodification in the Sierra Leone Hinterland," in *Magical Interpretations, Material Realities: Modernity, Witchcraft and the Occult in Postcolonial Africa*, ed. Henrietta L. Moore and Todd Sanders (New York: Routledge, 2001), 66.

49. Alexander Rödlach, *Witches, Westerners, and HIV: AIDS and Cultures of Blame in Africa* (Walnut Creek, CA: Left Coast Press, 2006), 55.

50. Ibid., 73–84.

51. Ibid., 119, 122, 144–149.

52. Cohn, *Europe's Inner Demons*, 153–155, 159–163.

53. Ibid., 147, 225–232.

54. Ibid., 208–219.

55. Venetia Newall, "The Jew as Witch Figure," in *The Witch Figure*, ed. Venetia Newall (London: Routledge & Kegan Paul, 1973), 95–124, esp. 111–114.

56. Cohn, *Europe's Inner Demons*, 1–15. Walter L. Wakefield and Austin P. Evans, eds., *Heresies of the High Middle Ages* (New York: Columbia University Press, 1991), 103.

57. Jacobus Sprenger and Heinrich Kramer, *Malleus Maleficarum: The Hammer of Witchcraft* (London: Folio Society, 1968), 48–53, 72–81, 127–133.

58. Alexander Eliot, *Myths* (New York: McGraw-Hill, 1976), 75, 195. Irène Aghion, Claire Barbillon, and François Lissarrague, *Gods and Heroes of Classical Antiquity* (New York: Flammarion, 1996), 263.

59. Karel van der Toorn, Bob Becking, and Pieter W. van der Horst, eds., *Dictionary of Deities and Demons in the Bible* (Leiden: E. J. Brill, 1995), 1163–1167, 1681–1682.

60. Katharine Briggs, *An Encyclopedia of Fairies* (New York: Pantheon Books, 1976), 183–184; idem, *The Vanishing People: Fairly Lore and Legends* (New York: Pantheon Books, 1978), 70, 81–82, 147, 168. Keith Thomas opens a window on the well-populated supernatural belief-world of sixteenth- and seventeenth-century England in *Religion and the Decline of Magic*, with ghosts and fairies treated on pp. 587–614.

61. Briggs, *Encyclopedia of Fairies*, 62–66; Briggs, *The Vanishing People*, 93–94.

62. Briggs, *The Vanishing People*, 95–96.

63. David M. Jacobs, *Secret Life* (New York: Simon & Schuster, 1992), 149–150.

64. Briggs, *Encyclopedia of Fairies*, 69–70; Briggs, *The Vanishing People*, 100–103.

65. Briggs, *Encyclopedia of Fairies*, 354–355, 386–387.

66. Ibid., 286–287, 394–395.

67. Michael P. Carroll, *The Cult of the Virgin Mary: Psychological Origins* (Princeton, NJ: Princeton University Press, 1986), 123–124, 156–158, 174–177; see other examples in Sandra L. Zimdars-Swartz, *Encountering Mary: Visions of Mary from La Salette to Medjugorje* (New York: Avon Books, 1992). Ingvald Raknem, *Joan of Arc in History, Legend and Literature* (Oslo: Universitetsforlaget, 1971), 19–22.

68. David Finkelhor, *Sexually Victimized Children* (New York: Free Press, 1979), 1–2. Debbie Nathan and Michael Snedeker, *Satan's Silence: Ritual Abuse and the Making of a Modern American Witch Hunt* (New York: BasicBooks, 1995), 3–7.

69. Nathan and Snedeker, *Satan's Silence*, 67–92.

70. Judith Herman, *Trauma and Recovery* (New York: Basic Books, 1992), 8–9, 28–32.

71. Ellen Bass and Laura Davis, *The Courage to Heal: A Guide for Women Survivors of Child Sexual Abuse* (New York: Harper & Row, 1988), 21, 42, 58–59, 86–90, 307–310. Richard Ofshe and Ethan Watters, *Making Monsters: False Memories, Psychotherapy, and Sexual Hysteria* (New York: Charles Scribner's Sons, 1994), 1–3.

72. Jennifer J. Freyd, *Betrayal Trauma: The Logic of Forgetting Childhood Abuse* (Cambridge, MA: Harvard University Press, 1996), 4, 9–11, 22.

73. Some reports of recovered memories of sexual abuse came from a former Miss America, Marilyn Van Derbur Atler ("The Darkest Secret," *People*, June 10, 1991, 88–94), and actress Roseann (Barr) Arnold ("A Star Cries Incest," *People*, October 7, 1991, 84–88).

74. Michelle Smith and Lawrence Pazder, *Michelle Remembers* (New York: Pocket Books, 1980).

75. Nathan and Snedeker, *Satan's Silence*, 107–159. Ofshe and Watters, *Making Monsters*, 177–204.

76. Jeffrey S. Victor, *Satanic Panic: The Creation of a Contemporary Legend* (Chicago: Open Court, 1973), 27–36, 330–354.

77. Elizabeth Loftus and Katherine Ketcham, *The Myth of Repressed Memory: False Memories and Allegations of Sexual Abuse* (New York: St. Martin's Press, 1994), 88–90, 150–171. Nathan and Snedeker, *Satan's Silence*, 1–7, 37–38, 88–91, 112–114, 116. Ofshe and Watters, *Making Monsters*, 1–8, 177–196.

78. Phillips Stevens Jr., "The Demonology of Satanism: An Anthropological View," in *The Satanism Scare*, ed. James T. Richardson, Joel Best, and David G. Bromley (Hawthorne, NY: Aldine de Gruyter, 1991), 21–22.

79. Arlette Farge and Jacques Revel, *The Vanishing Children of Paris: Rumor and Politics before the French Revolution* (Cambridge, MA: Harvard University Press, 1991), 18–28, 104–113.

80. Paula S. Fass, *Kidnapped: Child Abduction in America* (New York: Oxford University Press, 1997), 57–58, 95–96, 99, 106–110.

81. David H. Bennett, *The Party of Fear: From Nativist Movements to the New Right in*

American History (Chapel Hill: University of North Carolina Press, 1988), 35–41, 80–92. Richard Hofstadter, *The Paranoid Style in American Politics and Other Essays* (New York: Alfred A. Knopf, 1965), 19–23.

82. Bennett, *The Party of Fear*, 42–47. Maria Monk, *Awful Disclosures of the Hotel Dieu Nunnery*, in *Veil of Fear: Nineteenth-Century Convent Tales by Rebecca Reed and Maria Monk* (West Lafayette, IN: NotaBell Books / Purdue University Press, 1999).

83. Bennett, *The Party of Fear*, 162.

84. William F. Wu, *The Yellow Peril: Chinese Americans in American Fiction 1850–1940* (Hamden, CT: Archon Books, 1982), 30, 164–174. Herbert Aptheker, *American Negro Slave Revolts* (New York: International, 1974), 18, 53, 368–370. Dennis Rome, *Black Demons: The Media's Depiction of the African American Male Criminal Stereotype* (Westport, CT: Praeger, 2004), 19–22, 46–53.

85. Frederick K. Grittner, *White Slavery: Myth, Ideology, and American Law* (New York: Garland, 1990), 3–4, 61–76. Clifford Roe, *The Great War on White Slavery* (1911; New York: Garland, 1979), 27–81.

86. Jan Harold Brunvand, *Encyclopedia of Urban Legends* (Santa Barbara, CA: ABC-Clio, 2001), 277–278.

87. Bennett, *The Party of Fear*, 183–198, 286–310.

88. Bradford W. Wright, *Comic Book Nation: The Transformation of Youth Culture in America* (Baltimore: Johns Hopkins University Press, 2001), xvi, 88–90, 92–98, 157–164.

89. Wright, *Comic Book Nation*, 90–92, 156.

90. Loretta Schwartz-Nobel, *Poisoned Nation: Pollution, Greed, and the Rise of Deadly Epidemics* (New York: St. Martin's Press, 2007), xvi–xix, 85–101. Steven Novella, "The Anti-Vaccination Movement," *Skeptical Inquirer* 31, no. 6 (2007): 25–31.

91. Hanns Heinz Ewers, *Alraune*, in Ray Furness, ed., *The Daedalus Book of German Decadence: Voices of the Abyss* (New York: Daedalus / Hippocrene, 1994), 206–253.

92. Arlene Judith Klotzko, *A Clone of Your Own? The Science and Ethics of Cloning* (New York: Oxford University Press, 2004), xxi–xxiii, xxxi–xxxii, 7–13, 110–111, 122. Jane Maienschein, *Whose View of Life? Embryos, Cloning and Stem Cells* (Cambridge, MA: Harvard University Press, 2003), 123–155.

93. H. G. Wells, *Star Begotten*, in *28 Science Fiction Stories* (New York: Dover, 1952), 510–635, see esp. 537–542, 546–552, 563, 596–600, 612–615, 625.

Chapter 6. Secret Worlds and Promised Lands

1. E. A. Wallis Budge, *The Egyptian Heaven and Hell* (La Salle, IL: Open Court, 1974), 41–42, 48; idem, *Egyptian Religion: Egyptian Ideas of the Future Life* (Boston: Routledge & Kegan Paul, 1975), 176. Raymond O. Faulkner, *The Ancient Egyptian Book of the Dead* (New York: Macmillan, 1972), 10.

2. Jean Delumeau, *History of Paradise: The Garden of Eden in Myth and Tradition* (New York: Continuum, 1995), 6–10, 39–55, 109–115, 135–137. Katharine Briggs, *An Encyclopedia of*

Fairies (New York: Pantheon Books, 1976), 400–401. Edwin Bernbaum, *The Way to Shambhala* (Los Angeles: Jeremy P. Tarcher, 1989), 3. Valerie I. J. Flint, *The Imaginative Landscape of Christopher Columbus* (Princeton, NJ: Princeton University Press, 1992), 154.

3. Herman Pleij, *Dreaming of Cockaigne: Medieval Fantasies of the Perfect Life* (New York: Columbia University Press, 1997), 3, 89–90.

4. Hal Rammel, *Nowhere in America: The Big Rock Candy Mountain and Other Comic Utopias* (Urbana: University of Illinois Press, 1990), opposite of title page. Harry McClintock sings the song on the soundtrack of the movie *O Brother, Where Art Thou?* (Universal City, CA: Mercury Records 088170069–2, 2000).

5. Jesse Hutchinson Jr., "Uncle Sam's Farm," from *Union and Liberty! Music Heard on the Northern Home Front during the Civil War,* performed by D. C. Hall's New Concert and Quadrille Band (Troy, NY: Dorian Recordings, DOR-90197, 1994).

6. Lyman Tower Sargent, "Utopian Traditions: Themes and Variations," in Roland Schaer, Gregory Claeys, and Lyman Tower Sargent, eds., *Utopia: The Search for the Ideal Society in the Western World* (New York: New York Public Library / Oxford University Press, 2000), 11–14.

7. Roland Schaer, "Utopia: Space, Time, History," in Schaer et al., *Utopia,* 3–4.

8. Ruth Bloch, *Visionary Republic: Millennial Themes in American Thought, 1756–1800* (New York: Cambridge University Press, 1985), 75–93.

9. Alain Touraine, "Society as Utopia," in Schaer et al., *Utopia,* 22–23.

10. Chad Walsh, *From Utopia to Nightmare* (Westport, CT: Greenwood Press, 1962), 24–28.

11. Walsh, *From Utopia to Nightmare,* 129–134.

12. See John Passmore, *The Perfectibility of Man* (New York: Charles Scribner's Sons, 1970).

13. Peter Worsley, *The Trumpet Shall Sound* (New York: Schoken Books, 1968), 80–85.

14. James Mooney, *The Ghost-Dance Religion and the Sioux Outbreak of 1890* (Chicago: University of Chicago Press, 1965), 19, 29.

15. Hélène Clastres, *The Land-without-Evil: Tupí-Guaraní Prophetism* (Urbana: University of Illinois Press, 1995), viii.

16. Norman Cohn, "How Time Acquired a Consummation," in *Apocalypse Theory and the Ends of the World,* ed. Malcolm Bull (Cambridge, MA: Blackwell, 1995), 21–37.

17. Camille Flammarion, *Popular Astronomy* (London: Chatto & Windus, 1907), 78–80.

18. Anthony F. C. Wallace, "Revitalization Movements," *American Anthropologist,* n.s., 58 (1956): 264–281.

19. Paul Boyer, *When Time Shall Be No More: Prophecy Belief in Modern American Culture* (Cambridge, MA: Harvard University Press, 1992), 11.

20. Bernard McGinn, *Antichrist: Two Thousand Years of the Human Fascination with Evil* (San Francisco: HarperSanFranciso, 1994), 256–257, 260.

21. David Redles, *Hitler's Millennial Reich: Apocalyptic Belief and the Search for Salvation* (New York: New York University Press, 2005), 1–13.

22. Peter J. S. Duncan, *Russian Messianism: Third Rome, Revolution, Communism and After* (New York: Routledge, 2000), 48–61.

23. Richard T. Hughes, *Myths America Lives By* (Urbana: University of Illinois Press, 2003), 5–8.

24. Daniel Wojcik, *The End of the World as We Know It: Faith, Fatalism, and Apocalypse in America* (New York: New York University Press, 1997), 34–35, 38–39. Boyer, *When Time Shall Be No More*, 96. Hughes, *Myths America Lives By*, 87–88.

25. Wojcik, *The End of the World as We Know It*, 165–170.

26. Martin W. Lewis, *Green Delusions: An Environmentalist Critique of Radical Environmentalism* (Durham, NC: Duke University, 1992), 3.

27. Patrick Lucanio, *Them or Us: Archetypal Interpretations of Fifties Alien Invasion Films* (Bloomington: Indiana University Press, 1987), 22–46. David Seed, *American Science Fiction and the Cold War: Literature and Film* (Edinburgh, Scotland: Edinburgh University Press, 1999), 133–134.

28. Michael Barkun, *A Culture of Conspiracy: Apocalyptic Visions in Contemporary America* (Berkeley: University of California Press, 2003), 39–40.

29. Norman Cohn, *Europe's Inner Demons: An Enquiry Inspired by the Great Witch-Hunt* (New York: Basic Books, 1975), x. The seventeenth-century cleric Robert Kirk wrote a pioneering book about fairies entitled *The Secret Commonwealth*. Philip Lamy, *Millennium Rage: Survivalists, White Supremacists, and the Doomsday Prophecy* (New York: Plenum Press, 1996), 109.

30. H. E. Hunt, "The 30 Greatest Conspiracy Theories," pts. 1 and 2, *Telegraph* (UK), http://www.telegraph.co.uk/news/newstopics/howaboutthat/3483477/The-30-greatest-conspiracy-theories-part-1.html; http://www.telegraph.co.uk/news/newstopics/howaboutthat/3483652/The-30-greatest-conspiracy-theories-part-2.html.

31. Barkun, *A Culture of Conspiracy*, 3–4.

32. Boyer, *When Time Shall Be No More*, 312.

33. Wojcik, *The End of the World*, 146.

34. Barkun, *A Culture of Conspiracy*, 16–21.

35. Jodi Dean, *Aliens in America: Conspiracy Cultures from Outerspace to Cyberspace* (Ithaca, NY: Cornell University Press, 1998), 7–12.

36. For overviews of UFO contactees, see J. Gordon Melton, "The Contactees: A Survey," in *The Gods Have Landed*, ed. James R. Lewis (Albany: State University of New York Press, 1995), 1–13, and Jerome Clark, "Contactees," in *The UFO Encyclopedia* (Detroit: Omnigraphics, 1998), 243–254.

37. Desmond Leslie and George Adamski, *The Flying Saucers Have Landed* (New York: British Book Centre, 1953), 194–195. Truman Bethurum, *Aboard a Flying Saucer* (Los Angeles: DeVorss & Co., 1954).

38. Howard Menger, *From Outer Space to You* (Clarksburg, WV: Saucerian Press, 1959), 126–127.

39. Ibid., 162. Orfeo Angelucci, *Secret of the Saucers* (Amherst, WI: Amherst Press, 1955), 13, 24.

40. George Adamski, *Flying Saucers Farewell* (New York: Abelard-Schuman, 1961), 110.

41. Angelucci, *Secret of the Saucers*, 44. G. W. Van Tassel, *Into This World and Out Again* (Los Angeles: DeVorss & Co., 1956), 43–44.

42. George Hunt Williamson and Alfred C. Bailey, *The Saucers Speak! A Documentary Report of Interstellar Communication by Radio Telegraphy* (Los Angeles: New Age, 1954), 77.

43. Angelucci, *Secret of the Saucers*, 46, 123.

44. Adamski, *Flying Saucers Farewell*, 26. Reinhold O. Schmidt, *Edge of Tomorrow: The Reinhold O. Schmidt Story* (N.p., Author, 1963), 42. [AU: City and state?] Van Tassel, *Into This World*, 77–78. Angelucci, *Secret of the Saucers*, 45.

45. George W. Van Tassel, *I Rode a Flying Saucer* (Los Angeles: New Age, 1952), 30–31. Ashtar, *In Days to Come* (Los Angeles: New Age, 1955), 28–29.

46. Angelucci, *Secret of the Saucers*, 31. George Adamski, *Inside the Space Ships* (New York: Abelard-Schuman, 1955), 137. Daniel W. Fry, *To Men of Earth* (1954; reprint, Merlin, OR: Merlin, 1973), 82–83, 104–107.

47. Van Tassel, *Into This World*, 42–43.

48. Ibid., 42. Angelucci, *Secret of the Saucers*, 47. Williamson and Bailey, *The Saucers Speak!* 98.

49. Gloria Lee, *Why We Are Here!* (Palos Verdes Estates, CA: Cosmon Research Foundation, 1959), 153.

50. Williamson and Bailey, *The Saucers Speak!* 118.

51. Adamski, *Flying Saucers Farewell*, 26. Menger, *From Outer Space to You*, 27. Angelucci, *Secret of the Saucers*, 30.

52. Lee, *Why We Are Here!* 151–152.

53. Williamson and Bailey, *The Saucers Speak!* 118.

54. Angelucci, *Secret of the Saucers*, 143.

55. Thomas E. Bullard, *UFO Abductions: The Measure of a Mystery* (Mount Ranier, MD: Fund for UFO Research, 1987), 1:108–109.

56. John E. Mack, *Passport to the Cosmos: Human Transformation and Alien Encounters* (New York: Crown, 1999), 93–96.

57. Whitley Strieber, *Communion* (New York: Beech Tree Books / William Morrow & Co., 1987), 69–70. John E. Mack, *Abduction: Human Contact with Aliens* (New York: Charles Scribner's Sons, 1994), 39–40. David M. Jacobs, *Secret Life: Firsthand Accounts of Alien Abductions* (New York: Simon & Schuster, 1992), 136, 140.

58. Bullard, *UFO Abductions*, 1:157. Kenneth Ring, *The Omega Project: Near-Death Experiences, UFO Encounters, and Mind at Large* (New York: William Morrow & Co., 1992), 151–168.

59. Budd Hopkins, *Witnessed: The True Story of the Brooklyn Bridge UFO Abductions* (New York: Pocket Books, 1996), 4–5, 376–382.

60. Mack, *Abduction*, 409; Mack, *Passport to the Cosmos*, 17–18, 52, 130, 218, 277, 280. For the quotation see John E. Mack's obituary in the *Independent* (UK), http://www.independent.co.uk/news/obituaries/john-e-mack-542964.html.

61. Mack, *Abduction*, 3.

62. Mack, *Passport to the Cosmos*, 279.

63. Leo Sprinkle, "UFO Contactees: Captive Collaborators or Cosmic Citizens?" in *1980 MUFON UFO Symposium Proceedings*, ed. Walter H. Andrus Jr. and Dennis W. Stacy (Seguin, TX: Mutual UFO Network, 1980), 64. Strieber, *Communion*, 294–295. Ring, *Omega Project*, 192–193, 218–222, 228–231, 240.

64. See Mircea Eliade, *Cosmos and History: The Myth of the Eternal Return* (New York: Harper Torchbooks, 1959), viii, xi, 5–6, 24–25, 54, 85–92.

65. "Swarm of Mysterious Rockets Is Seen over Capital of Sweden," *New York Times*, August 12, 1946, 1. "Two Swedes Escape a 'Ghost Rocket,'" *New York Times*, August 14, 1946, 11.

66. Leon Davidson, *Flying Saucers: An Analysis of the Air Force Project Blue Book Special Report No. 14*, 4th ed. (White Plains, NY: Author, 1971), 93–94, B2.

67. Frank Allnutt, *Infinite Encounters* (Old Tappan, NJ: Spire Books, 1978), 116–117, 120–121, 169. William M. Alnor, *UFO Cults and the New Millennium* (Grand Rapids, MI: Baker Books, 1998), 92–93, 152–153. Clifford Wilson, *UFOs and Their Mission Impossible* (New York: Signet, 1974), 211–215.

68. "Pat Robertson Says All UFO Believers Should Be Stoned!" at http://www.mnmufon.org/nuts.htm.

69. "Mantell Incident," in Clark, *Encyclopedia*, 606–607.

70. For various incidents at sea, see M. K. Jessup, *The Case for the UFO* (New York: Citadel Press, 1955), 119–134, 162–167. For the Stendec case, see H. T. Wilkins, *Flying Saucers on the Attack* (New York: Citadel Press, 1954), 139–140. And for the solution, see "Nova Discovers Plane Thought to Have Been Intercepted by ETs 50 Years Ago," http://www.100megsfree4.com/farshores/nstendec.htm.

71. For the *Ourang Madan* case, see Wilkins, *Flying Saucers on the Attack*, 251, and Roy Bainton, "Cargo of Death," *Fortean Times*, September 1999, 28–31.

72. Donald E. Keyhoe, *The Flying Saucers from Outer Space* (New York: Henry Holt & Co., 1953), 209.

73. Donald E. Keyhoe, *The Flying Saucer Conspiracy* (New York: Henry Holt & Co., 1955), 13–23.

74. Gord Heath, "What Really Happened to Lt. Gene Moncla? The Missing Kinross F-89 Mystery Endures through Time," *UFO*BC Quarterly* 8, no. 1 (2003): 7–14.

75. Jacques Vallee, *Messengers of Deception: UFO Contacts and Cults* (Berkeley, CA: And/Or Press, 1979), 19, 217–218.

76. John A. Keel, *UFOs: Operation Trojan Horse* (New York: G. P. Putnam's Sons, 1970), 218, 305.

77. Ibid., 290.

78. Bullard, *UFO Abductions*, 1:87, 257.

79. David M. Jacobs, *Secret Life* (New York: Simon & Schuster, 1992), 107–131, 153–167.

80. Jacobs, *The Threat*, 185, 226–253.

81. Budd Hopkins, *Intruders: The Incredible Visitations at Copley Woods* (New York: Random House, 1987), 148–149.

82. Donald Keyhoe, *The Flying Saucers Are Real* (New York: Fawcett Publications, 1950), 82–83, 158–163. Keyhoe, *Flying Saucers: Top Secret* (New York: G. P. Putnam's Sons, 1960), 89–90, 118–119.

83. Keyhoe, *Flying Saucer Conspiracy*, 310–303, 312–315.

84. Ibid., 7.

85. Keyhoe, *Flying Saucers from Outer Space*, 12.

86. Donald E. Keyhoe, *Aliens from Space* (New York: Doubleday & Co., 1973), 79–91.

87. Lee Davidson and Joe Bauman, "Toxic Utah: A Land Littered with Poisons," *Deseret News*,

February 12, 2001, http://www.deseretnews.com/dn/sview/1%2C3329%2C2500.0322%2C00.html.

88. William L. Moore, "UFOs: Uncovering the Ultimate Answers," in *MUFON 1983 UFO Symposium Proceedings*, ed. Walter H. Andrus, Jr., and Dennis W. Stacy (Seguin, TX: Mutual UFO Network, 1983), 93.

89. Stanton T. Friedman and William L. Moore, "The Roswell Incident: Beginning of the Cosmic Watergate," in *1981 MUFON Symposium Proceedings*, ed. Walter H. Andrus Jr. and Dennis W. Stacy (Seguin, TX: Mutual UFO Network, 1981), 132–153.

90. Friedman and Moore, "The Roswell Incident," 135. Kevin D. Randle and Donald R. Schmitt, *UFO Crash at Roswell* (New York: Avon Books, 1981), 26–33.

91. Randle and Schmitt, *UFO Crash at Roswell*, 31.

92. Ibid., 91–93.

93. Stanton T. Friedman, "Update on Operation Majestic-12," in *MUFON 1989 International UFO Symposium Proceedings*, ed. Walter H. Andrus (Seguin, TX: Mutual UFO Network, 1989), 82–87, 102–107.

94. Milton William Cooper, *Behold a Pale Horse* (Flagstaff, AZ: Light Technology, 1991), 196–235.

95. Barkun, *Culture of Conspiracy*, 6.

96. Valdemar Valerian, *The Matrix: Understanding Aspects of Covert Interaction with Alien Culture, Technology and Planetary Power Structures* (Stone Mountain, GA: Arcturus Book Service, 1988), 63.

97. "Dark Side," in *The UFO Encyclopedia*, 2nd ed., ed. Jerome Clark (Detroit: Omnigraphics, 1998), 303–310. See also Christa Tilton, *The Bennewitz Papers* (Tulsa: Crux Publications, 1991). Dennis Stacy, "MUFON Las Vegas Symposium," *MUFON UFO Journal* no. 256 (August 1989): 8–10.

98. Cooper, *Behold a Pale Horse*, 165.

99. Don Ecker, "Freedom of Disinformation," *Fortean Times*, no. 122 (June 1999): 31.

100. Philip J. Corso, *The Day after Roswell* (New York: Pocket Books, 1997), 4, 115.

101. Michael E. Salla, *Exopolitics: Political Implications of the Extraterrestrial Presence* (Tempe: Dandelion Books, 2004), 72–74.

102. Jim Marrs, *The Rise of the Fourth Reich: The Secret Societies That Threaten to Take over America* (New York: William Morrow, 2008), 50–91. Robert Sheaffer, "Nazi Saucers and Antigravity," *Skeptical Inquirer* 33, no. 1 (2009): 13–15.

103. David Icke, *Children of the Matrix* (Wildwood, MO: Bridge of Love Publications, 2001), xxi–xxiii.

104. Robert Sheaffer, "Hurricane Osama?" *Skeptical Inquirer* 29, no. 1 (2005): 17–18.

105. Ed Pilkington, "We're Not Alone, Says Former Nasa Astronaut," *Guardian* (Manchester), July 26, 2008, http://www.guardian.co.uk/science/2008/jul/26/spaceexploration/print.

106. "The Million Fax on Washington to End the UFO Truth Embargo," Paradigm Research Group press release, October 1, 2008, http://www.paradigmresearchgroup.org/main.html.

107. "The 30 Greatest Conspiracy Theories," pt. 1.

108. See, for example, Steven M. Greer, *Hidden Truth—Forbidden Knowledge* (Crozet, VA: Crossing Point Publications, 2006), 319–325.

Chapter 7. Other than Ourselves

1. Timothy K. Beal, *Religion and Its Monsters* (New York: Routledge, 2002), 4.

2. Rudolf Otto, *The Idea of the Holy* (New York: Oxford University Press, 1969), 1–40.

3. Sigmund Freud, "The Uncanny," in *Collected Papers* (London: Hogarth Press, 1948), 4:369–370, 383–384, 391, 394. David D. Gilmore, *Monsters: Evil Beings, Mythical Beasts, and All Manner of Imaginary Terror* (Philadelphia: University of Pennsylvania Press, 2003), 174–175.

4. Edith Hall, *Inventing the Barbarian: Greek Self-Definition through Tragedy* (Oxford: Clarendon Press, 1980), 80, 121.

5. François Hartog, *The Mirror of Herodotus: The Representation of the Other in the Writing of History* (Berkeley: University of California Press, 1988), 51, 61, 121, 134, 171, 191, 197, 200.

6. John Block Friedman, *The Monstrous Races in Medieval Art and Thought* (Cambridge, MA: Harvard University Press, 1981), 9–21.

7. Roger Bartra, *Wild Man in the Looking Glass: The Mythic Origins of European Otherness* (Ann Arbor: University of Michigan Press, 1994), 85–125. Hayden White, "The Forms of Wildness: Archaeology of an Idea," in *The Wild Man Within*, ed. Edward Dudley and Maximilian E. Novak (Pittsburgh: University of Pittsburgh Press, 1972), 16.

8. Phillips Stevens Jr., "The Demonology of Satanism: An Anthropological View," in *The Satanism Scare*, ed. James T. Richardson, Joel Best, and David G. Bromley (New York: Aldine de Gruyter, 1991), 21–24.

9. Philippe Burrin, "Nazi Antisemitism: Animalization and Demonization," in *Demonizing the Other: Antisemitism, Racism, and Xenophobia*, ed. Robert S. Wistrich (Amsterdam: Harwood Academic, 1999), 226–227.

10. Richard VanDerBeets, *The Indian Captivity Narrative: An American Genre* (Lanham, MD: University Press of America, 1984), 1–3, 17, 19–21, 31.

11. Dennis Rome, *Black Demons: The Media's Depiction of the African American Male Criminal Stereotype* (Westport, CT: Praeger, 2004), 21–22, 46. Rudyard Kipling, "The Young British Soldier," in *Complete Verse* (New York: Doubleday, 1987), 416.

12. David H. Bennett, *The Party of Fear: From Nativist Movements to the New Right in American History* (Chapel Hill: University of North Carolina Press, 1988), 80–92.

13. James Morgan Read, *Atrocity Propaganda 1914–1919* (New Haven, CT: Yale University Press, 1941), 41–43, 210–216; John Horne and Alan Kramer, *German Atrocities 1914: A History of Denial* (New Haven: Yale University Press, 2001), 204–211.

14. James S. Romm, *The Edges of the Earth in Ancient Thought: Geography, Exploration, and Fiction* (Princeton, NJ: Princeton University Press, 1992), 55–58.

15. Hartog, *Mirror of Herodotus*, 26. Hall, *Inventing the Barbarian*, 52.

16. Bartra, *Wild Man in the Looking Glass*, 15–16.

17. White, "Forms of Wildness," 11–12.

18. Ibid., 28. Bartra, *Wild Man in the Looking Glass*, 63–74, 104.

19. Michel de Montaigne, "On Cannibals," *Essays* (New York: Penguin Books, 1993), 108–110, 113–114. Bartra, *Wild Man in the Looking Glass*, 173–174.

20. Ter Ellingson, *The Myth of the Noble Savage* (Berkeley: University of California Press, 2001), 81–82, 178–192.

21. Auguste Comte, "Introduction" to *Cours de philosophie positive*, in *Auguste Comte and Positivism: The Essential Writings*, ed. Gertrud Lenzer (New York: Harper Torchbooks, 1975), 71–75.

22. Edward B. Tylor, *Primitive Culture* (New York: Brentano's, 1924), 27, 284–285.

23. Paul Israel, *Edison: A Life of Invention* (New York: John Wiley & Sons, 1998), 153–156, 363–378.

24. David E. Nye, *America as Second Creation: Technology and Narratives of New Beginnings* (Cambridge, MA: MIT Press, 2003), 9–13.

25. Leon Stover, *The Prophetic Soul: A Reading of H. G. Wells's Things to Come* (Jefferson, NC: McFarland & Co., 1987), 296–297.

26. Isaac Asimov, *Futuredays: A Nineteenth-Century Vision of the Year 2000* (New York: Henry Holt & Co., 1986), 36, 66.

27. Arthur C. Clarke, *Profiles of the Future: An Inquiry into the Limits of the Possible* (1962; London: Pan Books, 1983), 254–255.

28. Ray Kurzweil, *The Singularity Is Near: When Humans Transcend Biology* (New York: Viking Press, 2005), 9, 20–21. For some of Freeman Dyson's predictions, see Clarke, *Profiles of the Future*, 248–250.

29. Isaac Asimov, "The Last Question," in *The Best Science Fiction of Isaac Asimov* (Garden City, NY: Doubleday & Co., 1986), 209–221, quotation from 221.

30. For examples of cyclical history or inherent limitations to progress, see Thomas Robert Malthus, "An Essay on the Principles of Population," in *Population, Evolution, and Birth Control*, ed. Garrett Hardin (San Francisco: W. H. Freeman & Co., 1969), 4–16; Arnold J. Toynbee, *A Study of History* (New York: Oxford University Press, 1946), 1:67, 140, 187, 244–246, 276, 307, 379–383; Gunther S. Stent, *The Coming of the Golden Age: A View of the End of Progress* (Garden City, NY: Natural History Press, 1969), 87, 94, 121, 136, 138; Francis Fukuyama, *The End of History and the Last Man* (New York: Free Press, 1992), 294, 310–312, 319–320, 328, 336.

31. "Gilgamesh (Old Babylonian Version)," in *Myths from Mesopotamia*, trans. Stephanie Dalley (New York: Oxford University Press, 1991), 150.

32. Romm, *Edges of the Earth in Ancient Thought*, 121, 123, 166.

33. Alexander Pope, *Essay on Man*, 1:123–126, in *Poems of Alexander Pope* (New Haven, CT: Yale University Press, 1970), 509.

34. Michele Carlton, "Children of Kelly Witnesses Firmly Believe Their Father Shot at Entities," *MUFON UFO Journal* no. 481 (February 2003): 9–10.

35. Joseph Mali, *The Rehabilitation of Myth: Vico's "New Science"* (New York: Cambridge University Press, 1992), 13, 53–54, 79–82, 164–168, 182–184.

36. William Wordsworth, "The Tables Turned" and William Blake, "Milton," in *English Romantic Poetry and Prose*, ed. Russell Noyes (New York: Oxford University Press, 1956), 224, 259. Walt Whitman, "When I Heard the Learn'd Astronomer," *Leaves of Grass* (Albany: New York University Press, 1965), 271. Alfred Lord Tennyson, "In Memoriam," lvi, in *Poetic and Dramatic Works of Alfred Lord Tennyson* (Boston: Houghton Mifflin & Co., 1898), 176.

37. Leo Marx, *The Machine in the Garden: Technology and the Pastoral Ideal in America* (New York: Oxford University Press, 1970), 11–16. On the ambivalent relationship of Dickens with the railroad, see Michael R. Trimble, "Post-Traumatic Stress Disorder: History of a Concept,"

in *Trauma and Its Wake: The Study and Treatment of Post-Traumatic Stress Disorder*, ed. Charles R. Figley (New York: Brunner / Mazel, 1985), 7; Andrew Sanders, *Dickens and the Spirit of the Age* (Oxford: Clarendon Press, 1999), 60–66; Ewald Mengel, ed., *The Railway through Dickens's World* (New York: Peter Lang, 1989), 22.

38. Howard E. McCurdy, *Space and the American Imagination* (Washington, DC: Smithsonian Institution Press, 1997), 99–101.

39. John Yewell, Chris Dodge, and Jan De Sirey, eds., *Confronting Columbus: An Anthology* (Jefferson, NC: McFarland & Co., 1992), x–xiii, 1–14, 65–75, 109–124, 149–158.

40. Barry Commoner, *The Closing Circle: Nature, Man, and Technology* (New York: Alfred A. Knopf, 1971), 193.

41. Donella H. Meadows et al., *The Limits to Growth: A Report for The Club of Rome's Project on the Predicament of Mankind* (New York: Universe Books, 1972), 23–24.

42. See Henry I. Miller and Gregory Conko, *The Frankenfood Myth: How Protest and Politics Threaten the Biotechnology Revolution* (Westport, CT: Praeger, 2004); Paul R. Gross and Norman Levitt, *Higher Superstition: The Academic Left and Its Quarrels with Science* (Baltimore: Johns Hopkins University Press, 1994), 2–12.

43. Leon R. Kass, *Life, Liberty and the Defense of Dignity: The Challenge for Bioethics* (San Francisco: Encounter Books, 2002), 260.

44. President's Council on Bioethics, *Beyond Therapy: Biotechnology and the Pursuit of Happiness* (Washington, DC: President's Council on Bioethics, 2003), 286–301.

45. Tom Bissell, "A Comet's Tale: On the Science of Apocalypse," *Harper's Magazine* (February 2003): 33–47.

46. Howard E. McCurdy, *Space and the American Imagination* (Washington, DC: Smithsonian Institution Press, 1997), 139–161. Marina Benjamin, *Rocket Dreams: How the Space Age Shaped Our Vision of a World Beyond* (New York: Free Press, 2003), 15, 36–41.

47. Jodi Dean, *Aliens in America: Conspiracy Culture from Outer Space to Cyberspace* (Ithaca, NY: Cornell University Press, 1998), 19–20.

48. See, for example, Margaret McLean, "Who Owns the Moon?" *Santa Clara University*, http://www.scu.edu/ethics/publications/iie/v10n1/moon.html; Leonard David, "Reclaiming the Moon," *Space.com*, http://www.space.com/scienceastronomy/solarsystem/moon_nss_020 604.html; David Grinspoon, "Is Mars Ours?" *Slate*, http://www.slate.com/id/2093579, and Paul York, "The Ethics of Terraforming," *Philosophy Now* (October–November 2002): 6–9.

49. H. G. Wells, "Of a Book Unwritten ('The Man of the Year Million')," in David Y. Hughes and Harry M. Geduld, eds., *A Critical Edition of the War of the Worlds* (Bloomington: Indiana University Press, 1993), 293–294.

50. Early science fiction literature popularized enlarging brains as part of the human future, like Hugo Gernsback's "Ralph 124C 41+" from 1912, and the possibility that too much technology would lead to physical decline, as in David H. Keller's "The Revolt of the Pedestrians" in 1928. See David Kyle, *A Pictorial History of Science Fiction* (New York: Hamlyn , 1976), 44, 64. An episode of the 1960s TV series *The Outer Limits* included "The Sixth Finger," wherein a Welsh coal miner entered an evolution-accelerating machine and appeared the next day with an enlarged and balding head, also the beginnings of a sixth finger and the dexterity to play Bach like a master. He soon became psychokinetic and then appeared with an enormous cranium and

a desire to evolve into a pure vortex of thought, though his girlfriend pulled the lever backward and returned him to his initial state.

51. Hunter S. Thompson, *Generation of Swine, Gonzo Papers* (New York: Simon & Schuster, 1988), 2:27.

52. An offshoot of the Disclosure project is an effort by Stephen Greer to promote advanced energy technologies allegedly made possible from recovered UFOs and well known to the government but sequestered from public usage out of a desire to preserve the economic status quo. See Ross Fale, "Keeping UFOs Off the National Radar," *UFO Digest*, December 22, 2008, http://www.ufodigest.com/news/1208/off-radar.html.

Chapter 8. Explaining UFOs: An Inward Look

1. David Sivier, "Visions before Midnight: Witchcraft, Folklore and the Prehistory of the Abduction Phenomenon," *Magonia*, no. 94 (January 2007): 13.

2. Robert E. Bartholomew and George S. Howard, *UFOs and Alien Contact: Two Centuries of Mystery* (Amherst, NY: Prometheus Books, 1998), 21–64. Nigel Watson, *The Scareship Mystery: A Survey of Phantom Airship Scares 1909–1918* (Corby, Northamptonshire: Domra Publications, 2000).

3. "The Stephenville Lights: What Actually Happened," *Skeptical Inquirer* 33, no. 1 (2009): 56–57.

4. Alvin H. Lawson, "What Can We Learn from Hypnosis of Imaginary Abductees?" in *1977 MUFON UFO Symposium Proceedings*, ed. Walter H. Andrus Jr. (Seguin, TX: Mutual UFO Network, 1977), 107–135.

5. Kevin D. Randle, Russ Estes, and William P. Cone, *The Abduction Enigma: The Truth Behind the Mass Alien Abductions of the Late Twentieth Century* (New York: Forge Books, 1999), 359–363.

6. Martin Kottmeyer, "Entirely Unpredisposed," *Magonia*, no. 35 (January 1990): 5–7.

7. Bertrand Méheust, *Soucoupes volantes et folklore* (Paris: Mercure de France, 1985); Michel Meurger, *Alien Abduction: L'Enlèvement extraterrestre de la fiction à la croyance* (Amiens: Encrage, 1995).

8. Peter Rogerson, "Sex, Science, and Salvation," *Magonia*, no. 49 (June 1994): 14. In fact Rogerson has the order of influence turned around—the book of fiction most likely borrows its abduction motifs from *The Interrupted Journey*.

9. David Kestenbaum, "Panel Says Some UFO Reports Worthy of Study," *Science* 281 (1998): 21.

10. Lester Grinspoon and Alan D. Persky, "Psychiatry and UFO Reports," in *UFOs—A Scientific Debate*, ed. Carl Sagan and Thornton Page (Ithaca, NY: Cornell University Press, 1972), 235–236.

11. Donald I. Warren, "Status Inconsistency Theory and Flying Saucer Sightings," *Science* 170 (1970): 599–603.

12. Robert E. Bartholomew, Keith Basterfield, and George S. Howard, "UFO Abductees and Contactees: Psychopathology or Fantasy Proneness?" *Professional Psychology: Research and*

Practice 22 (1991): 217. Clancy, *Abducted*, 132–133. Martin Kottmeyer, "Abduction: The Boundary Deficit Hypothesis," *Magonia*, no. 32 (1988): 3–7.

13. Lawson, "What Can We Learn," 115–131; Susan A. Clancy, *Abducted: How People Come to Believe They Were Kidnapped by Aliens* (Cambridge, MA: Harvard University Press, 2005), 102–103.

14. Leonard S. Newman and Roy F. Baumeister, "Toward an Explanation of the UFO Abduction Phenomenon: Hypnotic Elaboration, Extraterrestrial Sadomasochism, and Spurious Memories," *Psychological Inquiry* 7 (1996): 100, 122–123.

15. Michael A. Persinger, "Neuropsychological Profiles of Adults Who Report 'Sudden Remembering' of Early Childhood Memories: Implications for Claims of Sex Abuse and Alien Visitation/Abduction Experiences," *Perceptual and Motor Skills* 75 (1992): 259–266.

16. Elizabeth Loftus and Katherine Ketcham, *The Myth of Repressed Memory: False Memories and Allegations of Sexual Abuse* (New York: St. Martin's Press, 1994), 94–100. Richard Ofshe and Ethan Watters, *Making Monsters: False Memory, Psychotherapy, and Sexual Hysteria* (New York: Charles Scribner's Sons, 1994), 5, 25–44.

17. For the story of the child abuse moral panic, see Ofshe and Watters, *Making Monsters*, and Debbie Nathan and Michael Snedeker, *Satan's Silence: Ritual Abuse and the Making of a Modern American Witch Hunt* (New York: BasicBooks, 1995). For the Paul Ingram case, see Ofshe and Watters, *Making Monsters*, 166–175, and Lawrence Wright, *Remembering Satan: A Tragic Case of Recovered Memory* (New York: Vintage Books, 1994).

18. Nicholas P. Spanos, *Multiple Identities and False Memories: A Sociocognitive Perspective* (Washington, DC: American Psychological Association, 1996), 19–20.

19. Ibid., 3.

20. Steven Jay Lynn, Judith Pintar, Jane Stafford, Lisa Marmelstein, and Timothy Lock, "Rendering the Implausible Plausible: Narrative Construction, Suggestion, and Memory," in *Believed-In Imaginings: The Narrative Construction of Reality*, ed. Joseph de Rivera and Theodore R. Sarbin (Washington, DC: American Psychological Association, 1998), 128–130. Susan A. Clancy, Richard J. McNally, Daniel L. Schacter, Mark F. Lenzenweger, and Roger K. Pitman, "Memory Distortion in People Reporting Abduction by Aliens," *Journal of Abnormal Psychology* 111 (2002): 456. For further treatments of sociocultural contributions, see Clancy, *Abducted*, 33–38, 57–63, 101–102, 128–136. Nicholas P. Spanos, Patricia A. Cross, Kirby Dickson, and Susan C. DuBreuil, "Close Encounters: An Examination of UFO Experiences," *Journal of Abnormal Psychology* 102 (1993): 631. Randle, Estes, and Cone, *The Abduction Enigma*, 359–363.

21. June O. Parnell, "Measured Personality Characteristics of Persons Who Claim UFO Experiences," *Psychotherapy in Private Practice* 6 (1989): 163. June O. Parnell and R. Leo Sprinkle, "Personality Characteristics of Persons Who Claim UFO Experiences," *Journal of UFO Studies*, n.s., 2 (1990): 55. Mark Rodeghier, Jeff Goodpaster, and Sandra Blatterbauer, "Psychological Characteristics of Abductees: Results from the CUFOS Abduction Project," *Journal of UFO Studies*, n.s., 3 (1991): 72. Clancy, *Abducted*, 134. Susan J. Blackmore, "Alien Abductions, Sleep Paralysis and the Temporal Lobe," *European Journal of UFO and Abduction Studies* 1 (2000): 115. Troy A. Zimmer, "Social Psychological Correlates of Possible UFO Sightings," *Journal of Social Psychology* 123 (1984): 204. Denzler, *Lure of the Edge*, 174–184. Discussions covering the full range of psychological characteristics of UFO abductees are available in Stuart Appelle, Steven

Jay Lynn, and Leonard Newman, "Alien Abduction Experiences," in *Varieties of Anomalous Experience: Examining the Evidence,* ed. Etzel Cardeña, Steven Jay Lynn, and Stanley Krippner (Washington, DC: American Psychological Association, 2000), 253–283; Stuart Appelle, "The Abduction Experience: A Critical Evaluation of Theory and Evidence," *Journal of UFO Studies,* n.s., 6 (1995–1996): 29–78; and Thomas E. Bullard, "False Memories and UFO Abductions," *Journal of UFO Studies,* n.s., 8 (2003): 92–102, 136–144.

22. Spanos et al., "Close Encounters," 628.

23. Duncan John Andrew Day, *Psychological Correlates of the UFO Abduction Experience: The Role of Beliefs and Indirect Suggestions on Abduction Accounts Obtained during Hypnosis* (Ph.D. diss., Concordia University, Montreal, 1998), 119, 144, 149–150.

24. Clancy et al., "Memory Distortion in People Reporting Abduction by Aliens," 458–460. Negative results for fantasy proneness emerged from studies by Kenneth Ring and Christopher J. Rosing, "The Omega Project: A Psychological Survey of Persons Reporting Abductions and Other UFO Encounters," *Journal of UFO Studies,* n.s., 2 (1990): 70; Rodeghier et al., "Psychological Characteristics of Abductees," 70; Spanos et al., "Close Encounters," 629; Caroline C. McLeod, Michael L. O'Connell, Robert L. Colasanti, and John E. Mack, "Anomalous Experience and Psychopathology: The Question of Alien Abduction," 38 (available through the John E. Mack Institute, Boulder, CO); Peter Hough and Paul Rogers, "Individuals Who Report Being Abducted by Aliens: Investigating the Differences in Fantasy Proneness, Emotional Intelligence and the Big Five Personality Factors," *Imagination, Cognition and Personality* 27 (2007–2008): 139–161.

25. Christopher C. French, Julia Santomauro, Victoria Hamilton, Rachel Fox, and Michael A. Thalbourne, "Psychological Aspects of the Alien Contact Experience," *Cortex* 44 (2008): 1387–1395.

26. Ted Bloecher, Aphrodite Clamar, and Budd Hopkins, *Final Report on the Psychological Testing of UFO "Abductees"* (Mount Rainier, MD: Fund for UFO Research, 1985), 18–31. Parnell and Sprinkle, "Personality Characteristics of Persons Who Claim UFO Experiences," 51–55. Kenneth Ring, *The Omega Project: Near-Death Experiences, UFO Encounters, and Mind at Large* (New York: William Morrow & Co., 1992), 145.

27. Spanos et al., "Close Encounters," 627–628.

28. Kathryn Gow, Janine Lurie, Stuart Coppin, Ari Popper, Anthony Powell, and Keith Basterfield, "Fantasy Proneness and Other Psychological Correlates of UFO Experience," *European Journal of UFO and Abduction Studies* 2 (2001): 53, 55, 61–63.

29. Bloecher et al., *Final Report on the Testing of UFO "Abductees,"* 22–24. Parnell and Sprinkle, "Personality Characteristics of Persons Who Claim UFO Experiences," 55. Clancy, *Abducted,* 129–130.

30. Alexander G. Keul and Ken Phillips, "The UFO—An Unidentified Form of Creativity?" *Journal of Transient Aerial Phenomena* 5 (1988): 37; Persinger, "Neuropsychological Profiles," 261; Ring and Rosing, "The Omega Project: A Psychological Survey of Persons Reporting Abductions and Other UFO Encounters," 71–72; John E. Mack, *Abduction: Human Encounters with Aliens* (New York: Charles Scribner's Sons, 1994), 112, 145, 178, 202, 219, 267, 340; Jo Stone-Carmen, "A Descriptive Study of People Reporting Abduction by UFOs," in *Alien Discussions,* ed. Andrea Pritchard et al. (Cambridge, MA: North Cambridge Press, 1994), 310, 313.

31. Randle, Estes, and Cone, *The Abduction Enigma*, 97–101.

32. Spanos et al., "Close Encounters," 631.

33. Budd Hopkins, "UFO Abductions—The Skeleton Key," in *MUFON 1988 International UFO Symposium Proceedings*, ed. Walter H. Andrus Jr. and Richard H. Hall (Seguin, TX: Mutual UFO Network, 1988), 104.

34. Ruth Benedict, *Patterns of Culture* (1934; New York: Mentor Books, 1959), 79–80, 121–155.

35. Richard Hofstadter, *The Paranoid Style in American Politics and Other Essays* (New York: Alfred A. Knopf, 1965), 4, 10–38.

36. Martin Kottmeyer develops an extensive case for paranoia as an underlying psychological theme of UFO belief in three series of articles published in *Magonia:* The first series, "A Universe of Spies," no. 39 (April 1991): 8–14; "Eye in the Sky," no. 40 (August 1991): 3–8; and "Eye-Yi-Yi," no. 41 (November 1991): 5–9, treats the pervasive imagery of alien surveillance. The second series, "What's Up, Doc?" no. 44 (October 1992): 3–7; "Swinging through the Sixties," no. 45 (March 1993): 7–12, 19; "Shams and Shepherds," no. 46 (June 1993): 8–12, treats UFO-related fears of contamination and injury as further evidence for a paranoid bent among UFO believers. A third series, "Alienating Fancies: The Influencing Machine Fantasy in Ufology and the Extraterrestrial Mythos," no. 49 (June 1994): 3–10; and the second part, in no. 50 (September 1994), 3–6, traces the suspicions of external control common in paranoid ideation as they appear in the technological terms of UFO belief.

37. Kottmeyer, "Ufology Considered as an Evolving System of Paranoia," in *Cyberbiological Studies of the Imaginal Component in the UFO Contact Experience*, ed. Dennis Stillings (St. Paul, MN: Archaeus Project, 1989), 51–60.

38. Frederick Jackson Turner, *The Frontier in American History* (New York: Henry Holt & Co., 1920), 2–3, 30, 37.

39. For an extensive discussion of American characteristics in the nineteenth century, see Henry Steele Commager, *The American Mind* (New Haven, CT: Yale University Press, 1963), 3–40.

40. David E. Nye, *America as Second Creation: Technology and Narratives of New Beginnings* (Cambridge, MA: MIT Press, 2003), 46–50.

41. Richard Hofstadter, *Anti-Intellectualism in American Life* (New York: Alfred A. Knopf, 1966), 6–7, 33–35, 47–51.

42. Howard E. McCurdy, *Space and the American Imagination* (Washington, DC: Smithsonian Institution Press, 1997), 143–150.

43. For a discussion of common fallacies of thinking, see Michael Shermer, *Why People Believe Weird Things: Pseudo-Science, Superstition, and Bogus Notions of Our Time* (New York: MJF Books, 1997), 44–61.

44. Michael Busby, *Solving the 1897 Airship Mystery* (Gretna, LA: Pelican, 2004), 351.

45. These subtitles come from the 1993, 1995, 1996, and 2002 MUFON Symposium Proceedings. Twelve of the thirty-five proceedings since 1971 have included the word "science" or "scientific" in the subtitle.

46. Etzel Cardeña, Steven Jay Lynn, and Stanley Krippner, eds., *Varieties of Anomalous Experience: Examining the Scientific Evidence* (Washington, DC: American Psychological Association, 2000), 4.

47. David Hume, "Of Miracles," from *An Enquiry concerning Human Understanding*, sec. 10, pt.1 (New York: Longmans, Green & Co., 1898), 94.

48. Karl R. Popper, *Conjectures and Refutations: The Growth of Scientific Knowledge* (New York: Harper Torchbooks, 1968), 33–39.

49. Jacques Vallee, *Forbidden Science: Journals 1957–1969* (Berkeley, CA: North Atlantic Books, 1992), 41–42.

50. James E. McDonald, "Statement," in Committee on Science and Astronautics, *Symposium on Unidentified Flying Objects, Hearings before the Committee on Science and Astronautics*, 90th Cong., 2d sess., July 29, 1968, 18–85 (Washington, DC: U.S. Government Printing Office, 1968), 34.

51. J. Allen Hynek, "UFOs Merit Scientific Study," *Science*, n.s., 154 (October 21, 1966): 329.

52. Ibid., 329.

53. Shermer, *Why People Believe Weird Things*, 48–55.

54. Kent Jeffrey, "Roswell—Anatomy of a Myth," *MUFON UFO Journal*, no. 350 (June 1997): 3–17.

55. See Jeffrey, 3–4, and letters to the *MUFON UFO Journal*, no. 352 (August 1997): 19–20, and no. 353 (September 1997): 20.

56. William J. Birnes, "The Double Life of Walter Haut," *UFO Magazine*, July 2007, 32–35.

57. "'Houston, This Is Discovery, We Still Have the Alien Spacecraft under Observance,'" *Ufoseek*, http://www.ufoseek.org/nasaufo.htm.

58. Anthony Bragalia, "UFOs and the States of Matter," *The UFO Iconoclast(s)*, February 12, 2009, http://ufocon.blogspot.com/2009/02/ufos-and-states-of-matter-by-anthony.html.

59. Brent Raynes, *Visitors from Hidden Realms: The Origin and Destiny of Humanity as Told by Star Elders, Shamans, and UFO Visitors* (Memphis: Eagle Wing Books, 2004), 24.

60. Stephen Bassett, "Disclosure in the Age of Secrecy," *UFO Magazine* (U.S.), April–May 2004, 26.

61. For examples of misleading, false, or oversimplified statements by skeptics in their attempts to explain the Hill abduction case, see Kathleen Marden, "Pseudoskeptics' Deception about the Betty and Barney Hill UFO Encounter," *MUFON UFO Journal*, no. 489 (January 2009): 3–6.

62. Kevin Christopher, "Mexican Air Force UFOs Likely Equipment Artifacts," *Skeptical Inquirer* 28, no. 4 (2004): 5. George Knapp, "Knappster: Usual Scientific Explanations Lacking in Mexican UFO Case," *Las Vegas Mercury*, http://www.lasvegasmercury.com/2004/MERC-Jun-03-Thu-2004/24005082.html.

63. Bronislaw Malinowski, *Magic, Science, and Religion* (Garden City, NY: Doubleday Anchor Books, 1954), 87.

64. J. B. S. Haldane, *Possible Worlds and Other Essays* (London: Chatto & Windus, 1928), 286.

65. Kottmeyer, "Ufology Considered as an Evolving System of Paranoia," 52.

66. Michael Swords, "Extraterrestrial Hybridization Unlikely," *MUFON UFO Journal*, no. 247 (November 1988): 6–10.

67. Thomas E. Bullard, *UFO Abductions: The Measure of a Mystery* (Mount Ranier, MD: Fund for UFO Research, 1987), 1:36, 106–108, 115.

68. Linda Dégh, *Legend and Belief: Dialectics of a Folklore Genre* (Bloomington: Indiana University Press, 2001), 91, 252. Jan Harold Brunvand, *The Vanishing Hitchhiker: American Urban Legends and Their Meanings* (New York: W. W. Norton & Co., 1981), 11, 47–48, 168–169.

69. Ronald Reagan caused a knowing stir when he suggested to Mikhail Gorbachev in 1985 that if confronted by an alien invasion threat, the people of earth would have to unite. UFO believers took his statement not as a rhetorical what-if but as concrete proof that the government knew such a threat existed (see Tom Vesey, "Md. Students Hail the Chief," *Washington Post*, December 5, 1985). "The Presidents UFO Website: Reagan UFO Story (The Alien Invasion)," http://www.presidentialufo.com/ronald-reagan/99-reagan-ufo-story.

70. David Seed, *American Science Fiction and the Cold War: Literature and Film* (Edinburgh: Edinburgh University Press, 1999), 132–34.

71. Nahum Z. Medalia and Otto N. Larsen, "Diffusion and Belief in a Collective Delusion: The Seattle Windshield Pitting Epidemic," *American Sociological Review* 23 (1958): 180–186. Donald E. Keyhoe, *The Flying Saucer Conspiracy* (New York: Henry Holt & Co., 1955), 132–133.

72. William J. Birnes, "Publisher's Note," *UFO Magazine* (U.S.), August–September 2005, 4.

73. Clancy, *Abducted*, 142–155.

74. Brenda Denzler, *The Lure of the Edge: Scientific Passions, Religious Beliefs, and the Pursuit of UFOs* (Berkeley: University of California Press, 2001), 137, 159.

75. Daniel S. Gillmor, ed., *Scientific Study of Unidentified Flying Objects* (New York: Bantam Books, 1969), 290–291.

76. "The Anomaly Foundation Solves the 'Manises' UFO Case: 20 Years of Mystery Are Over," *Anomaly Foundation*, http://www.anomalia.org/manisen.htm. The full study is in Juan Antonio Fernández Peris, *El Expediente Manises* (Santander, Spain: Fundación Anomalía, 2000).

77. Martin Kottmeyer, "The Eyes Still Speak," *REALL News* 6, no. 5 (1998): 2, 6–9. The "Bellero Shield" episode is available on DVD in *The Outer Limits: The Complete Original Series*, vol. 1 (Hollywood: Metro-Goldwyn-Mayer Studios, 2007).

78. Jerome Clark, "Hill Abduction Case," in *The UFO Encyclopedia*, 2nd ed. (Detroit: Omnigraphics, 1998), 1:501–502.

79. On cryptomnesia, see Antonia Mills and Steven Jay Lynn, "Past-Life Experiences," in *Varieties of Anomalous Experience*, ed. Etzel Cardeña, Steven Jay Lynn, and Stanley Crippner (Washington, DC: American Psychological Association, 2000), 287–288; Barry L. Beyerstein and James R. P. Ogloff, "Hidden Memories: Fact or Fancy?" in *Child Sexual Abuse and False Memory Syndrome*, ed. Robert A. Baker (Amherst, NY: Prometheus Books, 1998), 20–21.

80. Jerome Clark provides a detailed critique of the psychosocial approach in *The UFO Encyclopedia*, 749–759.

81. Carol Zaleski, *Otherworld Journeys: Accounts of Near-Death Experience in Medieval and Modern Times* (New York: Oxford University Press, 1987), 184–205.

82. Gregory Shushan, *Conceptions of the Afterlife in Early Civilizations: Universalism, Constructivism and Near-Death Experience* (New York: Continuum International, 2009), 1–5, 193–201.

83. Martin Kottmeyer, "Entirely Unpredisposed," *Magonia*, no. 35 (January 1990): 5–7.

84. Pascal Boyer, *The Naturalness of Religious Ideas: A Cognitive Theory of Religion* (Berkeley: University of California Press, 1994), 4–5, 100–113, 123–124, 256–257.

85. Ibid., 113–124.

86. Thomas S. Kuhn, *The Structure of Scientific Revolutions* (Chicago: University of Chicago Press, 1970), 10–11, 17–18, 24, 52–53, 65.

87. Phillip S. Duke, *The AIDS-ET Connection* (Omaha: Cosmos Press, 1999).

Chapter 9. Explaining UFOs: Something Yet Remains

1. Kary Mullis, *Dancing Naked in the Mind Field* (New York: Vintage Books, 1998), 131, 136.

2. James Renner, "Strangers in the Night," *Cleveland Scene*, March 21, 2004, 3.

3. Michael D. Swords, *Grassroots UFOs: Case Reports from the Timmerman Files* (Mount Rainier, MD: Fund for UFO Research, 2005), xi–xv.

4. Report from the Timmerman files courtesy of Michael D. Swords.

5. Mullis, *Dancing Naked in the Mind Field*, 130–136. Bill Chalker, "The Raccoon and the Nobel Prize," *MUFON UFO Journal*, no. 420 (April 2003): 6–7.

6. For the Project Blue Book report, see Kevin D. Randle, *Project Blue Book Exposed* (New York: Marlowe & Co., 1997), 151–163. Detailed interviews with witnesses by Thomas Tulien and James Klotz provided the basis for the Minot case segment in the "Peter Jennings Reports" UFO special on ABC, February 24, 2005, and their research is the subject of a forthcoming book. Transcriptions from the Sign Oral History Project interviews were provided to me courtesy of Tom Tulien.

7. D. Felton, *Haunted Greece and Rome: Ghost Stories from Classical Antiquity* (Austin: University of Texas Press, 1999), 34–35. Ronald C. Finucane, "Historical Introduction: The Example of Early Modern and Nineteenth-Century England," in *Hauntings and Poltergeists: Multidisciplinary Perspectives*, ed. James Houran and Rense Lange (Jefferson, NC: McFarland & Co., 2001), 9–17.

8. R. C. Finucane, *Ghosts: Appearances of the Dead and Cultural Transformation* (Amherst, NY: Prometheus Books, 1996), 169.

9. J. Allen Hynek, *The UFO Experience: A Scientific Inquiry* (Chicago: Henry Regnery Co., 1972), 23.

10. *Project Blue Book Special Report No. 14 (Analysis of Reports of Unidentified Aerial Objects)* (Wright-Patterson Air Force Base, Ohio: Air Technical Intelligence Center, 1955), 91–94; reprinted version of Leon Davidson, ed., *Flying Saucers: An Analysis of the Air Force Project Blue Book Special Report No. 14* (New York: Flying Saucer News, n.d.). Martin Kottmeyer, "Gill Again," *Magonia* 54 (November 1995): 11.

11. Allan Hendry, *The UFO Handbook* (Garden City, NY: Doubleday & Co., 1979), 284.

12. Linda Dégh, *Legend and Belief: Dialectics of a Folklore Genre* (Bloomington: Indiana University Press, 2001), 42, 62, 66–67, 77. Linda Dégh and Andrew Vázsonyi, "The Memorate and the Proto-Memorate," *Journal of American Folklore* 87 (1974): 231.

13. Frederic C. Bartlett, *Remembering: A Study in Experimental and Social Psychology* (London: Cambridge University Press, 1964), 171–176, 213–214.

14. Gordon W. Allport and Leo J. Postman, *The Psychology of Rumor* (New York: Holt, Rinehart & Winston, 1965), 75–105.

15. Dégh, *Legend and Belief*, 41–42, 69.

16. Linda Dégh and Andrew Vázsonyi, "Legend and Belief," in *Folklore Genres*, ed. Dan Ben-Amos (Austin: University of Texas Press, 1976), 96–97, 116–118; "The Hypothesis of Multi-Conduit Transmission in Folklore," in *Narratives in Society: A Performer-Centered Study of Narration*, ed. Linda Dégh (Helsinki: Suomalainen Tiedeakatemia, 1995), 176–177, 208–210.

17. Bill Ellis, *Aliens, Ghosts, and Cults: The Legends We Live* (Jackson: University Press of Mississippi, 2001), 11–12.

18. Linda Dégh and Andrew Vázsonyi, "The Crack in the Red Goblet, or Truth in Modern Legend," in Dégh, *Narratives in Society*, 152–156.

19. Thomas E. Bullard, "What's New in UFO Abductions? Has the Story Changed in 30 Years?" in *MUFON 1999 International UFO Symposium Proceedings*, ed. Walter H. Andrus Jr. and Irena Scott (Seguin, TX: MUFON, 1999), 181.

20. Linda Dégh, "Processes of Legend Formation," 227.

21. Ellis, *Aliens, Ghosts, and Cults*, 8.

22. Compare the satanic ritual abuse accounts in Michelle Smith and Lawrence Pazder, *Michelle Remembers* (New York: Pocket Books, 1980); Judith Spencer, *Suffer the Child* (New York: Pocket Books, 1989); Robert S. Mayer, *Satan's Children* (New York: Avon Books, 1991); Lauren Stratford, *Satan's Underground* (Gretna, LA: Pelican, 1991); Gail Carr Feldman, *Lessons in Evil, Lessons from the Light: A True Story of Satanic Abuse and Spiritual Healing* (New York: Crown, 1993); Judith Spencer, *Satan's High Priest: A True Story* (New York: Pocket Books, 1997); Jeanne Marie Lorena and Paula Levy, *Breaking Ritual Silence: An Anthology of Ritual Abuse Survivor Stories* (Gardnerville, NV: Trout & Sons, 1998).

23. Bullard, "What's New in UFO Abductions?" 180–184.

24. Budd Hopkins, "*Communion* Cover Error Creates a Type of Scientific Control," *MUFON UFO Journal*, no. 455 (March 2006): 3–5.

25. Lauri Honko, "Memorates and the Study of Folk Belief," *Journal of the Folklore Institute* 1 (1969): 15–18.

26. David J. Hufford, *The Terror That Comes in the Night: An Experience-Centered Study of Supernatural Assault Traditions* (Philadelphia: University of Pennsylvania Press, 1982), 1–11, 25, 48–53.

27. Hufford, *Terror*, 15, 248–249; Hufford, "Beings without Bodies: An Experience-Centered Theory of the Belief in Spirits," in *Out of the Ordinary: Folklore and the Supernatural*, ed. Barbara Walker (Logan: Utah State University Press, 1995), 13.

28. Hufford, "Beings without Bodies," 18.

29. Hufford, *Terror*, x, xvi–xix. For studies of ghosts, ESP, and near-death experiences with a focus on the experience, see Gillian Bennett, *Traditions of Belief: Women, Folklore and the Supernatural Today* (New York: Penguin Books, 1987); Leea Virtanen, *That Must Have Been ESP! An Examination of Psychic Experiences* (Bloomington: Indiana University Press, 1990); Kenneth Ring, *Life at Death: A Scientific Investigation of the Near-Death Experience* (New York: Quill, 1982).

30. William James, *The Varieties of Religious Experience* (New York: Collier Books, 1961), 73–75, 386.

31. James McClenon, *Wondrous Events: Foundations of Religious Belief* (Philadelphia: University of Pennsylvania Press, 1994), 238–248.

32. Hufford, *The Terror That Comes in the Night*, 169.

33. Dorothy B. Vitaliano, *Legends of the Earth* (Bloomington: Indiana University Press, 1973), 218–251. Paul Barber, *Vampires, Burial, and Death: Folklore and Reality* (New Haven, CT: Yale University Press, 1988), 1–4, 110–111, 132, 161–162. Adrienne Mayor, *The First Fossil Hunters: Paleontology in Greek and Roman Times* (Princeton, NJ: Princeton University Press, 2000), 3–4, 193–202.

34. For the Jackalope, see *Journal of Laboratory and Clinical Medicine* 147 (2006): 52.

35. Linda Dégh, "UFOs and How Folklorists Should Look at Them," *Fabula* 18 (1977): 242–248.

36. J. Allen Hynek, "Swamp Gas Plus Ten . . . And Counting," in *1976 MUFON Symposium Proceedings*, ed. N. Joseph Gurney (Seguin, TX: Mutual UFO Network, 1976), 78.

37. Hendry, *UFO Handbook*, 45–46.

38. Jan Vansina, *Oral Tradition: A Study in Historical Methodology* (Chicago: Aldine, 1965), 45–46, 111–112, 120–121, 183–186.

39. Luise White, *Speaking with Vampires: Rumor and History in Colonial Africa* (Berkeley: University of California Press, 2000), 3–10, 30–43.

40. Don Ecker, "Freedom of Disinformation," *Fortean Times* no. 122 (June 1999): 31.

41. Bullard, "What's New in UFO Abductions?" 173–175, 186.

42. William K. Hartmann, "Process of Perception, Conception, and Reporting," in *Scientific Study of Unidentified Flying Objects*, ed. Daniel S. Gillmor (New York: E. P. Dutton & Co., 1969), 574–575.

43. Martin Jasek, *Giant UFO in the Yukon Territory* (Delta, B.C.: UFO*BC, 2000), esp. 1–2, 28–31.

44. In 1972 the molecular biologist Gunther Stent proposed that an important reason why scientists reject a new discovery, even one that will later become accepted, is prematurity. "A discovery is premature," he said, "if its implications cannot be connected by a series of simple logical steps to contemporary canonical knowledge" (Gunther S. Stent, "Prematurity in Scientific Discovery, in *Prematurity in Scientific Discovery*, ed. Ernest B. Hook [Berkeley: University of California Press, 2002], 24). Even if UFOs met other scientific standards for evidence, acceptance would still be likely to falter over this criterion. The gap between UFO evidence and UFO implications remains too wide to overcome scientific caution.

45. Heldervelez, "Explaining the O'Hare Airport UFO," *Physics Forums*, November 22, 2008, http://www.physicsforums.com/showthread.php?t=274003.

46. Jacques Vallee, *Confrontations: A Scientist's Search for Alien Contact* (New York: Ballantine Books, 1990), 231–244.

47. Giuseppi Cocconi and Philip Morrison, "Searching for Interstellar Communications," *Nature* 184 (September 19, 1959): 846.

Select Bibliography

Adamski, George. *Inside the Space Ships*. New York: Abelard-Schuman, 1955.

———. *Flying Saucers Farewell*. New York: Abelard-Schuman, 1961.

Aghion, Irène, Claire Barbillon, and François Lissarrague. *Gods and Heroes of Classical Antiquity*. New York: Flammarion, 1996.

Aldrich, Jan L. *Project 1947: A Preliminary Report*. N.p.: UFO Research Coalition, 1997.

Allnutt, Frank. *Infinite Encounters*. Old Tappan, NJ: Spire Books, 1978.

Allport, Gordon W., and Leo J. Postman. *The Psychology of Rumor*. New York: Holt, Rinehart & Winston, 1965.

Alnor, William M. *UFO Cults and the New Millennium*. Grand Rapids: Baker Books, 1998.

Angelucci, Orfeo. *Secret of the Saucers*. Amherst, WI: Amherst Press, 1955.

"The Anomaly Foundation Solves the 'Manises' UFO Case: 20 Years of Mystery Are Over." *Anomaly Foundation*. http://www.anomalia.org/manisen.htm.

Appelle, Stuart. "The Abduction Experience: A Critical Evaluation of Theory and Evidence." *Journal of UFO Studies*, n.s., 6 (1995–1996): 29–78.

Appelle, Stuart, Steven Jay Lynn, and Leonard Newman. "Alien Abduction Experiences." In *Varieties of Anomalous Experience: Examining the Scientific Evidence*, edited by Etzel Cardeña, Steven Jay Lynn, and Stanley Krippner, 253–282. Washington, DC: American Psychological Association, 2000.

Ashtar. *In Days to Come*. Los Angeles: New Age Co., 1955.

Asimov, Isaac. *Futuredays: A Nineteenth-Century Vision of the Year 2000*. New York: Henry Holt & Co., 1986.

Auchettl, John. *The Knowles Family Encounter*. Melbourne: Victorian UFO Research Society, 1989.

Baker, Carey H. "The Fyffe, Alabama, Experience." In *MUFON 1990 International UFO Symposium Proceedings*, edited by Walter H. Andrus Jr., 86–91. Seguin, TX: Mutual UFO Network, 1990.

Balch, Robert W. "Waiting for the Ships: Disillusionment and the Revitalization of Faith in Bo and Peep's UFO Cult." In *The Gods Have Landed*, edited by James R. Lewis, 137–166. Albany: State University of New York Press, 1995.

Bannerman-Richter, Gabriel. *Mmoetia: The Mysterious Little People*. N.p.; Gabari, 1987.

Barker, Gray. 1953. "West Virginia 'Monster'—A Full Report." *Saucerian* 1 (September 1953): 8–21.

———. *They Knew Too Much about Flying Saucers*. New York: University Books, 1956.

Barkun, Michael. *A Culture of Conspiracy: Apocalyptic Visions in Contemporary America*. Berkeley: University of California Press, 2003.

Bartholomew, Robert E., Keith Basterfield, and George S. Howard. "UFO Abductees and Contactees: Psychopathology or Fantasy Proneness?" *Professional Psychology: Research and Practice* 22 (1991): 215–222.

Bartholomew, Robert E., and George S. Howard. *UFOs and Alien Contact: Two Centuries of Mystery*. Amherst, NY: Prometheus Books, 1998.

Bartlett, Frederic C. *Remembering: A Study in Experimental and Social Psychology*. London: Cambridge University Press, 1964.

Bartra, Roger. *Wild Men in the Looking Glass: The Mythic Origins of European Otherness*. Ann Arbor: University of Michigan Press, 1994.

Bascom, William. "The Forms of Folklore: Prose Narratives." In *Sacred Narrative*, edited by Alan Dundes, 5–29. Berkeley: University of California Press, 1984.

Bass, Ellen, and Laura Davis. *The Courage to Heal: A Guide for Women Survivors of Child Sexual Abuse*. New York: Harper & Row, 1988.

Bassett, Stephen. "Disclosure in the Age of Secrecy." *UFO Magazine* (U.S.), April–May 2004, 26–28.

Basterfield, Keith, Vladimir Godic, Pony Godic, and Mark Rodeghier. "Australian Ufology: A Review." *Journal of UFO Studies*, n.s., no. 2 (1990): 19–44.

Bateman, Stephen. *The Doome Warning All Men to the Judgemente*. [London]: Imprinted by Ralphe Nubery, 1581.

Baxter, John, and Thomas Atkins. *The Fire Came By: The Riddle of the Great Siberian Explosion*. Garden City, NY: Doubleday, 1976.

Beal, Timothy K. *Religion and Its Monsters*. New York: Routledge, 2002.

Bender, Albert K. *Flying Saucers and the Three Men*. Clarksburg, WV: Saucerian Books, 1962.

Benedict, Ruth. *Patterns of Culture*. 1934. Reprint, New York: Mentor Books, 1959.

Benjamin, Marina. *Rocket Dreams: How the Space Age Shaped Our Vision of a World Beyond*. New York: Free Press, 2003.

Bennett, David H. *The Party of Fear: From Nativist Movements to the New Right in American History*. Chapel Hill: University of North Carolina Press, 1988.

Berliner, Don. *UFO Briefing Document: The Best Available Evidence*. New York: Dell, 2000.

Berlitz, Charles, and William L. Moore. *The Roswell Incident*. New York: Grossett & Dunlap, 1980.

Bethurum, Truman. *Aboard a Flying Saucer*. Los Angeles: DeVorss & Co., 1954.

Bidney, David. "Myth, Symbolism, and Truth." In *Myth: A Symposium*, edited by Thomas A. Sebeok, 3–24. Bloomington: Indiana University Press, 1971.

Bieri, Robert. "Huminoids [*sic*] on Other Planets?" *American Scientist* 52 (1964): 452–458.

Bissell, Tom. "A Comet's Tale: On the Science of Apocalypse." *Harper's Magazine* (February 2003): 33–47.

Blackmore, Susan J. "Alien Abductions, Sleep Paralysis and the Temporal Lobe." *European Journal of UFO and Abduction Studies* 1 (2000): 113–118.

Blinderman, Barry, and Bill Conger. *The UFO Show*. Normal: University Galleries, Illinois State University, 2000.

Bloch, Ruth. *Visionary Republic: Millennial Themes in American Thought, 1756–1800*. New York: Cambridge University Press, 1985.

Bloecher, Ted. *Report on the UFO Wave of 1947*. N.p.: Author, 1967.

Bloecher, Ted, Aphrodite Clamar, and Budd Hopkins. *Final Report on the Psychological Testing of UFO "Abductees."* Mount Rainier, MD: Fund for UFO Research, 1985.

Blumrich, Josef F. *The Spaceships of Ezekiel*. New York: Bantam Books, 1974.

Bougard, Michel. *La chronique des O.V.N.I.* Paris: Jean-Pierre Delarge, 1977.

Bowen, Charles, ed. *The Humanoids*, FSR, special issue, October–November 1966. Expanded ed., Chicago: Henry Regnery, 1969.

Boyer, Pascal. *The Naturalness of Religious Ideas: A Cognitive Theory of Religion*. Berkeley: University of California Press, 1994.

Boyer, Paul. *When Time Shall Be No More: Prophecy Belief in Modern American Culture*. Cambridge, MA: Harvard University Press, 1992.

Branston, Brian. *Gods of the North*. New York: Vanguard Press, 1957.

Branton. *The Dulce Wars: Underground Alien Bases and the Battle for Planet Earth*. New Brunswick, NJ: Inner Light / Global Communications, 1999.

Briggs, Katharine. *An Encyclopedia of Fairies*. New York: Pantheon Books, 1976.

———. *The Vanishing People: Fairly Lore and Legends*. New York: Pantheon Books, 1978.

Bruni, Georgina. *You Can't Tell the People: The Definitive Account of the Rendlesham Forest Mystery*. London: Sidgwick and Jackson, 2000.

Brunvand, Jan Harold. *The Vanishing Hitchhiker: American Urban Legends and Their Meanings*. New York: W. W. Norton & Co., 1981.

———. *Encyclopedia of Urban Legends*. Santa Barbara, CA: ABC-Clio, 2001.

Bryan, C.D.B. *Close Encounters of the Fourth Kind: Alien Abductions, UFOs, and the Conference at M.I.T.* New York: Alfred A. Knopf, 1995.

Buck, William. *Ramayana*. New York: New American Library, 1978.

Budge, E. A. Wallis. *Egyptian Literature*. Vol. 1, *Legends of the Gods*. London: Kegan Paul, Trench, Trübner & Co., 1912.

———. *The Gods of the Egyptians*. 2 vols. New York: Dover, 1969.

———. *The Egyptian Heaven and Hell*. La Salle, IL: Open Court, 1974.

———. *Egyptian Religion: Egyptian Ideas of the Future Life*. Boston: Routledge & Kegan Paul, 1975.

Bullard, Thomas E. *UFO Abductions: The Measure of a Mystery*. 2 vols. Mount Ranier, MD: Fund for UFO Research, 1987.

———. "Folkloric Dimensions of the UFO Phenomenon." *Journal of UFO Studies*, n.s., 3 (1991): 1–57.

———. "A Comparative Study of Abduction Reports Update." In *Alien Discussions*, edited by Andrea Pritchard et al., 45–47. Cambridge, MA: North Cambridge Press, 1994.

———. *The Sympathetic Ear: Investigators as Variables in UFO Abduction Reports*. Mount Rainier, MD: Fund for UFO Research, 1995.

———. "Ancient Astronauts." In *Encyclopedia of the Paranormal*, edited by Gordon Stein, 25–32. Amherst, NY: Prometheus Books, 1996.

———. "Abduction Phenomenon." In *The UFO Encyclopedia*, 2nd ed., edited by Jerome Clark, 1–26. Detroit: Omnigraphics, 1998.

————."Anomalous Aerial Phenomena before 1800." In *The UFO Encyclopedia*, 2nd ed., edited by Jerome Clark, 121–138. Detroit: Omnigraphics, 1998.

————."Waves." In *The UFO Encyclopedia*, 2nd ed., edited by Jerome Clark, 1004–1023. Detroit: Omnigraphics, 1998.

————."What's New in UFO Abductions: Has the Story Changed in 30 Years?" In *MUFON 1999 International UFO Symposium Proceedings*, edited by Walter H. Andrus Jr. and Irena Scott, 170–199. Seguin, TX: MUFON, 1999.

————."False Memories and UFO Abductions." *Journal of UFO Studies*, n.s., 8 (2003): 85–160.

Burrin, Philippe. "Nazi Antisemitism: Animalization and Demonization." In *Demonizing the Other: Antisemitism, Racism, and Xenophobia*, edited by Robert S. Wistrich, 223–235. Amsterdam: Harwood Academic, 1999.

Busby, Michael. *Solving the 1897 Airship Mystery*. Gretna, LA: Pelican, 2004.

Butler, Brenda, Dot Street, and Jenny Randles. *Sky Crash: A Cosmic Conspiracy*. Sudbury, Suffolk: Neville Spearman, 1984.

Camerarius, Joachim. *The History of Strange Wonders, or The Epistle of One Friend to Another, of a Strange Fyre That Was Sene in the Aire both Longe and Brode almost through Al Germany. . . .* London: Imprinted by Roulande Hall, 1561.

Campbell, Joseph. *The Hero with a Thousand Faces*. Princeton, NJ: Princeton University Press, 1971.

Campbell, Mary B. *The Witness and the Other World: Exotic European Travel Writing, 400–1600*. Ithaca, NY: Cornell University Press, 1988.

"Canals on Mars All Nonsense." *St. Louis Republic*, feature section, February 13, 1916.

Cantril, Hadley. *The Invasion from Mars: A Study in the Psychology of Panic*. New York: Harper Torchbooks, 1966.

Cardeña, Etzel, Steven Jay Lynn, and Stanley Krippner, eds. *Varieties of Anomalous Experience: Examining the Scientific Evidence*. Washington, DC: American Psychological Association, 2000.

Carlton, Michele. "Children of Kelly Witnesses Firmly Believe Their Father Shot at Entities." *MUFON UFO Journal*, no. 481 (February 2003): 9–10.

Carpenter, John. "Gerald Anderson: Disturbing Revelations—A Series of Hoaxes Casts Doubt on an 'Eyewitness' Crashed Saucer Account." *MUFON UFO Journal*, no. 299 (March 1993): 6–9.

Carroll, Michael P. *The Cult of the Virgin Mary: Psychological Origins*. Princeton, NJ: Princeton University Press, 1986.

Cashman, Mark. "Is Anyone Looking at Us? The Mars Face after Global Surveyor." *UFO Magazine* (U.S.), August 1998, 4–9.

Cavendish, Richard. *Visions of Heaven and Hell*. London: Orbis, 1977.

Chalker, Bill. "Airship Sightings in New Zealand and Australia." In *UFO Encyclopedia*, edited by Jerome Clark, 42–44. Detroit: Omnigraphics, 1998.

————."The Raccoon and the Nobel Prize." *MUFON UFO Journal*, no. 420 (April 2003): 6–7.

Cheney, Margaret. *Tesla: Man Out of Time*. New York: Delta, 1998.

Childress, David Hatcher. *Extraterrestrial Archaeology*. Stella, IL: Adventures Unlimited Press, 1994.

Christopher, Kevin. "Mexican Air Force UFOs Likely Equipment Artifacts." *Skeptical Inquirer* 28, no. 4 (2004): 5.

Chryssides, George D. "Scientific Creationism: A Study of the Raelian Church." In *UFO Religions*, edited by Christopher Partridge, 45–61. New York: Routledge, 2003.

Cicero. *De senectute, de amicita, de divinatione* (Loeb Classical Library). Cambridge, MA: Harvard University Press, 1964.

Clancy, Susan A. *Abducted: How People Come to Believe They Were Kidnapped by Aliens.* Cambridge, MA: Harvard University Press, 2005.

Clancy, Susan A., Richard J. McNally, Daniel L. Schacter, Mark F. Lenzenweger, and Roger K. Pitman. "Memory Distortion in People Reporting Abduction by Aliens." *Journal of Abnormal Psychology* 111 (2002): 459–460.

Clark, Jerome, and Loren Coleman. *The Unidentified: Notes toward Solving the UFO Mystery.* New York: Warner Paperback Library, 1975.

———. "The Fall and Rise of the Extraterrestrial Hypothesis." In *MUFON 1988 International UFO Symposium Proceedings*, edited by Walter H. Andrus Jr. and Richard H. Hall, 59–72. Seguin, TX: MUFON, 1988.

———. *The UFO Encyclopedia: The Phenomenon from the Beginning*, 2nd ed., 2 vols. Detroit: Omnigraphics, 1998.

Clark, Jerome, and Marcello Truzzi. *UFO Encounters: Sightings, Visitations, and Investigations.* Lincolnwood, IL: Publications International, 1992.

Clarke, Arthur C. *Profiles of the Future: An Inquiry into the Limits of the Possible.* 1962. London: Pan Books, 1983.

Clarke, David. *The Angel of Mons: Phantom Soldiers and Ghostly Guardians.* Chichester, West Sussex: John Wiley & Sons, 2005.

Classic of the Mountains and Seas. New York: Penguin Books, 1999.

Clastres, Hélène. *The Land-Without-Evil: Tupí-Guaraní Prophetism.* Urbana: University of Illinois Press, 1995.

Cocconi, Giuseppi, and Philip Morrison. "Searching for Interstellar Communications." *Nature* 184 (September 19, 1959): 846.

Cohn, Norman. *Europe's Inner Demons: An Enquiry Inspired by the Great Witch-Hunt.* New York: Basic Books, 1975.

———. "How Time Acquired a Consummation." In *Apocalypse Theory and the Ends of the World*, edited by Malcolm Bull, 21–37. Cambridge, MA: Blackwell, 1995.

Collings, Beth, and Anna Jamerson. *Connections: Solving Our Alien Abduction Mystery.* Newberg, OR: Wild Flower Press, 1996.

Commager, Henry Steele. *The American Mind.* New Haven, CT: Yale University Press, 1963.

Commoner, Barry. *The Closing Circle: Nature, Man, and Technology.* New York: Alfred A. Knopf, 1971.

Comte, Auguste. *Auguste Comte and Positivism: The Essential Writings.* Edited by Gertrud Lenzer. New York: Harper Torchbooks, 1975.

Cooper, Milton William. *Behold a Pale Horse.* Flagstaff: Light Technology, 1991.

Corn, Joseph J., and Brian Horrigan. *Yesterday's Tomorrows: Past Visions of the American Future.* Baltimore: Johns Hopkins University Press, 1996.

Corso, Philip J. *The Day After Roswell*. New York: Pocket Books, 1997.

Cox, Harvey. *Fire from Heaven*. Reading, MA: Addison-Wesley, 1995.

Crowe, Michael J. *The Extraterrestrial Life Debate 1750–1900: The Idea of a Plurality of Worlds from Kant to Lowell*. New York: Cambridge: Cambridge University Press, 1986.

Cruttwell, N. G. "Flying Saucers over Papua." *FSR*, special issue, no. 4 (August 1971): 3–38.

Cumont, Franz. *After Life in Roman Paganism*. New York: Dover, 1959.

Cunningham, Andrew, and Ole Peter Grell. *The Four Horsemen of the Apocalypse: Religion, War, Famine and Death in Reformation Europe*. New York: Cambridge University Press, 2000.

Curran, Douglas. *In Advance of the Landing: Folk Concepts of Outer Space*. New York: Abbeville Press, 1985.

Dalley, Stephanie, trans. *Myths from Mesopotamia: Creation, the Flood, Gilgamesh, and Others*. New York: Oxford University Press, 1991.

Däniken, Erich von. "Chariots of the Gods?" In *In Search of the Gods*, 9–182. New York: Avinel Books, 1989.

Darrach, Jr., H. B., and Robert Ginna. "Have We Visitors from Space?" *Life*, April 7, 1952, 80–96.

Dash, Mike. "Springheeled Jack: To Victorian Bugaboo from Suburban Ghost." *Fortean Studies* 3 (1996): 7–125.

Daston, Lorraine, and Katherine Park. *Wonders and the Order of Nature 1150–1750*. New York: Zone Books, 1998.

Davidson, Hilda Ellis. *The Road to Hel: A Study of the Conception of the Dead in Old Norse Literature*. New York: Greenwood Press, 1968.

———. "The Wild Hunt." In *Supernatural Enemies*, edited by Davidson and Anna Chaudhri, 163–176. Durham, NC: Carolina Academic Press, 2001.

Davidson, Leon. *Flying Saucers: An Analysis of the Air Force Project Blue Book Special Report No. 14*. 4th ed. White Plains, NY: Author, 1971.

Davis, Isabel, and Ted Bloecher. *Close Encounter at Kelly and Others of 1955*. Evanston, IL: CUFOS, 1978.

Day, Duncan John Andrew. "Psychological Correlates of the UFO Abduction Experience: The Role of Beliefs and Indirect Suggestions on Abduction Accounts Obtained during Hypnosis." Ph.D. diss., Concordia University, Montreal, 1998.

Dean, Jodi. *Aliens in America: Conspiracy Cultures from Outerspace to Cyberspace*. Ithaca, NY: Cornell University Press, 1998.

Dégh, Linda. "UFOs and How Folklorists Should Look at Them." *Fabula* 18 (1977): 242–248.

———. "Processes of Legend Formation." In *Narratives in Society: A Performer-Centered Study of Narration*, edited by Linda Dégh, 226–235. Helsinki: Suomalainen Tiedeakatemia, 1995.

———. *Legend and Belief: Dialectics of a Folklore Genre*. Bloomington: Indiana University Press, 2001.

Dégh, Linda, and Andrew Vázsonyi. "The Memorate and the Proto-Memorate." *Journal of American Folklore* 87 (1974): 225–239.

———. "Legend and Belief." In *Folklore Genres*, edited by Dan Ben-Amos, 93–123. Austin: University of Texas Press, 1976.

———. "The Crack in the Red Goblet, or Truth in Modern Legend." In *Narratives in Society: A*

Performer-Centered Study of Narration, edited by Linda Dégh, 152–170. Helsinki: Suomalainen Tiedeakatemia, 1995.

———."The Hypothesis of Multi-Conduit Transmission in Folklore." In *Narratives in Society: A Performer-Centered Study of Narration,* edited by Linda Dégh, 173–212. Helsinki: Suomalainen Tiedeakatemia, 1995.

Delumeau, Jean. *History of Paradise: The Garden of Eden in Myth and Tradition.* New York: Continuum, 1995.

Denzler, Brenda. *The Lure of the Edge: Scientific Passions, Religious Beliefs, and the Pursuit of UFOs.* Berkeley: University of California Press, 2001.

Dhalla, Maneckji Nusservanji. *Zoroastrian Theology.* New York: AMS Press, 1972.

Dick, Steven J. *Plurality of Worlds: The Origins of the Extraterrestrial Life Debate from Democrates to Kant.* New York: Cambridge University Press, 1982.

———. *The Biological Universe: The Twentieth Century Extraterrestrial Life Debate and the Limits of Science.* New York: Cambridge University Press, 1996.

Dick, Thomas. *Celestial Scenery.* Brookfield, MA: E. & L. Merriam, 1838.

Dickinson, Terence. *The Zeta Reticuli Incident.* Milwaukee, WI: AstroMedia Corporation, 1976.

Documents Describing UFO/Helicopter Overflights of U.S.A.F. Bases in 1975, Obtained by Citizens against UFO Secrecy. Evanston, IL: CUFOS, n.d.

Donovan, Roberta, and Keith Wolverton. *Mystery Stalks the Prairie.* Raynesford, MT: THAR Institute, 1976.

Doty, William G. *Mythography: The Study of Myth and Ritual.* Tuscaloosa: University of Alabama Press, 1986.

Duke, Phillip S. *The AIDS-ET Connection.* Omaha: Cosmos Press, 1999.

Eberhart, George M., ed. *The Roswell Report: A Historical Perspective.* Chicago: CUFOS, 1991.

Ecker, Don. "Freedom of Disinformation." *Fortean Times,* no. 122 (June 1999): 28–31.

Ecker, Vicki. "A Clone of Their Own," *UFO Magazine* (U.S.), February–March 2001, 44–51.

Eliade, Mircea. *Cosmos and History: The Myth of the Eternal Return.* New York: Harper Torchbooks, 1959.

———. *Patterns in Comparative Religion.* Cleveland: Meridian Books, 1963.

———. *Shamanism: Archaic Techniques of Ecstasy.* Princeton, NJ: Princeton University Press, 1972.

Eliot, Alexander. *Myths.* New York: McGraw-Hill Book Co., 1976.

Ellingson, Ter. *The Myth of the Noble Savage.* Berkeley: University of California Press, 2001.

Ellis, Bill. *Raising the Devil: Satanism, New Religions, and the Media.* Lexington: University Press of Kentucky, 2000.

———. *Aliens, Ghosts, and Cults: The Legends We Live.* Jackson: University Press of Mississippi, 2001.

Erdész, Sándor. "The World Conception of Lajos Ámi, Storyteller." *Acta Ethnographica* 10 (1961): 327–344.

Evans, David S. "The Great Moon Hoax." *Sky and Telescope* 62, no. 3 (1981): 196–198; no. 4 (1981): 308–311.

Evans, Hilary. *Visions, Apparitions, Alien Visitors: A Comparative Study of the Entity Enigma.* Wellingborough, Northamptonshire: Aquarian Press, 1984.

Evans-Pritchard, E. E. *Witchcraft, Oracles and Magic among the Azande*. Oxford: Clarendon Press, 1937.

Evanzz, Karl. *The Messenger: The Rise and Fall of Elijah Muhammad*. New York: Vintage Books, 2001.

Ewers, Hanns Heinz. "Alraune." In *The Daedalus Book of German Decadence: Voices of the Abyss*, edited by Ray Furness, 206–253. New York: Daedalus / Hippocrene, 1994.

Fairchild, Hoxie Neale. *The Romantic Quest*. Philadelphia: Albert Saifer, 1931.

Fawcett, Lawrence, and Barry J. Greenwood. *Clear Intent: The Government Coverup of the UFO Experience*. Englewood Cliffs, NJ: Prentice-Hall, 1984.

Felton, D. *Haunted Greece and Rome: Ghost Stories from Classical Antiquity*. Austin: University of Texas Press, 1999.

Fernandes, Joaquim, and Fina D'Armada. *Heavenly Lights: The Apparition of Fátima and the UFO Phenomenon*. Victoria, BC: EcceNova Editions, 2005.

Festinger, Leon, Henry W. Riecken, and Stanley Schachter. *When Prophecy Fails*. New York: Harper Torchbooks, 1964.

Finkelhor, David. *Sexually Victimized Children*. New York: Free Press, 1979.

Finucane, R. C. *Ghosts: Appearances of the Dead and Cultural Transformation*. Amherst, NY: Prometheus Books, 1996.

———. "Historical Introduction: The Example of Early Modern and Nineteenth-Century England." In *Hauntings and Poltergeists: Multidisciplinary Perspectives*, edited by James Houran and Rense Lange, 9–17. Jefferson, NC: McFarland & Co., 2001.

Flammarion, Camille. *Urania*. Boston: Estes & Lauriat, 1890.

———. *La planète Mars et ses conditions d'habitabilité: Synthèse générale de toutes les observations*. Paris: Gauthier-Villars et Fils, t.1, 1892; t.2, 1909.

———. *Popular Astronomy*. London: Chatto & Windus, 1907.

Flint, Valerie I. J. *The Imaginative Landscape of Christopher Columbus*. Princeton, NJ: Princeton University Press, 1992.

Florescano, Enrique. *The Myth of Quetzalcoatl*. Baltimore: Johns Hopkins University Press, 1999.

Fontenelle, Bernard le Bovier de. *Conversations on the Plurality of Worlds*. Berkeley: University of California Press, 1990.

Fort, Charles. *The Books of Charles Fort*. New York: Henry Holt, 1959.

Fowler, Raymond E. *Unidentified Flying Objects, Hearing by Committee on Armed Services of the House of Representatives, Eighty-Ninth Congress, Second Session, April 5, 1966*. Washington, DC: U.S. Government Printing Office, 1966.

———. *The Andreasson Affair: The Documented Investigation of a Woman's Abduction aboard a UFO*. Englewood Cliffs, NJ: Prentice-Hall, 1979.

———. *Casebook of a UFO Investigator*. Englewood Cliffs, NJ: Prentice-Hall, 1981.

———. *The Andreasson Affair, Phase Two: The Continuing Investigation of a Woman's Abduction by Alien Beings*. Englewood Cliffs, NJ: Prentice-Hall, 1982.

———. *The Allagash Abductions*. Tigard, OR: Wild Flower Press, 1993.

Freud, Sigmund. "The Uncanny." In *Collected Papers*. Vol. 4. London: Hogarth Press, 1948.

Freyd, Jennifer J. *Betrayal Trauma: The Logic of Forgetting Childhood Abuse*. Cambridge, MA: Harvard University Press, 1996.

Friedman, John Block. *The Monstrous Races in Medieval Art and Thought*. Cambridge, MA: Harvard University Press, 1981.

Friedman, Stanton T. "Update on Operation Majestic-12." In *MUFON 1989 International UFO Symposium Proceedings*, edited by Walter H. Andrus, 82–112. Seguin, TX: Mutual UFO Network, 1989.

Friedman, Stanton T., and William L. Moore. "The Roswell Incident: Beginning of the Cosmic Watergate." In *1981 MUFON Symposium Proceedings*, edited by Walter H. Andrus Jr. and Dennis W. Stacy, 132–153. Seguin, TX: Mutual UFO Network, 1981.

Fry, Daniel W. *To Men of Earth*. 1954. Merlin, OR: Merlin, 1973.

Frye, Northrop. *The Anatomy of Criticism*. New York: Atheneum, 1966.

Fukuyama, Francis. *The End of History and the Last Man*. New York: Free Press, 1992.

Fuller, John G. *Incident at Exeter: Unidentified Flying Objects over America Now*. New York: G. P. Putnam's Sons, 1966.

———. *The Interrupted Journey*. 1966. New York: Berkley Medallion Books, 1974.

Gardiner, Eileen, ed. *Visions of Heaven and Hell before Dante*. New York: Italica Press, 1989.

Gervase of Tilbury. *Otia Imperialia: Recreation for an Emperor*. Oxford: Clarendon Press, 2002.

Gillmor, Daniel S., ed. *Scientific Study of Unidentified Flying Objects*. New York: Bantam Books, 1969.

Gilmore, David D. *Monsters: Evil Beings, Mythical Beasts, and All Manner of Imaginary Terror*. Philadelphia: University of Pennsylvania Press, 2003.

Goode, Erich, and Nachman Ben-Yehuda. *Moral Panics: The Social Construction of Deviance*. Cambridge, MA: Blackwell, 1994.

Gould, Stephen Jay. *Dinosaurs in a Haystack: Reflections in Natural History*. New York: Harmony Books, 1994.

Gow, Kathryn, Janine Lurie, Stuart Coppin, Ari Popper, Anthony Powell, and Keith Basterfield. "Fantasy Proneness and Other Psychological Correlates of UFO Experience." *European Journal of UFO and Abduction Studies* 2 (2001): 45–66.

Green, Roger Lancelyn. *Into Other Worlds: Space-Flight in Fiction from Lucian to Lewis*. New York: Abelard-Schuman, 1958.

Greer, Steven M. *Extraterrestrial Contact: The Evidence and Implications*. Afton, VA: Crossing Point, 1999.

———. *Disclosure: Military and Government Witnesses Reveal the Greatest Secrets in Modern History*. Crozet, VA: Crossing Point, 2001.

Griffith, George. "Stories of Other Worlds." In *Science Fiction by the Rivals of H. G. Wells*, edited by Alan K. Russell, 117–188. Secaucus, NJ: Castle Books, 1979.

Grinspoon, Lester, and Alan D. Persky. "Psychiatry and UFO Reports." In *UFOs—A Scientific Debate*, edited by Carl Sagan and Thornton Page, 233–246. Ithaca, NY: Cornell University Press, 1972.

Grittner, Frederick K. *White Slavery: Myth, Ideology, and American Law*. New York: Garland, 1990.

Gross, Loren E. *UFOs: A History*. Fremont, CA: Author, 1982–2006.

Gross, Paul R., and Norman Levitt. *Higher Superstition: The Academic Left and Its Quarrel with Science*. Baltimore: Johns Hopkins University Press, 1994.

Grosso, Michael. "UFOs and the Myth of the New Age." *ReVision* 11, no. 3 (1989): 5–13.

Guiteras-Holmes, C. *Perils of the Soul: The World View of a Tzotzil Indian*. New York: Free Press of Glencoe, 1961.

Haldane, J.B.S. *Possible Worlds and Other Essays*. London: Chatto & Windus, 1928.

Hall, Edith. *Inventing the Barbarian: Greek Self-Definition through Tragedy*. Oxford: Clarendon Press, 1980.

Hall, Richard H. *The UFO Evidence*. Washington, DC: National Investigations Committee on Aerial Phenomena, 1964.

———. *The UFO Evidence: A Thirty-Year Report*. Vol. 2. Lanham, MD: Scarecrow Press, 2000.

Hansen, Terry. *The Missing Times: News Media Complicity in the UFO Cover-up*. Bloomington, IN: X-Libris Corp., 2000.

Hardy, David. *The Encyclopedia of Science Fiction Movies*. Minneapolis: Woodbury Press, 1984.

Hartland, Edwin Sidney. *The Science of Fairy Tales: An Inquiry into Fairy Mythology*. London: Walter Scott, 1891.

Hartmann, William K. "Processes of Perception, Conception, and Reporting." In *Scientific Study of Unidentified Flying Objects*, edited by Daniel S. Gillmor, 567–590. New York: Bantam Books, 1969.

Hartog, François. *The Mirror of Herodotus: The Representation of the Other in the Writing of History*. Berkeley: University of California Press, 1988.

Heath, Gord. "What Really Happened to Lt. Gene Moncla? The Missing Kinross F-89 Mystery Endures through Time." *UFO B.C. Quarterly* 8, no. 1 (Winter 2003): 7–14.

Heide, George Hans. "Dwarfs in German Folk Legends: An Inquiry into the Human Qualities of These Creatures." Ph.D. diss., University of California at Los Angeles, 1976.

Heilbroner, Robert. *Visions of the Future: The Distant Past, Yesterday, Today, and Tomorrow*. New York: Oxford University Press, 1995.

Hendry, Alan. *The UFO Handbook*. Garden City, NY: Doubleday & Co., 1979.

Hickson, Charles, and William Mendez. *UFO Contact at Pascagoula*. Tucson: Wendelle C. Stevens, 1983.

Hind, Cynthia. *UFOs Over Africa*. Madison, WI: Horus House Press, 1996.

Hoffmann, Bill, and Cathy Burke. *Heaven's Gate: Cult Suicide in San Diego*. New York: Harper Paperbacks, 1997.

Hofstadter, Richard. *The Paranoid Style in American Politics and Other Essays*. New York: Alfred A. Knopf, 1965.

———. *Anti-Intellectualism in American Life*. New York: Alfred A. Knopf, 1966.

Honko, Lauri. "Memorates and the Study of Folk Belief." *Journal of the Folklore Institute* 1 (1969): 5–19.

———. "The Problem of Defining Myth." In *Sacred Narrative*, Alan Dundes, 41–52. Berkeley: University of California Press, 1984.

Hopkins, Budd. *Missing Time: A Documented Study of UFO Abductions*. New York: Richard Marek, 1981.

———. *Intruders: The Incredible Visitations at Copley Woods*. New York: Random House, 1987.

———. "UFO Abductions—The Skeleton Key." In *MUFON 1988 International UFO Symposium*

Proceedings, edited by Walter H. Andrus Jr. and Richard H. Hall, 104–112. Seguin, TX: Mutual UFO Network, 1988.

———. *Witnessed: The True Story of the Brooklyn Bridge UFO Abductions.* New York: Pocket Books, 1993.

———."*Communion* Cover Error Creates a Type of Scientific Control." *MUFON UFO Journal*, no. 455 (March 2006): 3–5.

Horn, Michael. "Meier Contacts." In *Encyclopedia of Extraterrestrial Encounters*, edited by Ronald D. Story, 337–342. New York: New American Library, 2001.

Horne, John, and Alan Kramer. *German Atrocities 1914: A History of Denial.* New Haven, CT: Yale University Press, 2001.

Hornung, Erik. *The Ancient Egyptian Books of the Afterlife.* Ithaca, NY: Cornell University Press, 1999.

Hoskin, Michael, ed. *The Cambridge Illustrated History of Astronomy.* New York: Cambridge University Press, 1997.

Howe, Linda Moulton. *An Alien Harvest.* Littleton, CO: Linda Moulton Howe Productions, 1989.

———. *Glimpses of Other Realities.* Vol. 1, *Facts and Eyewitnesses.* Huntingdon Valley, PA: Linda Moulton Howe Publications, 1993.

———. "1994 Animal Mutilation Research Grant: Summary of Case Studies." In *MUFON 1995 International UFO Symposium*, edited by Walter H. Andrus Jr. and Irena Scott, 136–147. Seguin, TX: MUFON, 1995.

———. *Glimpses of Other Realities.* Vol. 2, *High Strangeness.* New Orleans: Paper Chase Press, 1998.

Hufford, David J. *The Terror That Comes in the Night: An Experience-Centered Study of Supernatural Assault Traditions.* Philadelphia: University of Pennsylvania Press, 1982.

———. "Traditions of Disbelief." *New York Folklore* 8 (1982): 47–55.

———. "Beings without Bodies: An Experience-Centered Theory of the Belief in Spirits." In *Out of the Ordinary: Folklore and the Supernatural*, edited by Barbara Walker, 11–45. Logan: Utah State University Press, 1995.

Hughes, Robert. *Heaven and Hell in Western Art.* New York: Stein & Day, 1968.

Hultkrantz, Åke. *The Religions of the American Indians.* Berkeley: University of California Press, 1979.

Hume, David. "Of Miracles." In *An Enquiry concerning Human Understanding*, sec. 10, pt. 1. New York: Longmans, Green & Co., 1898.

Huygens, Christian. *The Celestial Worlds Discover'd.* London: Frank Cass & Co., 1968.

Hynek, J. Allen. "UFOs Merit Scientific Study." *Science* 154, no. 3746 (1966): 329.

———. *The UFO Experience.* Chicago: Henry Regnery, 1972.

———. "Swamp Gas Plus Ten . . . And Counting." In *1976 MUFON Symposium Proceedings*, edited by N. Joseph Gurney, 76–83. Seguin, TX: Mutual UFO Network, 1976.

———. *The Hynek UFO Report.* New York: Dell, 1977.

———. "Tracking the Hessdalen Lights." *IUR* 10, no. 2 (March–April 1985): 10–11.

Hynek, J. Allen, Philip J. Imbrogno, and Bob Pratt. *Night Siege: The Hudson Valley UFO Sightings.* New York: Ballantine Books, 1987.

Icke, David. *Children of the Matrix*. Wildwood, MO: Bridge of Love Publications, 2001.

Ikenga-Metuh, Emefie. *Comparative Studies of African Traditional Religions*. Onitsha, Nigeria: IMICO, 1987.

Israel, Paul. *Edison: A Life of Invention*. New York: John Wiley & Sons, 1998.

Jacobs, David M. *The UFO Controversy in America*. Bloomington: Indiana University Press, 1975.

———. *Secret Life: Firsthand Accounts of UFO Abductions*. New York: Simon & Schuster, 1992.

———. *The Threat*. New York: Simon & Schuster, 1998.

James, William. *The Varieties of Religious Experience*. New York: Collier Books, 1961.

Jasek, Martin. *Giant UFO in the Yukon Territory*. Delta, B.C.: UFO*BC, 2000.

Jeffrey, Kent. "Santilli's Controversial Autopsy Movie: A Comprehensive Review." *MUFON UFO Journal*, no. 335 (March 1996): 3–13.

———. "Roswell—Anatomy of a Myth." *MUFON UFO Journal*, no. 350 (June 1997): 3–17.

Jeremias, Alfred. *The Babylonian Conception of Heaven and Hell*. London: David Nutt, 1902.

Jessup, M. K. *The Case for the UFO*. New York: Citadel Press, 1955.

———. *UFO and the Bible*. New York: Citadel Press, 1956.

———. *The Expanding Case for the UFO*. New York: Citadel Press, 1957.

Johnson, Donald M. "The 'Phantom Anesthetist' of Mattoon: A Field Study of Mass Hysteria." *Journal of Abnormal and Social Psychology* 40 (1945): 175–186.

Jones, Harold Spencer. *Life on Other Worlds*. New York: Mentor Books, 1964.

Joseph, Lawrence E. *Gaia: The Growth of an Idea*. New York: St. Martin's Press, 1990.

Jung, C. G. *Flying Saucers: A Modern Myth of Things Seen in the Skies*. New York: Harcourt, Brace & Co., 1959.

Kass, Leon R. *Life, Liberty and the Defense of Dignity: The Challenge for Bioethics*. San Francisco: Encounter Books, 2002.

Keel, John A. *UFOs: Operation Trojan Horse*. New York: G. P. Putnam's Sons, 1970.

———. *The Mothman Prophecies*. New York: Signet Books, 1976.

Keen, Montague. "Doubt and Deviousness in the UK Crop Circle Scene." In *MUFON 1992 International UFO Symposium Proceedings*, edited by Walter H. Andrus Jr., 38–52. Sequin, TX: MUFON, 1992.

Keith, Jim. *Black Helicopters over America: Strikeforce for the New World Order*. Lilburn, GA: IllumiNet Press, 1994.

Kestenbaum, David. "Panel Says Some UFO Reports Worthy of Study." *Science* 281 (1998): 21.

Keul, Alexander G., and Ken Phillips. "The UFO—An Unidentified Form of Creativity?" *Journal of Transient Aerial Phenomena* 5 (1988): 36–45.

Keyhoe, Donald E. *The Flying Saucers Are Real*. New York: Fawcett Publications, 1950.

———. *The Flying Saucers from Outer Space*. New York: Henry Holt & Co., 1953.

———. *The Flying Saucer Conspiracy*. New York: Henry Holt & Co., 1955.

———. *Flying Saucers: Top Secret*. New York: G. P. Putnam's Sons, 1960.

———. *Aliens from Space*. New York: Doubleday & Co., 1973.

Klass, Philip J. *UFOs Explained*. New York: Random House, 1974.

———. *UFOs—The Public Deceived*. Buffalo, NY: Prometheus Press, 1983.

———. "The MJ-12 Papers, Pt. 2." *Skeptical Inquirer* 12, no. 3 (1988): 279–289.

———. "New Evidence of MJ-12 Hoax." *Skeptical Inquirer* 14, no. 2 (1989–1990): 135–140.

———. *The Real Roswell Crashed-Saucer Coverup.* Amherst, NY: Prometheus Books, 1997.

Klotzko, Arlene Judith. *A Clone of Your Own? The Science and Ethics of Cloning.* New York: Oxford University Press, 2004.

Knapp, George. "Area 51, Robert Lazar, and Disinformation: A Reevaluation." In *MUFON 1993 International UFO Symposium Proceedings,* edited by Walter H. Andrus Jr. and Irena Scott, 216–238. Seguin, TX: Mutual UFO Network, 1993.

———. "Knappster: Usual Scientific Explanations Lacking in Mexican UFO Case." *Las Vegas Mercury,* June 3, 2004. http://www.lasvegasmercury.com/2004/MERC-Jun-03-Thu -2004/24005082.html.

Kottmeyer, Martin. "Ufology Considered as an Evolving System of Paranoia." In *Cyberbiological Studies of the Imaginal Component in the UFO Contact Experience,* edited by Dennis Stillings, 51–60. St. Paul, MN: Archaeus Project, 1989.

———. "Abduction: The Boundary Deficit Hypothesis." *Magonia,* no. 32 (1988): 3–7.

———. "Entirely Unpredisposed." *Magonia,* no. 35 (1990): 3–10.

———. "A Universe of Spies." *Magonia,* no. 39 (April 1991): 8–14.

———. "Eye in the Sky." *Magonia,* no. 40 (August 1991): 3–8.

———. "Eye-Yi-Yi." *Magonia,* no. 41 (November 1991): 5–9.

———. "What's Up, Doc?" *Magonia,* no. 44 (October 1992): 3–7.

———. "Swinging through the Sixties." *Magonia,* no. 45 (March 1993): 7–12, 19.

———. "Shams and Shepherds." *Magonia,* no. 46 (June 1993): 8–12.

———. "The Saucer Error." *REALL News* 1, no. 4 (1993). http://www.debunker.com/texts/ SaucerError.html.

———. "Alienating Fancies: The Influencing Machine Fantasy in Ufology and the Extraterrestrial Mythos." *Magonia,* pt. 1, no. 49 (June 1994): 3–10; pt. 2, no. 50 (September 1994): 3–6.

———. "The Eyes That Spoke." *REALL News* 2, no. 7 (1994). http://www.reall.org/newsletter/ v02/n07/index.html.

———. "The Exeter File." Pts. 1 and 2. *REALL News* 4, no. 2 (1996), http://www.reall.org/newsletter/v04/n09/exeter.html; 4, no. 10 (1996), http://www.reall.org/newsletter/v04/n10/ exeter2.html.

———. "The Eyes Still Speak." *REALL News* 6, no. 5 (1998): 2, 6–9. http://www.reall.org/news letter/v06/n05/eyes-still-speak.html.

Krauss, Franklin Brunel. *An Interpretation of the Omens, Portents and Prodigies Recorded by Livy, Tacitus, and Suetonius.* Philadelphia: Author, 1930.

Kren, Thomas, and Roger S. Wieck. *The Visions of Tondal, from the Library of Margaret of York.* Malibu, CA: J. Paul Getty Museum, 1990.

Kuhn, Thomas S. *The Structure of Scientific Revolutions.* Chicago: University of Chicago Press, 1970.

Kurzweil, Ray. *The Singularity Is Near: When Humans Transcend Biology.* New York: Viking Press, 2005.

Kyle, David. *The Illustrated Book of Science Fiction Ideas and Dreams.* New York: Hamlyn, 1977.

Lammer, Helmut, and Marion Lammer. *MILABs: Military Mind Control and Alien Abductions.* Lilburn, GA: IllumiNet Press, 1999.

Lampe, G.H.W."Miracles and Early Christian Apologetics." In *Miracles*, edited by C.F.D. Moule, 203–218. London: A. R. Mowbray & Co., 1965.

Lamy, Philip. *Millennium Rage: Survivalists, White Supremacists, and the Doomsday Prophecy.* New York: Plenum Press, 1996.

Langton, Edward. *Essentials of Demonology: A Study of Jewish and Christian Doctrine, Its Origin and Development.* London: Epworth Press, 1949.

Laufer, Berthold. *Prehistory of Aviation.* Chicago: Field Museum of Natural History, 1928.

Lauren, Phoebe. *Star Children among Us.* West Palm Beach, FL: Garev Publishing International, 2004.

Lawson, Alvin H."What Can We Learn from Hypnosis of Imaginary Abductees?" In *1977 MU-FON UFO Symposium Proceedings*, edited by Walter H. Andrus Jr., 107–135. Seguin, TX: Mutual UFO Network, 1977.

———."'Alien' Roots: Six UFO Entity Types and Some Possible Earthly Ancestors." In *1979 MUFON UFO Symposium Proceedings*, edited by Walter H. Andrus Jr., 152–176. Seguin, TX: Mutual UFO Network, 1979.

———. "Perinatal Imagery in UFO Abduction Reports." *Journal of Psychohistory* 12 (1984): 211–239.

Layne, Meade."Welcome, Kareeta!" *Round Robin* 2, no. 10 (1946): 3–7.

———. *The Ether-Ship Mystery and Its Solution.* San Diego: Borderland Sciences Research Foundation, 1950.

Lear, John. "Lear's Aliens: Original Statement" (as posted on *Paranet*, December 29, 1987). http://www.ufomind.com/area51/people/lear/original.html.

Lee, Gloria. *Why We Are Here!* Palos Verdes Estates, CA: Cosmon Research Foundation, 1959.

Le Goff, Jacques. *The Birth of Purgatory.* Chicago: University of Chicago Press, 1984.

León-Portilla, Miguel. *Aztec Thought and Culture.* Norman: University of Oklahoma Press, 1963.

Leonard, George H. *Somebody Else Is on the Moon.* New York: David McKay, 1976.

Leslie, Desmond, and George Adamski. *The Flying Saucers Have Landed.* New York: British Book Centre, 1953.

Levinsohn, Florence Hamlish. *Looking for Farrakhan.* Chicago: Ivan R. Dee, 1997.

Lévi-Strauss, Claude. *The Savage Mind.* Chicago: University of Chicago Press, 1966.

———."The Structural Study of Myth." In *Myth: A Symposium*, edited by Thomas A. Sebeok, 81–106. Bloomington: Indiana University Press, 1971.

Lewis, James R., ed. *The Gods Have Landed: New Religions from Other Worlds.* Albany: State University of New York Press, 1995.

———, ed. *Encyclopedic Sourcebook of UFO Religions.* Amherst, NY: Prometheus Books, 2003.

Lewis, Martin W. *Green Delusions: An Environmentalist Critique of Radical Environmentalism.* Durham, NC: Duke University Press, 1992.

Lieb, Michael. *Children of Ezekiel: Aliens, UFOs, the Crisis of Race, and the Advent of End Times.* Durham, NC: Duke University Press, 1999.

Lind, Tom. *Catalogue of UFO Periodicals.* Hobe Sound, FL: Author, 1982.

Lindell, Jeffrey A."Supernatural Belief Traditions: The Traditions of Belief and Disbelief and the Role of the Memorate in Illustrative Dialogue." Folklore seminar paper, Indiana University, Bloomington.

Littrell, Helen, and Jean Bilodeux. *Raechel's Eyes*. 2 vols. Columbus, NC: Granite, 2005.

Loftus, Elizabeth, and Katherine Ketcham. *The Myth of Repressed Memory: False Memories and Allegations of Sexual Abuse*. New York: St. Martin's Press, 1994.

Long, Greg. *Examining the Earthlight Theory: The Yakima UFO Microcosm*. Chicago: J. Allen Hynek Center for UFO Studies, 1990.

Loomis, C. Grant. *White Magic*. Cambridge, MA: Mediaeval Academy of America, 1948.

Lore, Gordon I. R., and Harold H. Deneault Jr. *Mysteries of the Skies: UFOs in Perspective*. Englewood Cliffs, NJ: Prentice-Hall, 1968.

Lorenzen, Coral, and Jim Lorenzen. *Flying Saucer Occupants*. New York: Signet Books, 1967.

———. *Encounters with UFO Occupants*. New York: Berkley Medallion Books, 1976.

Lorenzi, Lorenzo. *Devils in Art: Florence, from the Middle Ages to the Renaissance*. Florence, Italy: Centro Di, 1997.

Lowell, Percival. *Mars*. Boston: Houghton, Mifflin & Co., 1895.

———. *Mars as the Abode of Life*. New York: Macmillan, 1908.

Luomala, Katharine. "The Menehune of Polynesia and Other Mythical Little People of Oceania." Bulletin 203, Bernice P. Bishop Museum, Honolulu, 1951.

Lüthi, Max. "Aspects of the Märchen and the Legend." In *Folklore Genres*, edited by Dan Ben-Amos, 17–33. Austin: University of Texas Press, 1981.

Lynn, Richard. *Eugenics: A Reassessment*. Westport, CT: Praeger, 2001.

Lynn, Steven Jay, Judith Pintar, Jane Stafford, Lisa Marmelstein, and Timothy Lock. "Rendering the Implausible Plausible: Narrative Construction, Suggestion, and Memory." In *Believed-In Imaginings: The Narrative Construction of Reality*, edited by Joseph de Rivera and Theodore R. Sarbin, 123–143. Washington, DC: American Psychological Association, 1998.

Maccabee, Bruce. "Still in Default." In *MUFON 1986 UFO Symposium Proceedings*, Walter H. Andrus Jr. and Richard Hall, 130–160. Seguin, TX: Mutual UFO Network, 1986; updated version at http://brumac.8k.com.

———. "The Fantastic Flight of JAL 1628." *IUR* 12, no. 2 (1987): 4–21.

———. "Even More Remarkable (UFOs in History: The U.S.S. *Supply* Sighting of Remarkable Meteors)." In *MUFON 2003 International UFO Symposium Proceedings*, edited by Barbra Maher, 55–70. Morrison, CO: MUFON, 2003. Updated at "Meteors? Even More Remarkable," http://brumac.8k.com/RemarkableMeteors/Remarkable.html.

Mack, John E. *Abduction: Human Encounters with Aliens*. New York: Charles Scribner's Sons, 1994.

———. *Passport to the Cosmos: Human Transformation and Alien Encounters*. New York: Crown, 1999.

McClenon, James. *Deviant Science: The Case of Parapsychology*. Philadelphia: University of Pennsylvania Press, 1984.

———. *Wondrous Events: Foundations of Religious Belief*. Philadelphia: University of Pennsylvania Press, 1994.

McCurdy, Howard E. *Space and the American Imagination*. Washington, DC: Smithsonian Institution Press, 1997.

McDannell, Colleen, and Bernhard Lang. *Heaven: A History*. New Haven, CT: Yale University Press, 1988.

McDonald, James E. "Statement." In *Symposium on Unidentified Flying Objects, Hearings before the Committee on Science and Astronautics,* Committee on Science and Astronautics, 90th Cong., 2d sess., July 29, 1968, 18–85. Washington, DC: U.S. Government Printing Office, 1968.

McLeod, Caroline C., Michael L. O'Connell, Robert L. Colasanti, and John E. Mack. "Anomalous Experience and Psychopathology: The Question of Alien Abduction." Unpublished study, John E. Mack Institute, Boulder, CO.

MacManus, Dermot. *The Middle Kingdom: The Faerie World of Ireland.* Gerrards Cross, Bucks: Colin Smythe, 1973.

Maienschein, Jane. *Whose View of Life? Embryos, Cloning and Stem Cells.* Cambridge, MA: Harvard University Press, 2003.

Mali, Joseph. *The Rehabilitation of Myth: Vico's "New Science."* New York: Cambridge University Press, 1992.

Malinowski, Bronislaw. *Magic, Science and Religion and Other Essays.* Garden City, NY: Anchor Books, 1954.

Malthus, Thomas Robert. "An Essay on the Principles of Population." In *Population, Evolution, and Birth Control,* edited by Garrett Hardin, 4–16. San Francisco: W. H. Freeman & Co., 1969.

Marx, Leo. *The Machine in the Garden: Technology and the Pastoral Ideal in America.* New York: Oxford University Press, 1970.

Mbiti, John S. *Concepts of God in Africa.* London: SPCK, 1970.

Medalia, Nahum Z., and Otto N. Larsen. "Diffusion and Belief in a Collective Delusion: The Seattle Windshield Pitting Epidemic." *American Sociological Review* 23 (1958): 180–186.

Méheust, Bertrand. *Science-Fiction et Soucoupes Volantes.* Paris: Mercure de France, 1978.

———. *Soucoupes Volantes et Folklore.* Paris: Mercure de France, 1985.

Melton, J. Gordon. "The Contactees: A Survey." In *The Gods Have Landed,* edited by James R. Lewis, 1–13. Albany: State University of New York Press, 1995.

Menger, Howard. *From Outer Space to You.* Clarksburg, WV: Saucerian Press, 1959.

Menzel, Donald H. *Flying Saucers.* Cambridge, MA: Harvard University Press, 1953.

———. "UFOs—The Modern Myth." In *UFOs—A Scientific Debate,* edited by Carl Sagan and Thornton Page, 123–182. Ithaca, NY: Cornell University Press, 1972.

Menzel, Donald H., and Lyle G. Boyd. *The World of Flying Saucers: A Scientific Examination of a Major Myth of the Space Age.* Garden City, NY: Doubleday & Co., 1963.

Mercier, A. *Communications avec Mars.* Orléans, France: Imprimerie Orléanaise, 1899.

Meurger, Michel. *Alien Abduction: L'Enlèvement extraterrestre de la fiction à la croyance.* Amiens: Encrage Édition, 1995.

Meyer, Kuno, ed. *The Voyage of Bran, Son of Febal, to the Land of the Living.* London: David Nutt, 1895.

Michel, Aimé. "The Valensole Affair." *FSR* 11, no. 6 (1965): 7–9.

Mode, Heinz. *Fabulous Beasts and Demons.* London: Phaidon Press, 1975.

Monk, Maria. "Awful Disclosures of the Hotel Dieu Nunnery." *Veil of Fear: Nineteenth-Century Convent Tales by Rebecca Reed and Maria Monk.* West Lafayette, IN: NotaBell Books/Purdue University Press, 1999.

Montaigne, Michel de. "On Cannibals." *Essays.* New York: Penguin Books, 1993.

Montell, William Lynwood. *Ghosts along the Cumberland*. Knoxville: University of Tennessee Press, 1975.

Mooney, James. *The Ghost-Dance Religion and the Sioux Outbreak of 1890*. Chicago: University of Chicago Press, 1965.

Moore, William L. "UFOs: Uncovering the Ultimate Answers." In *MUFON 1983 UFO Symposium Proceedings*, edited by Walter H. Andrus Jr. and Dennis W. Stacy, 83–100. Seguin, TX: Mutual UFO Network, 1983.

Morris, Simon Conway. *Life's Solution: Inevitable Humans in a Lonely Universe*. New York: Cambridge University Press, 2003.

Moss, Rosalind. *The Life after Death in Oceania and the Malay Archipelago*. London: Oxford University Press, 1925.

Muchembled, Robert. *Damned: An Illustrated History of the Devil*. San Francisco: Chronicle Books, 2004.

MUFON UFO Journal, special issue, no. 237 (January 1988): 3–16.

Muhammad, Elijah. *Message to the Blackman in America*. Chicago: Muhammad's Temple No. 2, 1965.

Mullis, Kary. *Dancing Naked in the Mind Field*. New York: Vintage Books, 1998.

Nathan, Debbie, and Michael Snedeker. *Satan's Silence: Ritual Abuse and the Making of a Modern American Witch Hunt*. New York: BasicBooks, 1995.

Needham, Rodney. *Primordial Characters*. Charlottesville: University Press of Virginia, 1978.

Neeley, Robert G., Jr. *UFOs of 1896/1897: The Airship Wave*. Mount Ranier, MD: Fund for UFO Research, 1985.

Neihardt, John G. *Black Elk Speaks*. New York: Pocket Books, 1972.

Nesheim, Eric, and Leif Nesheim. *Saucer Attack!* Los Angeles: Kitchen Sink Press, 1997.

Newman, Leonard S., and Roy F. Baumeister. "Toward an Explanation of the UFO Abduction Phenomenon: Hypnotic Elaboration, Extraterrestrial Sadomasochism, and Spurious Memories." *Psychological Inquiry* 7 (1996): 99–126.

Nickell, Joe. "The Flatwoods UFO Monster." *Skeptical Inquirer* 24, no. 6 (2000): 15–19.

Nisbet, Lee. "The Origins and Evolution of CSICOP: Science Is Too Important to Be Left to Scientists." *Skeptical Inquirer* 25, no. 6 (2001): 50–52.

Nye, David E. *America as Second Creation: Technology and Narratives of New Beginnings*. Cambridge, MA: MIT Press, 2003.

Nyman, Joseph. "The Familiar Entity and Dual Reference in the Latent Encounter." *MUFON UFO Journal*, no. 251 (March 1989): 10–12.

Obsequens, Julius. *A Book of Prodigies*. In *Summaries, Fragments, Obsequens*, vol. 14, Loeb Classical Library Livy, 238–319. Cambridge, MA: Harvard University Press, 1959.

Ofshe, Richard, and Ethan Watters. *Making Monsters: False Memories, Psychotherapy, and Sexual Hysteria*. New York: Charles Scribner's Sons, 1994.

O'Neil, Paul. "The Week of the Flying Saucers: A Well-Witnessed Invasion—By Something." *Life*, April 1, 1966, 24–31.

Otto, Rudolf. *The Idea of the Holy*. New York: Oxford University Press, 1969.

Padgett, J. Michael. *The Centaur's Smile: The Human Animal in Early Greek Art*. Princeton, NJ: Princeton University Art Museum, 2003.

Palmer, Susan Jean. "Women in the Raelian Movement." In *The Gods Have Landed*, edited by James R. Lewis, 105–135. Albany: State University of New York Press, 1995.

Parnell, June O. "Measured Personality Characteristics of Persons Who Claim UFO Experiences." *Psychotherapy in Private Practice* 6 (1989): 159–165.

Parnell, June O., and R. Leo Sprinkle. "Personality Characteristics of Persons Who Claim UFO Experiences." *Journal of UFO Studies*, n.s., 2 (1990): 45–58.

Partridge, Christopher, ed. *UFO Religions*. New York: Routledge, 2003.

Patch, Howard Rollin. *The Other World, According to Descriptions in Medieval Literature*. New York: Octagon Books, 1980.

Peebles, Curtis. *Watch the Skies! A Chronicle of the Flying Saucer Myth*. Washington, DC: Smithsonian Institution Press, 1994.

Persinger, Michael A. "Neuropsychological Profiles of Adults Who Report 'Sudden Remembering' of Early Childhood Memories: Implications for Claims of Sex Abuse and Alien Visitation/Abduction Experiences." *Perceptual and Motor Skills* 75 (1992): 259–266.

Pflock, Karl T. *Roswell: Inconvenient Facts and the Will to Believe*. Amherst, NY: Prometheus Books, 2001.

Pickering, William H. *Mars*. Boston: Richard G. Badger, 1921.

Pleij, Herman. *Dreaming of Cockaigne: Medieval Fantasies of the Perfect Life*. New York: Columbia University Press, 1997.

Popper, Karl R. *Conjectures and Refutations: The Growth of Scientific Knowledge*. New York: Harper Torchbooks, 1968.

Pratt, Bob. *UFO Danger Zone*. Madison, WI: Horus House Press, 1996.

President's Council on Bioethics. *Beyond Therapy: Biotechnology and the Pursuit of Happiness*. Washington, DC: President's Council on Bioethics, 2003.

Pritchard, Andrea, David E. Pritchard, John E. Mack, Pam Kasey, and Claudia Yapp, eds. *Alien Discussions: Proceedings of the Abduction Study Conference Held at MIT*. Cambridge, MA: North Cambridge Press, 1994.

Proctor, Richard A. *Other Worlds Than Ours: The Plurality of Worlds Studied under the Light of Recent Scientific Researches*. New York: D. Appleton & Co., 1880.

Pugh, Randall Jones. "Broad Haven School Report." *FSR* 23, no. 1 (1977): 3–5.

Pugh, Randall Jones, and F. W. Holiday. *The Dyfed Enigma*. London: Faber & Faber, 1979.

Raknem, Ingvald. *Joan of Arc in History, Legend and Literature*. Oslo: Universitetsforlaget, 1971.

Rammel, Hal. *Nowhere in America: The Big Rock Candy Mountain and Other Comic Utopias*. Urbana: University of Illinois Press, 1990.

Randle, Kevin D. *Project Blue Book Exposed*. New York: Marlowe & Co., 1997.

Randle, Kevin D., and Donald R. Schmitt. *UFO Crash at Roswell*. New York: Avon Books, 1991.

———. *The Truth About the UFO Crash at Roswell*. New York: M. Evans & Co., 1994.

Randle, Kevin D., Russ Estes, and William P. Cone. *The Abduction Enigma: The Truth Behind the Mass Alien Abductions of the Late Twentieth Century*. New York: Tom Doherty Associates, 1999.

Randles, Jenny. *The Pennine UFO Mystery*. London: Granada, 1983.

———. *Star Children*. London: Robert Hale, 1994.

———. *Alien Contact: The First Fifty Years*. New York: Sterling, 1997.

Ranke, Kurt. "Einfache Formen." *Journal of the Folklore Institute* 4 (1967): 17–31.

Rasmussen, Knud. *Myter og Sagn fra Grønland.* 3 vols. Kjøbenhavn: Gyldendal, 1921–1925.

———. *Eskimo Folk-Tales.* Copenhagen: Gyldendal, 1921.

Raynes, Brent. *Visitors from Hidden Realms: The Origin and Destiny of Humanity as Told by Star Elders, Shamans, and UFO Visitors.* Memphis: Eagle Wing Books, 2004.

Read, James Morgan. *Atrocity Propaganda 1914–1919.* New Haven, CT: Yale University Press, 1941.

Redfern, Nicholas. *Cosmic Crashes: The Incredible Story of UFOs That Fell to Earth.* London: Simon & Schuster, 1999.

———. *Body Snatchers in the Desert: The Horrible Truth at the Heart of the Roswell Story.* New York: Paraview Pocket Books, 2005.

Ridge, Francis L. *Regional Encounters.* Evansville, IN: UFO Filter Center, 1994.

Ring, Kenneth. *Life at Death: A Scientific Investigation of the Near-Death Experience.* New York: Quill, 1982.

———. *The Omega Project: Near-Death Experiences, UFO Encounters, and Mind at Large.* New York: William Morrow & Co., 1992.

Ring, Kenneth, and Christopher J. Rosing. "The Omega Project: A Psychological Survey of Persons Reporting Abductions and Other UFO Encounters." *Journal of UFO Studies,* n.s., 2 (1990): 59–98.

Rodeghier, Mark, Jeff Goodpaster, and Sandra Blatterbauer. "Psychological Characteristics of Abductees: Results from the CUFOS Abduction Project." *Journal of UFO Studies,* n.s., 3 (1991): 59–90.

Rodeghier, Mark, and Mark Chesney. "Who's the Dummy Now? The Latest Air Force Report." *IUR* 22, no. 3 (1997): 7–10.

Roe, Clifford. *The Great War on White Slavery.* 1911. New York: Garland, 1979.

Rogerson, Peter. "Fairyland's Hunters: Notes Towards a Revisionist History of Abductions." Pts. 1 and 2. *Magonia* 46 (June 1993): 3–7; 47 (October 1993): 4–8.

Rome, Dennis. *Black Demons: The Media's Depiction of the African American Male Criminal Stereotype.* Westport, CT: Praeger, 2004.

Romm, James S. *The Edges of the Earth in Ancient Thought: Geography, Exploration, and Fiction.* Princeton, NJ: Princeton University Press, 1992.

Rommel, Kenneth, Jr. *Operation Animal Mutilation.* Albuquerque: Department of the District Attorney, First Judicial District, State of New Mexico, 1980.

Ross, Andrew, ed. *Science Wars.* Durham, NC: Duke University Press, 1996.

Roth, John E. *American Elves: An Encyclopedia of Little People from the Lore of 380 Ethnic Groups of the Western Hemisphere.* Jefferson, NC: McFarland & Co., 1997.

Ruppelt, Edward J. *The Report on Unidentified Flying Objects.* Garden City, NY: Doubleday, 1956.

Sadakata, Akira. *Buddhist Cosmology: Philosophy and Origins.* Tokyo: Kōsei, 1997.

Sagan, Carl, and Thornton Page, eds. *UFOs—A Scientific Debate.* Ithaca, NY: Cornell University Press, 1972.

Salas, Robert, and James Klotz. *Faded Giant: The 1967 Missile/UFO Incidents.* N.p.: Privately printed, 2004

Saler, Benson, Charles A. Ziegler, and Charles B. Moore. *UFO Crash at Roswell: The Genesis of a Modern Myth*. Washington, DC: Smithsonian Institution Press, 1997.

Saliba, John A. "Religious Dimensions of UFO Phenomena." In *The Gods Have Landed*, James R. Lewis, 15–64. Albany: State University of New York Press, 1995.

Salisbury, Frank B. *The Utah UFO Display*. Old Greenwich, CT: Devin-Adair, 1974.

Salla, Michael E. *Exopolitics: Political Implications of the Extraterrestrial Presence*. Tempe, AZ: Dandelion Books, 2004.

Saunders, David R., and R. Roger Harkins. *UFOs? Yes! Where the Condon Committee Went Wrong*. New York: World, 1968.

Schaer, Roland, Gregory Claeys, and Lyman Tower Sargent, eds. *Utopia: The Search for the Ideal Society in the Western World*. New York: New York Public Library / Oxford University Press, 2000.

Schmidt, Reinhold O. *Edge of Tomorrow: The Reinhold O. Schmidt Story*. N.p.: Author, 1963.

Schmitt, Don. "The Belleville Sightings." Pts. 1 and 2. *IUR* 12, no. 6 (1987): 4–8; 13, no. 1 (1988): 17–19.

Schussler, John F. *The Cash-Landrum UFO Incident*. LaPorte, TX: Geo Graphics, 1998.

Sconce, Jeffrey. *Haunted Media: Electronic Presence from Telegraphy to Television*. Durham, NC: Duke University Press, 2000.

Scully, Frank. *Behind the Flying Saucers*. New York: Henry Holt & Co., 1950.

Seed, David. *American Science Fiction and the Cold War: Literature and Film*. Edinburgh: Edinburgh University Press, 1999.

Séguy, Marie Rose. *The Miraculous Journey of Mahomet*. New York: George Braziller, 1977.

Serviss, Garrett P. *Edison's Conquest of Mars*. Burlington, Ontario: Apogee Books, 2005.

Sheaffer, Robert. *The UFO Verdict: Examining the Evidence*. Buffalo, NY: Prometheus Books, 1981.

Sheehan, William. *The Planet Mars: A History of Observation and Discovery*. Tucson: University of Arizona Press, 1996.

Shermer, Michael. *Why People Believe Weird Things: Pseudo-Science, Superstition, and Bogus Notions of Our Time*. New York: MJF Books, 1997.

Sherwood, John C. *Flying Saucers Are Watching You*. Clarksburg, WV: Saucerian Publications, 1967.

Shklovskii, I. S., and Carl Sagan. *Intelligent Life in the Universe*. San Francisco: Holden-Day, 1966.

Simmons, Michael. "Once Upon a Time in the West." *Magonia*, no. 20 (August 1985): 3–7.

Simpson, George Gaylord. *This View of Life*. New York: Harcourt, Brace & World, 1964.

Sitchin, Zecharia. *The 12th Planet*. New York: Stein & Day, 1976.

Smith, Michelle, and Lawrence Pazder. *Michelle Remembers*. New York: Pocket Books, 1989.

Smith, Toby. *Little Gray Men: Roswell and the Rise of a Popular Culture*. Albuquerque: University of New Mexico Press, 2000.

Smith, Willy. "Over Pennsylvania: The Enigmatic Captain Killian Case, February 24, 1959." *IUR* 23, no. 1 (1998): 13–14, 29–30.

Spanos, Nicholas P. *Multiple Identities and False Memories: A Sociocognitive Perspective*. Washington, DC: American Psychological Association, 1996.

Spanos, Nicholas P., Patricia A. Cross, Kirby Dickson, and Susan C. DuBreuil. "Close Encounters: An Examination of UFO Experiences." *Journal of Abnormal Psychology* 102 (1993): 624–632.

Spencer, John, and Ann Spencer. *Fifty Years of UFOs*. London: Boxtree, 1997.

Sprenger, Jacobus, and Heinrich Kramer. *Malleus Maleficarum: The Hammer of Witchcraft*. London: Folio Society, 1968.

Sprinkle, R. Leo. "UFO Contactees: Captive Collaborators or Cosmic Citizens?" In *1980 MUFON UFO Symposium Proceedings*, edited by Walter H. Andrus and Dennis W. Stacy, 54–70. Seguin, TX: Mutual UFO Network, 1980.

Steiger, Brad, ed. *Project Blue Book*. New York: Ballantine Books, 1976.

Stent, Gunther S. *The Coming of the Golden Age: A View of the End of Progress*. Garden City, NY: Natural History Press, 1969.

Stephens, Walter. *Demon Lovers: Witchcraft, Sex, and the Crisis of Belief*. Chicago: University of Chicago Press, 2002.

Stevens, Phillips, Jr. "The Demonology of Satanism: An Anthropological View." In *The Satanism Scare*, edited by James T. Richardson, Joel Best, and David G. Bromley, 21–39. New York: Aldine de Gruyter, 1991.

Stevens, Wendelle C., and Paul Dong. *UFOs over Modern China*. Tucson: UFO Photo Archives, 1983.

Stone-Carmen, Jo. "A Descriptive Study of People Reporting Abduction by UFOs." In *Alien Discussions*, edited by Andrea Pritchard, David E. Pritchard, John E. Mack, Pam Kasey, and Claudia Yapp, 309–314. Cambridge, MA: North Cambridge Press, 1994.

Story, Ronald D., ed. *The Encyclopedia of Extraterrestrial Encounters*. New York: New American Library, 2001.

Stover, Leon. *The Prophetic Soul: A Reading of H. G. Wells's Things to Come*. Jefferson, NC: McFarland & Co., 1987.

Strassberg, Richard E., ed. *A Chinese Bestiary: Strange Creatures from the Guideways through Mountains and Seas*. Berkeley: University of California Press, 2002.

Strieber, Whitley. *Communion*. New York: Beech Tree Books / William Morrow, 1987.

———. *Transformation: The Breakthrough*. New York: William Morrow & Co., 1988.

Sturluson, Snorri. *The Prose Edda*. Berkeley: University of California Press, 1964.

Surrock, Peter A. *The UFO Enigma: A New Review of the Physical Evidence*. New York: Warner Books, 1999.

Swords, Michael D. "Extraterrestrial Hybridization Unlikely." *MUFON UFO Journal*, no. 247 (November 1988): 6–10.

———. "Science and the Extraterrestrial Hypothesis in Ufology." *Journal of UFO Studies*, n.s., 1 (1989): 67–102.

———. "The University of Colorado UFO Project: The 'Scientific Study of UFOs.'" *Journal of UFO Studies*, n.s., no. 6 (1995–1996): 149–184.

———. "Project Sign and the Estimate of the Situation." *Journal of UFO Studies*, n.s., no. 7 (2000): 27–64.

———. *Grassroots UFOs: Case Reports from the Timmerman Files*. Mount Rainier, MD: Fund for UFO Research, 2005.

Terpening, Ronnie H. *Charon and the Crossing: Ancient, Medieval, and Renaissance Transforma-tions of a Myth.* Cranbury, NJ: Associated University Presses, 1985.

Thomas, Keith. *Religion and the Decline of Magic.* New York: Charles Scribner's Sons, 1971.

Thompson, Keith. "The Stages of UFO Initiations." *Magical Blend,* no. 18 (February–April 1988): 9–16.

Thompson, Stith. *Tales of the North American Indians.* Bloomington: Indiana University Press, 1968.

Tillyard, E. M.W. *The Elizabethan World Picture.* New York: Vintage Books, 1960.

Tilton, Christa. *The Bennewitz Papers.* Tulsa, OK: Crux Publications, 1991.

Todd, Dennis. *Imagining Monsters: Miscreations of the Self in Eighteenth-Century England.* Chi-cago: University of Chicago Press, 1995.

Toynbee, Arnold J. *A Study of History.* Abridged. Vols. 1–2. New York: Oxford University Press, 1946.

Tromp, Nicholas J. *Primitive Conceptions of Death and the Nether World in the Old Testament.* Rome: Pontifical Biblical Institute, 1969.

Tulien, Thomas. "The 1952 Nash/Fortenberry Sighting Revisited." *IUR* 27, no. 1 (2002): 20–23, 27–28. http://www.nicap.org/nash-tulien.htm.

Tumminia, Diana, and R. George Kirkpatrick. "Unarius: Emergent Aspects of an American Fly-ing Saucer Group." In *The Gods Have Landed,* edited by James R. Lewis, 85–104. Albany: State University of New York Press, 1995.

Turner, Frederick Jackson. *The Frontier in American History.* New York: Henry Holt & Co., 1920.

Turner, Karla. *Into the Fringe: A True Story of Alien Abduction.* New York: Berkley Books, 1992.

Tylor, Edward B. *Primitive Culture.* New York: Brentano's, 1924.

U.S. Congress. House Committee on Science and Astronautics. *Symposium on Unidentified Fly-ing Objects, Hearings before the Committee on Science and Astronautics.* 90th Cong., 2d sess., July 29, 1968, 18–85. Washington, DC: U.S. Government Printing Office, 1968.

Valerian, Valdemar. *The Matrix: Understanding Aspects of Covert Interaction with Alien Culture, Technology and Planetary Power Structures.* Stone Mountain, GA: Arcturus Book Service, 1988.

Vallee, Jacques. *Anatomy of a Phenomenon.* Chicago: Henry Regnery, 1965.

———. *Passport to Magonia: From Folklore to Flying Saucers.* Chicago: Henry Regnery, 1969.

———. *The Invisible College.* New York: E. P. Dutton & Co., 1975.

———. *Messengers of Deception: UFO Contacts and Cults.* Berkeley, CA: And/Or Press, 1979.

———. *Confrontations: A Scientist's Search for Alien Contact.* New York: Ballantine Books, 1990.

———. *Forbidden Science: Journals 1957–1969.* Berkeley, CA: North Atlantic Books, 1992.

———. *UFO Chronicles of the Soviet Union.* New York: Ballantine Books, 1992.

VanDerBeets, Richard. *The Indian Captivity Narrative: An American Genre.* Lanham, MD: Uni-versity Press of America, 1984.

van der Toorn, Karel, Bob Becking, and Pieter W. van der Horst, eds. *Dictionary of Deities and Demons in the Bible.* Leiden: E. J. Brill, 1995.

van Gennep, Arnold. *The Rites of Passage.* Chicago: University of Chicago Press, 1960.

Van Horn, William. "Press Release." Hillsdale, MI: Author, 1966.

Van Tassel, G. W. *I Rode a Flying Saucer.* Los Angeles: New Age, 1952.

———. *Into This World and Out Again.* Los Angeles: DeVorss & Co., 1956.

———. *The Council of Seven Lights.* Los Angeles: DeVorss & Co., 1958.

Van Utrecht, Wim. "The Belgian 1989–1990 UFO Wave." In *UFOs 1947–1997,* edited by Hilary Evans and Dennis Stacy, 165–174. London: John Brown, 1997.

Victor, Jeffrey S. *Satanic Panic: The Creation of a Contemporary Legend.* Chicago: Open Court, 1993.

Wachtel, Nathan. *Gods and Vampires: Return to Chipaya.* Chicago: University of Chicago Press, 1994.

Wallace, Alfred Russel. *Man's Place in the Universe: A Study of the Results of Scientific Research in Relation to the Unity or Plurality of Worlds.* New York: McClure, Phillips & Co., 1903.

Wallace, Anthony F. C. "Revitalization Movements." *American Anthropologist,* n.s., 58 (1956): 264–281.

Walsh, Chad. *From Utopia to Nightmare.* Westport, CT: Greenwood Press, 1962.

Walsh, William. *Our Lady of Fátima.* Garden City, NY: Doubleday, 1954.

Walters, Ed, and Frances Walters. *The Gulf Breeze Sightings.* New York: William Morrow, 1990.

Walton, Travis. *The Walton Experience.* New York: Berkley Medallion Books, 1978.

Ward, Peter D., and Donald Brownlee. *Rare Earth: Why Complex Life Is Uncommon in the Universe.* New York: Copernicus Books, 2004.

Warren, Donald I. "Status Inconsistency Theory and Flying Saucer Sightings." *Science* 170 (1970): 599–603.

Warren, Larry, and Peter Robbins. *Left at East Gate.* New York: Marlowe & Co., 1997.

Warren, William Fairfield. *The Earliest Cosmologies.* New York: Eaton & Mains, 1909.

Watson, Nigel. *The Scareship Mystery: A Survey of Worldwide Phantom Airship Scares (1909–1918).* Corby, Northamptonshire: Domra Publications, 2000.

Watson, Nigel, Granville Oldroyd, and David Clarke. *The 1912–1913 British Phantom Airship Scare.* Mount Ranier, MD: Fund for UFO Research, 1987.

Webb, Stephen. *If the Universe Is Teeming with Aliens . . . Where Is Everybody? Fifty Solutions to the Fermi Paradox and the Problem of Extraterrestrial Life.* New York: Copernicus Books, 2002.

Wells, H. G. "The Things That Live on Mars." *Cosmopolitan,* March 1908, 334–342.

———. "Star Begotten." In *28 Science Fiction Stories,* 510–635. New York: Dover Publications, 1952.

———. *A Critical Edition of The War of the Worlds: H. G. Wells's Scientific Romance.* Introduction and notes by David Y. Hughes and Harry M. Geduld. Bloomington: Indiana University Press, 1993.

Wessinger, Catherine. *How the Millennium Comes Violently: From Jonestown to Heaven's Gate.* New York: Seven Bridges Press, 2000.

White, Hayden. "The Forms of Wildness: Archaeology of an Idea." In Edward Dudley and Maximilian E. Novak, 3–38. *The Wild Man Within.* Pittsburgh: University of Pittsburgh Press, 1972.

Whiting, C. E. *Studies in English Puritanism.* New York: Society for Promoting Christian Knowledge, 1931.

Wilkins, H. T. *Flying Saucers on the Attack*. New York: Citadel Press, 1954.

———. *Flying Saucers Uncensored*. New York: Citadel Press, 1955.

Williamson, George Hunt. *Secret Places of the Lion*. London: Neville Spearman, 1958.

Williamson, George Hunt, and Alfred C. Bailey. *The Saucers Speak! A Documentary Report of Interstellar Communication by Radio Telegraphy*. Los Angeles: New Age, 1954.

Wilson, Clifford. *UFOs and Their Mission Impossible*. New York: Signet, 1974.

Wilson, Colin. *Alien Dawn: An Investigation into the Contact Experience*. London: Virgin, 1998.

Winter, Frank H. "The Strange Case of Madame Guzman and the Mars Mystique." *Griffith Observer* 48, no. 2 (1984): 2–15.

Wojcik, Daniel. *The End of the World as We Know It: Faith, Fatalism, and Apocalypse in America*. New York: New York University Press, 1997.

Wood, Robert M. "Validating the New Majestic Documents." In *MUFON 2000 International UFO Symposium Proceedings*, edited by Walter H. Andrus Jr. and Irena Scott, 164–192. Seguin, TX: Mutual UFO Network, 2000.

Wood, Ryan S. "The First Roswell: Evidence for a Crash Retrieval in Cape Girardeau Missouri in 1941." In *MUFON 2001 International UFO Symposium Proceedings*, edited by Barbara Maher and Irene Scott, 129–146. Morrison, CO: Mutual UFO Network, 2001.

Worsley, Peter. *The Trumpet Shall Sound: A Study of "Cargo" Cults in Melanesia*. New York: Schoken Books, 1968.

Wright, Bradford W. *Comic Book Nation: The Transformation of Youth Culture in America*. Baltimore: Johns Hopkins University Press, 2001.

Wright, Dan. "Five Themes: Further Findings of the Abduction Transcription Project." In *MUFON 1997 International UFO Symposium Proceedings*, edited by Walter H. Andrus Jr. and Irena Scott, 43–88. Seguin, TX: MUFON, 1997.

Wright, Lawrence. *Remembering Satan: A Tragic Case of Recovered Memory*. New York: Vintage Books, 1994.

Wu, William F. *The Yellow Peril: Chinese Americans in American Fiction 1850–1940*. Hamden, CT: Archon Books, 1982.

Yewell, John, Chris Dodge, and Jan De Sirey, eds. *Confronting Columbus: An Anthology*. Jefferson, NC: McFarland & Co., 1992.

York, Paul. "The Ethics of Terraforming." *Philosophy Now*, no. 38 (October–November 2002): 6–9.

Zaleski, Carol. *Otherworld Journeys: Accounts of Near-Death Experiences in Medieval and Modern Times*. New York: Oxford University Press, 1987.

Zeidman, Jennie. *A Helicopter-UFO Encounter over Ohio*. Evanston, IL: CUFOS, 1979.

Zimdars-Swartz, Sandra L. *Encountering Mary: Visions of Mary from La Salette to Medjugorje*. New York: Avon Books, 1992.

Zimmer, Troy A. "Social Psychological Correlates of Possible UFO Sightings." *Journal of Social Psychology* 123 (1984): 199–206.

Index